“All the pretty girls are in Halstons.”

—*The Andy Warhol Diaries*,

Sunday, March 12, 1978

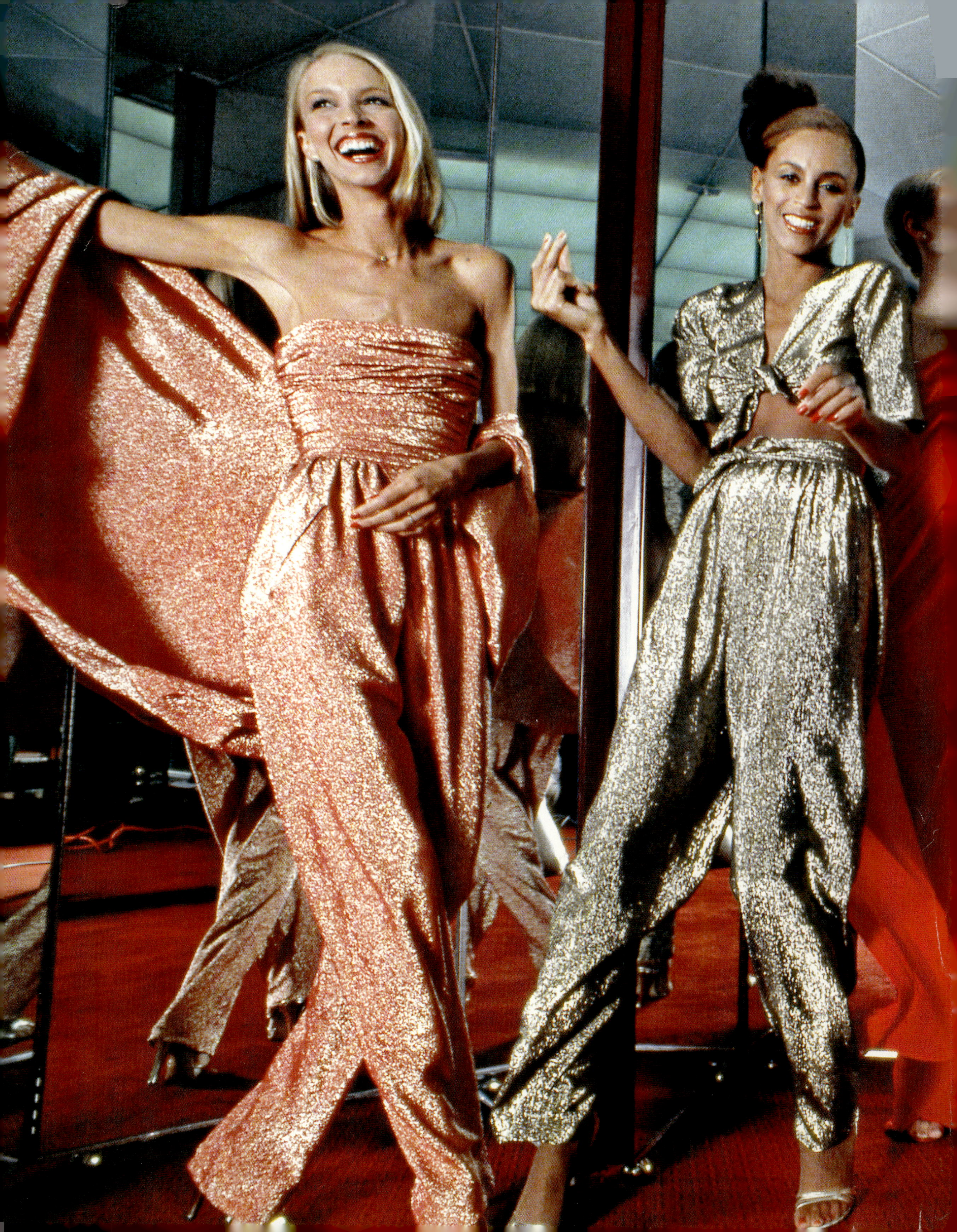

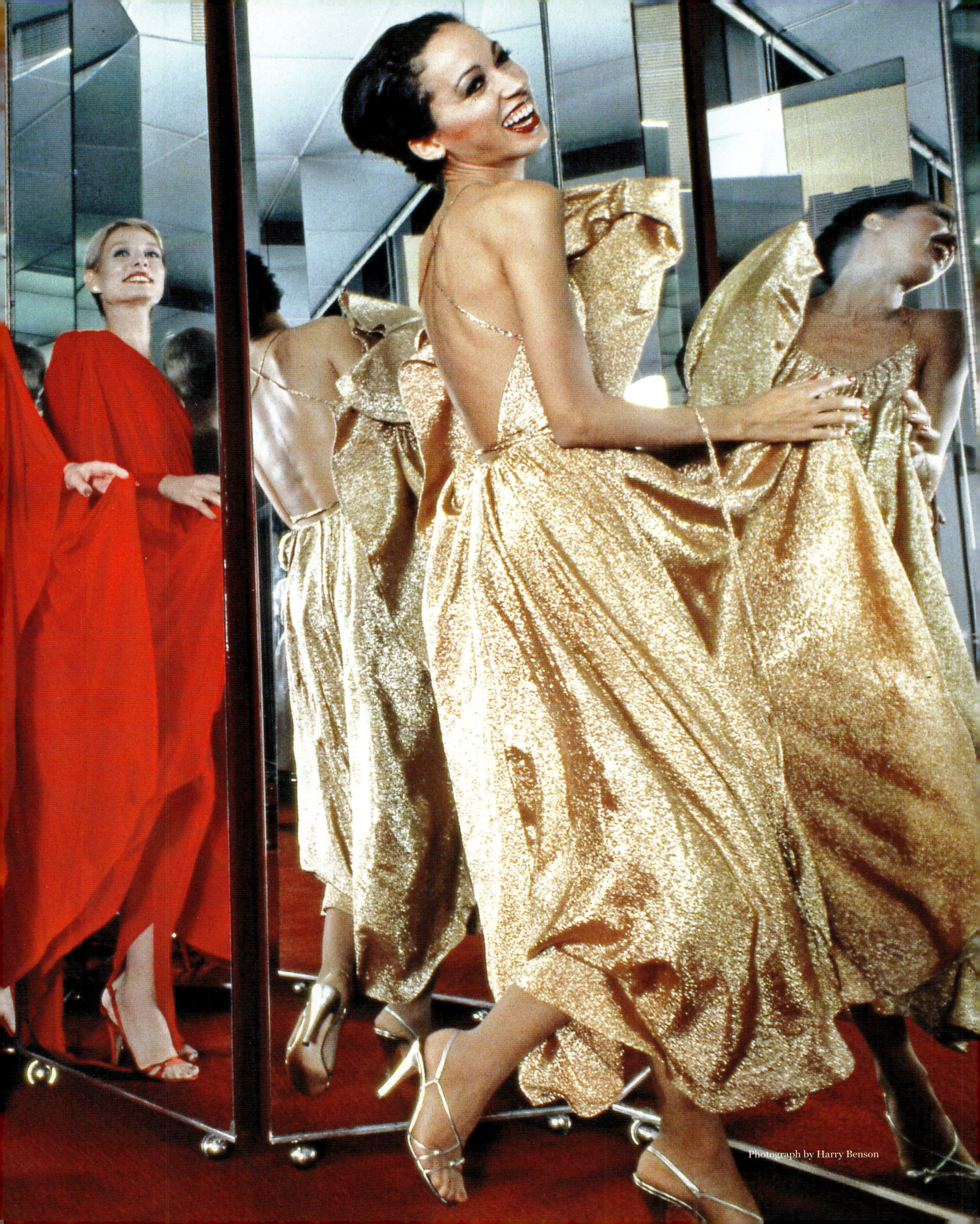

Photograph by Harry Benson

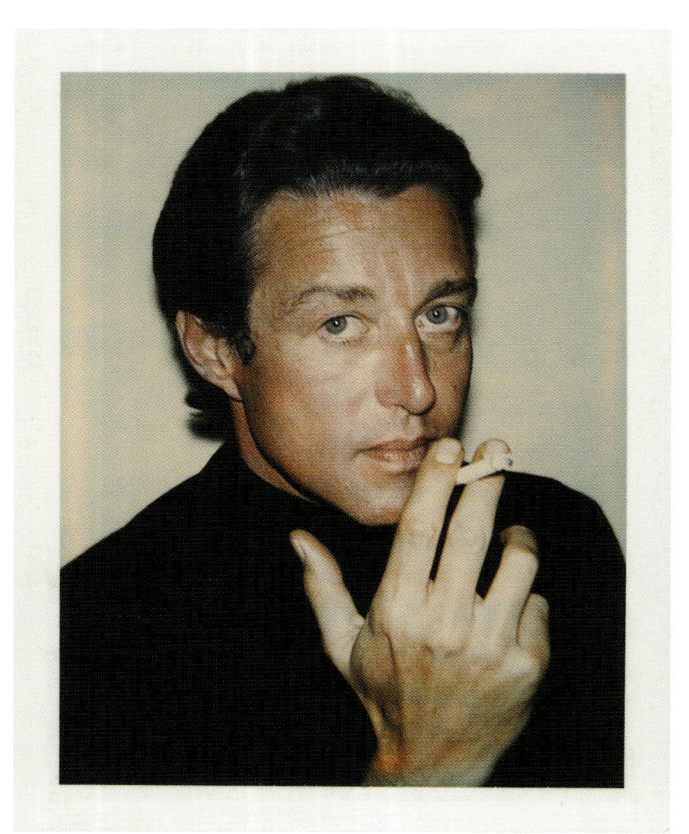

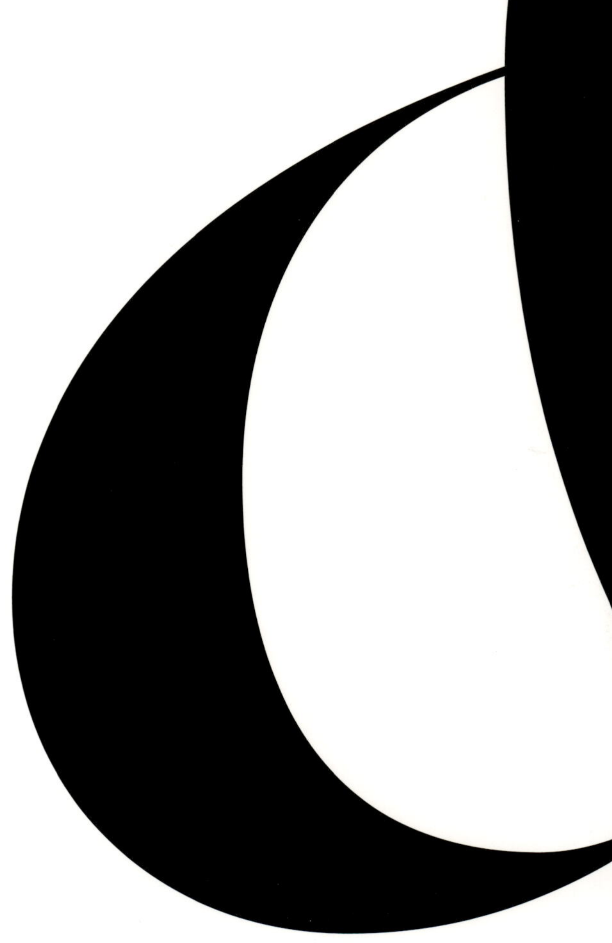

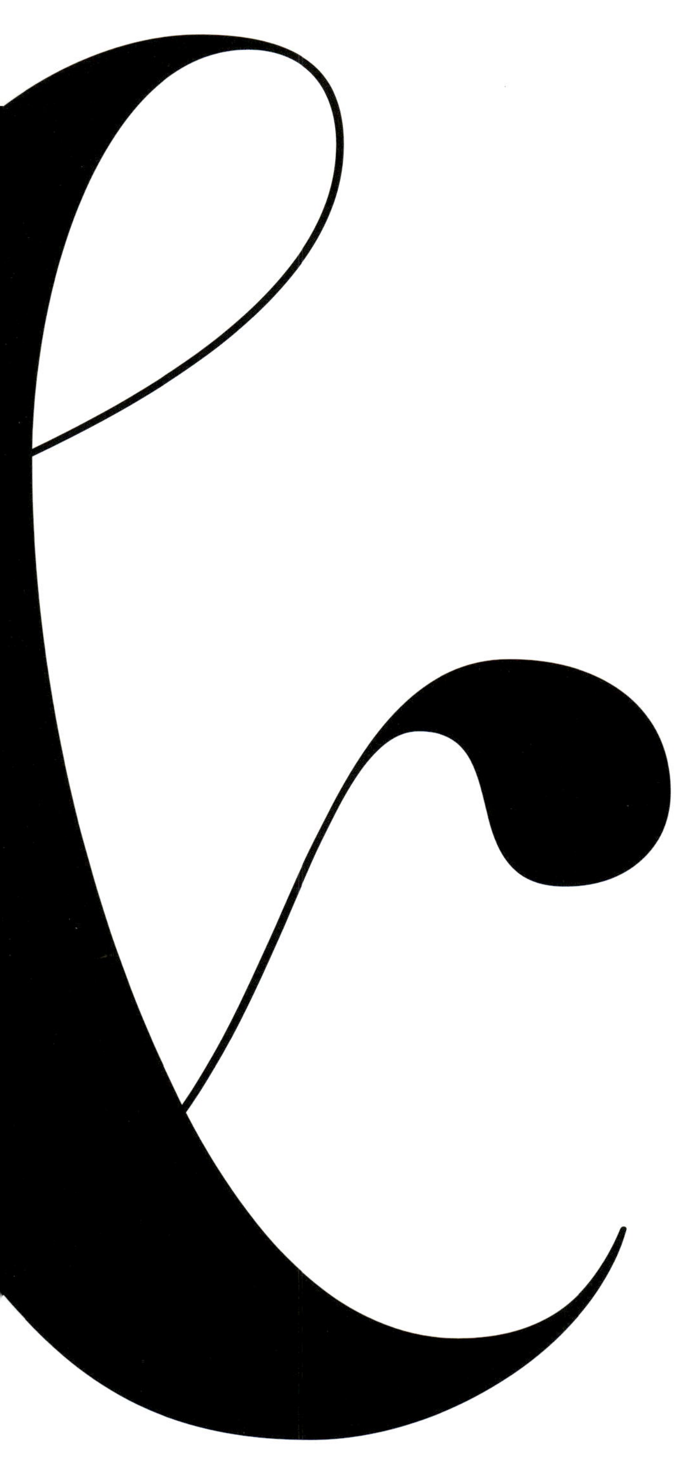

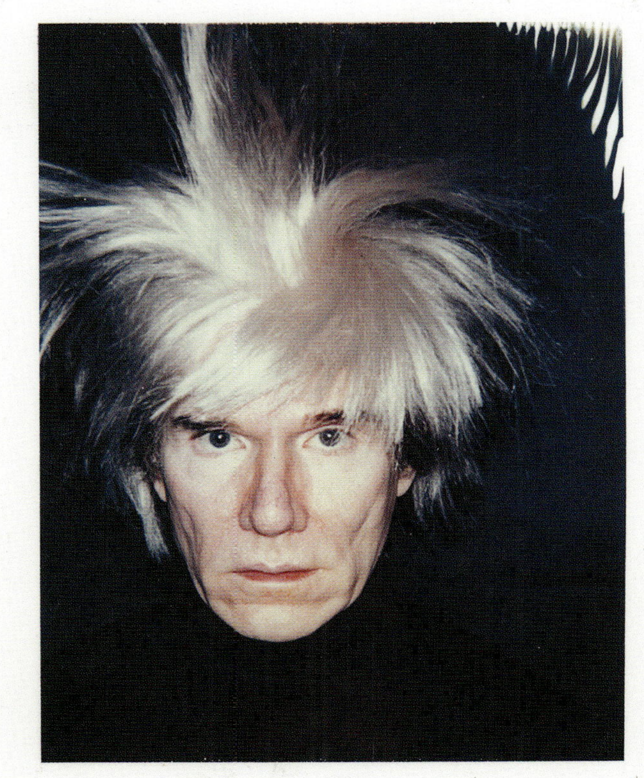

Edited by
Abigail Franzen-Sheehan

Essays by
Lesley Frowick
Geralyn Huxley
Corinne LaBalme
Valerie Steele

With contributions by
Nicholas Chambers
Pat Cleveland
Patrick Moore
Chris Royer
Eric C. Shiner
Diane von Furstenberg
Signe Watson
Matt Wrbican

The Andy Warhol Museum, Pittsburgh
Abrams, New York

HALSTON & WARHOL

SILVER & SUEDE

THE ANDY WARHOL MUSEUM

CONTENTS

11 FOREWORD
Eric C. Shiner

13 SPONSOR STATEMENT

14 MEMORIES OF UNCLE HALSTON
Lesley Frowick

20 THE INIMITABLE HALSTON
Valerie Steele

28 VICTOR HUGO AND HALSTON:
FASHION UNDER GLASS . . . VENEZUELAN STYLE
Corinne LaBalme

32 CAMEOS AND CATWALKS:
FASHION IN WARHOL'S FILM AND VIDEO
Geralyn Huxley

38 INTERVIEW WITH PAT CLEVELAND
Conducted by Kilolo Luckett

46 INTERVIEW WITH DIANE VON FURSTENBERG
Conducted by Eric C. Shiner and Signe Watson

49 TIMELINES
Nicholas Chambers, Abigail Franzen-Sheehan, Patrick Moore, Chris Royer, Signe Watson, and Matt Wrbican

50 1930s–40s

58 1950s

80 1960s

116 1970s

184 1980s

235 Notes to Pages 54–232
235 Credits
236 Index
239 Acknowledgments

Halston
Sketch, ca. 1972
The Halston collection at the Museum at FIT

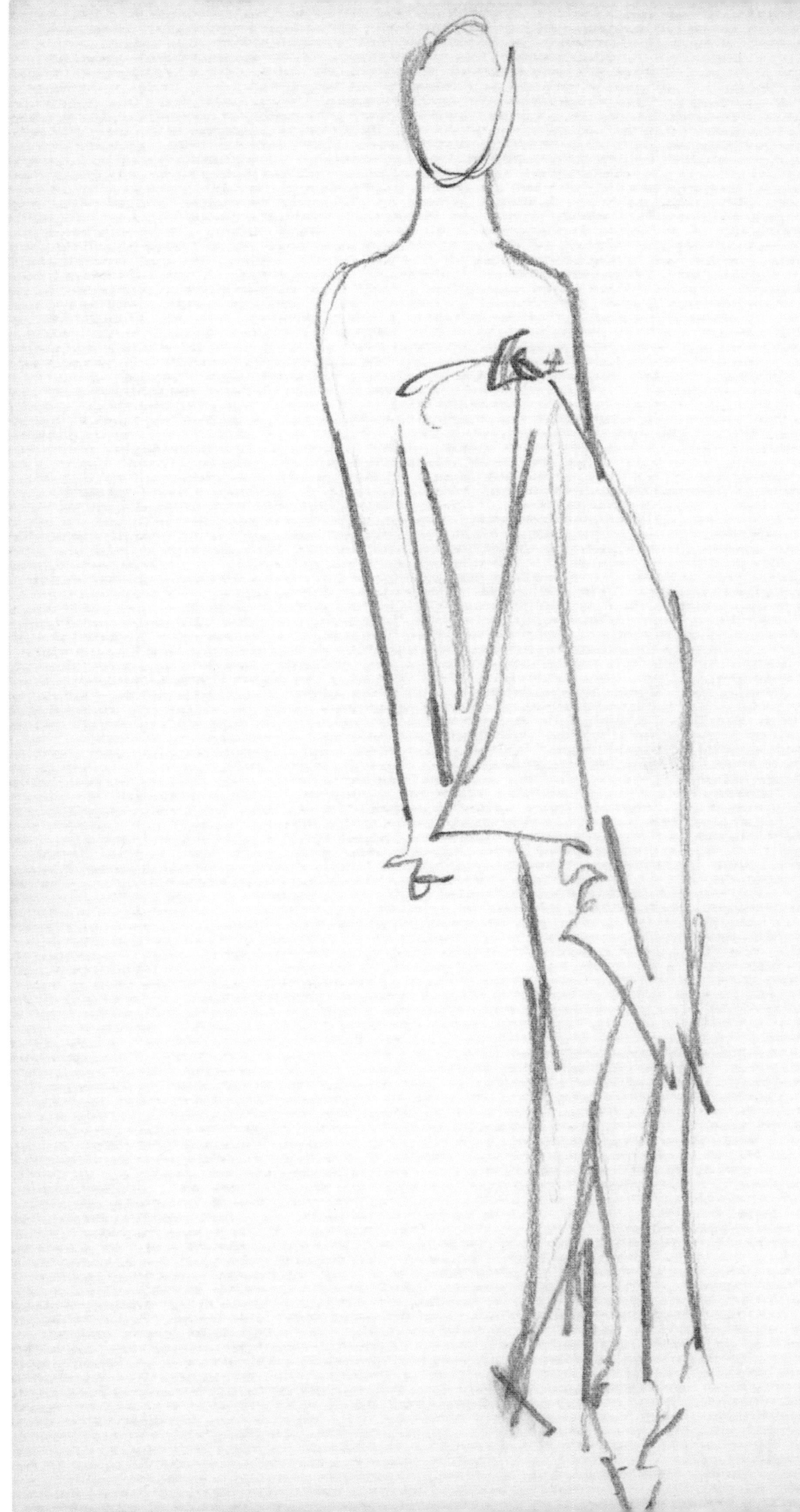

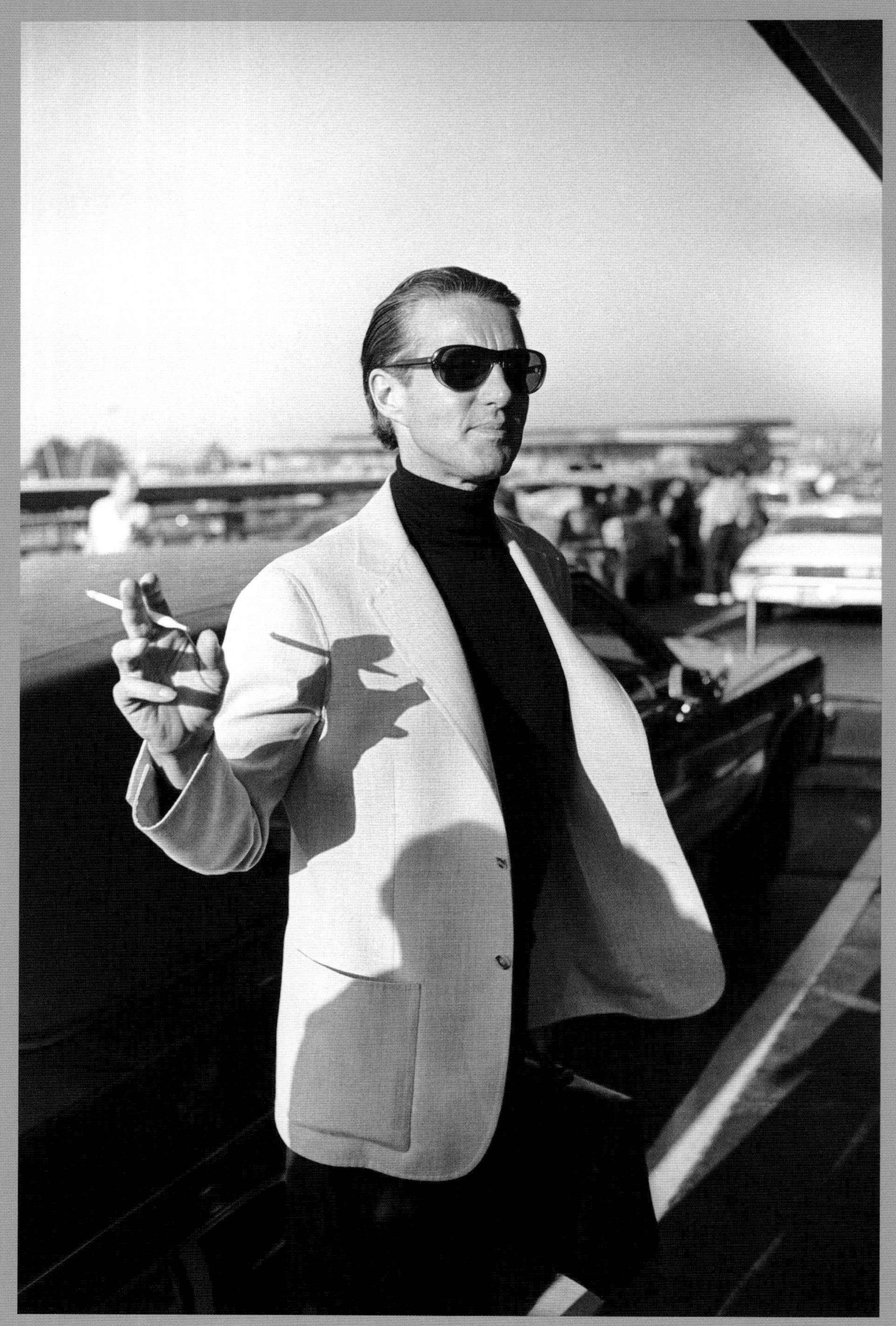

FOREWORD

Warhol and Halston are iconic names in American culture—luxury brands, if you will—but also deeply resonant of an era when experimentation and audacity were the hallmarks of a new kind of art. Any mention of the two men evokes nostalgia for a darkly glittering social scene centered on Studio 54; but this pop-culture image is reductive. The story of Warhol and Halston is far more complex, and it is the intention of *Halston and Warhol: Silver and Suede* to strip away some of the clichés that have built up around these two men.

Halston and Andy Warhol were both unashamedly businessmen, selling their vision of American culture. In the case of Halston, his pared-down designs brought into focus the kind of casual glamour personified by Jackie Kennedy. Warhol's work, steeped in the fashion world, where he initially worked as a commercial illustrator, and in the movie-star images that had been his childhood refuge, lived in an entirely new intersection between fine and commercial art. Both men had an uncanny ability to illuminate the point in American culture where the simplistic optimism of the 1950s became something edgier and more interesting during the 1960s and 1970s.

Although Warhol's and Halston's worlds extended far beyond Studio 54, the nightclubs and parties of New York were indeed where fashion and art mixed. The vision of nightlife that gay American men created in the 1970s influenced the highest reaches of New York society and ricocheted around the world through the network of jet setters that Warhol and Halston joined. These two men, from Pittsburgh and Des Moines, respectively, found themselves at the very center of a new high/low culture they had helped create.

This publication would not have come together without the leadership and dedication of The Andy Warhol Museum's Director of Publications, Abigail Franzen-Sheehan. I am grateful for her careful oversight of this project and am indebted to each of the contributors: Lesley Frowick, Geralyn Huxley, Corinne LaBalme, Valerie Steele, Pat Cleveland, Diane von Furstenberg, Kilolo Luckett, Chris Royer, Signe Watson, Patrick Moore, and Matt Wrbican.

Finally, I must thank PNC Financial Services for making this exhibition possible. PNC has a long history of supporting The Andy Warhol Museum's exhibition program. It is our honor to be associated with a company that so generously celebrates American culture.

Eric C. Shiner
Director, The Andy Warhol Museum

Halston, 1980
Photograph by Dustin Pittman

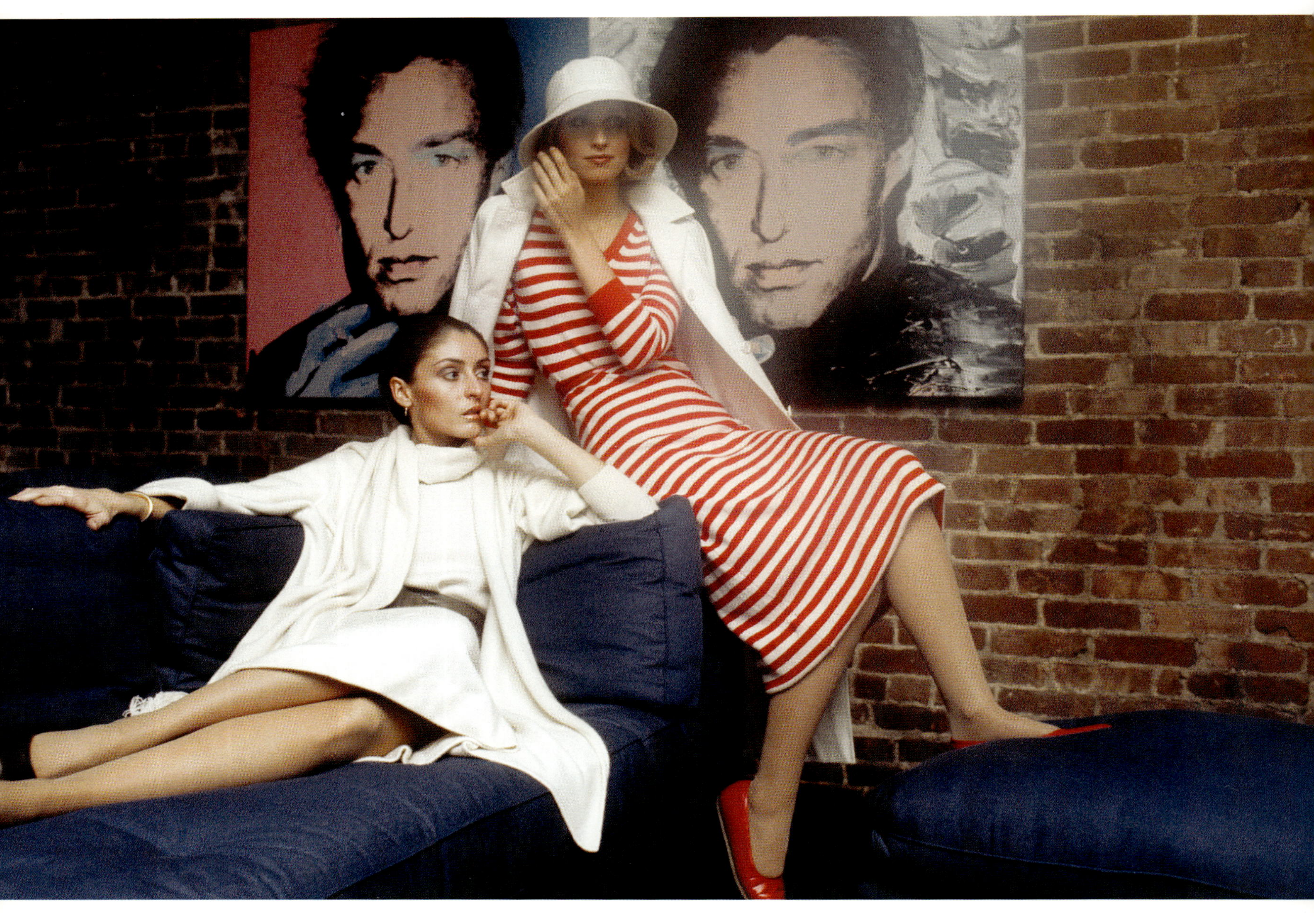

Shirley Ferro and Chris Royer modeling dresses from Halston's Spring 1975 ready-to-wear collection in front of Warhol's portraits of Halston in the designer's townhouse, October 16, 1974
Photograph by Pierre Schermann
Condé Nast Archive/CORBIS

SPONSOR STATEMENT

The marriage of high fashion and art has fascinated for decades and continues to impact American culture. *Halston and Warhol: Silver and Suede* brings two masters of their crafts together in a distinctive exhibition that examines their influence on each other as friends, entrepreneurs, and artists.

PNC Financial Services is pleased to continue our own unique collaboration with The Andy Warhol Museum as presenting sponsor for *Halston and Warhol: Silver and Suede*. As PNC enters new regions through acquisitions or growth, we seek to do something distinctive to showcase our legacy of supporting the arts and our strong commitment to the communities we serve. A friendship and mutually beneficial relationship with The Warhol was born eight years ago and continues to grow today.

Over the years, PNC has exported Warhol exhibitions throughout the regions we serve—to institutions ranging from the Corcoran Museum in Washington, D.C., and the Indianapolis Museum of Art to the Birmingham Museum of Art and the Museum of Art Fort Lauderdale. PNC believes that culturally engaging programs such as this exhibition and its accompanying publication strengthen the tremendous cultural vitality of our regions.

We are delighted to continue our partnership with The Warhol and hope you enjoy the vibrant display of *Halston and Warhol: Silver and Suede*.

Donna C. Peterman
Executive Vice President and Chief Communications Officer
The PNC Financial Services Group
Member, The Andy Warhol Museum Board of Directors

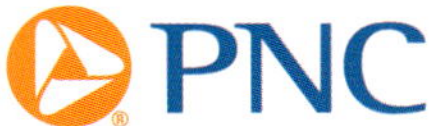

MEMORIES OF UNCLE HALSTON

Lesley Frowick

I was in New York, hunting for a job, when Halston first asked me to dinner. I had longed for such a date. Halston was my father's brother. They had the same stature, the same voice, some of the same mannerisms; they were both strong men who, when you were in their presence, made perceived problems somehow melt away. My father worked in the diplomatic corps and took us to live abroad for most of my childhood, leaving only sporadic opportunities to see Uncle Halston. But he and I had always admired each other. After our dinner of filet mignon, he asked me, "What do you want to be when you grow up?" I answered, "I am still trying to figure it out." He proposed that I work for him—an offer I could not pass up. Within the month my bags were packed. Even now, years removed, I am charmed that he was willing to devote so much time to me. Halston's gift of endless professional advice, as well as a rent-free place to live while I studied at the International Center for Photography, was even more generous than I could understand at the time.

My uncle and I shared many things, not the least of which was the same birthday, April 23. After Halston invited me into his world he always made a point of celebrating our birthdays together. On order for dessert were always two cakes; the first one was presented with candles and fanfare: "The angel's food cake—is for me," he said. He then delighted in exclaiming, "And the devil's food cake—is for Lesley!" followed by a distinctive Halston roar of laughter.

On my first day of work in 1982, I got off the elevator on the twenty-first floor of the Olympic Tower and immediately sensed Halston's style and aesthetic perfectionism. The mirrored walls and softly lit reception area, the orchids strategically positioned on tables, the Halston fragrance in the air, and the black-clad assistants silently popping in and out from closed doors were magical to me.

I was led by an assistant to the design room and given a desk, close to Halston's office. You couldn't really call it an office though; it was more like his domain. For midtown Manhattan, it was a luxurious space with a million-dollar view. On a clear day you could see the Central Park Zoo. An oversize red lacquer table was situated on the 51st Street side of the room, with the spires of St. Patrick's Cathedral as a backdrop. Huge sterling-silver Elsa Peretti Heart and Bean sculptures sat in the middle of the table, along with the orchid sprays. Sitting at the table in his customary mirrored sunglasses, surrounded by mirrors, Halston could be quite intimidating to new clients and staff if he so desired. Halston Enterprises occupied the entire floor and consisted of a primary design space (about 1,000 square feet, lined with mirrors and glass, overlooking Fifth Avenue), together with a workroom space, the JCPenney division, and Halston's domain.

Each day was scripted to the minutest detail. Lisa Zaye, who succeeded Faye Robson as Halston's administrative assistant, announced his imminent arrival. In anticipation, Bill Dugan,[1] Halston's right-hand man, double checked with staff to verify that all of the details of scheduling and fittings were in order. Another staffer placed on Halston's desk a new pad of legal paper and a fresh box of black Pentel markers for note taking and sketching. The

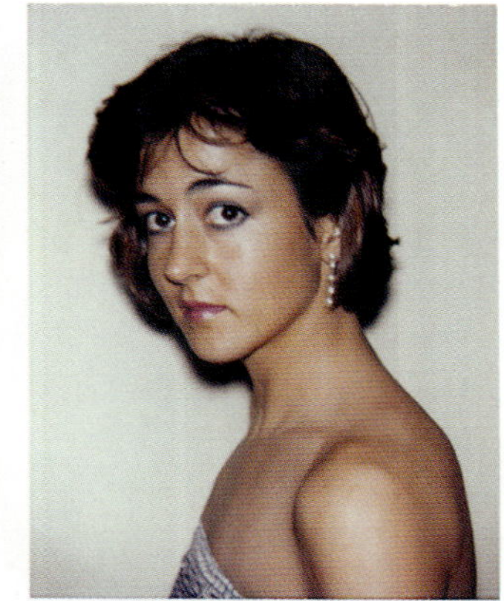

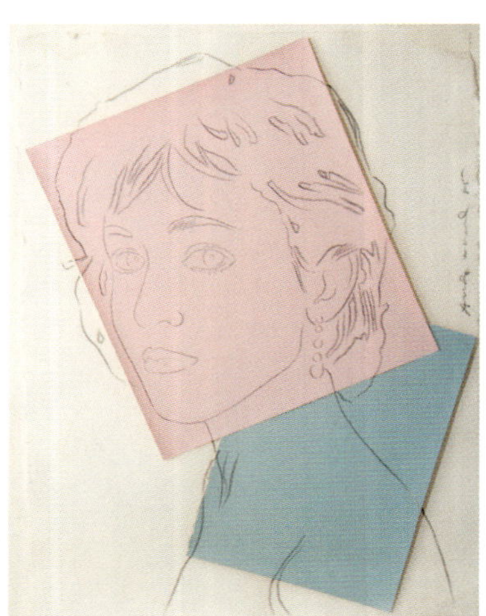

TOP
Andy Warhol
Lesley Frowick (Halston's niece), 1985
Polaroid™ Polacolor ER
4 ¼ × 3⅜ in. (10.8 × 8.6 cm)
The Andy Warhol Museum, Pittsburgh; Contribution The Andy Warhol Foundation for the Visual Arts, Inc., 2000.2.61

BOTTOM
Andy Warhol
Lesley Frowick, 1985
Screen print and collage on paper
Sheet: 23 × 31 in. (58.4 × 78.7 cm)
Courtesy the Lesley Frowick Collection

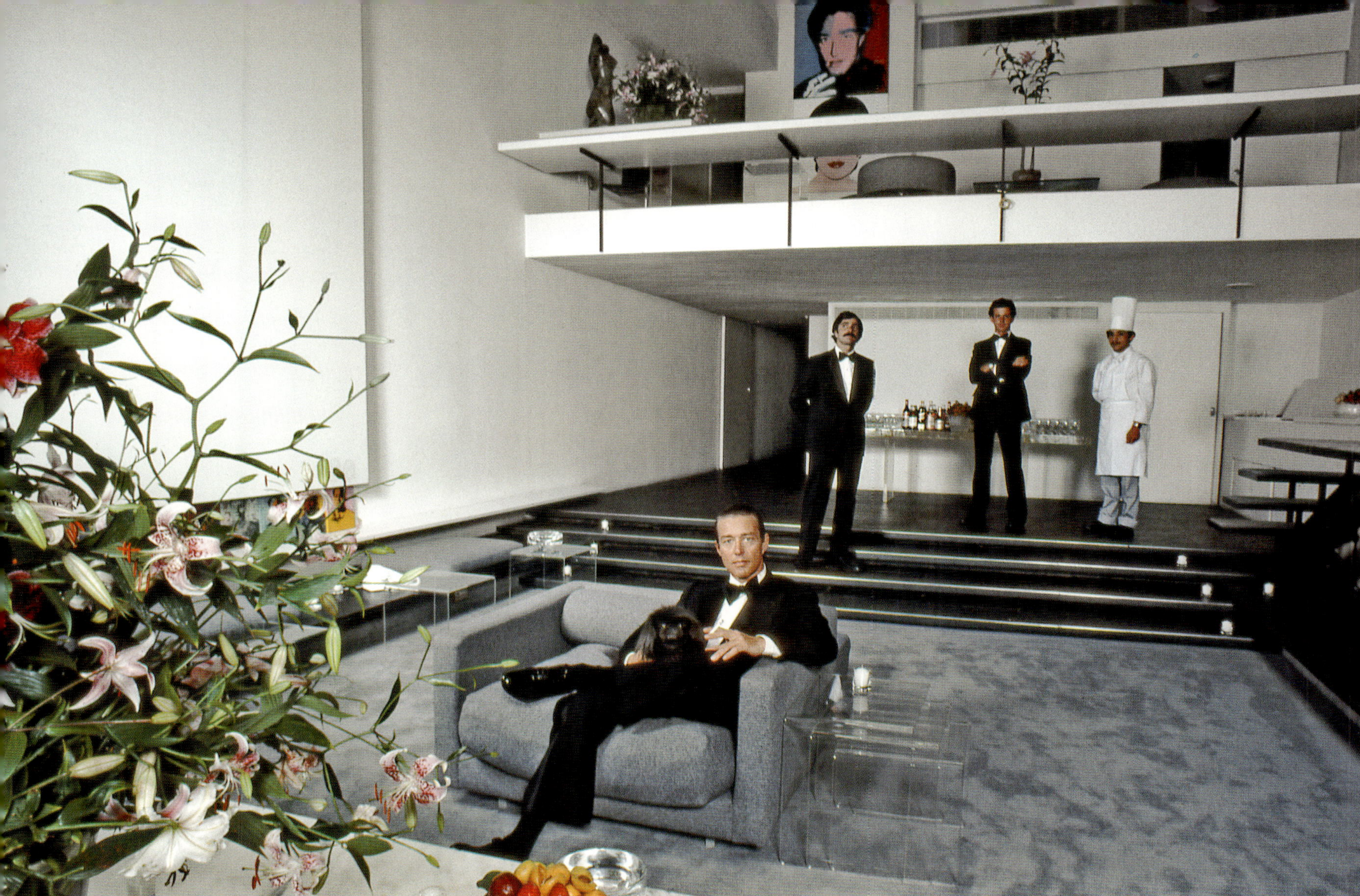

log of calls and appointments was reviewed and all the prototypes for fittings were prepared neatly on the garment rack in the design room. Everything down to his dry cleaning was readied in the proper spot. All employees were required to wear black so there were no visual distractions in the mirrors while he designed. He wanted absolute order and efficiency. Halston abhorred clutter.

Hermès briefcase in hand, Halston always arrived perfectly groomed and tan, emanating the scent of Z-14, with his overcoat gracefully draped over his shoulders. Briefings by Lisa, telephone calls, and meetings were finished in the morning to clear the decks for designing during the rest of the day. He continually sketched ideas, whether at his desk having conversations with people or at home in his living room on 63rd and Park. His legal-size sketchpad, which worked best for his large hands, was never too far from reach.

I was put through the paces immediately, thrown in to assist on multiple projects, including preparations for the Resort '84 collection, fittings for the Martha Graham Legion of Honor extravaganza in Paris, and designs for the JCPenney lines. Tape measure in hand and notebook nearby, Halston showed me how to take the perfect measurements of a female body—shoulders, bust, waist, and hips. He entrusted me to provide these dimensions for all the women in his personal entourage for the upcoming Paris trip. The clothes from his latest Fall collection were being altered to fit each of us. We were to be seen wearing his designs at every official event in Paris.

For the most part, my role was to support Halston or Bill. If they asked for anything to inspire or complement a new design, the design-room drones (me included) were expected to find it. I accompanied the clothing, with Halston's designated illustrations, to shoots at Hiro's and other fashion photographers' studios.[2] I learned to prepare the garments with a steam iron and matched correct garments and accessories to the selected models. I also performed a light amount of styling during the shoots.

While trying to learn the ropes I often stopped just to watch Halston work. I thought his hands were beautiful—no one could tie an obi into the perfect square-knot bow as gracefully as he.

Halston in his Paul Rudolph–designed Manhattan townhouse
Photograph by Harry Benson

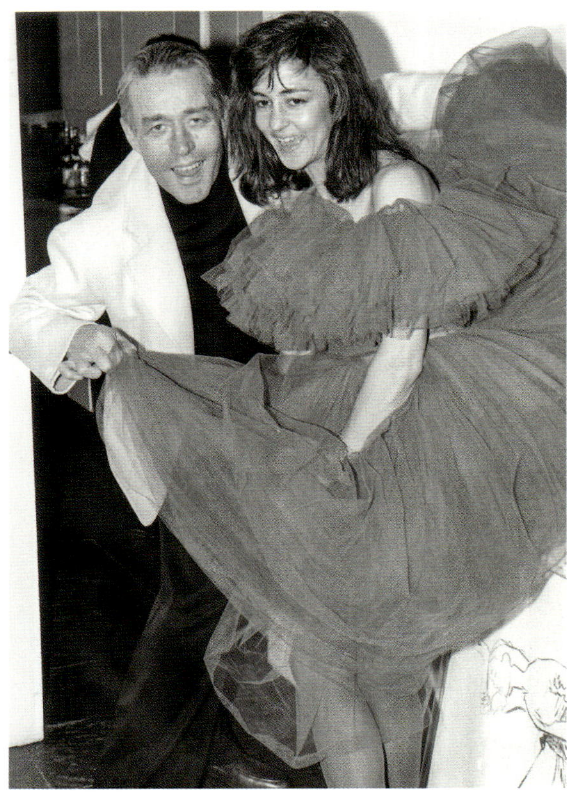

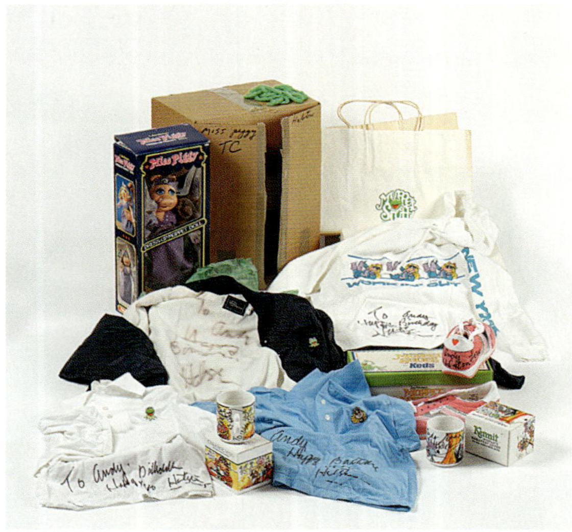

TOP
Halston and Lesley Frowick celebrating their birthdays, April 23, 1988
Courtesy the Lesley Frowick Collection

BOTTOM
Andy Warhol
Time Capsule 471, 1980–83
Miscellaneous Muppet souvenirs signed by Halston and given to Warhol on his birthday
The Andy Warhol Museum, Pittsburgh; Contribution The Andy Warhol Foundation for the Visual Arts, Inc., TC471

With clients who needed his guidance, he employed a gentle touch. The MTO (made-to-order) side of his business was a lens onto Halston's impeccable manners and charm. After a lively fitting in which clients usually were cajoled into buying far more than they needed, he treated them to lunches of lobster salad and entertained them with his saucy humor. These interactions were always very orderly, respectful, and carefully planned.

Halston loved a woman who kept her figure. I recall one fitting with Lucille Ball, who was in great shape and whose measurements hadn't altered a bit from prior fittings. The numbers on file suggested there were no less than forty designs ready on the rack for her in the MTO room. As DD Ryan and I assisted Ms. Ball with slipping the outfits on and off, Halston waited in his grand room to see how his various creations fit. She tried on both fancy and casual wear. The color selection and basic styles were theoretically perfect for her, but some, he agreed, didn't suit her. He had no problem saying, "That doesn't work on you," but he always offered alternate suggestions.

From season to season Halston's atelier functioned with a familiar rhythm, which was ramped up before a show. The long platform was positioned at a strategic vantage point so that the press could shoot both the models in front of the spires of St. Patrick's and the VIP section of guests. The gentle lighting and soft jazz music created a sexy atmosphere. Drawings by the house illustrator[3] were pinned to a corkboard to choreograph the flow of garments in progression. The picture in his head came to life as Halston rearranged the illustrations on the board in a game of strategy and speed: a stream of casuals, then new colors, and then fancy dresses and sparkly beaded dresses culminating in a wedding gown.

The beaded gowns were the real showstoppers. For the beadwork, Halston worked with the Kahn family business in India. Naeem Kahn[4] got his start working for Halston as an assistant. He personally escorted the Halston garments to the factory in India for beading and delivered them back safely. I recall one harrowing moment when Naeem arrived late with the garment bags—on the eve of the show. We anxiously removed them for the house model to don for prior approval. Halston had to see the final beaded product, which concluded the show, before deciding on the order of preceding fashions. Everyone waited for orders, which then had to be executed very quickly with the models. Even when we dressed the models to exact specification, Halston always wanted to put on the final touches himself, often altering a piece just as the young woman stepped onto the catwalk.

Featuring a United Nations of models—black, white, blonde, redhead, rail thin, and larger proportioned—Halston's fashion shows broke every social barrier. In a moment of campiness years earlier, he invited the vaudevillian Pat Ast to the catwalk; modeling a plus-size hand-painted caftan, she sang a show tune as she marched down the aisle flapping her fan. His regular models included Karen Bjornson, Nancy North, and Chris Royer, who were American blondes; Marisa Berenson, a brunette of European descent; and Naomi Sims, Alva Chinn, and Pat Cleveland, all African Americans with very different looks.

His group of "regulars" became widely sought after. Additional models were hired from Wilhelmina. During a casting call, Halston looked for self-assuredness and someone who had a natural movement. He also had two house models, who modeled at the collections and did some print work as well as the day-to-day fittings. Halston strove for absolute control over his presence—the way he groomed his models and himself, and how he chose his words, whether to inspire, sting, manipulate, or praise. He made "suggestions" that, when delivered, were understood as commands. "Don't you think it would be better to tie it this way?" It was always done to his liking. He could put people on edge or at ease.

From the outside it appeared that Halston and Warhol were always at ease with each other. They were very close and spent a great deal of time together. They were invited to all the same parties, and between them they either dressed or painted all the stars in attendance. Halston appreciated Warhol's business sense, his campiness, and his creative output. That said, his nickname for Andy had a witty bite: "The Coal Miner's Daughter," after the title of the Loretta Lynn biopic starring Sissy Spacek. The movie had just come out, and since Andy was from Pittsburgh, a place Halston associated with coal mining, the nickname stuck.

Halston purchased many of Warhol's artworks and recommended to many of his clients that they commission portraits from Warhol. His own commissioned portraits by Warhol were hung strategically to accentuate the soaring three-story height of his living room. Works by Warhol came into and went out of Halston's house on a regular basis. Newer pieces seemed to find a temporary home propped up along the walls of the living space. At one point I remember a dozen *Mao* paintings lined up in a row in the large room. The bulk of his collection was held in a spare room on the third floor, adjacent to the room where I lived for a year. Halston also collected works by friends such as Marisol, Hiro, Arman, Isamu Noguchi, and Larry Rivers, but there were more Warhols than works by any other artist.

His New York townhouse, designed by the architect Paul Rudolph, was pristine and virtually devoid of furniture. I remember asking, early on, "Don't you want some furniture in here, like a French country armoire or some snazzy Louis XIV chairs?" His reply was swift and firm, "I don't wish to live in the past, my life is now and modern." I believe that was one of his mantras. The ever-revolving collection of art was Halston's preferred decoration. He honored Rudolph's philosophy of allowing the house's architectural elements, enhanced with monochromatic tones, to predominate.

Halston's domestic help provided all the required comforts. Mohammed was Halston's loyal butler, and Viola his devoted cook. She made sure that he had just what he needed—the perfect cup of tea and toast served on his plain white Limoges china. Viola was a very sweet, church-going woman who reminded me of my grandmother Hallie Mae (Halston's mother). She always sported a smile and had something nice to say. There was extreme mutual respect between them. She knew Halston's culinary likes and dislikes and cooked solid American meals. Halston loved her fried chicken, remarking, "She can really drag a chicken through a pan." Cooking mostly at the Olympic Tower kitchen, she prepared the meals exactly the way he liked; they were sent home with him in the evening or bundled up in large black tote bags for his weekend trips to Montauk.

Viola did the lion's share of the cooking, but all who knew Halston can attest to the fact that he liked to cook, too. His copy of *The New York Times Cook Book* was completely dog-eared. After he saw me trying to mash ground meat with a wooden spoon, he demonstrated how to gently pat it so that "the veins can be seen as though it just came out of the grinder, ever so slightly handled," in order to make the perfect hamburger. He purchased locally grown beefsteak tomatoes and cut them into thick slices lengthwise to show the "beautiful design of Mother Nature." Garlic never crossed his threshold; he thought it too pedestrian. Instead, for dinner he liked to dress up a baked potato with a heaping tablespoon of Beluga caviar and complement it with a bib lettuce and endive salad. He appreciated food as much for its taste as for its presentation. Like everything surrounding Halston, it had to look pretty.

Warhol's house in Montauk also went under Halston's beautification treatment. Halston rented the seaside compound for a number of years and filled the space with furnishings and friends. I was lucky to spend many weekends there, relaxing, eating, laughing, and, often in the evenings, watching movies.

One weekend in the summer of 1984, Halston brought out a videotape recording of *Entertainment Tonight*. The episode featured Miss Piggy shopping for a wedding dress from Halston's Resort Collection. We all got a big kick out of the concept, but Halston took it to the next level. With the group's assistance he drafted a letter to Miss Piggy and Kermit the Frog, congratulating them on their nuptials. Partially to acknowledge the nod to his collection, but also as a good marketing move, Halston offered Kermit a selection of his licensed grooming products, including a bronzing gel that "could perhaps enhance your remarkable skin tone" and a bottle of Z-14 to "give an added boost to your already confident posture." In return, Jim Henson reciprocated with a box full of Muppets memorabilia. It was a timely offering—very close to Andy's birthday. Halston gave all the various Muppet mugs, T-shirts, and dolls in boxes to Andy as a gift, signing each one "To Andy Happy Birthday love Halston" on the actual item. Andy used to love to sign anything, thus turning it into "art." I was delighted to find out during the making of this publication that Andy saved these items in his *Time Capsules*.

On another August weekend, two years later, Andy, Jon Gould, and Keith Haring came to Montauk to celebrate Andy's birthday (August 6, 1986), which, unbeknownst to any of us, would be his last. Halston and I schemed as to what we would do with the weekend visitors. He said Andy wouldn't take a walk on the beach unless he was completely covered, due to his skin sensitivity. Sure enough, Warhol emerged wearing a long-sleeve shirt, parasol in hand, and zinc ointment on his face, ready for a stroll on the sand. Later we prepared dinner—breaded flounder, homemade French fries, and thick-sliced tomatoes—and played a surprise birthday game of pin-the-tail-on-the-donkey afterward. Everyone got a spin, and, as I recall, we allowed Andy to win.

In the morning, seated at a table in the sun-drenched kitchen, Halston did an interview with Keith for *Interview* magazine. It was an education for me, as I didn't know much about him other than that he was a young, wild artist who kept getting into trouble for painting graffiti in the subways. After Keith, Andy, and Jon left, Halston bought dozens of terra-cotta pots and painted them with gold felt-tip pens in astonishing graffiti designs. Apparently Keith had inspired him. I think he was testing himself to see if he could do it, too. He was too shy to let them be seen in public, so chances are the pots were cast aside when he moved from Montauk.

Few people know how devoted Halston was to his family. He invited relatives to many gatherings at the beach and always asked the extended family to dinner when they were visiting New York. And for anyone in the family getting married—nieces, sisters, and in-laws—Halston designed the wedding gown. He created a goddess-style dress for my stepmother, Ann. It had layers of diaphanous chiffon, in light shades of beige, pulled together at the waist with a leather obi. He knew her measurements so he just sent it to her wrapped up in a box—couture fit in ready-to-wear speed.

Although Halston derived pleasure making so many women happy with his dresses and designs, the management of the business he had built brought him a great challenge. When he sold his company to Norton Simon in 1973, he was able at first to retain a certain guarantee of design control. However, by the mid-1980s, the company had been bought and sold numerous times over, leaving Halston with less control over his own brand at each turn. He tried to maintain the power of positive thinking in spite of legal problems. My uncle was losing the thing he loved most, working and creating under his own name. In October 1984, Halston left the offices at the Olympic Tower and did not return.

The blows continued to strike. One evening in 1987 I was invited to the traditional Sunday dinner at Halston's. I remember arriving and having Halston buzz me in from his upstairs suite; Mohammed was off for the night. I fixed myself a drink in the kitchen and called up the stairs with some idle conversation. I didn't realize Halston was composing himself on the mezzanine. Immediately I could detect tension in his voice, "You didn't hear the news?! Andy died." He was noticeably upset, but I didn't believe what he was saying. Fred Hughes had telephoned and told him the improbable; Andy had died from complications following his gallbladder surgery. During a recent visit, Andy had mentioned his pain and the impending surgery, but he conjectured that he couldn't die from such a simple procedure. We were all in shock.

The evening proceeded with sad discussions and speculations as to how this could have happened. Halston brought up the sad irony that Andy had miraculously survived being shot multiple times, "but a gallbladder operation was just routine." Halston talked of all the serigraphs that Andy had created to be auctioned at a benefit for Martha Graham's school of dance and how the auction might unravel without Andy.

I was convinced that it was a postmodern ruse; surely Andy would pop out onto the altar during his memorial service at St. Patrick's Cathedral, eventually scheduled for April Fool's Day. I liked Andy. He was quiet, funny, and curious. When Halston and I celebrated our birthdays, he gave us both presents. My last gift from him was an "I.O.U. one art." I never got a chance to cash it in.

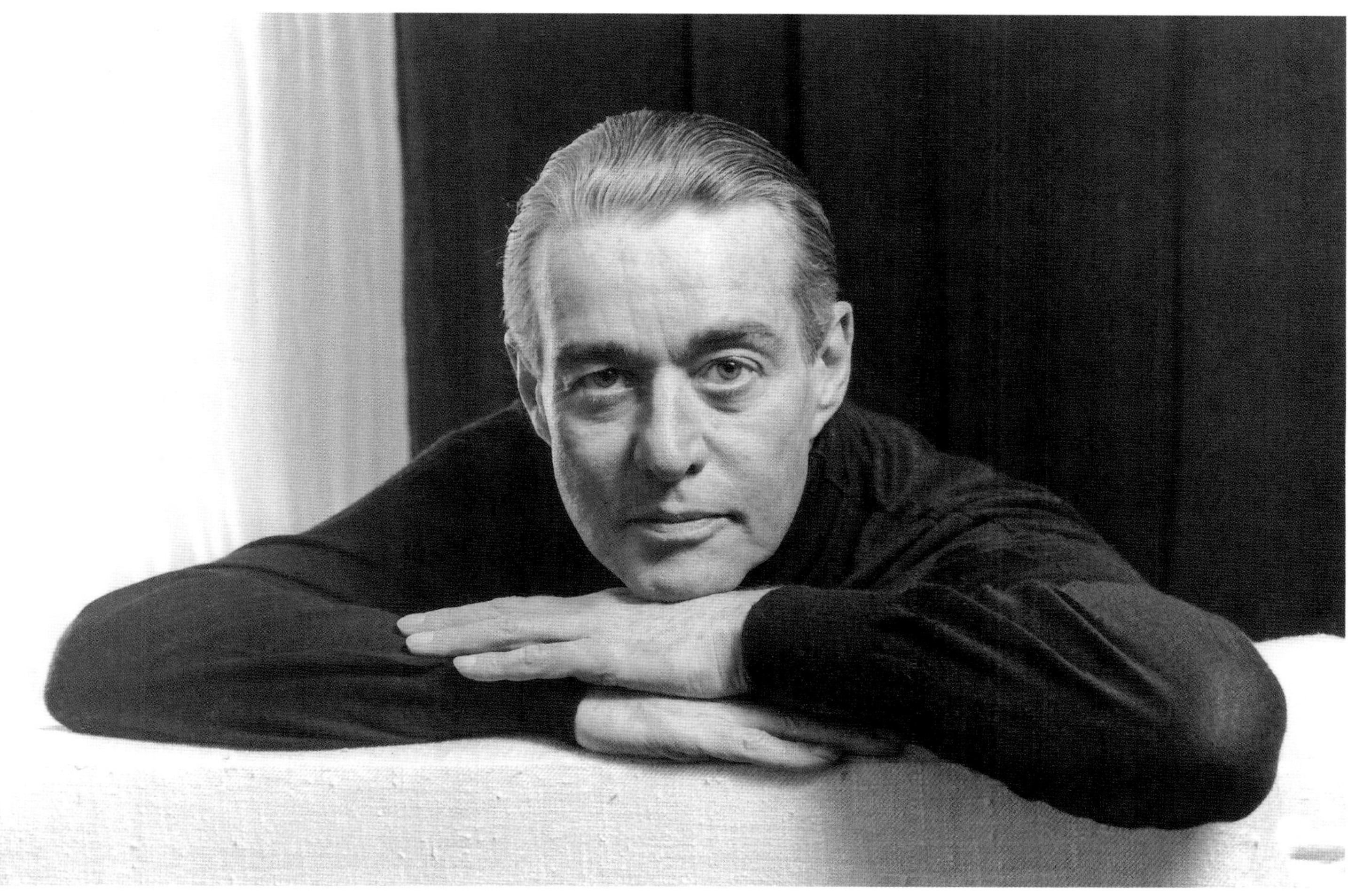

Andy's death was so sad, so sudden and without warning. It wasn't until the memorial service that it truly sunk in—a great friend and artist was really gone.

On reflection, I am so glad that I was able to be at my uncle's side during those difficult days. Ultimately I could do very little but lend my emotional support when his offices were taken over. Halston withdrew from designing and moved to California to live his final days with his doting family. I picked up my own photography work and, as the young do, I carried on.

But now, decades later, Halston's contribution to American style is celebrated—from his early window displays and his simple pillbox hat, to his iconic Ultrasuede shirtdress and sparkly sequined stage designs. My uncle left an indelible mark on fashion history and gave me the best seat in the house to watch the show. I will always remember what a determined, generous, funny, and expansive person he was. He put forth his best effort to make the world, and especially the people of his inner circle, as beautiful and comfortable as he could. As he would say, "I spoiled all of you."

Halston, last portrait at his home in New York, 1988
Photograph by Lesley Frowick
Courtesy the Lesley Frowick Collection

NOTES

1. Bill Dugan worked for Halston for twelve years. He left in the mid-1980s to start his own design business. He and his wife, the former Halston model Nancy North, opened a salon on 58th Street, off of Fifth Avenue, and coproduced two collections a year under the name W. S. Dugan Studio in the early 1990s. The line was picked up by Wilkes Bashford, Bergdorf Goodman, Saks Fifth Avenue, and Linda Dresner.
2. Halston usually hired Hiro for his shoots. Born in 1930, Yasuhiro Wakabayashi, known as Hiro, is an American commercial photographer. Hiro worked as an assistant to Richard Avedon in 1956 before launching his own career. He worked as a staff photographer at *Harper's Bazaar* from 1956 to 1975 and was named Photographer of the Year by the American Society of Magazine Photographers in 1969. Hiro is represented by Pace/MacGill Gallery in New York. See Richard Avedon, ed., *Hiro: Photographs* (New York: Bulfinch Press, 1999).
3. Joe Eula's illustrations are famously synonymous with Halston and document his designs throughout the 1970s. During my tenure in the offices, after Eula, the principal illustrator was Pui Yee with his assistant, Nancy Stone.
4. Naeem Kahn became well known after Michelle Obama wore a gown of his design to the Obama administration's first state dinner on November 24, 2009.

THE INIMITABLE HALSTON

Valerie Steele

"You're only as good as the people you dress," said Halston. Indeed, he repeated this statement so often that *Women's Wear Daily* described it as his "motto."[1] Halston was not only the most famous American fashion designer of the 1970s but also the country's first true celebrity designer. Tall and endowed with movie-star good looks, he counted Liza Minnelli, Elizabeth Taylor, Babe Paley, Bianca Jagger, and Andy Warhol among his friends and clients. It wasn't just that his clothes were featured in *Vogue* and *Women's Wear Daily* and on the covers of *Time* and *Newsweek*, Halston himself was on the cover of *People*, along with his friends "Liz and Liza."[2]

Always enamored of fashion, "Mr. Halston" began his career as a milliner, making his mark as the man who designed the pillbox hat that Jacqueline Kennedy wore to her husband's inauguration. This was an incredible coup for a milliner, but at the same time he recognized that hats were becoming less and less fashionable. With the help of Bergdorf Goodman, he astutely moved into apparel. Halston opened his eponymous business in New York City in 1968—just as the world was becoming more sexually and socially liberated. With a salon on the Upper East Side, he quickly established a reputation among wealthy, stylish socialites such as Mrs. William (Babe) Paley and Jane Engelhard, for whom he created luxurious, but delightfully easy-to-wear, made-to-order clothes.

These were not the stiff and formal clothes associated with the French couture, but they were also not "kooky" costume-party sixties styles. Instead, Halston offered deceptively simple-looking, often bias-cut dresses, trousers, and tunics—sophisticated minimalist designs that revolutionized fashion, making other clothes look fussy and outdated.

Up until this time, most fashion designers, especially in America, had been kept very much in the "back room." Halston, however, socialized with his clients, who became friends, and each person's celebrity reinforced that of the others. He also surrounded himself with an entourage, including the famous "Halstonettes," a shifting group of friends and models such as Anjelica Huston, Pat Cleveland, Chris Royer, and Elsa Peretti, who wore his clothes and popularized his style. Andy Warhol, who was equally attracted to celebrity, evolved a similar strategy, bringing together wealthy uptown art-world patrons and his own motley of downtown "Superstars."

In the 1970s, Halston went from one success to another. His clothes were prominently featured in the famous Versailles fashion show of 1973, in which a small group of American designers (Halston, Stephen Burrows, Anne Klein, and Bill Blass) triumphed over their French competitors, with a much younger, hipper, and more modern style of clothing and presentation. The same year, Halston negotiated a business arrangement with Norton Simon, in which the conglomerate bought Halston's name in exchange for an annual salary that rose from $150,000 to $500,000, as well as $7 million in stock options.[3] Over the course of the 1970s, even as Yves Saint Laurent, France's greatest and most influential designer, flourished, Halston retained his unique appeal. In 1976, the front page of *W* magazine explicitly compared Halston's "clean" style with Saint Laurent's "fantasy" fashions.

Halston
Dress, 1972
Ultrasuede
The Museum at FIT, 82.193.4; Gift of Mrs. Sidney Merians

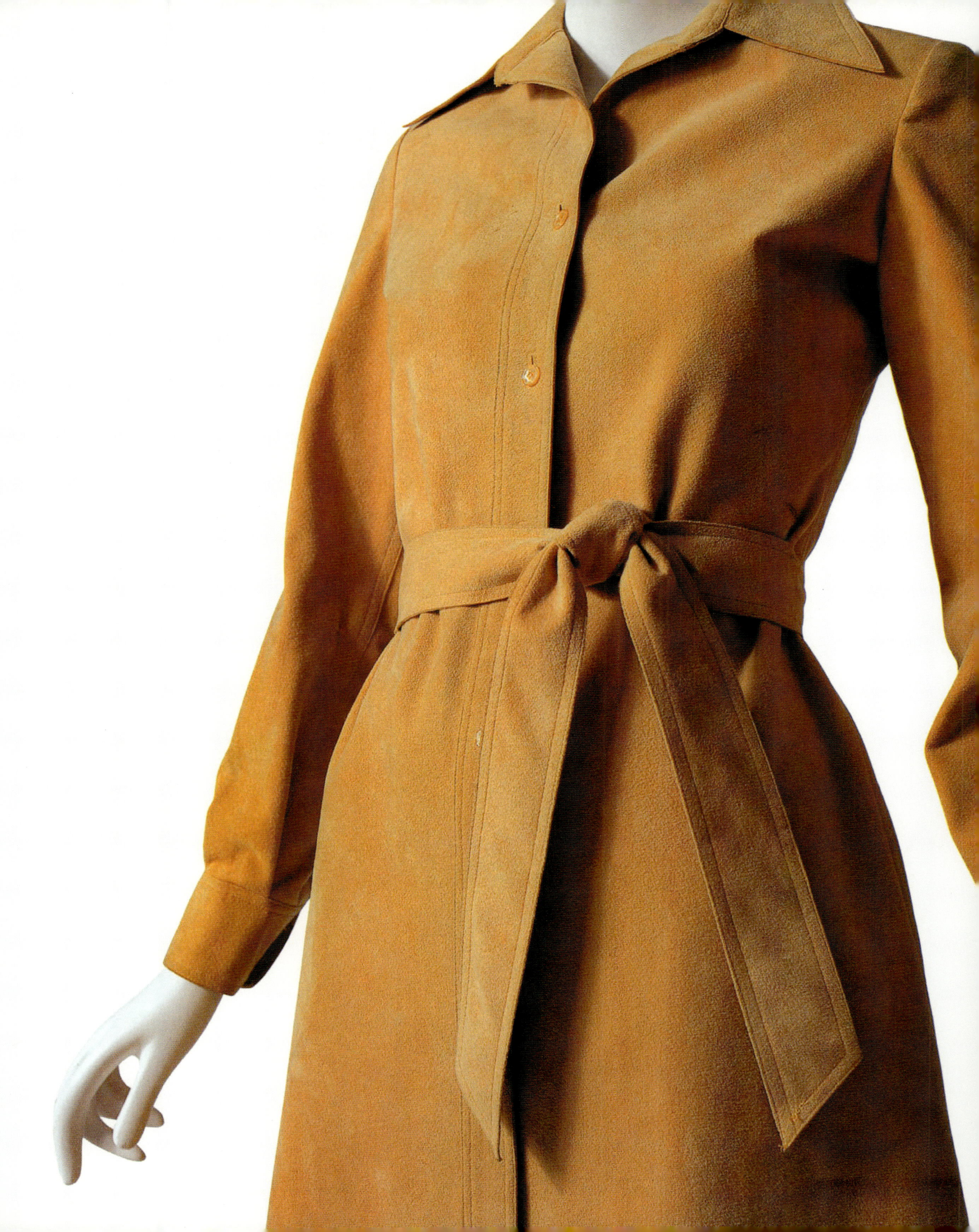

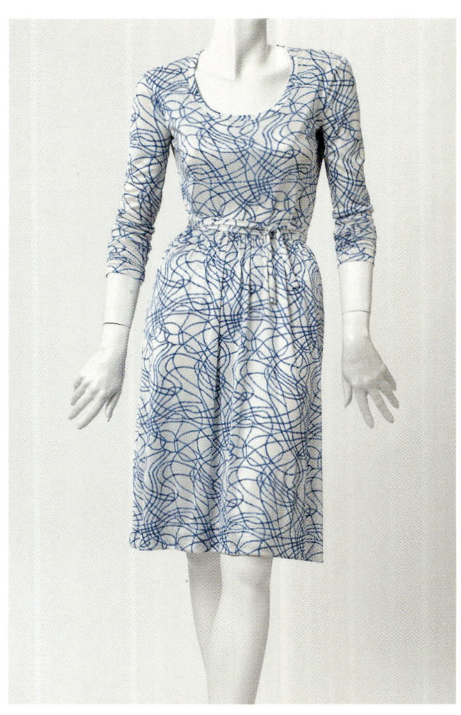
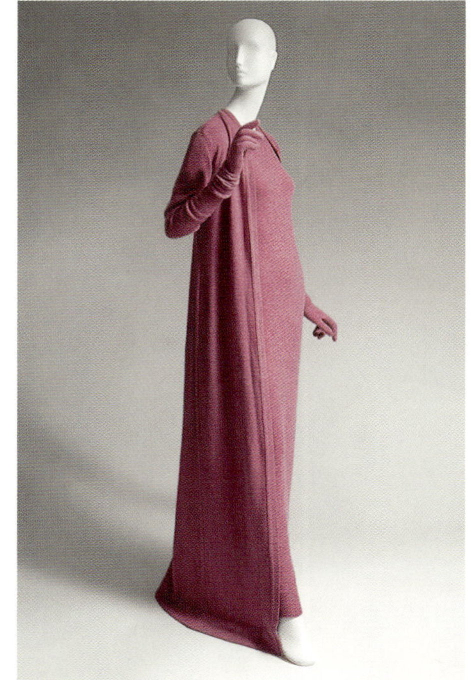
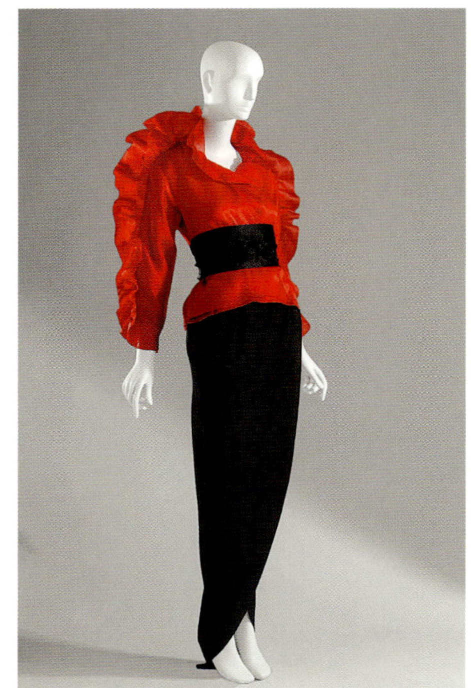
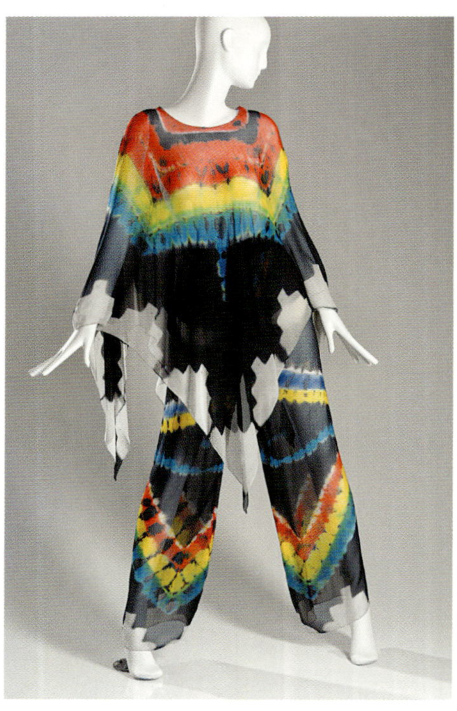
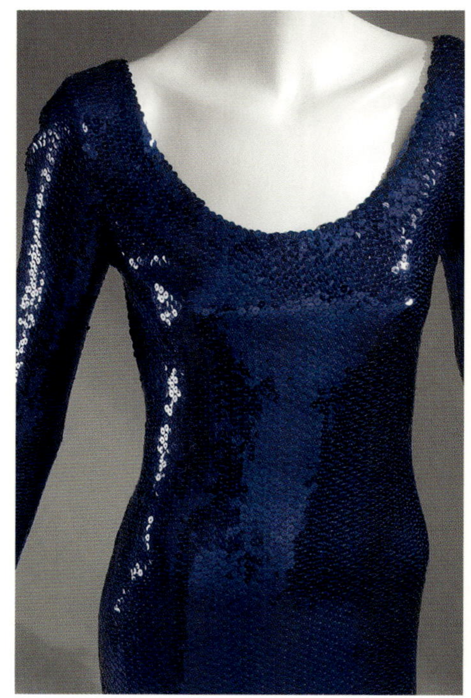
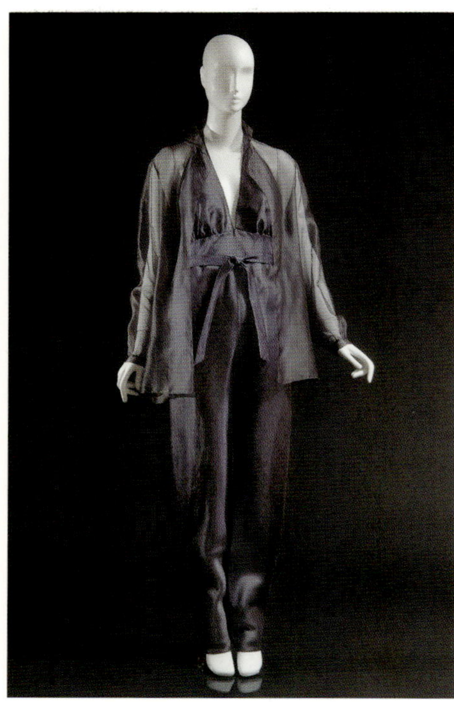

TOP
Halston
Two-piece dress, Halston V line, 1975
Poly-rayon
Photograph by Eve Prime
Collection of Chris Royer

BOTTOM
Halston
Ensemble, ca. 1974
Chiffon
The Museum at FIT, 80.7.17;
Gift of Lauren Bacall

TOP
Halston
Ensemble, 1972–73
Cashmere
The Museum at FIT, 88.29.2;
Gift of Elizabeth Pickering Kaiser

BOTTOM
Halston
Evening dress, 1972
Jersey, sequins
The Museum at FIT, 74.107.30;
Gift of Lauren Bacall

TOP
Halston
Two-piece evening dress, Spring 1981
Silk organza and crepe
The Museum at FIT, 2007.56.16;
Gift of Elizabeth Graham Weymouth

BOTTOM
Halston
Set, ca. 1972
Silk organza
The Museum at FIT, 82.237.12;
Gift of Lauren Bacall

Although Halston never received formal training in fashion design, he was brilliant at draping, and his taste and timing were impeccable. He made many important contributions to fashion, among them the Ultrasuede shirtdress, the bias-cut tube dress, the pajama, the cashmere sweater set, the caftan, the asymmetrical-neck dress, the sarong-tie dress, the halter dress, the jumpsuit, and the one-shoulder dress.[5] Obviously, Halston did not "invent" garments such as the shirtdress, caftan, or sweater set, which had long existed, but he put his own personal stamp on them and made them newly fashionable.

The shirtdress, for example, had been a classic of American fashion since the 1940s, when the pioneering sportswear designer Claire McCardell made it central to "the American look." But over time, it had become boring and unfashionable. Although Halston did not significantly redesign the shirtdress, in 1972 he reinvigorated it by utilizing the new machine-washable polyurethane material Ultrasuede. Halston's Ultrasuede shirtdress was immediately successful with high-end clients. Within a few years, more than 50,000 dresses had been sold, at prices that rose from $180 to $360 a piece. In 1975, *Esquire* dubbed it "the most popular pricey dress of all time."[6] Looking back more than a decade later, the fashion editor Grace Mirabella recalled, "For a lot of women it bridged the gap between what was ladylike and what was comfortable. It got them out of their tight, frilly clothes and into something *sportif*."[7]

Halston's clothes were elegant, but they were also "as casual as sportswear,"[8] and "as easy and light as a sweater."[9] In fact, Halston made the cashmere sweater set a signature style by experimenting with the fashion classic—for example, by transforming a sweater into a sweater dress and then a floor-length gown, with the cardigan turned into a luxurious coat. He made cashmere pullovers, T-shirts, and trousers—not just sweaters (which was what most people made from knitted cashmere). Cashmere is expensive, but not that expensive, and it is relatively easy to clean and care for. Many women copied Halston's personal style of tying a cashmere sweater around the neck. By 1974, he was dubbed "The Cashmere King."[10] As he said, "Cashmere feels good, it's easy . . . and it goes from day to night."[11]

One of the most significant aspects of Halston's style was the fact that many of his clothes were cut on the bias (with the fabric grain running diagonally), a technique that allows the garment to drape seductively around the body's curves. Designers had known about bias cutting since the nineteenth century, and many of the "body-worshipping" dresses of the 1930s were cut on the bias, in particular, those of the great couturière Madeleine Vionnet. Halston revived the technique in the 1970s, saying, "I just think bias is more sexy. . . . And since we are into such a sexy night period . . . I just find the bias cut the perfect answer. . . . There is nothing more of a turn-on than a fabric which hits the body the way the bias does."[12]

Halston's tube dresses, first introduced in 1974, were made completely on the bias, all in one piece, with a single seam spiraling around the body. This couture technique could be applied to a range of materials and garments, although it was much more difficult to produce ready-to-wear clothes this way. For custom-made clothes, Halston even cut sashes on the bias without seams, which necessarily wasted a great deal of expensive material, and all the details were hand-sewn.

One of Halston's most famous looks was the sarong-style strapless dress. The sarong is an ancient, non-Western style, essentially a rectangle of fabric. It had been adopted by Hollywood in the 1930s, but Halston discovered it accidentally. "We were on vacation in his house on Fire Island," Chris Royer later told the *New York Times*. "I was wrapped up in a big bath towel, and he said, 'come here,' and turned me around and that's how he came up with the design."[13] Since Americans were not used to clothing that was wrapped and tied, adjustments were made so that the sarong dress would not fall down.

The caftan was another traditional garment that Halston brought back into fashion. Originating in the Middle East, the caftan had been introduced into Europe from the Ottoman Empire as early as the thirteenth century. In the 1960s, hippies traveling in North Africa had brought back caftans, and the designer Rudi Gernreich had proposed it as a "unisex" garment. From Halston's perspective, the caftan provided an opportunity to dress women of all sizes and ages in an elegant, "timeless" design. Whereas many of his designs looked best on tall, slender women, he emphasized, "The caftan did the most for every woman, especially the heavier woman."[14] For example, when Halston and Warhol collaborated on a controversial performance at the 1972 Coty awards, the 200-pound Pat Ast jumped out of a birthday cake wearing a black sequined caftan. Halston also made caftans for clients as physically different as Elizabeth Taylor and Martha Graham.

Halston's clothes married a minimalist aesthetic with luxurious materials. Deceptively simple-looking, his dresses, caftans, pajamas, and tunics were all made of comfortable fabrics such as hammered silk satin, silk charmeuse, silk chiffon, and the finest multi-ply cashmere. Even Ultrasuede, which was a practical

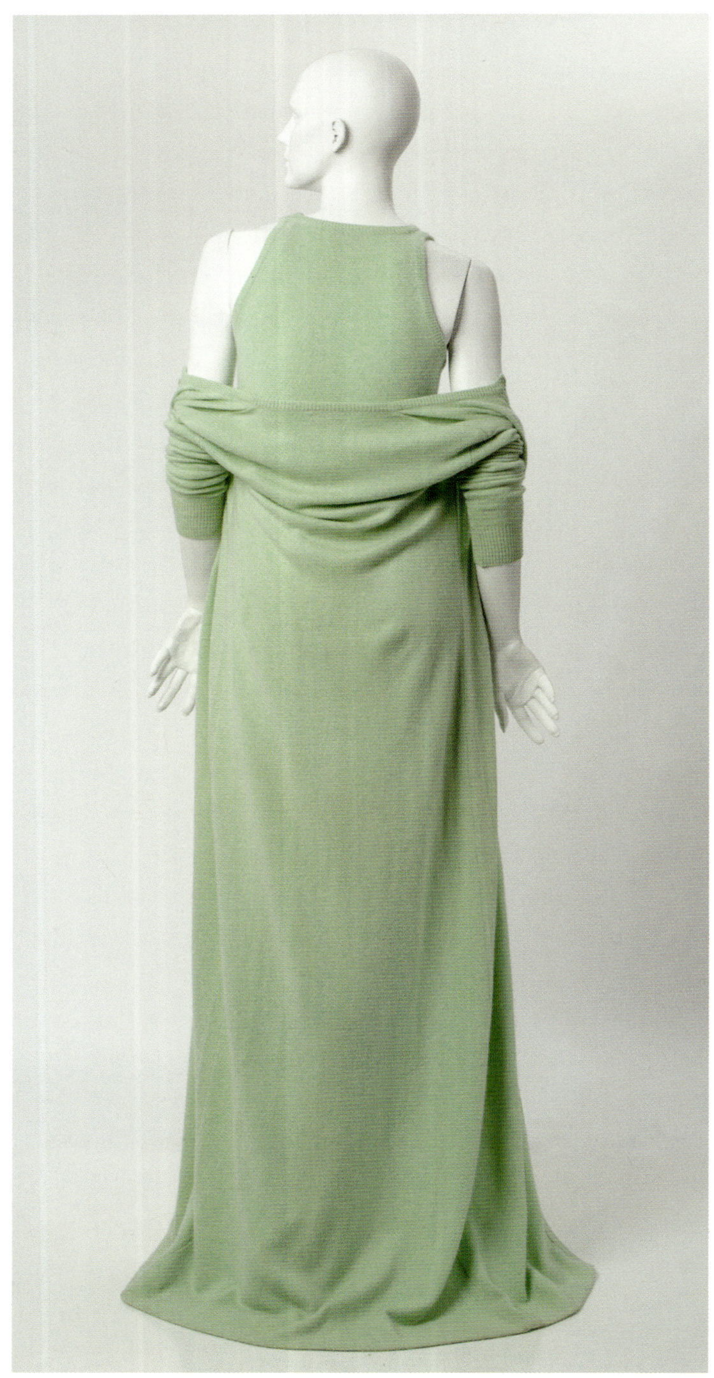

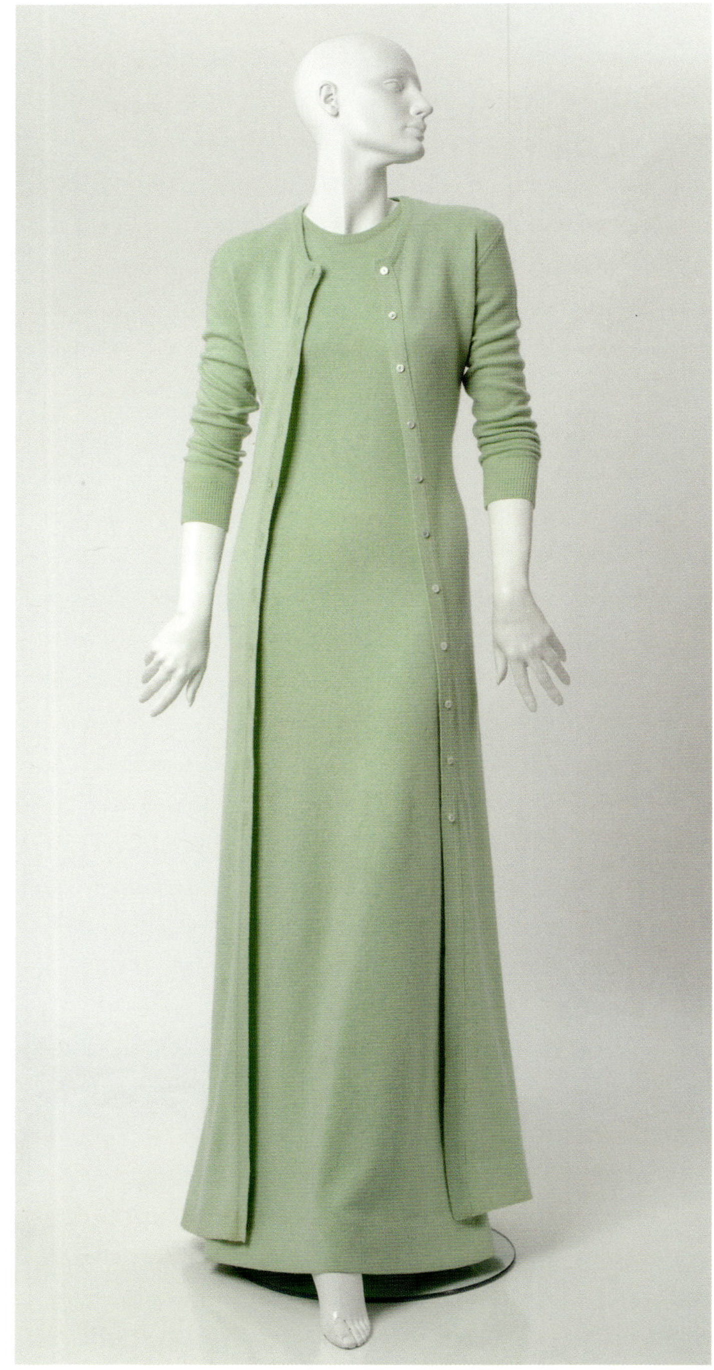

ABOVE
Halston
Sleeveless dress and cardigan set,
Made to Order, 1972
Cashmere
Photograph by Eve Prime
Collection of Chris Royer

OPPOSITE
Halston
Evening dress, 1972–73
Silk jersey
The Museum at FIT, 76.69.17; Gift of Lauren Bacall

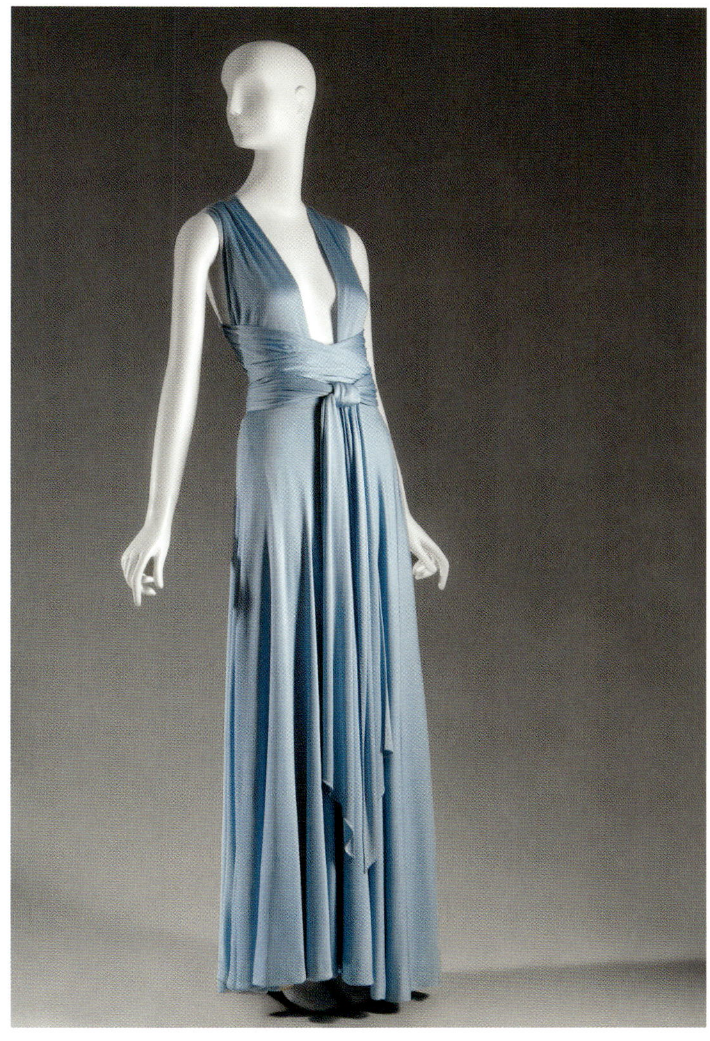

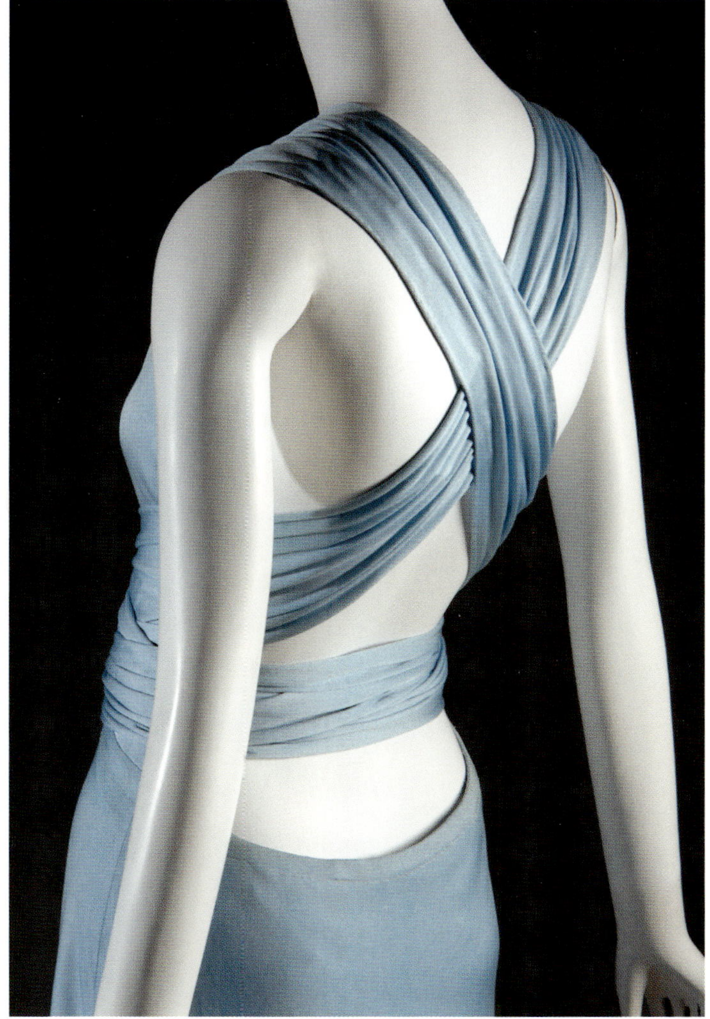

synthetic, had a lavish feel and the appeal of novelty. Halston eliminated superfluous trimmings and fastenings, but he was prepared to spend tens of thousands of dollars to experiment with materials and surface decoration for samples. Having launched a particular style in his custom-made collection, he often presented a similar style in his ready-to-wear line, capturing both the elite customer and the average woman who aspired to be fashionable.

Then, in time-honored celebrity fashion, Halston lost it all. By the early 1980s, sales were down, as trendsetters moved on to other designers like Calvin Klein. In 1982, a little more than ten years after Halston sold his company and the rights to his name to Norton Simon Industries, he agreed to design Halston III exclusively for the department store JCPenney in a six-year, multimillion-dollar licensing deal. Halston announced the decision to design clothing for women at budget-friendly prices. (Later, men's, children's, and home-furnishings lines were added.) When questioned about the rationale for fitting the JCPenney lines within the Halston brand, he recalled his all-American roots in Des Moines and mentioned that as a child he often shopped at JCPenney.

The announcement had a devastatingly negative effect on the designer's upscale Halston Originals line. Almost immediately, Bergdorf Goodman dropped Halston, a particularly cruel blow to the designer, whose fashion career in New York had begun at the very same store. Other high-end retailers agreed that Halston's association with JCPenney was detrimental to his market appeal and followed Bergdorf's lead. "High-low" collaborations are common in fashion today, but in 1982 the Halston III JCPenney line immediately moved the Halston name from "class" to "mass." Ultimately, he lost control of Halston Enterprises and was banished from its Olympic Tower offices.

In 1991, a year after Halston's death, the curators Richard Martin and Harold Koda organized an important exhibition at the Fashion Institute of Technology, *Halston: Absolute Modernism*, which made a strong case for Halston's importance as "a designer of essential form."[15] The Halston Archives and Study Room at the Fashion Institute of Technology were dedicated in 1993, and The Museum at FIT holds probably the world's greatest collection of Halston's clothes.

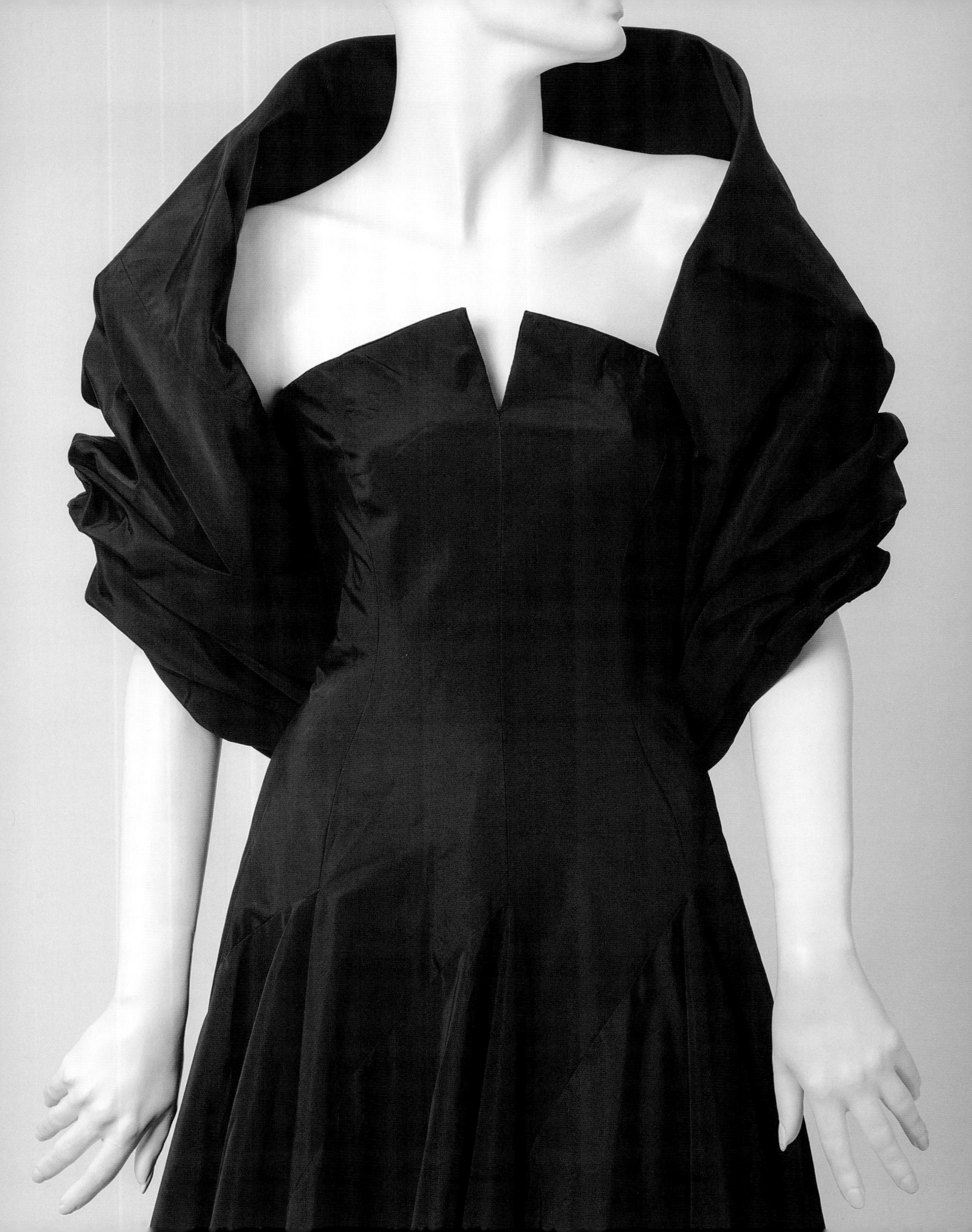

Yet sadly, Halston is remembered largely for his ignominious fall. He is a kind of cautionary tale about what can go wrong in a person's life and career. Although his significance in the history of fashion is not comparable to Andy Warhol's in the history of art (whose is?), Halston was unquestionably one of the most important modernist designers of the twentieth century, not only in America, but also in the world.

It is impossible to imagine the 1970s without Halston. But in retrospect, it is equally clear that his influence far transcends that decade. To give only three examples: Donna Karan's luxuriously simple styles continued his heritage, as did Tom Ford's slinky body-conscious designs for Gucci; and Narciso Rodriguez, probably today's greatest exemplar of seductive minimalism, is a great admirer of Halston's "clean and pure look."[16] From another perspective, Halston's prescient awareness of the power of "lifestyle branding" has also borne fruit in the empires of Ralph Lauren and Calvin Klein. But perhaps Halston's wholehearted embrace of the cult of celebrity may be his most lasting contribution to the culture of fashion. In this respect, his connection with Andy Warhol is especially significant. The 1997 exhibition, *The Warhol Look*, brilliantly demonstrated that throughout his life, Andy Warhol was deeply invested in glamour, style, and fashion.[17] So also was Halston, who was never simply a designer of women's clothing.

Glamour goes beyond fashion. Derived from an ancient Scottish word for "magic" and, by extension, "a deceptive or bewitching beauty or charm," glamour is the link between fashion and celebrity. In the context of Hollywood, glamour involves the image of the star; it is an artificial aura surrounding those who are photographed and talked about in the media.[18] Just as Warhol became famous far beyond the confines of the art world, so too did Halston break out of the fashion system to become part of pop culture. For both Halston and Warhol, the arc of fame has lasted for much longer than fifteen minutes. And, because this intersection of fashion, celebrity, media, and glamour remains so potent today, Halston and Warhol were prescient.

Halston
Evening dress with matching shrug/shawl, Made to Order, 1983
Silk taffeta; skirt cut on bias with eight inserts, figure 8 bias shrug/shawl
Photograph by Eve Prime
Collection of Chris Royer

NOTES

1. Francisca Stanfill, "Halston: 'I'm rather cozy,'" *Women's Wear Daily*, October 30, 1978, 5.
2. *People*, June 20, 1977, cover.
3. Steven Bluttal and Patricia Mears, *Halston* (London: Phaidon, 2001), 16–17.
4. Halston and Warhol's primary link was Halston's friend and lover, Victor Hugo, whom Warhol referred to as "Halston's 'art advisor,'" in Pat Hackett, ed., *The Andy Warhol Diaries* (New York: Warner Books, 1989), 3.
5. See Ena Szoda, "Halston: An Analysis of the Design and Style of Roy Halston Frowick through the Costume Collection and the Halston Archives of The Museum at the Fashion Institute of Technology," MA thesis, FIT, 1998. See also Elaine Gross and Fred Rottman, *Halston: An American Original* (New York: HarperCollins, 1999).
6. Jerry Bowles, "Will Halston Take Over the World?" *Esquire* (August 1975): 69.
7. Grace Mirabella, "The Halston Effect," *Mirabella* (July 1990): 71.
8. Patricia Bosworth, "The Halston Looks: From the Pillbox to the Herd Dress," *New York Times Magazine*, February 11, 1973, sect. 6, 75.
9. Edith Loew Gross, "Halston: Style . . . And Something More," *Vogue* (June 1980): 162.
10. Eugenia Sheppard, "The Cashmere King," *New York Post*, June 11, 1974, 41.
11. "New York Premiere: Cashmere," *Women's Wear Daily*, April 30, 1976, 1.
12. Halston, quoted in Gross and Rottman, *Halston*, 113–14.
13. Chris Royer, quoted in "The Way We Dressed," *New York Times*, Section IX, "Styles of the Times," March 14, 1993, sect. 6, 7.
14. Angela Taylor, "Halston's Groupies: 'Sweeticakes,'" *New York Times*, May 19, 1976, 49.
15. Richard Martin and Harold Koda, quoted in Gross and Rottman, *Halston*, 223.
16. Narciso Rodriguez, quoted in Gross and Rottman, *Halston*, 225.
17. Mark Francis and Margery King, *The Warhol Look: Glamour, Style, Fashion* (Boston: Little, Brown, 1997).
18. Valerie Steele, "Fashion," in Joseph Rush, ed. *Glamour* (San Francisco: San Francisco Museum of Modern Art in association with Yale University Press, 2004), 38–39.

VICTOR HUGO AND HALSTON: FASHION UNDER GLASS . . . VENEZUELAN STYLE

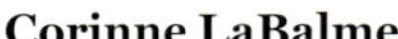

Corinne LaBalme

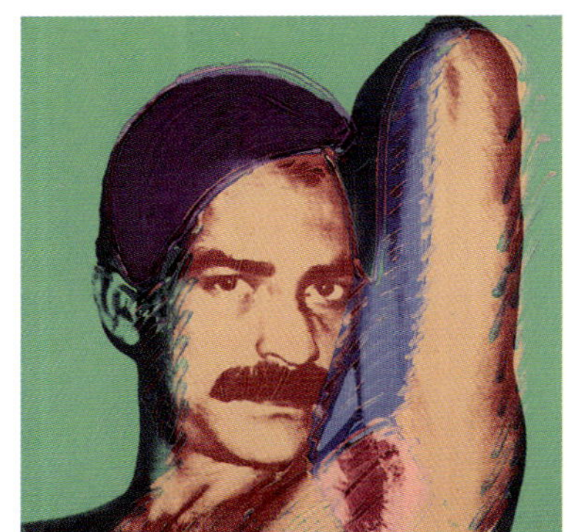

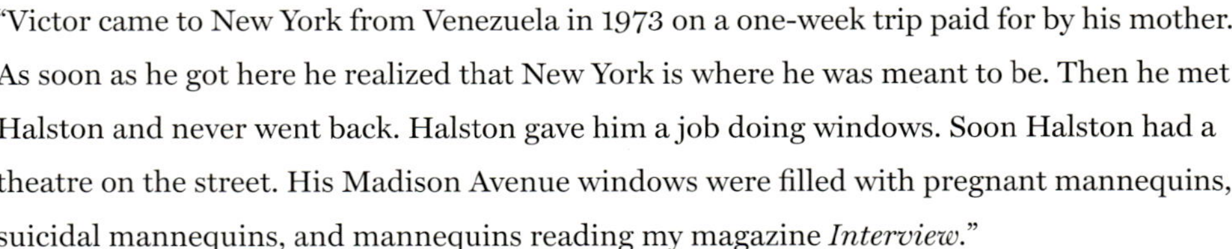

"Victor came to New York from Venezuela in 1973 on a one-week trip paid for by his mother. As soon as he got here he realized that New York is where he was meant to be. Then he met Halston and never went back. Halston gave him a job doing windows. Soon Halston had a theatre on the street. His Madison Avenue windows were filled with pregnant mannequins, suicidal mannequins, and mannequins reading my magazine *Interview*."

—Andy Warhol

In 1976 I joined Halston's ten-person entourage (which included a private cook and an Ivy League lawyer) as a serf-of-all-work with a sigh of relief, having spent a summer learning just how little art history degrees counted on the New York job market. At the time, Halston was a proto-Superstar, occupying most of a townhouse on Madison Avenue at 68th Street, with a duplex boutique, a couture showroom, nineteenth-century-style ateliers for evening and daywear, a storeroom packed with rolls of shimmery charmeuse, and a rabbit warren of dimly lit, Donghia-decorated offices for Halston's inner inner circle on the penthouse floor.

Did I say ten people?

There was an eleventh presence lurking on the scene—a dark, dashing enigma with no fixed office space—who to my ingénue eyes was by far the most glamorous. Victor Hugo wasn't his real name, but there wasn't much real about Victor except his Groucho Marx moustache and his XL man-parts, legendary on the bathhouse circuit. Artist, Factory fixture, Warhol confidant, and part-time prostitute, he swept into Halston's Paul Rudolph mansion in 1972 and slept there until he was kicked out years later, apparently for staging an unauthorized orgy. In the meantime, he'd taken over Halston's window displays, and part of my vaguely stated job description was supplying his props.

Victor never requested normal, seasonal items like Easter baskets or Christmas trees. His Thanksgiving display was a poultry apocalypse with chewed-up turkey bones scattered across the floor. Patty Hearst, machine gun in hand, robbed banks in impeccable Ultrasuede. Bald, marshmallow-white mannequins brandished whips and chains in their undies and, given their increasingly risky lifestyle, it was no surprise when they got knocked up. After very public pregnancies (plastic trash bags serving as pseudo-uteri), one of them bloodily miscarried with Texas Chainsaw-esque splatter in medias Madison Avenue. (That window managed to offend so many Upper East Side shoppers that it disappeared overnight.)

At this point, it would be nice to offer some pithy words of Victor's own about his guerrilla street theater, but despite our weekly conferences, I never understood much after "Darling . . ." Victor's Spanglish was overlaid with an impenetrable Caracas accent and—as he was the kind of guy who accessorized his T-shirts with Miss America tiaras—the macho,

ABOVE
Andy Warhol
Victor Hugo, 1978
Acrylic and silkscreen ink on linen
40 × 40 in. (101.6 × 101.6 cm)
The Andy Warhol Museum, Pittsburgh; Founding Collection, Contribution The Andy Warhol Foundation for the Visual Arts, Inc., 1998.1.577

OPPOSITE
Andy Warhol
Victor Hugo, 1981
Gelatin silver print
8 × 10 in. (20.3 × 25.4 cm)
The Andy Warhol Museum, Pittsburgh; Contribution The Andy Warhol Foundation for the Visual Arts, Inc., 2001.2.527

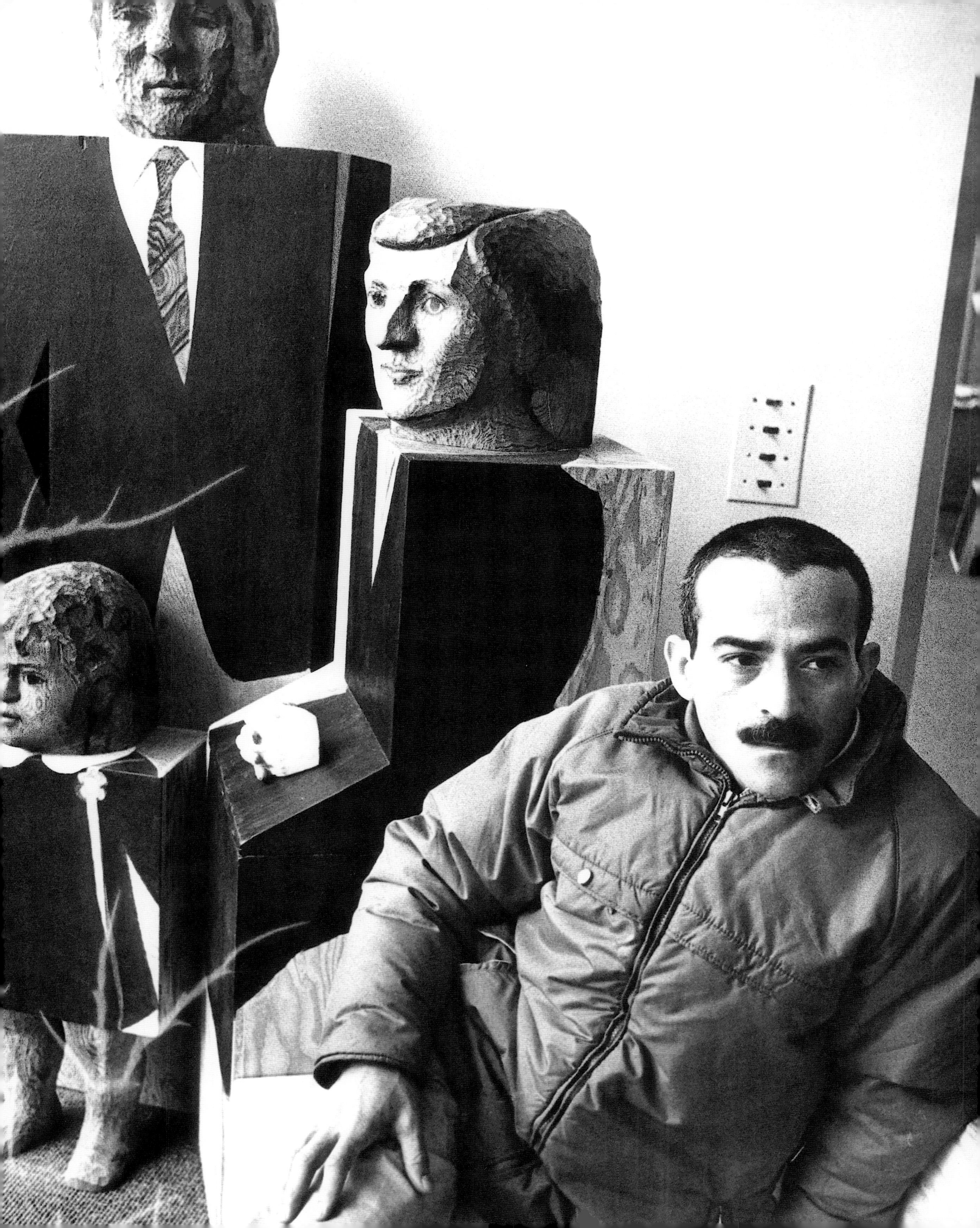

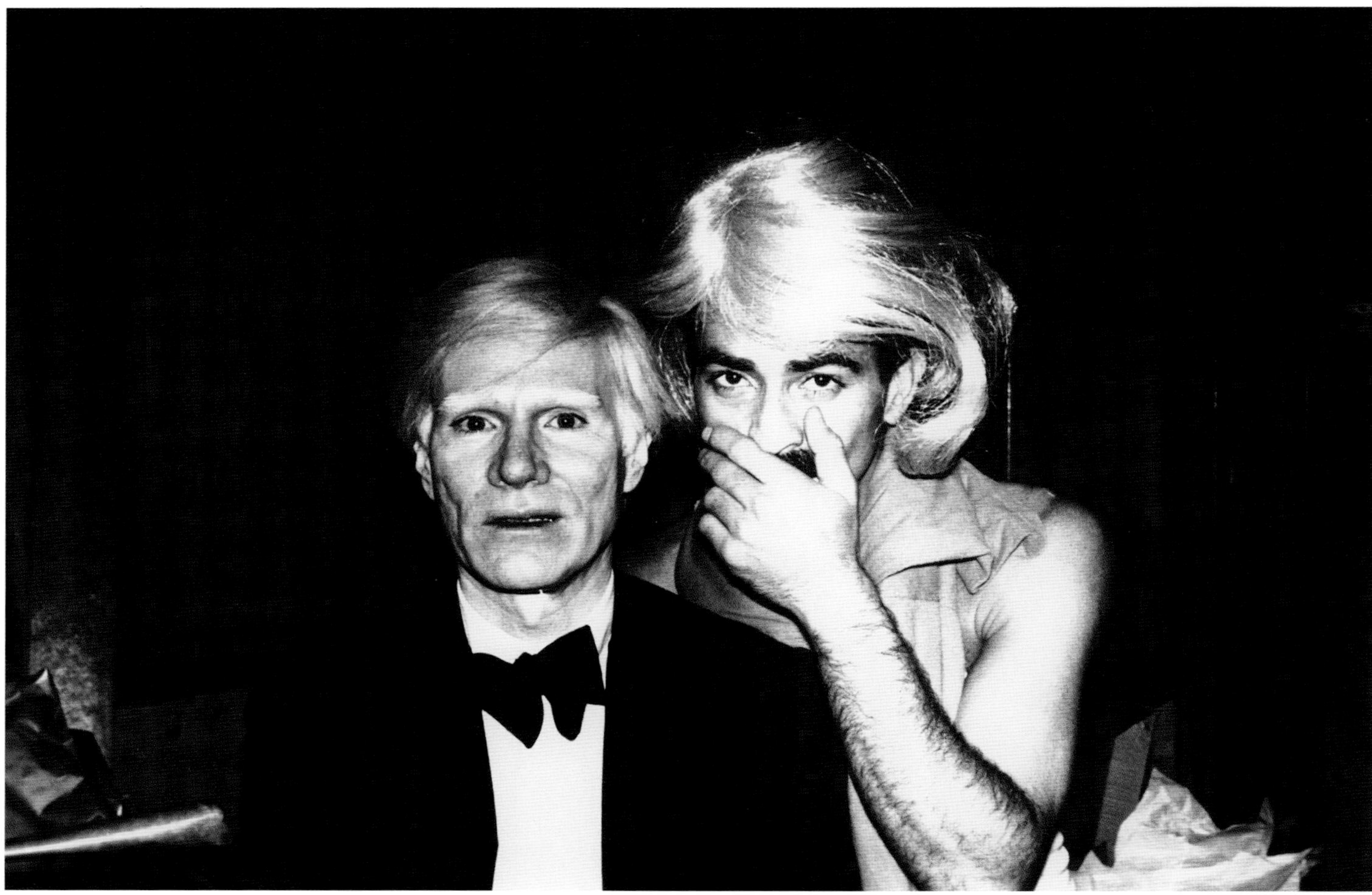

Central American boys in the mail room were no help at all when it came to translation, preferring to cross themselves and retreat to the next zip code whenever Victor crossed their path.

So Victor drew me pictures of what he wanted. Like the elephant. That was one of the few times I disappointed him. Though his heart was set on a live one, he cheerfully made do with a pink, bejeweled papier mâché animal on loan. I remained his "darling," perhaps because I held the purse strings on Halston's not-so-petty cash for household expenses. It was Victor who decided that Halston's budget-minded Soave Bolla wine should be replaced by Dom Pérignon. Obligingly, I ordered case after case until Halston threw a Midwestern thrifty fit about the sky-high liquor bills.

Just spilt Champagne . . . but it shows Victor's influence. Halston was an innovator on many fronts—think of the breakthrough perfume bottle, the JCPenney contract—but he was also a creature who clung slavishly to routine. He needed the same models for each fashion show, the same bratwurst from Schaller and Weber, the same Bob Lester orchids on his desk, the same scented Rigaud candles, the same black pens, the same white legal pads for his sketches. The slightest deviation from the norm enraged him. Victor, on the other hand, was 100 percent deviant.

And that's why Victor Hugo deserves more than a mere footnote in the Halston hagiology. While the exquisite bias-cut gowns that Halston constructed during his 1970s glory days stand up to the best of Balenciaga, they were timeless, rather than timely, creations. (Even Halston's employees got confused between last season's couture and next season's cruise wear.) Halston created dresses that would never go out of style, but Victor's dangerous windows gave the label contemporary street cred. Victor referred to these as his "weekly paintings," and they linked Halston to the Warhol cultural mystique; in fact, in 1975, Victor "carpeted" the boutique floor with copies of Warhol's *THE Philosophy of Andy Warhol (From A to B and Back Again)*. Though delighted to shock la bourgeoisie, Victor was relatively tame chez Halston. Over at the Factory, he was fully engaged with the *Oxidation* paintings and the notorious *Male Landscape* project. Halston regulars like

Andy Warhol
Andy and Victor Hugo, 1982
Gelatin silver print
8 × 10 in. (20.3 × 25.4 cm)
The Andy Warhol Foundation for the Visual Arts, Inc., FL06.00041

Happy Rockefeller, Barbara Walters, and Jackie Onassis never knew what they missed on the anatomical art front.

Victor introduced Halston to Warhol, and the formation of that terribly trendy triangle coincided with the onset of Halston's decline as a serious designer and his beatification as a pop phenom. There were other factors, of course. A new and thoroughly addictive style of nightlife took hold when Steve Rubell and Ian Schrager opened Studio 54 in 1977. The troublesome implications of selling the Halston "brand" to a super-straight, corporate cartel were just starting to surface as well. And since the medical profession had not yet determined the minimum daily requirement for cocaine, Halston's coterie self-diagnosed and snorted as much—or more—than they could safely inhale.

In January 1978, Halston moved his operation to the twenty-first floor of the Olympic Tower, kick starting a hubris-fueled Greek tragedy that Euripides could have scripted in ancient Athens. The fully mirrored offices were built to intimidate, and Halston—or "H," as we were now encouraged to call him—had morphed into a black-clad, tantrum-prone Darth Vader-ish figure, eyes shielded by mirrored sunglasses, who staggered into the studio on vampire time. The staff now dressed in black uniforms, meted out on a caste system. As I was now No. 9 on the roster, I got Halston V polyester instead of silk. (It still looks good.)

Visits from East 68th Street buddies whose passports had "Transexual Transylvania" visas were less welcome at the Olympic Tower, and thus, I gradually lost contact with Victor. He was still around though, offering artistic input on a freelance basis. Only Victor could have come up with the idea to spray paint the office foliage more "green" before a fashion show, an ill-fated initiative still referred to by Manhattan botanists as the "Great Fifth Avenue Fern Massacre."

Eventually, I forsook Victor Hugo for Victor Caraballo, another handsome Hispanic Halston protégé, who set up his eponymous design studio on 17 West 17th Street, only three blocks from Victor Hugo's Chelsea loft. The Victors didn't mix much socially, and without any conscious poaching, our client list soon included Halston/54 refugees like Altovise Davis, Lucie Arnaz, Peter Allen, and John DeLorean. I moved to Paris in the early 1980s and lost touch with the Halston crew.

In a quote that Victor Hugo must have overheard somewhere: *Joo anlee gut feefteen meenutees darling.* He certainly made the most of his, and I sincerely hope he's designing the 3-D window displays in Hades, and drinking Dom Pérignon *à volonté.* Any other scenario would be a waste of his talents.

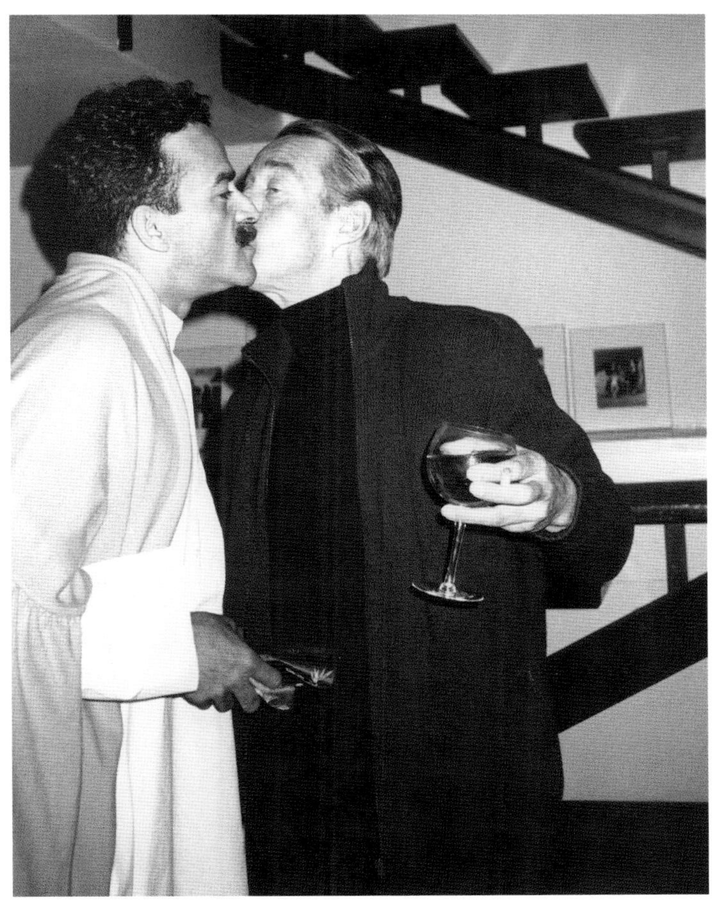

NOTE

Epigraph: Andy Warhol and Bob Colacello, *Andy Warhol's Exposures* (New York: Grosset & Dunlap, 1979), 42.

Andy Warhol
Halston and Victor Hugo, n.d.
Gelatin silver print
10 × 8 in. (25.4× 20.3 cm)
The Andy Warhol Museum, Pittsburgh; Contribution The Andy Warhol Foundation for the Visual Arts, Inc., 2001.2.705

CAMEOS AND CATWALKS: FASHION IN WARHOL'S FILM AND VIDEO

Geralyn Huxley

"Fashion was alpha and omega to Andy Warhol's visual world." —Richard Martin

Andy Warhol's nascent notion of glamour was inspired by the costumes of the Hollywood stars he watched as a boy. His early movie-fed fantasies allowed him to escape the poverty of his surroundings, his sensitivity and loneliness, and his discontent with his own appearance. As a child he collected photographs of his idols, and as a man he collected their clothing and ultimately transformed himself into a star in his own right. Glamour and fashion added excitement and romance to Warhol's life and allowed him to continually change his persona, a strategy that helped him achieve the lifestyle he always craved. Warhol's acute attention to style is reflected in much of his work, especially the moving images he created from 1963 until his death in 1987.

As Warhol matured during college and his early years in New York, his experience of fashion was expanded through working in commercial illustration and creating window displays for department stores and shops, most notably for Bonwit Teller & Co. In 1958, Warhol created a window for the Gilded Lily, the Madison Avenue shop of the clothing designer Joan "Tiger" Morse. In the 1960s, Tiger had a fashionable shop called Kaleidoscope on East 58th Street and managed the Cheetah boutique on Broadway and 53rd Street, next to the famous psychedelic club of the same name. She turned her fashion shows into parties and "happenings." One such show, staged around the swimming pool at the Henry Hudson Baths on West 57th Street, involved models using the diving board as a runway; later, drunken guests joined in, jumping into the pool with their clothes on. In 1966 Tiger opened a new space called Teeny Weeny at Madison Avenue and East 73rd Street, which showcased the futuristic fashions she made from materials such as plastic, synthetics, glass, paper, and found objects. Warhol called Tiger "an original" and shot footage of her in her boutique. He included it in his twenty-five-hour film ***** [Four Stars]*, which comprised more than eighty half-hour reels of color film shot between August 1966 and September 1967. It was shown one time on December 15–16, 1967.

Warhol, ever the keen observer, was always perceptive to style in others. Describing the look of the 1960s, he wrote: "The kids at the Dom [a nightclub on St. Mark's Place] looked really great, glittering and reflecting in vinyl, suede, and feathers, in skirts and boots and bright-colored mesh tights, and patent leather shoes, and silver and gold hip-riding miniskirts, and the Paco Rabanne thin plastic look with the linked plastic disks in the dresses, and lots of bell bottoms and poor-boy sweaters, and short, short dresses that flared out at the shoulders and ended 'way above the knee.'"[1] In the 1960s, Warhol also adopted a new look for himself, changing his persona as a commercial illustrator—baggy suit, white shirt, and bow tie—to that of a painter and a filmmaker. Like "the kids," he dressed in a leather jacket, boots, sunglasses, and the ubiquitous striped French sailor top with a boat neck and

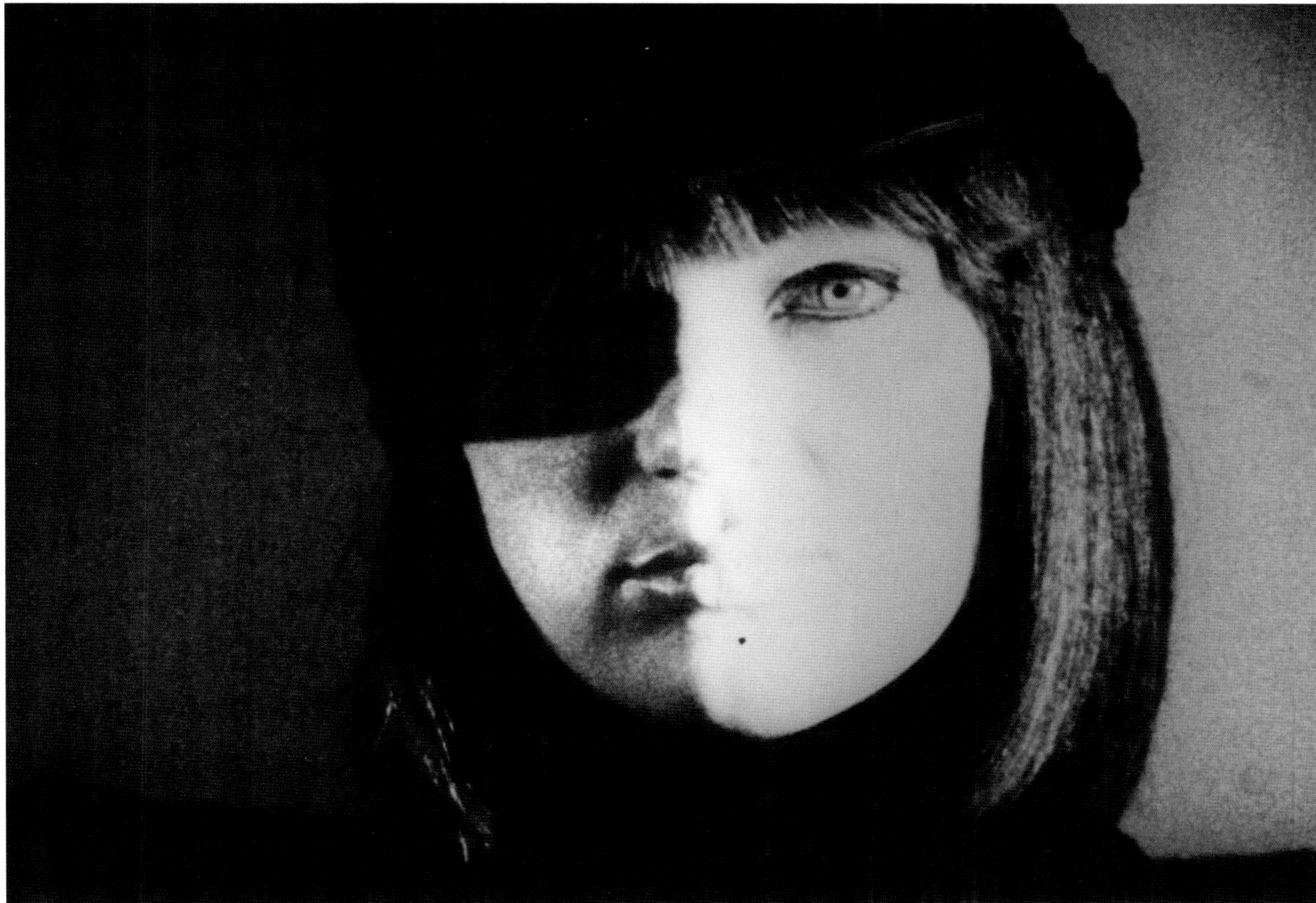

three-quarter sleeves. He sprayed his wig space-age silver. With this attire, he fit in with the beauties who populated his world.

Always drawn to stylish women, Warhol starred models in his films of the 1960s, elevating many of them to the rank of "Superstar" in homage to the Hollywood icons of his youth. And they, too, contributed to the new look through their exposure in film and print. In addition to the famous Superstars Edie Sedgwick, Baby Jane Holzer, and Nico, the Velvet Underground chanteuse, other marvelous models were part of the Warhol Factory scene.

In 1965, Donyale Luna was the subject of two of Warhol's *Screen Tests* and appeared in *Camp*. One of the first African American models, Luna met Warhol through the photographer David McCabe, who discovered her on the street in her hometown of Detroit. She later graced the pages of *Paris Match*, *Harper's Bazaar*, *Vogue*, and other high-fashion magazines. In her *Screen Tests*, she poses and preens, fluttering and voguing nonstop in front of Warhol's camera.

Andy Warhol
Screen Test: Ivy Nicholson
[ST232], 1965
16mm film, black and white, silent,
4.5 minutes at 16 frames per second
The Andy Warhol Museum, Pittsburgh

Before becoming a member of the Factory circle, Superstar Ivy Nicholson had been an extremely successful fashion model and cover girl in both Europe and America, appearing as an haute couture diva on the covers of magazines such as *Elle*, *Cosmopolitan*, and *Harper's Bazaar*. Warhol made the first of her seven *Screen Tests* in the fall of 1964 and thought she was "an original."[2] In the March 19, 1965, issue of *Life* magazine, an article titled "Underground Clothes" touted "bizarre styles to match avant-garde movies" and "reel swingers in provocative togs." Nicholson modeled clothes onto which were projected her Warhol film portrait. Warhol shot dozens of reels of film of her, including them in films such as *Couch*, *Soap Opera*, and *Loves of Ondine*. However, most were shown only as part of ****.[3]

Susan Bottomly, also known by her Superstar name International Velvet, was only a teenager when she appeared on the cover of *Mademoiselle* and met Warhol. As her modeling career took off

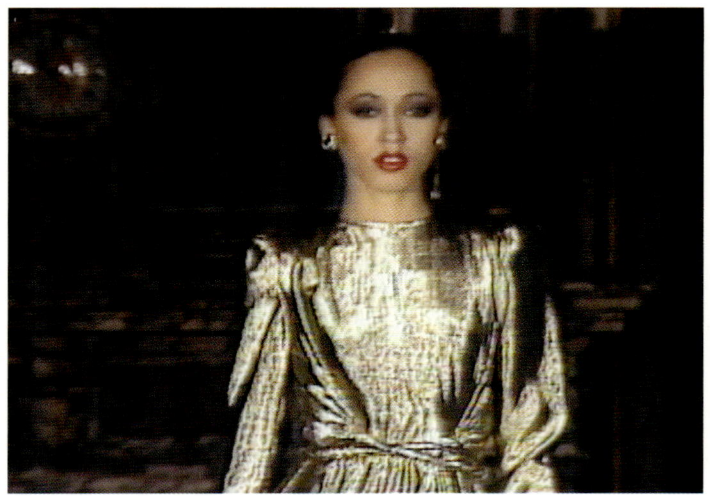

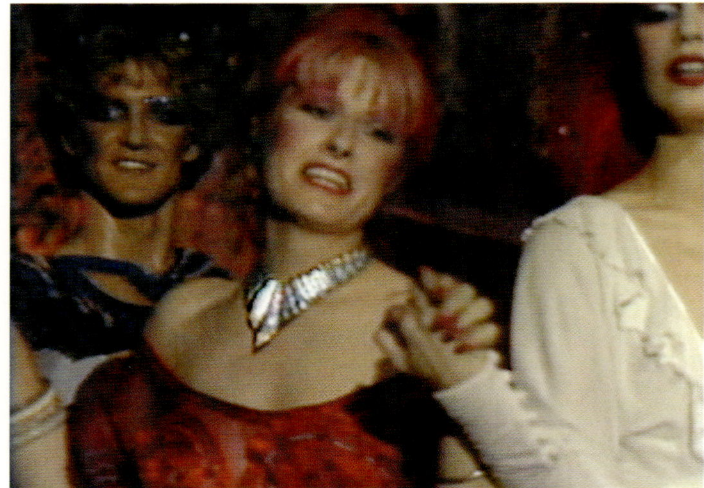

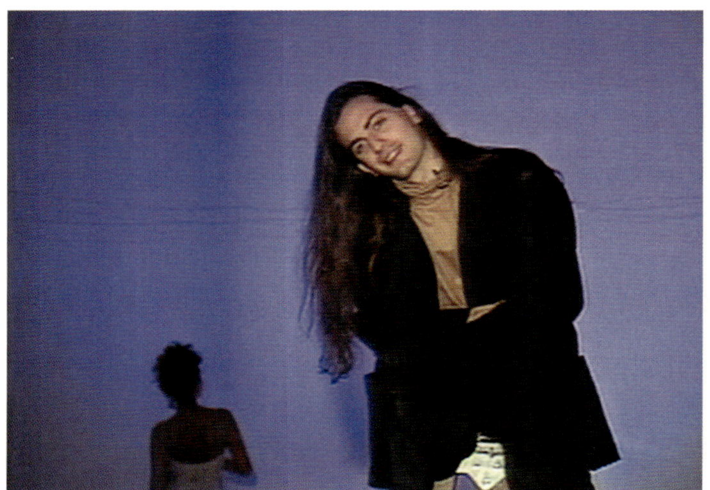

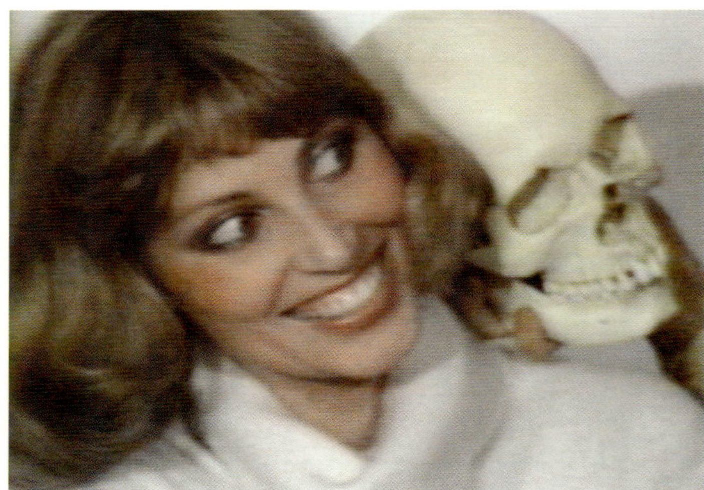

TOP LEFT
Andy Warhol
Pat Cleveland in *Andy Warhol's T.V.*
[season 1, episode 17], 1982
¾ in. videotape, color, sound,
30 minutes
The Andy Warhol Museum, Pittsburgh

BOTTOM LEFT
Andy Warhol
Marc Jacobs in *Andy Warhol's Fifteen Minutes* [episode 2], 1987
1 in. videotape, color, sound, 30 minutes
The Andy Warhol Museum, Pittsburgh

TOP RIGHT
Andy Warhol
Zandra Rhodes in *Andy Warhol's T.V.*
[season 1, episode 4], 1980
¾ in. videotape, color, sound, 30
minutes
The Andy Warhol Museum, Pittsburgh

BOTTOM RIGHT
Andy Warhol
Evelyn Kuhn in *Factory Diary*
December 15, 1976
½ in. reel-to-reel videotape, color, sound,
75 minutes
The Andy Warhol Museum, Pittsburgh

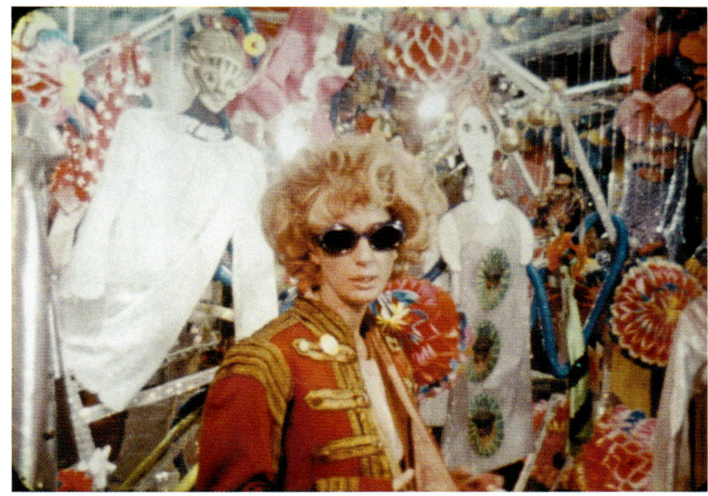

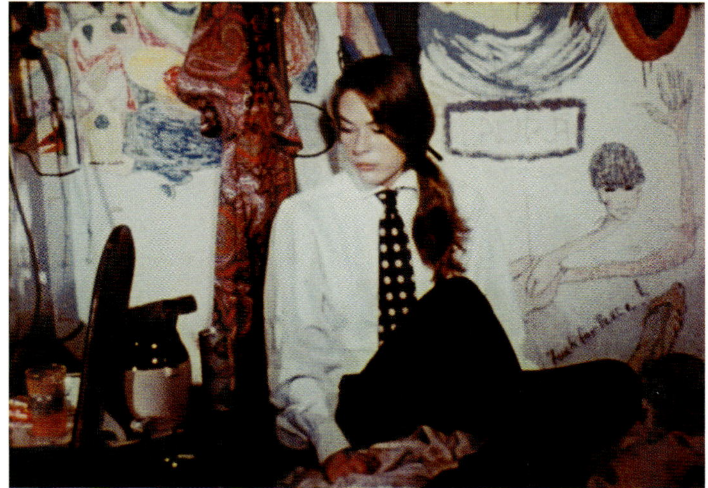

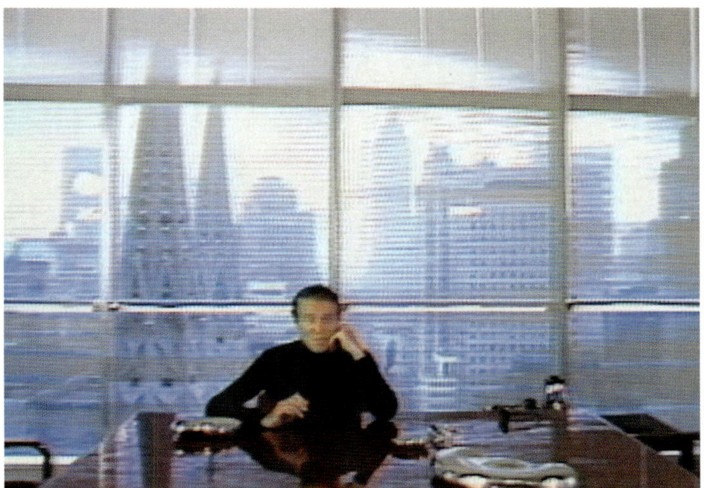

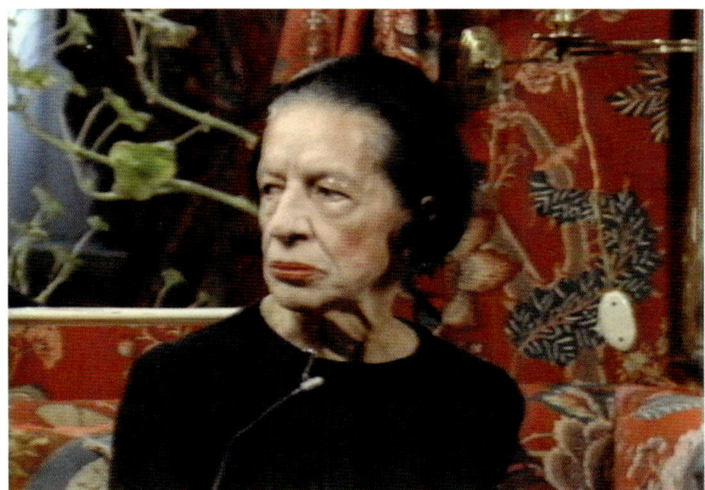

TOP LEFT
Andy Warhol
Tiger Morse, 1967
16mm film, color, sound, 34 minutes
The Andy Warhol Museum, Pittsburgh

BOTTOM LEFT
Andy Warhol
Halston in *Fashion*, 1979
¾ in. videotape, color, sound, 30 minutes
The Andy Warhol Museum, Pittsburgh

TOP RIGHT
Andy Warhol
Mary Waronov in *The Chelsea Girls*, 1966
16mm film, black & white and color, sound, 204 minutes in double screen
The Andy Warhol Museum, Pittsburgh

BOTTOM RIGHT
Andy Warhol
Diana Vreeland in *Fashion: The Empress and the Commissioner*, 1980
¾ in. videotape, color, sound, 30 minutes
The Andy Warhol Museum, Pittsburgh

she appeared in several Warhol films, including *The Chelsea Girls*. In 1965, Warhol hosted the opening of the chic mod boutique Paraphernalia, on the corner of 67th Street and Madison Avenue. The next year, in an unreleased film titled *Paraphernalia*, his frenetic camera filmed the young Bottomly in the shop, vamping with a whip and dressed in a black-and-white zigzag-patterned sequin dress, fishnet stockings, and extra-long dangly earrings made of crystal beads and glittering balls. Unlike in commercial fashion photography, Warhol's films of models and other subjects emphasized their performative reality. Whether his stationary camera lingered, as in his *Screen Tests*, or whether it never rested, zooming in and out, as in *Paraphernalia*, it always sought the essence of the person.

Warhol largely left off making films in the late 1960s. He did not, however, abandon the moving image. In 1965 he had been seduced by the new medium of video when he was loaned a prototype Norelco home-video camera. As consumer video equipment became more available in the 1970s, he embraced it with the characteristic enthusiasm he showed for all new trends. Warhol wanted to constantly document his surroundings, so as to not miss any angle of life; therefore, he recorded multiple views of the same content with a still camera, an audiotape recorder, and a video camera. He wrote, "What I liked was chunks of time all together, every real moment. . . . I only wanted to find great people and let them be themselves and talk about what they usually talked about and I'd film them for a certain length of time and that would be the movie."[4] The endless supply of relatively inexpensive (compared to film) videotape finally allowed him to do just that.

He purchased equipment and began to shoot in a diaristic manner at his home and around his studio. Warhol often asked Vincent Fremont, his assistant who worked on all the studio's video projects, and cameraman Michael Netter to document various offsite events. One of the most memorable sessions is Fremont's documentation of a 1975 shoot by Peter Beard for Warhol's *Interview* magazine, in which German supermodel Veruschka, enacting her own concept, wore a flowing white dress and stood as still as a statue on a chair in the middle of traffic on a busy New York street.

The *Factory Diaries*, as these recordings came to be called, were used not only to facilitate the production of *Interview*, which by this time had evolved from a film journal to a fashion fanzine, but also to document Warhol's working process. A case in point involves Warhol's 1976 portrait commission from the 1960s supermodel Evelyn Kuhn, whom he had met at a restaurant. The whole process of generating a source image for the painting—Warhol snapping dozens of Polaroid photos, Kuhn going through her poses, and bystanders Peter Beard and Jonas Mekas photographing and filming with their own cameras—was recorded by the studio's cameras. As if in a house of mirrors, well before the days of *Matrix*-style 360-degree camera work, the totality of the experience, almost "every real moment," was captured.

By this time, Warhol was more immersed than ever in the world of fashion. When his friend Halston wanted a fabulous presentation for the 1972 Coty American Fashion Critics' Awards ceremony at Lincoln Center, Warhol was glad to oblige. He produced an "Onstage Happening by Andy Warhol," including Superstars Candy Darling, Jane Holzer, Donna Jordan, and Jane Forth among "the Halstonettes," a group of models and debutantes who wore Halston couture while dancing and singing to wildly blaring music. "Before it was over, the smell of frying bacon wafted through the auditorium as social arbiter Nan Kempner cooked breakfast onstage on a real electric stove while dressed in a sequined evening gown. For the finale a huge wood-and-cardboard birthday cake was pushed out on the stage"[5] and Halston's assistant Pat Ast sang a refrain of "Happy Birthday to Me." The posh international audience of press, buyers, shop owners, manufacturers, and designers was stunned. The staid world of runway shows was never the same again.

As the 1970s progressed, Warhol continued to be involved with Halston's circle. When the artist and Fremont began working on an experimental project to develop soap operas, their first attempt, *Vivian's Girls*, was cast with Halston's models, including Nancy North, Karen Bjornson, and Pat Cleveland. Another effort was an untitled domestic drama starring Ast and Michael Sklar, who was also featured in Warhol's film *Trash* (1970), directed by Paul Morrissey.

By 1978, fashion video was becoming popular. Even Bloomingdale's had an in-house video studio, where every major designer filmed their collections in order to present them via video on the selling floor and on local cable television. Warhol loved fashion and he loved Bloomingdale's. He loved what they were doing with video and he had always wanted his own television show, so he hired the director Don Munroe and, with Fremont, created Andy Warhol T.V. Productions. By 1979, in the role of executive director, Warhol launched a ten-episode cable series called *Fashion*, intended to be the television equivalent of *Interview* magazine but with an emphasis on the fashion designer as celebrity and on the fashion show as the newest kind of TV entertainment.

Using his connections in the industry, Warhol was able to focus on behind-the-scenes subjects, creating episodes such as "Models & Photographers" and "Make-up." He devoted an entire episode to his friend Diana Vreeland, the former editor-in-chief of *Vogue* and Special Consultant to The Costume Institute of The Metropolitan Museum of Art. Warhol's episode on Halston documented the designer's 1979 Fall/Winter made-to-order and Originals/Resort collections. The entire show, including the runway segments, was shot in Halston's glass-walled Olympic Tower showrooms. In another episode, "Fashion Flowers," which examines flowers and style trends, several florists were interviewed. Tommy Pashun's segment was taped largely in Halston's house on East 63rd Street and focused on the designer's orchid collection, which cost him $150,000 yearly to maintain.

Within a year of the premiere of his series, Warhol had become a fixture on the fashion scene. He was featured as a guest, along with Halston, Martha Graham, and Liza Minnelli, on the first episode of the longest-running fashion series ever, CNN's *Style with Elsa Klensch*. His contacts and friends in the industry, his television shows, *Interview* magazine, and all of the parties and events he attended served him well. He was able to generate more work (and income) for himself by producing industrial videos for the designers he met, including Henry Grethel, Nicole Miller, and Carlos Falchi, and for brands such as Bottega Veneta.

Andy Warhol's T.V., the artist's second series, which lasted for twenty-seven episodes, premiered in 1980. Warhol became a frequent presence on the shows. One episode consisted exclusively of a conversation between Warhol and the artist Larry Rivers. Most episodes included fashion segments, but the show's scope was expanded from that of the first series to a wider variety of subjects. Warhol purchased time slots on New York City's Manhattan Cable to air the shows, which featured designers such as Giorgio Armani, Zandra Rhodes, Carolina Herrera, Kansai Yamamoto, Perry Ellis, Koos van den Akker, and Sonia Rykiel. The next season, commissioned by Madison Square Garden Network in 1983, maintained the same format but was produced in a more energetic TV-magazine style, emphasizing trendy topics and new stars. Designers highlighted were Issey Miyake, Donna Karan, Louis Dell'Olio, Bob Mackie, Fernando Sánchez, and Fabrice Simon.

Warhol's final series, *Andy Warhol's Fifteen Minutes*, a fast-paced show coproduced with the young music-video cable network MTV, debuted in 1985. The show's unofficial motto was "Today you only get fifteen seconds of fame. So make it good." In the brief five episodes that were produced before Warhol's death, young designers such as Marc Jacobs, Isabel and Ruben Toledo, and Stephen Sprouse were presented along with trendy clubs, celebrities, movie stars, musicians, and artists.

Finally confident in the onscreen persona he had been cultivating, Warhol became more than just a passive guest on his television show; he embraced the role of host, appearing in every episode. And, in a remarkable personal achievement, the man who had always been self-conscious and unhappy about his looks became a model, represented by the Zoli and Ford agencies. Warhol's last taping for the program was also his last public appearance—and it was as a model. Although feeling ill, he gallantly braved a cold dressing room and a less-than-stellar wardrobe to model with Miles Davis in a fashion show at the Tunnel nightclub. The next day Warhol entered the hospital and never returned. The final episode of his show, which aired shortly after his unexpected death, did not include the Tunnel footage but instead contained portions of Warhol's memorial service at St. Patrick's Cathedral.

Warhol considered cable television "the ultimate America" and, in many ways, his television shows were the culmination of his ambitions to transform himself into a success and an idol. His lifelong awareness of style and attention to his personal appearance had helped him finally realize and participate in the deified lifestyle of the stars he had sought after since his youth. By the time of his death, he was no longer an onlooker, no longer constrained to the occasional cameo appearance; he had become a performer turned outward toward the world—striding the catwalk himself.

NOTES

Epigraph: Richard Martin, who succeeded Diana Vreeland at The Costume Institute of The Metropolitan Museum of Art, began his talk at "Warhol's Worlds," the inaugural conference of The Andy Warhol Museum in 1995, with these words. Richard Martin, "Pre-Pop and Post-Pop: Andy Warhol's Fashion Magazines," in *Who Is Andy Warhol?*, edited by Colin MacCabe (London: British Film Institute; Pittsburgh: Andy Warhol Museum, 1997), 41.

1. Andy Warhol and Pat Hackett, *POPism: The Warhol '60s* (New York: Harcourt Brace Jovanovich, 1990), 163.
2. Ibid., 178.
3. Callie Angell, *Andy Warhol Screen Tests: The Films of Andy Warhol Catalogue Raisonné* (New York: Abrams, 2006), 141.
4. Warhol and Hackett, *POPism*, 110.
5. Steven Gaines, *Simply Halston: The Untold Story* (New York: Putnam, 1991), 145.

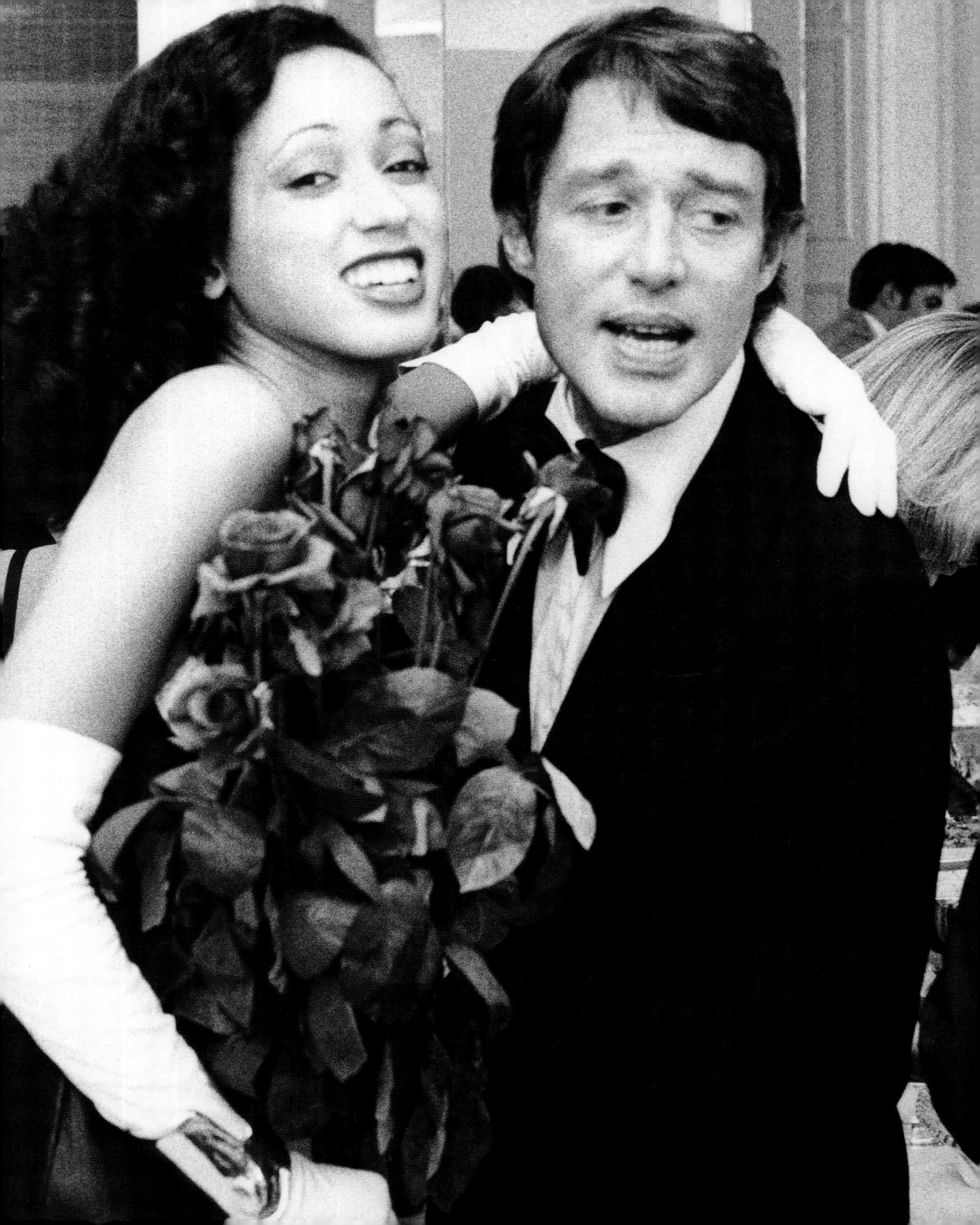

INTERVIEW WITH PAT CLEVELAND

Conducted by Kilolo Luckett

Legendary supermodel Pat Cleveland was born in 1950 in New York City. She grew up in a modest home surrounded by a family deeply rooted in the arts. Cleveland was raised by her mother, an accomplished painter who goes by the name Lady Bird Strickland. Her father was Johnny Johnston, a saxophonist. Cleveland studied at the High School of Art and Design and at the Fashion Institute of Technology (FIT). As a teenager, she modeled for *Ebony* Fashion Fair and designed her own clothes. In the late-1960s she was discovered by *Vogue* editor Carrie Donovan. Cleveland's unique look and iconic style had a tremendous impact on the fashion world and led to a modeling career that spanned almost half a century. Cleveland has written an autobiography about her life in fashion.

KL: How did your career begin?

PC: I wanted to be a designer before I was a model. I used to make my own clothes; nothing fit me properly because of my slim build. I was sewing and dressing up, and going out at night to dance at the Cheetah and other clubs. I went to school for art and design and then studied at FIT, but I didn't finish because I was having such a wonderful career in modeling, which had begun in my early teens.

I remember being "discovered." I was crossing town, walking through the subway on 42nd Street after school with my girlfriend Frances, when she noticed a woman following us. The lady looked really nice, so I stopped to let her catch up with us. She was very chic looking. It turns out she was Carrie Donovan's assistant at *Vogue* magazine. Her first words to me were, "Oh my, you are so wonderful looking!" She had an English accent, which intrigued me. She asked where I had gotten my outfit, I told her I had made it. Then she gave me her calling card and asked me to come to *Vogue* with my designs to show then to Carrie Donovan. Well, of course, I went home so excited and in a whirlwind got on the project right away, sketching outfits and sewing them with help from my mom. I was fifteen years old when they wrote a small article about me, and at seventeen they photographed me and gave me a spread in the magazine as "an up-and-coming designer." Then I was given the opportunity to create line of clothes for Henri Bendel, which was a dream come true for me.

My mother was the one who had sent photos of me to modeling agencies and magazines. *Ebony* magazine responded right away; I was invited to meet Mrs. Johnson at the Waldorf Astoria.[1] She was wonderful to me, promoting and protecting me in a very maternal way. My mother and I were invited to travel with the *Ebony* Fashion Fair, me as a model and she as my chaperone. We saw every city in every state of America. I met the crème de la crème of black fashion society: doctors, lawyers, judges, teachers, and university professors. In the 1960s that Fashion Fair show sent a very powerful message to black society, that they were able to have the luxury of high fashion in their lives. I traveled with beautiful, talented black models for three months on a greyhound bus. We were invited into luxurious homes and met all types of people—stars such as Muhammad Ali, Redd Foxx, Bill Cosby, Sammy

Pat Cleveland and Halston at the party at Halston's studio following the Coty Awards, October 19, 1972
Photograph by Ron Galella
WireImage/Getty Images

Davis Jr., jazz musicians, and all of these wonderful people in show business. There was live jazz onstage, and that's the music I learned to walk to.

Halston saw me during the Fashion Fair in New York. Later, when we were friends, he reminded me, "You know, you don't remember, but I saw you first—before any of the other designers." At the beginning of my career, I didn't know who he was, even though he was already on the map creating hats for the likes of Jackie Kennedy. At that time he was at Bergdorf's, creating hats for society ladies, and Mrs. Johnson was one of his clients.

KL: I've heard that Mrs. Johnson had an extensive collection of clothes from all different designers. Is that true?

PC: Yes. There was an exhibition called *Inspiring Beauty: 50 Years of Ebony Fashion Fair* at the Chicago History Museum. It was a wonderful display that showcased couture fashion by European and American designers. Mrs. Johnson bought the entire collection of most of the designers.

KL: So Halston had seen you as a teenager, but when did you two truly meet?

PC: I first spoke to Halston when I was at a party with the designer Stephen Burrows. Stephen and Halston knew each other. Stephen, Giorgio di Sant'Angelo,[2] Halston, and Andy were all at the party, and became good friends later. There were different camps at the party, and everyone was out to show off, trying to be number one. I was sitting with Stephen and Giorgio, who said, "You should go over there and talk to that guy [Halston]. He's a designer, too." So I did. Halston was very positive and said he would love to have me in his show. My friend Donna Jordan, who was also at the party, was one of Andy's first Superstars.[3] She was a great show off and very risqué. Most of the fashion designers said, "Oh, don't talk to Andy's group of friends, they're trashy." But I knew Donna because we both went to the same art school, so I went over and said hello, and that's how I met Andy.

Another friend of mine, Antonio Lopez,[4] used to go down to this club on Sheridan Square in the West Village to dance. Donna and Andy would be there, too. Everybody was so shocked that I socialized with Andy because he was considered underground—he had friends who were drug addicts and drag queens. Everyone loves drag queens now, but he was socializing with people that some thought were at "the bottom of the barrel." But Andy seemed to be able to read people for who they really were, people who were crying out to be loved. He could see interesting things in all kinds of people. He was visionary.

KL: Could you talk about an early show in which you modeled for Halston?

PC: One that comes to mind included Anjelica Huston, Naomi Sims, Elsa Peretti,[5] and Pat Ast.[6] Pat was the first large-size model, and she was working in the back room of Halston's studio, which was on East 68th Street at that time. It was a salon apartment. Halston asked Angelo Donghia to decorate the space to look like an indoor jungle. Donghia was popular then for creating exotic interiors with large plants and patterned fabrics and wallpapers. So there we were, immersed in that jungle interior, walking through a private audience of two rows of society ladies, VIP journalists, and a few film and stage stars. In the evening Halston would turn the lights down low and have parties, inviting all the society women and friends. They would dress in the kaftans and evening attire created by him. It seemed he was dressing all the women on the "best-dressed" lists.

Halston was very handsome; he was sleek, slim, and sophisticated. All the society women were in love with him. Halston took his time speaking and was so forgiving of some women's imperfections. He'd rather build them up than tear them down. A "girlfriend" might gossip, "she's so and so." Halston would reply, "Well, you know that's how it is, darling," not playing into the gossip but giving good advice—he was actually trying to help his friends become more refined because he knew they could miss out on a lot of opportunities by not being restrained. He knew what a lady was and could remind them when they were not being ladylike. He really did have very good taste for things and for behaviors as well. His talent was bringing out the best in a person, and what he saw in you was the magic.

KL: What was it like to be part of Halston's professional and personal inner circle?

PC: "Pivot, turn, pivot, turn"—he loved to say "pivot, turn" because that is what I did a lot of, just to show the clothes. I remember working with him as he created a garment. He would take a bolt of fabric, roll it out like a carpet, and then hold up the fabric to my body in a certain place and know exactly how the cloth would fall on the bias; then he would step back, look at it, and say to his assistant, "Pin it"; but then sometimes he would change his mind and say, "Oh, she doesn't want that up there, she wants it right here, and we'll show a little bit of this. Pin it." It was like being in a dance with him, really. I would move in the dress and he would say, "Let me see, does that feel good on you? Okay, we'll do that."

As a friend, Halston was protective of me. If I had to go home late at night he would accompany me in his limo and take me to my door. Halston was chivalrous. I got to know Halston best at Andy Warhol's beach house in Montauk, which Halston rented for many summers. I remember when we were there; Halston was really good about eating. His food was so clean. He had this wonderful maid that he adored—she was a part of his lifeline in New York City. But when we went to Montauk, she didn't come along, so we'd all try to cook.

KL: What was that like?

PC: Halston always had carrot and celery sticks in water in the refrigerator, and we sort of lived off of those during the weekend, until one of us would be brave enough to cook, like his friend Victor Hugo. He was good at making a red sauce for pasta. One weekend, I decided to buy Halston a pasta machine and make him pasta, but there was no place to put it in the kitchen, so Victor and I ended up trying to make the pasta in the laundry room. What a mess! Flour everywhere. Halston was in the other room by the fireplace, waiting for us to make dinner. So I finally squeezed out the pasta; we were all starving by that time. Then I told Halston I would make the sauce. "NO, NO," he said, "let Victor make the sauce!" I wasn't a very good cook at the time but I had good intentions.

The house at Montauk was peaceful. There were rooms dedicated to his friends. There was the Martha Graham room; and there was a little Liza Minnelli house. I usually slept in the Martha Graham room. Sleeping in a bed that Martha Graham has slept in—well, it always inspired me to dance.

KL: And did you?

PC: I'd always come out into the living room dancing, while Halston was sitting in the chaise lounge. He loved listening to music, and he loved watching me dance through the house. He was funny. He would imitate the caterpillar from *Alice in Wonderland*, puffing his cigarette in a very relaxed manner, dressed in casual cashmere, and he would say, "Who are you?" "Who are you?" and blow smoke rings into the air.

KL: You mentioned music. What kind of music did Halston play?

PC: Oh, he loved smooth jazz. If you put on smooth jazz, it seemed like he could sink back into a dream world. He always loved jazz, you know, he had a thing for that.

KL: And what was your interaction like with Halston and Warhol back in New York?

PC: I remember getting Halston to go dancing with me at Studio 54—it was his very first time there—just the two of us, kind of incognito. Steve Rubell was my friend, and he let us in for free. But my world with Andy and Halston was really back at the beach house. I called it "their" house because it was Andy's house but Halston took it over. Andy would take pictures of me out at the house in Montauk, and I would take pictures of Andy and Halston, very casual photos.

My fun times with Andy were very private, doing films with him and Antonio, or in Montauk on the weekends. Andy would bring all of these old horror monster movies to the house. I remember us watching *The Blob* together. We would all sit on the floor in front of the fireplace and watch old, tacky, B movies. Andy loved B movies; I think he wanted to be a B-movie maker. I was in *Vivian's Girls* (1973), one of Warhol's films.

KL: What was it like being with Andy?

PC: Andy was different in social situations than when he was watching movies. Movies made him excited. Andy would blurt things out loudly, "Did you see that?!" He would never speak like that in front of other people; he would whisper and be more discrete. He was such a matchmaker, always trying to encourage me to be interested in these mega-powerful guys: "Go over there and say hello, it'll be good for you." "No thank you," I would say.

I remember once being in Paris with Andy and Antonio. We went out to a private party, and after the party someone suggested we go to a bordello, one of the oldest in Paris. We went out of curiosity. Downstairs was a little, dark room with wooden walls and red lights. First we had dinner there, and then we were invited upstairs to look at all the ladies, but I stayed downstairs and waited for them. They didn't do anything; they just liked to look. Andy and Antonio did the Toulouse-Lautrec thing, the nightlife, going out in the streets of Paris to see the denizens of the night.

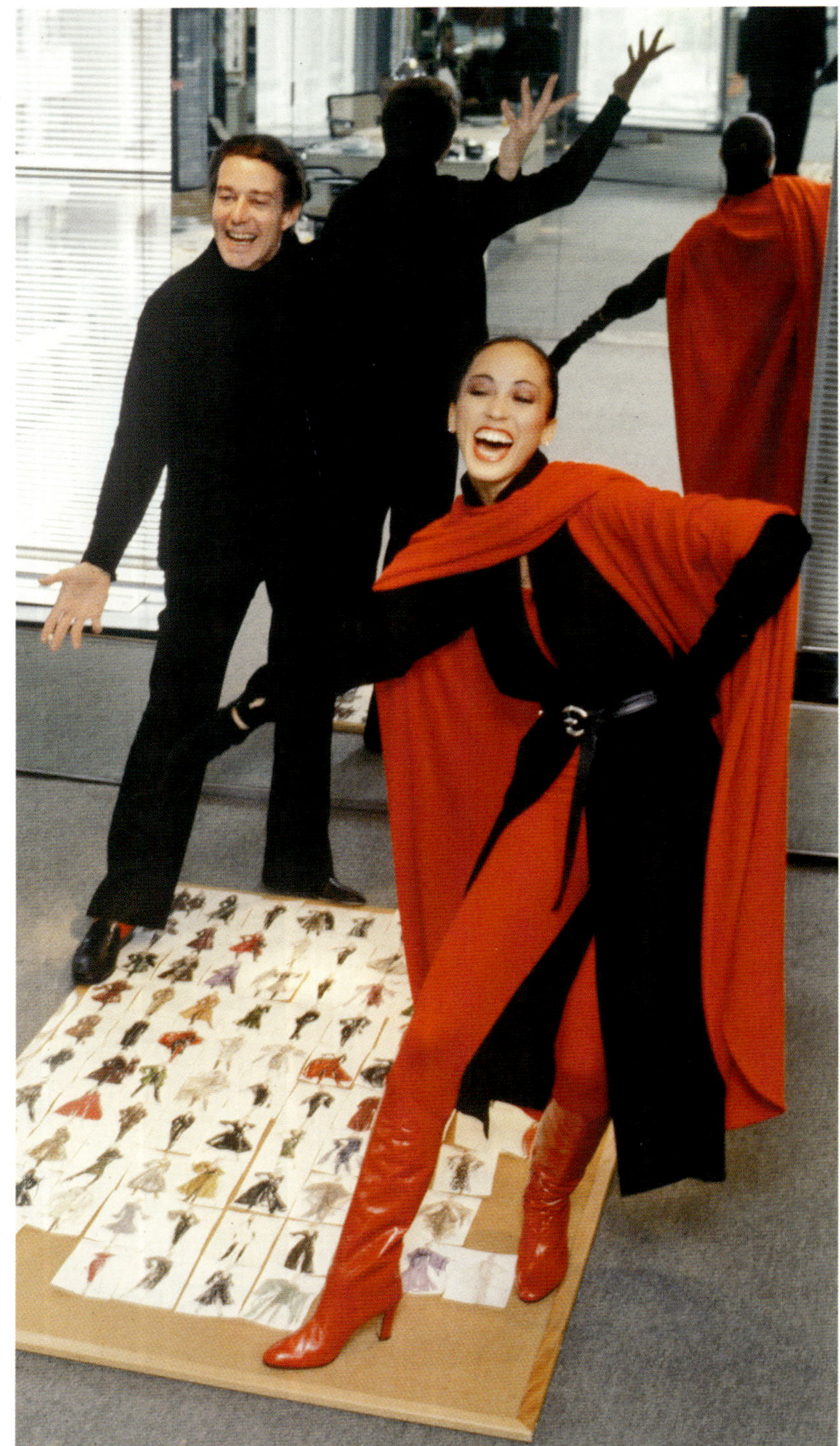

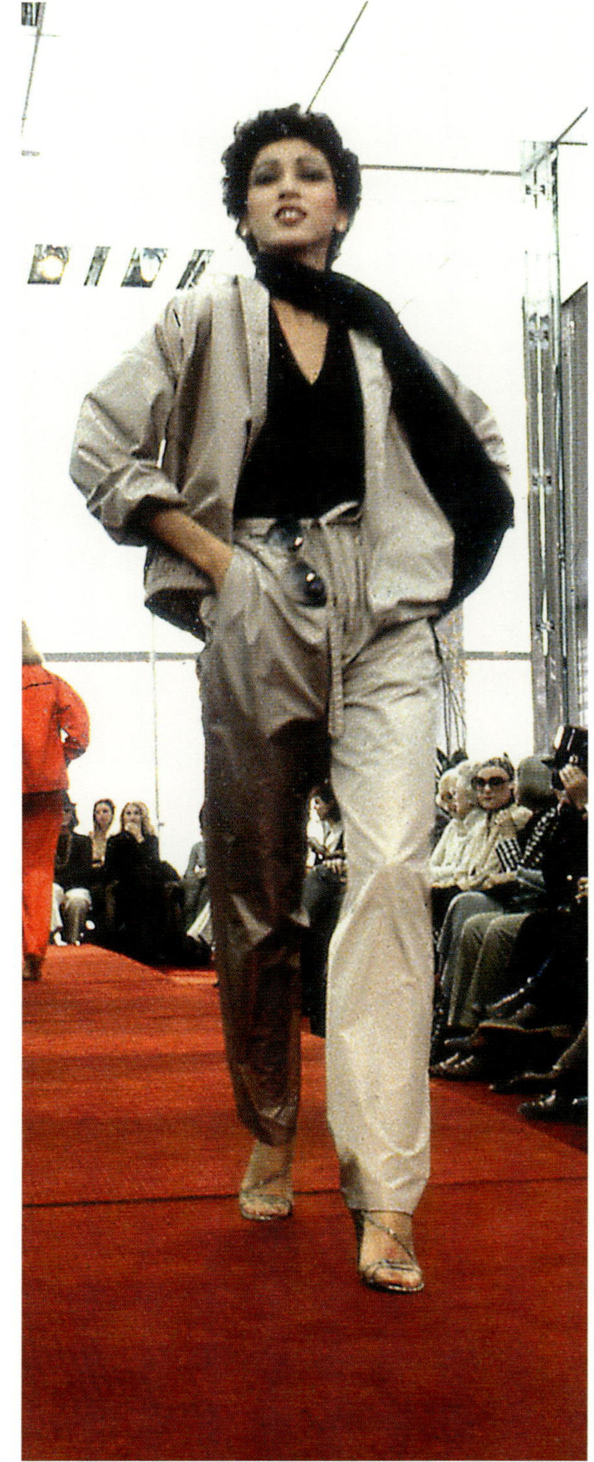

LEFT
Halston and Pat Cleveland in Halston's showroom
Photograph by Harry Benson

RIGHT
Pat Cleveland modeling Halston sportswear
Photograph by Rose Hartman

KL: You spent a lot of time with Halston in his home. Did you ever spend time with Warhol there as well?

PC: Andy came over to Halston's house all the time. They were such buddies. Andy's portraits of Halston hung on the mezzanine, and the entire house was full of Andy's work.

KL: How were fashion and art related in the 1970s?

PC: The spirit of the people made art. They were all in love with each other. They were in each other's houses and in each other's beds telling each other stories about who they wanted to be. Halston became an American icon of fashion and Warhol became an icon of art. But they didn't seem iconic then. Andy was just out there doing his thing, and he just kept doing it because he loved it; that was his livelihood.

KL: Do you think they had any inclination, back then, that their work would have such a significant impact on contemporary society?

PC: Of course they did. They were working toward fame; they loved fame and famous people, and they loved to party, make art, and be in each other's houses, presence, and minds.

KL: How do you think each one's work influenced the other?

PC: They had a certain kind of penetrating attitude about winning. They were both star-struck and much admired by women in society and the arts. Andy painted portraits of women, and Halston dressed them.

KL: Were there particular women with whom both Halston and Warhol shared close friendships?

PC: They both enjoyed the company of Liza Minnelli and Elizabeth Taylor. Halston was in awe of Elizabeth Taylor. She used to recite poetry to him in the back of the limo. Halston, Liz, and I would sit in the back seat going somewhere, and he would ask her to recite something. I remember she recited the entire "Owl and the Pussycat," by Edward Lear. Halston begged her to do it again, and she did. He loved it.

Halston liked to have parties. He'd invite famous artists and musicians. Once the Beatles came to his house. Halston really appreciated his house butler, Mohammed Soumaya. In the midst of his own parties at his home he would say, "Let's go in the kitchen with Mohammed," especially when the party got too busy. We'd go hang out in the kitchen, Halston's sanctuary. Halston dressed Mohammed just like he dressed himself. Mohammed was dedicated to Halston.

KL: We have been talking about the later 1970s and 1980s when Halston, Warhol, and you were very successful, but what led up to this success for you? What was it like modeling in the 1960s and early 1970s when there were not many models of color?

PC: It was difficult sometimes being the odd one, a new breed. During my mother's time, interracial relationships were very much prohibited. I grew up in an artistic Black American culture, just three generations of women out of slavery. People were suffering in this country because of racial prejudices, and all they wanted was equality, but it seemed I was lucky I had the chance to be free because I had that other half, being half Swedish.

KL: Was there a time when you felt like you really broke through into high fashion? When you felt, "Okay, I'm here, I've arrived?" That feeling seems to come across in your rhythm, the way you walk on the runway.

PC: It's energy. It's a culture. I thought, "Okay, I'm here, I have to show you that there is something worthwhile that you need to look at."

KL: Did you see any impact of the civil-rights movement on fashion, on art, and in your social circle?

PC: There were all kinds of people preaching love: Martin Luther King, the Beatles, Mahatma Gandhi. Being criminalized because of your skin color did not go down well in the art world. There aren't as many inhibitions in the art world, and that's why, in the 1960s, some designers and artists started supporting the civil-rights movement. In 1968 or 1969 it started changing for black models.

KL: Why was Versailles '73 such a pivotal moment in fashion history?

PC: Versailles '73 was the fashion show that put American designers on the international fashion map. The established French haute couture creators showed along with the American ready-to-wear fashion designers for a benefit to save Versailles. It was really revolutionary. Black girls from Seventh Avenue were not getting the breaks because there were limited opportunities in editorial work. But then something happened: Music influenced the fashion world, and designers loved how black girls could move the clothes like no one else, especially to the new sounds of R&B, known as soul music, which was very popular and powerful at the time. The American designers decided, "Okay, this is what we like." Stephen Burrows and Halston had the most African-American girls, along with Oscar de la Renta, so they decided to fly all the black models to Paris for the Versailles show. The French were used to show girls, but when they saw the American black models, they fell in love with us because we had the new music in our soul and we were symbolic of free America. Suddenly, the art and fashion worlds couldn't get enough of black models and performers. Designers and artists had a platform, and they made a difference because they recognized something beautiful in diversity.

KL: Did you ever talk to Halston or Warhol about any of this?

PC: I feel that Warhol's *Race Riot* images tried to make people wake up and see how they were treating each other. Halston had Naomi Sims; she was like a billboard. She was so important because she was very symbolic. And Donyale Luna, too. They made such a difference and don't get enough credit for what they did.

My attitude (like that of many of the black models) was one of determination. Life is a dance—you have to move and represent the energy of your true soul and use the energy and the blessings, whatever talent you have.

Notes

1. In 1958, Mrs. Eunice W. Johnson produced the *Ebony* Fashion Fair, a traveling fashion show featuring African-American models. It brought high-end designer fashion and couture to black communities and readers of *Jet* and *Ebony* magazines. Mr. John H. Johnson was the founder of Johnson Publishing Company, which started in 1942, and the owner of *Ebony* and *Jet*. *Ebony* was *Life* magazine to African Americans, and *Jet* was similar to *Reader's Digest*.
2. Giorgio di Sant'Angelo was an Italian-born fashion designer.
3. Model Donna Jordan was known for her famous white-blonde hair and eyebrows, and gap-tooth smile.
4. Antonio Lopez was a fashion illustrator who was good friends with Pat Cleveland and spent time with her in Paris.
5. Elsa Peretti, who designed jewelry and gifts for Tiffany & Co., also modeled for Halston and created the design for his signature Halston perfume bottle. Halston accessorized his models in her diamonds-by-the-yard necklaces, her silver loop belts, and other signature pieces.
6. Pat Ast, an actress who appeared in some of Warhol's films, also worked and modeled for Halston.

Andy Warhol
Pat Cleveland, n.d.
Gelatin silver print
10 x 8 in. (25.4 x 20.3 cm)
The Andy Warhol Museum, Pittsburgh; Contribution The Andy Warhol Foundation for the Visual Arts, Inc., 2001.2.53

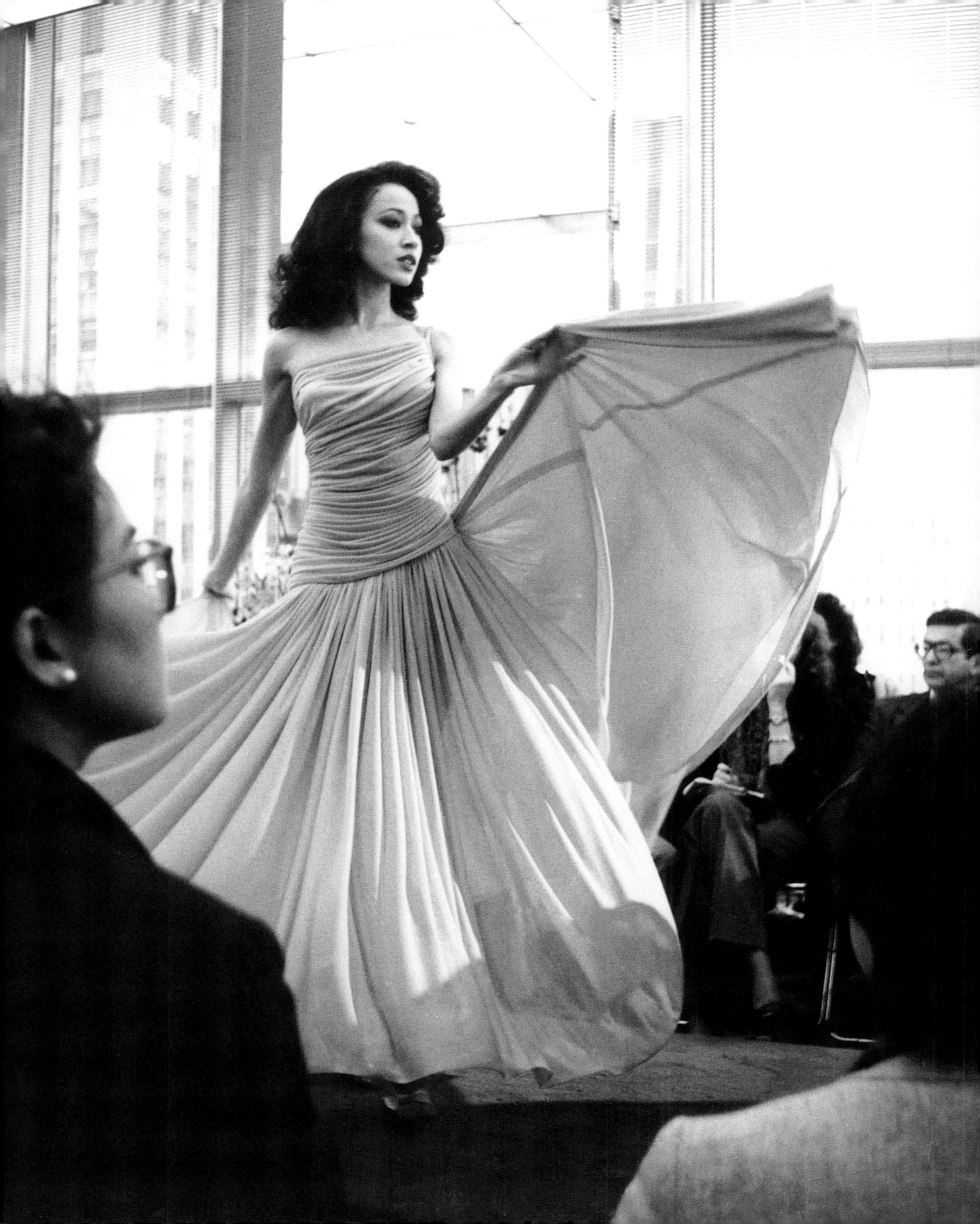

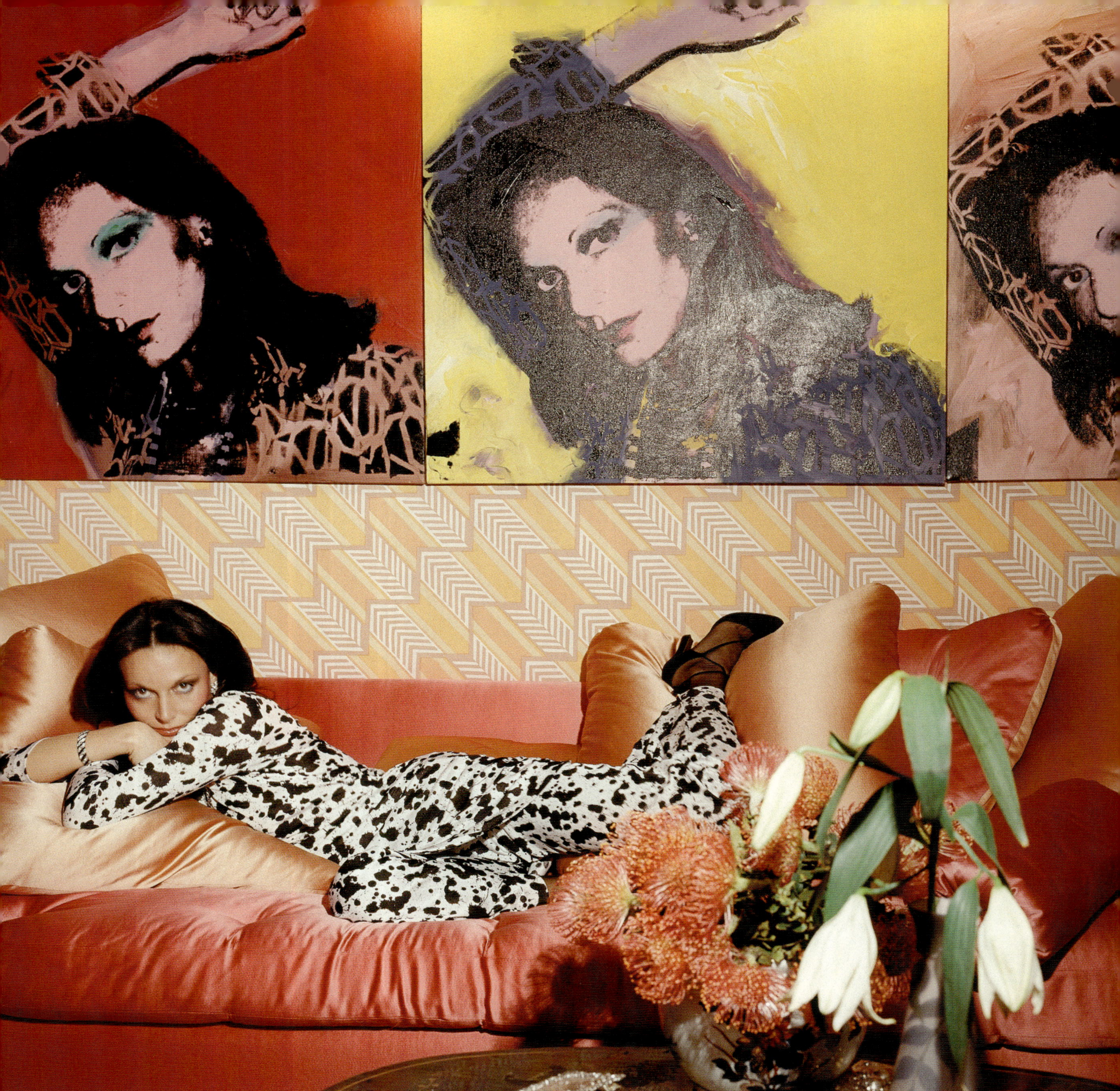

Diane von Furstenberg at home,
ca. 1976
Photograph by Horst P. Horst
Condé Nast Archive/CORBIS

INTERVIEW WITH DIANE VON FURSTENBERG

Conducted by Eric C. Shiner and Signe Watson

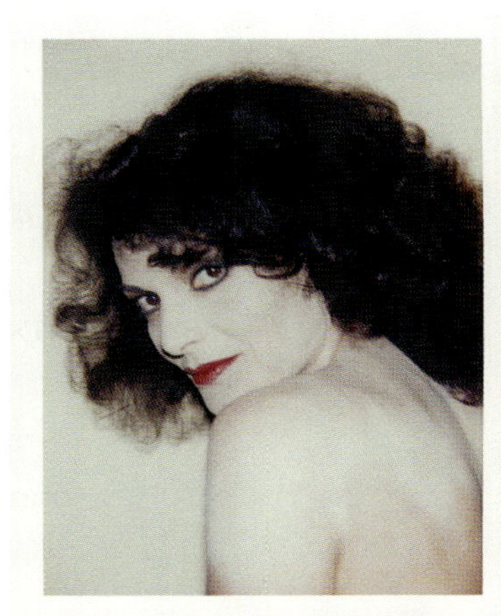

Andy Warhol
Diane von Furstenberg, 1984
Polaroid™ Polacolor ER
4¼ × 3⅜ in. (10.8 × 8.6 cm)
The Andy Warhol Museum, Pittsburgh; Contribution The Andy Warhol Foundation for the Visual Arts, Inc., 2000.2.200

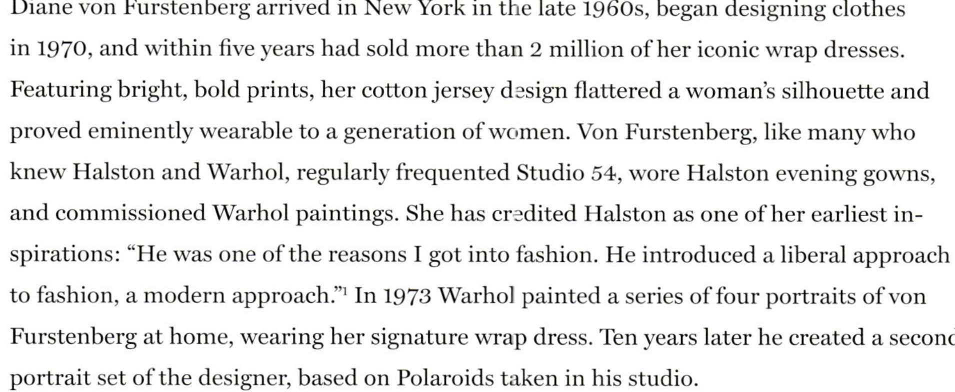

Diane von Furstenberg arrived in New York in the late 1960s, began designing clothes in 1970, and within five years had sold more than 2 million of her iconic wrap dresses. Featuring bright, bold prints, her cotton jersey design flattered a woman's silhouette and proved eminently wearable to a generation of women. Von Furstenberg, like many who knew Halston and Warhol, regularly frequented Studio 54, wore Halston evening gowns, and commissioned Warhol paintings. She has credited Halston as one of her earliest inspirations: "He was one of the reasons I got into fashion. He introduced a liberal approach to fashion, a modern approach."[1] In 1973 Warhol painted a series of four portraits of von Furstenberg at home, wearing her signature wrap dress. Ten years later he created a second portrait set of the designer, based on Polaroids taken in his studio.

ES and SW: It must have been a heady time in New York in the early 1970s. Halston was photographed for the cover of *Newsweek* in 1972, and you were on the cover of both *Newsweek* and Warhol's *Interview* in 1976. What did you think of Halston's fashion at the time?

DvF: I loved Halston's work and wore his dresses many times. The week that we were both on the covers of *Newsweek* and *Time* was also the week of my first visit to the White House. I was invited by Luis Estévez[2] to be his escort to a formal ball with the president and first lady. Estévez was Mrs. Ford's favorite designer. I did not make evening dresses, so I asked Halston for a dress appropriate for such an occasion. Halston gave me a black strapless gown. I remember dancing with President Ford and being terrified that one of us was going to step on my dress and lose it!

ES and SW: The *Newsweek* cover described you as "the most marketable woman since Coco Chanel." Being at the center of celebrity culture, going to Studio 54, were you aware of the headiness of the times? Do you think that environment was advantageous to you as a designer and business woman?

DvF: New York was full of energy at the time. I was living an American dream. I felt free and in charge, and had become the woman I wanted to be. I loved seeing so many women wearing my dresses on the streets and in the restaurants. I used to have fun counting how many I saw in a day. It really was a high for a young European girl. It was exhilarating!

In terms of celebrity culture, I think Warhol started the idea of creating a celebrity persona [outside of film], and this trend kept on growing. I think it is helpful to be a celebrity or to have celebrities wear your clothes, but, in the end, it is still the design that counts.

ES and SW: Warhol and Halston each entertained diverse artists, collaborators, and friends in his salon or studio. Can you speak to their social and creative interactions?

DvF: Warhol and Halston were always in the same circle, or intersecting circles, always around each other, but they didn't compete against the other. Each one had a court. It was so much fun—a moveable feast of art, design, and fashion. I think we all felt we had invented freedom.

ES and SW: It seems you and Halston were at the forefront of a design revolution in women's ready-to-wear, transforming high-end designs to more affordable off-the-rack clothes. Likewise, Warhol created a revolution of sorts in the art world, mixing high and low. Was that a conscious goal for you, and did Pop art and Andy influence your thinking?

DvF: I think Andy and I shared a notion of what it is to be young and free. We were doing what we felt like doing without constraints. My original designs were more about lifestyle than anything else. I wanted to create something that was effortless to wear while also being sexy. But yes, I was always conscious that clothes should be accessible, and I like that about my designs.

ES and SW: You created the wrap dress in knitted jersey; Halston created the shirtwaist dress in Ultrasuede. Both designs were luxurious but devoid of unnecessary fasteners and decoration. Integrity of material and the display of surface were important design elements. Can you talk about honesty in design?

DvF: I think honesty and substance have staying power. Time is what eventually tells what lasts and what does not. My little wrap dress is still a mystery to me. Its success has gone through so many generations. While I can't pinpoint exactly why it has been so successful, I do think there is honesty in its design. My wrap dress molds the body in ways that are incredibly flattering. People trust it. It is still a symbol of femininity today; it is still alive.

ES and SW: Halston was the first American designer invited to show his clothes in China in 1980, and Warhol traveled there in 1982. They were taking early steps in the globalization of American fashion and art. Fast forward to today, you have established stores in Beijing, Chengdu, and Shanghai; staged the Red Ball; and have had an exhibition at Pace Gallery in Beijing. Can you talk about the allure of China and how commerce, art, and fashion have merged in your own projects?

DvF: I think all of us were fascinated by China. I have been interested in China since childhood. I devoured Pearl S. Buck's books, fascinated by China's very old civilization. The country's mystery and seductiveness are so appealing to me. I feel very comfortable there.

In the same way that art and fashion fused with many of Warhol's and Halston's projects, I have incorporated the work of Chinese artist Zhang Haun into some of my presentations. His work is brilliant, and he and his wife have become my friends. Huan, like Warhol, did a portrait of me, and I have a huge Buddha of his in my garden. As Warhol and Halston showed us, work and friendship spill over. Art is so much a part of our time—and so is fashion. They continue to blend and always have.

ES and SW: If you could pinpoint the legacy of Halston and Warhol today, what are some of the lasting ideas they shared with you and/or with the larger community of art and design?

DvF: Warhol was a true visionary, Halston was a great designer. Both were able to take risks, and they were keen observers. I think they left us with the legacy of being responsible with our art. Art has both the obligation and privilege to reflect society.

NOTES

1. Diane von Furstenberg, quoted in the documentary *Ultrasuede: In Search of Halston* (2010), directed by Whitney Smith.
2. Luis Estévez is a Cuban designer best known for his eveningwear for prestigious clients, including Merle Oberon, Lana Turner, Rosalind Russell, Eva Gabor, Nancy Reagan, and Betty Ford.

TIMELINES

Nicholas Chambers, Abigail Franzen-Sheehan, Patrick Moore, Chris Royer, Signe Watson, and Matt Wrbican

Halston and Warhol traced parallel and improbable paths, rising from mundane circumstances to become big-city innovators and cultural icons that helped transform the age. Each pursued the American Dream—shaping a desired future through hard work. The points of intersection are many. Halston's innovative designs and Warhol's work embraced new materials and technology at every juncture. Both unabashedly marshaled the new plastics, synthetics, and machinery suddenly at their disposal. And yet, their successes were owed greatly to the humble basics and values of their pasts. Through hard work, Halston and Warhol created a distinctly modern American aesthetic in fashion and art.

Patricia Mears has assessed that American fashion is functional in its design, closely wedded to mass production and mass merchandizing, and innovative in its tiered approach of creating affordable designs for the middle class.[1] Halston understood the changing role of the twentieth-century woman: her inclusion in the workplace, ever-widening social circles, and active lifestyle required modern clothing options. As a master of ready-to-wear, he also understood that this new line of design would be realized in American garment factories and not in the couture salons of Paris and Milan. Halston took cues from the fashion greats, paring down flattering couture to sportswear and stylish separates that were priced accessibly for the middle class. He even licensed sewing patterns to *McCall's*.

While Andy Warhol's art was seemingly less affordable to the masses, his subject matter was taken directly from America's kitchens, supermarkets, newspaper piles, and magazines.[2] Warhol's method of reproduction mirrored the way images were presented in the media. The process of photographic silkscreen printing allowed him to borrow imagery directly from consumer culture, to maintain its photographic quality, and to mechanically reproduce the imagery in multiples, thus elevating the mundane to high art. The subjects—products, celebrities, news headlines, and advertisements—reflected society's predilections for consumption, while their repetition mimicked the numbing barrage of commercial images in the media. Through these means he forced the high-art establishment to reconsider what can constitute a work of art, in both subject matter and in the way it is made.

What follows are decade-by-decade timelines of Halston's and Warhol's lives, accompanied by significant designs and works. While the timelines are neatly divided into decades, some of the points of intersection defy this rule, crossing over larger time periods. The images are grouped loosely by theme, and at times the pairings function as a purely interesting visual juxtaposition. Explanations have been included where the connections are less obvious or are editorial in nature.

NOTES

1. Patricia Mears, *American Beauty, Aesthetics and Innovation in Fashion* (New York: Fashion Institute of Technology, 2009).
2. In his lifetime Warhol commanded exceedingly high sales prices for many of his paintings, but at the same time he wanted people to think of products like his album covers as works of art, thus providing an affordable art.

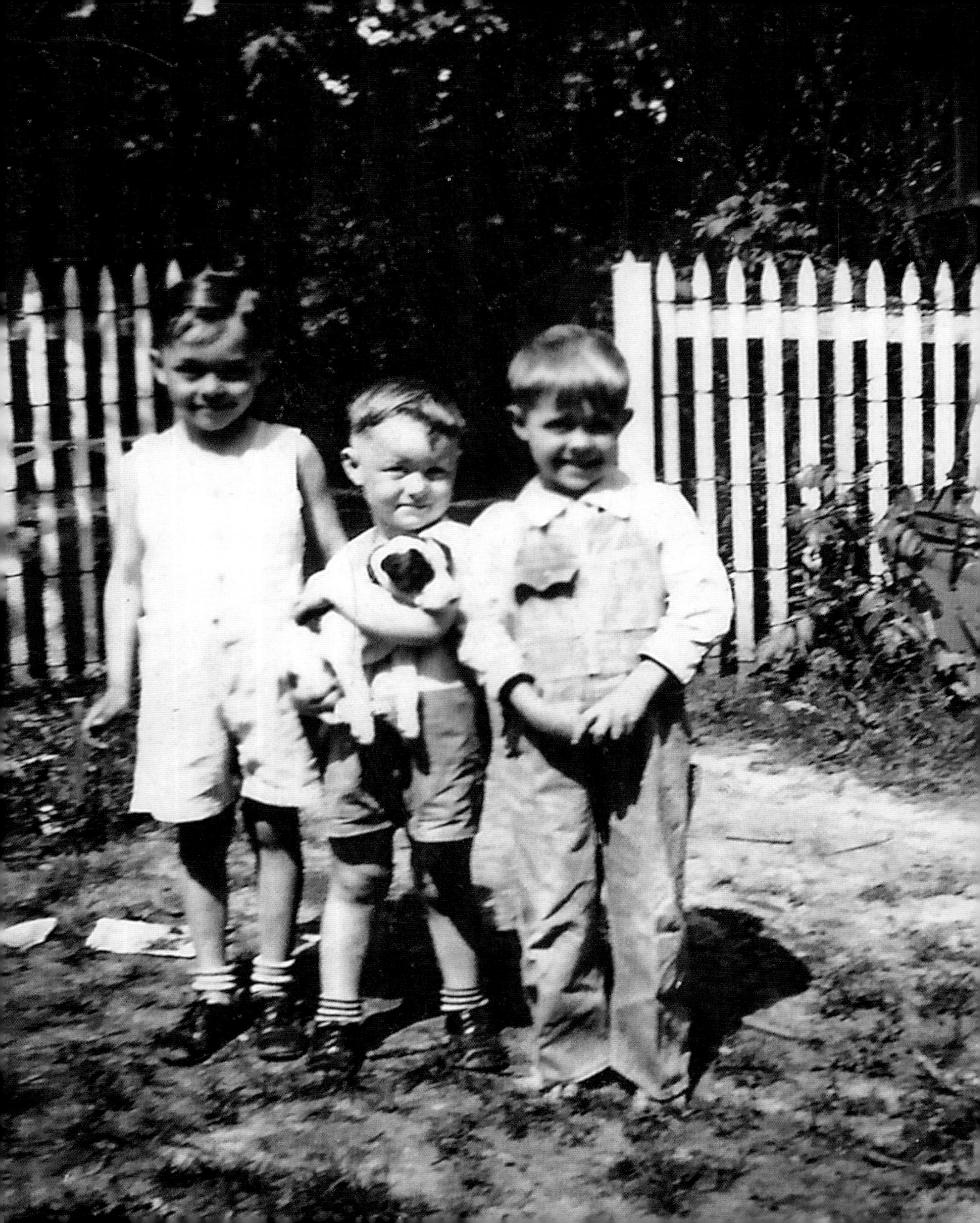

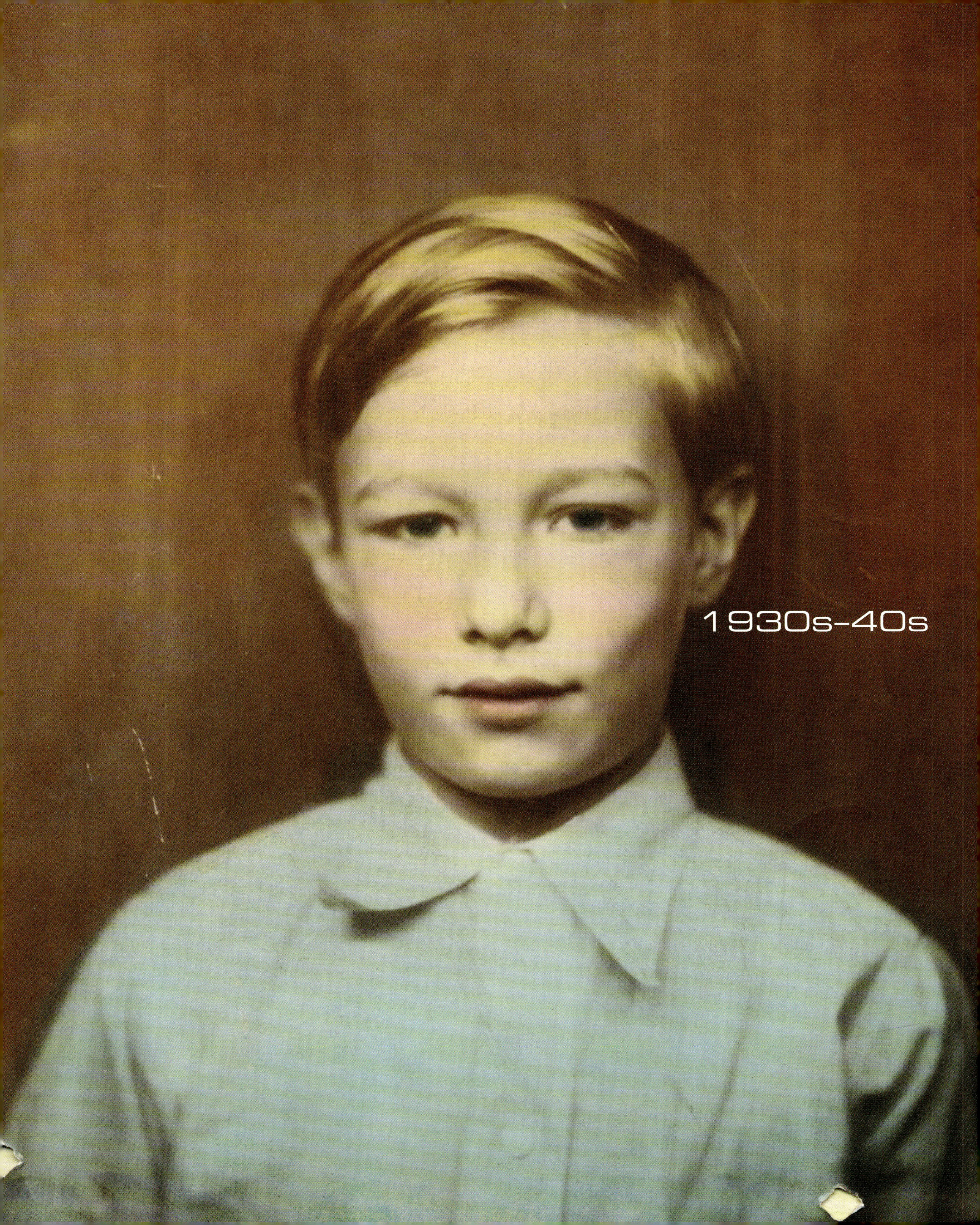

1930s–40s

1930s–40s

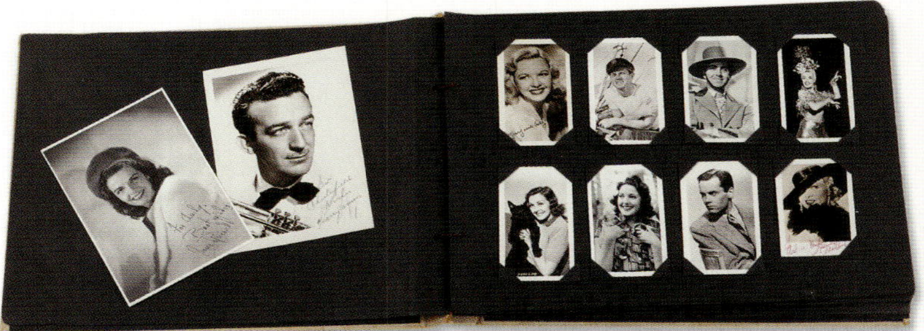

LEFT
Andy Warhol's childhood movie-star scrapbook, ca. 1938–41
Leather on board, paper, assorted photographs
11½ × 15¼ × 1 in. (29.2 × 38.7 × 2.5 cm)
The Andy Warhol Museum, Pittsburgh; Founding Collection, Contribution The Andy Warhol Foundation for the Visual Arts, Inc., TC689

WARHOL

1928
Andrew Warhola is born in Pittsburgh, Pennsylvania, on August 6 to Julia and Andrej Warhola, Carpatho-Rusyn immigrants from the village of Miková in present-day eastern Slovakia. He has two older brothers, Paul and John.

1934
After renting a succession of small apartments, the Warholas purchase a home at 3252 Dawson Street. Andy lives there until he moves to New York City in 1949.

1937
Andy becomes interested in photography and takes pictures with the family's Kodak Brownie camera. An area of the Warholas' basement is cleared for use as a darkroom.

From about 1937 to 1941, he attends free Saturday art classes at the Carnegie Institute.

After contracting rheumatic fever, Andy is stricken with St. Vitus dance (Sydenham chorea) and confined to home for more than two months, during which his mother encourages his interests in art, comics, and movies.

1939
Andy begins collecting photographs of movie stars.

HALSTON

1932
Roy Halston Frowick is born in Des Moines, Iowa, on April 23 to Hallie Mae (née Holmes) and James Edward (Ed) Frowick Jr. The Frowicks are of Norwegian descent. Ed is a certified public accountant and Hallie Mae is a housewife and sometime model for Halston's early millinery creations. Halston is the second of four children; his older brother is Robert and his younger siblings are Susan and Don.

1934
Roy is named "Healthiest City Baby" in the two- and three-year-old division at the Iowa State Fair.

1937
Halston enjoys his second appearance in a local newspaper when he presents his creation of a May Day flower basket to his neighbor Beverly Beaumont, "the prettiest girl in the neighborhood."

1939
Ed Frowick moves his family from their rented home at 1809 25th Street in Des Moines into his father's house at 2127 High Street.

Roy attends Callahan and Kirkwood elementary schools in Des Moines.

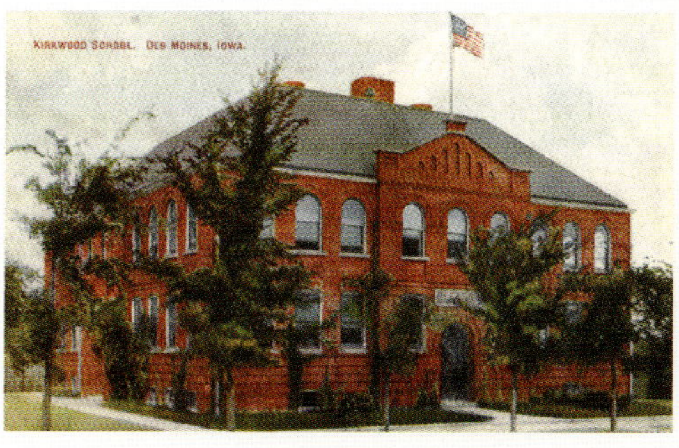

PREVIOUS SPREAD, LEFT
Halston in the middle with dog, brother Bobby, and a neighbor, ca. 1936
Courtesy the Lesley Frowick Collection

PREVIOUS SPREAD, RIGHT
Andy Warhol, ca. 1936
Hand-colored sepia print
6 × 4¾ in. (15.2 × 12.1 cm)
The Andy Warhol Museum, Pittsburgh; Founding Collection, Contribution The Andy Warhol Foundation for the Visual Arts, Inc., 1998.3.5218

RIGHT
Andy Warhol, ca. 1945
Sepia print on textured photographic paper
7 × 5 in. (17.8 × 12.7 cm)
The Andy Warhol Museum, Pittsburgh; Founding Collection, Contribution The Andy Warhol Foundation for the Visual Arts, Inc., 1998.3.5219

1942

Andy graduates from Holmes Elementary School and enters Schenley High School, where he receives the highest marks in his art classes.

Andrej Warhola dies after a lengthy illness. He had saved several thousand dollars to be used for Andy's education.

1945

On the standard IQ test, Andy receives a mark of 104, slightly above average. He is admitted to the Carnegie Institute of Technology (now Carnegie Mellon University) and enrolls in the Department of Painting and Design. His professors include Samuel Rosenberg and Robert Lepper.

1947

Andy works at a summer job in the display department at the Joseph Horne department store in downtown Pittsburgh; he also holds similar jobs at other stores in the city.

In 1947–48, he experiments with a blotted-line drawing technique that becomes a mainstay of his 1950s commercial work.

1948

Andy's painting *I Like Dance* and his print *Dance in Black and White* are included in the annual exhibition of the Associated Artists of Pittsburgh.

Andy serves as art editor for the student magazine *Cano*.

BELOW
Andy Warhol and unidentified coworkers at Joseph Horne Department Store, 1947
Gelatin silver print
3¾ × 4⅝ in. (9.5 × 11.7 cm)
The Andy Warhol Museum, Pittsburgh; Founding Collection, Contribution The Andy Warhol Foundation for the Visual Arts, Inc., 1998.3.5418.1

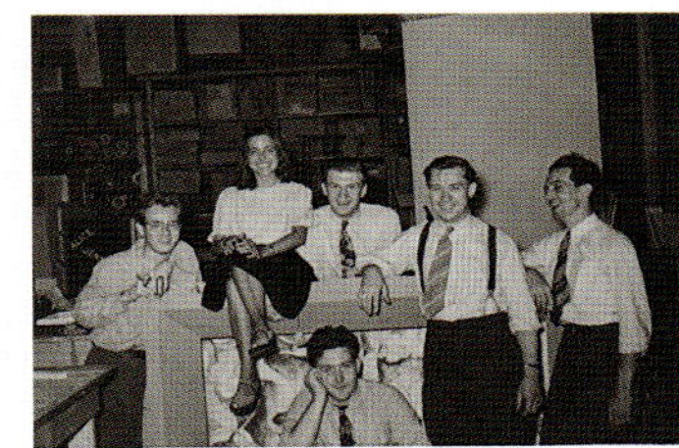

1949

Andy graduates from Carnegie Tech with a Bachelor of Fine Arts degree in pictorial design. Shortly thereafter, he moves to New York City.

He begins to work as a commercial artist, usually under the name Andy Warhol.

1941

At age nine, Roy creates some of his first costumes and headdresses, crafting them from chicken feathers, for his siblings and cousins at their family farm.

LEFT
Kirkwood Elementary School, Des Moines, Iowa

1943

The Frowick family relocates to Evansville, Indiana, after a brief period living in Carbondale, Illinois, where Ed works for Crab Orchard Lake Ordinance plants as a defense contractor auditor.

During the nine years the Frowicks live in Evansville, they reside in several rental homes, moving as Ed Frowick changes jobs.

Roy attends Hebron Elementary School and in sixth grade co-writes a play in which he performs several roles.

1944

As a seventh grader at the Washington School in Evansville, Roy choreographs the school musical.

RIGHT
Roy Halston Frowick, Benjamin Bosse High School, Evansville, Indiana, ca. 1948
Courtesy the Lesley Frowick Collection

1945

Hallie Mae proudly wears one of Roy's homemade creations—a red cloche hat with a Chore Boy scouring pad attached as a decorative pom-pom—to Easter Sunday church services.

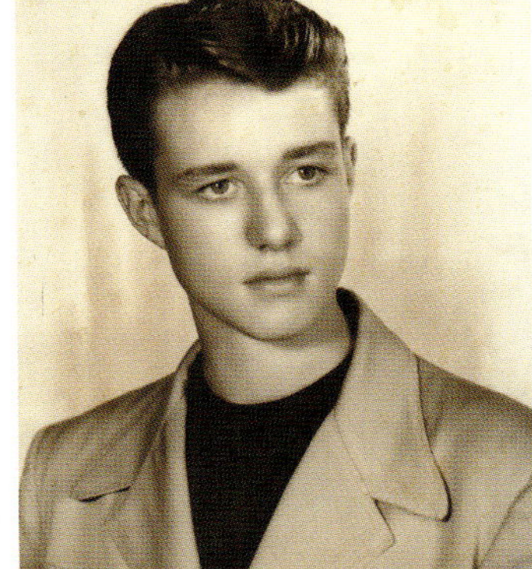

CHILDHOOD AND ASPIRATIONS

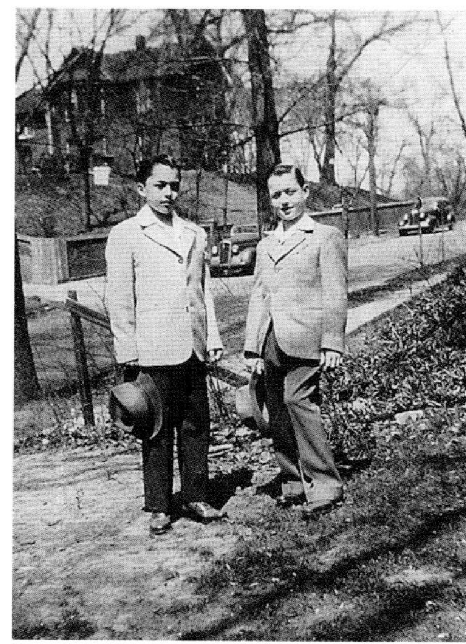

Bob and Roy Halston Frowick, Evansville, Indiana, 1942
Courtesy the Lesley Frowick Collection

"It's very strange, but very true. I always wanted to be in the fashion business; from the time I was about four or five years old. I was always fascinated with it, and always wanted to make things, and actually did make things when I was really young. And it was very difficult for me as a young man because I wasn't much encouraged in that world of fashion. Everybody discouraged you right down the pike, and you were not supposed to do what I was doing, which was making hats. I guess you had to be smaller and a little bit more fey."

—Halston, quoted in Elaine Gross and Fred Rottman, *Halston: An American Original*

"I never wanted to be a painter, I wanted to be a tap dancer."

—Andy Warhol, interview with Gretchen Berg, "Andy Warhol, My True Story," 1966

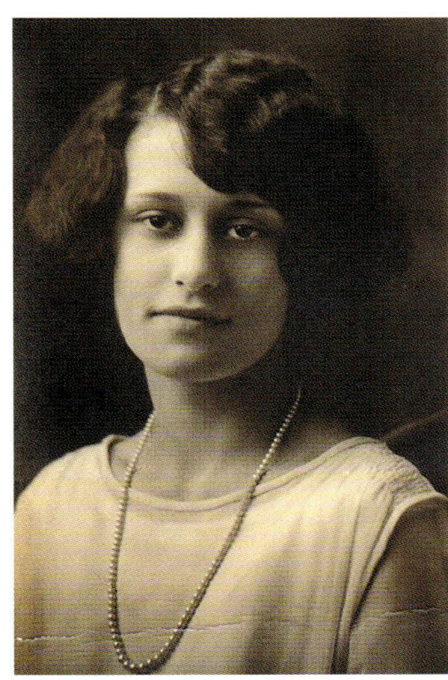

Andrew Warhola and Roy Halston Frowick were born four years apart in Midwestern America. Their humble beginnings belie the notorious and exciting careers these men pursued and built. The strenuous blue-collar environment of the steel industry in Pittsburgh and the rugged farmlands of Iowa, Indiana, and Illinois were the respective backdrops to their early creative interests.

Encouraged by their mothers, Warhol and Halston each showed an early aptitude for their talents. Julia Warhola often drew with her children, creating a contest of sorts. The son who created the best drawing, usually Andy, was awarded with a candy bar. Hallie Mae Frowick and Halston's siblings proudly wore the designer's early hat creations in public and allowed him to select their outfits.

Each family experienced its share of hardship. The untimely death of Andrej Warhola and the constant moving due to Ed Frowick's work placed strain on their families, while the economic pressures of the 1930s and the nation's involvement in World War II impacted all Americans. Both Pittsburgh and Evansville were hubs for war manufacturing: steel and munitions in the former and tank landing ships and fighter aircrafts in the latter.

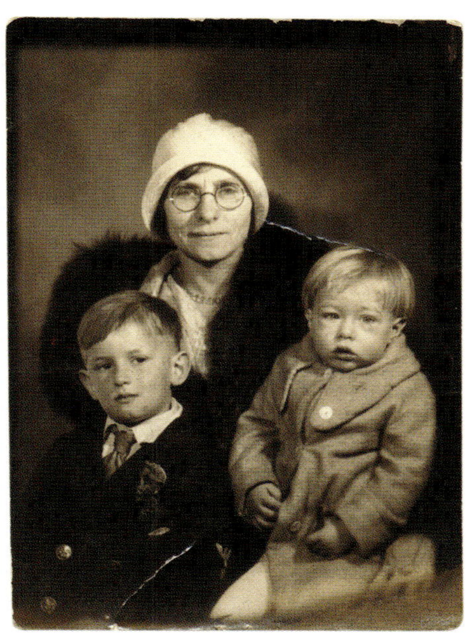

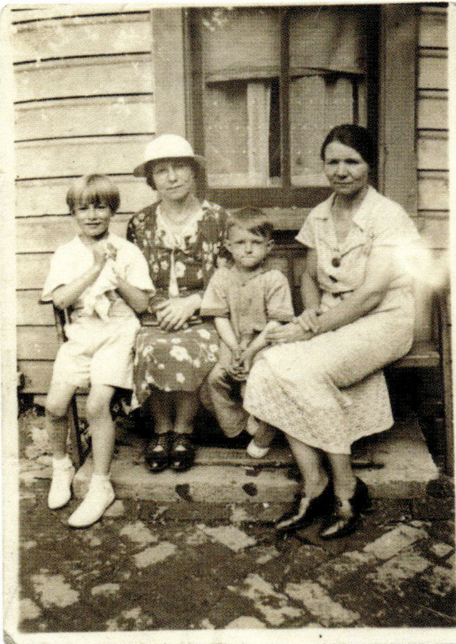

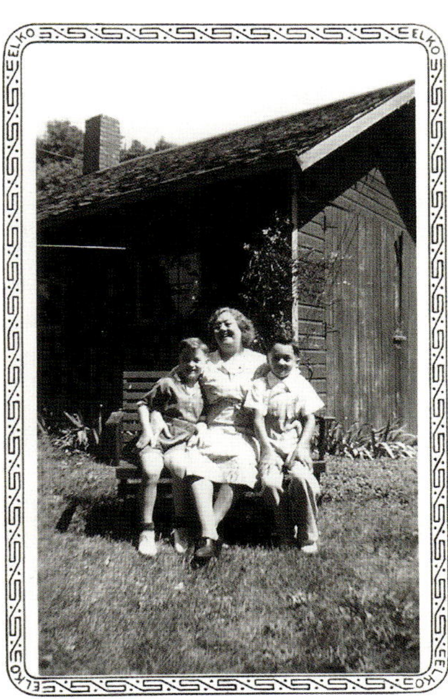

TOP
Hallie Mae Frowick photographed on her wedding day, Des Moines, Iowa, 1927
Courtesy the Lesley Frowick Collection

BOTTOM LEFT
Julia, John, and Andy Warhola, 1932
Sepia print
2¼ × 1⅝ in. (5.7 × 4.1 cm)
The Andy Warhol Museum, Pittsburgh; Founding Collection, Contribution The Andy Warhol Foundation for the Visual Arts, Inc., 1998.3.5247

BOTTOM MIDDLE
Andy Warhol, Julia Warhola, George Guke, and Mrs. Mary (Zavacky) Preksta, 1937
Sepia print
3⅝× 2⅜ in. (9.2 × 6 cm)
The Andy Warhol Museum, Pittsburgh; Founding Collection, Contribution The Andy Warhol Foundation for the Visual Arts, Inc., 1998.3.10540.1

BOTTOM RIGHT
Halston's grandmother Margaret Frowick, Roy, and Bobby, Des Moines, Iowa, 1937
Courtesy the Lesley Frowick Collection

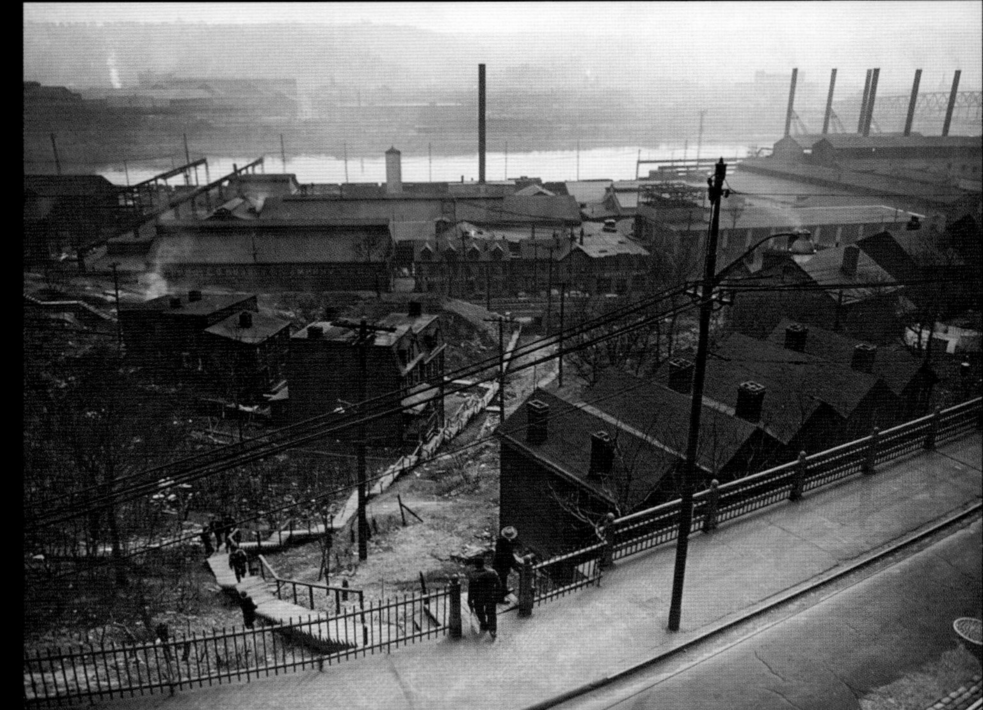

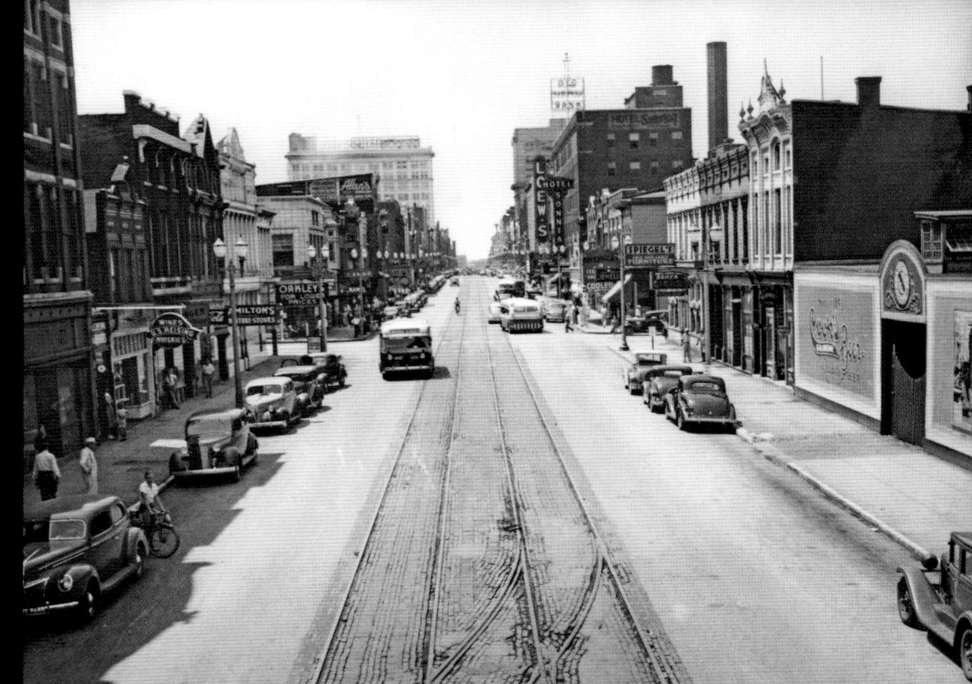

**f Pittsburgh steel mills from
l's childhood neighborhood,**

raph by the C. G. Hussey Co.
*Museum of Art Collection of Photographs,
the Carnegie Museum of Art*

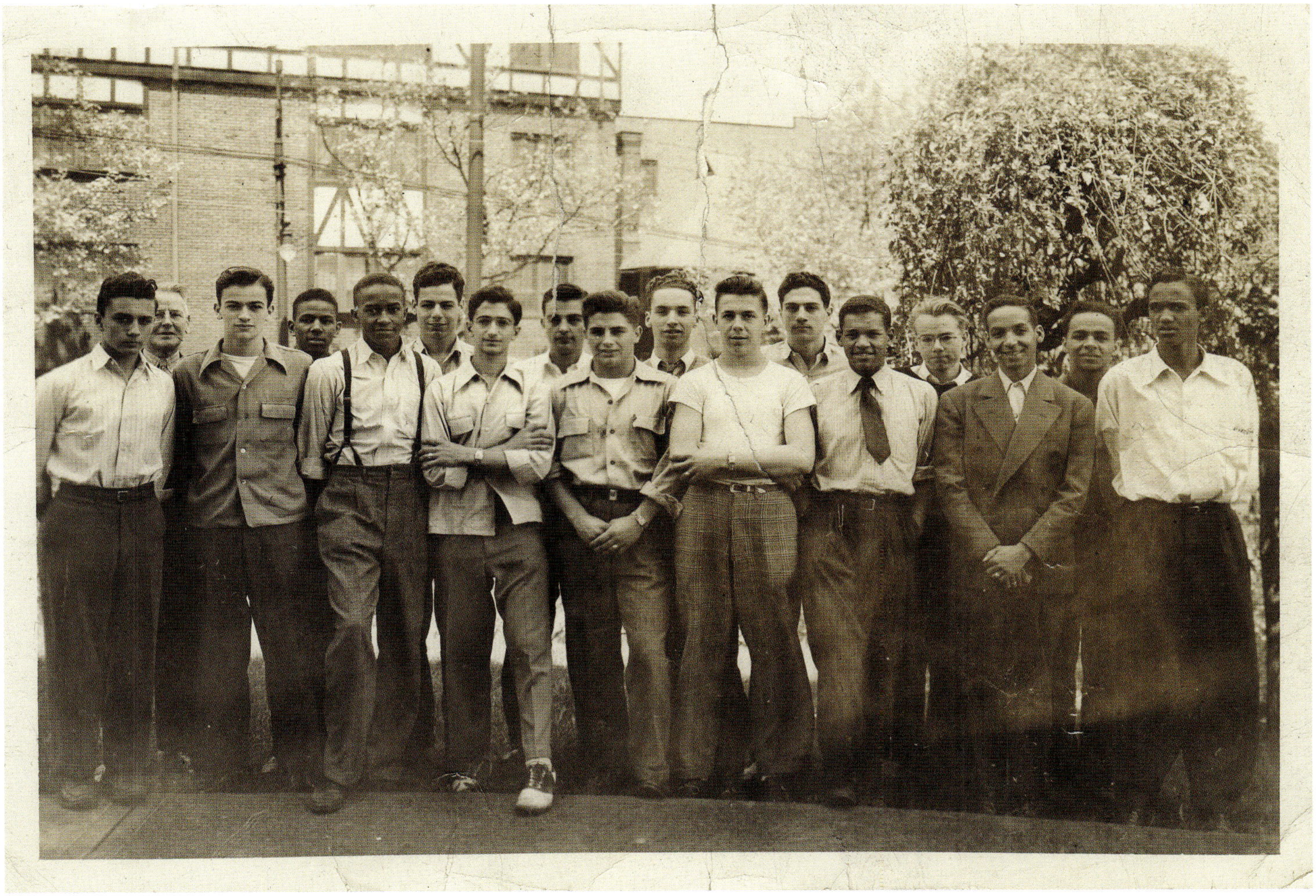

TOP
Photographer unknown
Homeroom picture of Andy Warhol's class at Schenley High School (Warhol is fourth from right), 1944–45
Gelatin silver print
$5 \times 7\frac{3}{16}$ in. (12.7 × 18.3 cm)
The Andy Warhol Museum, Pittsburgh; Founding Collection, Contribution The Andy Warhol Foundation for the Visual Arts, Inc., 1998.3.5412

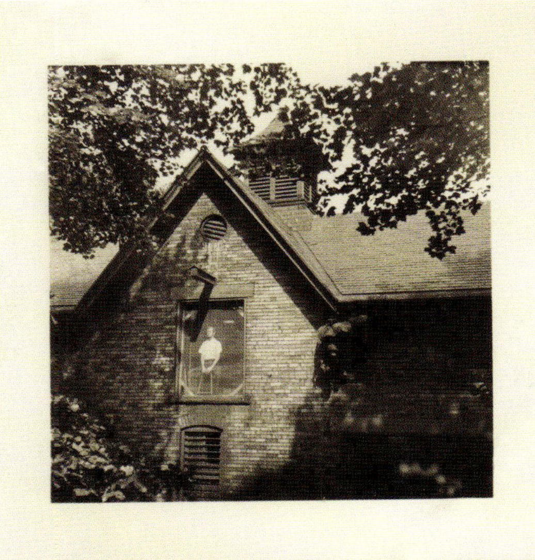

BOTTOM
Photographer unknown
Andy Warhol sitting in the window of a barn that served as a studio space for him and other students, ca. 1948
Gelatin silver print
2¾ × 2¾ in. (7 × 7 cm)
The Andy Warhol Museum, Pittsburgh; Founding Collection, Contribution The Andy Warhol Foundation for the Visual Arts, Inc., 1998.3.5223

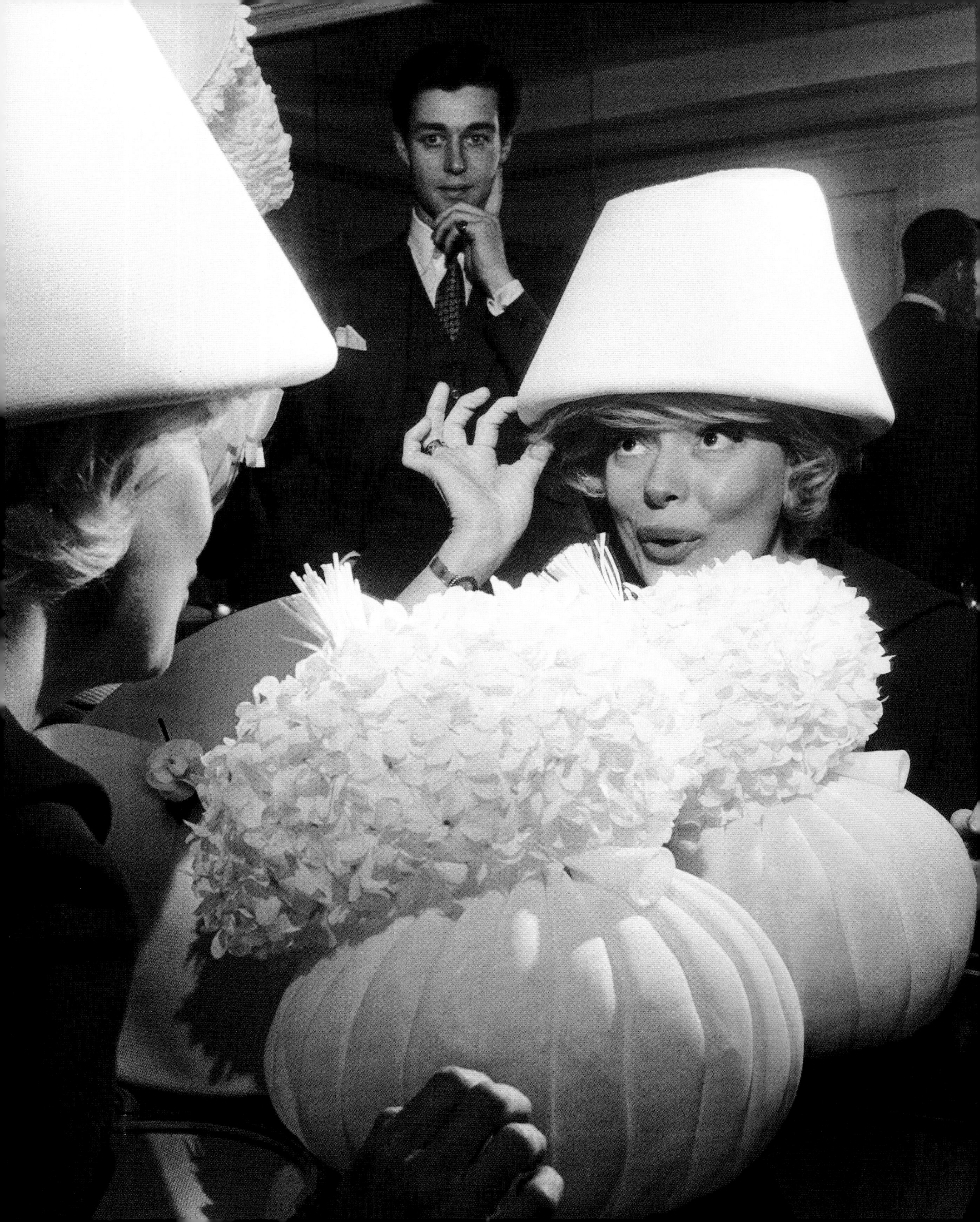

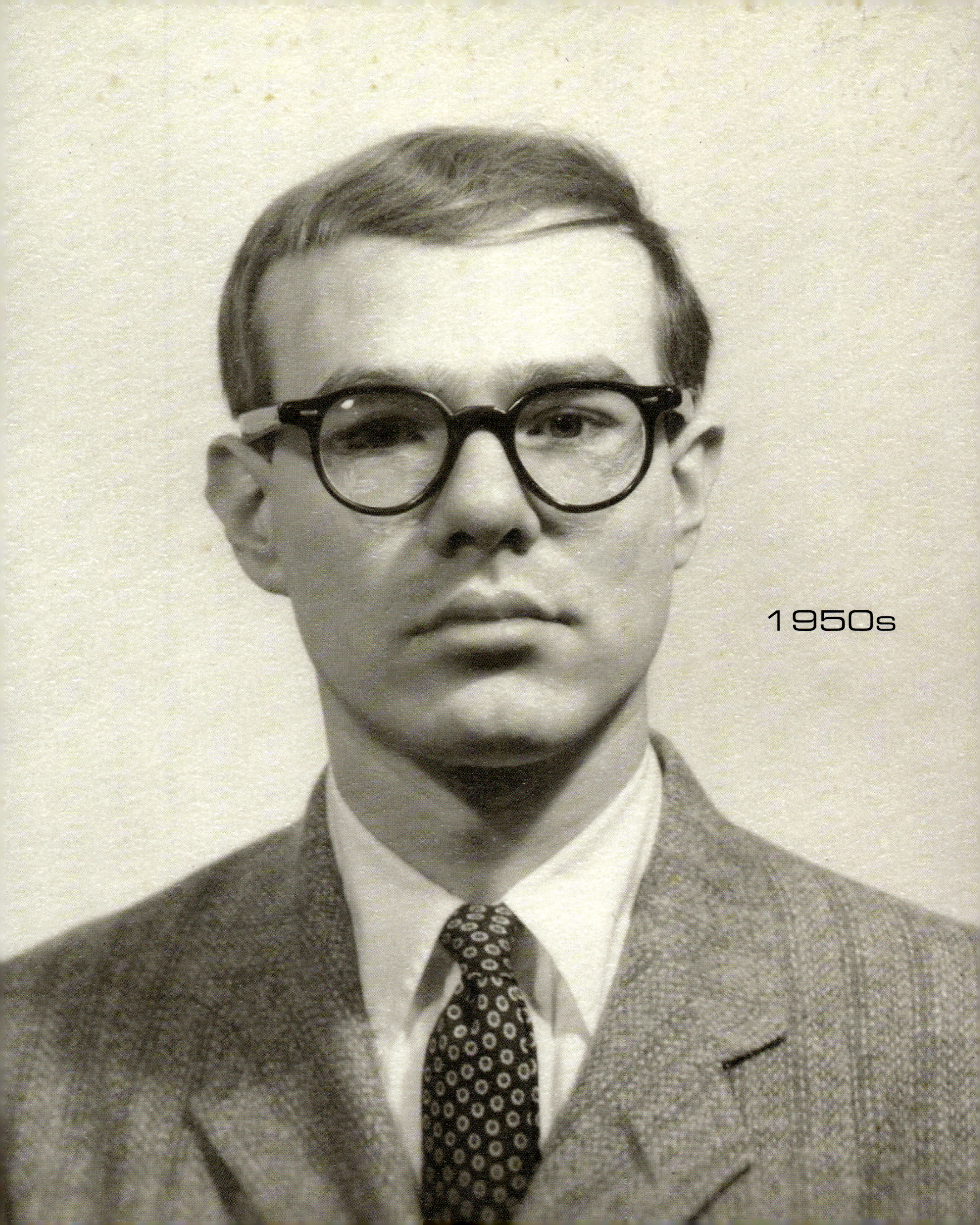

1950s

1950s

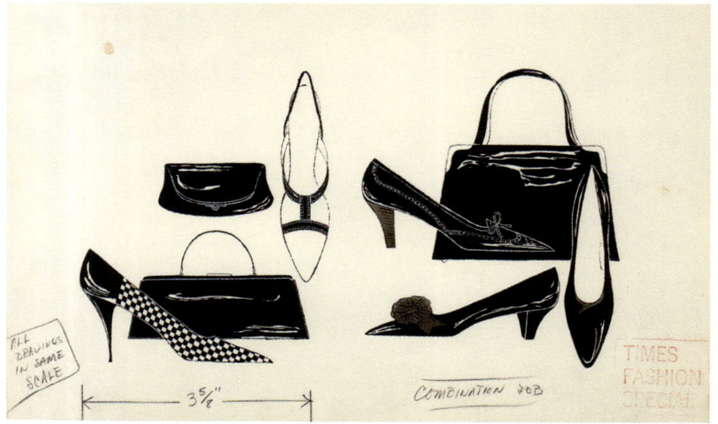

LEFT
Andy Warhol
Five Shoes and Three Purses, 1950s
Ink, graphite, and gouache on Strathmore Seconds paper
14¼ x 22 9/16 in. (36.2 x 57.3 cm)
The Andy Warhol Museum, Pittsburgh; Founding Collection, Contribution The Andy Warhol Foundation for the Visual Arts, Inc., 1998.1.1292

WARHOL

1951
Warhol is awarded an Art Directors Club Medal for his newspaper illustrations advertising the CBS radio feature "The Nation's Nightmare," one of numerous graphic-arts awards he receives throughout the 1950s.

1952
Warhol's first solo exhibition, *Fifteen Drawings Based on the Writings of Truman Capote*, is held at the Hugo Gallery in New York.

Julia Warhola moves to New York, where she lives with her son until 1971.

1954
Exhibits in both group and solo shows at the Loft Gallery in New York.

Self-publishes the illustrated book *25 Cats Name Sam and One Blue Pussy*, with text by Charles Lisanby. These and Warhol's other books are hand colored at "coloring parties" with friends and associates.

Begins frequenting Serendipity 3 on East 58th Street, a café known for its desserts.

HALSTON

1950
Graduates from Benjamin Bosse High School in Evansville, Illinois.

Purchases a black-and-white sleeveless dress and red heels for his sister Sue's thirteenth birthday, in July. He requests that Sue walk down Main Street in Evansville so he can watch people's reactions to the outfit he had styled for her.

1952
Attends Indiana University for a brief period and then returns home to Evansville. He takes a full-time job at International Harvester in the blueprint room, where he had held a summer job in high school.

After being laid off from International Harvester, Halston moves to Chicago and takes night classes in fashion illustration at the Art Institute of Chicago.

While taking classes, Halston also works as a window dresser at the Carson Pirie Scott department store.

In his free time, he designs and makes hats using a sewing machine he keeps in his apartment.

PREVIOUS SPREAD, LEFT
As Halston looks on, Carol Channing tries on a white Courrèges hat in Halston's studio at Bergdorf Goodman, March 3, 1960
Bettmann/CORBIS

PREVIOUS SPREAD, RIGHT
Andy Warhol (passport photograph), 1956
Gelatin silver print
2¾ × 2½ in. (7 × 6.4 cm)
The Andy Warhol Museum, Pittsburgh; Founding Collection, Contribution The Andy Warhol Foundation for the Visual Arts, Inc., 1998.3.14802

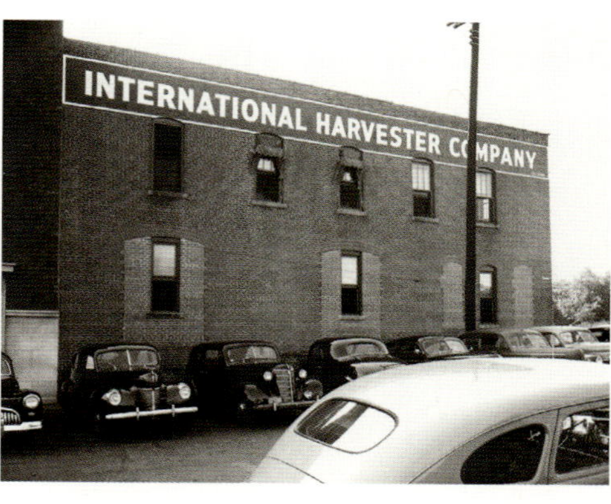

LEFT
International Harvester building in Evansville, Indiana, 1956
Courtesy the Donahue Collection

1955

Uses hand-carved rubber stamps to create repeated images, which are often hand colored. He employs this technique through the early 1960s.

The shoe company I. Miller selects Warhol to illustrate its weekly newspaper advertisements, which become a great success and run for about three years.

Creates window displays for the Bonwit Teller department store.

1956

Warhol's *Studies for a Boy Book* is exhibited at the Bodley Gallery in New York. During the 1950s, Warhol fills numerous sketchbooks with his drawings of young men.

A Warhol drawing of a shoe is included in the exhibition *Recent Drawings U.S.A.* at the Museum of Modern Art.

Warhol's gift of a drawing to the Museum of Modern Art in New York is rejected by the museum's director, Alfred Barr.

Takes a two-month trip around the world, visiting Japan, Cambodia, India, Egypt, and Italy with his friend Charles Lisanby. This is his first trip outside the United States.

RIGHT
Andy Warhol
Female Costumed Full Figure, 1950s
Ink, tempera, and Dr. Martin's Aniline dye on Strathmore Seconds paper
28½ × 22½ in. (72.4 × 57.2 cm)
The Andy Warhol Museum, Pittsburgh; Founding Collection, Contribution The Andy Warhol Foundation for the Visual Arts, Inc., 1998.1.970

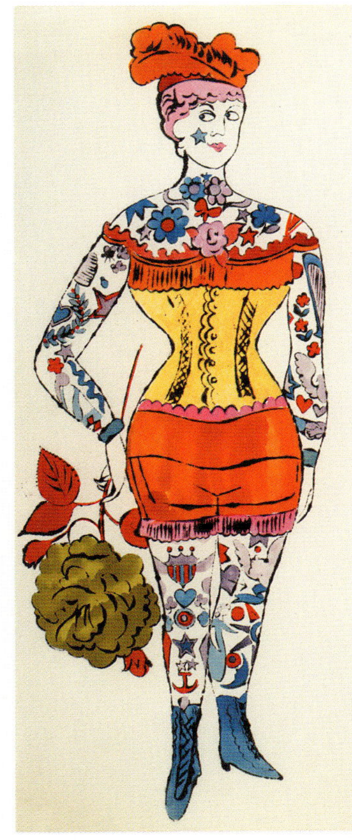

1957

Andy Warhol Enterprises is legally incorporated.

Warhol undergoes cosmetic surgery on his nose.

Warhol's series of drawings of gold shoes is featured in *Life* magazine.

1954–56

Opens a small millinery shop inside Andre Basil's hair salon at the Ambassador Hotel, one of Chicago's best locations. The wealthy clientele quickly takes to the flattering, sculptural designs by the new, young milliner. Early clients include Fran Allison, Hedda Hopper, Joan Crawford, Kim Novak, and Gloria Swanson.

1956

Peg Zwecker, fashion columnist for the *Chicago Daily News*, befriends Halston and begins promoting his talent in her column "Fashionably Speaking."

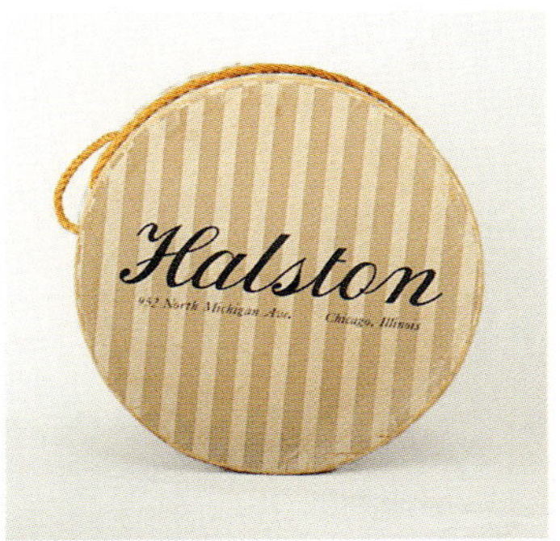

ABOVE
Halston hat box from shop at 952 Michigan Avenue, Chicago, ca. 1956
Courtesy the Lesley Frowick Collection

1957

Opens his own shop, the Boulevard Salon, on North Michigan Avenue. Receives national press coverage in *Women's Wear Daily*.

Begins to use his middle name as his business moniker.

1958

Moves to New York City when recruited to work with the pre-eminent French-born millinery designer Lilly Daché, whose salon is located at 78 East 56th Street.

1959

Begins designing millinery at Bergdorf Goodman, one of the premier retail meccas in the United States. Halston further expands his client base within New York's most fashionable social circles and fine-tunes his skill at providing service and care for his customers. His name becomes synonymous with inventive creations that are comfortable to wear and suited to the most current fashions.

November 1: The *New York Times* publishes an article, "Young New Talent a Feather in an Experienced Cap," about the twenty-seven-year-old Halston designing for Bergdorf Goodman's Custom Millinery Salon.

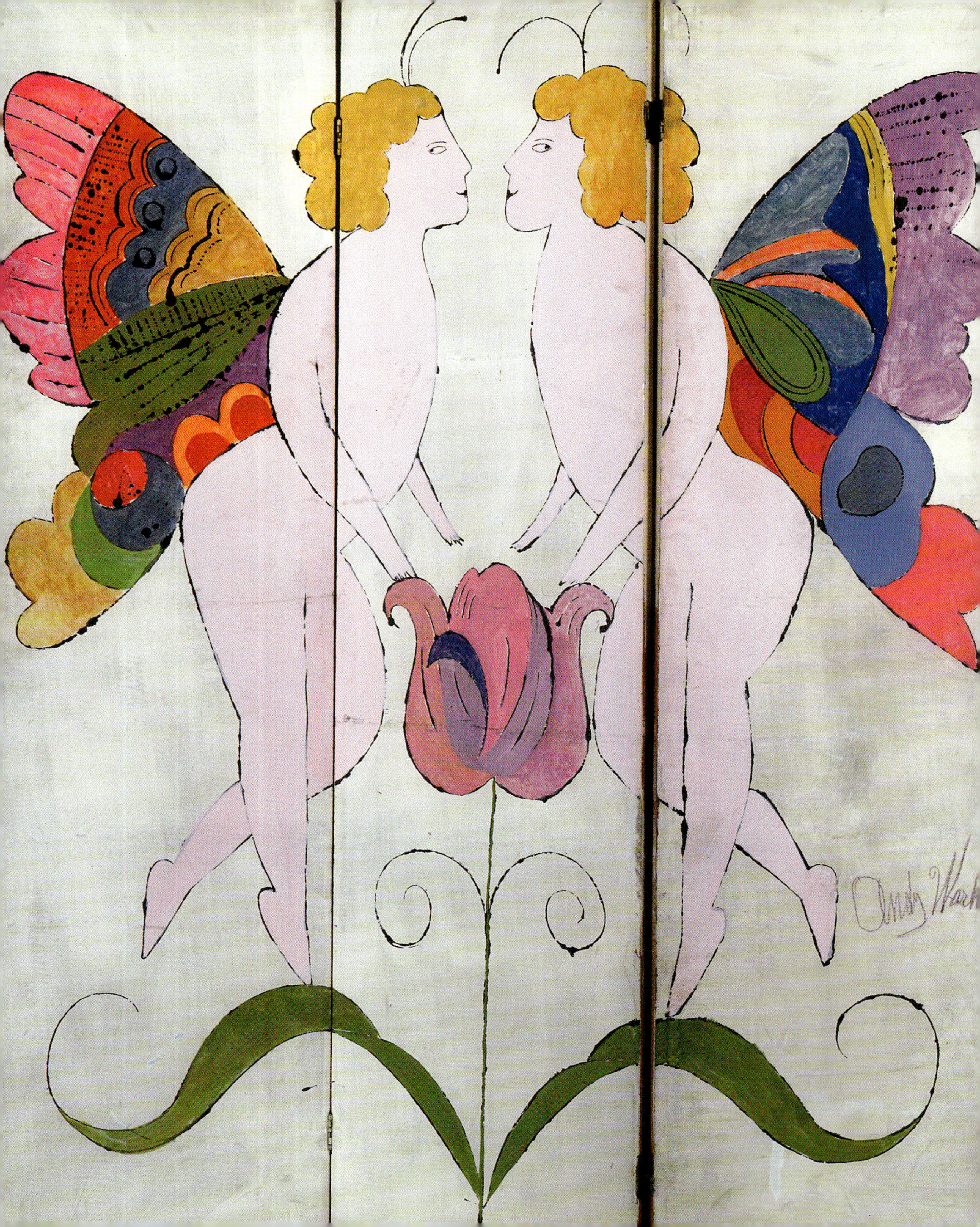

NEW YORK CITY

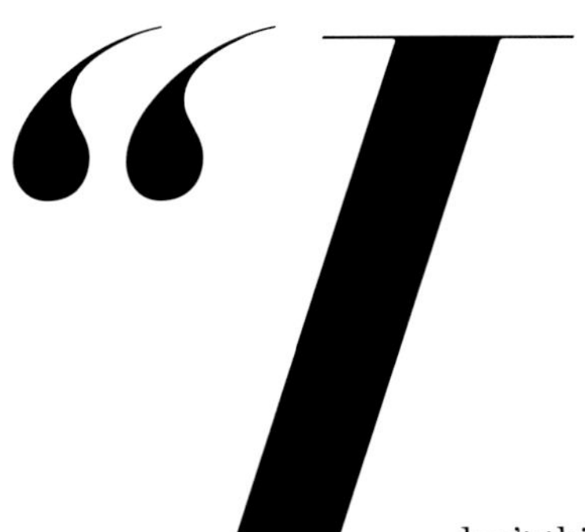

“I don’t think there’s any place in the world like New York City as far as street life goes. Here you can see every class, every race, every sex and every kind of fashion bumping up against each other. Everyone gets to mix and mingle and you can never guess what combinations you’re going to see next. The movies and T.V. like to separate everybody when they show New York, so you’ll see a whole New York movie made up of rich people getting in and out of limousines and spending their lives going to museums and eating lunches at stuffy restaurants. Or it’s white and clean and middle-class, with these helpful upstairs neighbors who are always sweet and eccentric and cooking these ‘old world’ meals. Or it’s a New York where criminals run the streets and every alley is filled with gangsters and everyone carries a gun or a switchblade and there’s a murder every three minutes. Or maybe it’s an ‘art’ movie where the boys wear makeup and the girls have crew-cuts and nobody has a personality like anyone you’ve ever met and everyone talks in this strange philosophic way and they’re all sleeping with each other for no reason. But the great thing is that all of this is true and in New York it’s all happening at the same time.”

—Andy Warhol, *America*

By the late 1950s New York City was home to both Warhol and Halston. Warhol took a straight path from Pittsburgh, moving to Manhattan with his friend the artist Phillip Pearlstein after graduating from Carnegie Institute of Technology. Halston arrived nine years later by way of Chicago.

Andy Warhol
Folding Screen, 1950s
Tempera and ink on cardboard and wooden screen
64½ × 50 in. (163.8 × 127 cm)
The Andy Warhol Museum, Pittsburgh; Founding Collection, Contribution The Andy Warhol Foundation for the Visual Arts, Inc., 1998.1.793

DEPARTMENT STORES

"When you think about it, department stores are kind of like museums."

—Andy Warhol, *America*

Interestingly, the world of department stores and ladies' fashion provided a launch pad for the careers of both men. Each worked briefly during college in jobs involving department-store window displays, learning concepts about staging, merchandising, and working for a brand. Warhol worked for the Joseph Horne department store in Pittsburgh while a student and then as an illustrator of backdrops, advertisements, and designs for Bonwit Teller, Bergdorf Goodman, and Tiffany's in New York. Halston cut his teeth at Carson Pirie Scott in Chicago before landing at Bergdorf Goodman in New York.

Warhol created a number of displays for the Fifth Avenue windows of Bonwit Teller. In the 1950s these installations included his fanciful illustrations on folding screens. In April 1961, Warhol hung a mini exhibition of his first Pop paintings of ads and comic strips as a backdrop for a new line of summer fashions.

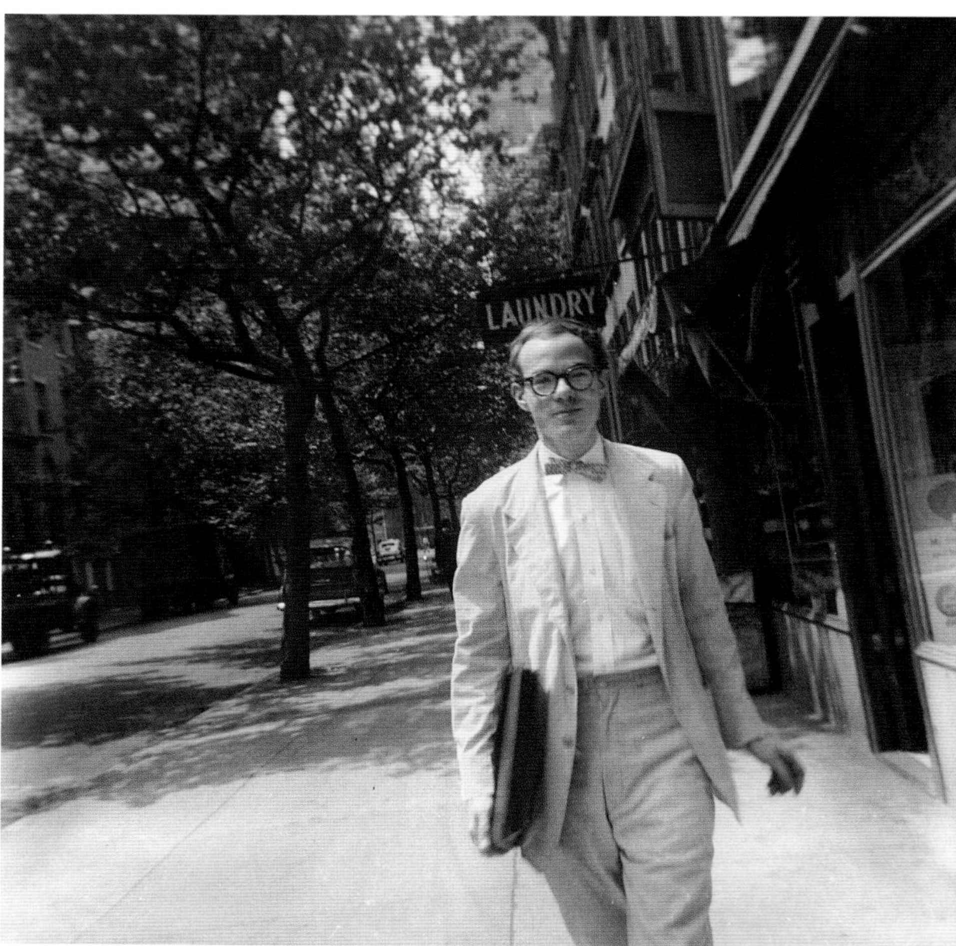

RIGHT
Leila Davis Singelis
Making the Rounds, 1950
Gelatin silver print
8³⁄₁₆ × 8 in. (20.8 × 20.3 cm)
The Andy Warhol Museum, Pittsburgh; Gift of Leila Davies Singelis, 1994.22.9.1

OPPOSITE
Virginia Roehl
Bonwit Teller window display designed by Andy Warhol, late 1950s
Gelatin silver print
10 × 8⅛ in. (25.4 × 20.6 cm)
The Andy Warhol Museum, Pittsburgh; Founding Collection, Contribution The Andy Warhol Foundation for the Visual Arts, Inc., 1998.3.3495

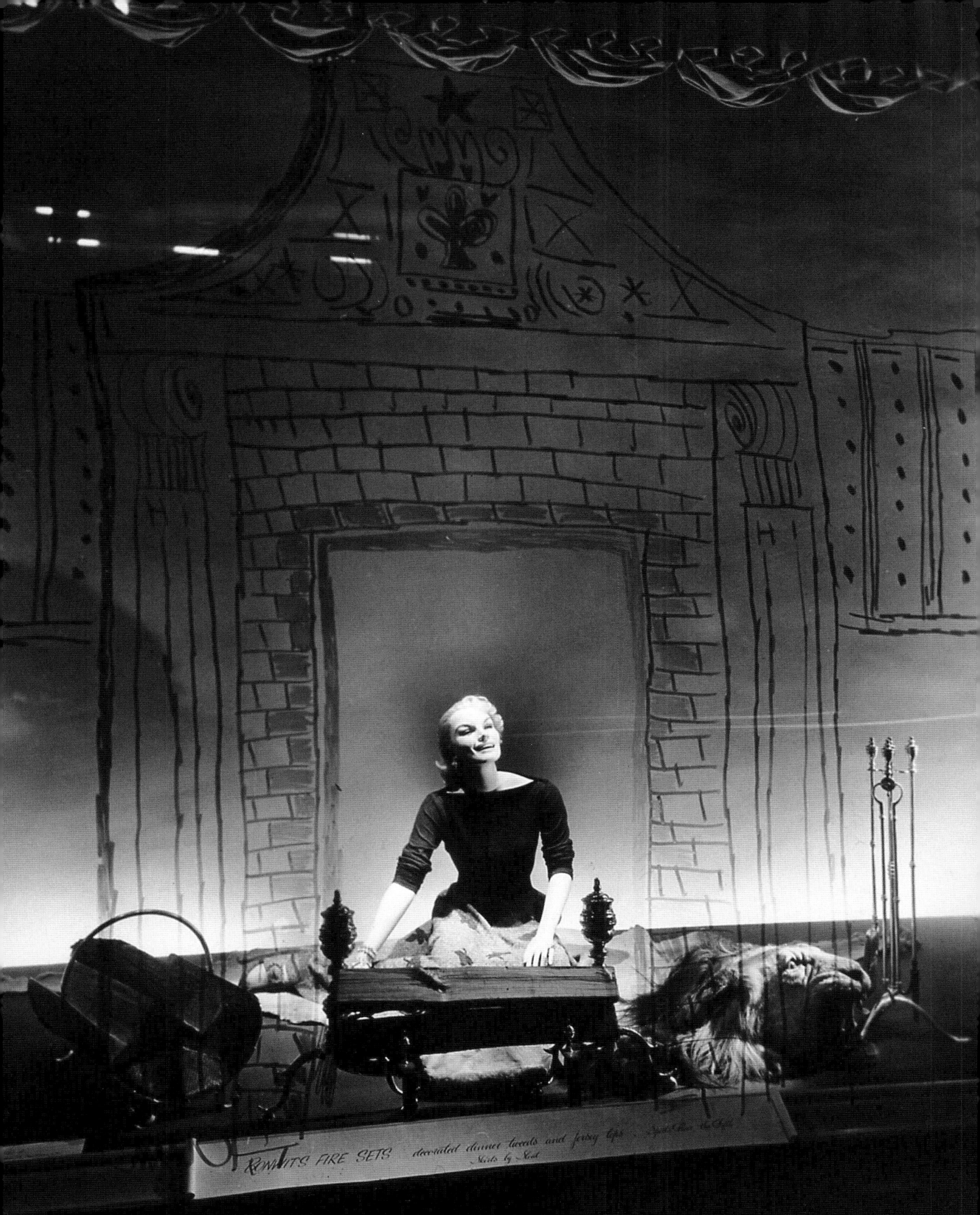
FIRE SETS
decorated dinner tweeds and jersey tops

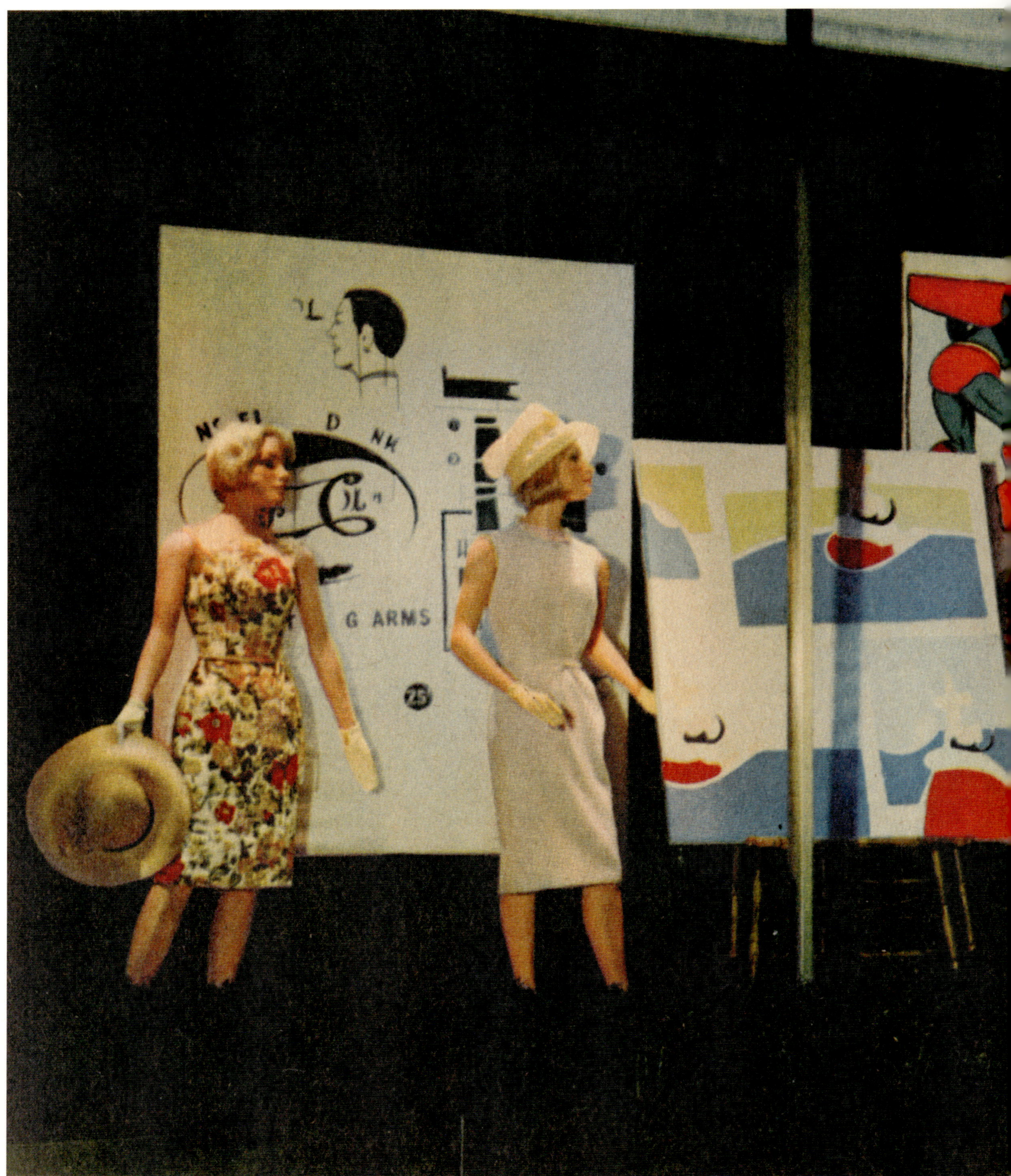
G ARMS
25

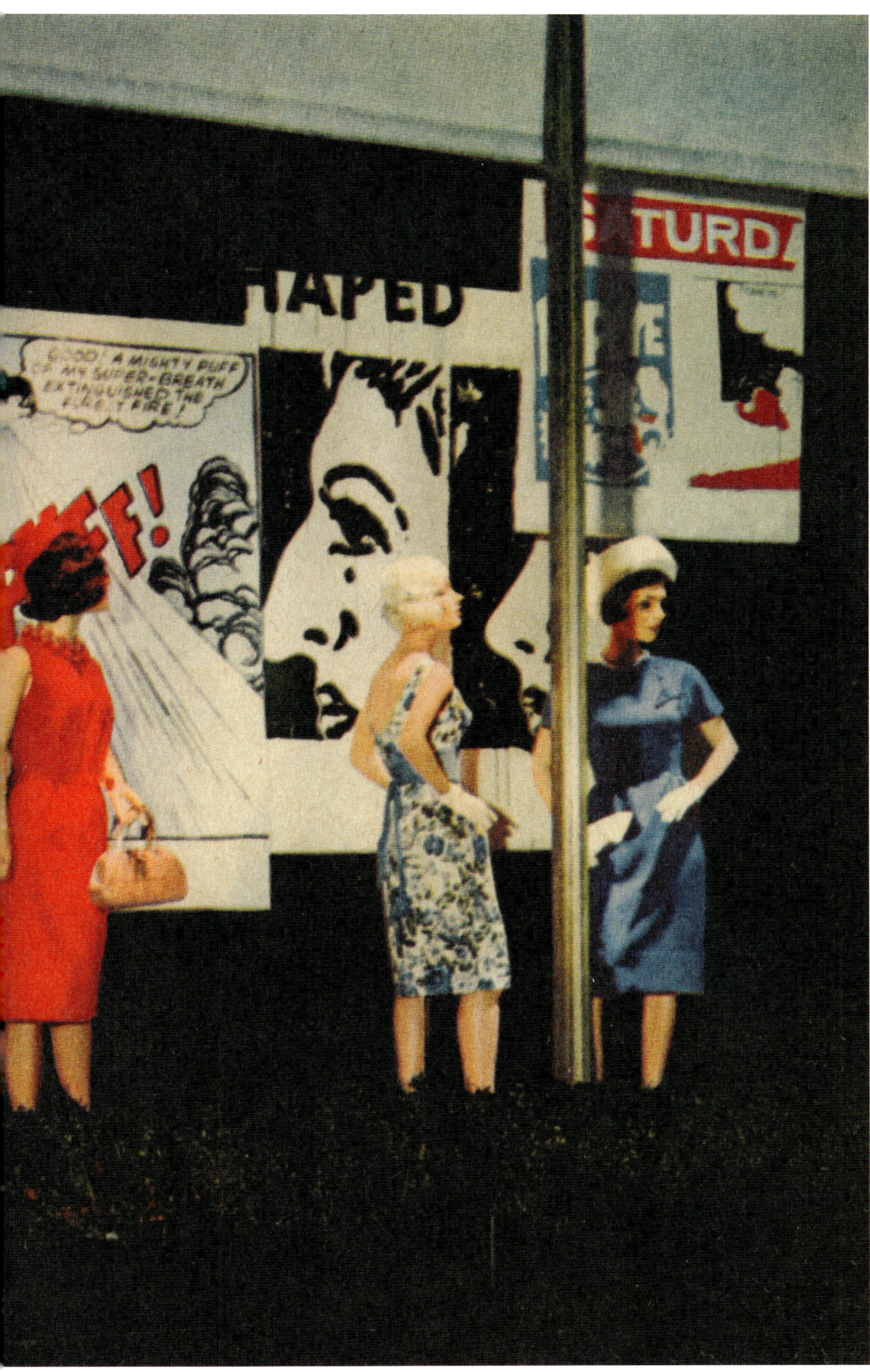

Bonwit Teller window display, New York, April 1961

The Andy Warhol Museum, Pittsburgh; Founding Collection, Contribution The Andy Warhol Foundation for the Visual Arts, Inc.

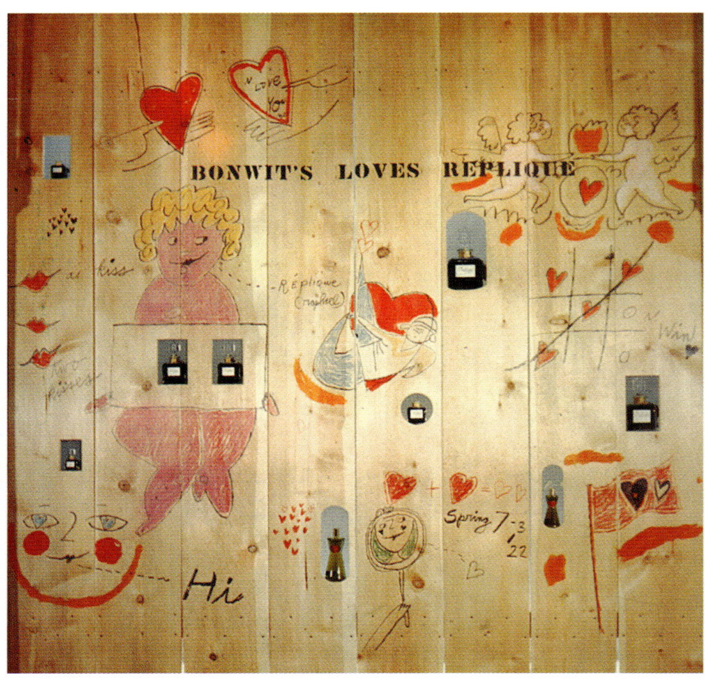

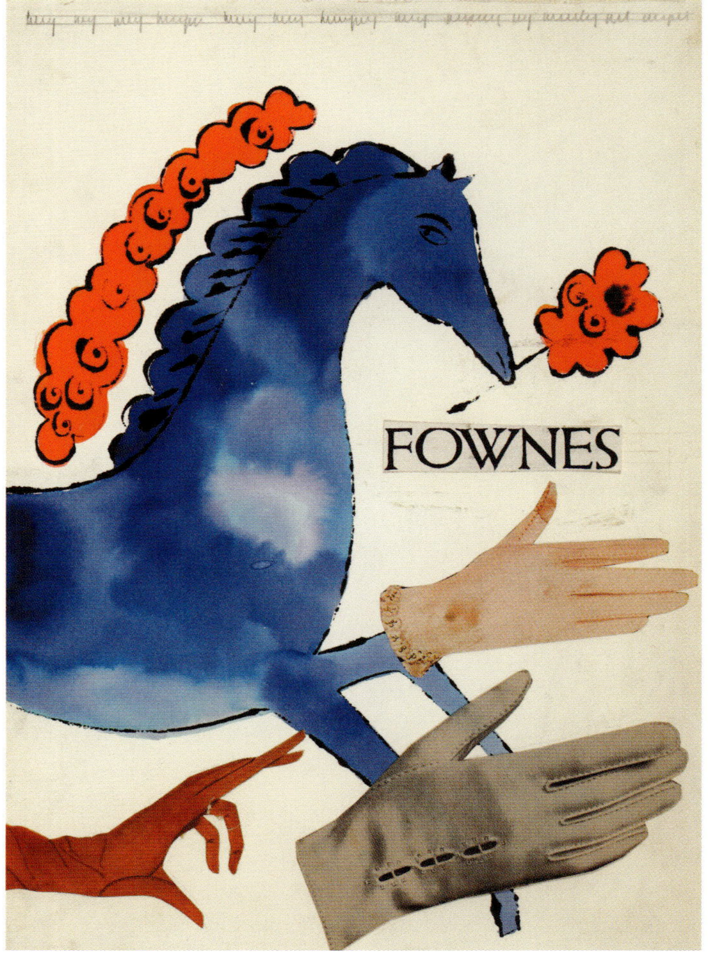

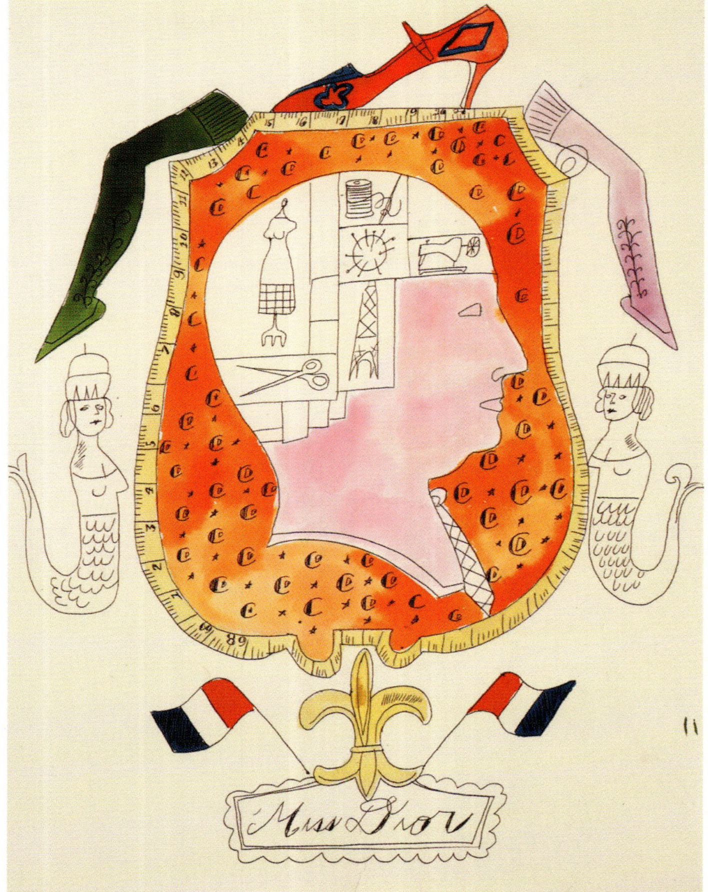

TOP LEFT
Printed card, Bonwit Teller window display by Andy Warhol, 1955
Printed ink on coated paper
9⅞ × 6 in. (25.1 × 15.2 cm)
The Andy Warhol Museum, Pittsburgh; Founding Collection, Contribution The Andy Warhol Foundation for the Visual Arts, Inc., 1998.3.3547

BOTTOM LEFT
Andy Warhol
"Miss Dior," 1950s
Ballpoint pen and watercolor on laid paper
23⅝ × 17⅞ in. (60 × 45.4 cm)
The Andy Warhol Museum, Pittsburgh; Founding Collection, Contribution The Andy Warhol Foundation for the Visual Arts, Inc., 1998.1.1182

TOP RIGHT
Andy Warhol
"Fownes," 1950
Ink, graphite, Dr. Martin's Aniline dye, and collage on Strathmore paper
15⅜ × 11⅜ in. (39.1 × 28.9 cm)
The Andy Warhol Museum, Pittsburgh; Founding Collection, Contribution The Andy Warhol Foundation for the Visual Arts, Inc.,

OPPOSITE
Andy Warhol
Folding Screen, 1950s
Tempera, ink, and gold leaf on cardboard and wooden screen
64½ × 50 in. (163.8 × 127 cm)
The Andy Warhol Museum, Pittsburgh; Founding Collection, Contribution The Andy Warhol Foundation for the Visual Arts, Inc., 1998.1.794

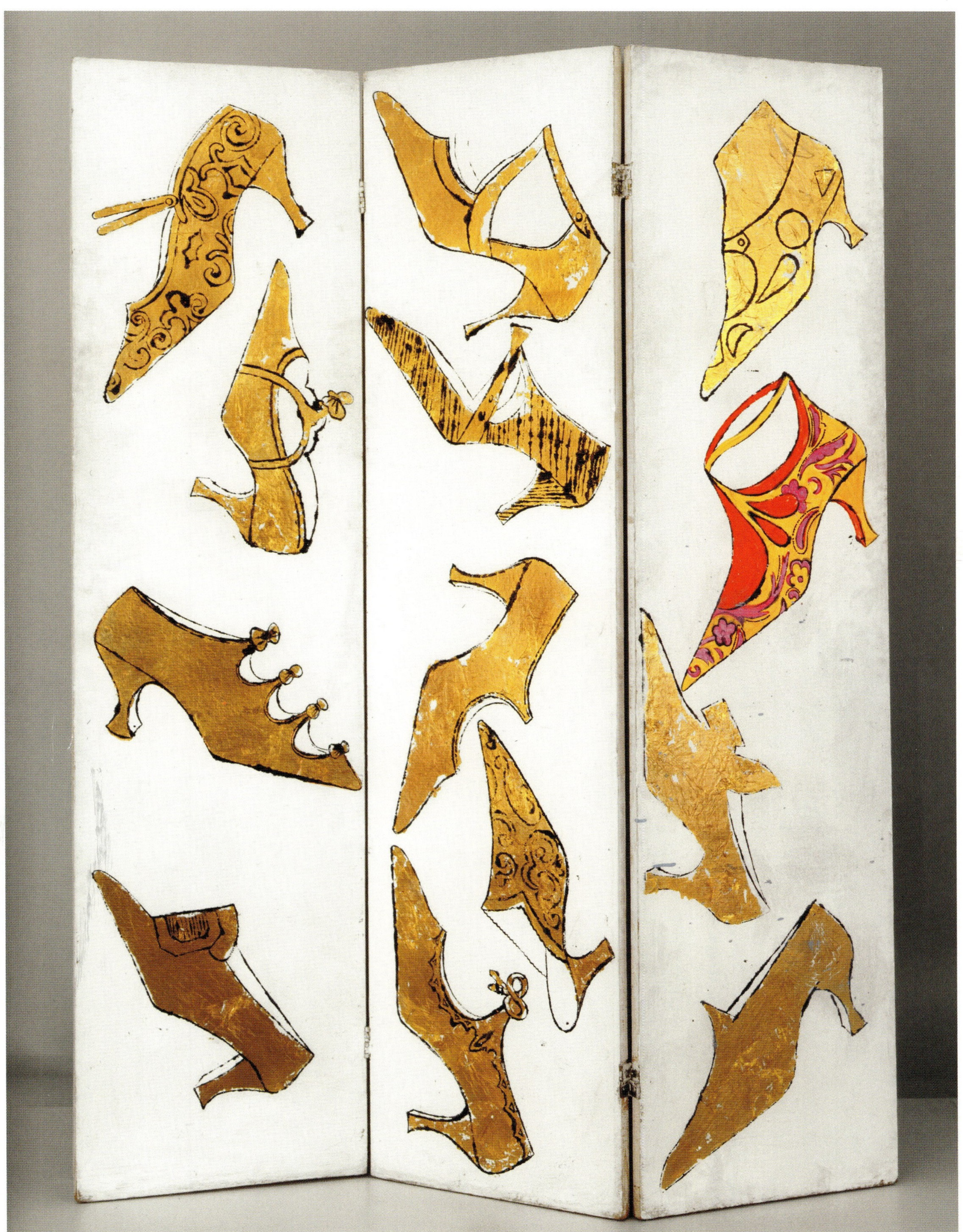

EARLY WORK

Warhol's success as a commercial artist was largely due to his ability to create art very quickly and his absolute willingness to respond to the revisions demanded by the art directors. One of the most well-known ad campaigns he helped create was for I. Miller shoes. By the end of the 1950s Warhol earned $70,000 a year, an incredible salary for such a young artist at that time.

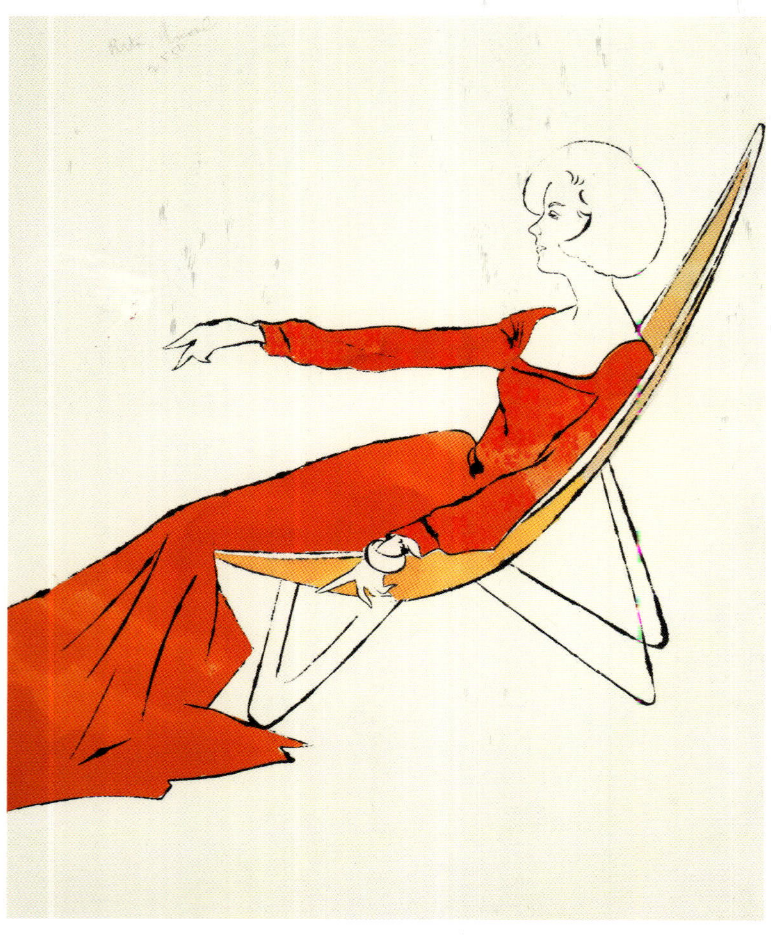

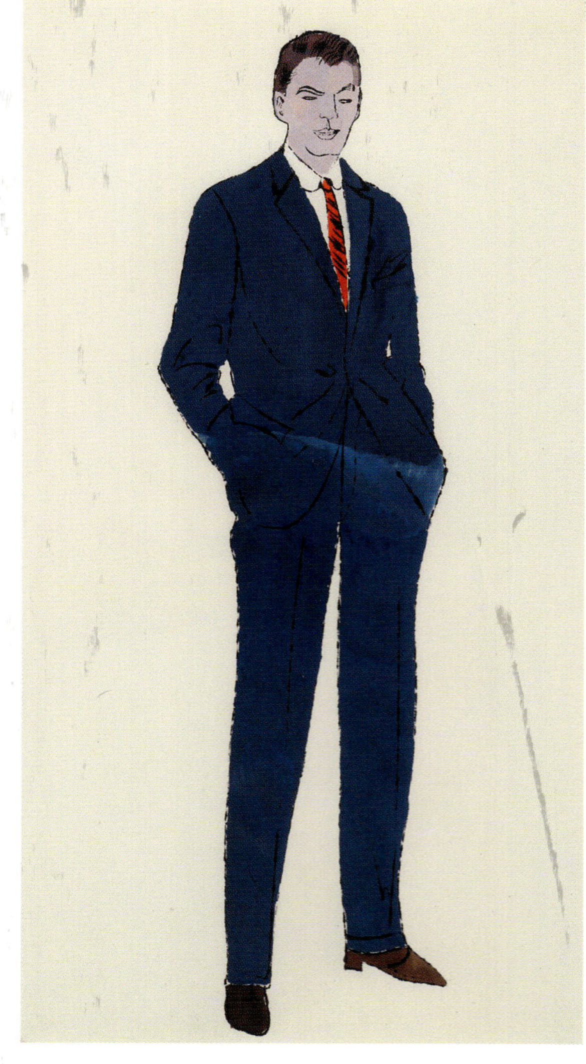

LEFT
Andy Warhol
Female Fashion Figure, 1950s
Ink and Dr. Martin's Aniline dye on Strathmore paper and board
22 × 17½ in. (55.9 × 44.5 cm)
The Andy Warhol Museum, Pittsburgh; Founding Collection, Contribution The Andy Warhol Foundation for the Visual Arts, Inc., 1998.1.1208

RIGHT
Andy Warhol
Male Fashion Figure, 1950s
Ink, watercolor, and tempera on Strathmore paper
26⅞ × 15 in. (68.3 × 38.1 cm)
The Andy Warhol Museum, Pittsburgh; Founding Collection, Contribution The Andy Warhol Foundation for the Visual Arts, Inc., 1998.1.1209

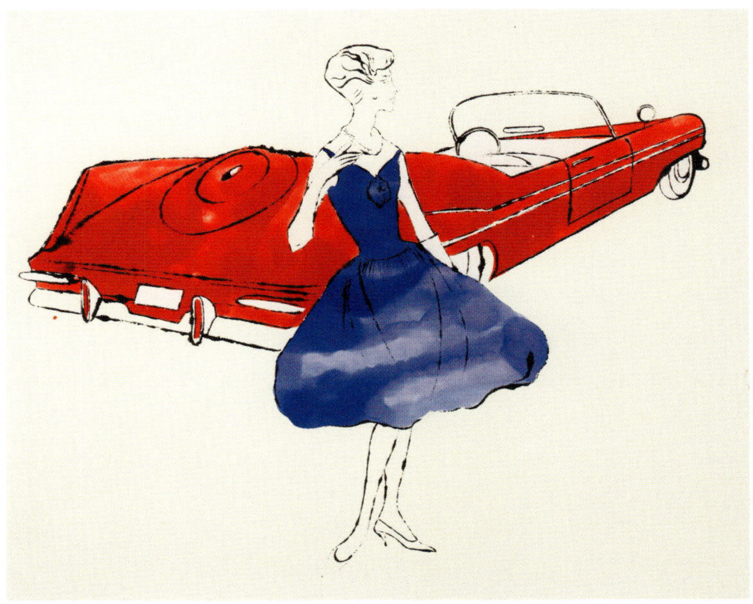

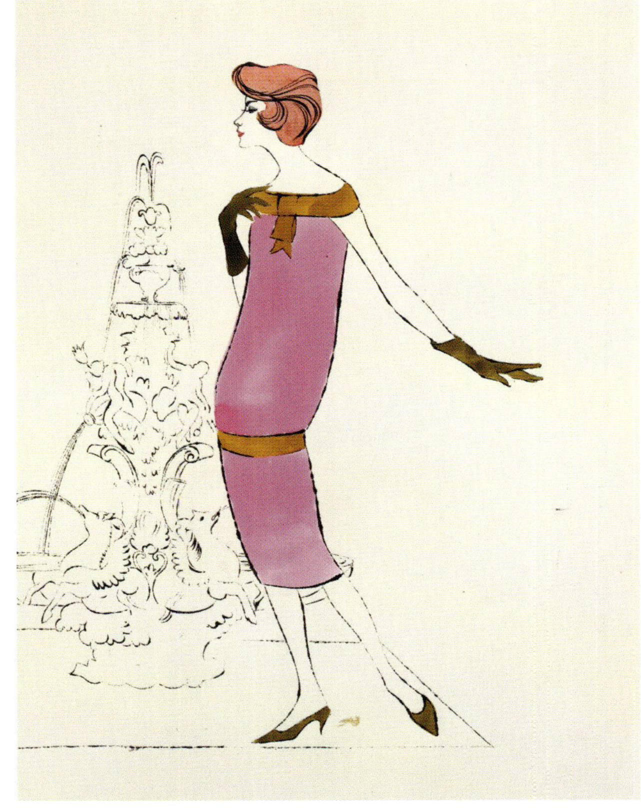

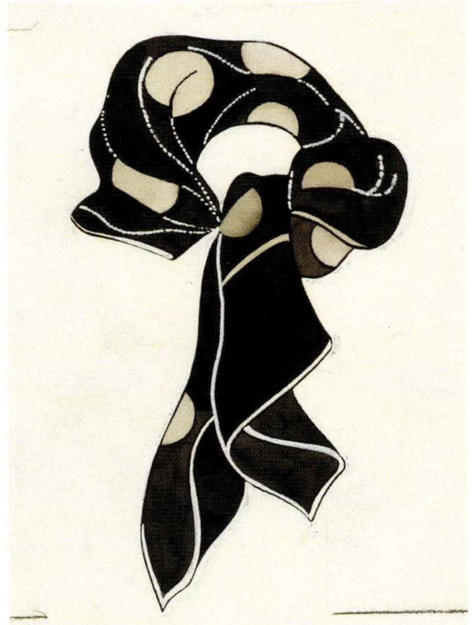

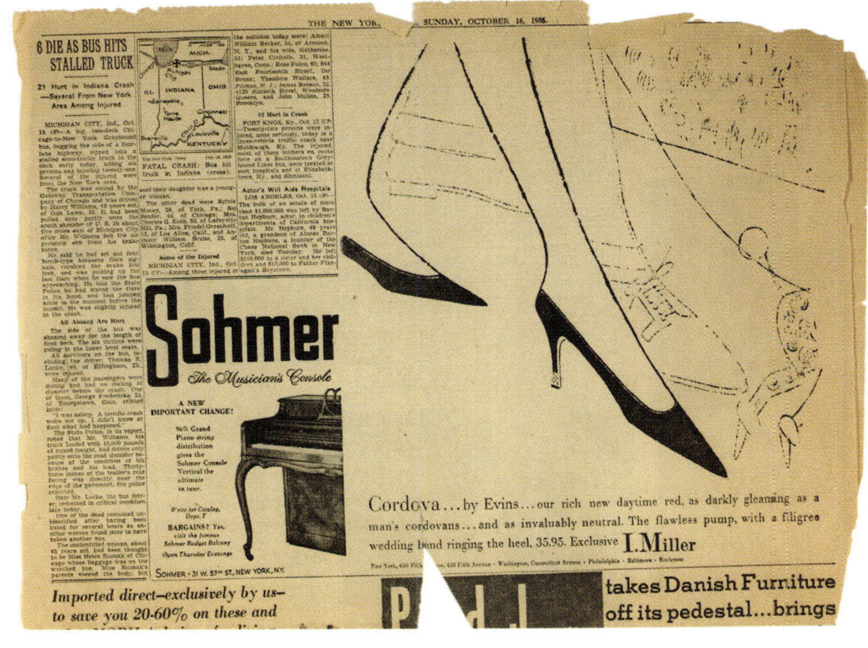

THE NEW YOR[K TIMES], SUNDAY, OCTOBER 16, 1955.

6 DIE AS BUS HITS STALLED TRUCK

21 Hurt in Indiana Crash —Several From New York Area Among Injured

FATAL CRASH: Bus hit truck in Indiana (cross).

All Aboard Are Hurt

Some of the Injured

22 Hurt in Crash

Actor's Will Aids Hospitals

Sohmer

The Musician's Console

A NEW IMPORTANT CHANGE!

96% Grand Piano string distribution gives the Sohmer Console Vertical the ultimate in tone.

Write for Catalog, Dept. T

BARGAINS? Yes, visit the famous Sohmer Budget Balcony

Open Thursday Evenings

SOHMER • 31 W. 57TH ST., NEW YORK, N.Y.

Cordova . . . by Evins . . . our rich new daytime red, as darkly gleaming as a man's cordovans . . . and as invaluably neutral. The flawless pump, with a filigree wedding band ringing the heel, 35.95. Exclusive I. Miller

Imported direct—exclusively by us— to save you 20-60% on these and

takes Danish Furniture off its pedestal . . . brings

TOP LEFT
Andy Warhol
Female Fashion Figure, 1950s
Ink and Dr. Martin's Aniline dye on Strathmore paper
20⅛ × 24⅞ in. (51.1 × 63.2 cm)
The Andy Warhol Museum, Pittsburgh; Founding Collection, Contribution The Andy Warhol Foundation for the Visual Arts, Inc., 1998.1.1194

BOTTOM LEFT
Andy Warhol
Silk Scarf, 1950s
Ink, graphite, and tempera on Strathmore paper
12⅛ × 9⅞ in. (30.8 × 25.1 cm)
The Andy Warhol Museum, Pittsburgh; Founding Collection, Contribution The Andy Warhol Foundation for the Visual Arts, Inc., 1998.1.1219

TOP RIGHT
Andy Warhol
Female Fashion Figure, 1950s
Ink and Dr. Martin's Aniline dye on Strathmore paper
26 5/16 × 19⅛ in. (66.8 × 48.6 cm)
The Andy Warhol Museum, Pittsburgh; Founding Collection, Contribution The Andy Warhol Foundation for the Visual Arts, Inc., 1998.1.1192

BOTTOM RIGHT
I. Miller advertisement
The Andy Warhol Museum, Pittsburgh; Founding Collection, Contribution The Andy Warhol Foundation for the Visual Arts, Inc., TC-12 234

HATS AND SHOES

Halston was adept at styling hats for women that were flattering and functional. The wealthy clients of his Chicago shop led him to a job offer in 1958 to work with Lilly Daché in New York City. Under her tutelage, Halston was introduced firsthand to the workings of a successful fashion operation of the highest caliber. He became acquainted with the Hollywood actresses and fashionable women, including Jackie Kennedy, who patronized Daché's 56th Street salon. By the end of the 1950s, Halston was invited to open his own salon in Bergdorf Goodman. At six feet two inches, and impressively handsome, Halston became the lure to the store for many elite customers.

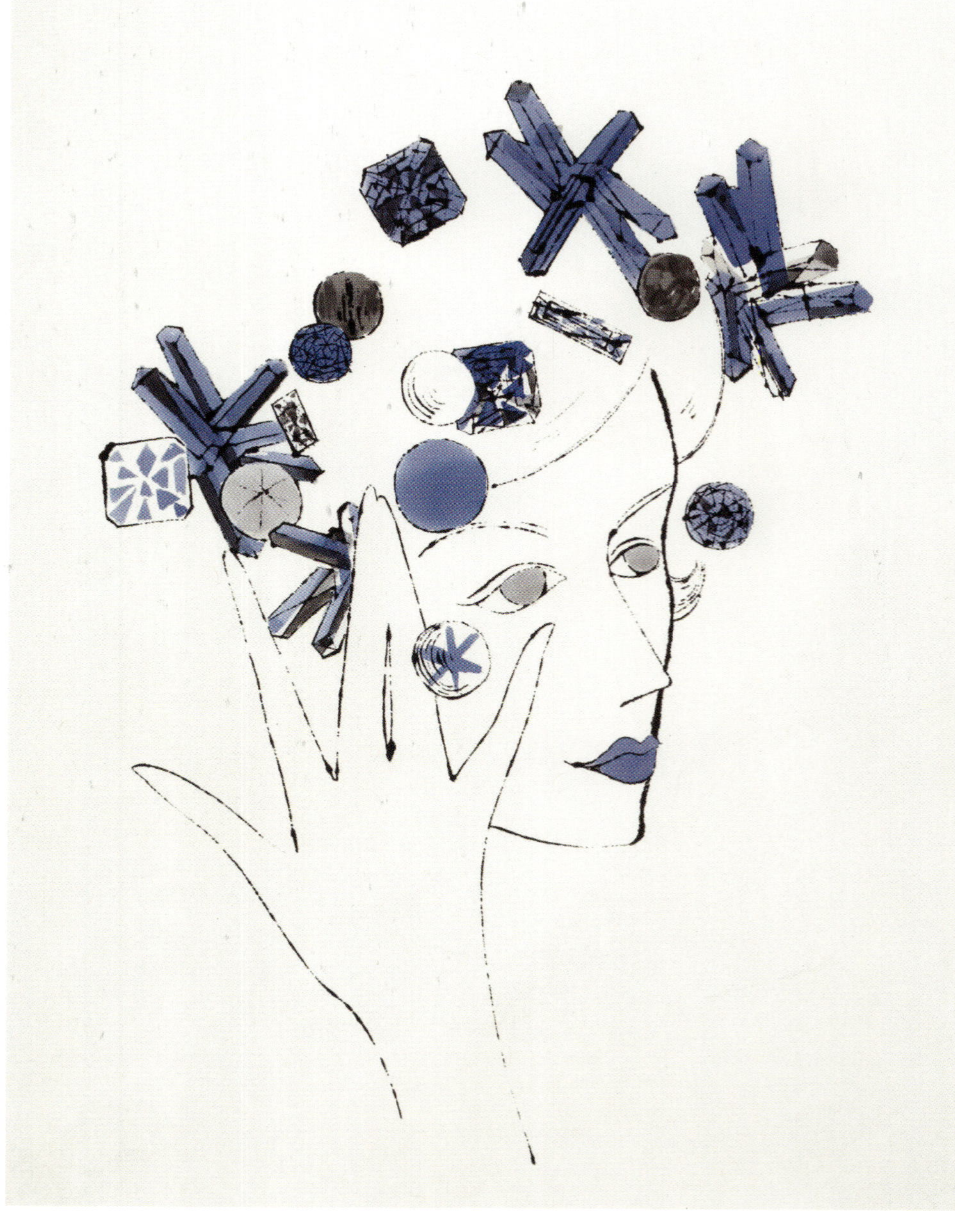

RIGHT
Andy Warhol
Female Head, 1950s
Ink and Dr. Martin's Aniline dye on Strathmore Seconds paper
22⅝ × 14¼ in. (57.5 × 36.2 cm)
The Andy Warhol Museum, Pittsburgh; Founding Collection, Contribution The Andy Warhol Foundation for the Visual Arts, Inc., 1998.1.853

OPPOSITE
A model wears Brussels lace on her eyelids and a cap by Halston, ca. 1960s
Photograph by Bert Stern
Condé Nast Archive/CORBIS

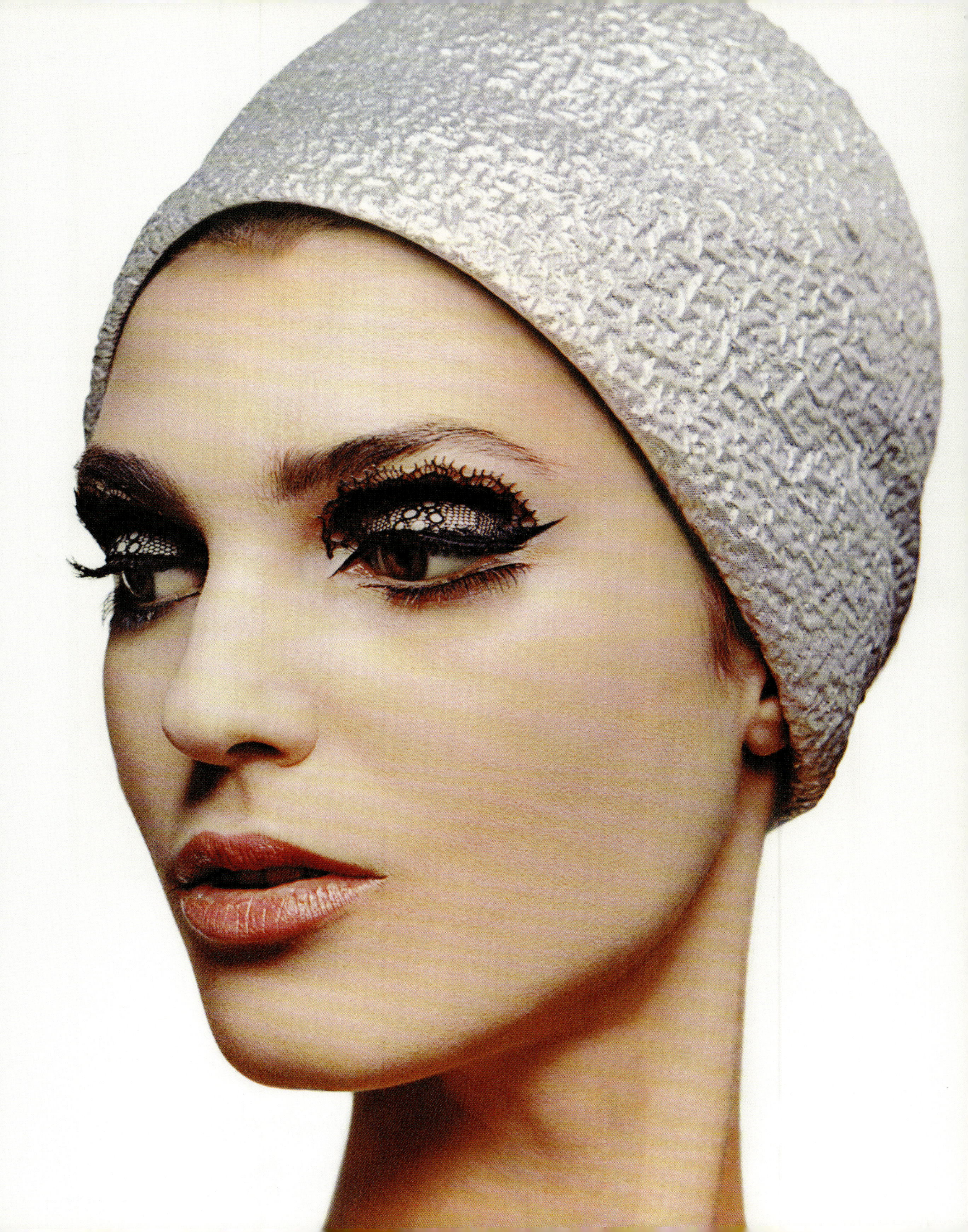

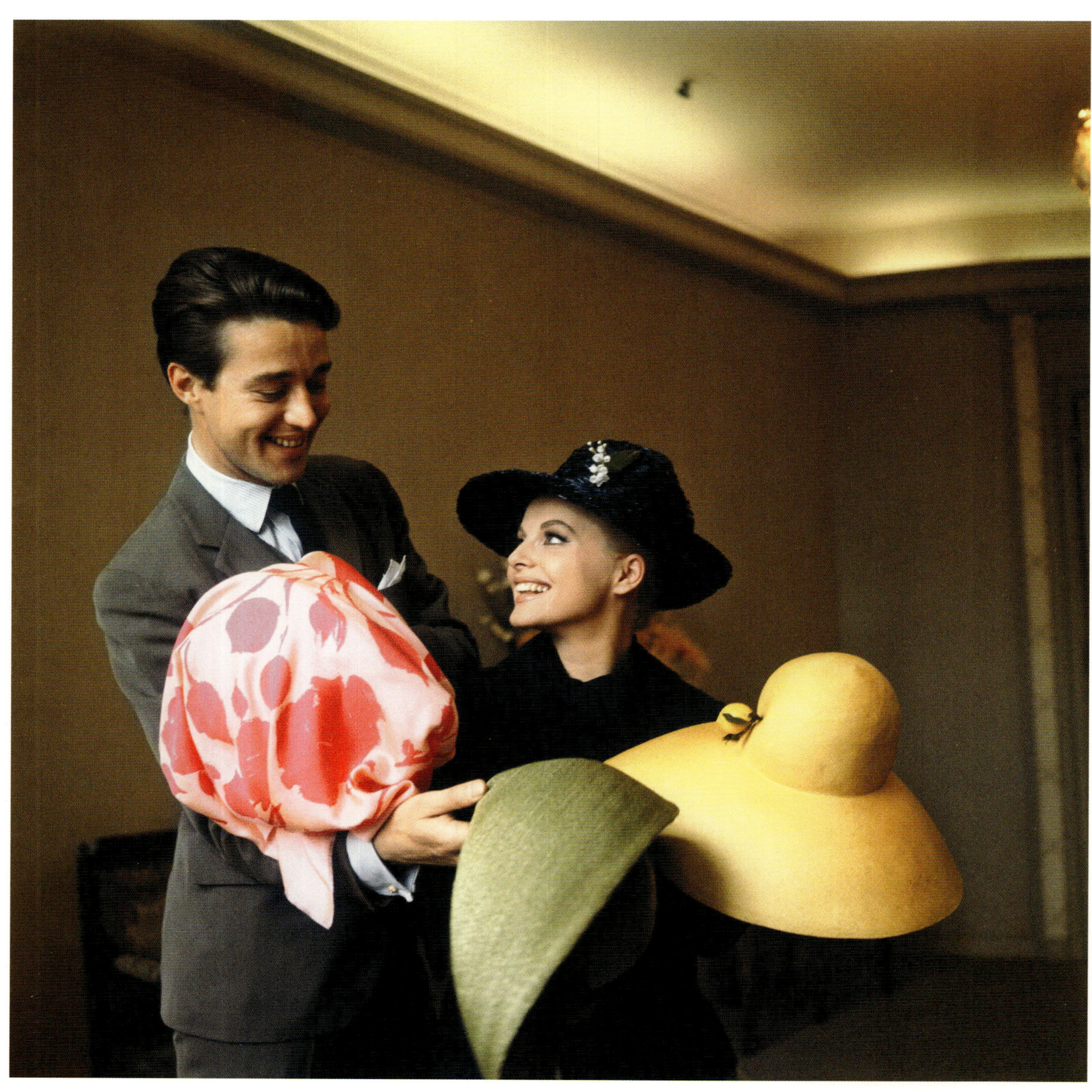

Italian actress Virna Lisi tries on hats at Bergdorf Goodman with assistance from Halston, March 21, 1964
Associated Press

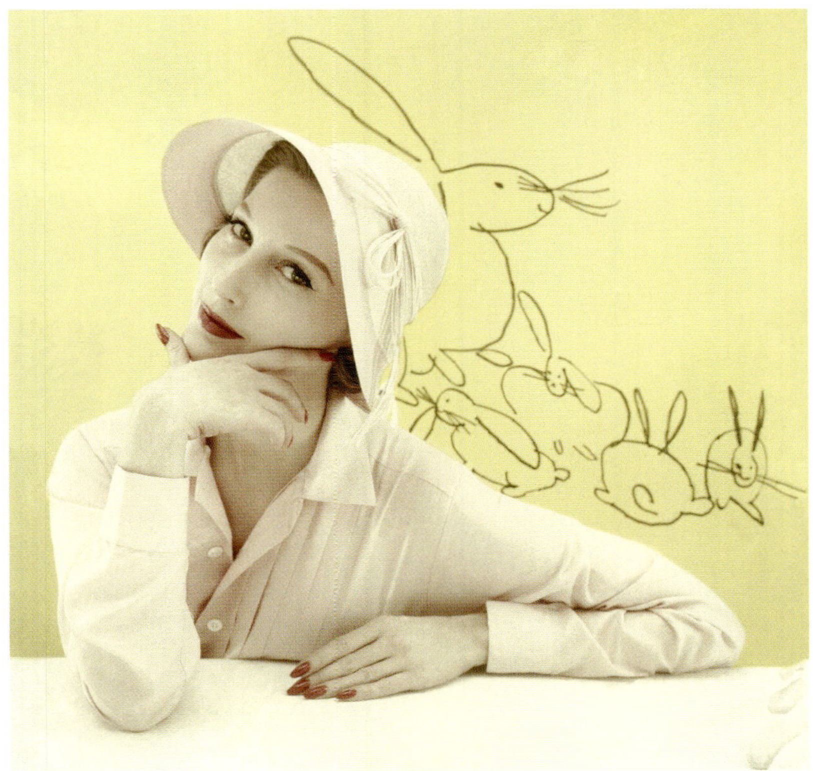

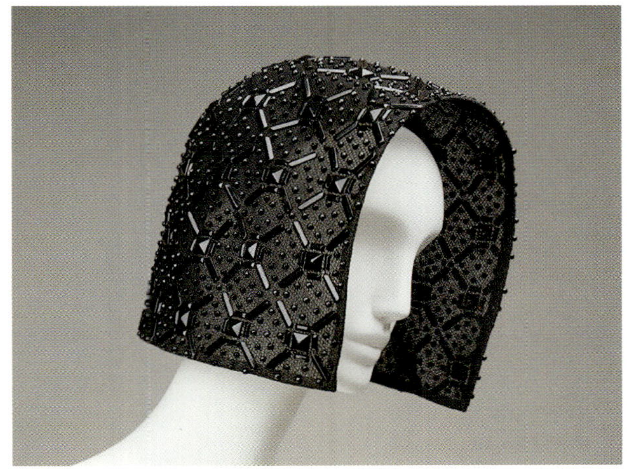

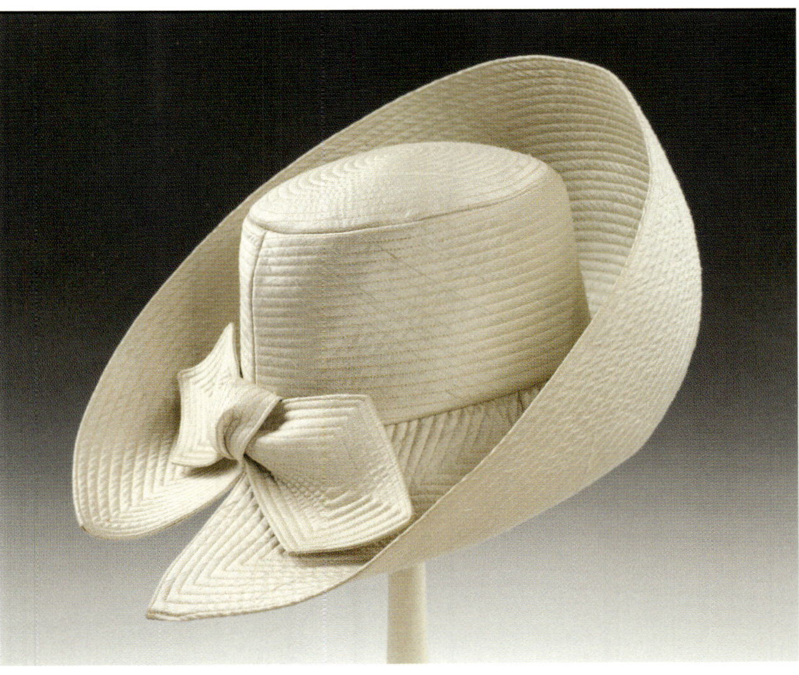

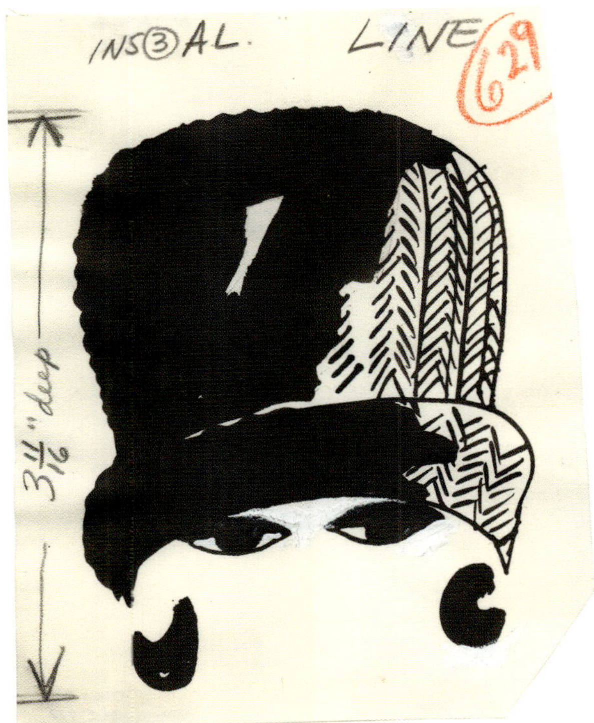

TOP LEFT
A Warhol drawing of rabbits serves as the backdrop for a model wearing a John Frederics straw hat with a Lady Manhattan Robaix silk broadcloth shirt and Dior makeup, ca. April 1, 1955
Photograph by Frances McLaughlin-Gill
Condé Nast

BOTTOM LEFT
Halston
For Bergdorf Goodman
Hat, ca. 1965
Silk
Brooklyn Museum Costume Collection at The Metropolitan Museum of Art, Gift of the Brooklyn Museum, 2009; Gift of Virginia Inness-Brown, 1986

TOP RIGHT
Halston
Hat, mid-1960s
Silk synthetic, plastic
The Metropolitan Museum of Art, New York. Gift of Paul Roebling in memory of Olga Bedin Roebling, 1988 (1988.138.3)

BOTTOM RIGHT
Andy Warhol
Eyes and Hat, n.d.
Ink on ivory paper
$7\frac{1}{8} \times 5\frac{5}{8}$ in. (18.1×14.3 cm)
The Andy Warhol Museum, Pittsburgh; Founding Collection, Contribution The Andy Warhol Foundation for the Visual Arts, Inc., 1998.1.1217

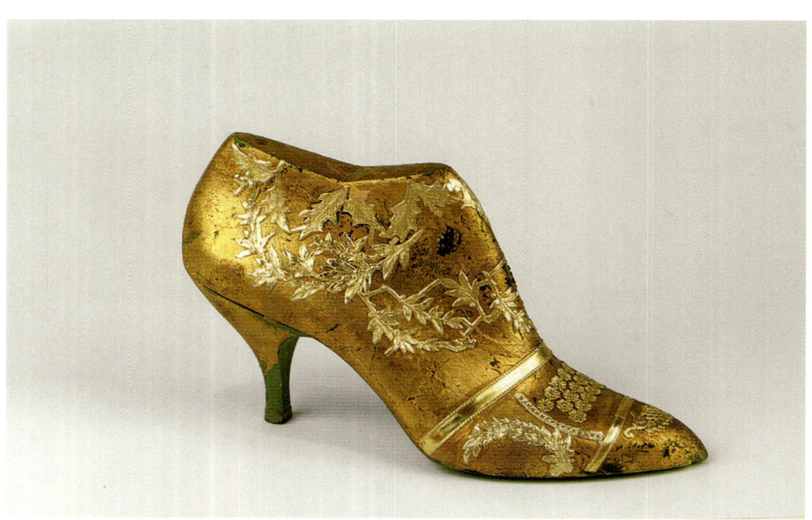

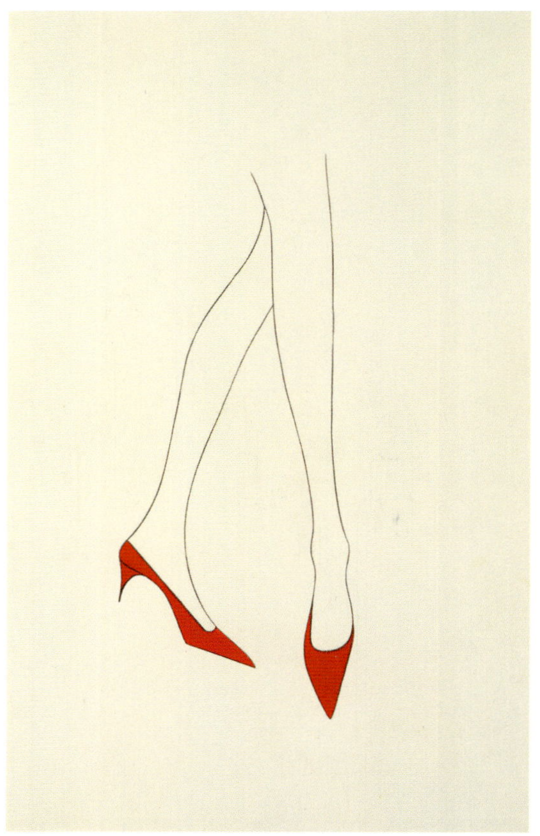

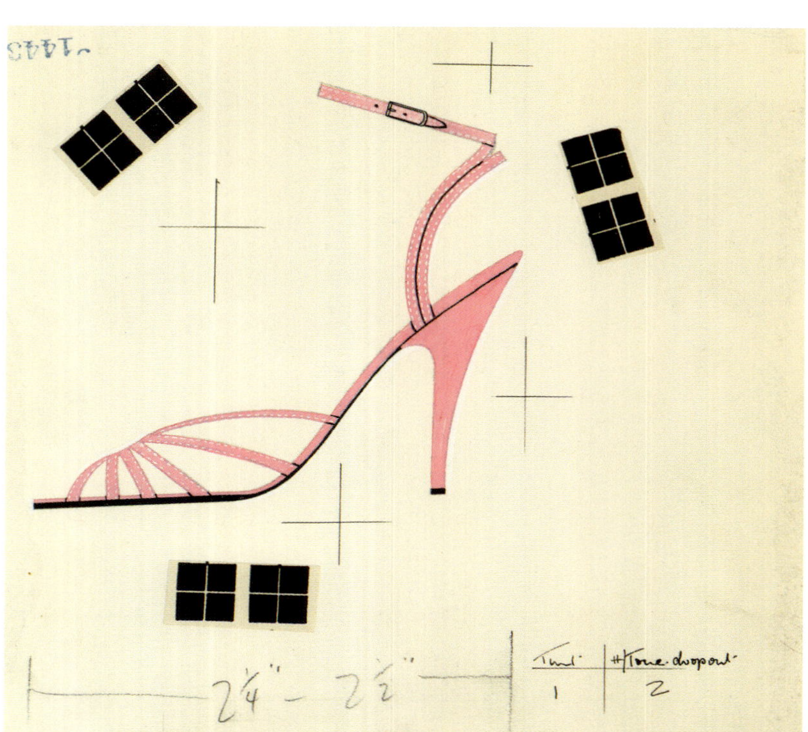

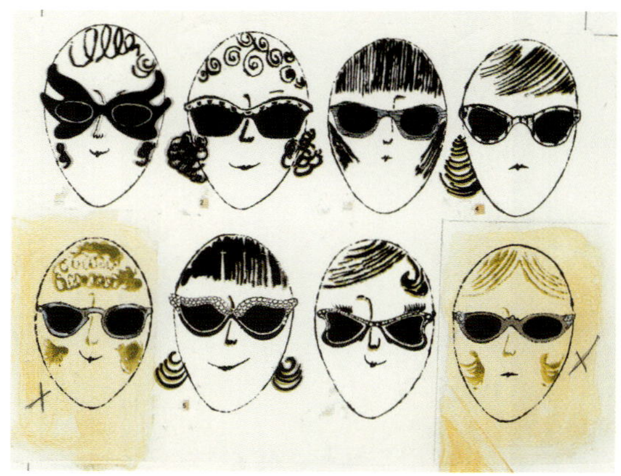

TOP LEFT
Andy Warhol
Shoe, 1950s
Gold leaf, tempera, and collage on wood shoe form
5 × 2¾ × 9 in. (12.7 × 7 × 22.9 cm)
The Andy Warhol Museum, Pittsburgh; Founding Collection, Contribution The Andy Warhol Foundation for the Visual Arts, Inc., 1998.1.704

BOTTOM LEFT
Andy Warhol
Sandal, 1950s
Ink and tempera with acetate overlay on Strathmore paper
15¾ × 22⅞ in. (40 × 58.1 cm)
The Andy Warhol Museum, Pittsburgh; Founding Collection, Contribution The Andy Warhol Foundation for the Visual Arts, Inc., 1998.1.1292

TOP RIGHT
Andy Warhol
Legs in Red High Heels, 1950s
Ink and Dr. Martin's Aniline dye on Strathmore paper
23 × 13½ in. (58.4 × 34.3 cm)
The Andy Warhol Museum, Pittsburgh; Founding Collection, Contribution The Andy Warhol Foundation for the Visual Arts, Inc., 1998.1.1268

BOTTOM RIGHT
Andy Warhol
Eight Female Heads Wearing Sunglasses, 1957
Ink and tempera with acetate overlay on Strathmore paper
15¾ × 22⅞ in. (40 × 58.1 cm)
The Andy Warhol Museum, Pittsburgh; Founding Collection, Contribution The Andy Warhol Foundation for the Visual Arts, Inc., 1998.1.1220

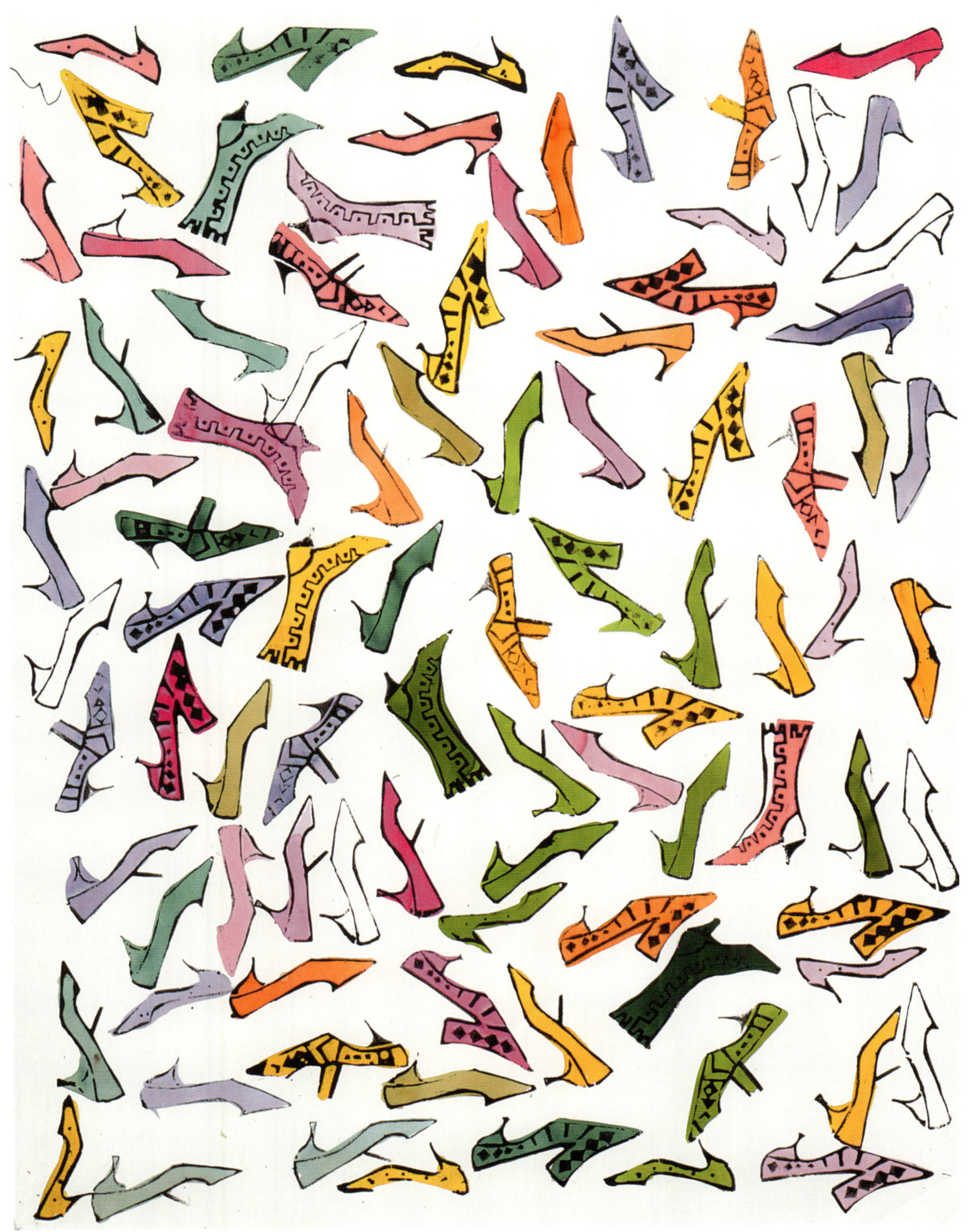

Andy Warhol
Stamped Shoes, ca. 1959
Ink and Dr. Martin's Aniline dye on sketchbook paper
$23\frac{7}{8} \times 17\frac{7}{8}$ in. (60.6 × 45.4 cm)
The Andy Warhol Museum, Pittsburgh- Founding Collection, Contribution The Andy Warhol Foundation for the Visual Arts, Inc., 1998.1.1460

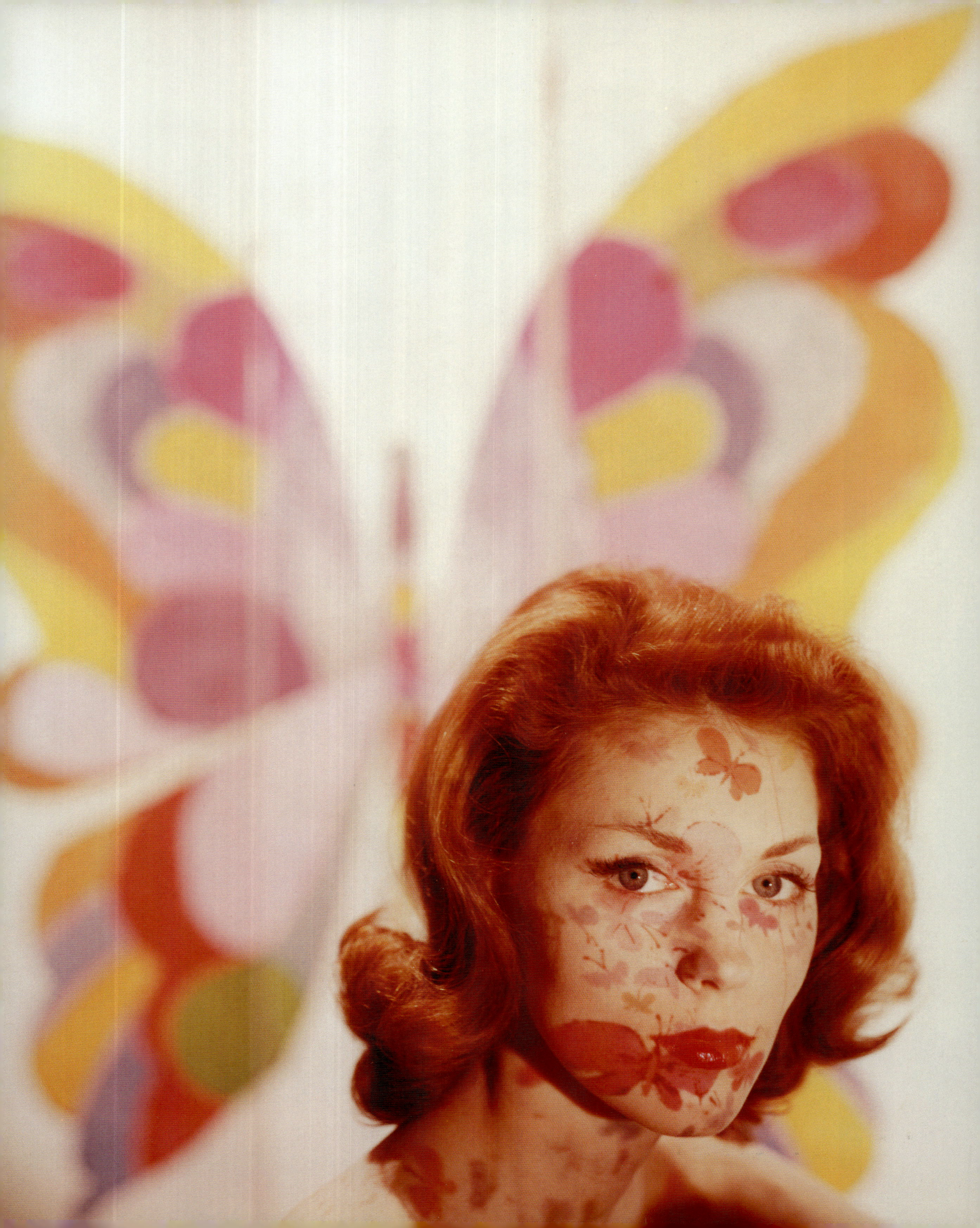

FASHION AND ENTERTAINMENT VENTURES

Warhol's experiments with photography took several forms during the 1950s. After meeting the fashion photographer Otto Fenn, in 1951, Warhol started to illustrate the backdrops for fashion sittings and window displays, culminating with his projections, in 1952, of several small, colorful drawings of butterflies and flowers onto fashion models photographed by Fenn.

Halston's hats found their way into the fashion shoot segment of Barbra Streisand's first television show in 1965. *My Name Is Barbra* was created in a deal with CBS, which gave Streisand complete creative control. She orchestrated the fashion sequence to be shot in the fur department of Bergdorf Goodman and hired Halston as an advisor. The show includes a sequence in which Streisand ironically performed "Give Me the Simple Life" (a 1945 poverty song) while wearing exotic hats and fur coats.

OPPOSITE
Otto Fenn
Unidentified model with butterfly screen projections, ca. 1952
Color photo acetate
9 15/16 × 7⅞ in. (25.2 × 20 cm)
The Andy Warhol Museum, Pittsburgh; Founding Collection, Contribution The Andy Warhol Foundation for the Visual Arts, Inc., 1998.3.1724.1

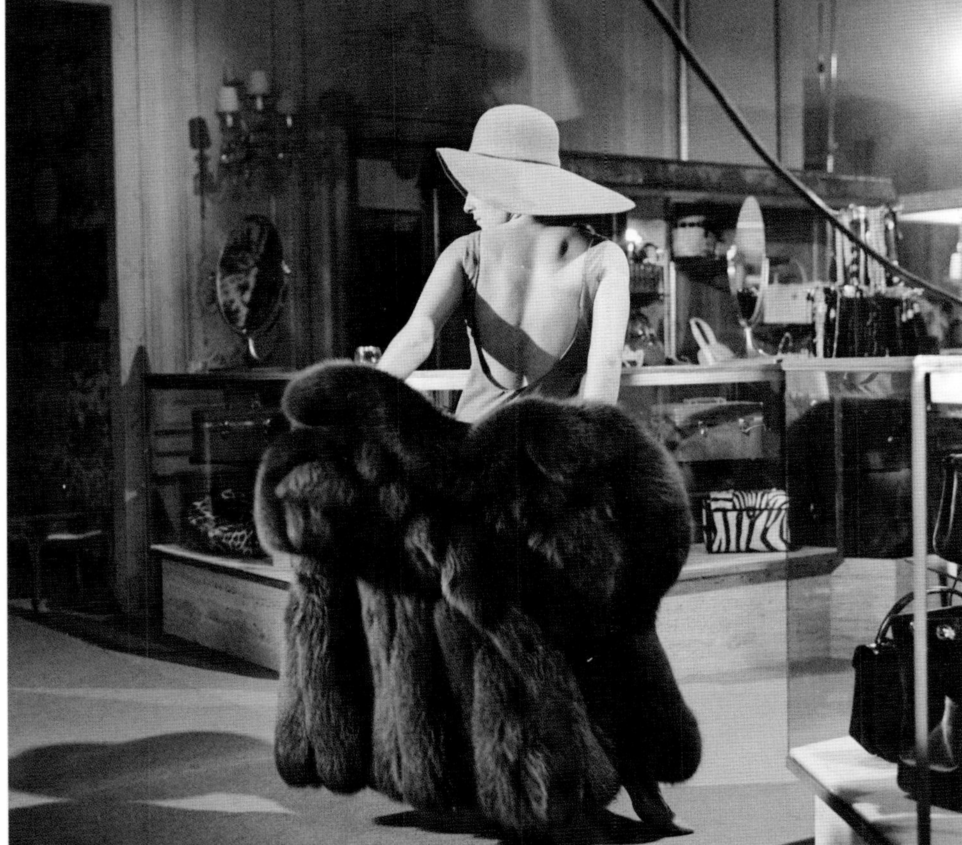

RIGHT
Barbra Streisand tries on a fur coat at Bergdorf Goodman while taping a scene for her *My Name Is Barbra* television special, April 21, 1965
CBS Photo Archive/Getty Images

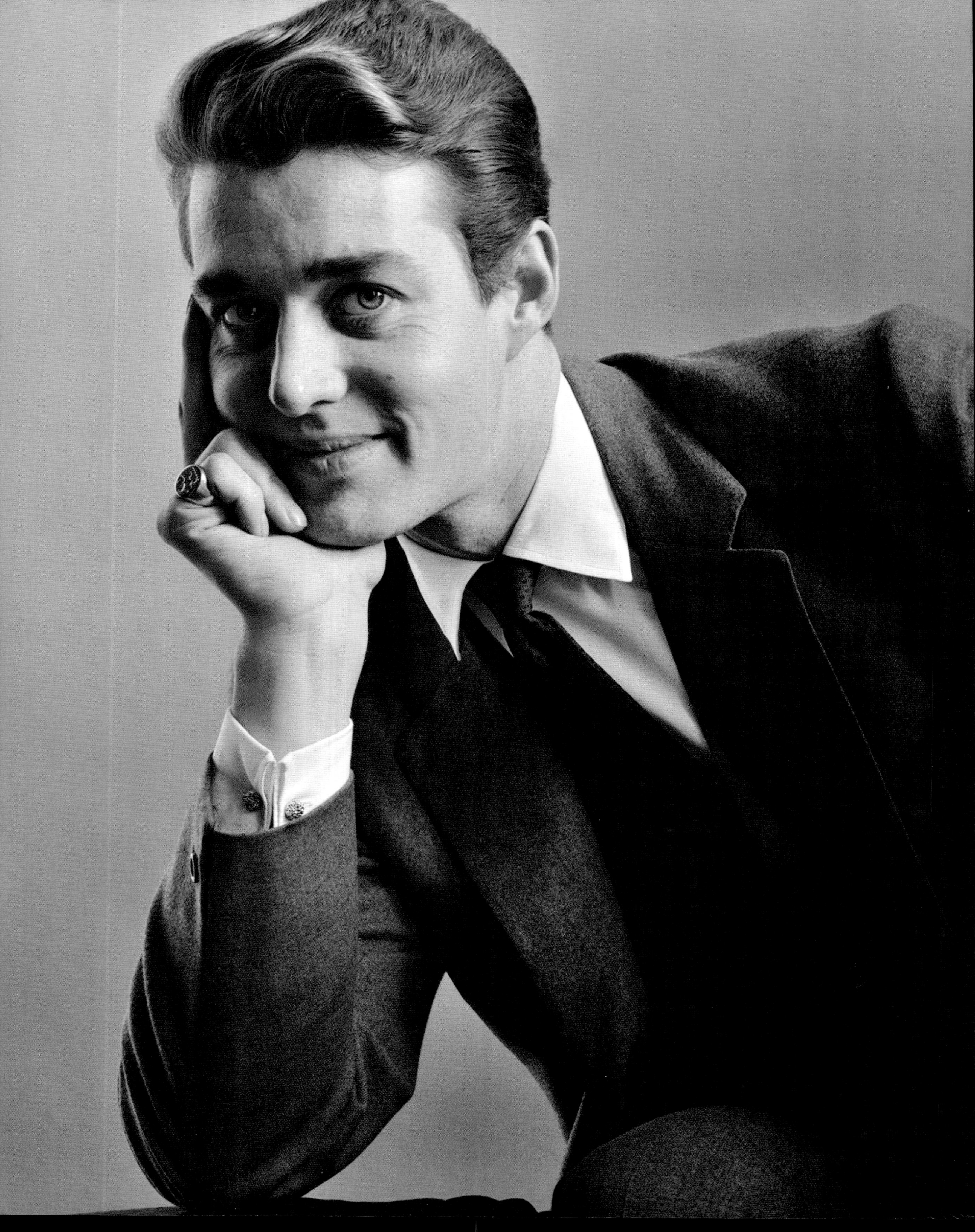

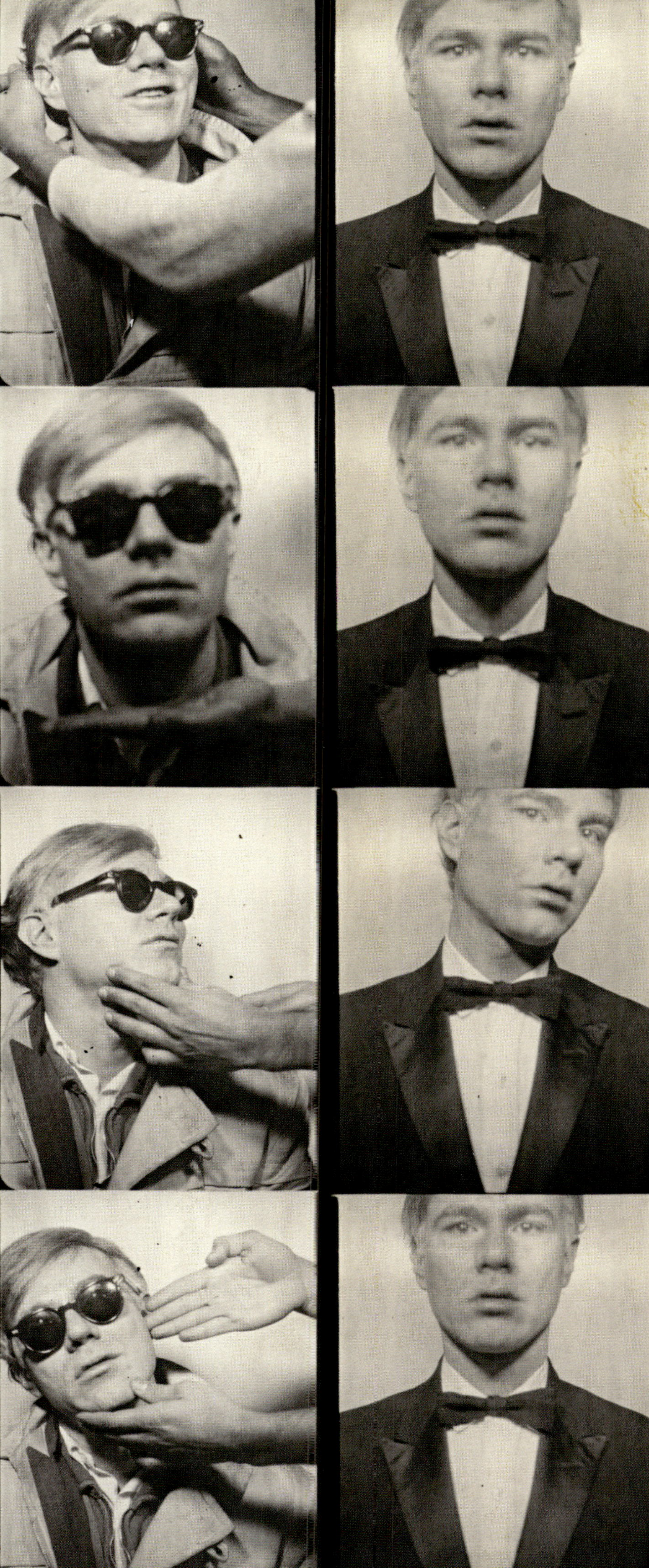

1960s

1960s

RIGHT
Andy Warhol
Campbell's Soup Can (Tomato Rice), 1961
Casein and wax crayon on linen
36¾ × 34¾ in. (93.3 × 88.3 cm)
The Andy Warhol Museum, Pittsburgh; Founding Collection, Contribution Dia Center for the Arts, 1997.1.19

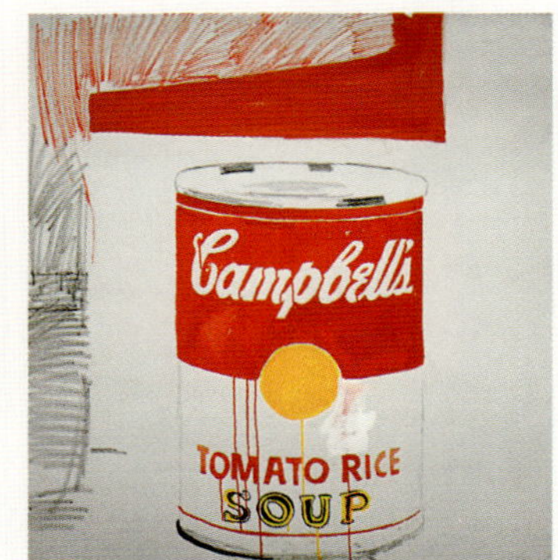

WARHOL

1960

Acquires a townhouse at 1342 Lexington Avenue, which accommodates his growing collections of art, furniture, and objects. It also gives him the space to create larger artworks.

Warhol's stage designs appear in performances of the Lukas Foss and Gian Carlo Menotti operetta *Introductions and Goodbyes* at the Festival of Two Worlds in Spoleto, Italy.

1961

Paints his first works based on comics and advertisements, using an opaque projector to enlarge the original image and then tracing the image onto a canvas and painting it.

Shows his paintings *Advertisement*, *Little King*, *Superman*, *Before and After*, and *Saturday's Popeye* with a display of dresses in a window of New York's Bonwit Teller department store.

1962

Uses rubber stamps to create *S & H Green Stamps* and other works, including portrait illustrations for *Harper's Bazaar*.

After creating a few series of works using hand-drawn silkscreens, he begins to use the photo-silkscreen technique.

HALSTON

1960

Harper's Bazaar features a hat designed by Halston on the cover. This is his first national magazine cover.

1961

Travels to Europe and sees the collections with Bergdorf Goodman's buyers.

Jacqueline Kennedy purchases a pillbox hat designed by Halston and wears it to the inauguration of her husband, John F. Kennedy, as President of the United States. The hat is an instant sensation across America. His millinery designs begin to be featured extensively in the pages and on the covers of *Vogue* and *Harper's Bazaar*.

1962

The Coty American Fashion Critics' Award, one of the most respected awards in the industry, is given to Halston for his innovative millinery designs. (Coty had started in France in the 1930s as a perfume company but quickly expanded with subsidiaries in London and New York. During World War II the company established the award program in New York to help American fashion gain recognition; only American designers were considered.)

PREVIOUS SPREAD, LEFT
Halston, 1966
Photograph by Neal Barr

PREVIOUS SPREAD, RIGHT
Andy Warhol
Self-Portrait, 1963–64
Photobooth photograph
7⅞ × 1⅝ in. (20 × 4.1 cm)
The Andy Warhol Museum, Pittsburgh; Founding Collection, Contribution The Andy Warhol Foundation for the Visual Arts, Inc., 1998.1.2749

PREVIOUS SPREAD, RIGHT
Andy Warhol
Self-Portrait (Tuxedo), 1964
Photobooth photograph
7⅞ × 1½ in. (20 × 3.8 cm)
The Andy Warhol Museum, Pittsburgh; Founding Collection, Contribution The Andy Warhol Foundation for the Visual Arts, Inc., 1998.1.2748

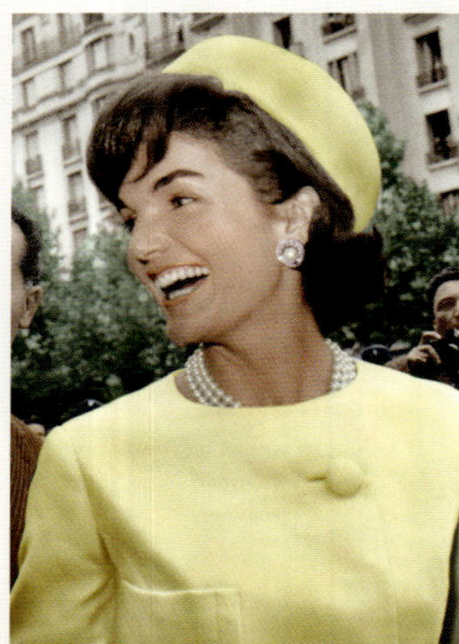

LEFT
Jacqueline Kennedy wears Alaskine (wool and silk), created by Oleg Cassini, and a pillbox hat by Halston during her official visit to Paris, 1961
RDA/Getty Images

RIGHT
Andy Warhol
S&H Green Stamps, ca. 1962
Acrylic stamped on sketchbook paper
23⅞ × 18 in. (60.6 × 45.7 cm)
The Andy Warhol Museum, Pittsburgh; Founding Collection, Contribution The Andy Warhol Foundation for the Visual Arts, Inc., 1998.1.2309

Experiments with instant photography, which becomes essential to his portrait process in the early 1970s.

Makes photographic silkscreen portraits of the teen idols Natalie Wood, Troy Donahue, and Warren Beatty. Begins his photo-silkscreen *Marilyn* paintings after Marilyn Monroe's death.

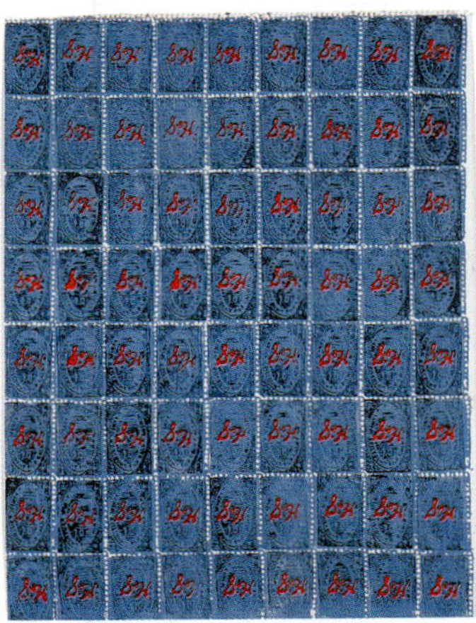

Warhol's hand-painted *Campbell's Soup Can* paintings are shown at the Ferus Gallery, Los Angeles.

Warhol is featured in a *Time* article on Pop artists.

1963

Makes multiple-image silkscreen portraits of the collector Ethel Scull and others based on photographs of his subjects taken in common photo booths.

Buys a 16mm movie camera and creates his first film, *Sleep*. This minimalist film shows John Giorno, a stockbroker-turned-poet, asleep, making very little movement for five hours and twenty-one minutes, at 16fps, a slower motion than the standard 24fps.

Designs costumes for a Broadway production of *The Beast in Me*, by James Thurber. The work is uncredited because he is not a union member.

Rents an abandoned firehouse near his home for use as a painting studio.

1964

Establishes his studio at 231 East 47th Street, soon to be known as "the Factory." The interior walls, floor, and ceiling are painted silver or covered with aluminum foil by Billy Name (Billy Linich), a theatrical lighting designer whom Warhol had met the year before.

Begins his *Flowers* paintings, which are shown at the Leo Castelli Gallery in New York this year and in Paris the next year.

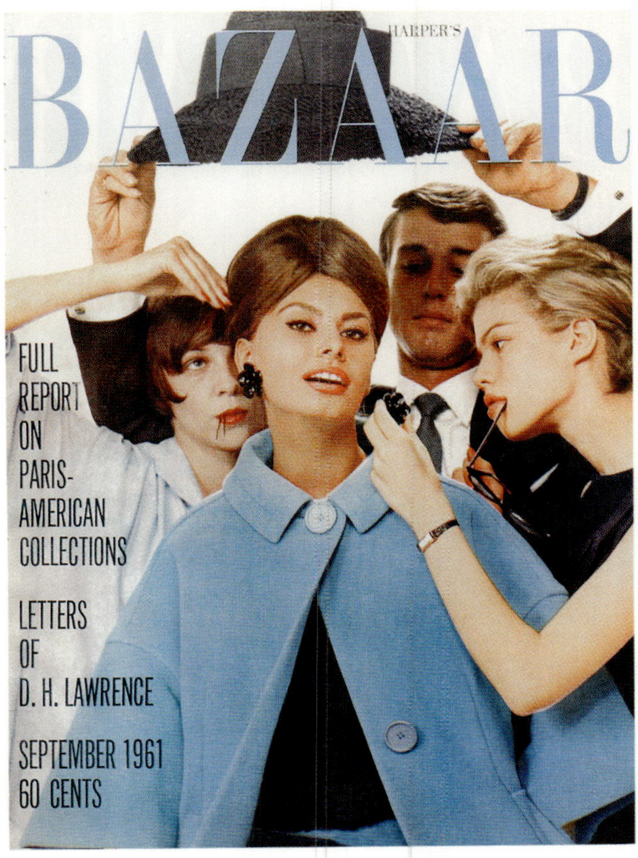

1963

The cover of the March issue of *Vogue* features a hat designed by Halston, photographed by Irving Penn.

1965

Barbra Streisand chooses Bergdorf Goodman as the setting for her first television special, *My Name Is Barbra*. She films one segment in the custom millinery salon, where she sings and dances from case to case trying on Halston's hats.

LEFT
Sophia Loren, hat by Halston, New York, May 26, 1961
Photograph by Richard Avedon

1960s

1965

Purchases a Norelco cassette recorder, which later becomes his constant companion.

Makes about ten films featuring Edie Sedgwick.

While in Paris for the opening of his *Flowers* exhibition at the Galerie Ileana Sonnabend, Warhol describes himself as a "retired artist" who plans to devote himself to film.

Film producer Lester Persky hosts the Fifty Most Beautiful People party at the Factory. Judy Garland, Rudolf Nureyev, Tennessee Williams, Allen Ginsberg, Montgomery Clift, and others attend. Glamorous and chic, it epitomizes Warhol's rising cultural standing.

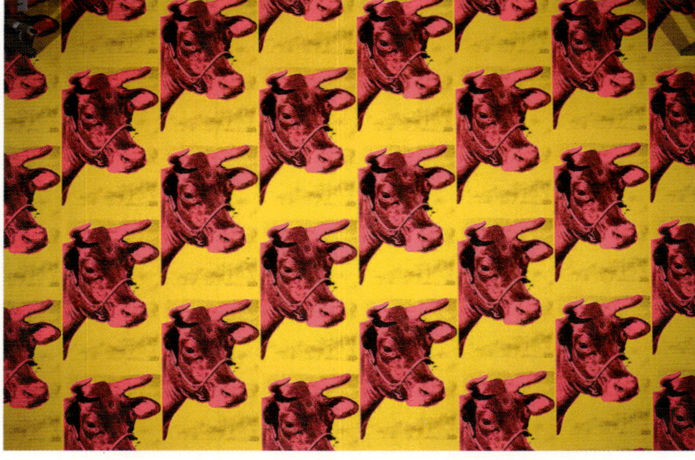

LEFT
Andy Warhol
Cow Wallpaper [Pink on Yellow], 1966
Screen print on wallpaper
Image (each): 46 × 28 in. (116.8 × 71.1 cm)
The Andy Warhol Museum, Pittsburgh, IA1994.7

1966

Produces *The Exploding Plastic Inevitable*, multimedia shows featuring the Velvet Underground, performance pieces, film, and light shows.

At the Leo Castelli Gallery, Warhol exhibits his *Cow* wallpaper in one room and fills a second, white-walled room with his floating *Silver Clouds*.

Makes the films *The Velvet Underground and Nico* and *The Chelsea Girls*. The latter is distributed widely and receives international media attention.

Warhol is a guest star in the Tristan Tzara play *The Gas Heart*, performed at Lilly Daché's place (known as "Gallery Daché") on East 56th Street.

Warhol and his Superstars begin to frequent the back room of the notorious bar-restaurant Max's Kansas City on Union Square.

November 28: Warhol attends Truman Capote's Black and White Ball, referred to as "the party of the decade."

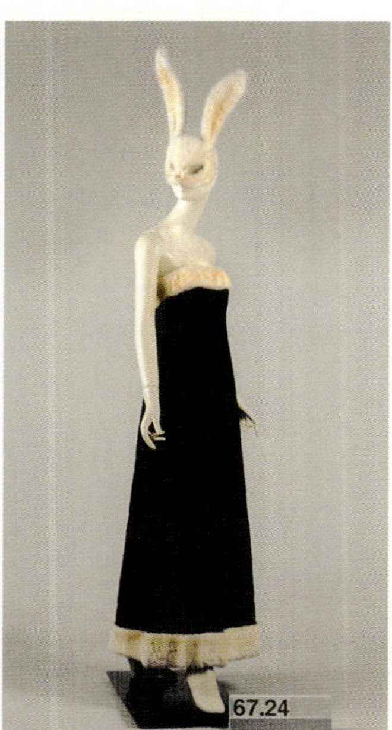

ABOVE
Halston
Velvet dress and white mink mask for Candice Bergen, Black and White Ball, 1966
Museum of the City of New York

1966

June: Shows his first apparel collection under the Halston name at Bergdorf Goodman. Eighteen pieces of clothing are modeled on the runway.

November 28: A number of guests wear masks designed by Halston at Truman Capote's Black and White Ball at the Plaza Hotel, including the guest of honor, *Washington Post* publisher Katherine Graham, and the actress Candice Bergen. The masquerade ball was attended by celebrities from the worlds of music, film, art, fashion, and literature, as well as a who's who of New York society.

1968

January 12: Leaves Bergdorf Goodman.

Signs a license agreement with Lin Mac Hat Company to sell a line of moderately priced hats under the label Halston USA.

April 25: Incorporates his own company, Halston Ltd. This label produces high-end hats. Important founding partners in Halston Ltd. are Joanne Creveling, Joel Schumacher, and Frances Stein.

September 26: Under the Halston Ltd. name, announces the launch of a ready-to-wear line, which is exclusive to department stores in major cities, and made-to-order lines. His first client is Mrs. William (Babe) Paley.

December 2: Shows his first clothing collection in his new showroom at 33 East 68th Street. The walls, ceiling, and furniture are draped in yards of batik-printed fabrics designed by Angelo Donghia.

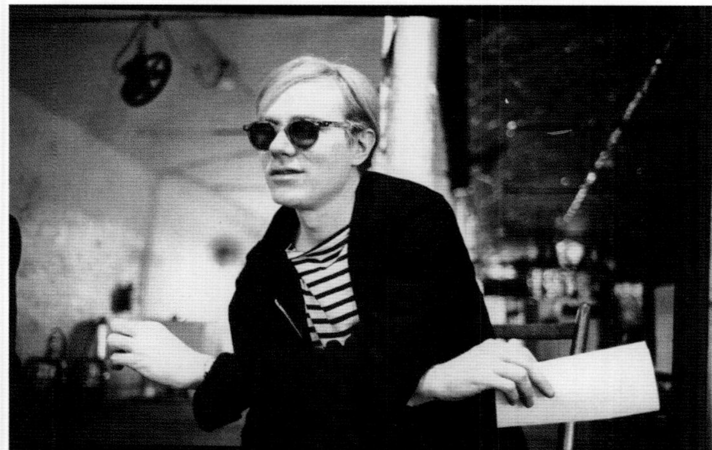

LEFT
Stephen Shore
Andy Warhol, 1965
Gelatin silver print
5 x 8 in. (12.7 x 20.3 cm)
The Andy Warhol Museum, Pittsburgh; Founding Collection, Contribution The Andy Warhol Foundation for the Visual Arts, Inc., 1998.3.14672

1968
January: Warhol moves the Factory to a white-walled office space on the sixth floor of 33 Union Square West.

June 3: Valerie Solanas, who appears in Warhol's film *I, a Man* and is the founder and sole member of S.C.U.M. (Society for Cutting Up Men), shoots Warhol in his studio.

The *Silver Clouds* are used as the set for Merce Cunningham's dance *RainForest*.

A retrospective of Warhol's work is held at the Moderna Museet, Stockholm, and travels throughout Scandinavia.

1969
The first issue of Warhol's *Interview* magazine is published.

Work by Warhol is included in the Metropolitan Museum of Art's exhibition *New York Painting and Sculpture: 1940–1970*.

Vincent Fremont begins to work for Warhol. He becomes a close associate on video and television projects, and eventually serves as his executive manager.

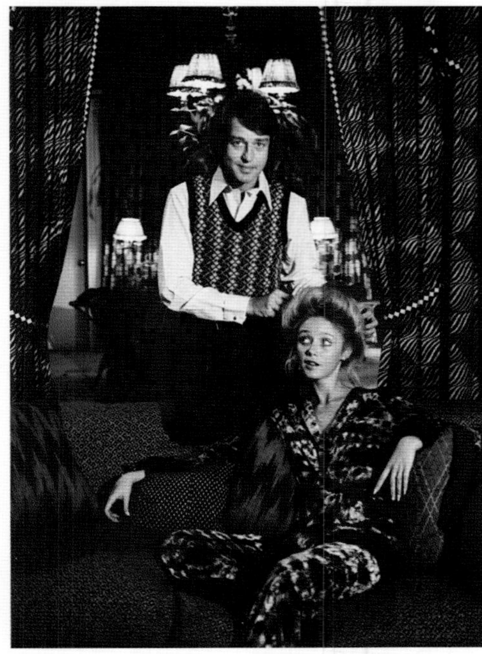

ABOVE
Halston, with the model Heidi Goldman wearing a Halston design, at his Manhattan townhouse, September 9, 1969
Photograph by David Gahr
Getty Images

1969
August: Replicating the design of his showroom on East 68th Street, Halston opens a boutique on the third floor of Bloomingdale's department store, located at 59th Street and Lexington Avenue. He designs the clothing and accessories sold in the boutique but outsources the manufacturing. In the two years following, Halston opens boutiques within major department stores in Houston and Denver.

October 13: Wins second Coty American Fashion Critics' Award for the total look of his first collection.

December 16: Underwrites a retrospective of the work of the fashion designer Charles James. The event is held at the Electric Circus, a nightclub on St. Mark's Place in the East Village. James briefly collaborates with Halston as a "fashion consultant–engineer."

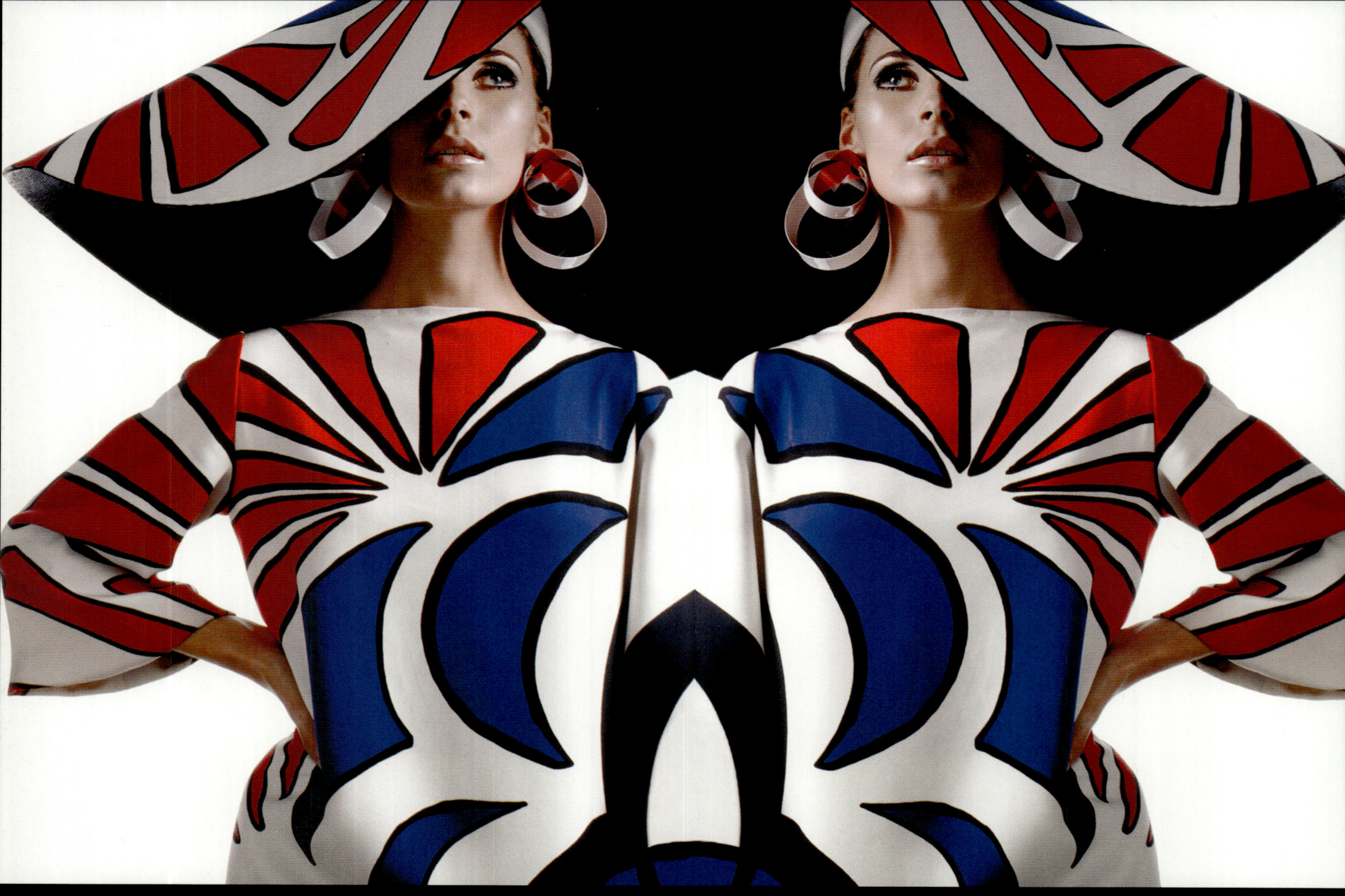

In this photo for the cover of *Harper's Bazaar*, model Astrid Shiller wears a dress by Burke-Amey and a hat by Halston, March 1967
Photograph by Neal Barr

EARLY SUCCESS

Warhol's red, white, and blue *Brillo* box, while a symbol of philosophical inquiry into the nature of art, is paired with a red, white, and blue Halston hat that was repeated in a mirror spread of *Vogue*. Both works were shown in multiples, referencing repetition, merchandising, and the nature of advertising.

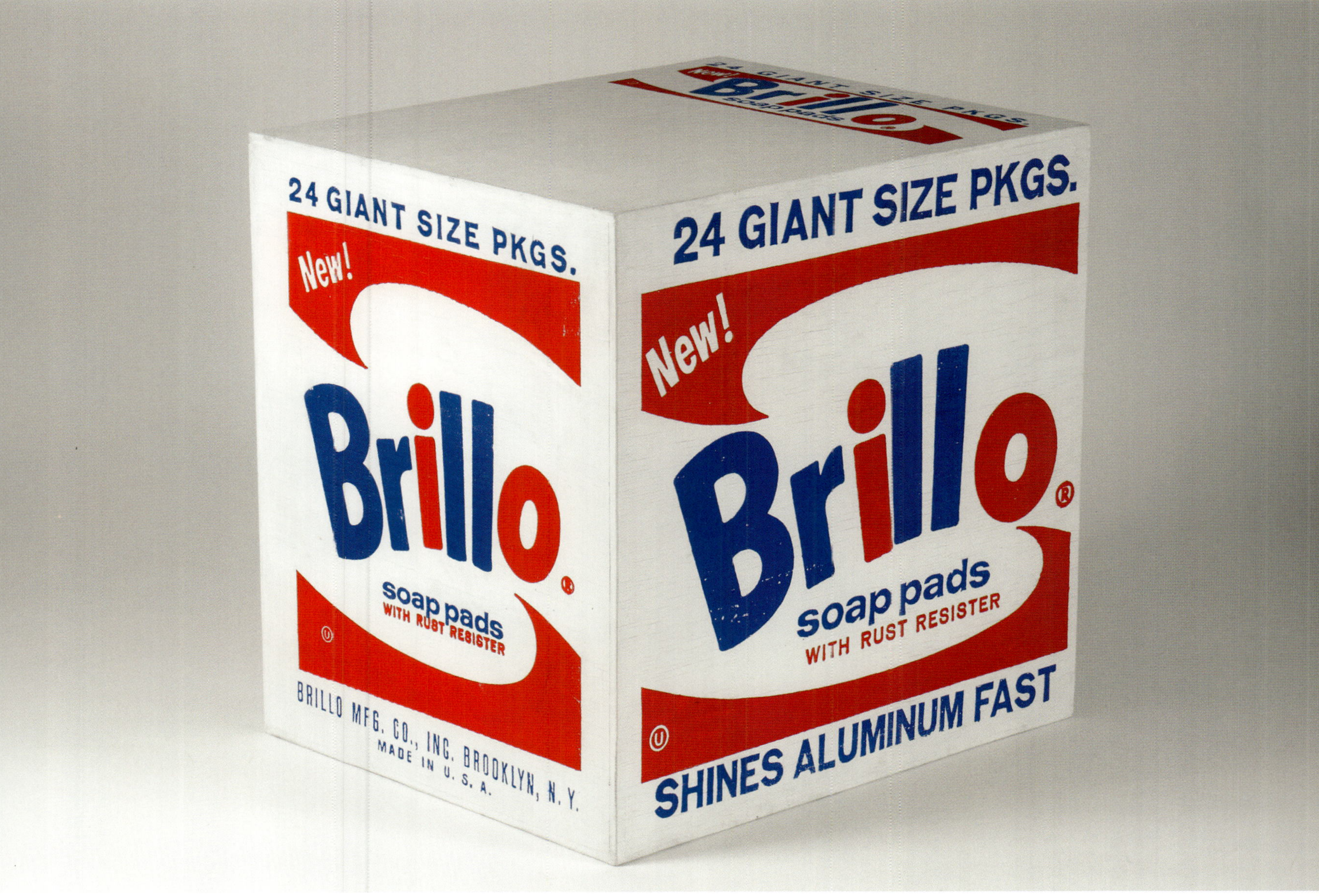

Andy Warhol
Brillo Soap Pads Box, 1964
Silkscreen ink and house paint on plywood
17 × 17 × 14 in. (43.2 × 43.2 × 35.6 cm)
The Andy Warhol Museum, Pittsburgh; Founding Collection, Contribution The Andy Warhol Foundation for the Visual Arts, Inc., 1998.1.710

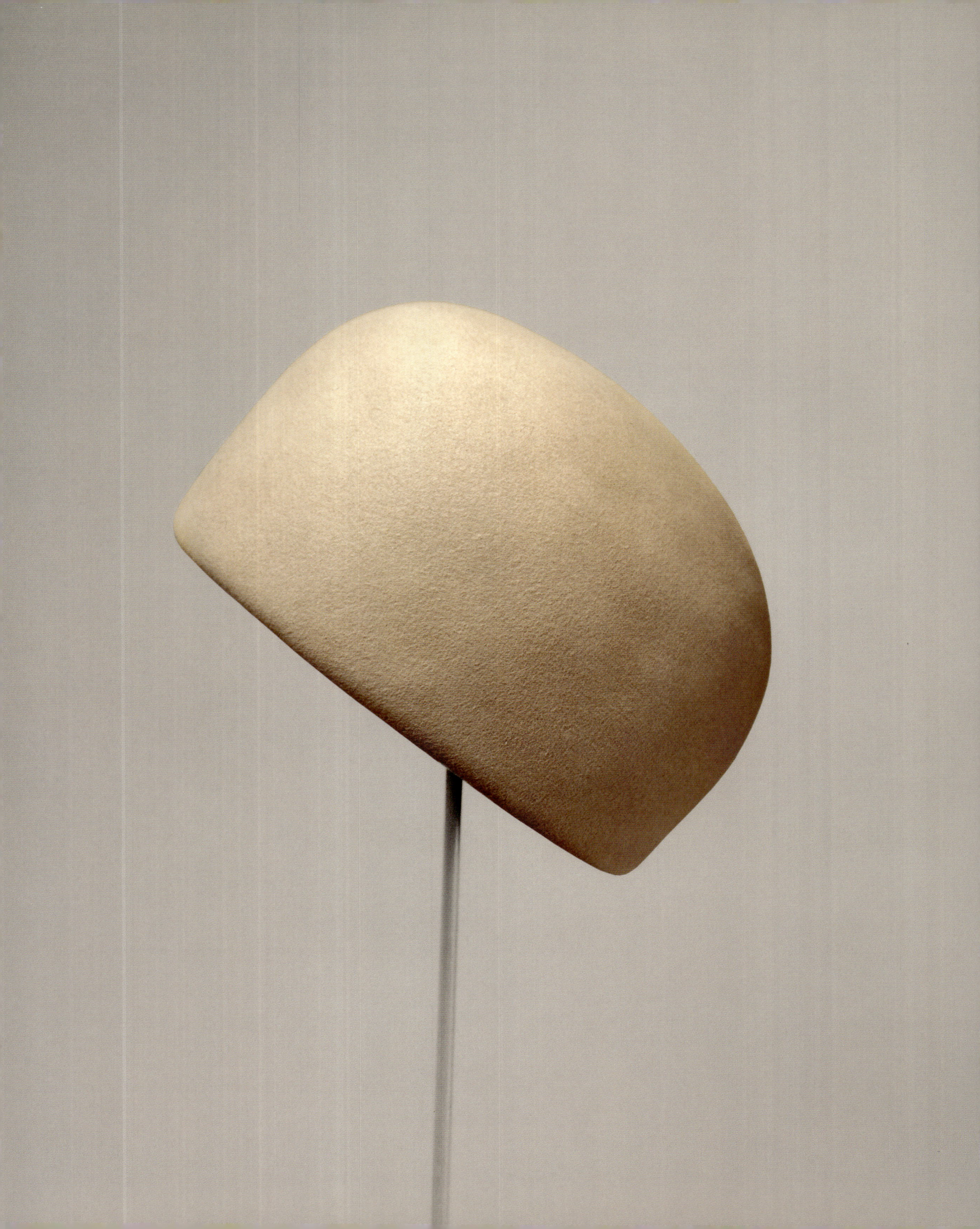

JACKIE AND THE PILLBOX HAT

Jacqueline Bouvier Kennedy Onassis (1929–1994) rose to prominence as the wife of the charismatic John F. Kennedy but soon demonstrated her own talents as hostess, style icon, mother, and arbiter of good taste. In her role as First Lady she was admired internationally for embodying elegance, and in the world of fashion she became a trendsetter who influenced designers, magazine editors, and the public at large. Halston's rank in American fashion design was immediately elevated when Jackie asked him to design her hat for the inauguration day celebrations in 1961. His pale pink pillbox hat was viewed by millions as Jackie's image was broadcast on television and circulated in print.

Deeply affected by the assassination of President John F. Kennedy in November 1963, Warhol began a large series of portraits of his widow. Based on images from newspapers and magazines, these portraits were shown individually and in groups. The initial exhibition of the *Jackies*, which entailed a single profile image repeated forty-two times, occurred at the Leo Castelli Gallery almost one year after the assassination.

Even long after the event, Warhol was amazed at the power that the image held: "As we walked through the galleries every person recognized Jackie. They didn't come too close. They stopped for a minute, looked, and whispered. You could hear her name in the air: 'Jackie. Jackie.' It's a very strange feeling. There is so much awe and respect for her. Being with her is like walking with a saint."

OPPOSITE
Halston
For Bergdorf Goodman
Pillbox hat, early 1960s
Felt
The John F. Kennedy Library

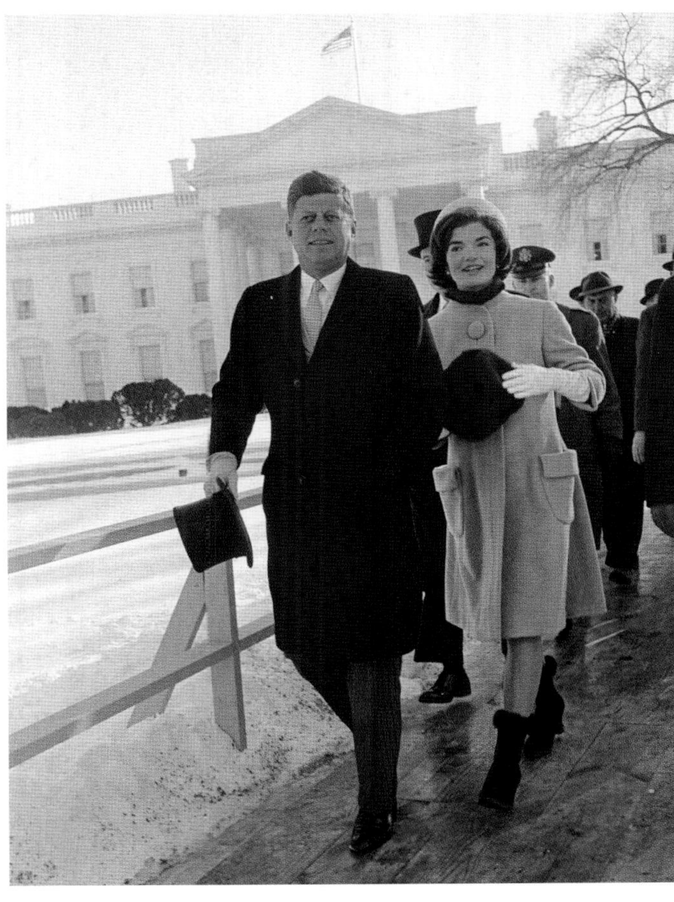

RIGHT
President Kennedy and his wife, Jackie, in front of the White House at the inauguration parade, January 20, 1961
Associated Press

OVERLEAF LEFT
Andy Warhol
Jackie, 1964
Spray paint and silkscreen ink on linen
20 × 16 × ¾ in. (50.8 × 40.6 × 1.9 cm)
The Andy Warhol Museum, Pittsburgh; Founding Collection, Contribution The Andy Warhol Foundation for the Visual Arts, Inc., 1998.1.89

OVERLEAF RIGHT
Andy Warhol
Jackie, 1964
Silkscreen ink on linen
20 × 16 in. (50.8 × 40.6 cm)
The Andy Warhol Museum, Pittsburgh; Founding Collection, Contribution The Andy Warhol Foundation for the Visual Arts, Inc., 1998.1.103

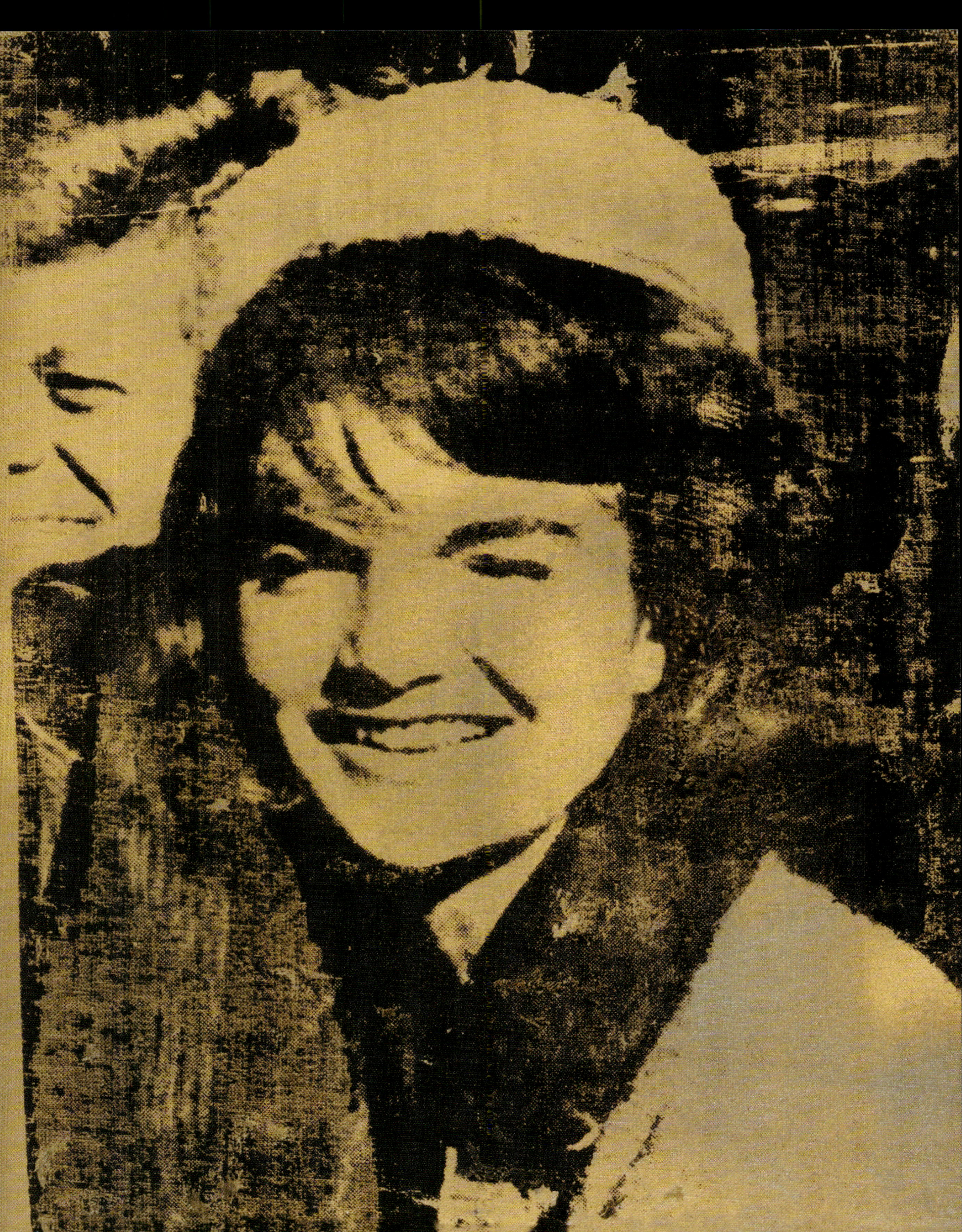

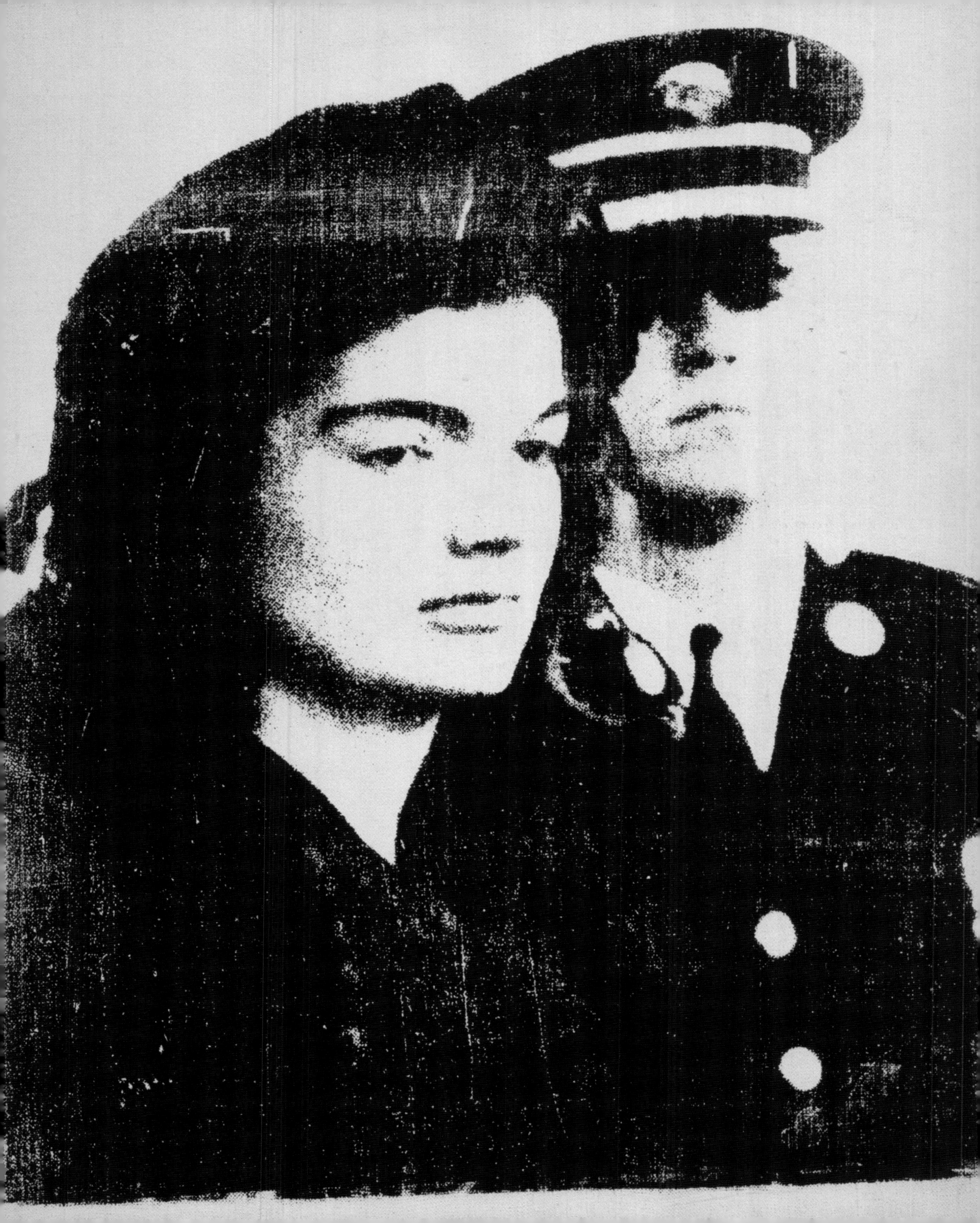

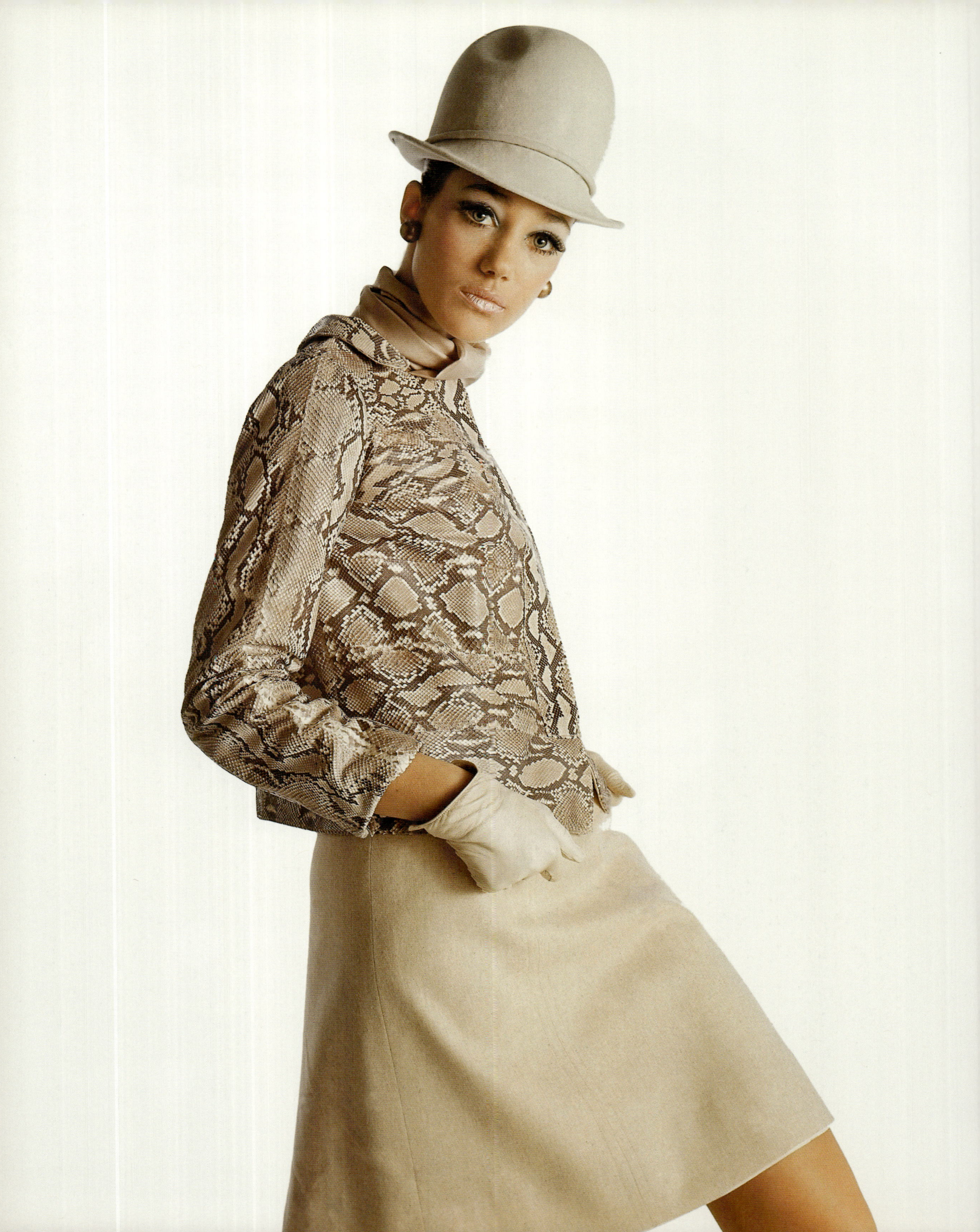

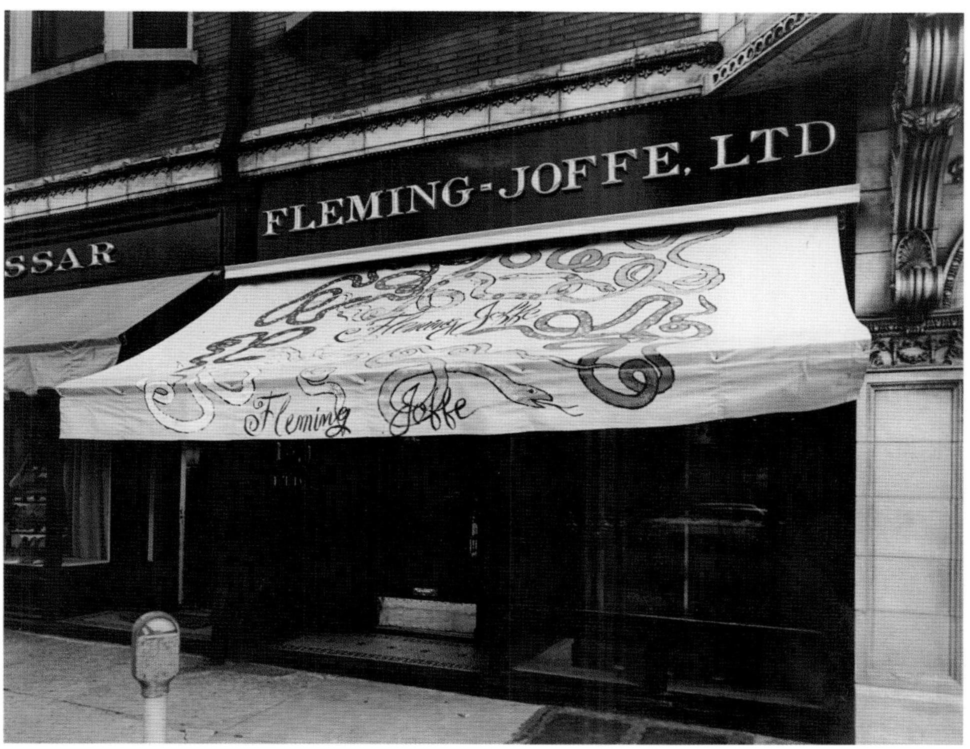

FLEMING-JOFFE, LTD.

Marisa Berenson, who later modeled for Halston throughout the 1960s and 1970s, is shown here wearing a Halston hat and a jacket made by Fleming-Joffe, a small leather-goods manufacturing company that sold exotic skins to the fashion industry. In the 1950s the owners of Fleming-Joffe, Arthur and Teddy Edelman, hired Warhol to create their advertising campaign. Warhol's whimsical drawings of Noa the Boa, the character he invented to sell these leather goods, are juxtaposed with Berenson in a snakeskin jacket. In Warhol's ad campaign the boa constrictor hobnobbed with society ladies such as Jackie Kennedy, who were also buying Halston hats.

Warhol hand painted an awning for the Fleming-Joffe showroom in St. Louis with multiple brightly colored images of the smiling snake. Inside the shop, he also painted shelf brackets and lighting fixtures with additional images of the reptile.

OPPOSITE
Marisa Berenson wears a Halston hat and a cobra jacket from Fleming-Joffe, ca. January 1966
Photograph by Bert Stern
Condé Nast Archive/CORBIS

ABOVE
W. C. Runder Photo Co., Inc., St. Louis, Missouri
Storefront (Fleming-Joffe, Ltd.), 1960
Gelatin silver print
8 × 10 in. (20.3 × 25.4 cm)
The Andy Warhol Museum, Pittsburgh; Gift of Teddy and Arthur Edelman, 1994.2.2

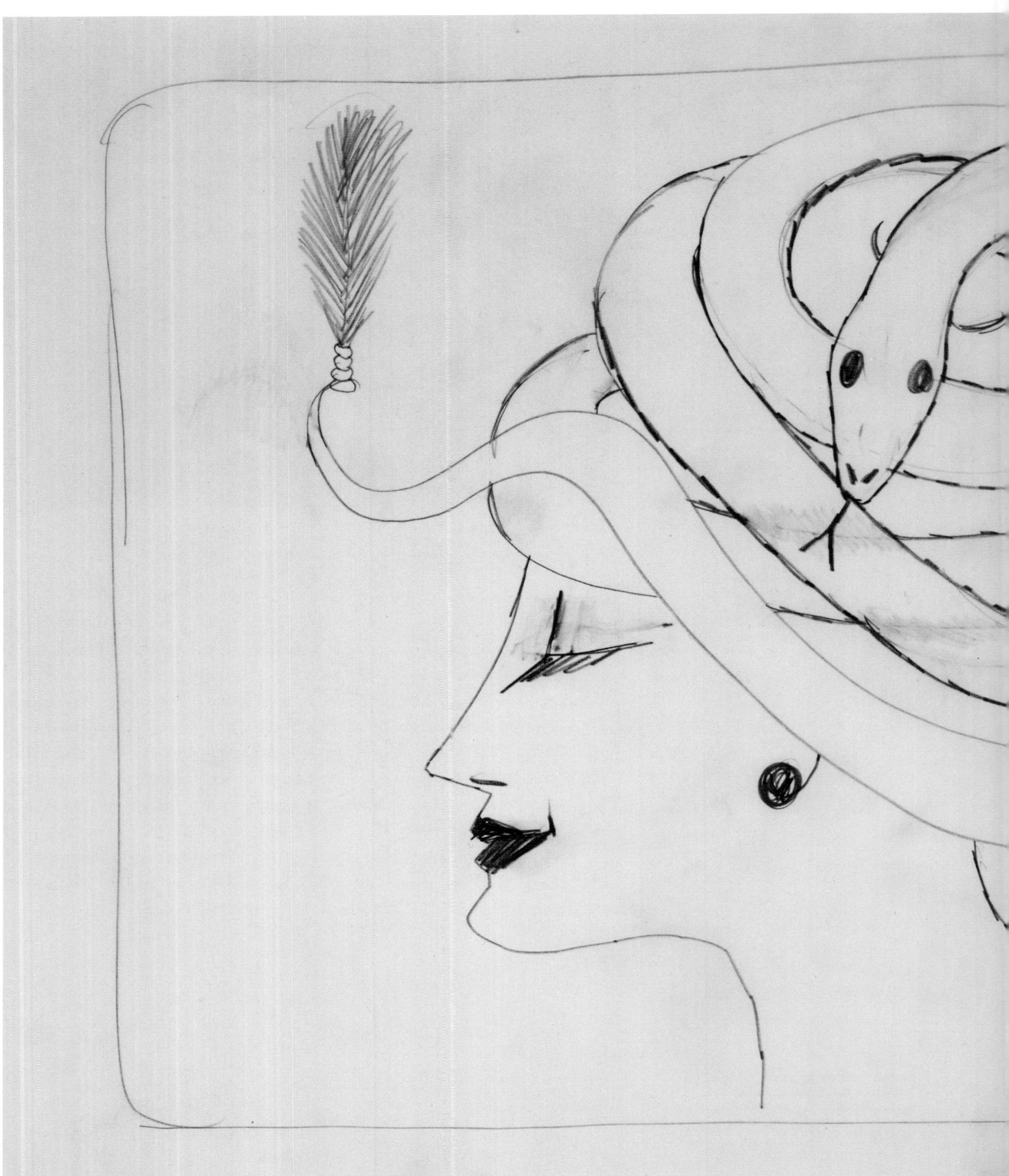

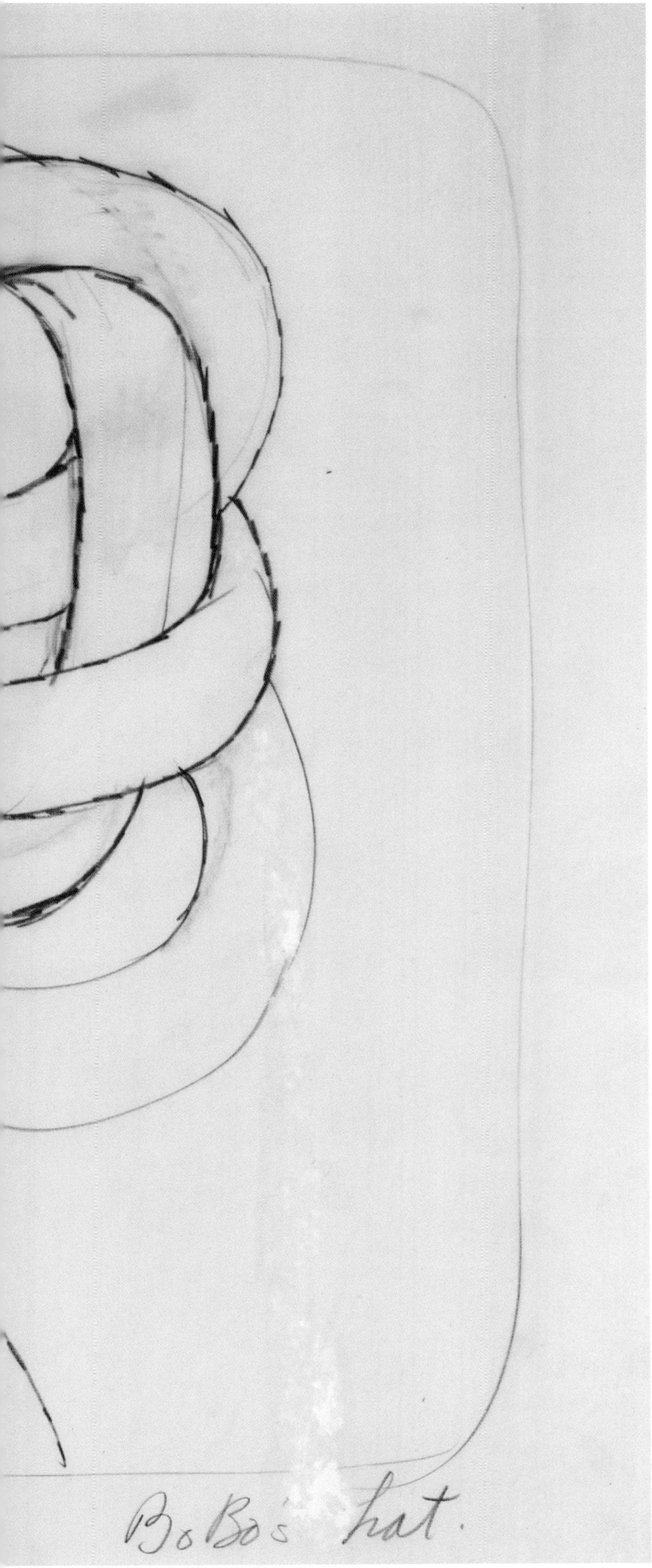

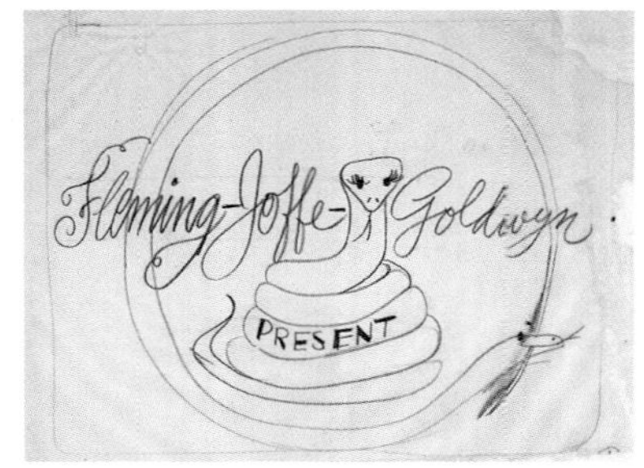

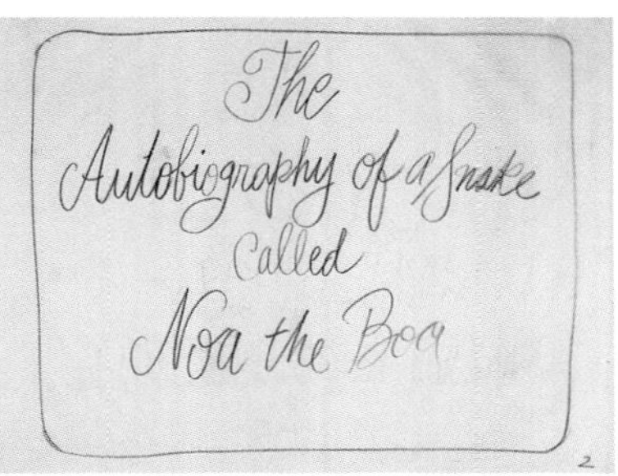

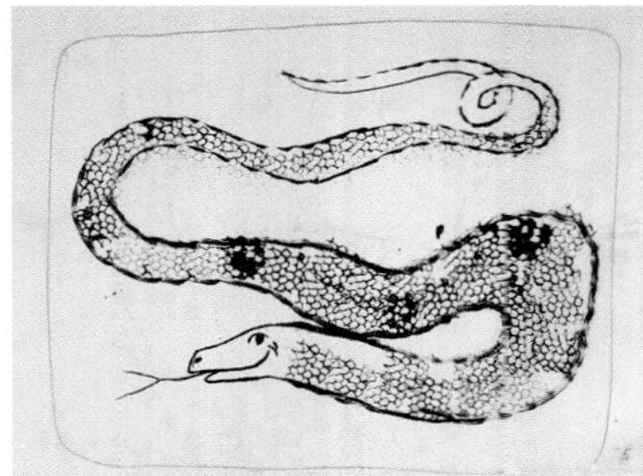

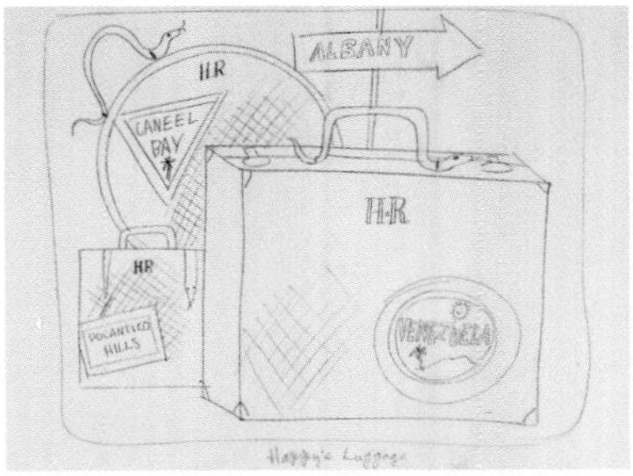

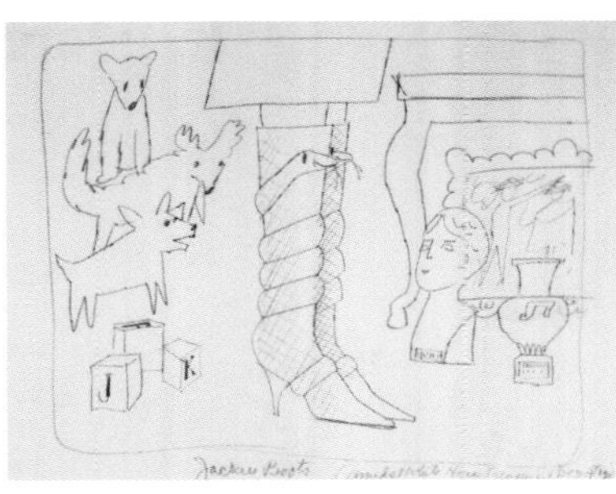

FAR LEFT
Andy Warhol
"BoBo's Hat," 1963
Graphite on tracing paper
18 ¾ × 23 ⅞ in. (47.6 × 60.6 cm)
1997.2.23

LEFT (TOP TO BOTTOM)
Andy Warhol
Introduction ("Fleming-Joffe-Goldwyn Present"), 1963
Graphite on tracing paper
18 ¾ × 24 in. (47.6 × 61 cm)
1997.2.1

Andy Warhol
Production title ("The Autobiography of a Snake Called Noa the Boa"), 1963
Graphite on tracing paper
18 ¾ × 24 in. (47.6 × 61 cm)
1997.2.2

Andy Warhol
Noa the Boa, 1963
Graphite and ink on tracing paper
18 ¾ × 23 ⅞ in. (47.6 × 60.6 cm)
1997.2.5

Andy Warhol
"Happy's Luggage," 1963
Graphite on tracing paper
18 ¾ × 23 ⅞ in. (47.6 × 60.6 cm)
1997.2.31

Andy Warhol
"Jackie's Boots . . . ," 1963
Graphite on tracing paper
18 ¾ × 23 ⅞ in. (47.6 × 60.6 cm)
1997.2.21

All works from The Andy Warhol Museum, Pittsburgh; Gift of Teddy and Arthur Edelman

WARHOL'S PROCESS

Warhol's Pop paintings appropriated images from newspapers, magazine advertisements, comic strips, and other mundane sources of popular culture. He enlarged the source image onto a blank canvas using a projector, traced the enlargement, and then painted the work by hand. *Make Him Want You* is an example of this early technique. In 1962 he developed the technique of photographic silkscreen, which allowed him to reproduce photographic imagery directly onto canvas. His *Elvis, Liz, Marilyn*, and other paintings of film stars became definitive emblems of American Pop art.

Warhol chose the source image for his painting of the actress Elizabeth Taylor from a publicity photograph of her 1960 film, *Butterfield 8*. At the time he created the first Taylor portrait she was at the height of stardom, but was also very ill with pneumonia. Warhol remembered: "I started those [pictures of Elizabeth Taylor] a long time ago, when she was so sick and everyone said she was going to die. Now I'm doing them all over, putting bright colors on her lips and eyes." Warhol signed a later editioned print of Elizabeth Taylor, "To Halston from Warhol"

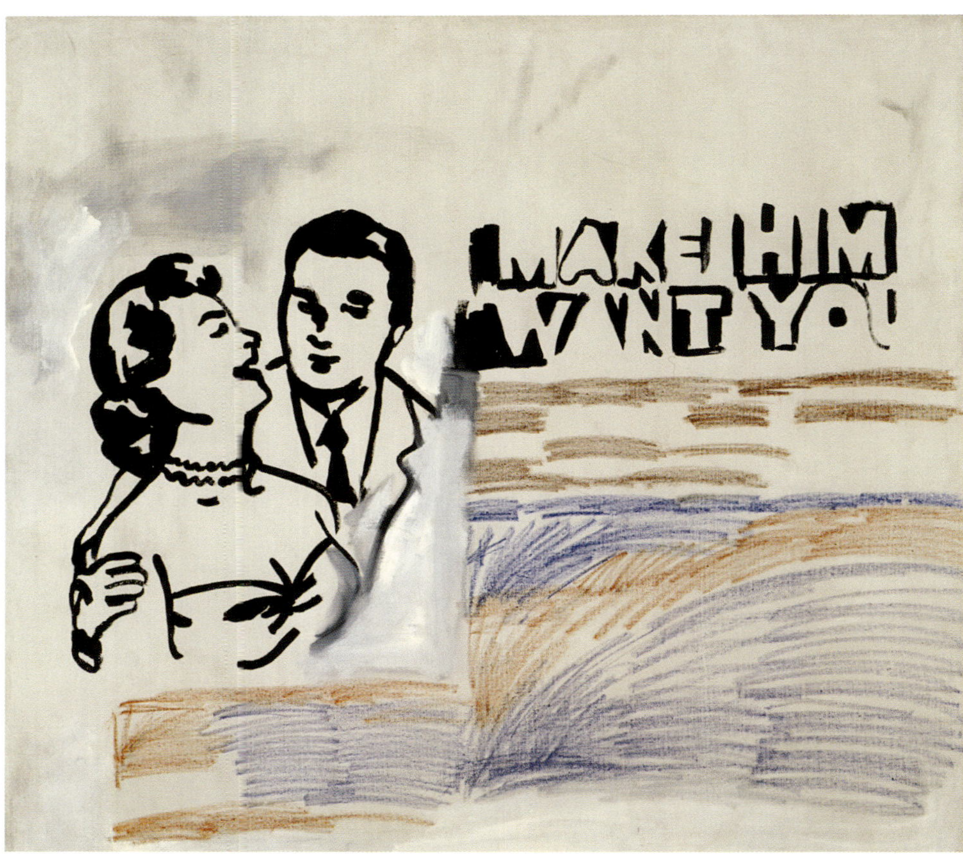

RIGHT
Andy Warhol
Make Him Want You, 1961
Casein, wax crayon, and oil paint on linen
33⅛ × 36⅛ in. (84.1 × 91.8 cm)
The Andy Warhol Museum, Pittsburgh; Founding Collection, Contribution Dia Center for the Arts, 1997.1.2

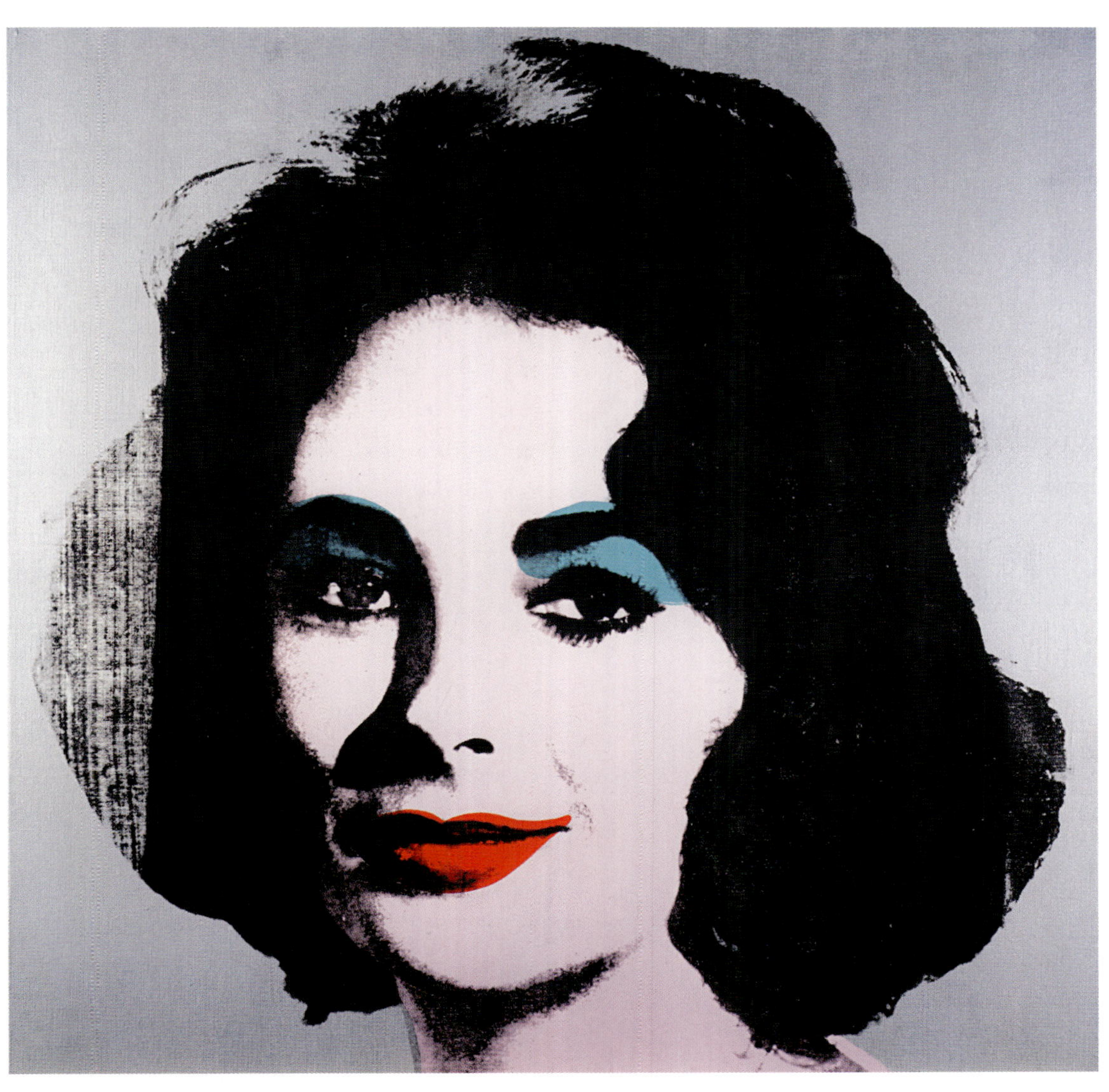

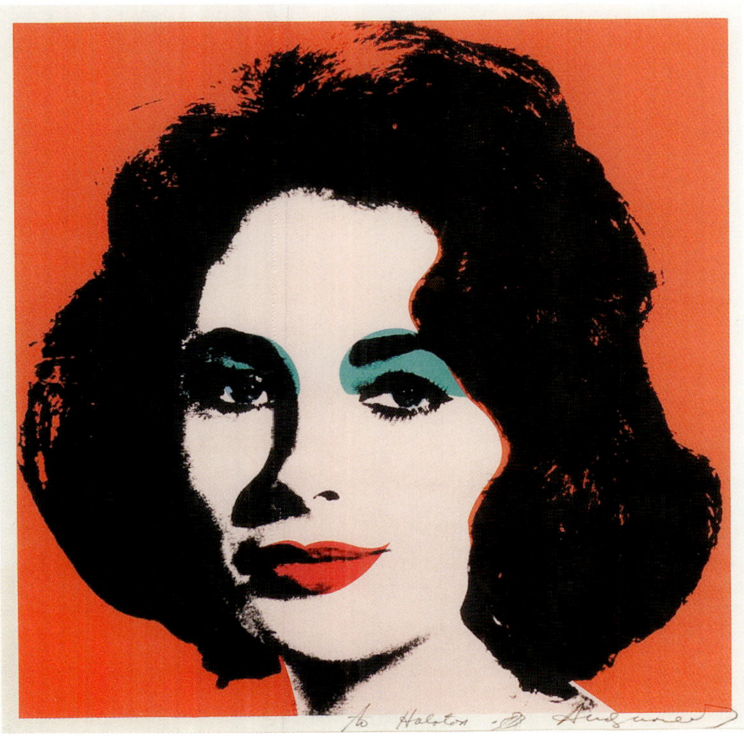

TOP
Andy Warhol
Silver Liz [Ferus Type], 1963
Silkscreen ink, acrylic, and spray paint on linen
40 × 40 in. (101.6 × 101.6 cm)
The Andy Warhol Museum, Pittsburgh; Founding Collection, Contribution The Andy Warhol Foundation for the Visual Arts, Inc., 1998.1.55

BOTTOM
Andy Warhol
Liz, 1964
Lithograph on paper
Sheet: 23⅛ × 23⅛ in. (58.7 × 58.7 cm)
Des Moines Art Center Permanent Collections; Gift of Roy Halston Frowick, New York, 1986.45

ASSISTANTS AND COLLABORATORS

Warhol and Halston each worked with many assistants throughout their careers to meet the demands of their clients. They met originally in 1960 through Halston's assistant and fashion illustrator, Joe Eula, who worked for many designers, performers, and musicians, illustrating album covers, concert posters, and books. Eula's illustrations in the 1970s became wedded to the Halston brand after Halston promoted him in 1970 to be his creative director. Eula's ability to draw quickly and to capture movement in clothing made him a favorite.

Warhol employed numerous assistants and collaborators throughout his career. Chuck Wein, shown here, was a close friend of Edie Sedgwick's. In 1965 Wein was instrumental in helping Warhol create a number of films featuring Sedgwick, including *Beauty No. 2*, *Poor Little Rich Girl*, and *Vinyl*. Other collaborators in Warhol's studio included Gerard Malanga, Billy Name, Billy Kluver, Jay Shriver, Rupert Jason Smith, Brigid Berlin, Ronnie Cutrone, Pat Hackett, Jed Johnson, Jonas Mekas, Paul Morrissey, John Giorno, and Ronald Tavel. Over the course of the 1960s dozens of other artists, musicians, writers, dealers, and friends were involved in different aspects of Warhol's practice.

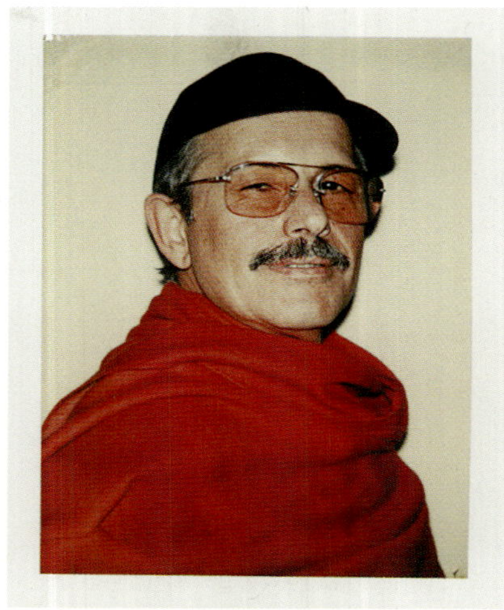

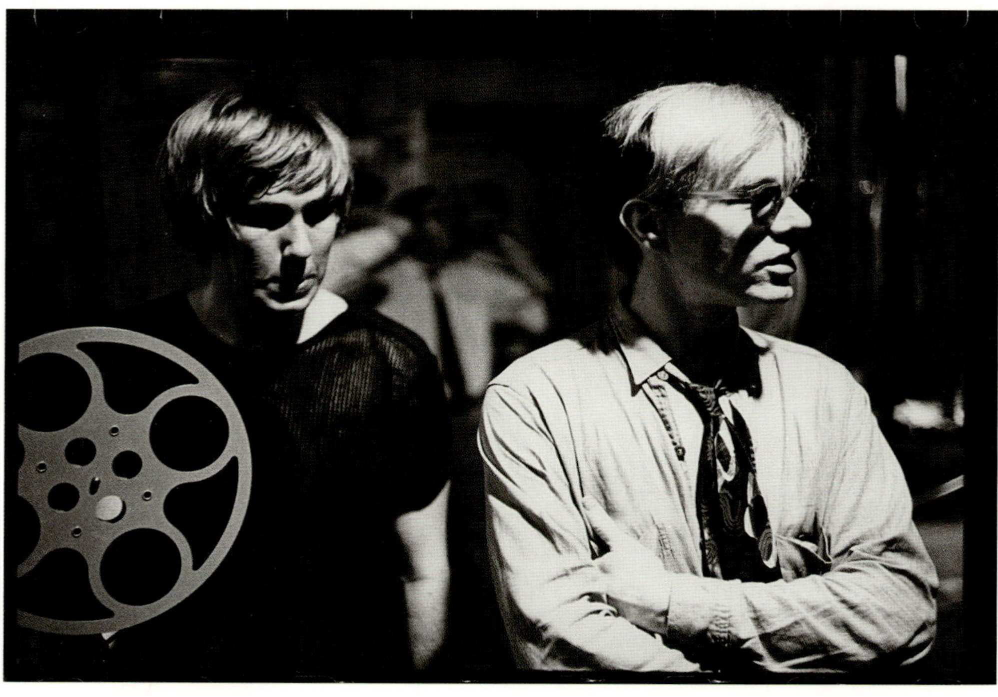

Andy Warhol
Joe Eula, 1977
Polaroid™ Polacolor Type 108
4¼ × 3⅜ in. (10.8 × 8.6 cm)
The Andy Warhol Museum, Pittsburgh; Contribution The Andy Warhol Foundation for the Visual Arts, Inc., 2000.2.839

Stephen Shore
Andy Warhol and Chuck Wein, 1965
Gelatin silver print
5 × 8 in. (12.7 × 20.3 cm)
The Andy Warhol Museum, Pittsburgh; Founding Collection, Contribution The Andy Warhol Foundation for the Visual Arts, Inc., 1998.3.1495

OPPOSITE
Joe Eula
Drawings of Halston designs, 1978
Pencil and watercolor
Collection of Chris Royer

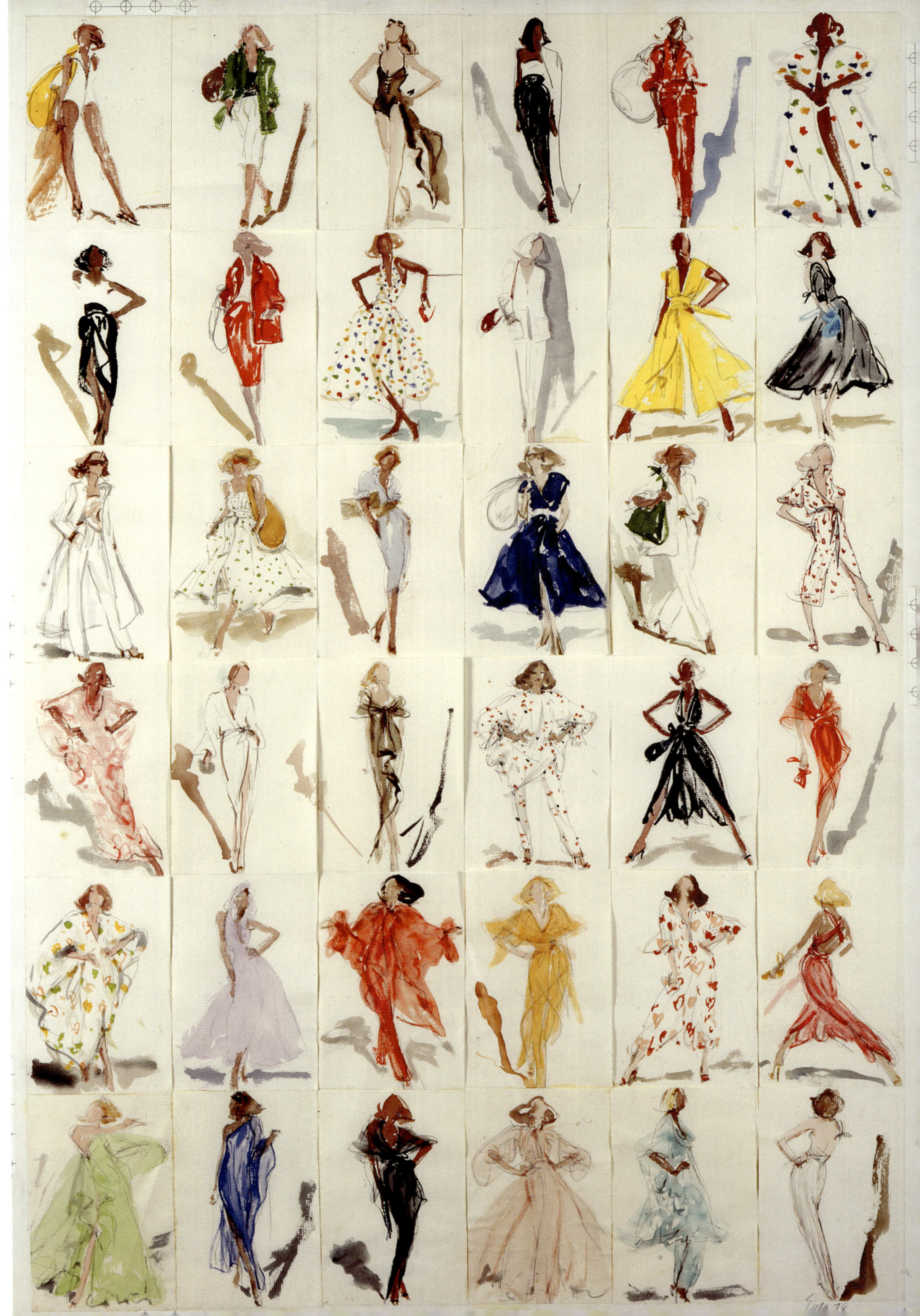
Eula 74

STUDIO AND SALON

Warhol premiered his new studio, which was painted silver and known as the Factory, to celebrate the first exhibition of his *Brillo* box sculptures in 1964. It quickly became "the" place to be in New York. Working with other artists, musicians, poets, and creative thinkers who hung out at the Factory, Warhol expanded into the realm of performance art with a traveling multimedia show called *The Exploding Plastic Inevitable*, featuring the Velvet Underground, a rock band that Warhol managed. The Factory's atmosphere of license, excess, and creativity transformed the traditional notion of an artist's studio as a barren garret into one of a permanent carnival, marked by openness, experimentation, and drama.

Angelo Donghia designed Halston's showroom at 33 East 68th Street. It was conceived as a performance space, like no other showroom in the fashion industry. The walls, ceiling, and furniture were swathed in yards of batik-printed fabrics by Donghia. The floors were covered in sisal. The accessories were evocative of exotic safari travel, including a rattan coffee table covered with animal horn vases and beaded necklaces. The result was a colorful and intimate environment for his clients. *Life* and *Look* magazines used the salon as a backdrop for fashion spreads, and Halston staged his first runway shows there. In this view, Liza Minelli lounges in a silk tie-dyed Halston pajama set.

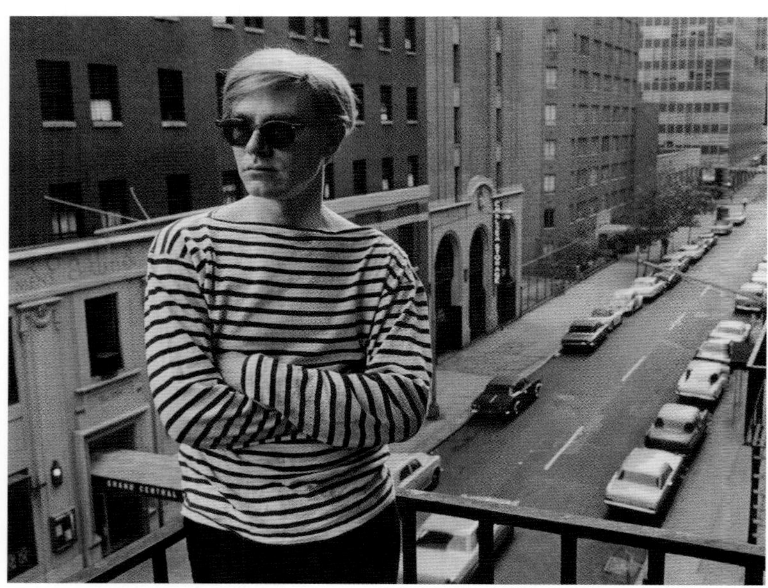

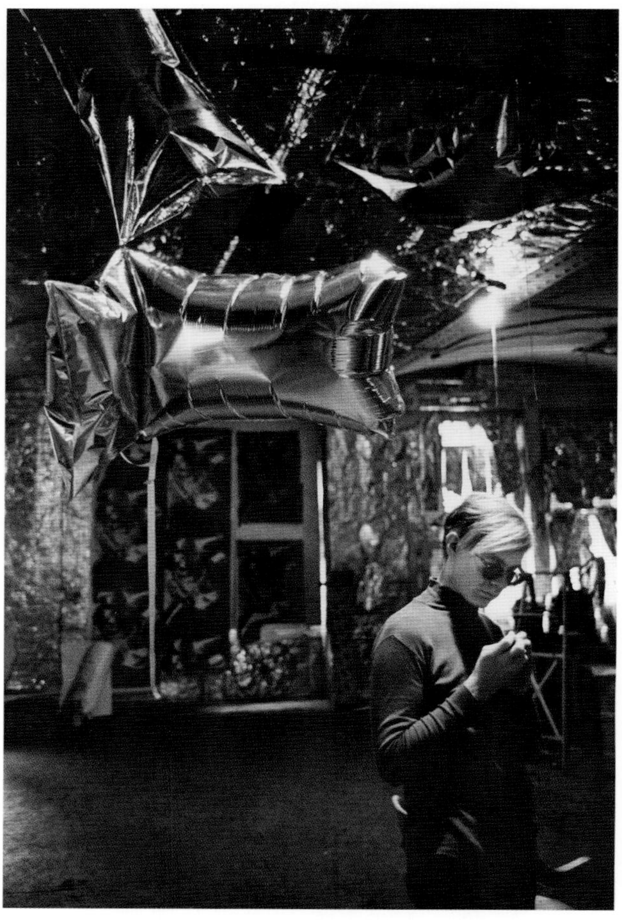

ABOVE
Stephen Shore
Andy Warhol, 1965–66
Gelatin silver print
8 × 10 in. (20.3 × 25.4 cm)
The Andy Warhol Museum, Pittsburgh; Founding Collection, Contribution The Andy Warhol Foundation for the Visual Arts, Inc., 1998.3.14529

RIGHT
Stephen Shore
Andy Warhol, 1965–66
Gelatin silver print
10 × 8 in. (25.4 × 20.3 cm)
The Andy Warhol Museum, Pittsburgh; Contribution Dia Center for the Arts, 1996.19.27

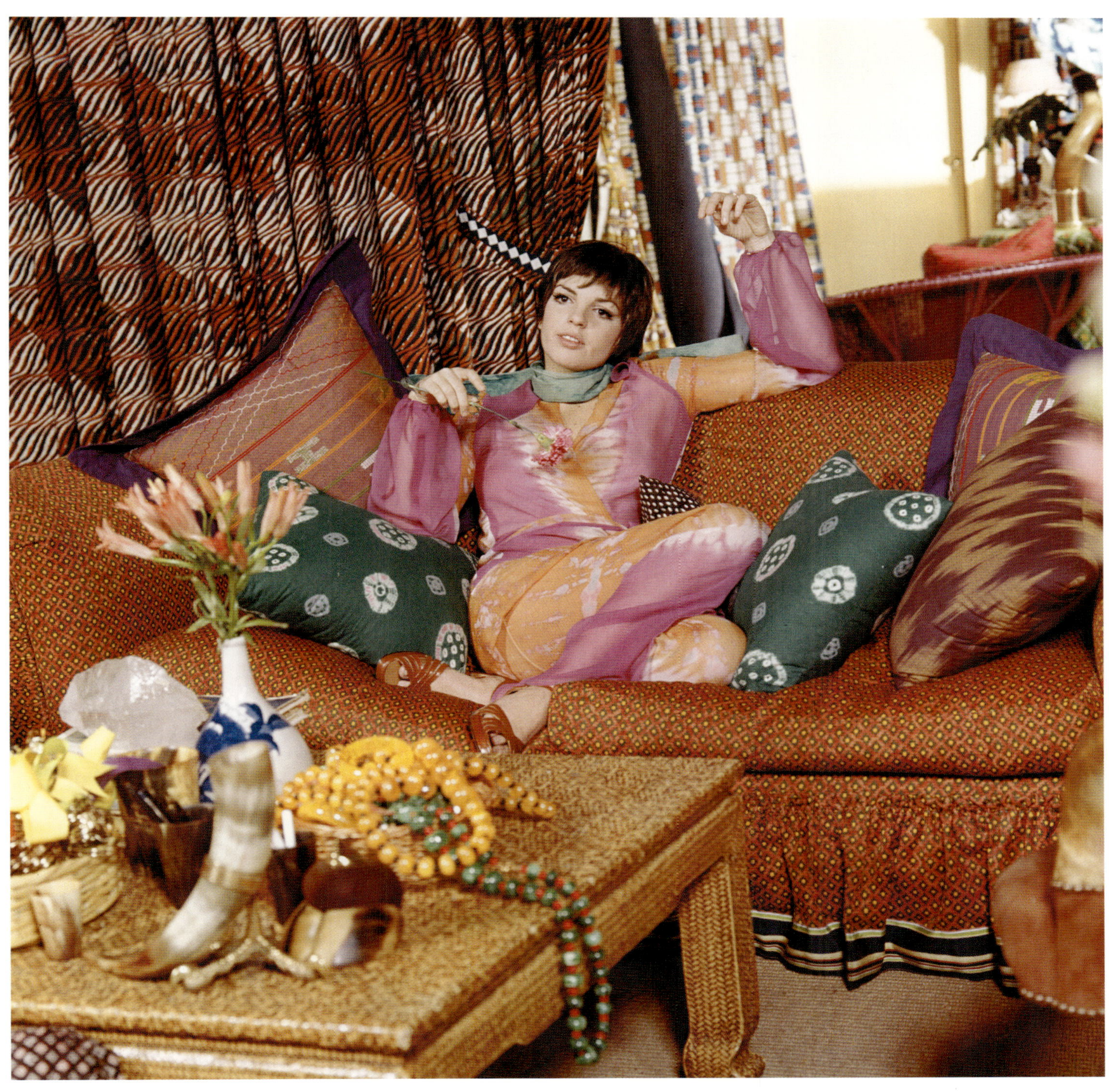

Liza Minnelli in Halston's showroom
Photograph by Ormond Gigli

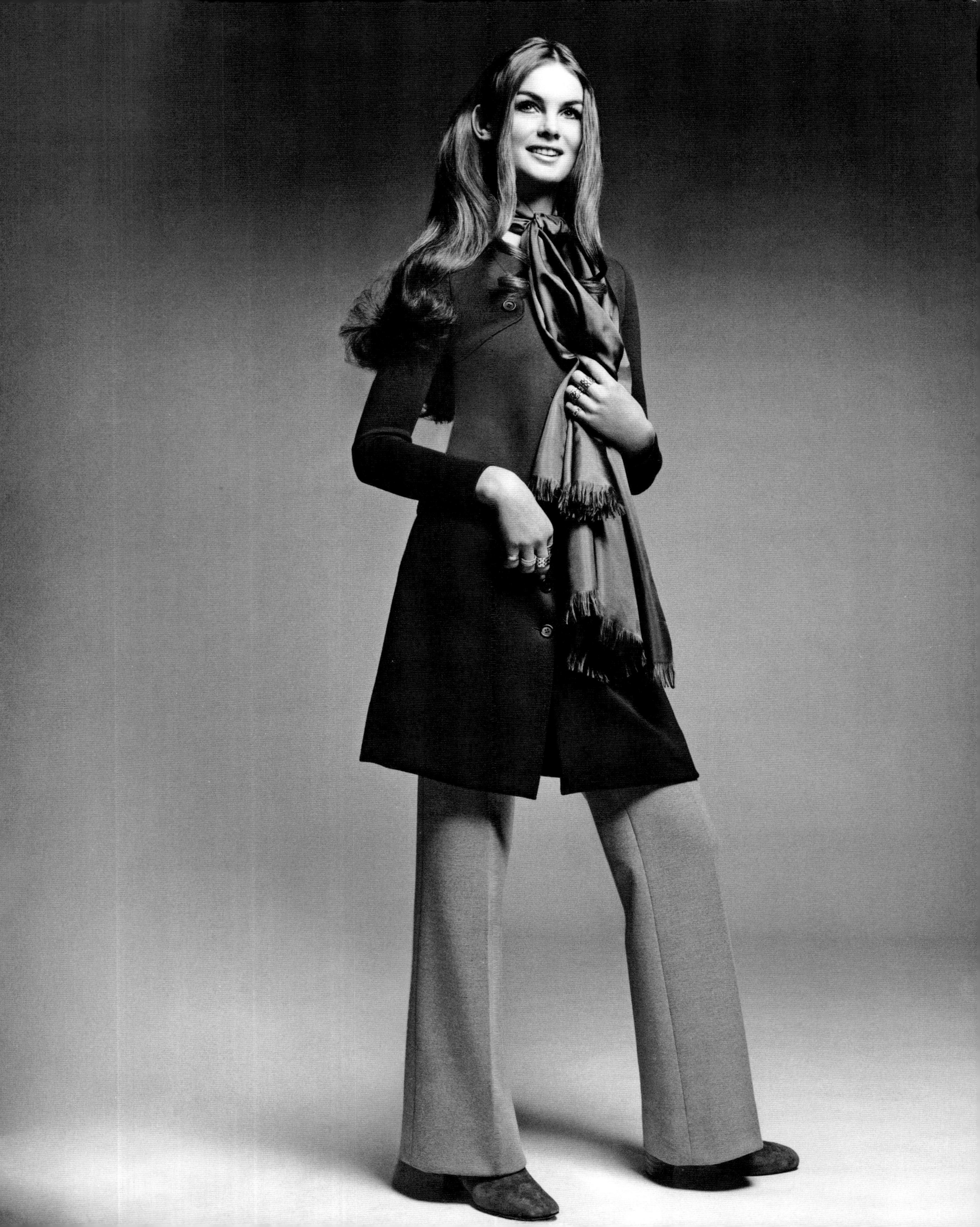

SUPERSTARS AND HALSTONETTES

Both Warhol and Halston had their entourages. Their openness to diverse people broadened the spectrum of who was celebrated in film, fashion, and art. Inspired by the Hollywood system of filmmaking, while also subverting it, Warhol created his own movie studio at the Factory, complete with underground Superstars. They were beautiful people without acting backgrounds, whom he selected to perform in his films. Halston's entourage was referred to as the "Halstonettes." As attested to in the essays and interviews in this book, Halston sought to represent new concepts of beauty through the wide range of race and nationality among the models in his shows.

Jean Shrimpton wearing an A-line jersey tunic and bell bottoms by Halston, a long fringed silk scarf, rings by Napier and Pakula, and suede boots by Charles Jourdan, ca. March 1969
Condé Nast Archive/CORBIS

OVERLEAF
Halstonettes, in black swimsuits of Halston's design, in Acapulco, February 22, 1977
Photograph by Lynn Karlin
Condé Nast Archive/CORBIS

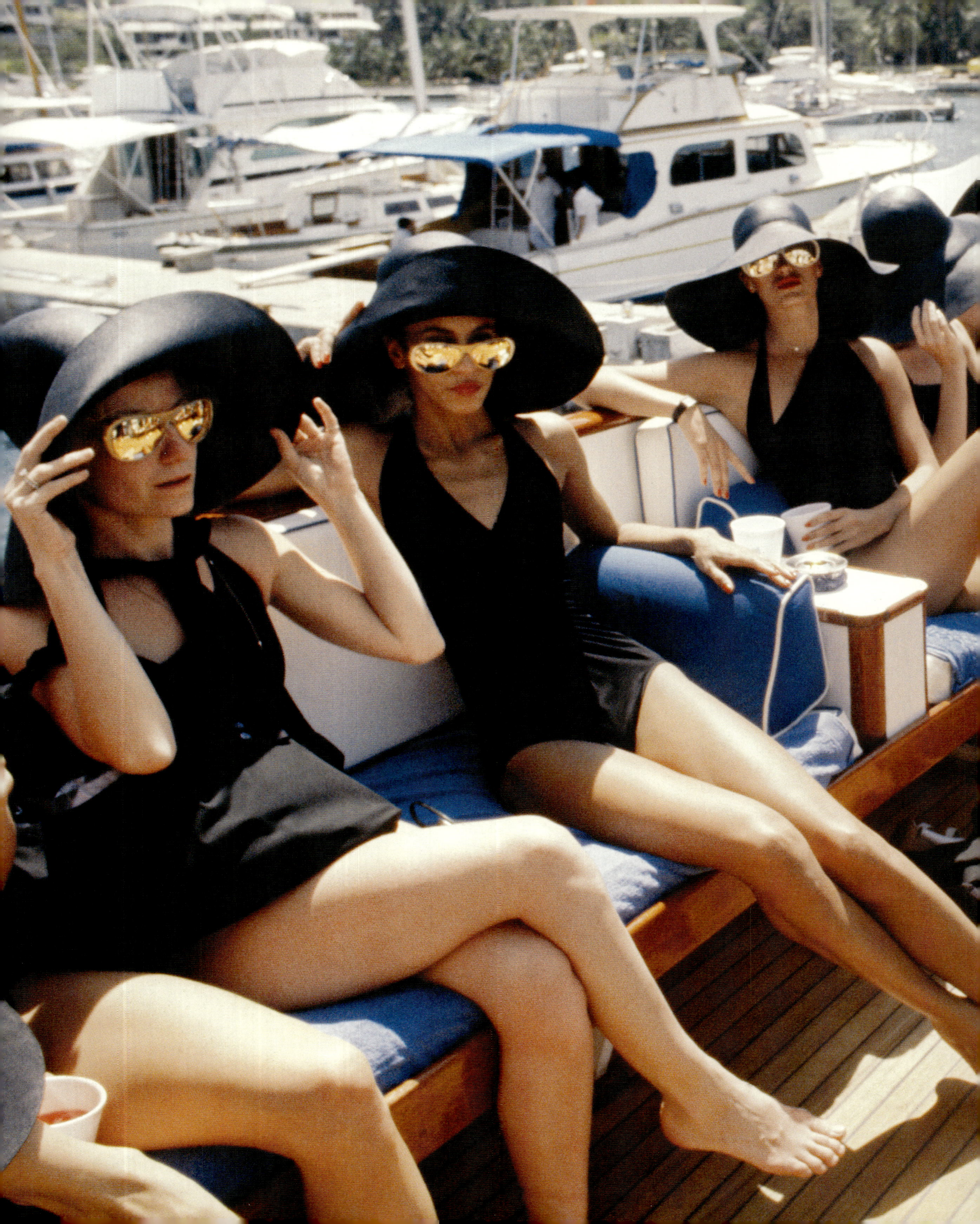

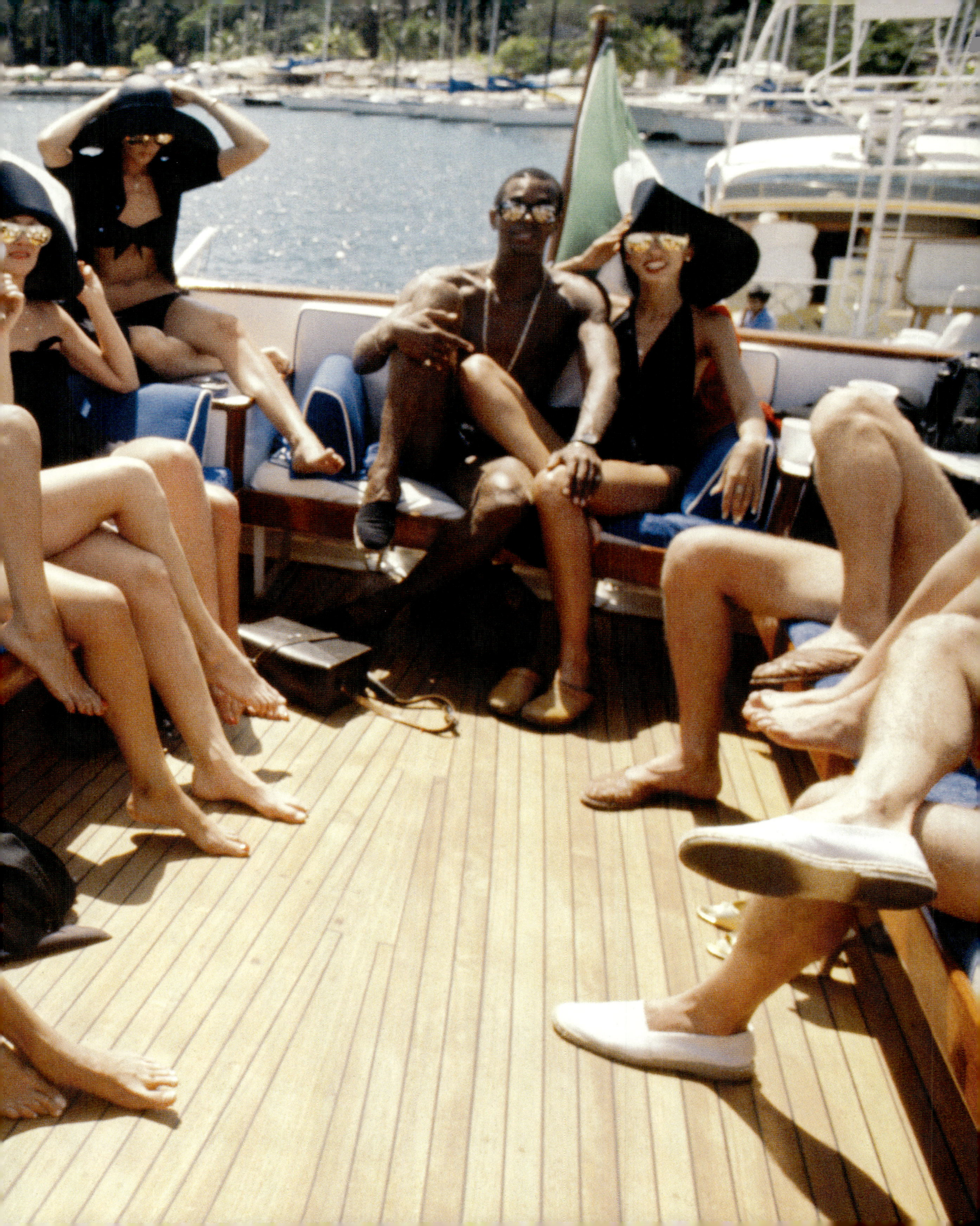

RIGHT
Andy Warhol attends a party in New York with Edie Sedgwick, 1965
Associated Press

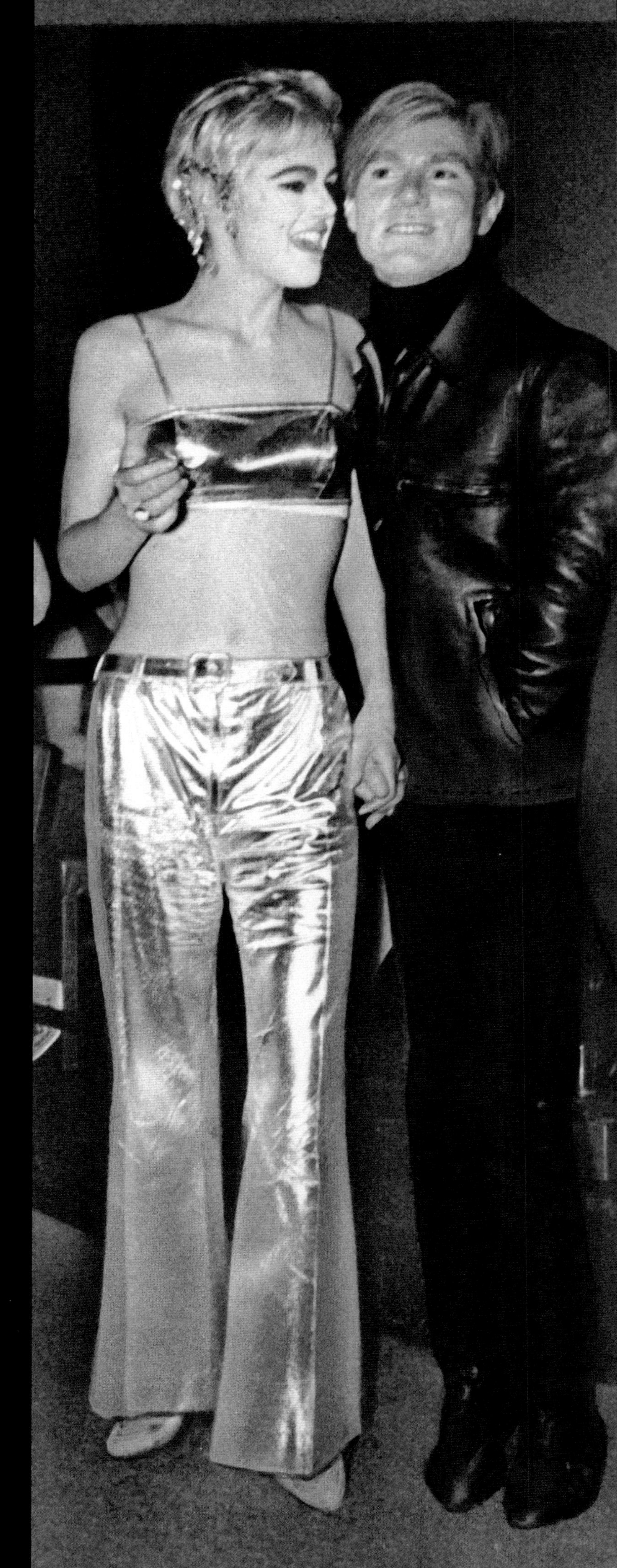

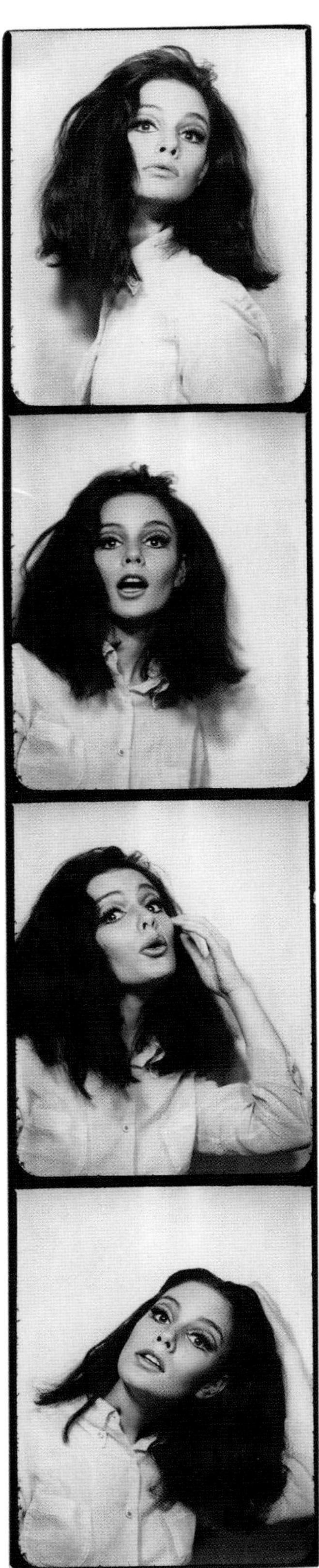

ABOVE
Andy Warhol
Susan Bottomly (International Velvet), ca. 1966
Photobooth photograph
8 × 1½ in. (20.3 × 3.8 cm)
The Andy Warhol Museum, Pittsburgh; Founding Collection, Contribution The Andy Warhol Foundation for the Visual Arts, Inc., 1998.1.2800

"Edie was incredible on camera. Just the way she moved. And she never stopped moving for a second. Even when she was sleeping, her hands were wide awake. She was all energy. She didn't know what to do with it when it came to living her life, but it was wonderful to film. The great stars are the ones who are doing something you can watch every second, even if it's just a movement inside their eye."

—Andy Warhol and Pat Hackett, *POPism: The Warhol '60s*

Perhaps none of the Superstars intrigued Warhol more than Edie Sedgwick, whose luminous personality made any event a success and led him to cast her in more than fifteen of his films. Warhol met Sedgwick in January 1965, shortly after she arrived in New York. A hip socialite from an old New England family ("right out of Gatsby," was how Warhol once described her), Edie was rich, glamorous, and smart, and she quickly became the center of the downtown Silver Factory scene. By the end of the year she was known as the "1965 Girl of the Year."

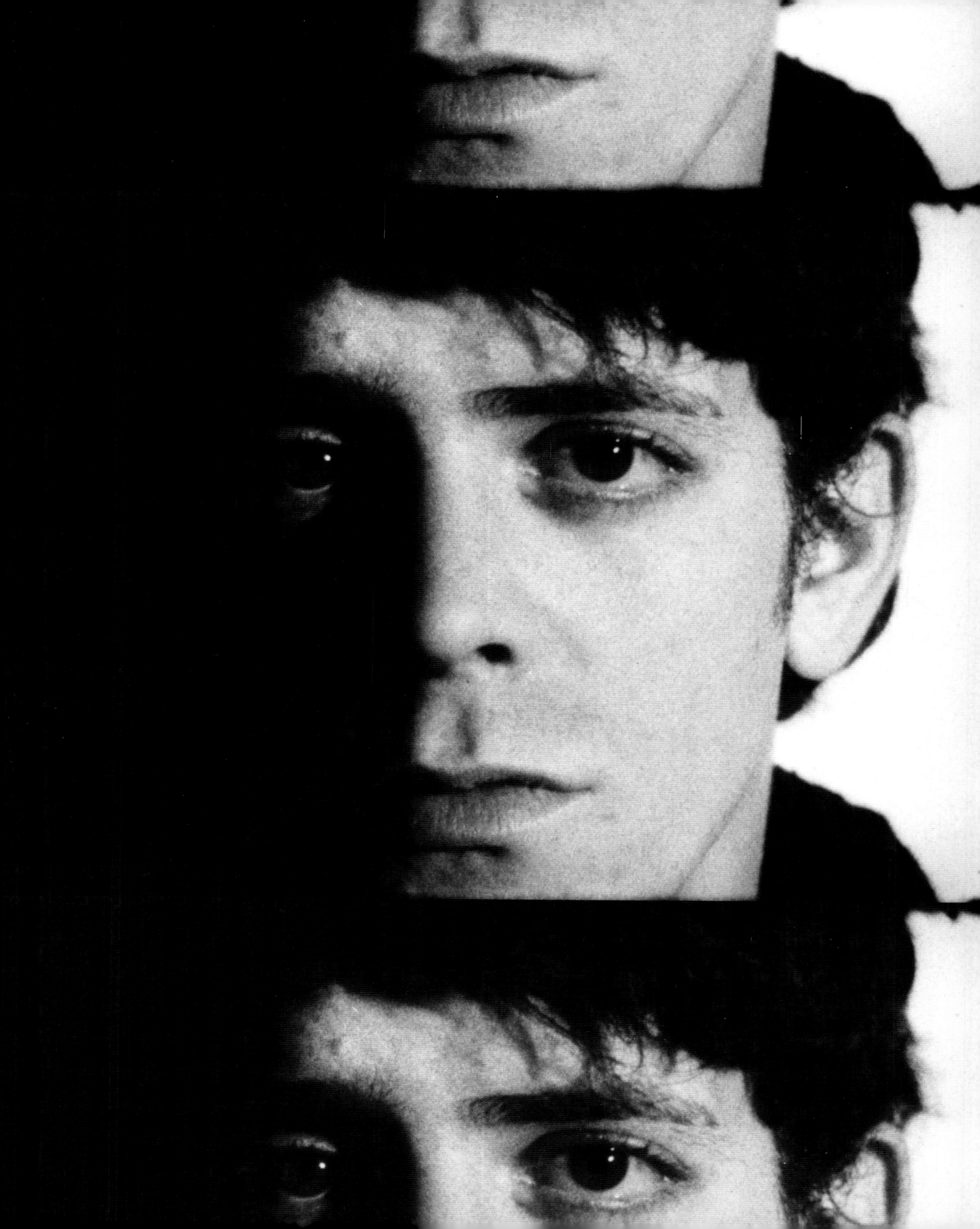

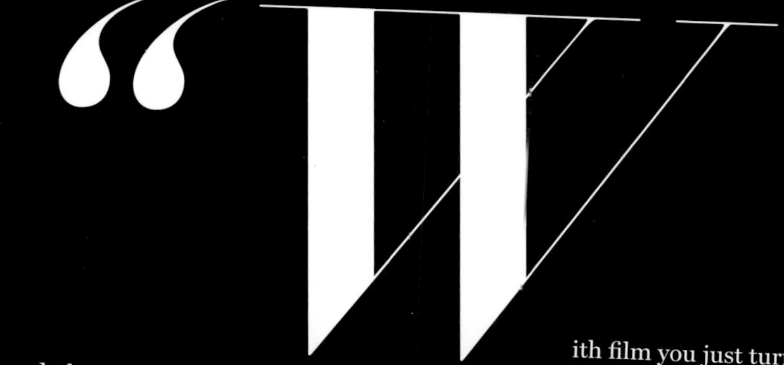

ith film you just turn on the camera and photograph something. I leave the camera running until it runs out of film because that way I can catch people being themselves. It's better to act naturally than to set up a scene and act like someone else. You get a better picture of people being themselves instead of trying to act like they're themselves."

—Andy Warhol, quoted by Gene Youngblood, *L.A. Free Press*, February 16, 1968

"I thought M.G.M., Paramount and 20th Century-Fox and R.K.O., all those studios, were taking too long to get in touch with me. I just went over to the Factory and just decided to get myself in film before it was too late because that seemed to me the thing to do. If you were a Warhol Superstar, you had made it, it seemed. I was right in the neighborhood."

—Jackie Curtis, quoted in Patrick S. Smith, *Andy Warhol's Art and Films*

BLACK AND WHITE BALL

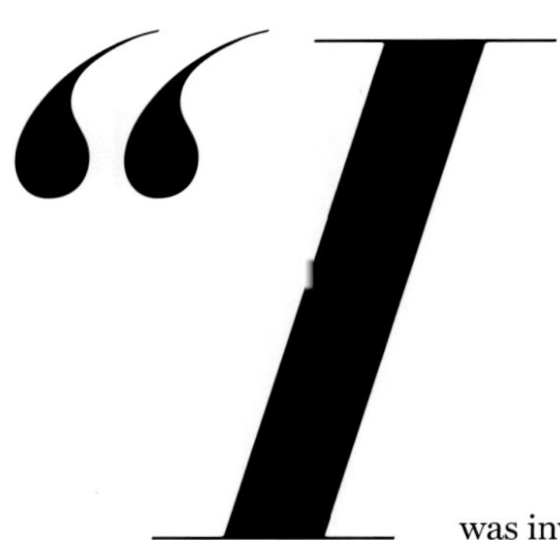

"I was invited to Truman Capote's Masked Ball in the Grand Ballroom of the Plaza Hotel. The media was calling it 'the party of the decade'—not only was this before the decade was over, it was before the party had started."

—Andy Warhol, *America*

Candice Bergen wore a Halston-designed bunny mask to Truman Capote's now-legendary Black and White Ball. The guest of honor, *Washington Post* publisher Katharine Graham, commissioned Halston to design a mask to match her evening gown. Halston created a mask for Mrs. William (Babe) Paley using rubies from her jewelry collection. Mrs. Charles Wrightsman and Mr. and Mrs. Alfred G. Vanderbilt also asked Halston to make masks for them. Most all of the guests donned masks of some sort, except for Warhol.

OPPOSITE
Guest of honor Katharine Graham and Truman Capote arrive at Capote's Black and White Ball at the Plaza Hotel in New York City,
November 28, 1966
Associated Press

OVERLEAF
Candice Bergen at Truman Capote's Black and White Ball,
November 28, 1966
Photograph by Elliott Erwitt
Magnum

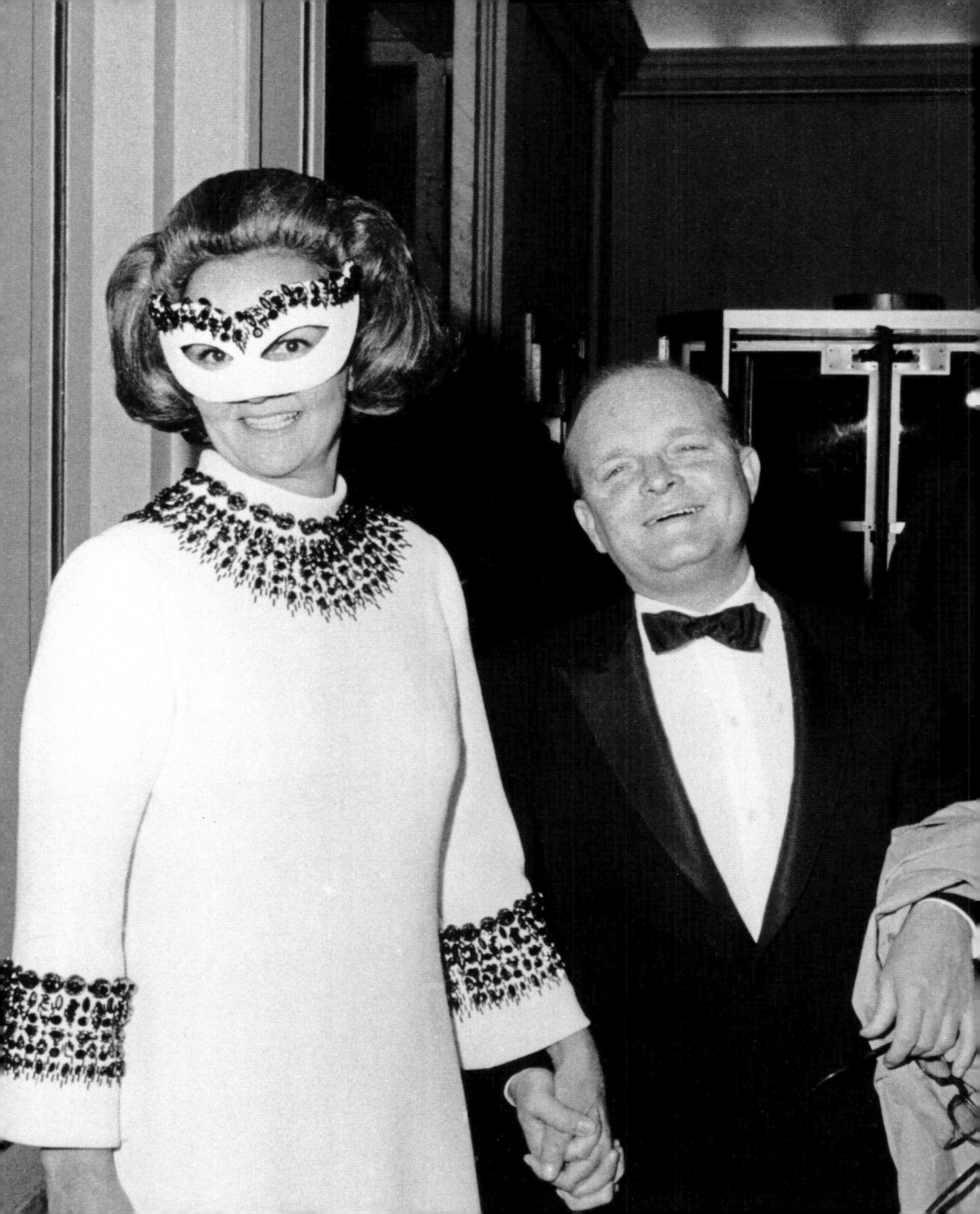

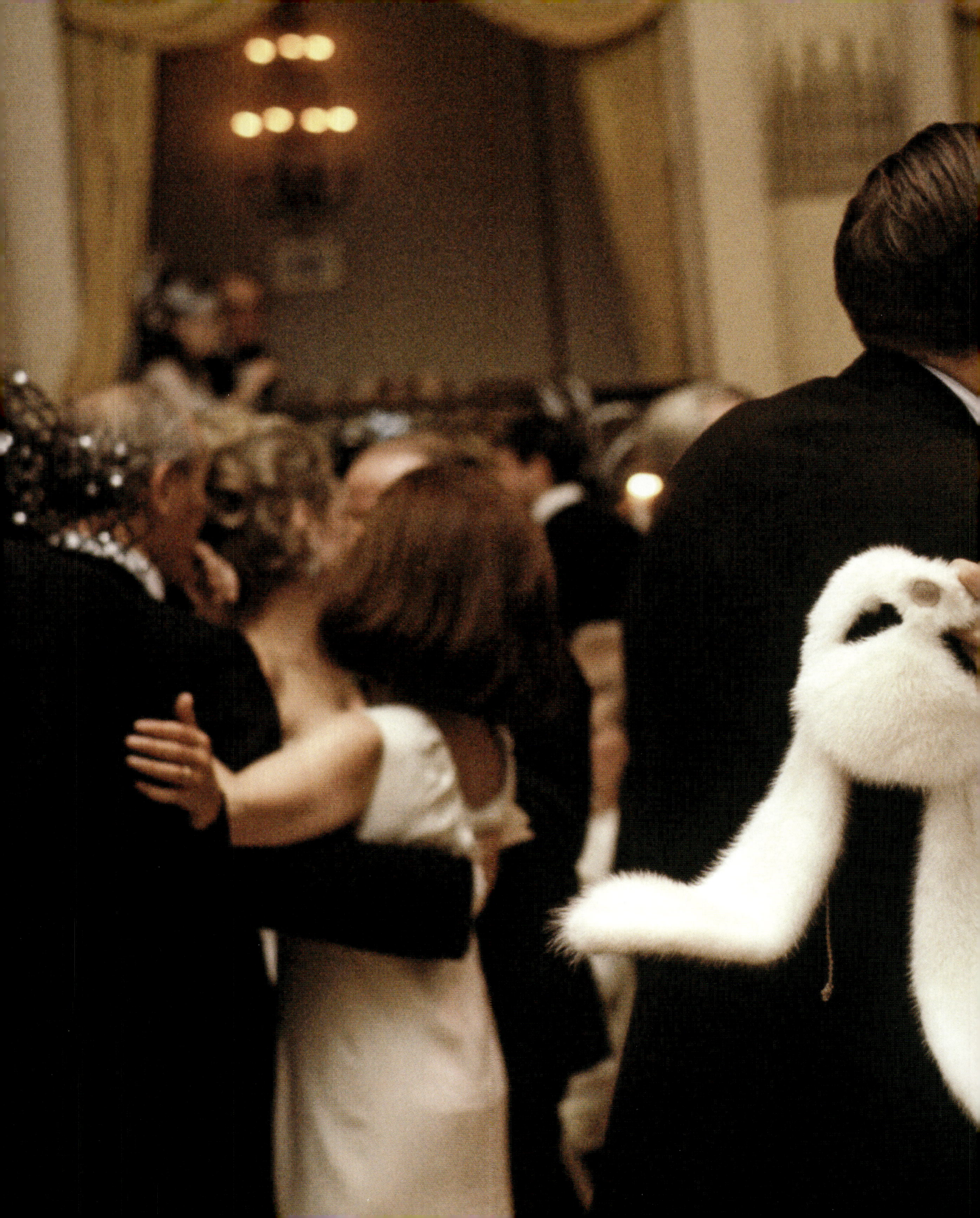

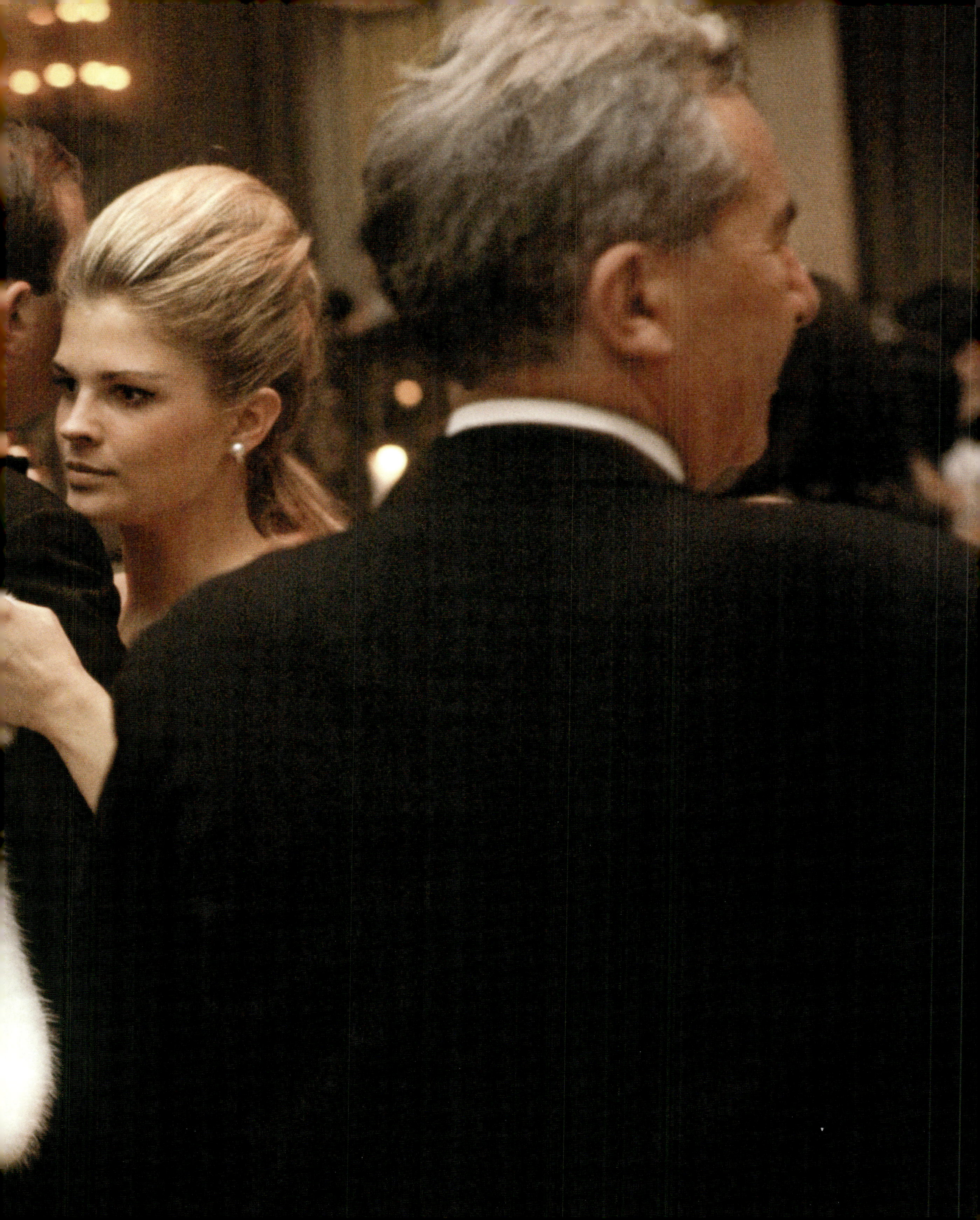

THE FACTORY AND BEYOND

"The Pop idea, after all, was that anybody could do anything, so naturally we were trying to do it all. Nobody wanted to stay in one category; we all wanted to branch out into every creative thing we could—that's why when we met the Velvet Underground at the end of '65, we were all for getting into the music scene, too."

—Andy Warhol and Pat Hackett, *POPism: The Warhol '60s*

Numerous parties, film screenings, and social events were held at the Silver Factory. Discarded pieces of furniture were rescued from the basement and given glamorous new life with a coat of silver paint; they doubled as both party furniture and film props. Everyone who came to New York in the 1960s claims to have visited the Silver Factory.

After attending a performance of the Velvet Underground in December 1965, Warhol offered to manage the rock group. He soon added Nico to the group as their chanteuse. They performed in New York and on tour in Warhol's performances *Up-Tight* and *The Exploding Plastic Inevitable* (*EPI*). *EPI* was a collaborative effort combining artistic talents in seemingly disparate media to create a frenzied mixture of film, live music, dance, and light show. After a brief tour, Warhol arranged a month-long residency for *EPI* at the Open Stage, above the Dom, an old Polish social club on St. Mark's Place in the East Village.

In November 1966 Warhol gave away the bride at the Mod Wedding at the Michigan State Fair Grounds during the Carnaby Street Fun Festival. WKNR radio ran a contest and chose the winning couple, Randi Rossi and Gary Norris, who would be married at the big event. *EPI* did the light show and films, and the Velvet Underground played throughout the ceremony. The ceremony also included a man smashing an old car with a sledgehammer and Warhol painting a young woman's paper dress with paint and ketchup as she modeled. Warhol gave the newlyweds a large inflatable replica of a Baby Ruth candy bar and an invitation to come to his studio to have their screen tests filmed. The event's youthful first-time promoters had conceived it as a last hurrah, since they had both just been drafted into the military.

OPPOSITE TOP LEFT
Andy Warhol and Nico, 1966
Gelatin silver print with typewritten paper slug
9 × 7⅛ in. (22.9 × 18.1 cm)
The Andy Warhol Museum, Pittsburgh; Founding Collection, Contribution The Andy Warhol Foundation for the Visual Arts, Inc., TC5.154a-b

OPPOSITE TOP RIGHT
Andy Warhol, Randy Rossi, and Nico, 1968
Gelatin silver print
10 × 8⅛ in. (25.4 × 20.6 cm)
The Andy Warhol Museum, Pittsburgh; Gift of Bill Rice and Treasure Ann Sachnoff, 1999.4.1

OPPOSITE BOTTOM
At a Factory Party, August 31, 1965
Among those pictured are Stephen Shore (on the couch, in sunglasses) and the filmmaker Shirley Clarke (on the couch, with camera). Warhol is visible at center rear, between the cow-print and Mylar wallpapers.
Photograph by Fred W. McDarrah
Getty Images

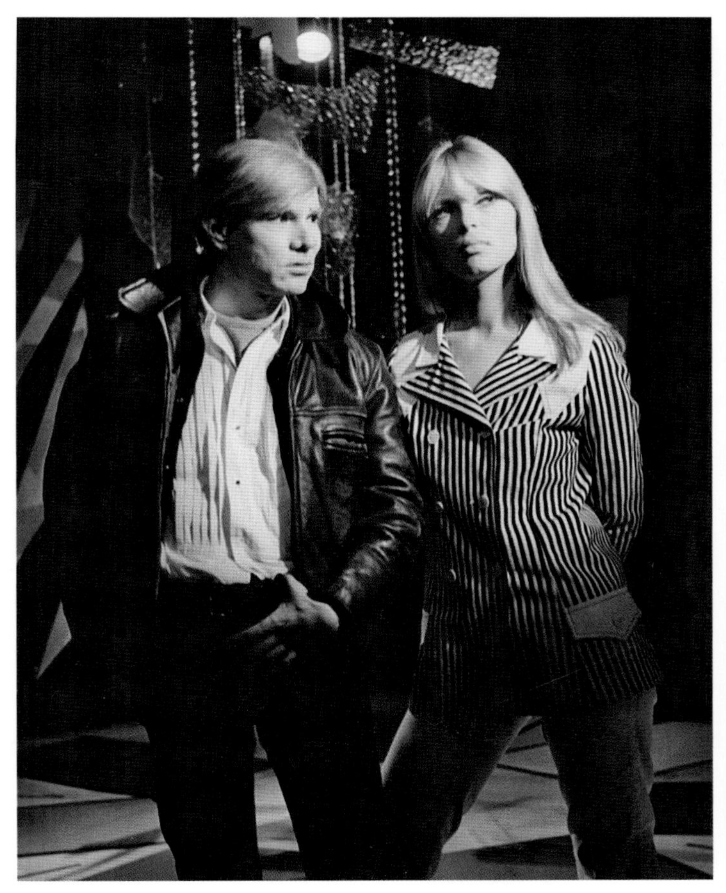

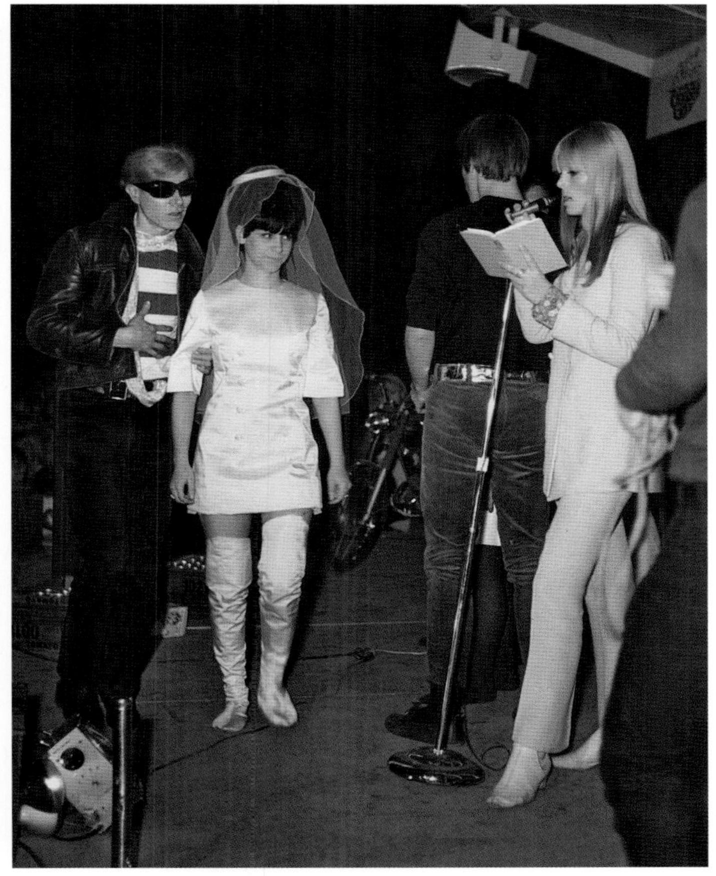

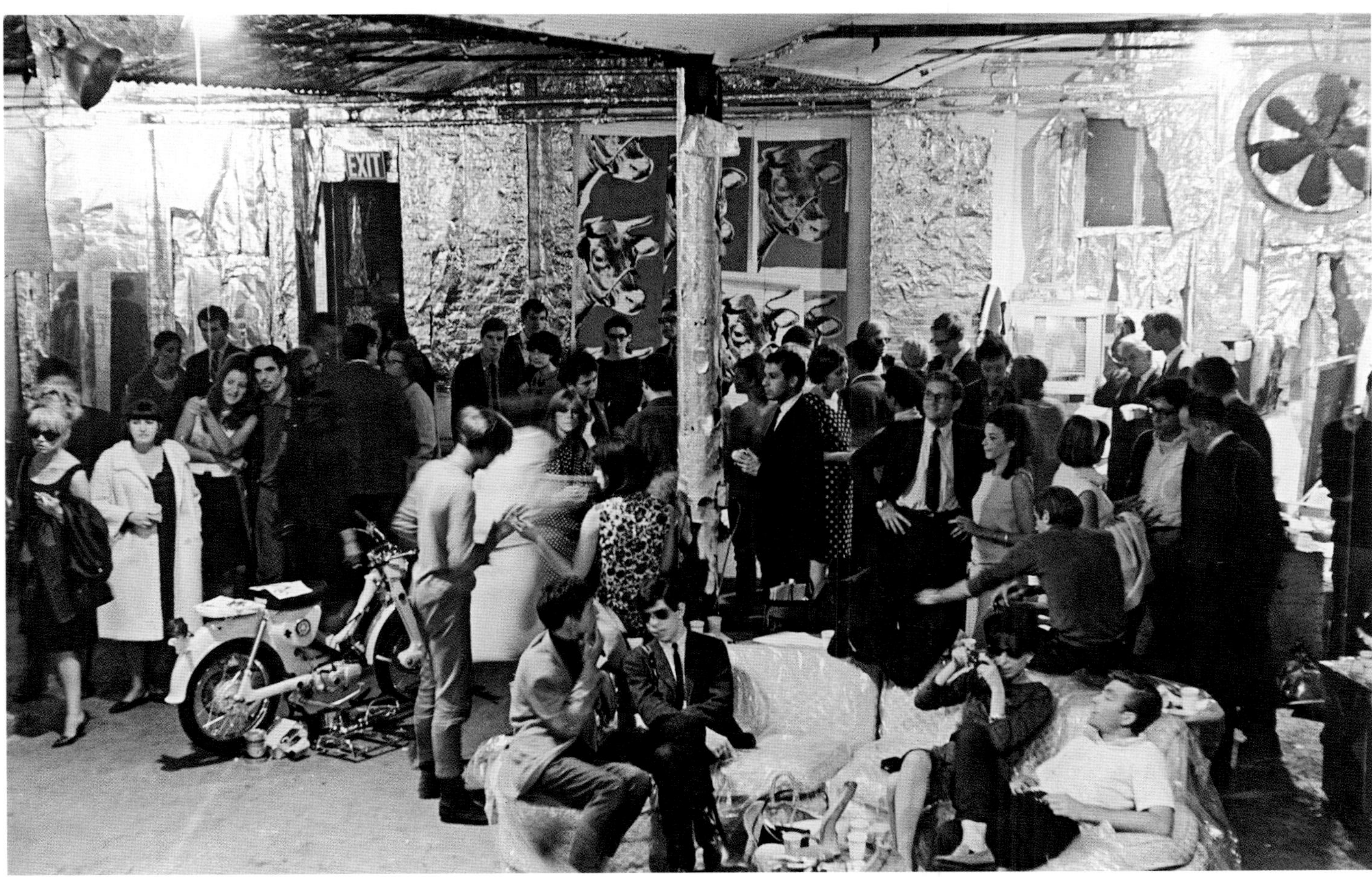
EXIT

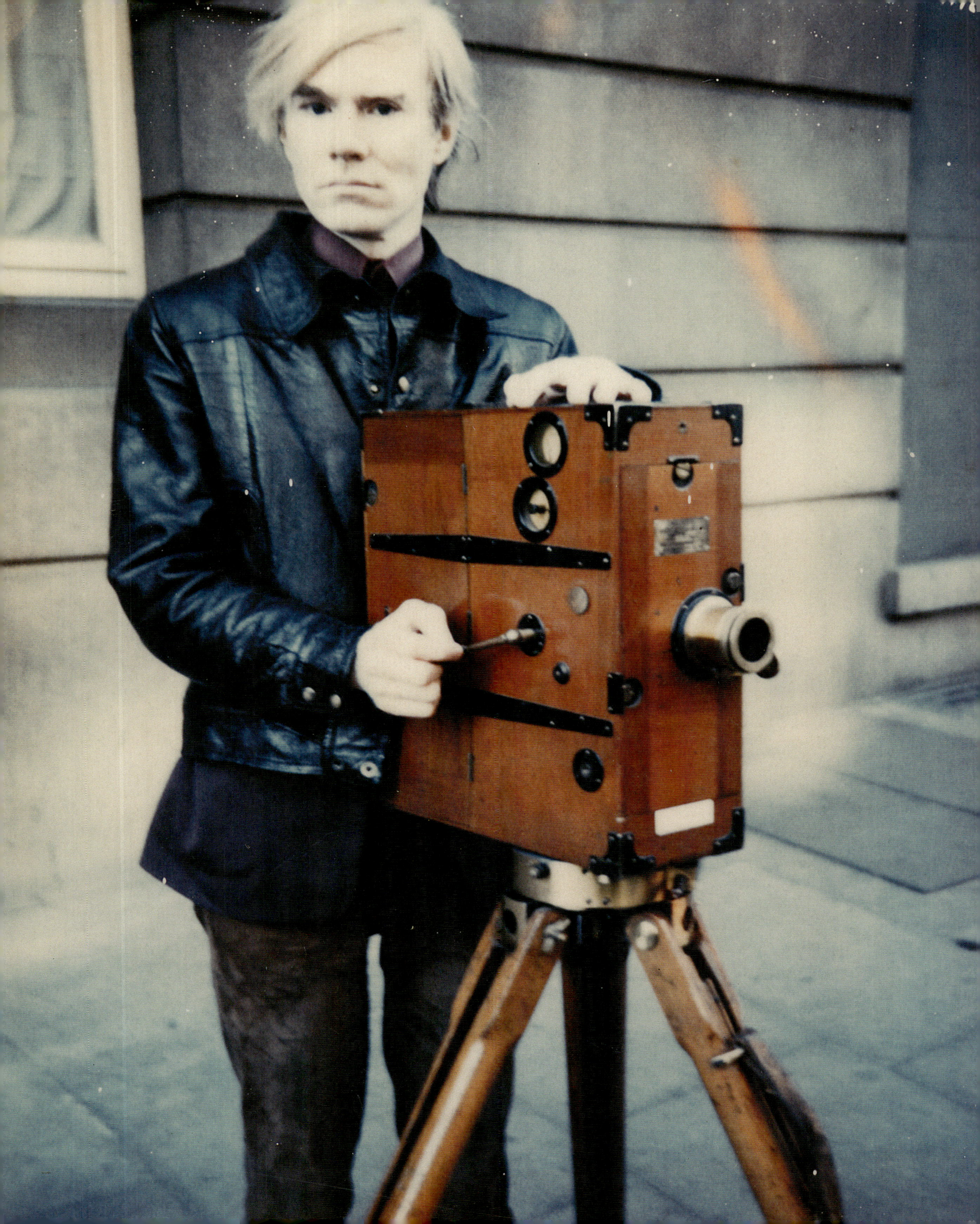

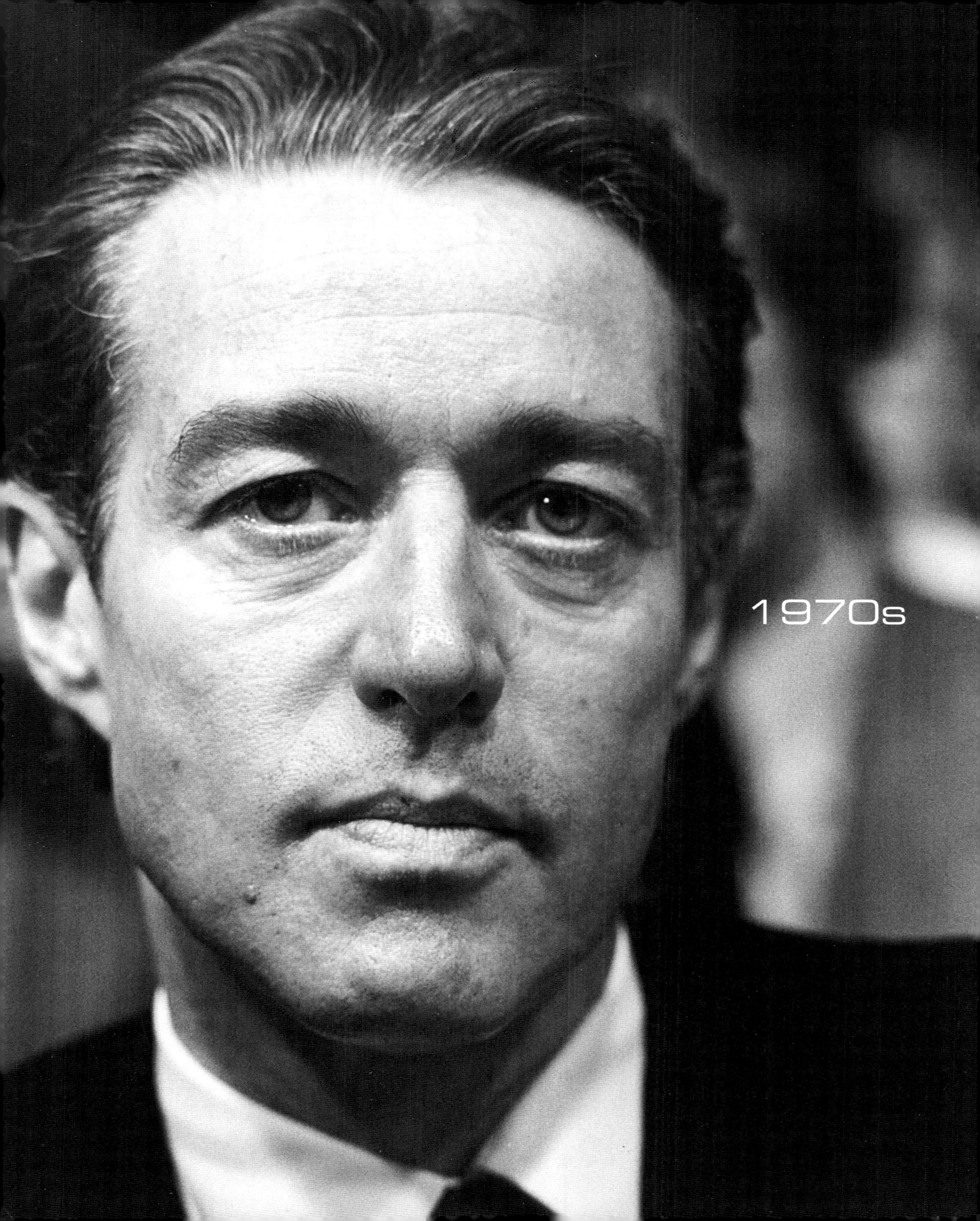

1970s

1970s

WARHOL

1970
Warhol's production of commissioned portraits increases in the early 1970s. Most are based on Polaroid photographs of his sitters, including collectors, friends, and celebrities.

Acquires a portable video camera and begins to work regularly with video.

The first monograph of his work, titled *Andy Warhol* and written by the art historian Rainer Crone, is published.

Bob Colacello and Glenn O'Brien begin to work for *Interview*. Each journalist eventually becomes the magazine's executive editor.

1971
With Vincent Fremont and Michael Netter, Warhol begins *The Factory Diaries*, a series of videotaped recordings of life at the studio.

Designs the cover of the Rolling Stones' *Sticky Fingers* album in collaboration with Craig Braun. Featuring an image of a male torso in jeans with a functioning zipper, the cover is nominated for a Grammy Award.

Warhol's play *Pork*, based on his tape recordings of the late 1960s, is performed in London and New York. It is edited and directed by Anthony J. Ingrassia and stars Anthony Zanetta as "B. Marlowe"—the pseudonym for Warhol in the recordings. Zanetta and two other members of the cast (Cherry Vanilla and Wayne County) later work for David Bowie's MainMan Production Company.

Warhol and Paul Morrissey acquire an isolated twenty-acre compound in Montauk, Long Island, for $225,000. Over the years, Truman Capote, Dick Cavett, Lee Radziwill, and other friends spend much time there.

HALSTON

1970
Joe Eula becomes Halston's creative director.

1971
Begins using Ultrasuede in his designs. Believing the material to be water repellent, he creates Ultrasuede raincoats.

October: Receives his third Coty American Fashion Critics' Award, a Winny Award for contributions to American Fashion.

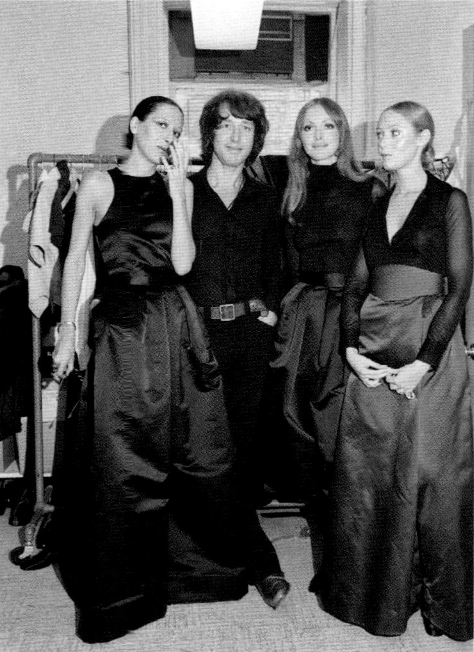

LEFT
Halston with models after a showing in New York City, June 15, 1970
Associated Press

PREVIOUS SPREAD, LEFT
Andy Warhol
Self-Portrait with Movie Camera
(detail), ca. 1971
Polaroid™ Polacolor Type 108
4¼ × 3⅜ in. (10.8 × 8.6 cm)
The Andy Warhol Museum, Pittsburgh; Founding Collection, Contribution The Andy Warhol Foundation for the Visual Arts, Inc., 1998.3.8902

PREVIOUS SPREAD, RIGHT
Halston, November 28, 1978
Photograph by Fred W. McDarrah
Getty Images

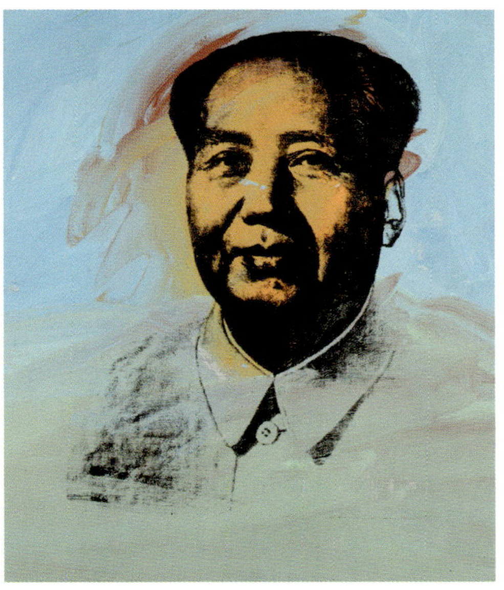

LEFT
Andy Warhol
Mao, 1973
Acrylic and silkscreen ink on linen
24 × 20 × 1 in. (61 × 50.8 × 2.5 cm)
The Andy Warhol Museum, Pittsburgh; Founding Collection, Contribution The Andy Warhol Foundation for the Visual Arts, Inc., 1998.1.160

1972

Begins *Mao* paintings, drawings, and prints.

After he publishes his print *Vote McGovern*, an endorsement of the presidential candidate, the Internal Revenue Service audits Warhol's taxes; he is audited annually until his death.

Warhol's mother dies in Pittsburgh. She had returned there from New York in 1971.

Creates "An Onstage Happening by Andy Warhol" for Halston's design show at the Coty American Fashion Critics' Awards. Warhol incorporates tap-dancing, juggling, and bongo-playing models. The socialite Nan Kempner cooks breakfast onstage in a Halston gown.

1973

Warhol and Vincent Fremont, the manager of Andy Warhol Studios, concentrate on developing ideas for improvised, experimental melodramas for what they term the *Soap Opera* project. The first, *Vivian's Girls*, uses Halston's models, including Pat Cleveland, Nancy North, and Karen Bjornson. It is modeled after the film *Stage Door* and Andy's *Chelsea Girls*. More characters are added to the cast: Candy Darling, Maxime de la Falaise, John Richardson, and Brigid Berlin. Andy changes the film's title to *Phoney*, a play on words—referring both to people who are always on the phone and to those who are phony.

Appears in the film *The Driver's Seat* with Elizabeth Taylor.

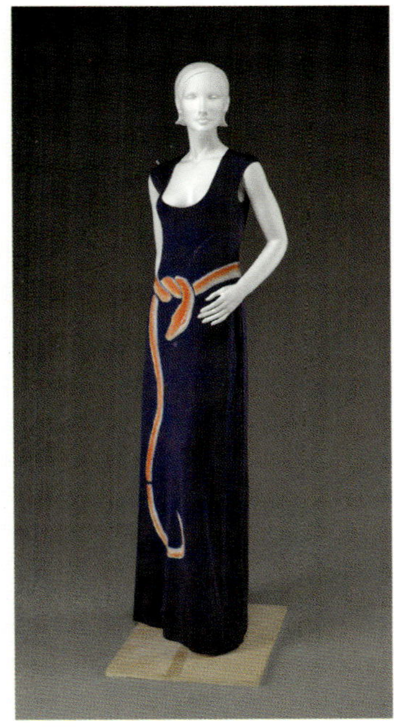

ABOVE
Halston
Evening dress with hand-painted snake, 1971
Resist-dyed silk jersey
Indianapolis Museum of Art, 1985.631

1972

Expands his showroom at 33 East 68th Street by leasing additional floors in the same building. On February 7, he opens a retail boutique on the ground floor to sell lower-priced apparel directly to consumers. In the second-floor salon, he showcases his ready-to-wear clothing to private customers. The space now contains sleek, low modern furniture covered in white Ultrasuede, mirrored panels, and Halston's signature white orchids. On the third floor, he meets with special clients who request made-to-order designs. Each floor sells fashion at a different price point.

Sometime in early 1972 Halston meets Victor Hugo. Both are avid fans of Pop art and Dada. Andy Warhol, Larry Rivers, Louise Nevelson, and Arman and his wife, Corice, become part of their circle.

Around this time Halston hires Stephen Sprouse to work with him. Sprouse leaves after two years to start his own line.

May: Forms a new partnership with Ben Shaw and Guido De Natale to create Halston Originals, a ready-to-wear fashion line distributed to only one store and one boutique in each major American city. Showrooms and offices are located at 550 Seventh Avenue, in the Garment District.

Shows first collection for Halston Originals.

Fall: Halston's Ultrasuede shirtdress, #704, becomes an instant success—a classically styled, easy-to-wear dress in a lightweight, luxurious, and machine-washable fabric.

August: Bergdorf Goodman opens a Halston boutique on the second floor, between the fur salon and the Givenchy boutique. Halston is pleased to have the boutique located on the same floor in Bergdorf's where his fashion career had been launched.

August 21: *Newsweek* runs a cover photo of the model Karen Bjornson in an Ultrasuede hat and outfit designed by Halston. The cover story, "The Ease and Elegance Designed by Halston," lauds Halston as "the premier fashion designer of all America."

October 19: Receives fourth Coty American Fashion Critics' Award.

1970s

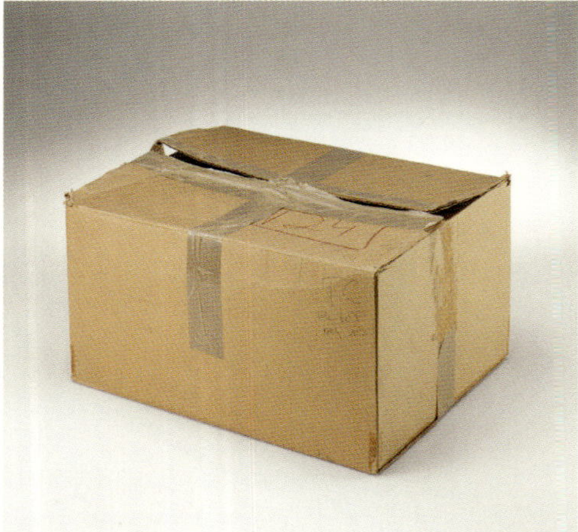

LEFT
Andy Warhol
Time Capsule 21, 1974
Mixed archival material
The Andy Warhol Museum, Pittsburgh; Founding Collection, Contribution The Andy Warhol Foundation for the Visual Arts, Inc., TC21.123

1974
Diane von Furstenberg and Halston each commission Warhol to create portraits.

Begins a series of *Time Capsules*: cardboard boxes that he fills with the materials of his everyday life, including mail, photos, art, clothing, and collectibles. Over the years he produces more than six hundred boxes, which are now an archival goldmine of his life and times. Documented in the *Time Capsules* is Warhol's incredible social life with friends, including Halston. Moves the Factory to 860 Broadway, which becomes known as "the office."

Acquires a townhouse at 57 East 66th Street. Jed Johnson decorates the house, which is filled with art and collectibles.

Sells ten *Mao* paintings to Halston.

1973
October: Sells his companies Halston Originals and Halston Ltd., his exclusive services as designer, and his trademarks to Norton Simon Inc. for $16 million. In this deal all businesses are consolidated under the name Halston Enterprises.

November 28: Halston is one of five American designers invited to present clothing alongside that of five French designers at the Palace of Versailles benefit fashion gala. The evening makes history as the first-ever joint fashion show of American and French designers. Halston, Anne Klein, Bill Blass, Oscar de la Renta, and Stephen Burrows represent the United States and Hubert de Givenchy, Pierre Cardin, Yves Saint Laurent, Emanuel Ungaro, and Marc Bohan for Christian Dior represent France.

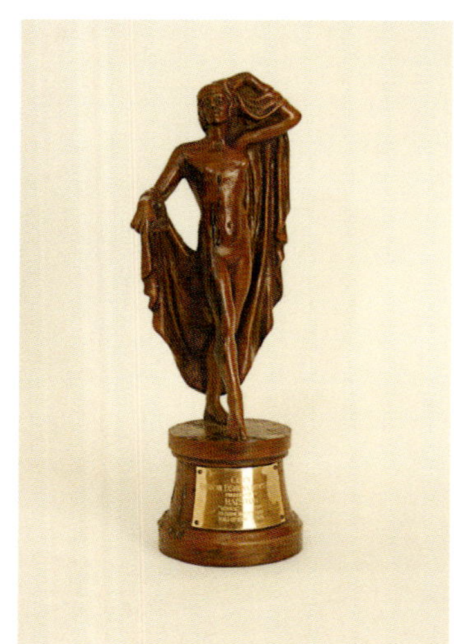

LEFT
Coty award given to Halston, 1974
Courtesy the Lesley Frowick Collection

1974
March: Purchases the Paul Rudolph–designed townhouse (commissioned by the previous owner) at 101 East 63rd Street. At the time, it is the only new townhouse that has been built in New York City since World War II. The three-story living room has a skylight in the ceiling and a twenty-seven-feet-tall glass atrium along the back wall. The minimalist gray-and-white interior contains integrated furniture designed by Rudolph, a dramatic floating staircase with no railing, and cantilevered balconies. Halston always has orchids in the entry and on the coffee table. The large expanses of white wall are usually left unadorned except for artwork by Warhol, which is hung on upper floors or in hallways.

Receives fifth Coty American Fashion Critics' Award, a Hall of Fame award.

Designs a short, floaty dress called the Skimp, which creates a lot of media attention when it is debuted in the Fall collection.

Works with Norton Simon Inc. to edit existing licenses and launches a massive new licensing program. New licenses are established for loungewear/robes, fur coats, menswear, and raincoats.

Agrees to license arrangement with Montgomery Ward for the design of uniforms for United States athletes participating in the

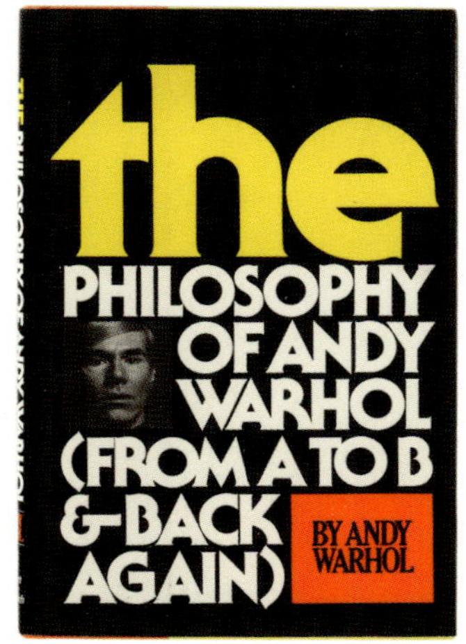

LEFT
Andy Warhol
THE Philosophy of Andy Warhol (from A to B and Back Again),
First Edition, 1975
Published by Harcourt Brace Jovanovich, New York and London
Printed ink on paper with buckram board cover and printed, coated paper jacket
8⅝ × 5¾ × 1 in. (21.9 × 14.6 × 2.5 cm)
The Andy Warhol Museum, Pittsburgh; Founding Collection, Contribution The Andy Warhol Foundation for the Visual Arts, Inc., 1998.3.2452.1a-b

1975

Makes *Ladies and Gentlemen* paintings, drawings, and prints depicting transvestites.

THE Philosophy of Andy Warhol (From A to B and Back Again) is published by Harcourt Brace Jovanovich.

The December issue of *Interview* is themed "Fashion as Fantasy." Tatum O'Neal appears on the cover and is featured trying on clothes in various designer showrooms, including Halston's.

1976

Makes *Skull* paintings, prints, and drawings and begins the *Hammer and Sickle* series, also in multiple mediums.

Begins dictating his diary to his secretary, Pat Hackett. In the fall, Warhol starts the daily habit of telephoning Hackett around 9:00 a.m. As Warhol talks, Hackett transcribes his monologue onto a legal pad. Warhol's initial intention is to use these entries primarily as a tax-expense record for the IRS. The diary is published posthumously and becomes a best-seller.

A retrospective of Warhol's drawings is held at the Württembergischer Kunstverein in Stuttgart, Germany.

---

summer 1975 Pan American Games in Mexico City, the summer 1976 Olympic Games in Montreal, and the winter 1976 Olympic Games in Innsbruck, Austria.

By November, Halston fires Ed Austin, who had been in charge of Halston Ltd. merchandising and displays, and gives Victor Hugo the role to design the Madison Avenue boutique windows. Hugo excels in producing inspiring and controversial visuals. He says, "I put windows on the map as a Pop artist. I looked at it as art. The windows became my paintings, my occupation." These displays become a highlight in the fashion press.

1975

Debuts his signature Sarong dress.

Halston commissions Elsa Peretti to design the bottle for his signature fragrance, which is launched through Max Factor. Peretti, who had modeled for Halston when she first arrived in New York and then became a close friend, bases the teardrop bottle on the organic, asymmetrical designs in her jewelry collection. Halston says, "I wanted a bottle that would be a collector's item" (*Women's Wear Daily*, June 4, 1976). The Halston name appears only on a small paper band that breaks away from the neck when the bottle is opened.

Elsa Peretti creates a gold-mesh bra for Halston's Fall collection, which becomes an important piece in her product line.

August: *Esquire* publishes an article posing the question: "Will Halston Take Over the World?"

In addition to the fragrance, new licenses are negotiated for Halston V sportswear, Halston VI blouses, bedding, carpets, men's clothing, men's sportswear, and dresses.

1976

March 22: Halston's high-cut Savage bathing suit appears on the cover of *Time*. The related article is titled "American Chic in Fashion."

June: Receives Fragrance of the Year award by the Fragrance Foundation.

Agrees to new licenses for hats, scarves, women's gloves and accessories, men's belts, swimwear, beachwear, men's shirts, eyeglasses, sunglasses, shoes, men's robes, men's pajamas, and men's swimsuits. He also begins designing home furnishings such as linens and floor coverings.

Designs uniforms for Braniff Airlines flight attendants. Organizes a weekend of parties and fashion shows in Acapulco, Mexico, to

1970s

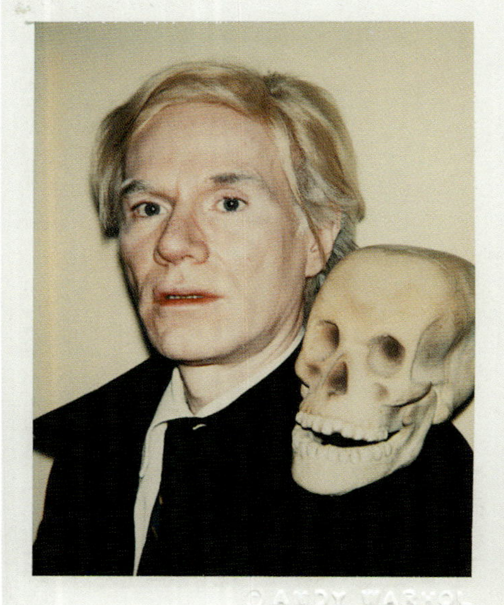

LEFT
Andy Warhol
Self-Portrait with Skull, 1977
Polaroid™ Polacolor Type 108
4 ¼ × 3⅜ in. (10.8 × 8.6 cm)
The Andy Warhol Museum, Pittsburgh; Founding Collection, Contribution The Andy Warhol Foundation for the Visual Arts, Inc., 1998.1.2866

1977
Makes *Torso* paintings and drawings. Victor Hugo models for some of the Polaroids that are used as source material for the paintings.

Andy Warhol's "Folk and Funk," an exhibition of Warhol's folk-art collection, is held at the Museum of American Folk Art in New York.

Begins to frequent the nightclub Studio 54 with his friends Halston, Bianca Jagger, and Liza Minnelli.

1977–78
Pays Victor Hugo to be his collaborator for his *Sex Parts* series.

1978
Makes *Self-Portraits* with skulls, *Shadows*, and *Oxidation* paintings.

A retrospective of Warhol's work is held at the Kunsthaus in Zurich, Switzerland.

Warhol meets Don Munroe through Marc Balet, the art director of *Interview* magazine. Munroe is the head of Bloomingdale's in-house video studio, where all the major fashion designers film their shows. Warhol has always wanted his own television studio, and so, with Munroe and Vincent Fremont, he creates Andy Warhol T.V. Productions.

Victor Hugo creates a number of sculptures using U.S. paper currency, including a fork, a knife, and a spoon, and gives a *50-Dollar Bills Paintbrush* to Warhol as a

---

introduce the new uniforms. Recognizing an opportunity, Braniff launches a new plane and partners with the Mexican government to promote the beach resort. Some 250 guests are flown in. Halston and the Halstonettes wear coordinating outfits throughout the weekend, including black bathing suits, oversize black broad-brimmed hats, and mirrored sunglasses.

Opens first retail store outside New York, at Chicago's Water Tower Place.

1977
Is nominated for a Tony Award in costume design for Liza Minnelli's costumes in *The Act*.

Licenses are negotiated for the design of women's foundations, men's ties, men's handkerchiefs, women's cosmetics, and women's handbags and belts.

June 30: Appears on the cover of *People* with Elizabeth Taylor and Liza Minnelli.

Encourages his friends to have their portraits done by Warhol; Liza Minnelli pays $70,000 for her portraits.

Hosts Bianca Jagger's white-themed birthday bash at Studio 54. Jagger rides across the dance floor on a white horse, wearing a white Halston dress, and releases white doves in the nightclub.

1978
January: Moves his office, workroom, and showroom to the new Olympic Tower building at 51st Street and Fifth Avenue.

Designs uniforms for staff and leaders of the Girl Scouts of America.

Designs winter uniforms for the New York City Police Department. The NYPD never manufactures the models for the jacket, pants, hat, coat, and boots.

June 26: Martha Graham wears a gown by Halston to the Martha Graham Benefit Gala held in her honor at Lincoln Center. Halston and Warhol attend. Halston, a longtime supporter and friend of Graham's, designs costumes

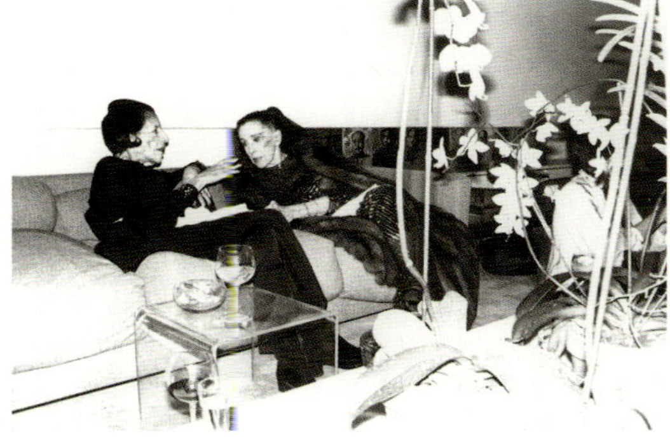

RIGHT
Andy Warhol
Diana Vreeland and Martha Graham, n.d.
Gelatin silver print
8 × 10 in. (20.3 × 25.4 cm)
The Andy Warhol Museum, Pittsburgh; Contribution The Andy Warhol Foundation for the Visual Arts, Inc., 2001.2.700

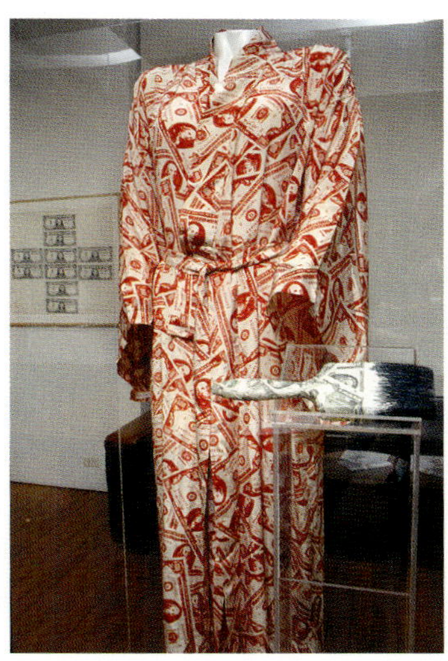

LEFT
Victor Hugo
50-Dollar Bills Paintbrush, 1978
Paper currency on paintbrush
The Andy Warhol Museum, Pittsburgh; Founding Collection, Contribution The Andy Warhol Foundation for the Visual Arts, Inc.

Halston
100-Dollar Bills Robe, ca. 1978
Printed silk
The Andy Warhol Museum, Pittsburgh; Founding Collection, Contribution The Andy Warhol Foundation for the Visual Arts, Inc.

Christmas gift. Hugo's use of money inspires Halston to design fabric printed with $100 bills. He is unable to market the clothing due to counterfeiting laws, but he creates for Warhol a kimono-style robe with matching pants.

1979

Andy Warhol: Portraits of the 70s is presented at the Whitney Museum of American Art in New York.The opening is the social event of the season, with guests including Leo Castelli, Ileana Sonnabend, Ivan Karp, Henry Geldzahler, Jane Holzer, Joe MacDonald, Halston, and Victor Hugo (all of whom are portrait subjects). Other people who have commissioned portraits also attend: Yves Saint Laurent, Hélène Rochas, Diane von Furstenberg, Sao Schlumberger, Marion Block, Kimio Powers, Gianni and Marella Agnelli, Freddy and Marcia Weisman, Mick Jagger, Kay Fortson, and Sidney and Frances Lewis.

Begins to produce the ten-episode video program *Fashion*, directed by Don Munroe. The first few episodes are shot at the Bloomingdale's video studio. The series focuses on individual designers and various other aspects of the fashion industry, including models, photographers, and assorted divas. Munroe goes on to direct all of Warhol's television projects.

Warhol's *Shadows* paintings are exhibited at the Heiner Friedrich Gallery in New York. In *New York* magazine, Warhol refers to the *Shadows* as "disco decor," a reference to his Studio 54 nightlife.

Andy Warhol's Exposures, with photographs by Warhol and text cowritten by Bob Colacello, is published by Grosset & Dunlap. The book features an entire chapter about Halston.

---

for many of her ballets, including "Clytemnestra," "Frescoes," and "Episodes," among others.

August 7: Hosts a surprise birthday party for Warhol at the restaurant 21.

August: Halston Enterprises announces the formation of a major new division, Halston Sportswear, which marks a new entry in the designer women's sportswear category. The first line is developed for Fall 1979 and proves to be very successful.

1979

June 2: Visits Montauk to consider renting Warhol's oceanfront house. Previous tenants have included Mick and Bianca Jagger and Lee Radziwill.

October: Receives a special citation by the Coty American Fashion Critics' Awards committee for his development of a total American look.

Designs uniforms for Avis Rent-A-Car.

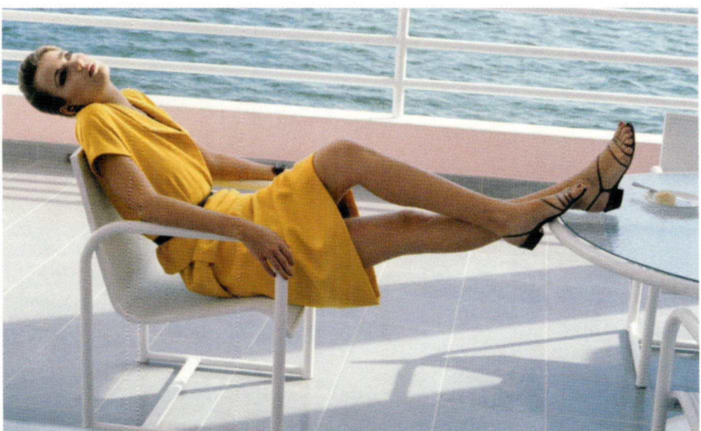

ABOVE
Eva Wallen lounging in a cap-sleeved jacket and skirt by Halston,
ca. April 1980
Condé Nast Archive/CORBIS

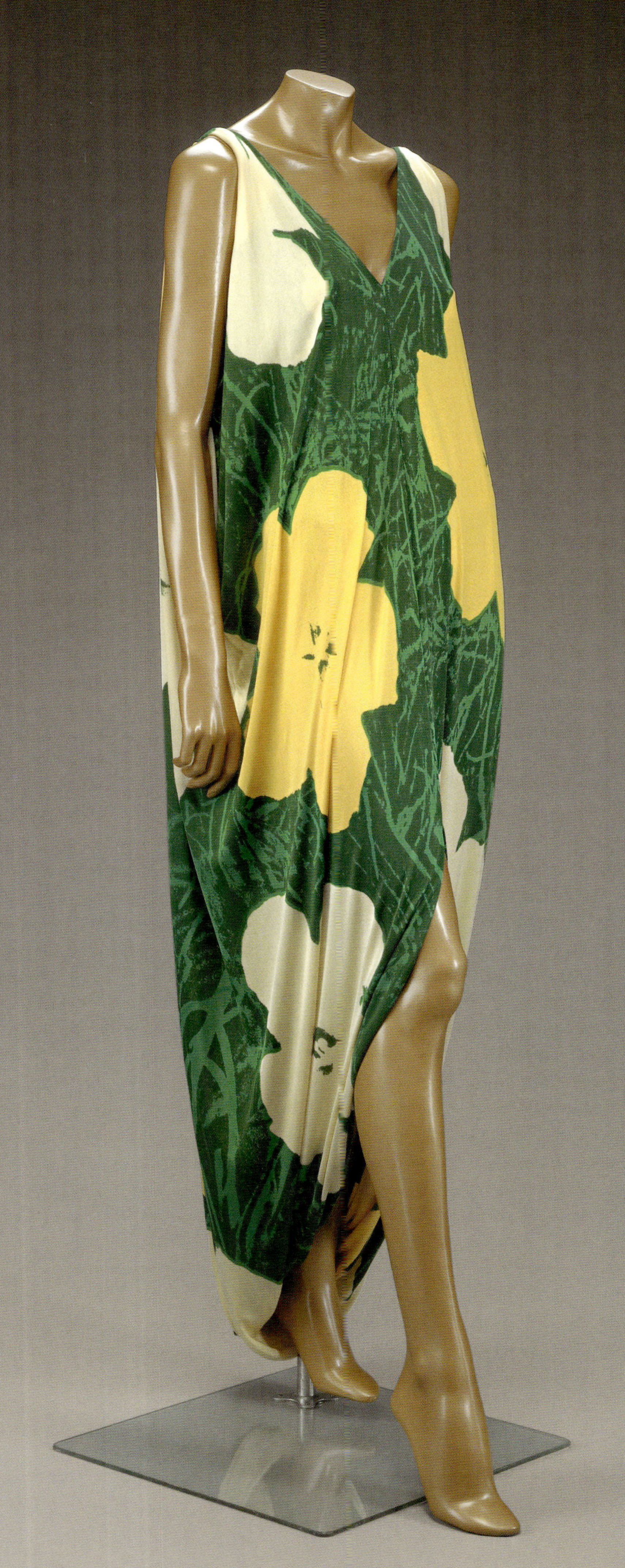

ART AND FASHION COLLABORATIONS

Warhol produced the same flower motif in hundreds of *Flower* paintings and prints. The paintings were created in multiple sizes—from miniature to monumental. He first displayed them at the Leo Castelli Gallery in 1964. Arranged in multiple formations, covering the walls in grids, the work simultaneously referenced abstraction, color theory, and decorative wallpaper. In 1970 Warhol returned to the flower motif to create print portfolios in editions of ten.

Given the repetitive and decorative nature of Warhol's motif, the work was naturally transformed into fabric. In 1972 Halston designed a dress using silk printed with the motif from Warhol's *Flower* paintings. Stephen Sprouse (Halston's assistant in 1972) later went on to design his own dresses using Warhol's *Camouflage* paintings printed on silk fabric.

OPPOSITE
Halston
Evening dress with print based on Warhol's *Flowers* painting, 1964–72
Silk knit
Indianapolis Museum of Art, 2010.227

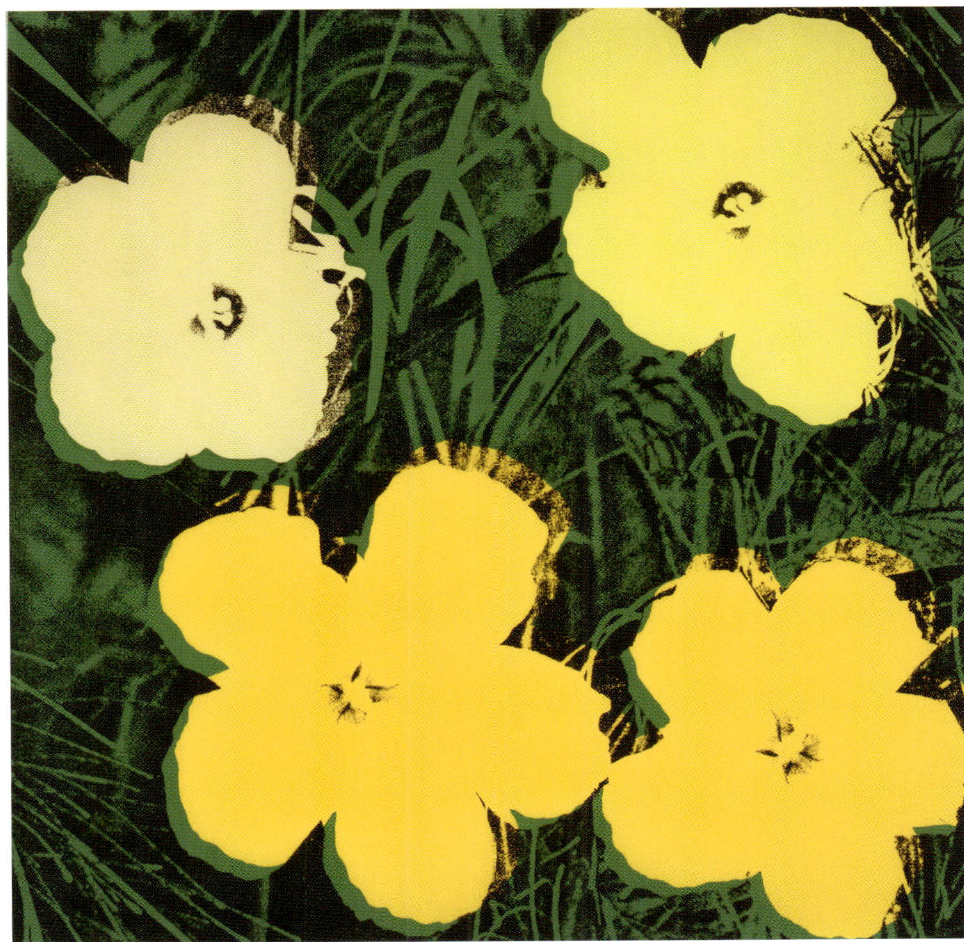

RIGHT
Andy Warhol
Flowers, 1970
Screen print on paper
36 × 36 in. (91.4 × 91.4 cm)
The Andy Warhol Museum, Pittsburgh; Founding Collection, Contribution The Andy Warhol Foundation for the Visual Arts, Inc., 1998.1.2395.9

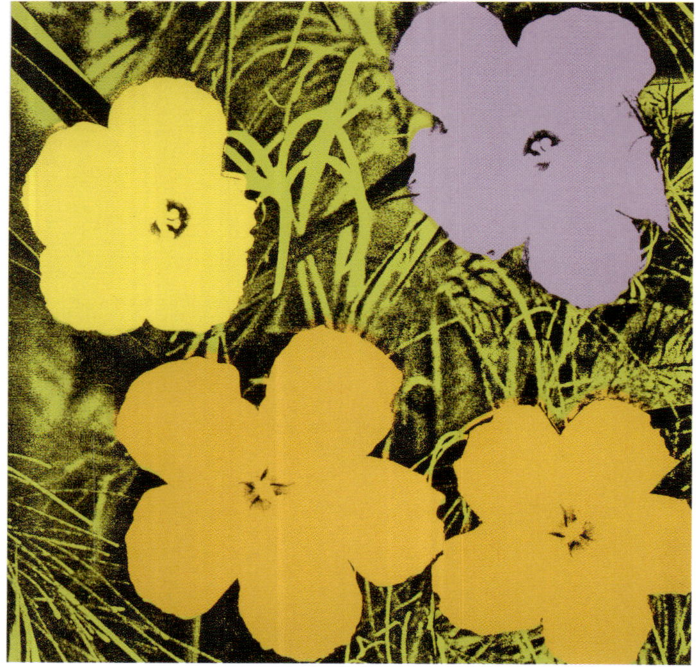

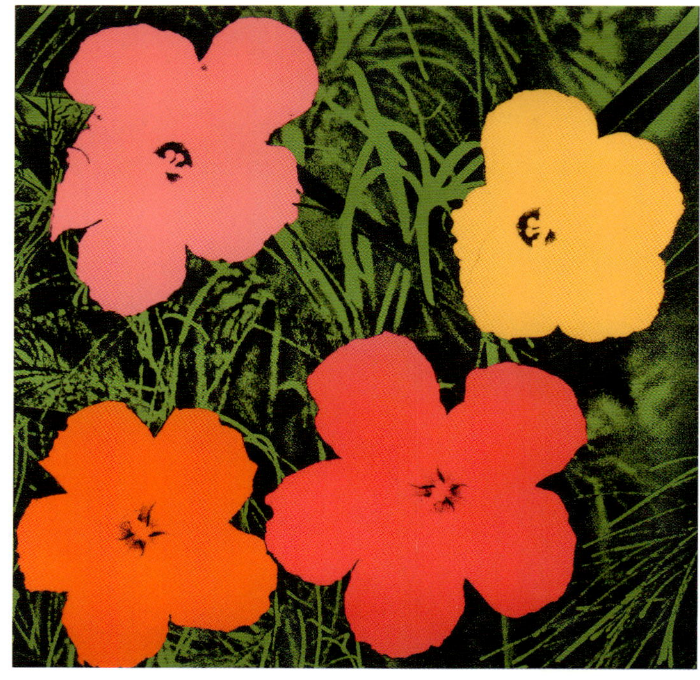

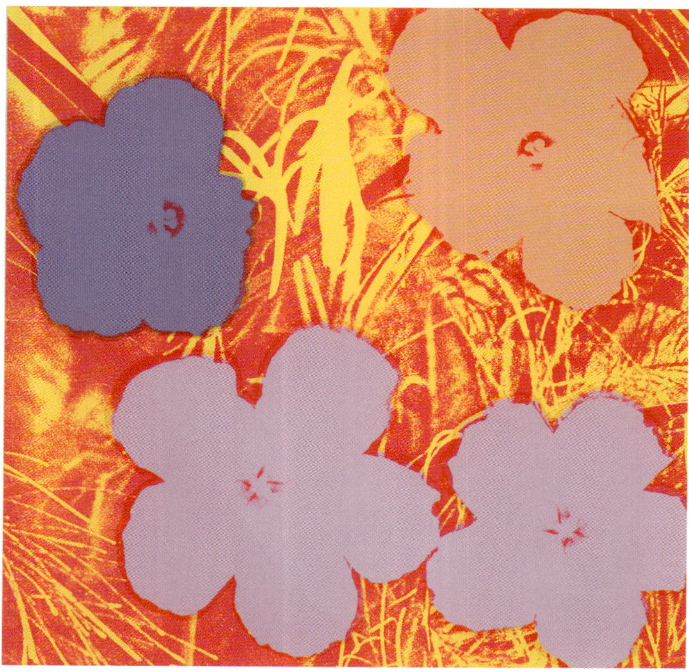

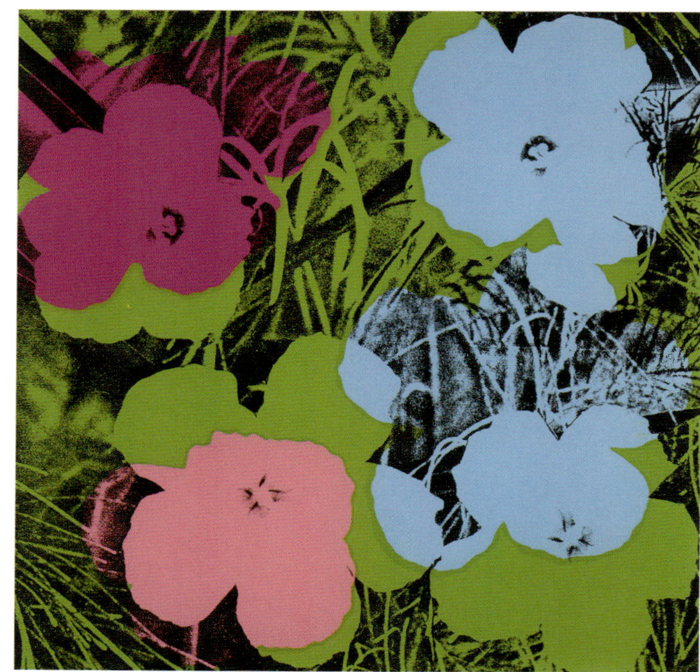

TOP LEFT
Andy Warhol
Flowers, 1970
Screen print on paper
36 × 36 in. (91.4 × 91.4 cm)
The Andy Warhol Museum, Pittsburgh; Founding Collection, Contribution The Andy Warhol Foundation for the Visual Arts, Inc., 1998.1.2395.4

BOTTOM LEFT
Andy Warhol
Flowers, 1970
Screen print on paper
36 × 36 in. (91.4 × 91.4 cm)
The Andy Warhol Museum, Pittsburgh; Founding Collection, Contribution The Andy Warhol Foundation for the Visual Arts, Inc., 1998.1.2395.6

TOP RIGHT
Andy Warhol
Flowers, 1964
Offset lithograph on paper
23⅛ × 23⅛ in. (58.7 × 58.7 cm)
The Andy Warhol Museum, Pittsburgh; Founding Collection, Contribution The Andy Warhol Foundation for the Visual Arts, Inc., 1998.1.2373

BOTTOM RIGHT
Andy Warhol
Flowers, 1970
Screen print on paper
36 × 36 in. (91.4 × 91.4 cm)
The Andy Warhol Museum, Pittsburgh; Founding Collection, Contribution The Andy Warhol Foundation for the Visual Arts, Inc., 1998.1.2395.1

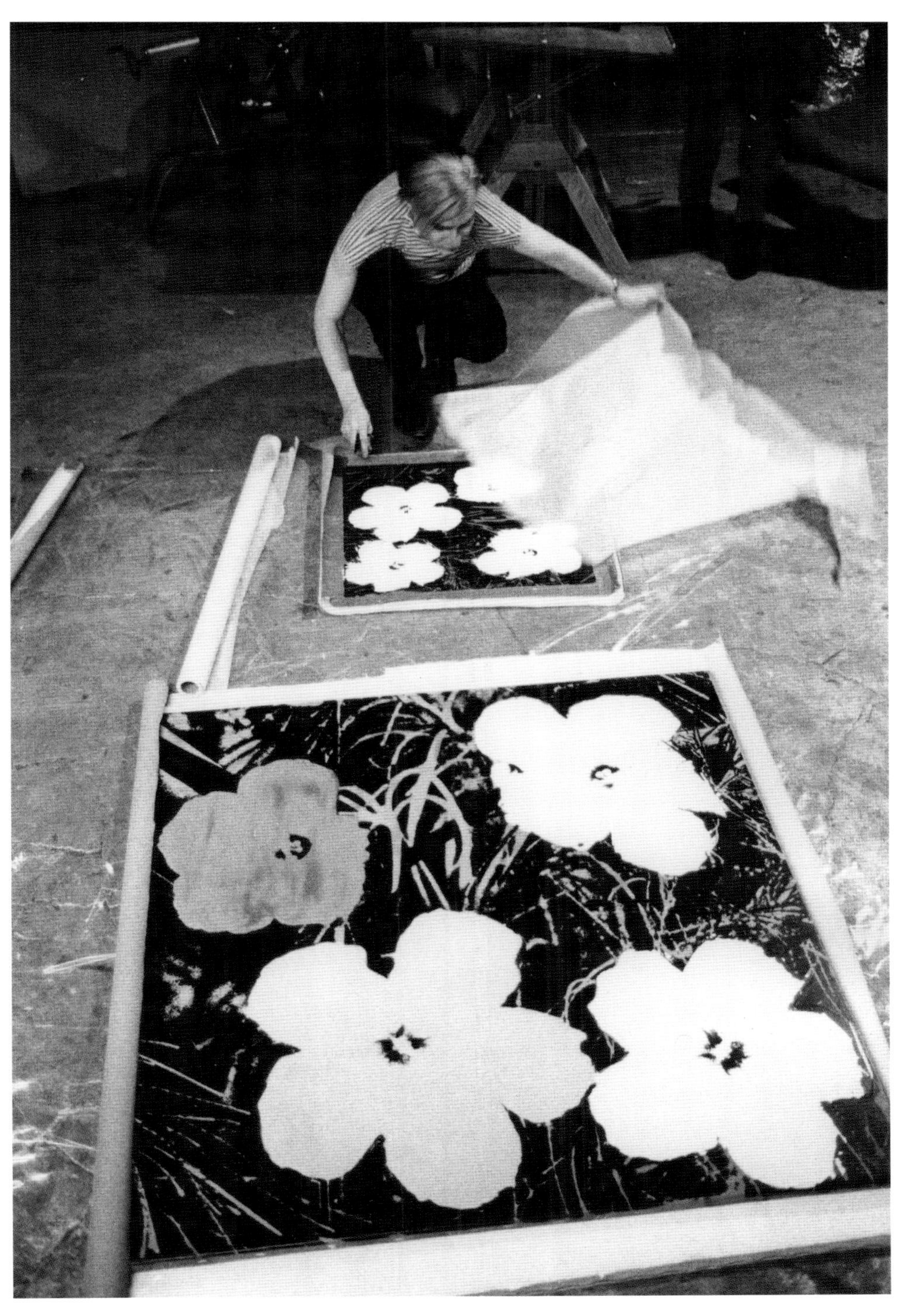

Stephen Shore
Andy Warhol, 1965
Gelatin silver print
8 × 5 in. (20.3 × 12.7 cm)
The Andy Warhol Museum, Pittsburgh; Founding Collection, Contribution The Andy Warhol Foundation for the Visual Arts, Inc., 1998.3.14674

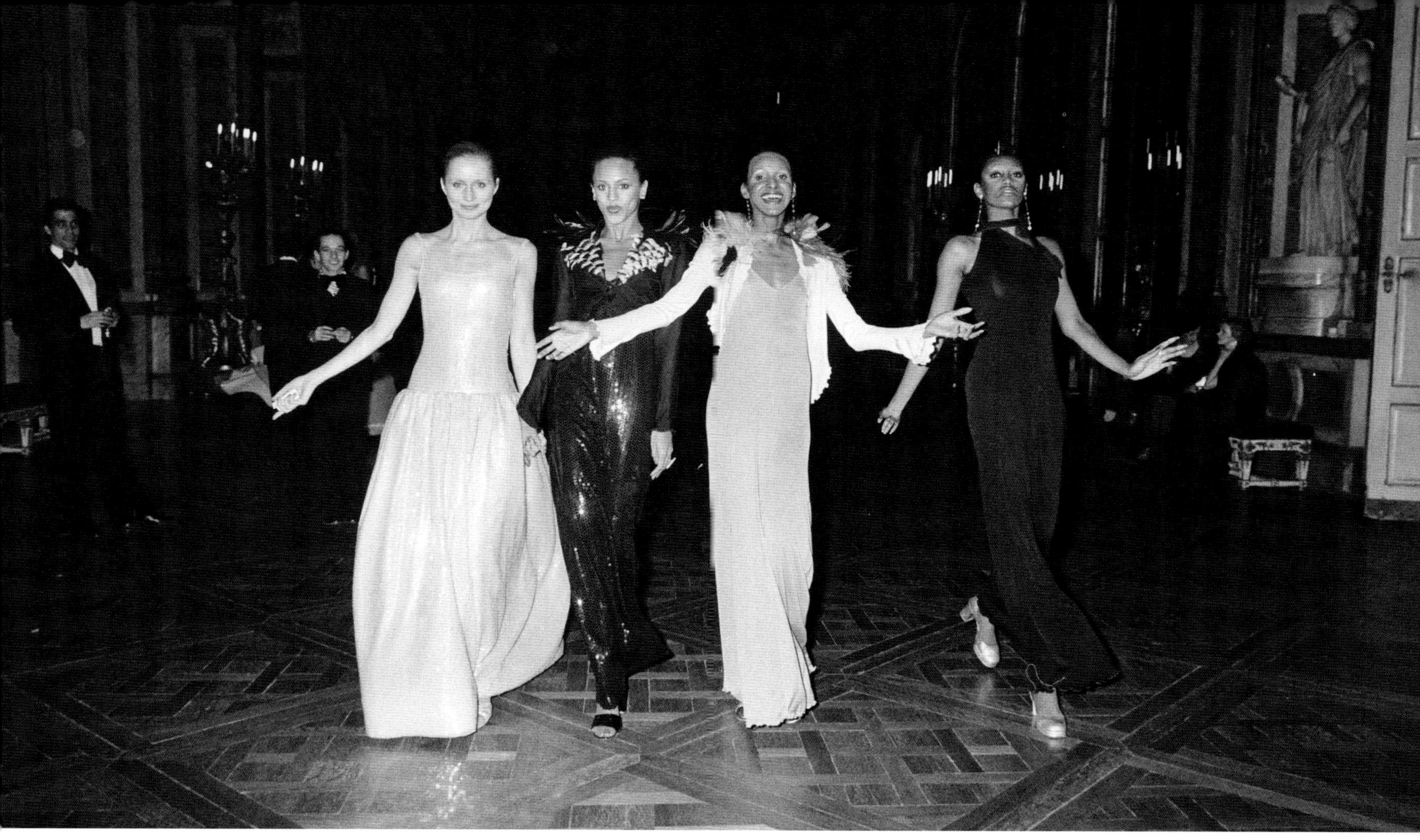

VERSAILLES 1973

Warhol attended the 1973 Palace of Versailles benefit fashion gala in Paris. What originated as a fundraiser for the restoration of the palace became a serious competition between French and American designers. The five French designers were Yves Saint Laurent, Hubert de Givenchy, Marc Bohan for Christian Dior, Pierre Cardin, and Emanuel Ungaro. The five Americans (selected by the French) were Halston, Anne Klein, Oscar de la Renta, Bill Blass, and Stephen Burrows. Josephine Baker performed for the French and Liza Minnelli for the Americans. The French had numerous props and elaborate backdrops, while the Americans used only a minimalist backdrop and lighting to accentuate the models, whose dancelike walking and modern look stole the show. For the Americans, to be embraced by the European hierarchy of fashion was a pivotal moment

Chris Royer wore this made-to-order "travel" outfit designed by Halston: a black cashmere dress with leather coat and boots. While incredibly chic, the outfit proved impractical. Royer remembers that she and the other Halstonettes were all freezing in the unheated foyers and marble-floored rooms of Paris.

Models at the gala night at the Opera of the Palace of Versailles, organized by French socialite Marie-Hélène de Rothschild, November 28, 1973
Chris Royer is on the far left wearing a mint green organza princess dress with sequins by Halston.
Photograph by Alain Dejean
Sygma/CORBIS

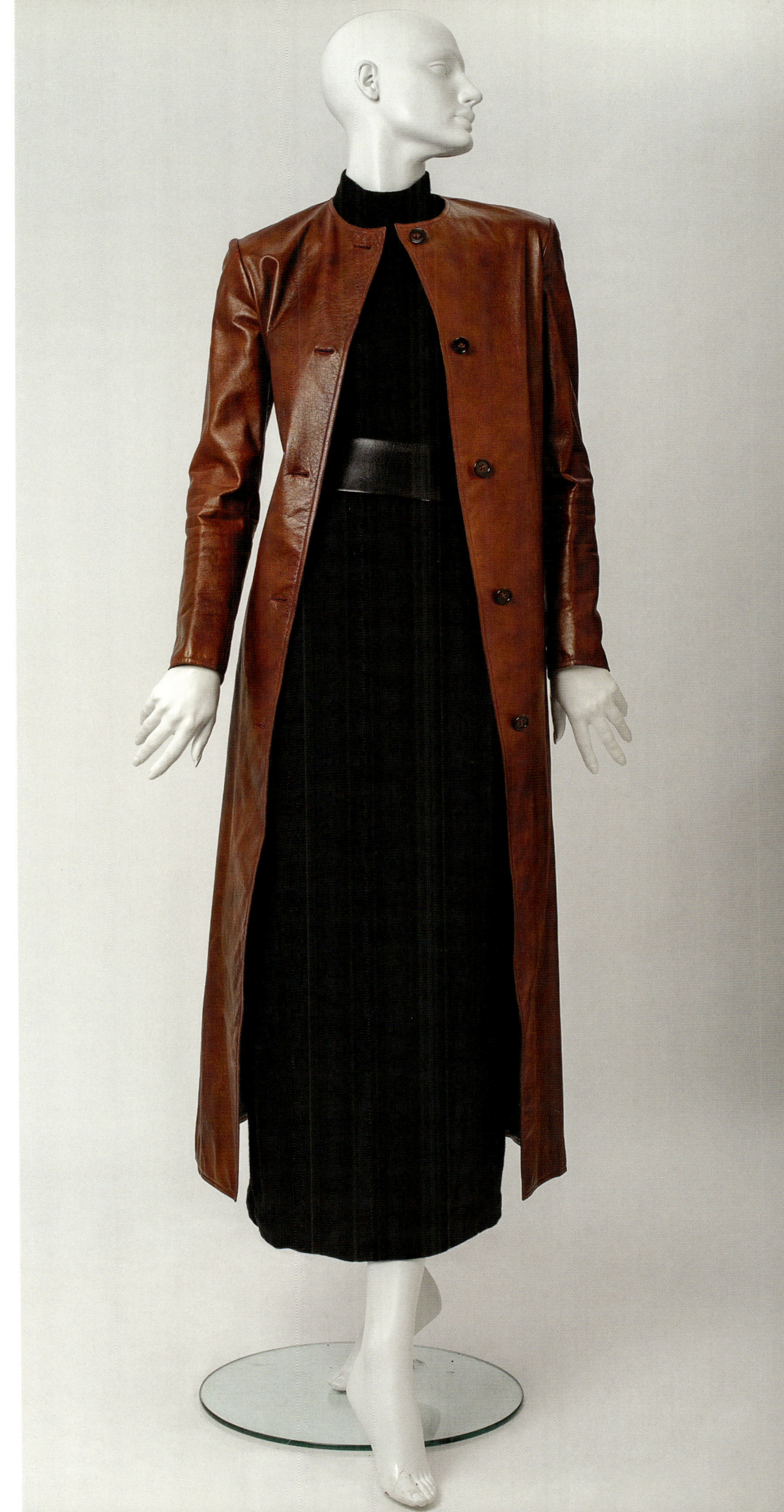

Halston
Midi-length collarless coat and midi-length sleeveless dress with mock turtleneck, Made to Order, 1973
Leather (coat, belt), cashmere (dress)
Photograph by Eve Prime
Collection of Chris Royer

SIGNATURE MATERIALS AND DESIGNS

"Women make fashion. Designers suggest, but it's what women do with the clothes that does the trick."

—Halston, interview with Eugenia Sheppard, *New York Post*, February 7, 1973

"Halston is the first All-American fashion designer. He never copies Paris. He just gives the American woman what she wants: simple clothes that are easy to care for—but look rich. He uses All-American colors like red, white, blue, green, yellow, orange, and purple. And lots of black. His colors always remind me of a box of crayons. He also uses All-American materials—like rayon. He put Ultrasuede on the map. He was smart enough to be the first person to use it. American women really loved it. They could throw their Halstons in the washing machine and stick them in the dryer."

—Andy Warhol, *Exposures*

"I admit to having worn suede and leather pants myself for a while, but you just never feel clean, and it's degenerate, anyway, to wear animal skins. . . . So I went back to blue jeans after my degenerate period."

—Andy Warhol, *THE Philosophy of Andy Warhol*

Mixing high and low, natural and synthetic, Halston was a master of material. Hammered silk, lamé, cashmere knit, iridescent taffeta, and silk charmeuse, as well as rayon matte jersey and Ultrasuede, were the hallmarks of his collections. Halston's choice of material provided richness and shape to his refined, minimalist forms.

Halston's signature designs—the shirtwaist dress, the caftan, the strapless dress, the full-length cardigan, the sarong, and the short-lived skimp, among others—were derived from Western and non-Western forms. His elongated cardigan in the softest six-ply cashmere with coordinating sheath underneath was drawn from the classic 1950s twinset; his best-selling shirtwaist dress in durable, no-wrinkle Ultrasuede was based on a man's collared shirt; his caftans in near-transparent silk chiffon were translated from Moroccan clothing. His narrow column of fabric tied simply at the bust echoed the drape of Grecian robes. Halston transformed the staple of everyman's wardrobe, the tailored business suit, into a soft, relaxed pantsuit for women. He reshaped pajamas in luxurious materials, and his customers donned them as eveningwear.

Lauren Hutton wears a "pajama" ensemble by Halston, with a long Indian-style tunic over matching narrow pants in gold lamé,
ca. September 1975
Photograph by Francesco Scavullo
Condé Nast Archive/CORBIS

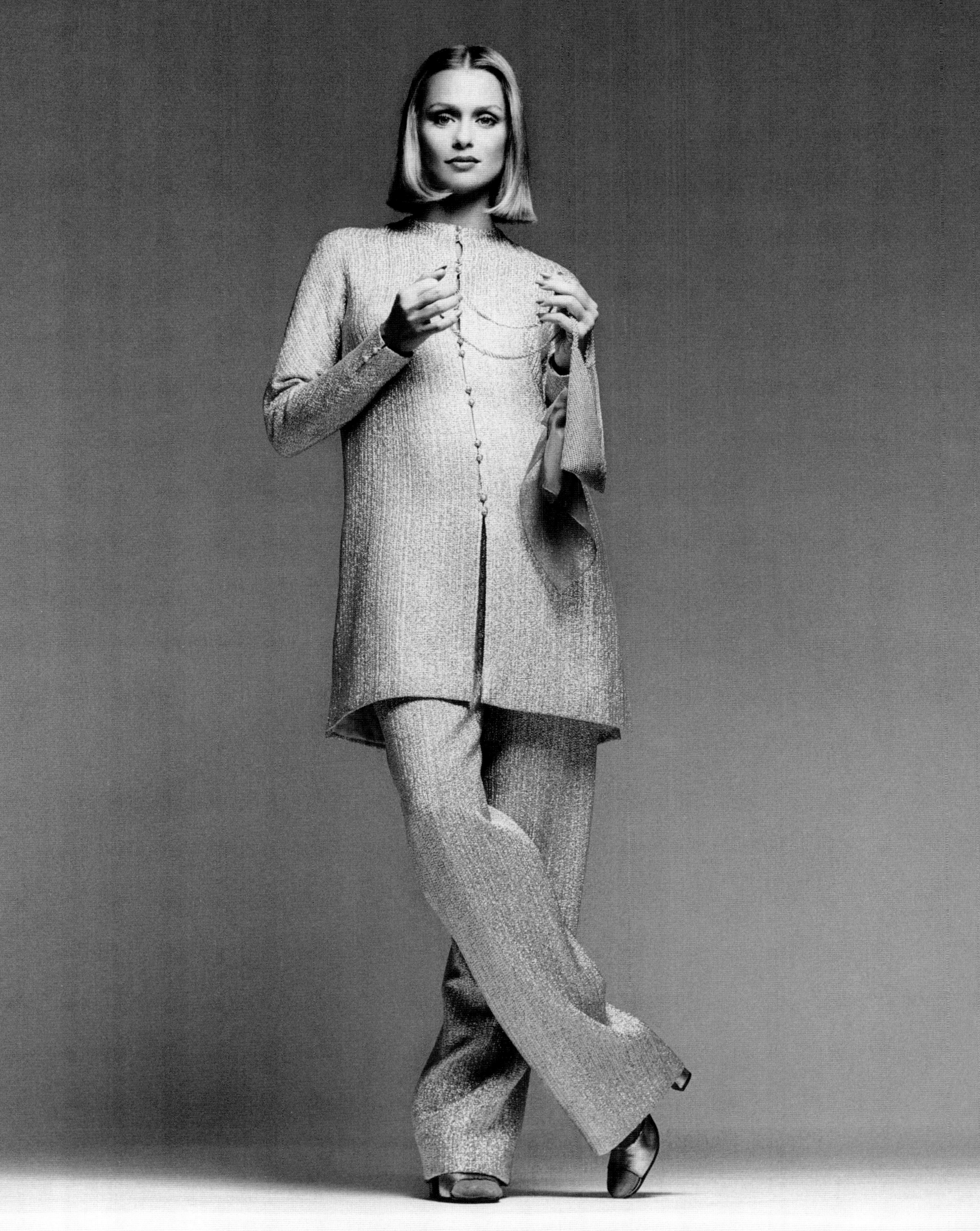

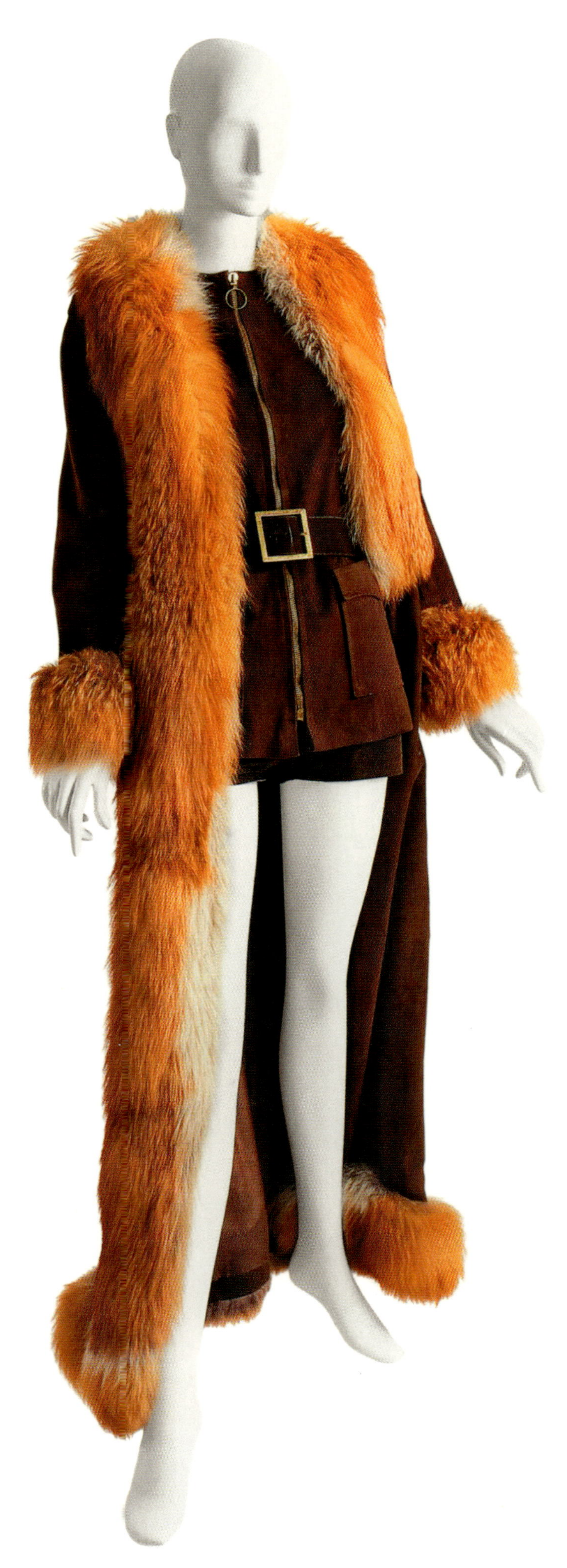

RIGHT
Halston
Ensemble, 1970–71
Brown suede, fur trim
The Museum at FIT, 88.29.39;
Gift of Elizabeth Pickering Kaiser

OPPOSITE
Halston
Dress, 1973
Ultrasuede
The Metropolitan Museum of Art.
Gift of Faye Robson, 1993 (1993.351)

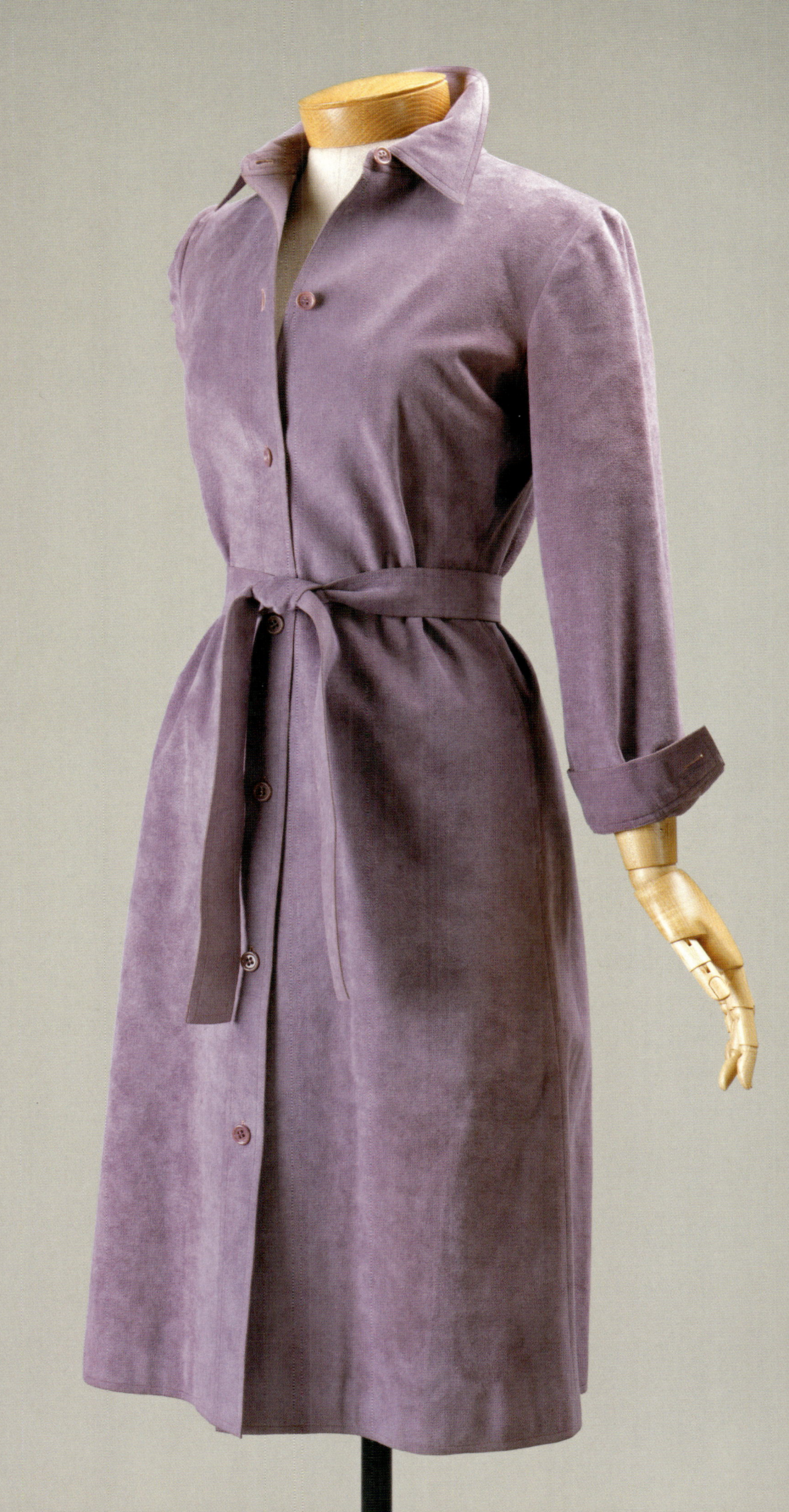

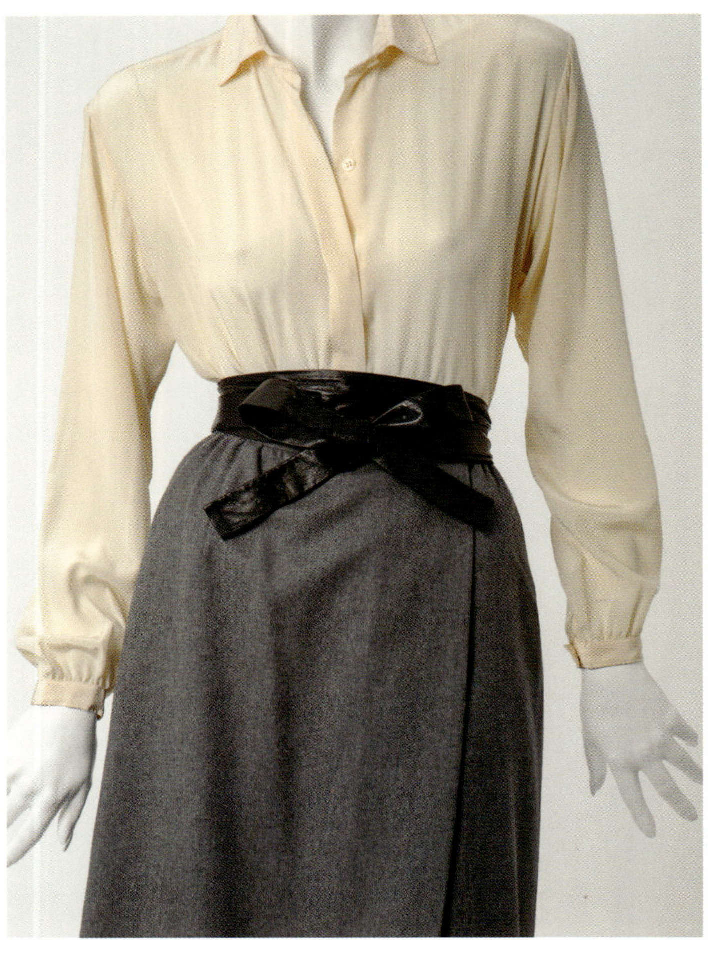

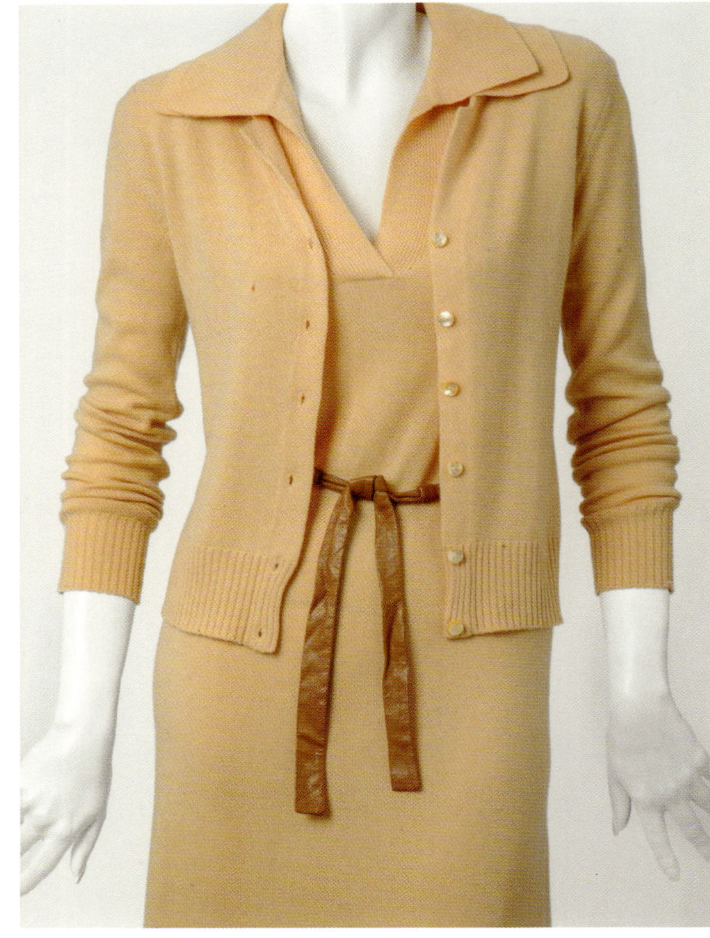

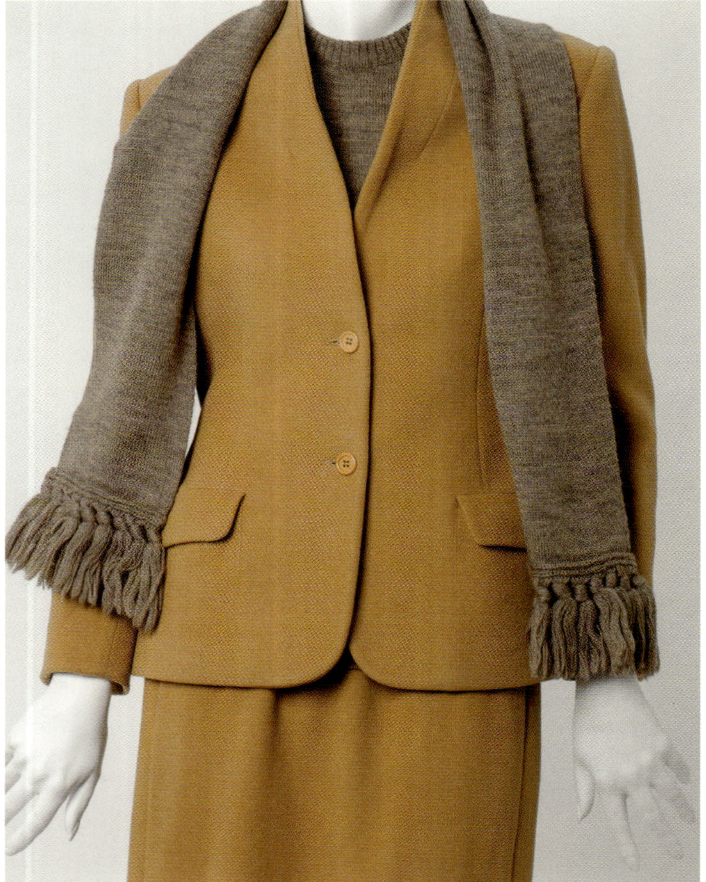

TOP LEFT
Halston
Suit with dirndl skirt, blouse, and obi belt, Fall/Winter 1979 sportswear line
Wool flannel (skirt), satin silk charmeuse (blouse), leather (belt)
Photograph by Eve Prime
Collection of Chris Royer

TOP RIGHT
Halston
Dress and sweater set,
Made to Order, 1972
Cashmere, leather
Photograph by Eve Prime
Collection of Chris Royer

BOTTOM LEFT
Halston
Suit with calla lily collar, sweater, and matching scarf, Fall/Winter 1979
Wool (suit), variegated wool tweed (sweater and scarf)
Photograph by Eve Prime
Collection of Chris Royer

OPPOSITE
Halston
Suit with matching coat and scarf,
Fall/Winter 1979 sportswear line
Mohair wool tweed
Photograph by Eve Prime
Collection of Chris Royer

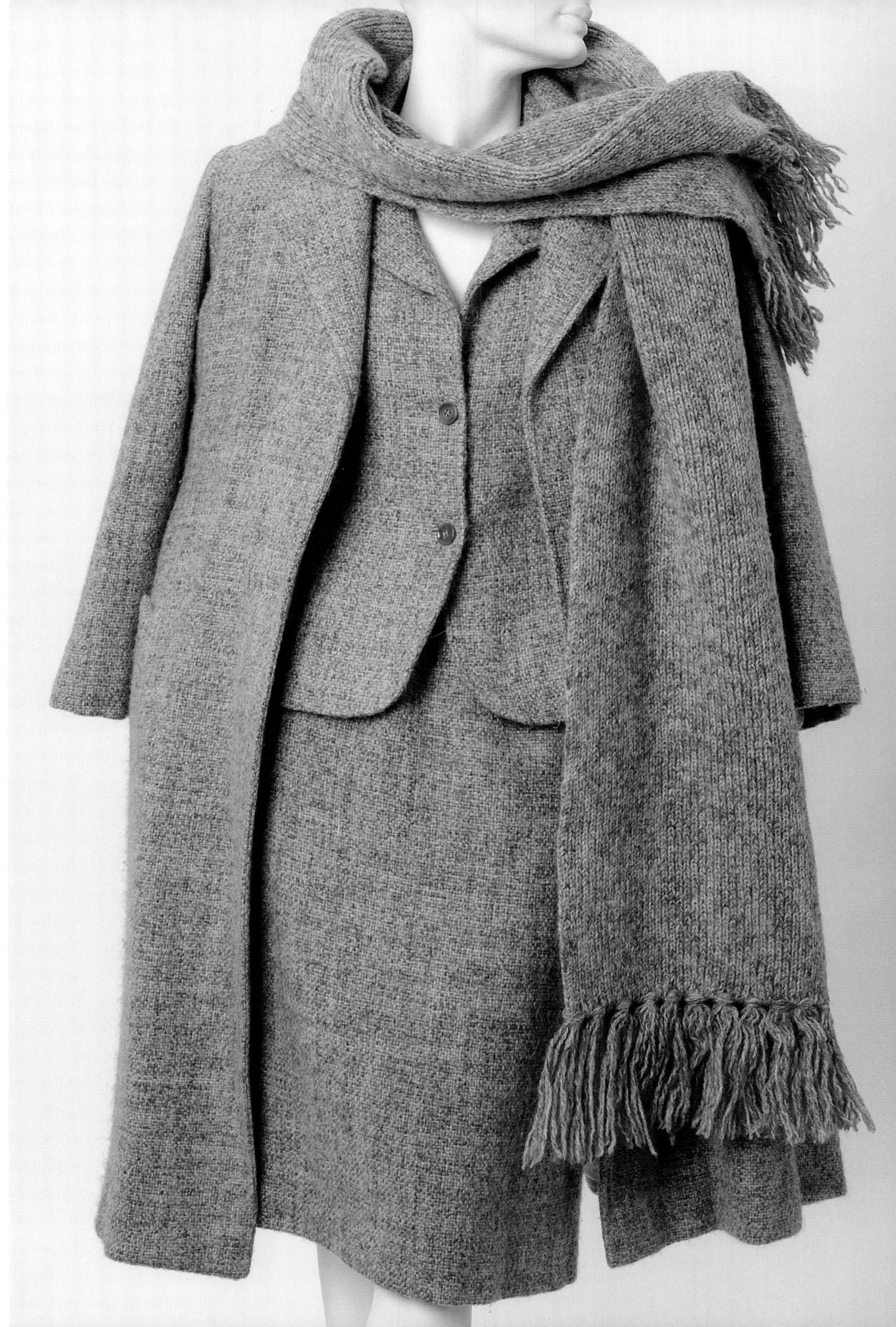

DRAPING

Halston was an excellent draper—he literally draped a house model with a bolt of fabric, pinning as he went, to figure out the proper drop, cross wrapping, and fit. As Pat Cleveland remembers, "He would hold up fabric to your body in a certain place and know exactly how the cloth would fall. He would step back, look at it, and say, 'Pin it' to the assistant. He'd pull it, move it around, and drape it, saying, 'Okay, pin it.'"

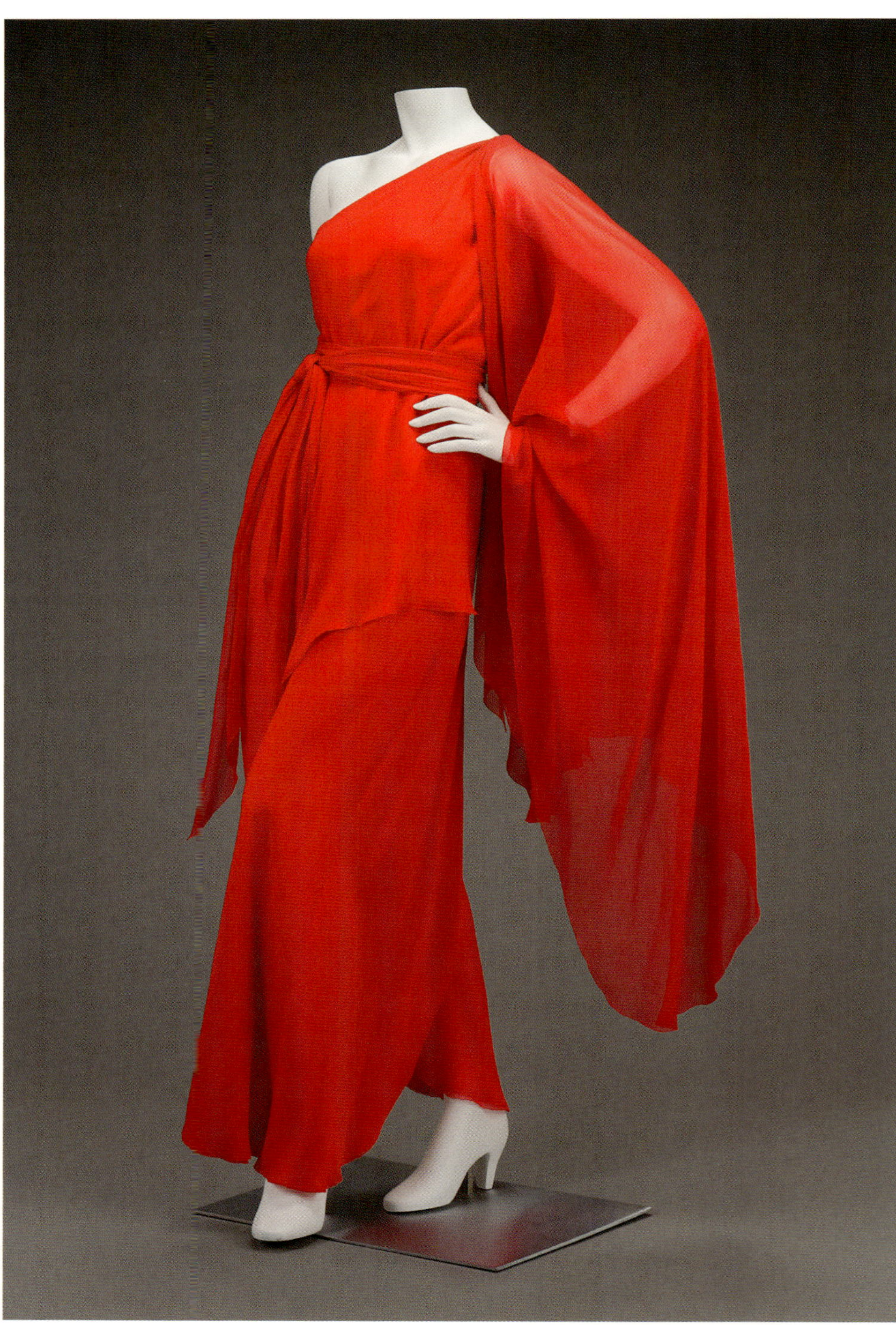

RIGHT
Halston
Evening ensemble: dress, 1970
Silk chiffon
Indianapolis Museum of Art, 1985.618

OPPOSITE
Halston drapes fabric around Carol Channing in his studio, May 25, 1977
He created her wardrobe for the revival of *Hello, Dolly!*
Bettmann/CORBIS

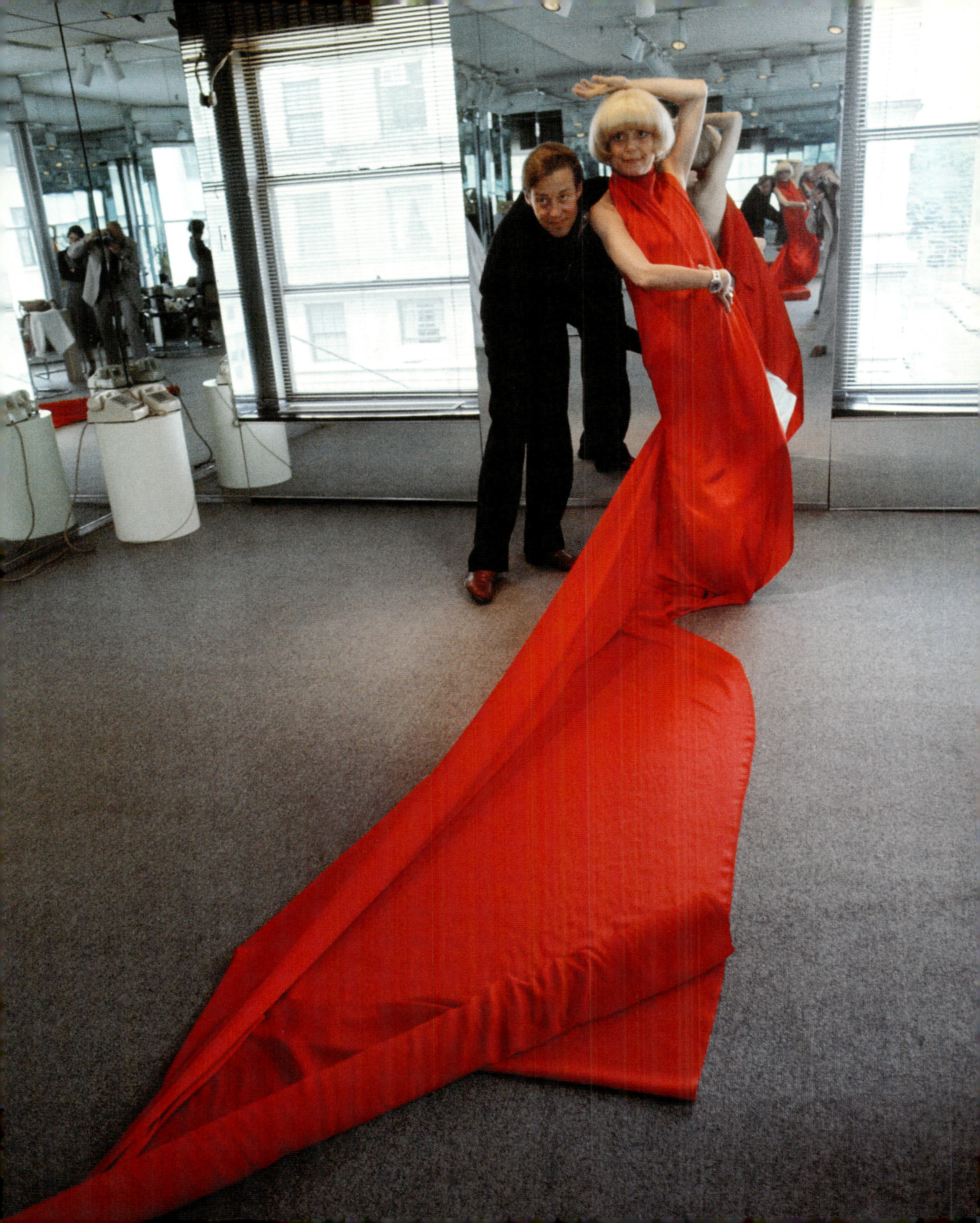

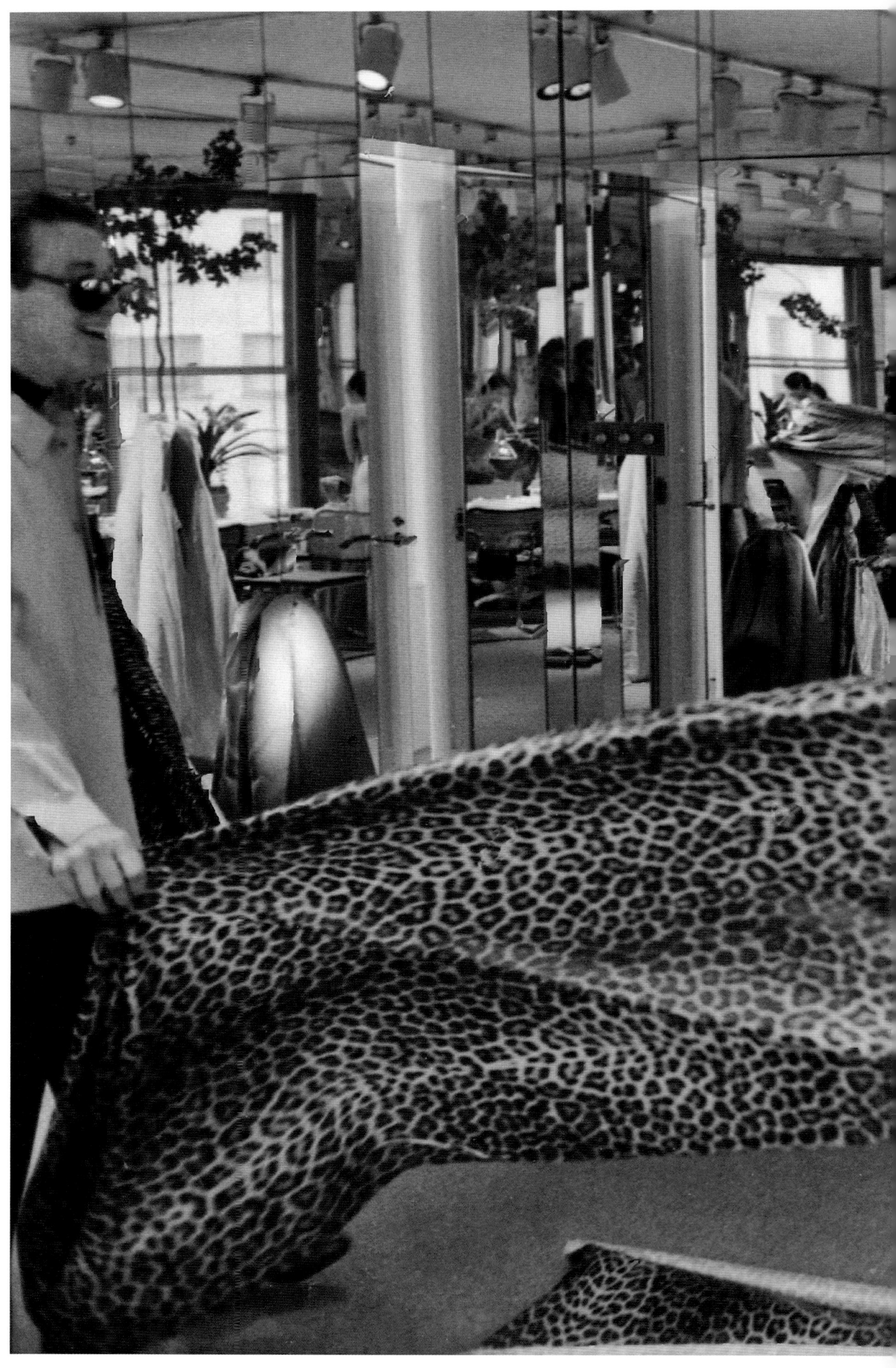

Bianca Jagger draped in leopard print in Halston's studio
Photograph by Harry Benson

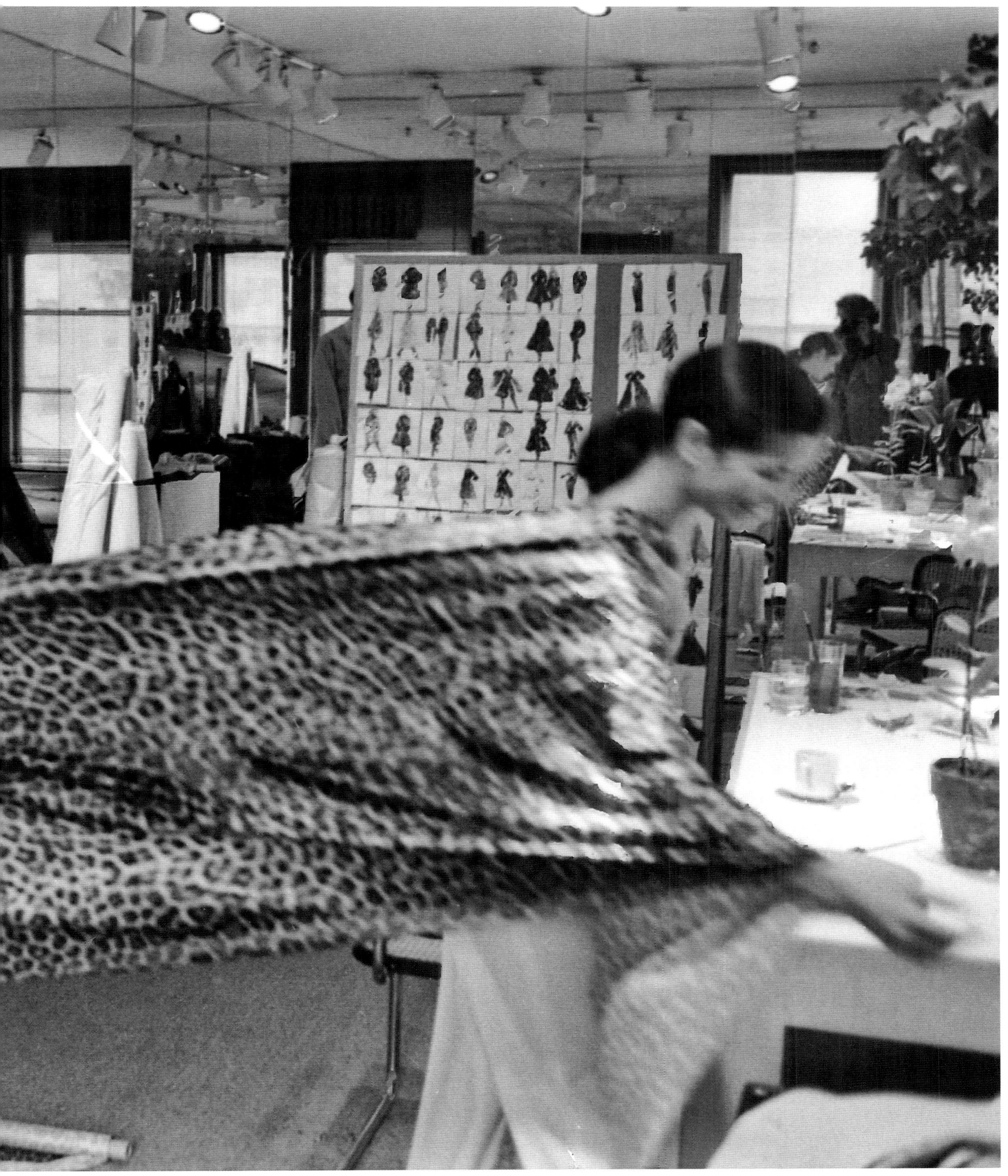

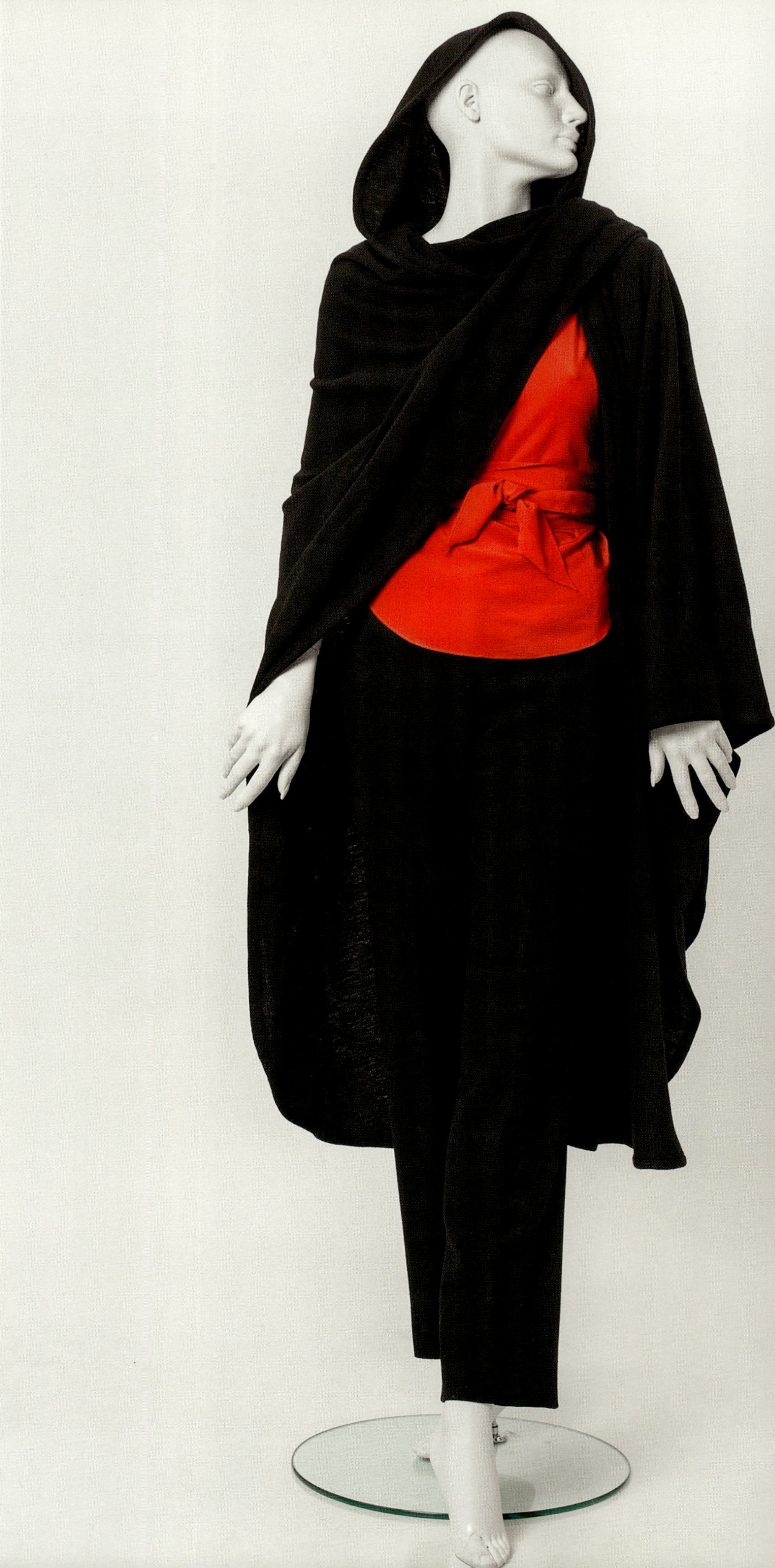

RIGHT
Halston
Cape with hood, matching pants, dolman-style top, and obi belt,
Fall/Winter 1979 sportswear line
Wool jersey (cape and hood), silk (top)
Photograph by Eve Prime
Collection of Chris Royer

OPPOSITE
Halston
Long goddess-style dress,
Made to Order, 1972
Cashmere
Photograph by Eve Prime
Collection of Chris Royer

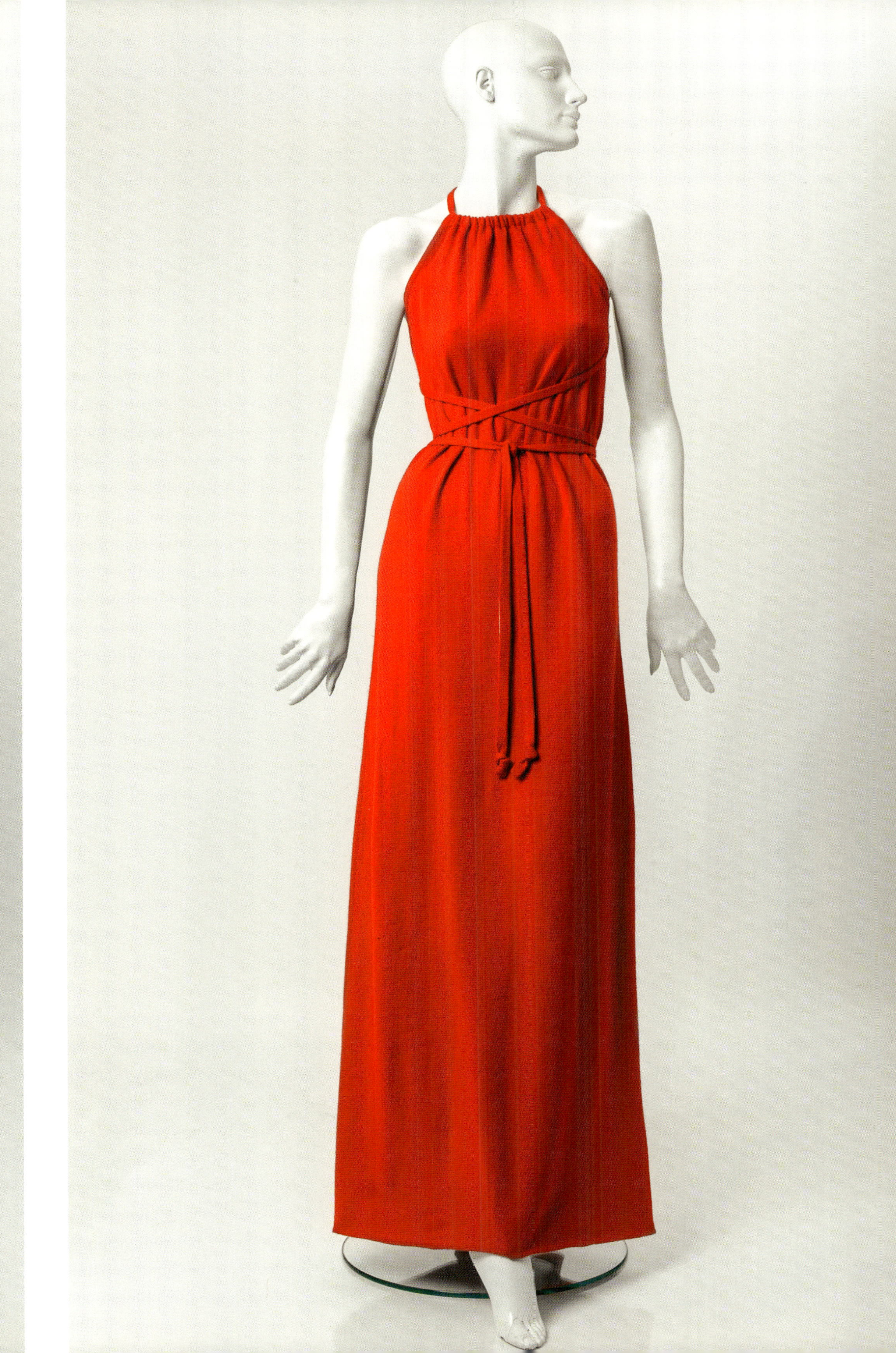

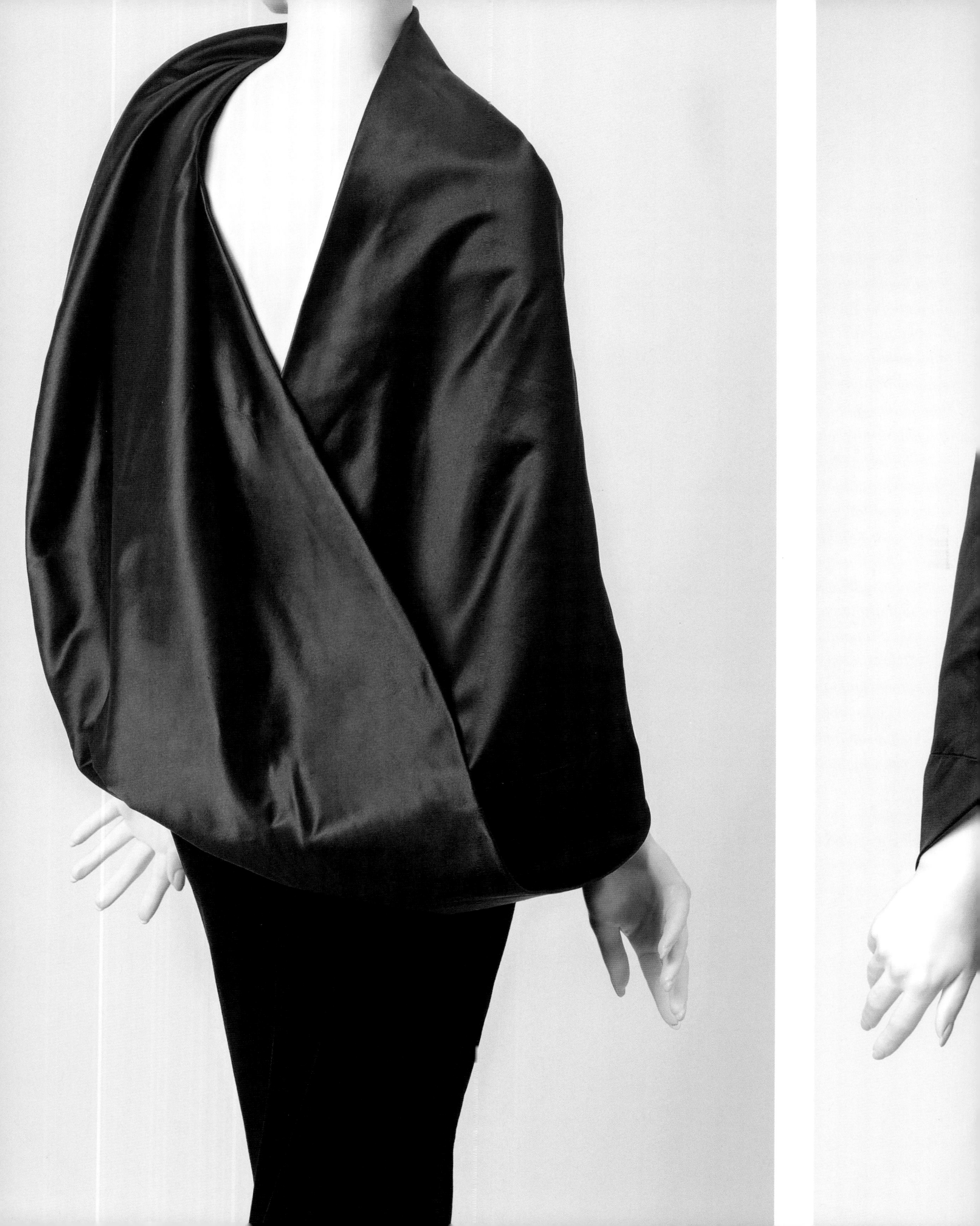

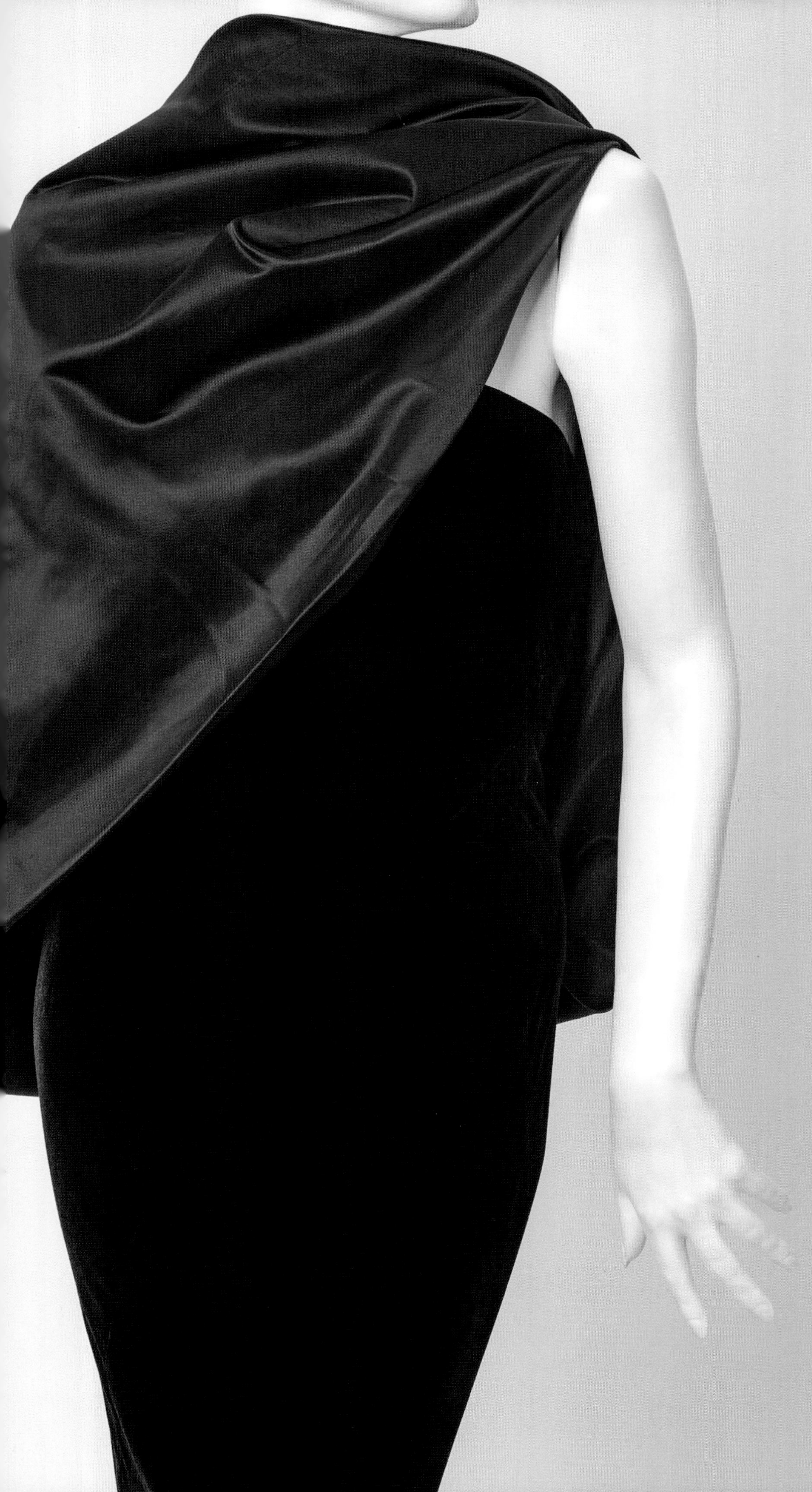

LEFT
Halston
Shrug/Shawl (back and front),
Made to Order, 1984
Silk, duchesse satin; figure 8 bias cut
Photograph by Eve Prime
Collection of Chris Royer

OVERLEAF LEFT
Halston
Evening ensemble: caftan, 1971
Tie-dyed silk chiffon
Indianapolis Museum of Art, 1984.96

OVERLEAF MIDDLE
Halston
Leopard-patterned evening ensemble, 1970
Crushed silk velvet, tie-dyed
Indianapolis Museum of Art, 1986.316

OVERLEAF RIGHT
Halston
Floor-length dress, 1975
Hand-painted silk
Indianapolis Museum of Art, 1985.619

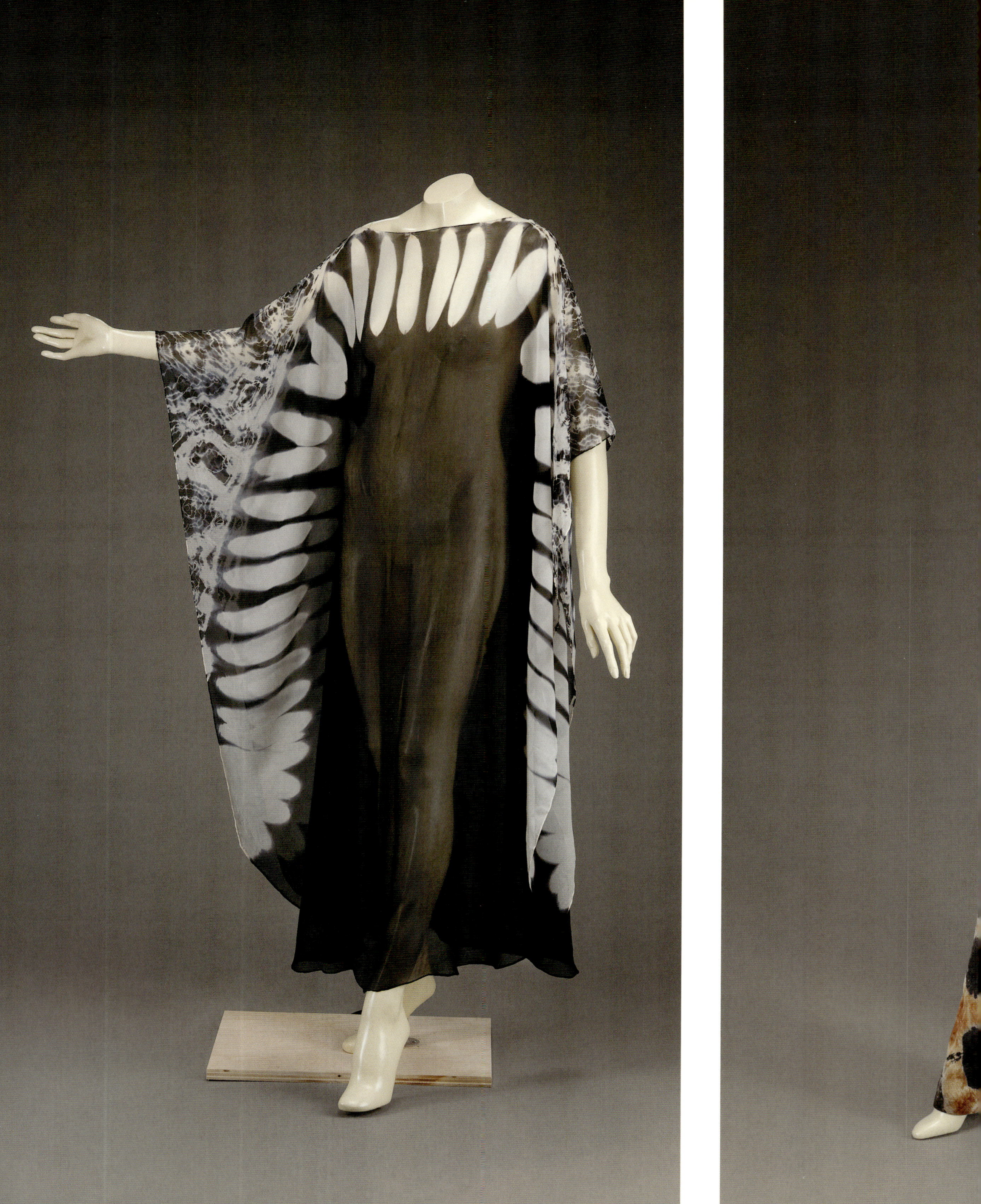

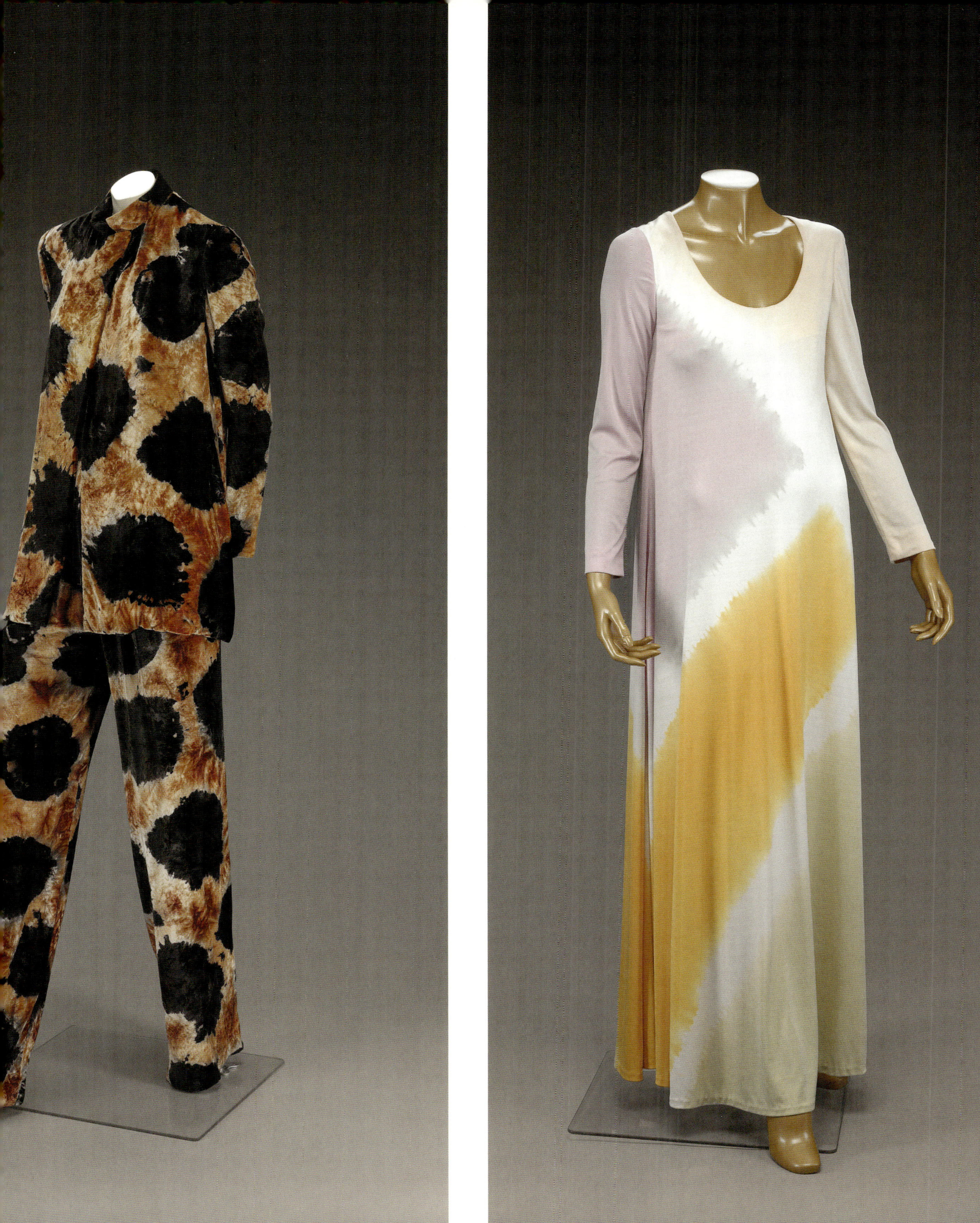

THE SARONG

In the summer of 1975, Halston had rented a house on Fire Island and invited his design team—including Elsa Peretti, Joe Eula, and Victor Hugo, as well as models and friends—to enjoy some rest and relaxation with him. Chris Royer gives the following account:

> One had to take a ferry boat to reach Fire Island, where no cars were allowed. Victor met me at the ferry and together we enjoyed a leisurely walk along a beautiful pristine beach until we reached the house. It was dazzling white, built in a sleek architectural style and set back from the ocean with a long flight of stairs leading to a very large deck. Huge floor-length mirrored sliding doors opened to the deck, replete with chic, wide white canvas lounge chairs placed around the deep-blue, azure pool. Looking into the distance, all one could see were miles and miles of a white sandy shore offset by a sparkling blue-green sea.
>
> We found Halston, on the deck, of course, sketching designs. That was his definition of rest and relaxation. His inspirations came from a variety of elements: nature and organic forms, art, and music, as well as the company he kept. His mind was constantly busy, busy, busy, thinking of new design concepts.
>
> After a walk on the beach, I put on my bathing suit and took a dip in the cool, inviting pool. When I finally came out I grabbed a large, white Fieldcrest bath towel to dry off. There was a stiff breeze, and so I decided to wrap the towel around me to keep warm. Halston was watching me, and all of a sudden a lightbulb appeared over his head! He pulled me over to the mirrored sliding doors and proceeded to drape the towel. He gathered and twisted it in such a way that the ends formed a knot with two rabbit-ear ties. Needless to say, it was no longer a white towel—it was an amazing creation. We smiled and looked at each other and said, "silk charmeuse!"

The actual Sarong dress was made from a tube pattern that was cut on the bias. The upper part had a built-in strapless bra to support the bust and keep the dress from sliding down, thus controlling the drape. It had to be intricately cut in order to obtain that simple, ultra-chic line that flattered the figure beneath.

Halston's iconic Sarong dress had its debut in the Spring of 1976. It boldly challenged the opulence of European fashion by defining an elegant American style. In August 1976, *Women's Wear Daily* did a piece titled the "Strapless Snatchers," featuring A-list celebrities such as Jackie and Natalie Wood, wearing the Sarong. In the following month, *W* magazine did a split cover showing two looks. The heading stated: "Here are two choices: the uncluttered shapes of Mr. Clean–Halston and the Lux Extravagance of Monsieur Fantasy–Yves Saint Laurent."

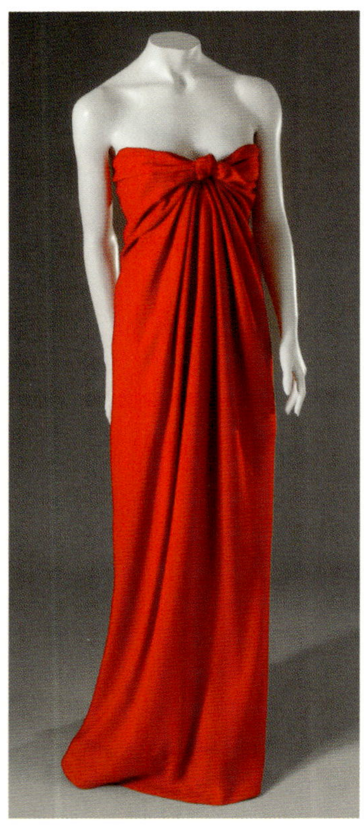

Halston
Evening dress, ca. 1976
Silk crepe
The Museum at FIT, 80.128.4; Gift of Celanese

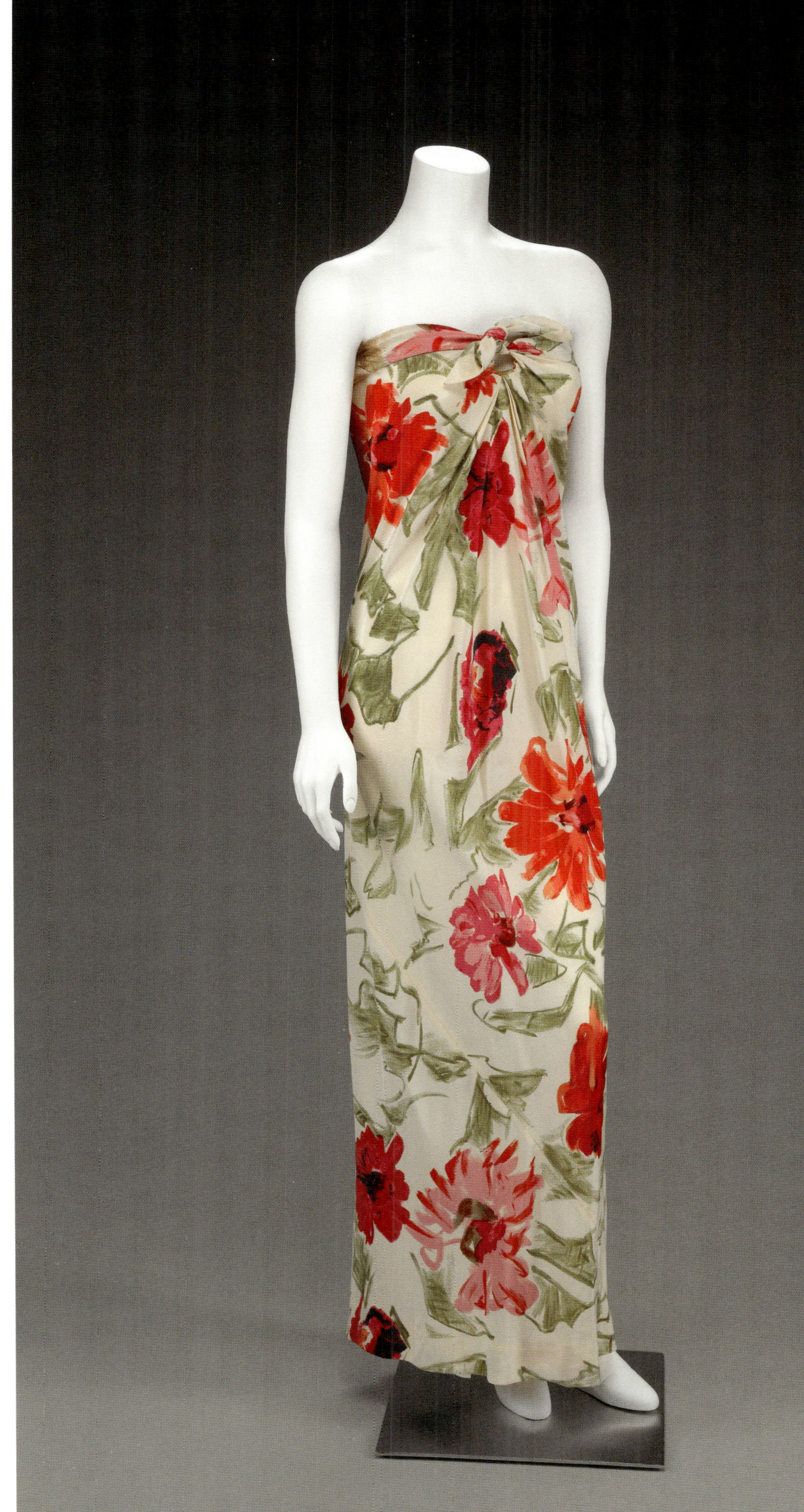

RIGHT
Halston
Evening sarong, 1977
Printed silk crepe de chine
Indianapolis Museum of Art, 1985.649

OVERLEAF
Halston
Sarong, Made to Order
Loungewear, 1981
Qiana/lycra
Photograph by Eve Prime
Collection of Chris Royer

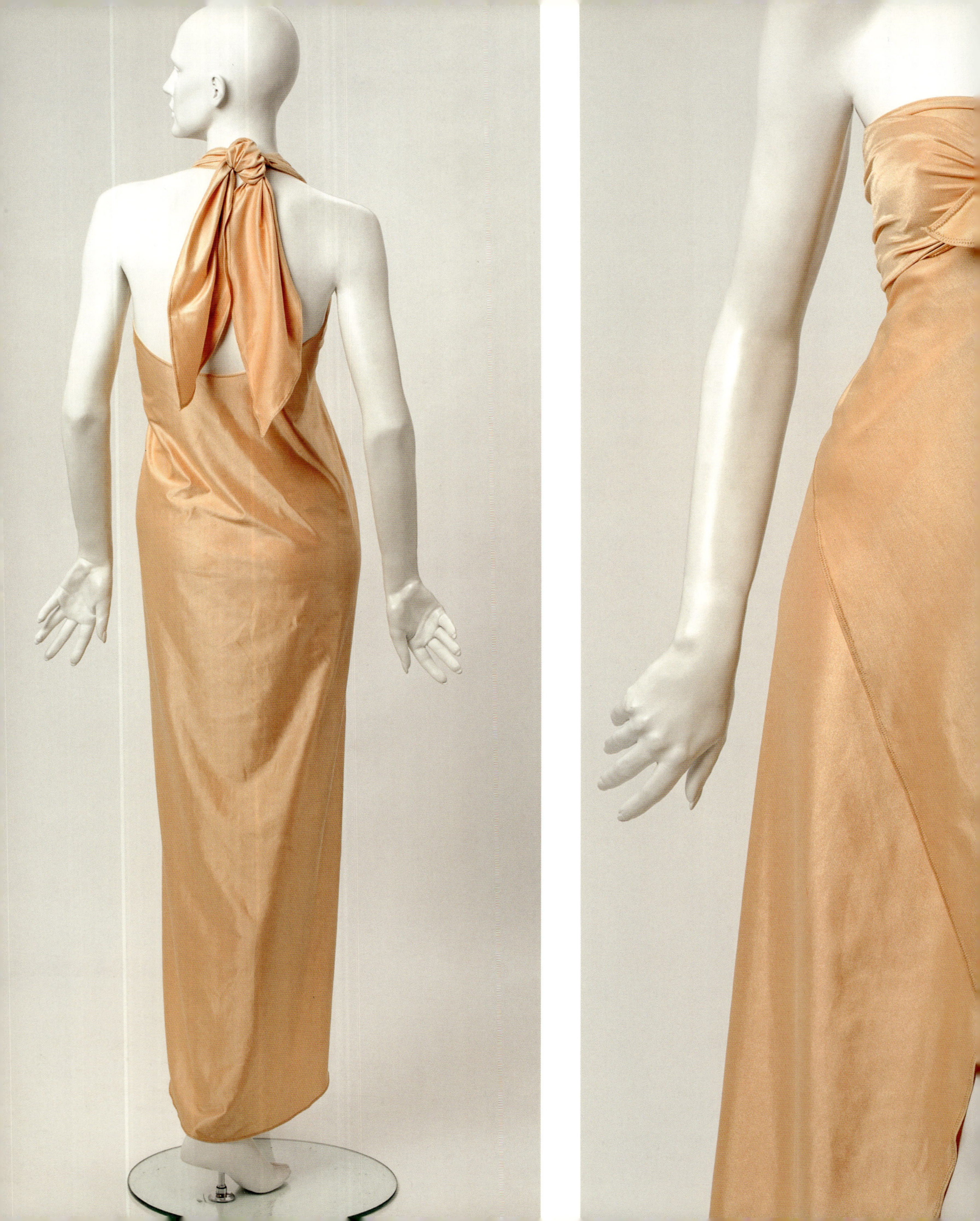

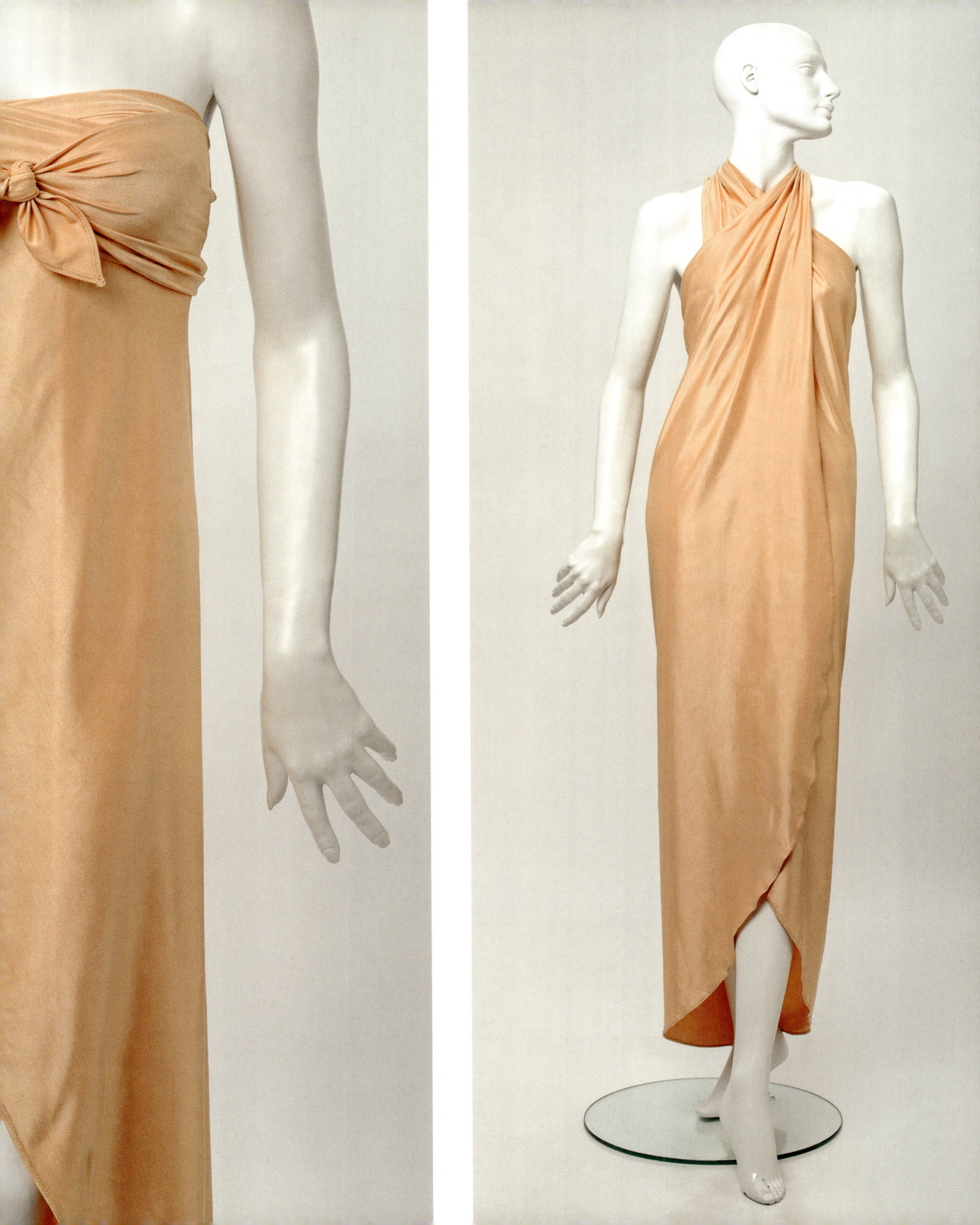

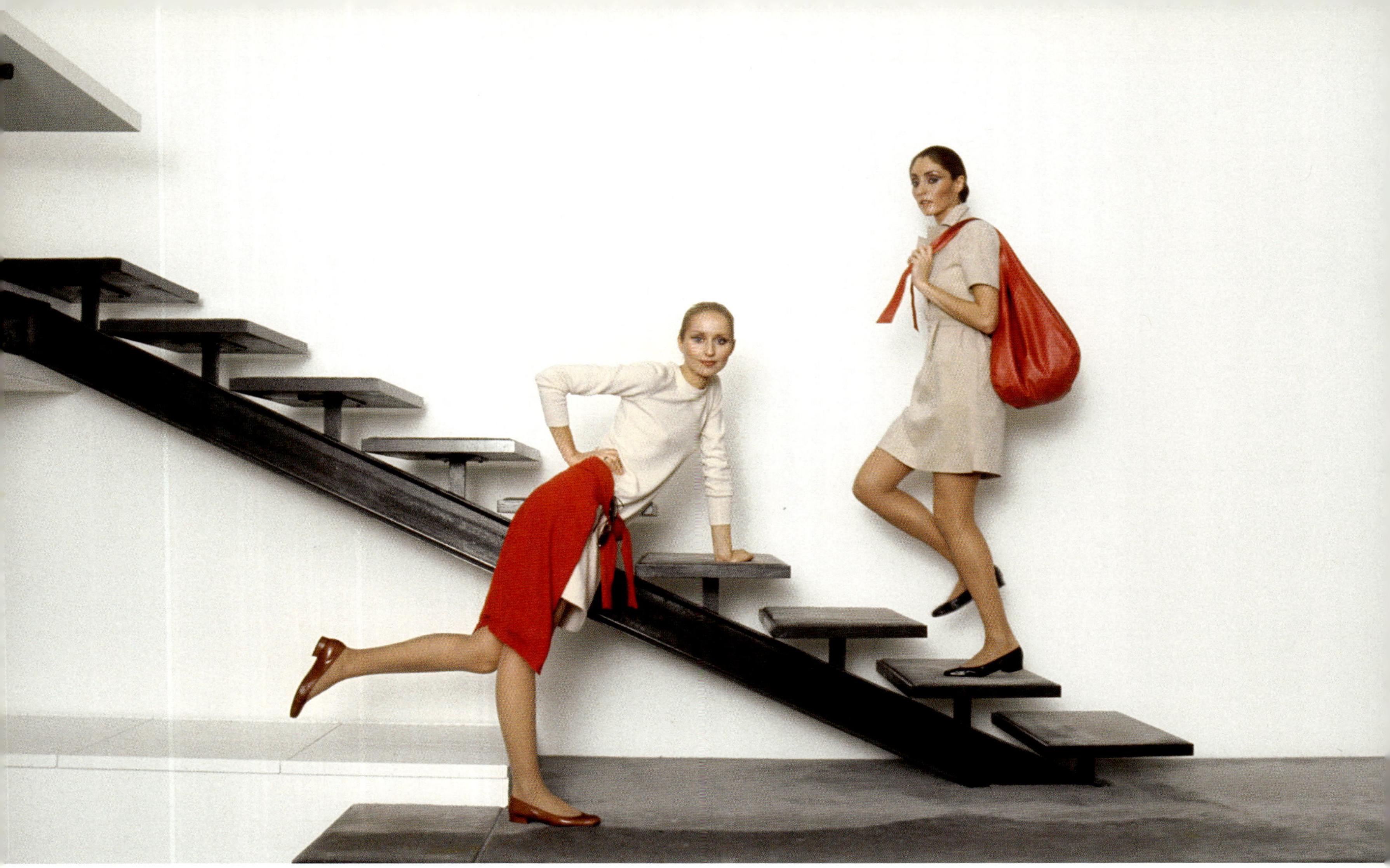

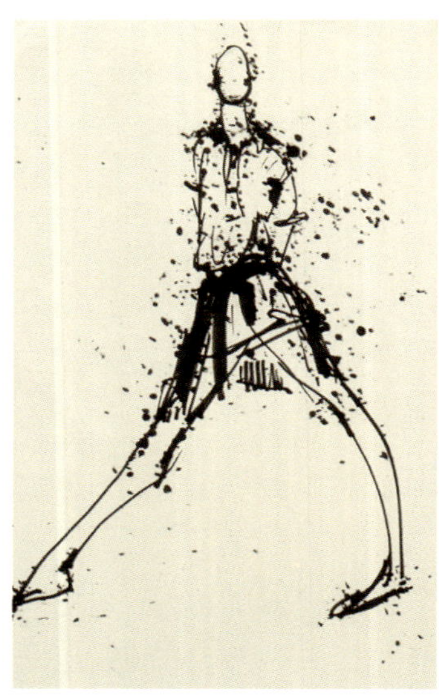

THE SKIMP

In the fall of 1974, Halston debuted the Skimp. Days earlier, Stephen Sprouse, who was working for Halston at the time, encouraged him in a late-night studio session to spontaneously chop off inches from his hemlines. Reportedly, Halston shouted "skimp it, skimp it!" as he lopped off excess fabric. His above-the-knee design sharply contrasted with the longer, fuller lengths being shown on other Fall runways. Credited with reinventing the mini skirt, Halston responded that the Skimp was "softer and floatier, more like a tunic."

TOP
Chris Royer in a white cashmere Skimp with a red cashmere sweater and Shirley Ferro in a buff Ultrasuede Skimp shirtdress with a red Bobby Breslo bag, posing in Halston's townhouse, October 16, 1974
Photograph by Pierre Schermann
Condé Nast Archive/CORBIS

BOTTOM
Joe Eula
Drawing of Halston's Skimp Dress, n.d.
Ink on paper
14 × 11 in. (35.6 × 27.9 cm)
Collection of Chris Royer

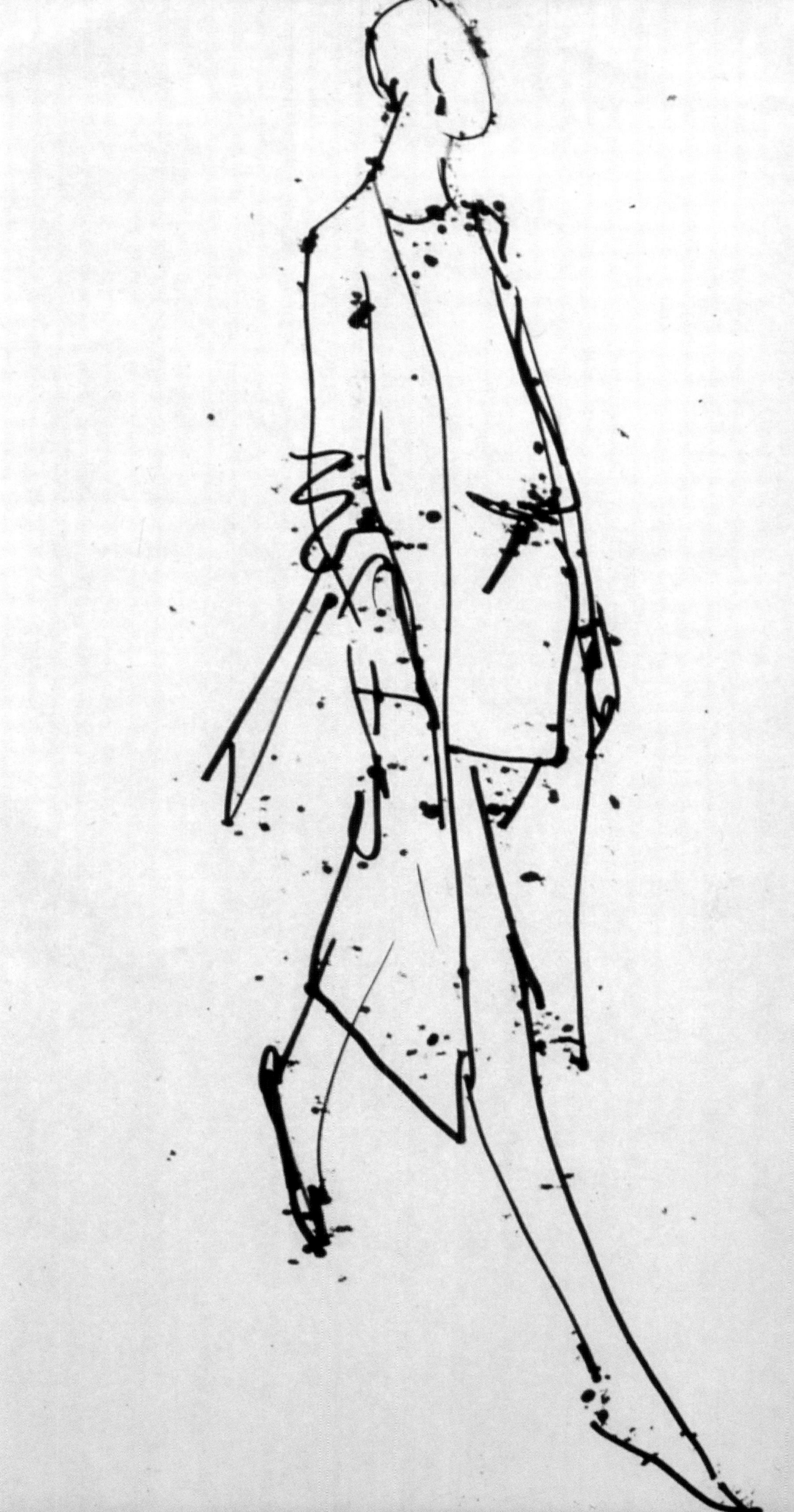

Joe Eula
Drawing of Halston's Skimp Dress, 1974
Ink on paper
14 × 11 in. (35.6 × 27.9 cm)
Collection of Chris Royer

FASHION AND PERFORMANCE

Against the backdrop of floor-to-ceiling views across Manhattan, Halston created a total environment at his Olympic Tower offices and showroom. The walls, movable partitions, and doors were mirrored. Warhol suggested the vibrant red color for the carpeting. Red lacquered Parsons tables throughout served multiple purposes, including a desk for Halston, on which stood a pair of Elsa Peretti silver candlesticks. A continuous supply of orchids was the only decoration in the bold, elegant, simply designed space. Warhol, who attended many of Halston's runway shows, commented, "All the mirrors. . . . Someday somebody is going to walk smack into a mirror there" (*Diaries*, March 13, 1978).

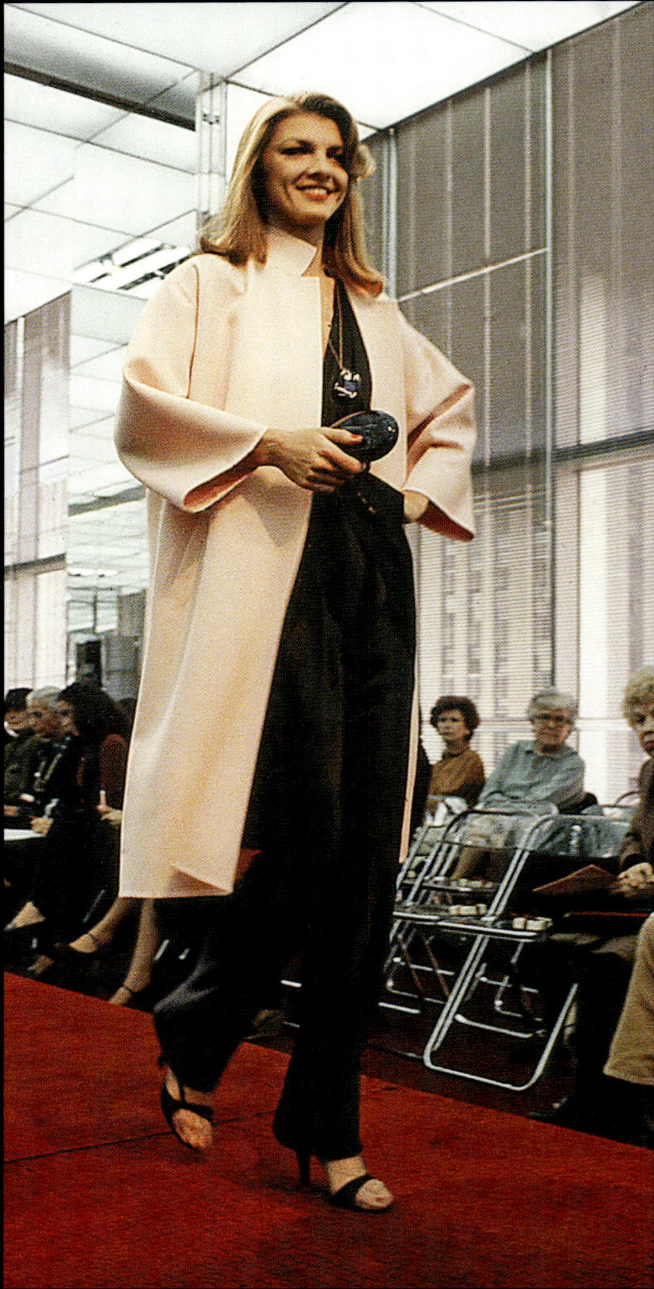

RIGHT
Model wearing a coat by Halston
Photograph by Rose Hartman

OPPOSITE (CLOCKWISE FROM TOP LEFT)
Andy Warhol
Liza Minnelli and Halston at Fashion Show (detail), ca. 1979
Gelatin silver print
8 × 10 in. (20.3 × 25.4 cm)
The Andy Warhol Foundation for the Visual Arts, Inc., FL06.00020

Andy Warhol
Unidentified Model (detail), n.d.
Gelatin silver print
8 × 10 in. (20.3 × 25.4 cm)
The Andy Warhol Museum, Pittsburgh; Contribution The Andy Warhol Foundation for the Visual Arts, Inc., 2001.2.52

Anjelica Huston models a peach gown with a matching coat from Halston's Spring 1973 collection, November 9, 1972
Photograph by John Rooney
Associated Press

Andy Warhol
Martha Graham, Carol Channing, and Unidentified Woman (detail), 1980
Gelatin silver print
8 × 10 in. (20.3 × 25.4 cm)
The Andy Warhol Museum, Pittsburgh; Contribution The Andy Warhol Foundation for the Visual Arts, Inc., 2001.2.243

Andy Warhol
Model at a fashion show at Halston's Olympic Tower showroom, New York, n.d.
Photograph from Time Capsule 577
8 × 10 in. (20.3 × 25.4 cm)
The Andy Warhol Museum, Pittsburgh; Founding Collection, Contribution The Andy Warhol Foundation for the Visual Arts, Inc., TC577.106.35

Andy Warhol
Female Fashion Model (Halston Show), n.d.
Gelatin silver print
9 15/16 × 8 in. (25.2 × 20.3 cm)
The Andy Warhol Museum, Pittsburgh; Contribution The Andy Warhol Foundation for the Visual Arts, Inc., 2001.2.51

OPPOSITE CENTER
Andy Warhol
Unidentified Fashion Models (Halston Show) (detail), n.d.
Gelatin silver print
9 15/16 × 8 in. (25.2 × 20.3 cm)
The Andy Warhol Museum, Pittsburgh; Contribution The Andy Warhol Foundation for the Visual Arts, Inc., 2001.2.54

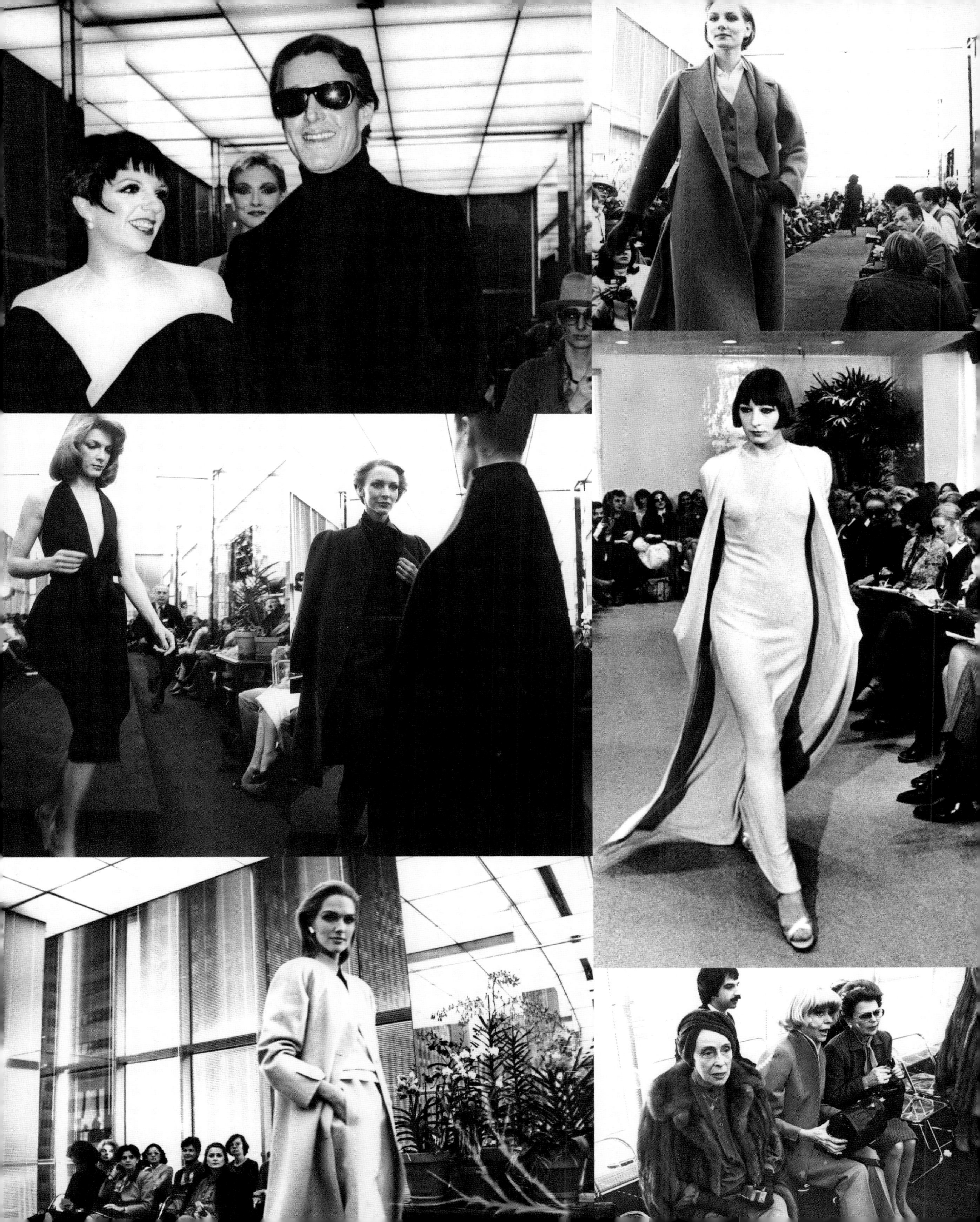

DIVERSITY

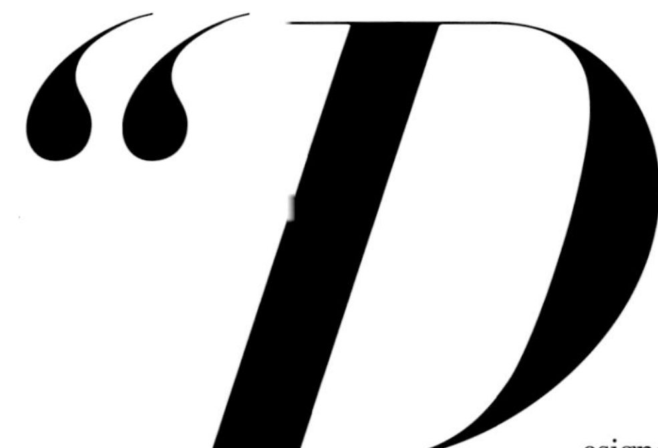

“Designers and artists had a platform, and they made a difference because they recognized something beautiful in diversity. . . . I feel that Warhol’s *Race Riot* images tried to make people wake up and see how they were treating each other. Halston had Naomi Sims; she was like a billboard. And Donyale Luna, too. They made such a difference and don’t get enough credit for what they did.”

—Pat Cleveland

Pat Cleveland wears an orange halter dress and pants ensemble from Halston’s Spring 1980 collection
Photograph by Dustin Pittman
Condé Nast Archive/CORBIS

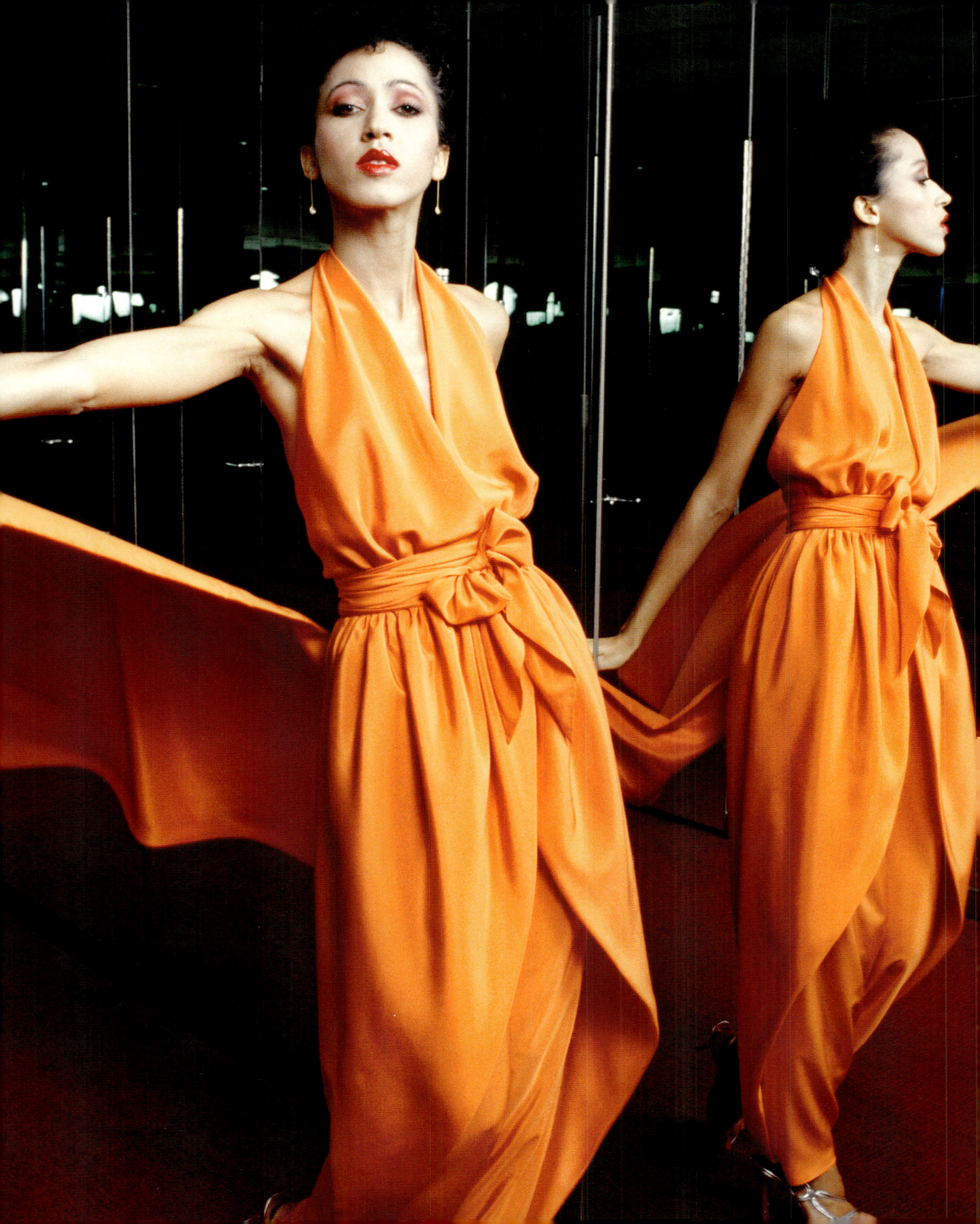

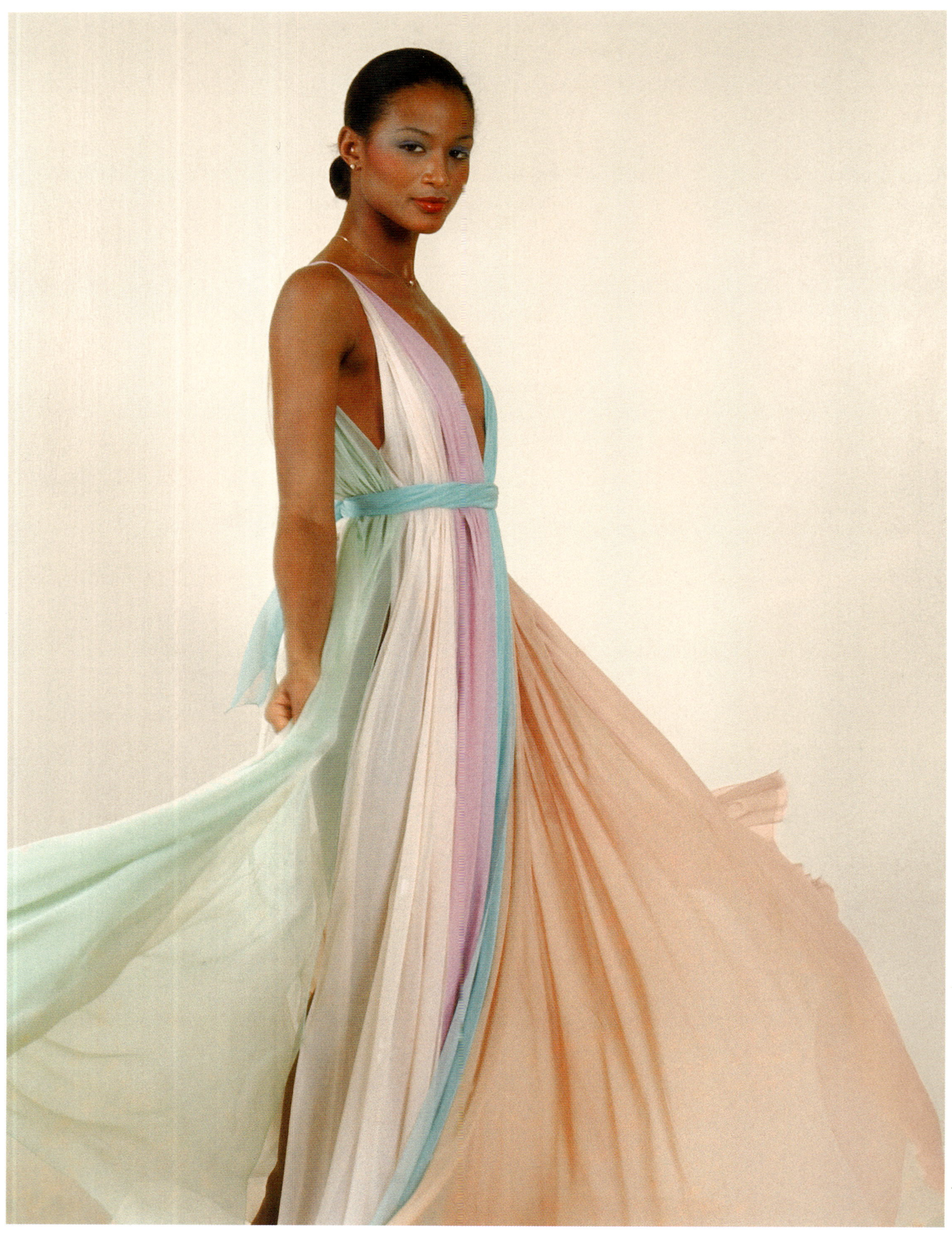

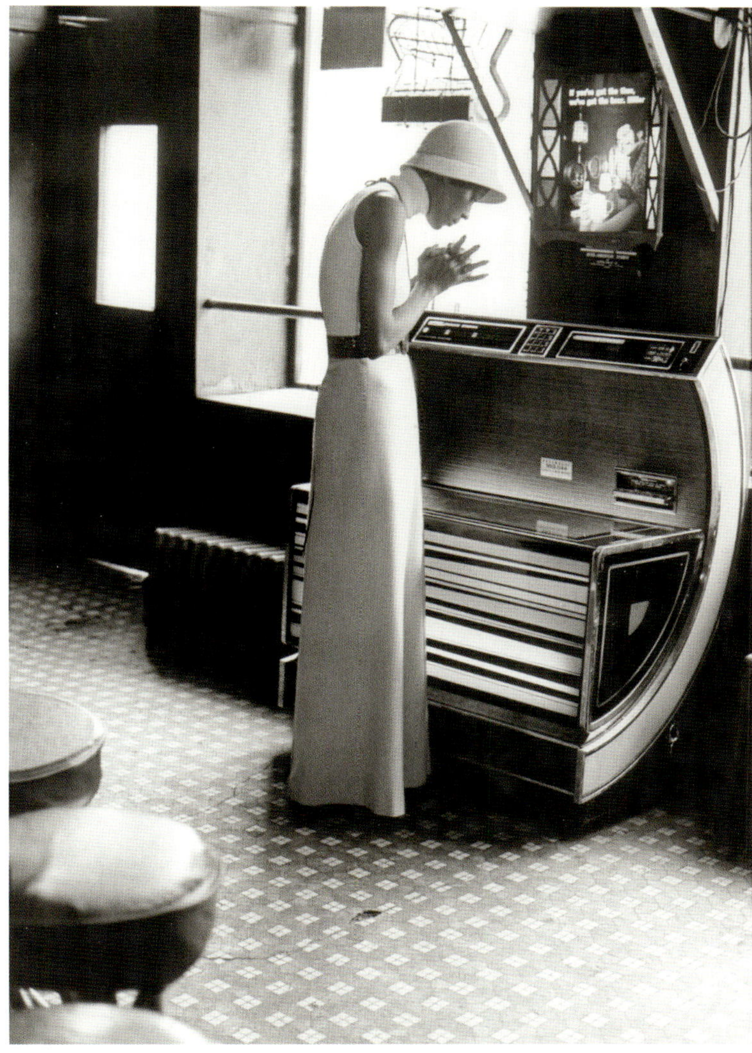

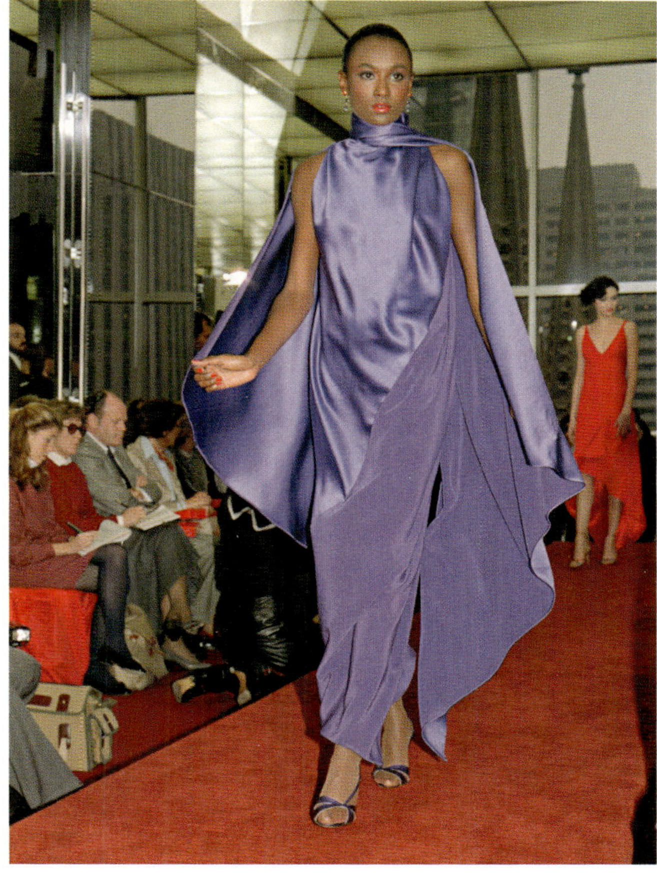

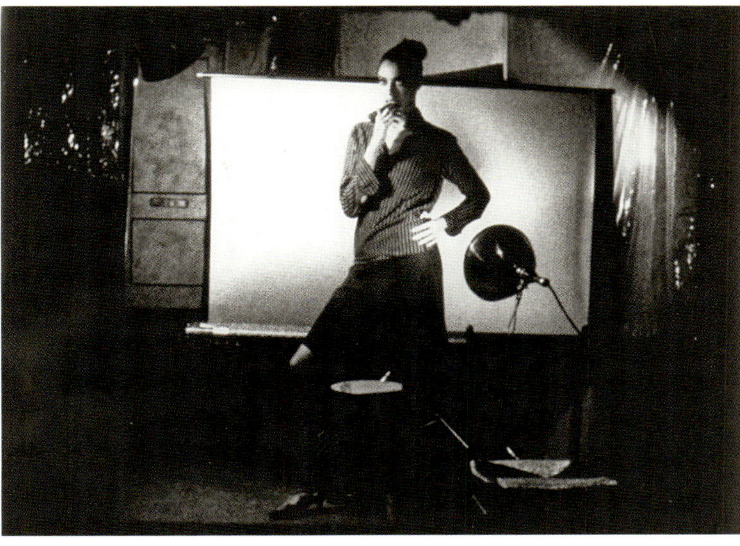

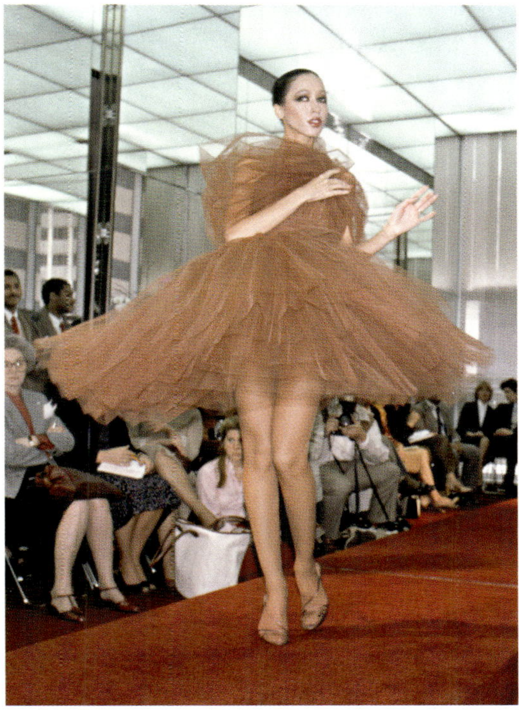

OPPOSITE
Beverly Johnson modeling a long pastel dress by Halston,
December 31, 1970
Photograph by Dirck Halstead
Time & Life Pictures/Getty Images

TOP LEFT
Model Naomi Sims at Harlem's Lucky Spot Restaurant, wearing a long belted dress by Halston, ca. 1972
Photograph by Berry Berenson
Condé Nast Archive/CORBIS

BOTTOM LEFT
Andy Warhol
Screen Test: Donyale Luna [ST196], 1965
16mm film, black and white, silent, 4.5 minutes at 16 frames per second
The Andy Warhol Museum, Pittsburgh

TOP RIGHT
Sleeveless gown with wrap from Halston's Spring/Summer collection,
November 11, 1983
Bettmann/CORBIS

BOTTOM RIGHT
Strapless tulle dance dress from Halston's Fall/Winter collection, April 1980
Associated Press

UNIFORMS AND COSTUMES

"You know, I do think I started this whole bluejeans-with-a-tuxedo-jacket thing because years ago after I wore that to a few big events and was photographed, all the kids began doing it and they're still doing it."

—Andy Warhol, *Diaries*, September 19, 1986

"Bought a 'fairy shirt' that has my name on it. It's just a list of names of people who're gay all over it like Thoreau, Alexander the Great, Halston, me."

—Andy Warhol, *Diaries*, July 2, 1977

"Andy liked to go uptown and downtown; and you didn't know where you were going to end up. Andy could dress any way he wanted, but we changed for the evening and wore full suits."
—Vincent Fremont, interview with Allison Unruh, March 2010

Warhol and Halston explored the boundaries between a uniform and a costume in their creative work and personal attire. While a uniform confers an immediate belonging to a set group, a costume implies a transformation into a performing or fictional character, whether in theater, dance, or film. Each man had his own personal uniform that his entourage adopted. In the 1960s Warhol often wore the uniform of a white-and-navy-blue-striped shirt, black jeans, black boots, and a leather jacket; his attire evolved in the 1970s to a sport coat, tie, and jeans. Halston's signature look was a black shirt and pants dressed up with a red scarf and white sport coat. Halston's employees were expected to wear black, and when out and about the Halstonettes always wore his latest line of fashions.

Halston designed uniforms for numerous organizations, both corporate and nonprofit, as well as fanciful costumes for performers, including Martha Graham's dance company and Liza Minnelli. Warhol explored the idea of costume in his transformation of himself and others. His wig, while part uniform, served also as costume, transforming the artist into an iconic character and making him instantly recognizable. In the mid-1980s he considered creating an edition of about forty framed wigs as a work of art but abandoned the idea after completing only two of them.

Manufactured by Paul Bochicchio, Inc., New York, NY
Warhol's wig (silver and brown), 1980s
Natural and synthetic hair on dyed cloth
19 × 16 × 1½ in. (48.3 × 40.6 × 3.8 cm)
The Andy Warhol Museum, Pittsburgh; Founding Collection, Contribution The Andy Warhol Foundation for the Visual Arts, Inc., 1998.3.6158.1

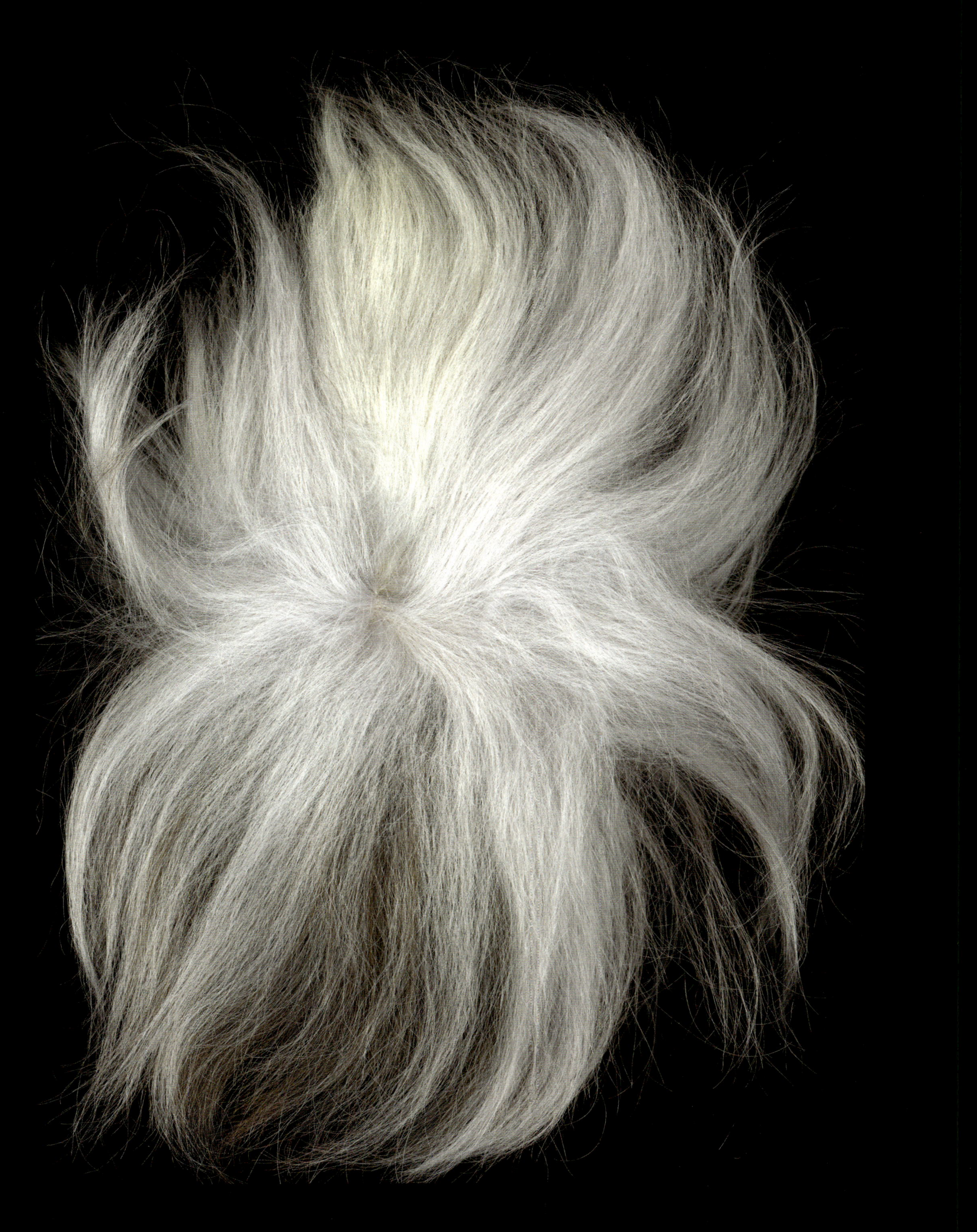

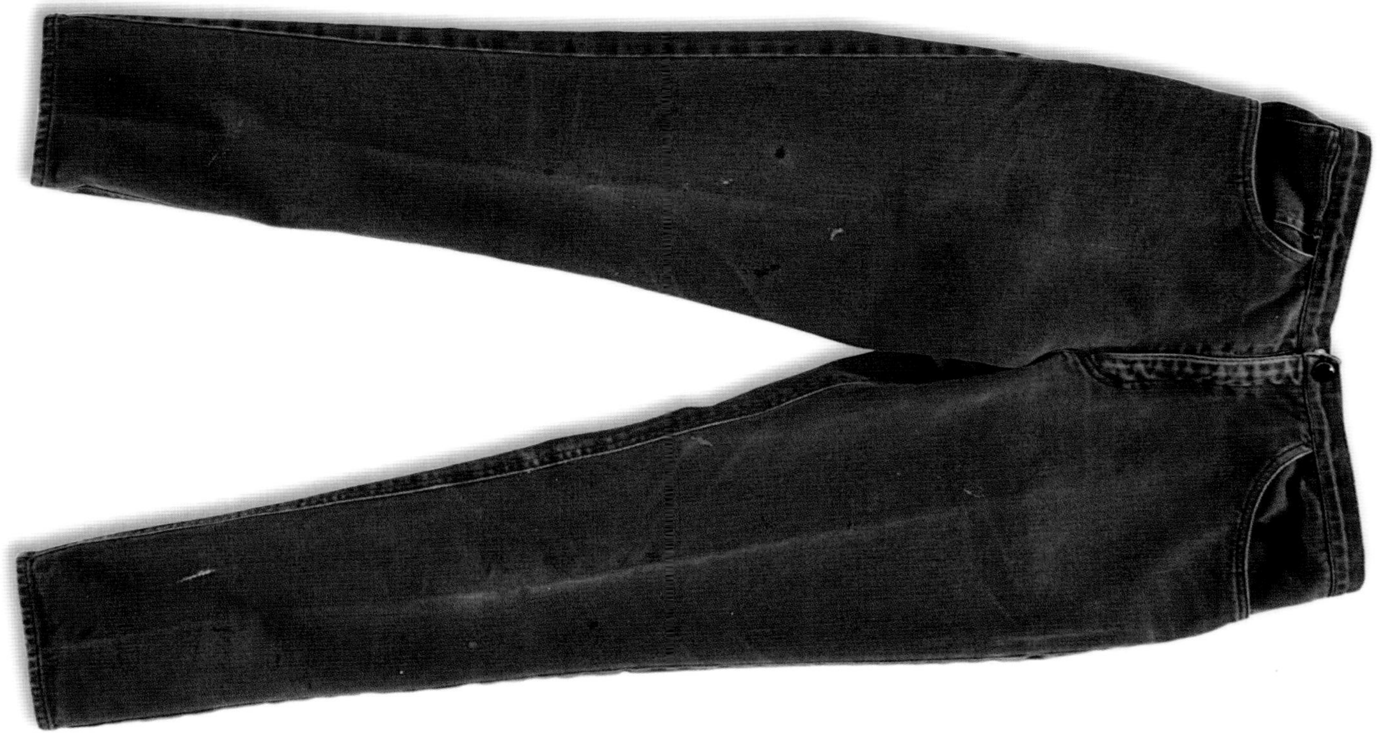

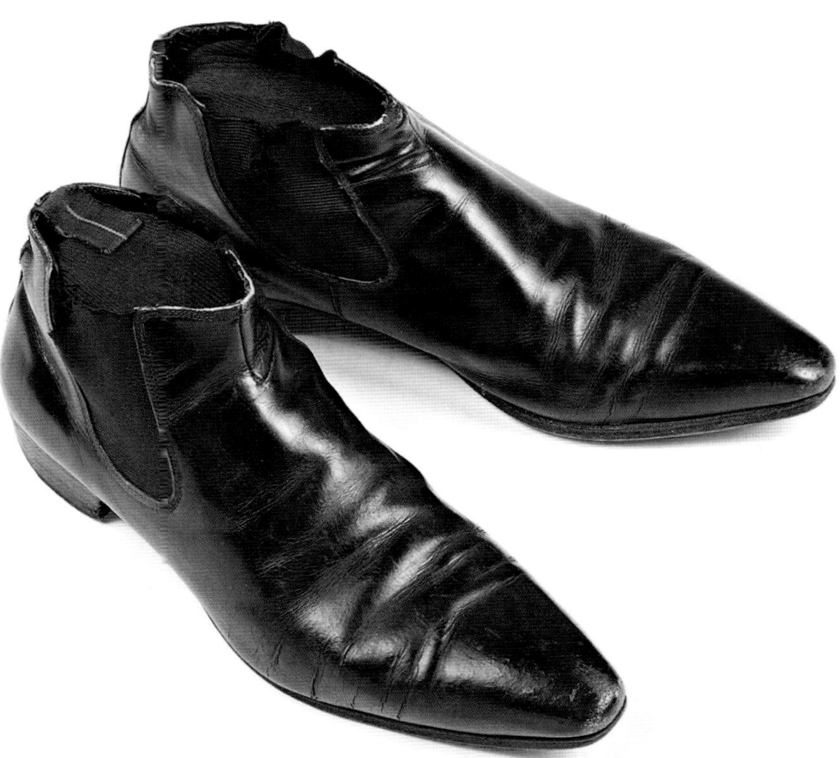

TOP
Warhol's jeans (faded black denim with paint splashes), 1965
Machine-sewn cotton
Waist: 28 in. (71.1 cm)
Inseam: 30 in. (76.2 cm)
The Andy Warhol Museum, Pittsburgh; Founding Collection, Contribution The Andy Warhol Foundation for the Visual Arts, Inc., 1998.3.5865.1

BOTTOM
Manufactured by Centenar[illegible] & Zinelli, Milan
Warhol's shoes (Beatle boots), 1965
Machine-sewn leather with elastic vents and leather soles
Size (European): 42 ½
The Andy Warhol Museum, Pittsburgh; Founding Collection, Contribution The Andy Warhol Foundation for the Visual Arts, Inc., 1998.3.5828a-b

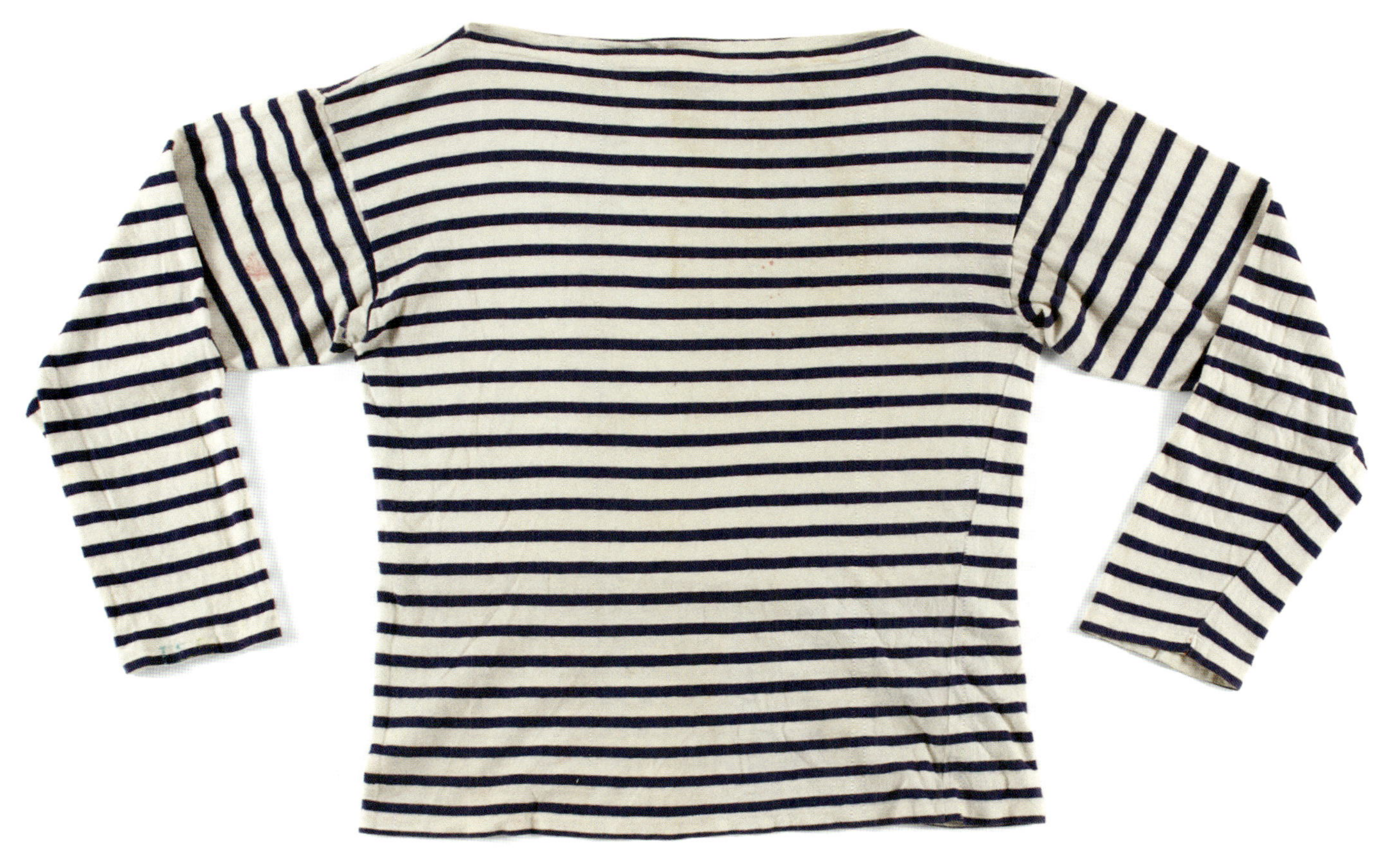

Warhol's shirt (striped, sailor-style jersey), 1965
Machine-sewn cotton knit
Nominal size (European): 3
The Andy Warhol Museum, Pittsburgh; Founding Collection, Contribution The Andy Warhol Foundation for the Visual Arts, Inc., 1998.3.6002.1

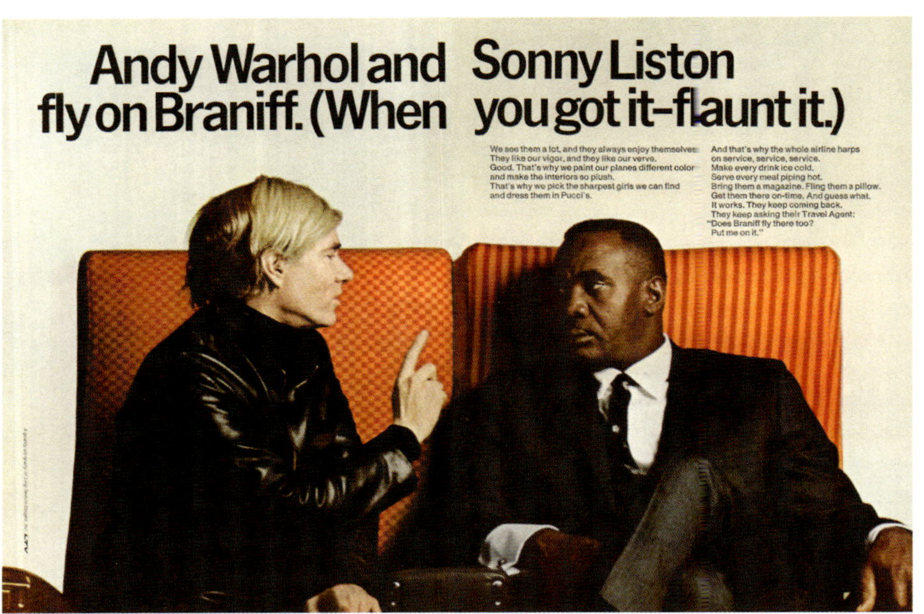

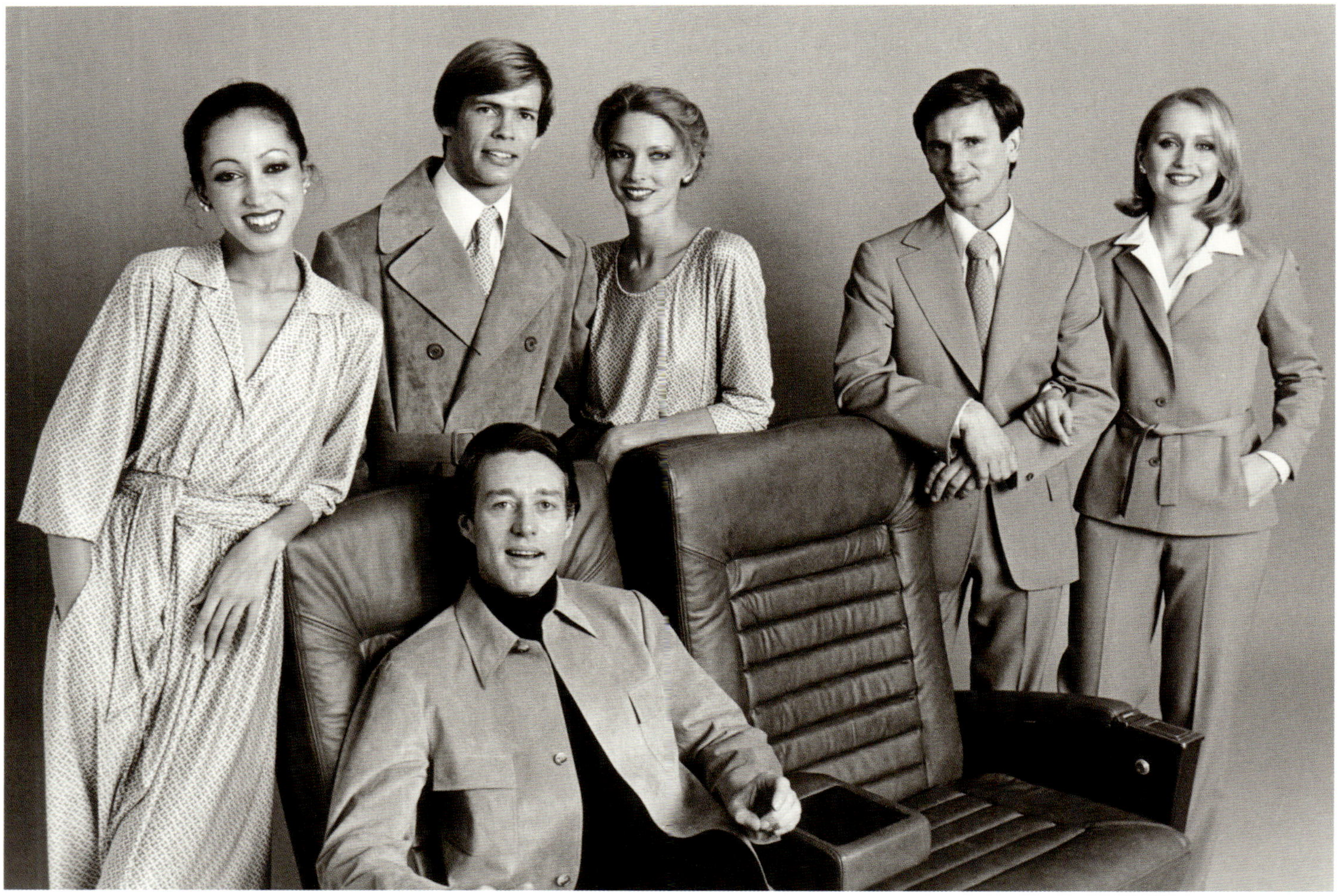

TOP
Advertisement (Andy Warhol and Sonny Liston for Braniff Airlines), 1969
Printed ink on coated paper
11½ × 8¼ in. each (29.2 × 21 cm)
The Andy Warhol Museum, Pittsburgh; Museum Purchase, 2001.9a–b

BOTTOM
Halston and models in Braniff uniforms, ca. 1975
Photograph by Hulton Archive/Stringer
Getty Images

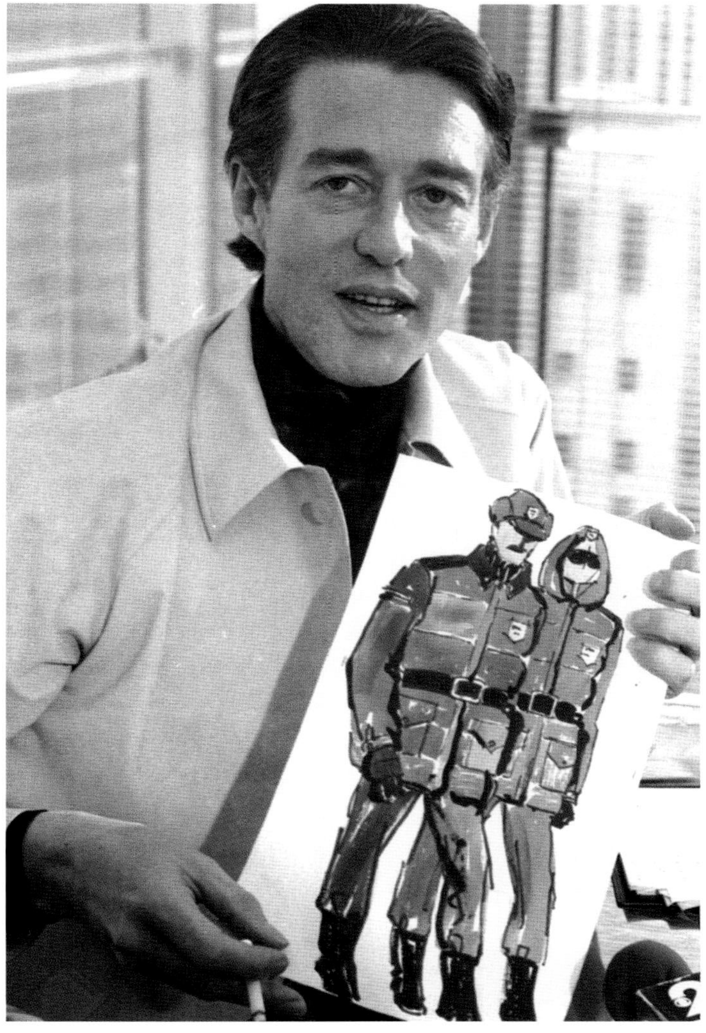

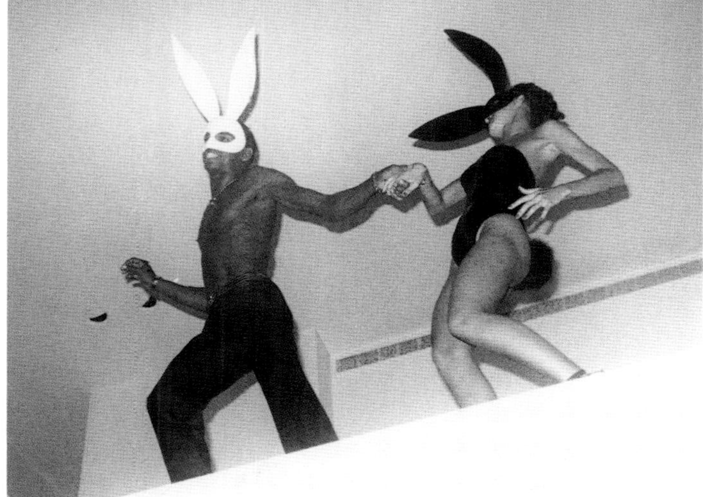

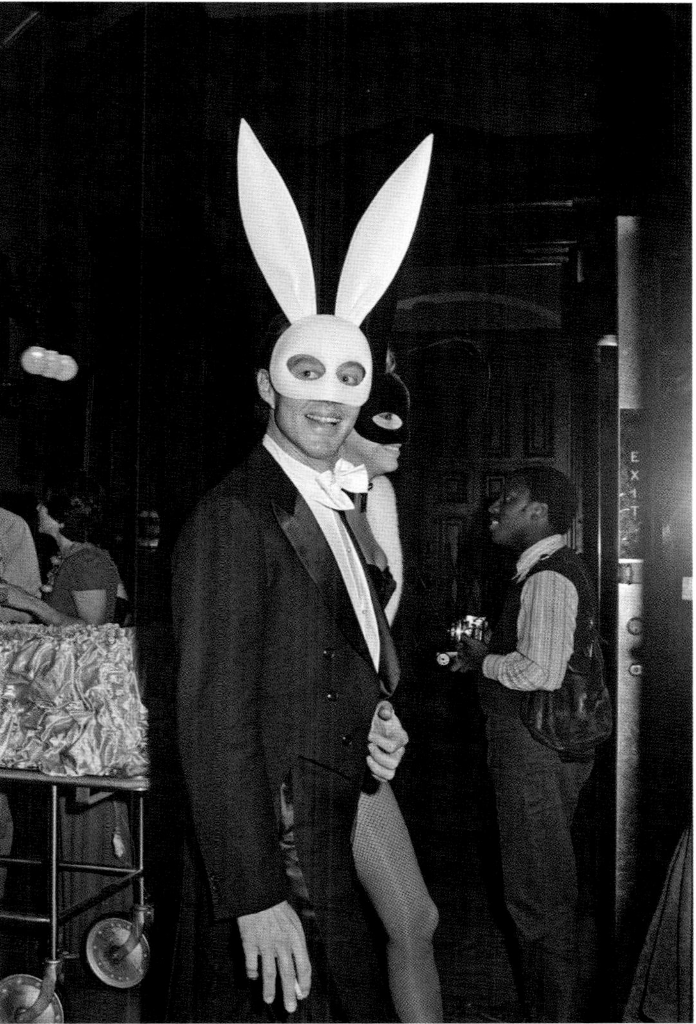

ABOVE
Halston with two of his designs for police uniforms, April 12, 1974
Photograph by Anthony Pescatore
NY Daily News Archive/Getty Images

TOP RIGHT
Andy Warhol
Unidentified Man and Woman, taken at Halston's townhouse, 101 E. 63rd Street, New York, n.d.
Gelatin silver print
8 × 10 in. (20.3 × 25.4 cm)
The Andy Warhol Museum, Pittsburgh; Contribution The Andy Warhol Foundation for the Visual Arts, Inc., 2001.1.651

BOTTOM RIGHT
Halston at Magic, Fantasy, and Dreams, a costume ball benefit for the Skowhegan School of Painting and Sculpture, October 24, 1971
Photograph by Nick Machalaba
Condé Nast Archive/CORBIS

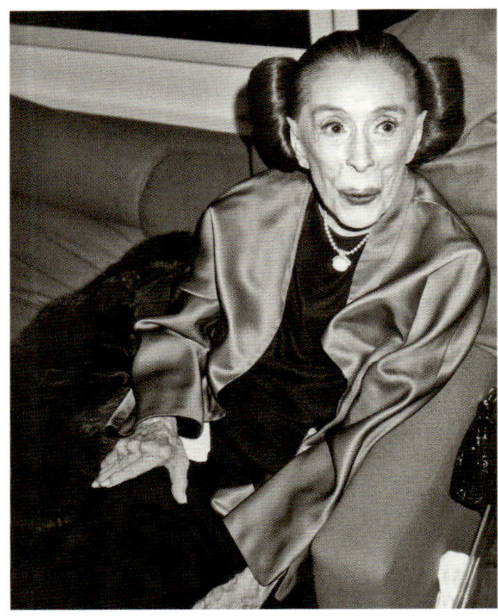

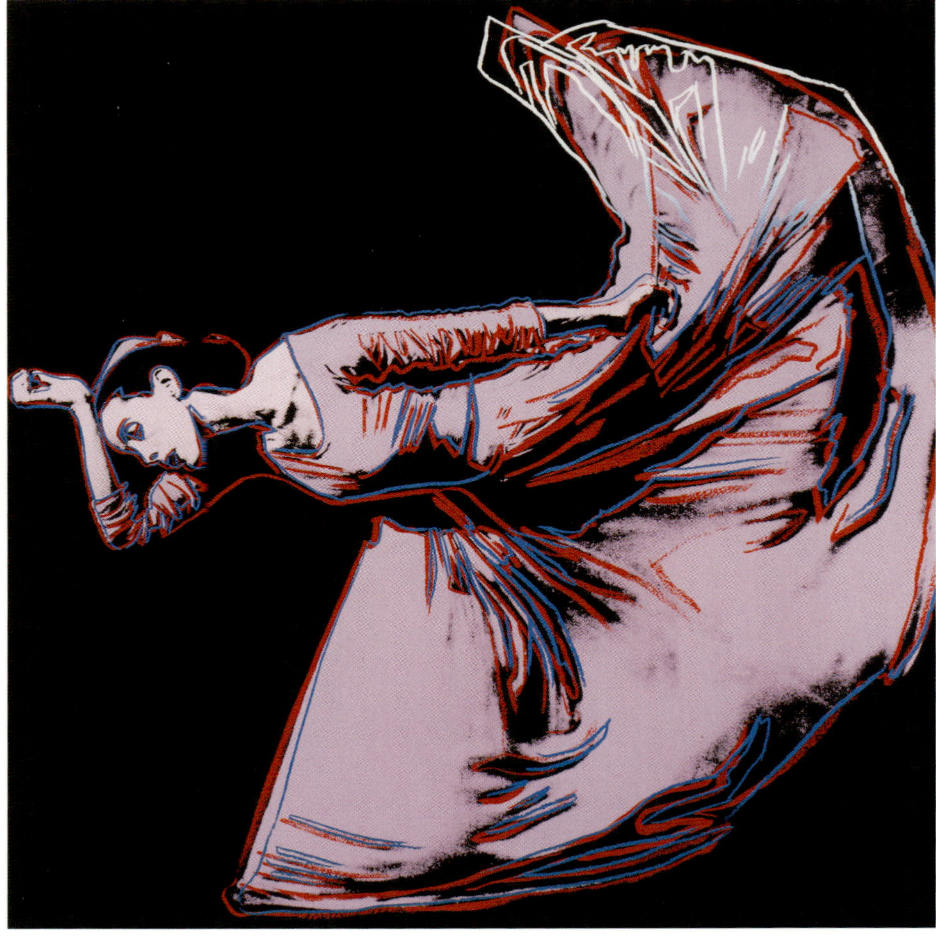

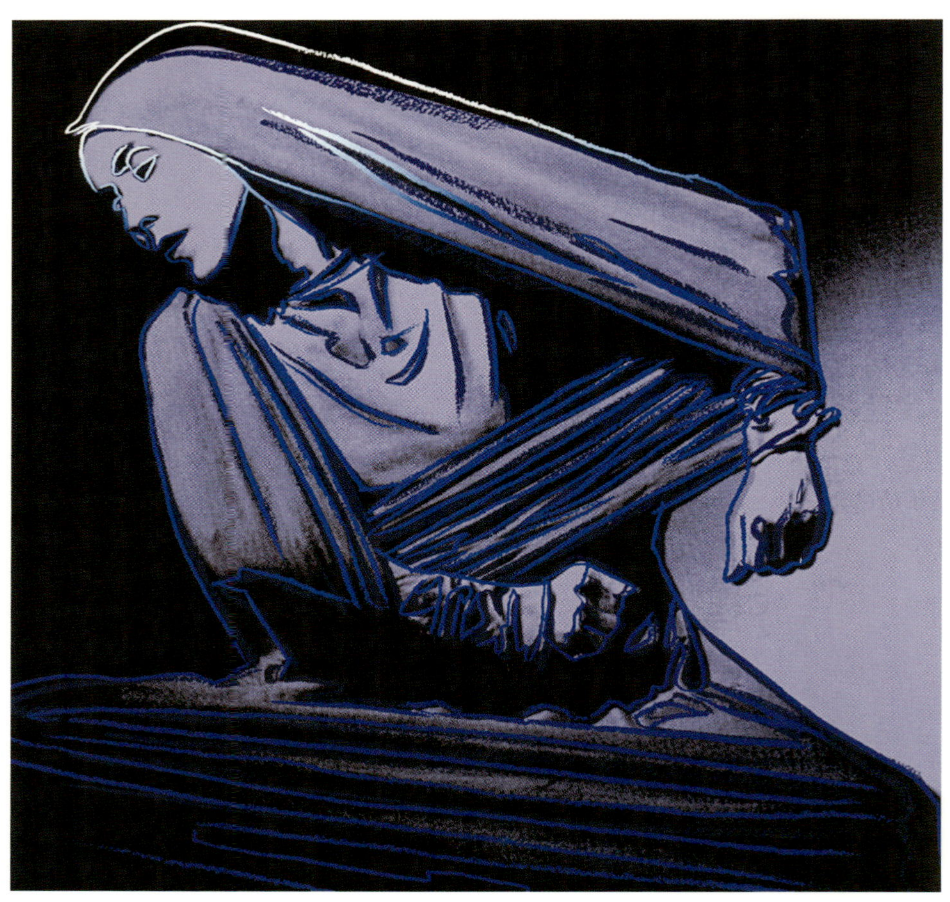

TOP LEFT
Andy Warhol
Martha Graham, n.d.
Gelatin silver print
10 × 8 in. (25.4 × 20.3 cm)
The Andy Warhol Museum, Pittsburgh; Contribution The Andy Warhol Foundation for the Visual Arts, Inc., 2001.2.82

TOP RIGHT
Andy Warhol
Martha Graham: Letter to the World (The Kick), 1986
Screen print on Lenox Museum Board
36 × 36 in. (91.4 × 91.4 cm)
The Andy Warhol Museum, Pittsburgh; Founding Collection, Contribution The Andy Warhol Foundation for the Visual Arts, Inc., 1998.1.2495.3

BOTTOM RIGHT
Andy Warhol
Martha Graham: Lamentation, 1986
Screen print on Lenox Museum Board
36 × 36 in. (91.4 × 91.4 cm)
The Andy Warhol Museum, Pittsburgh; Founding Collection, Contribution The Andy Warhol Foundation for the Visual Arts, Inc., 1998.1.2495.2

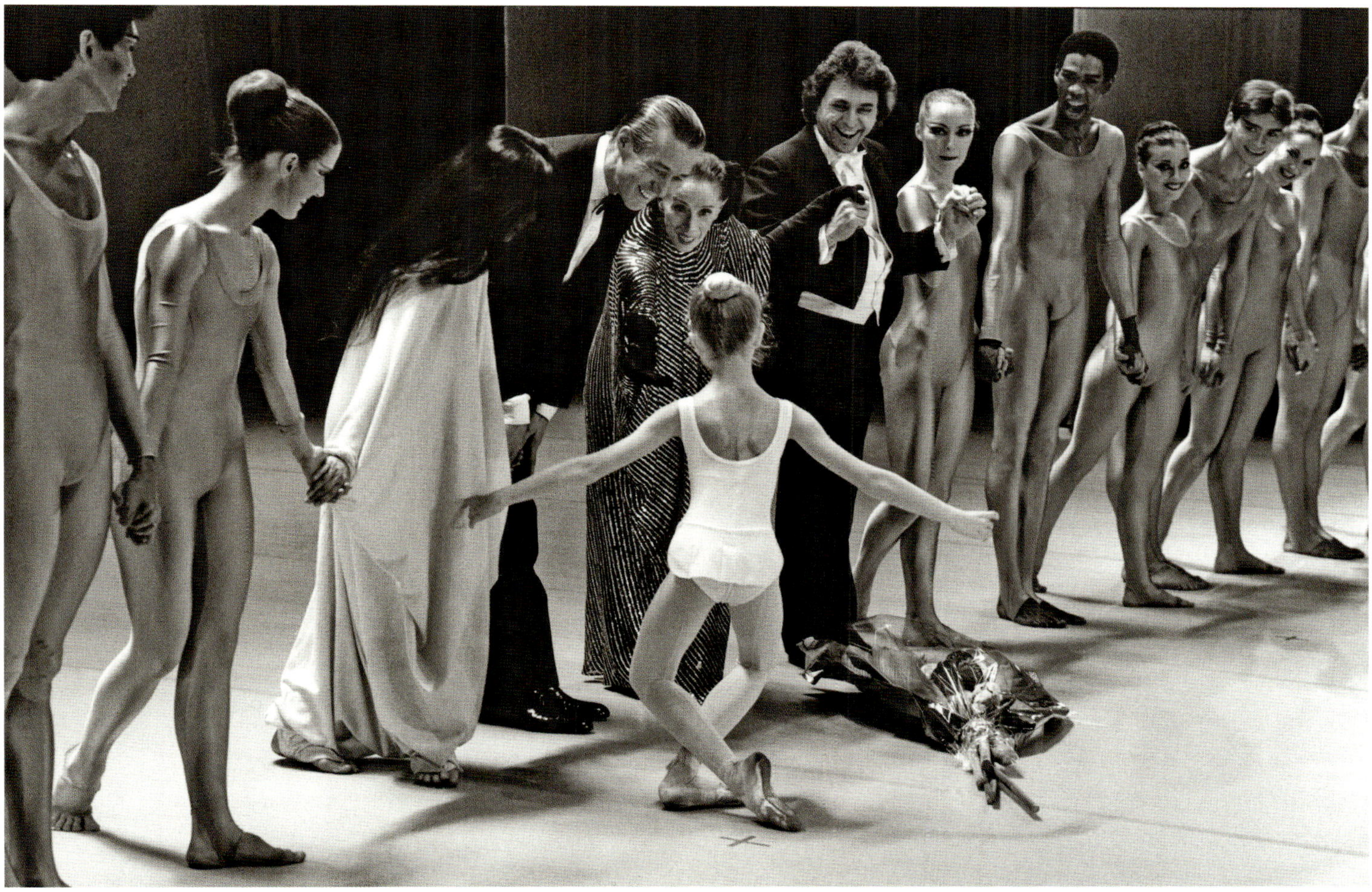

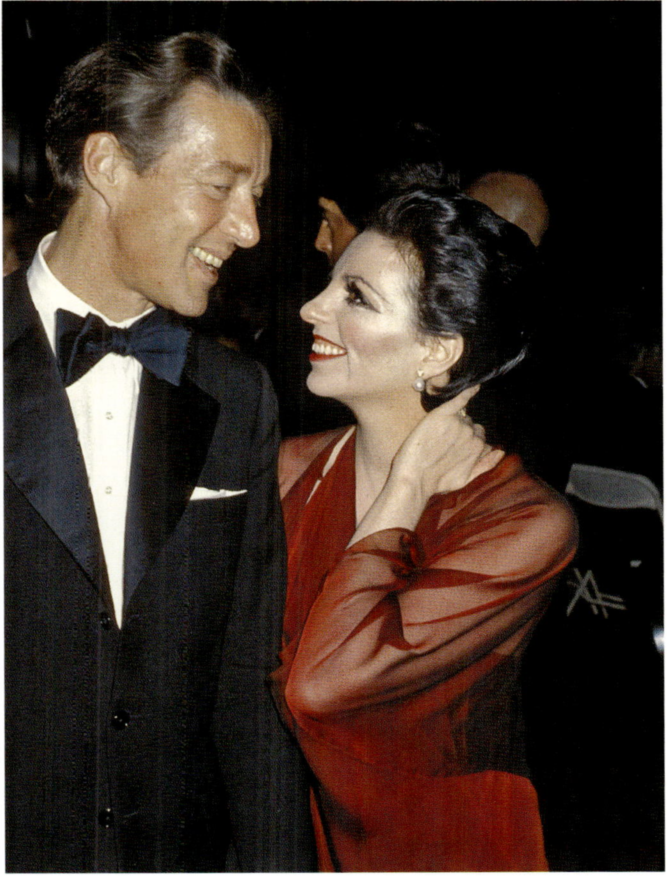

TOP
During a curtain call, a young ballerina curtsies for Martha Graham and Halston
Photograph by Peter Turnley
CORBIS

BOTTOM
Halston and Liza Minnelli attend the Martha Graham Dance Company Benefit Gala on June 26, 1978, at the Metropolitan Opera House, Lincoln Center, in New York City
Photograph by Ron Galella
WireImage/Getty Images

PERFUME AND ACCESSORIES

"I really love wearing perfume . . . I switch perfumes all the time. If I've been wearing one perfume for three months, I force myself to give it up, even if I still feel like wearing it, so whenever I smell it again it will always remind me of those three months. I never go back to wearing it again; it becomes part of my permanent smell collection."

—Andy Warhol, *THE Philosophy of Andy Warhol*

In association with Max Factor, a division of Norton Simon Industries, Halston extended his brand to luxury fragrances in 1975. He asked Elsa Peretti, his close friend and former model, to design the bottle for his signature scent, Halston. The result was a sensuous, organic form derived from shapes in her jewelry designs for Tiffany & Co. Halston was intimately involved with every step of the development process, from testing essential oils through the package design. He insisted that his name appear nowhere on the tear-drop-shaped bottle except for on the small paper band around the neck that broke away when the bottle was opened for the first time. Halston perfume generated $85 million in worldwide sales within the first two years and ranked as one of the top ten luxury scents for more than a decade.

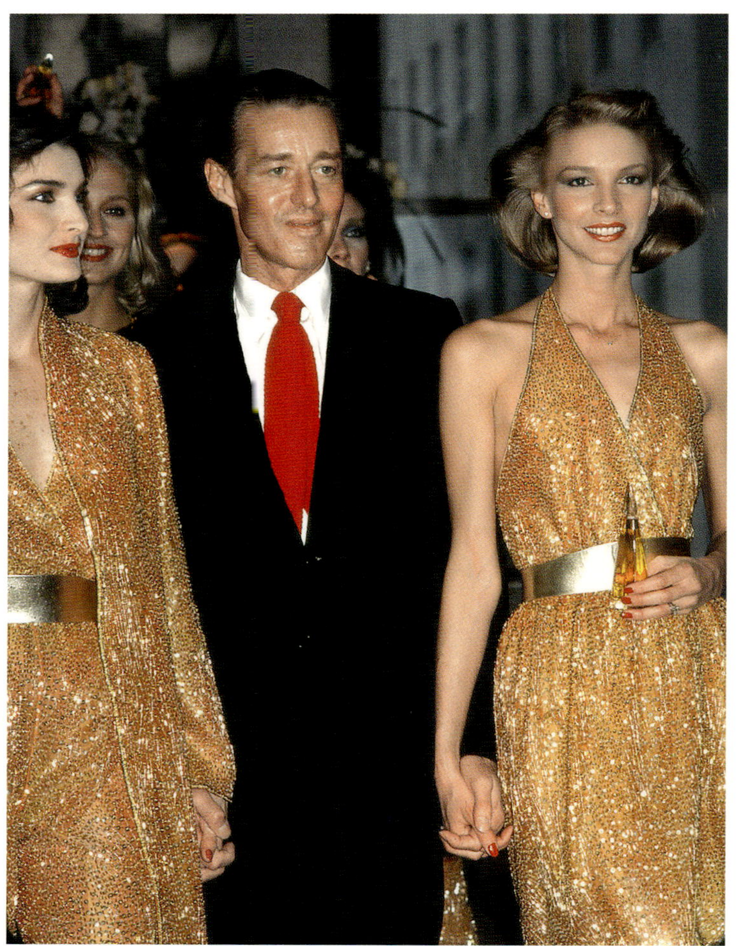

Halston with models promoting perfume
Photograph by Rose Hartman

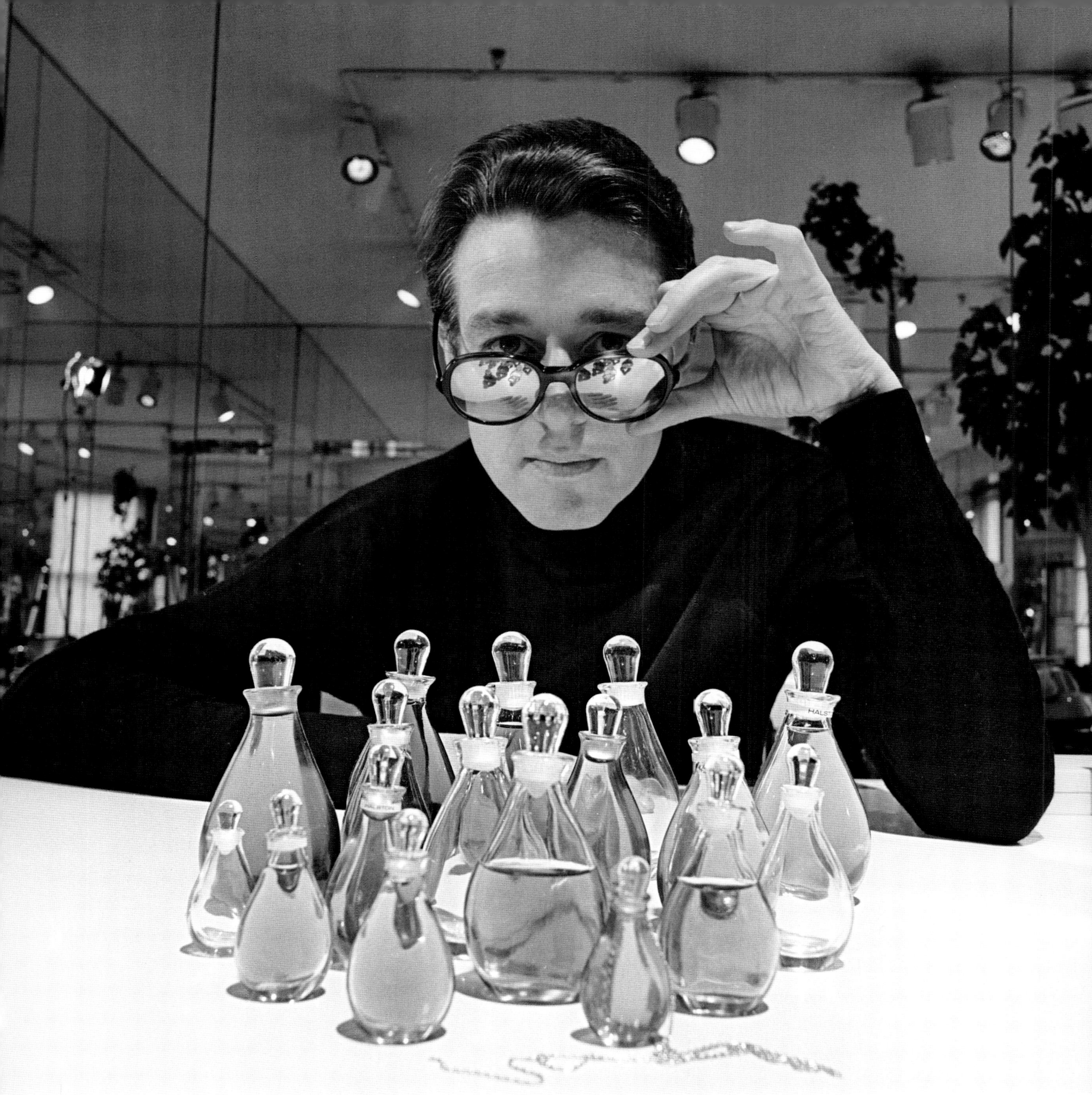

Halston in his showroom with an assortment of perfume bottles, New York, January 2, 1975
Photograph by Arnold Newman
Getty Images

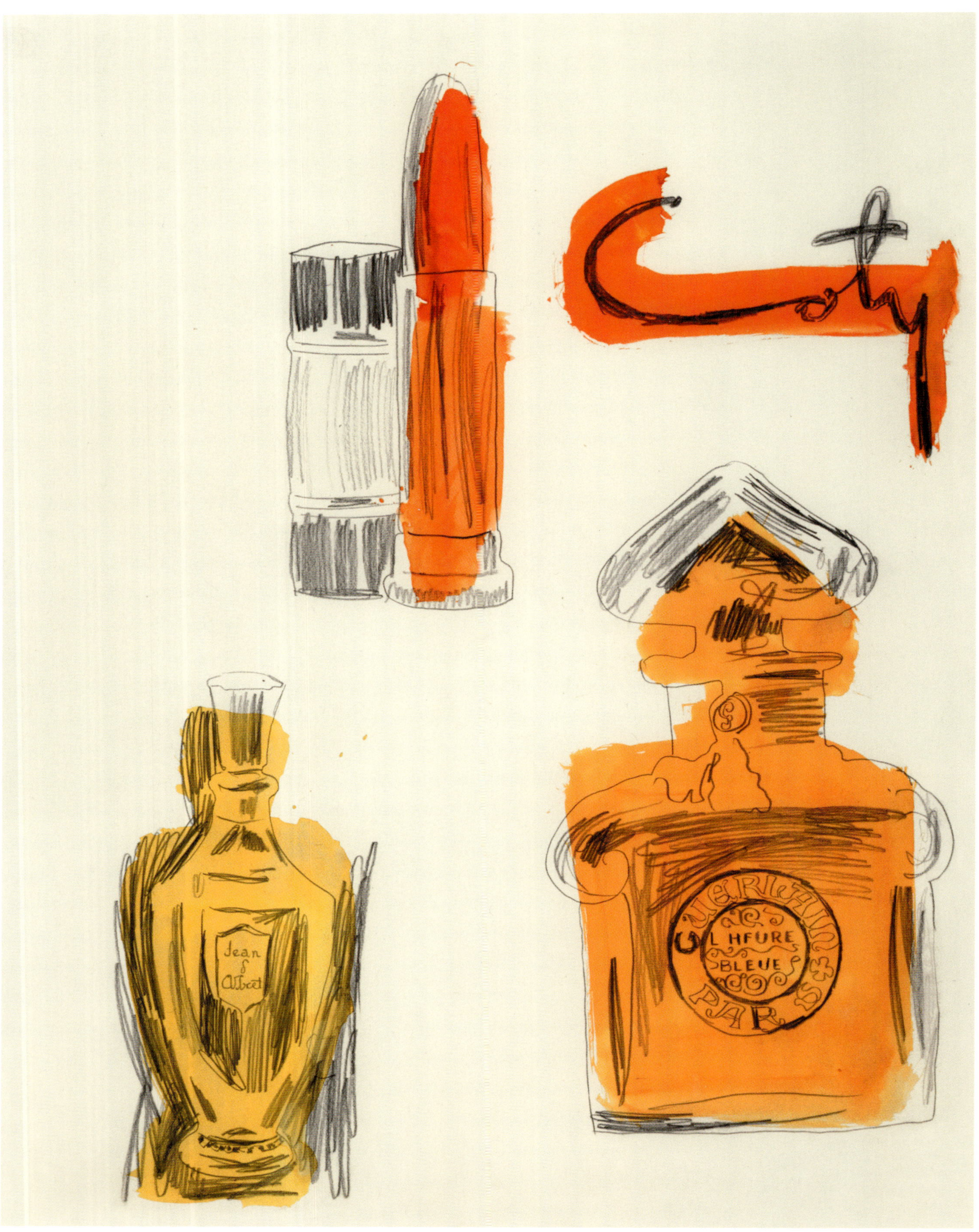
Coty
Jean
L HFURE
BLEUE
PARIS

Spanning multiple decades, Warhol created numerous works that featured perfume. Having made paintings of Coca-Cola bottles in the early 1960s, he then produced a sculpture from the brand's bottles (whose shape was refined by the renowned designer Raymond Loewy) that he coated with silver paint. Warhol went a step further by filling one hundred of these silver bottles with a perfume that he rakishly labeled "You're In"/"Eau d'Andy" and capping them off. The Coca-Cola Company was not pleased and sent him a letter to cease and desist.

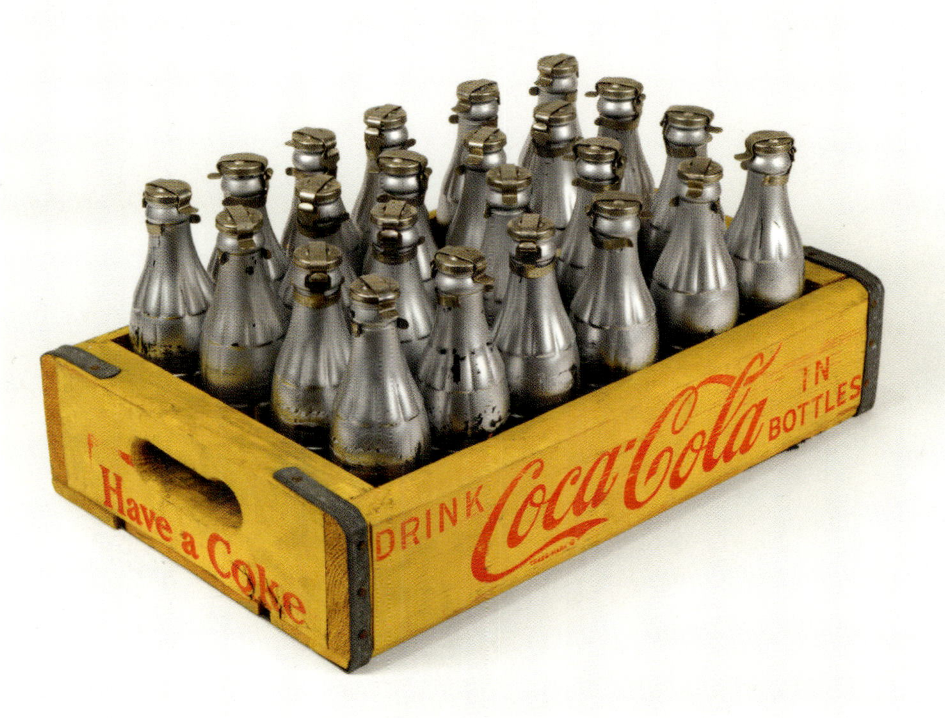

OPPOSITE
Andy Warhol
Perfume Bottles and Lipstick, ca. 1962
Graphite and Dr. Martin's Aniline dye on Strathmore paper
29 × 23 in. (73.7 × 58.4 cm)
The Andy Warhol Museum, Pittsburgh; Founding Collection, Contribution The Andy Warhol Foundation for the Visual Arts, Inc., 1998.1.2320

ABOVE
Andy Warhol
You're In, 1967
Spray paint on glass bottles in printed wooden crate
8½ × 18 × 11 in. (21.6 × 45.7 × 27.9 cm)
The Andy Warhol Museum, Pittsburgh; Founding Collection, Contribution The Andy Warhol Foundation for the Visual Arts, Inc., 1998.1.789a–y

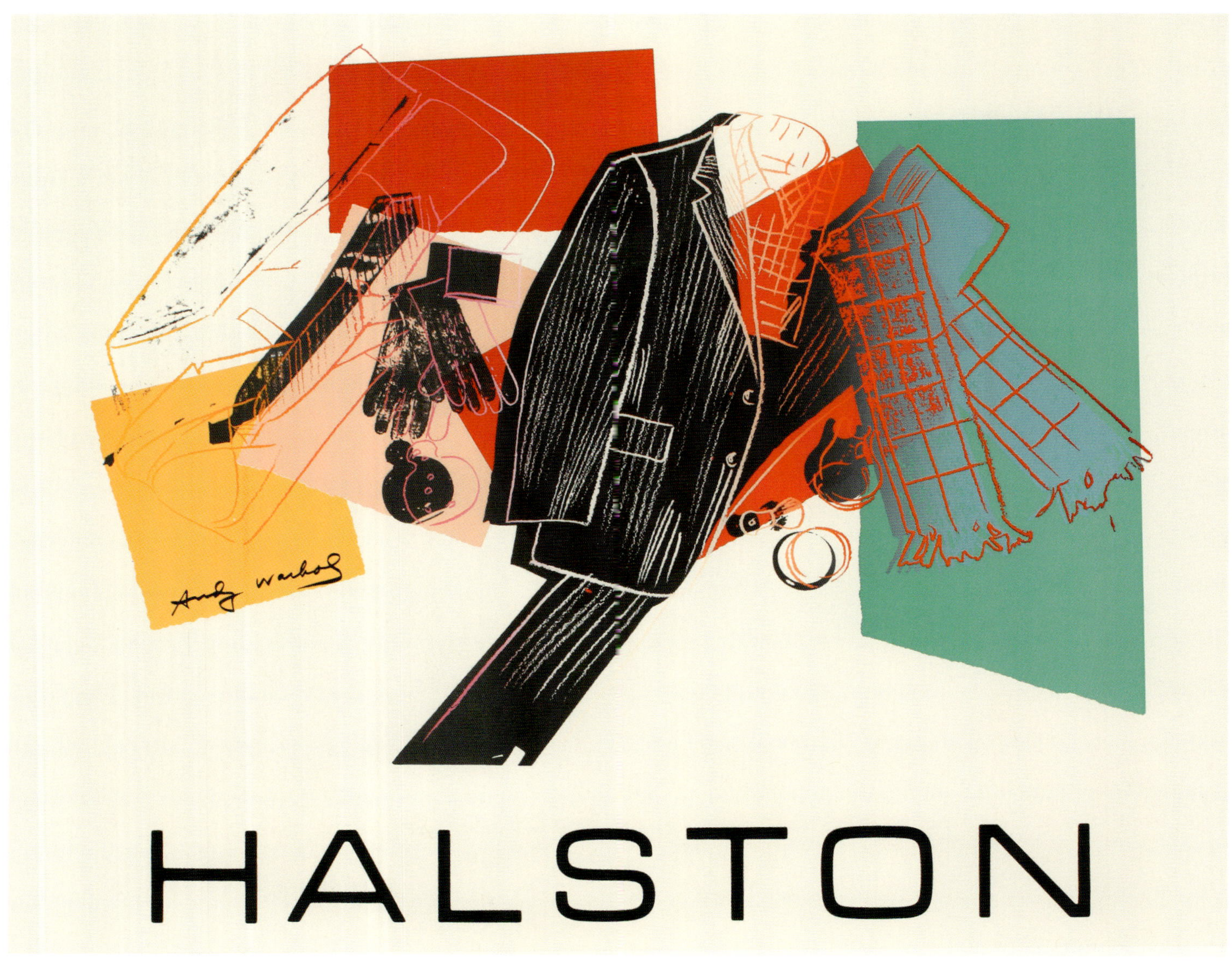

Many of the accessories that became synonymous with Halston in the 1970s, such as his cashmere scarves, were reimagined in this early 1980s ad series. Halston commissioned Warhol to create the campaign. Warhol incorporated Halston's metallic shoes into the fashion-accessory layout, as well as Halston's silver-studded treatment for women's belts and fashion apparel. In addition, he displayed the iconic silver compact, lipstick, and perfumes that Elsa Peretti designed for Halston's cosmetics and fragrance collection.

Andy Warhol
Poster (Halston Advertising Campaign: Men's Wear), 1982
Printed ink on paper
22 ½ × 28 ⅝ in. (57.2 × 72.7 cm)
Collection of The Andy Warhol Museum, Pittsburgh; Contribution The Andy Warhol Foundation for the Visual Arts, Inc., T146

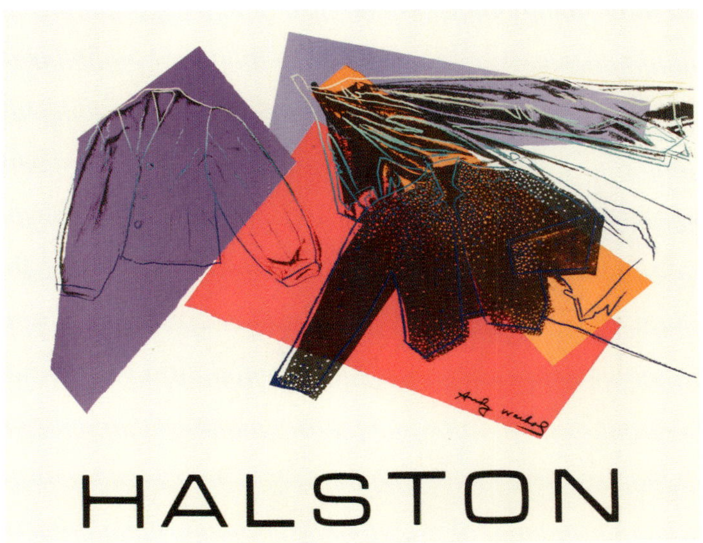

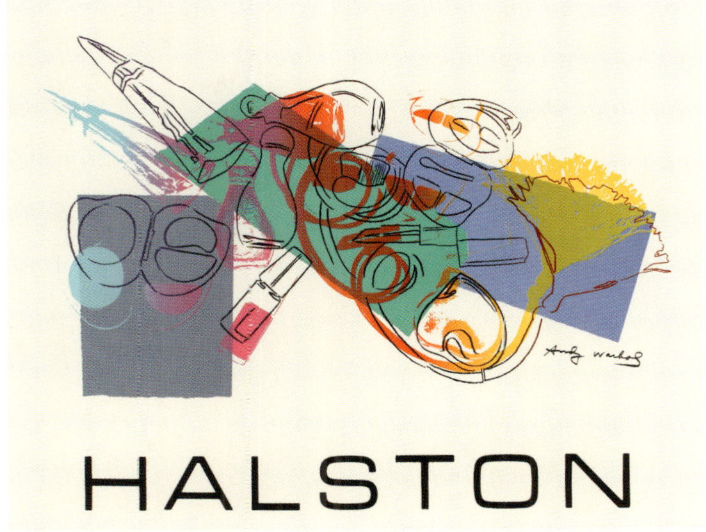

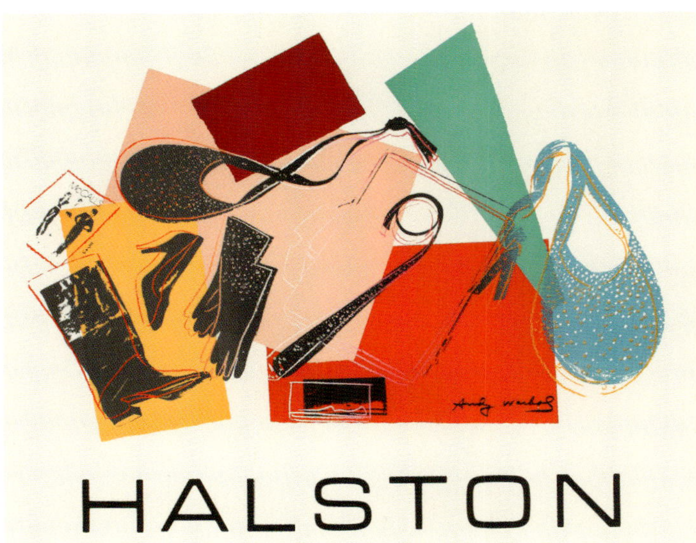

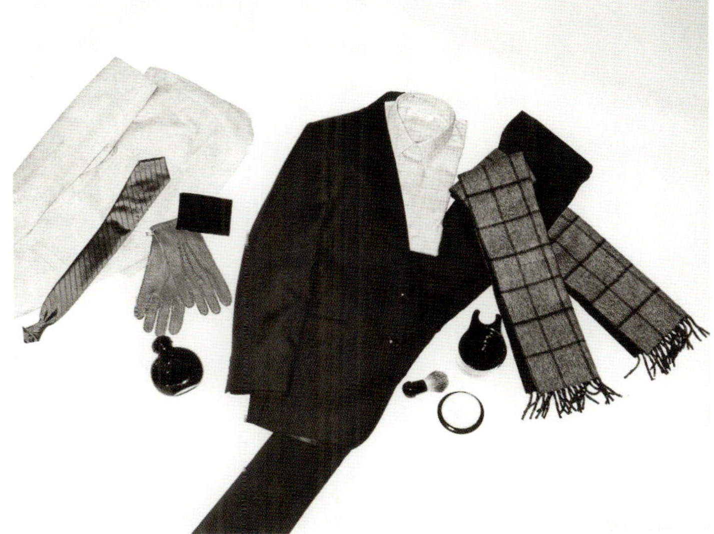

TOP LEFT
Andy Warhol
Poster (Halston Advertising Campaign: Jackets), 1982
Printed ink on paper
22½ × 25⅝ in. (57.2 × 65.1 cm)
The Andy Warhol Museum, Pittsburgh; Contribution The Andy Warhol Foundation for the Visual Arts, Inc., T147

BOTTOM LEFT
Andy Warhol
Poster (Halston Advertising Campaign: Women's Wear), 1982
Printed ink on paper
22½ × 28⅝ in. (57.2 × 72.7 cm)
The Andy Warhol Museum, Pittsburgh; Contribution The Andy Warhol Foundation for the Visual Arts, Inc., T145

TOP RIGHT
Andy Warhol
Poster (Halston Advertising Campaign: Makeup and Perfume), 1982
Printed ink on paper
22½ × 28⅝ in. (57.2 × 72.7 cm)
The Andy Warhol Museum, Pittsburgh; Contribution The Andy Warhol Foundation for the Visual Arts, Inc., T148

BOTTOM RIGHT
Andy Warhol
Halston Ad Campaign: Men's Wear, 1982
Gelatin silver print
8 × 10 in. (20.3 × 25.4 cm)
The Andy Warhol Museum, Pittsburgh; Contribution The Andy Warhol Foundation for the Visual Arts, Inc., 2001.2.638

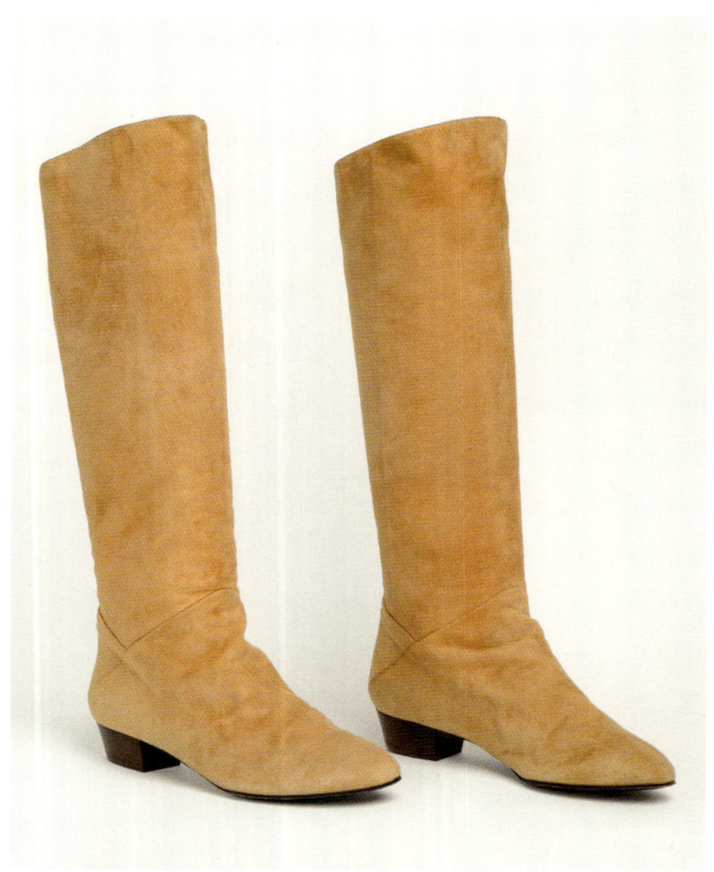

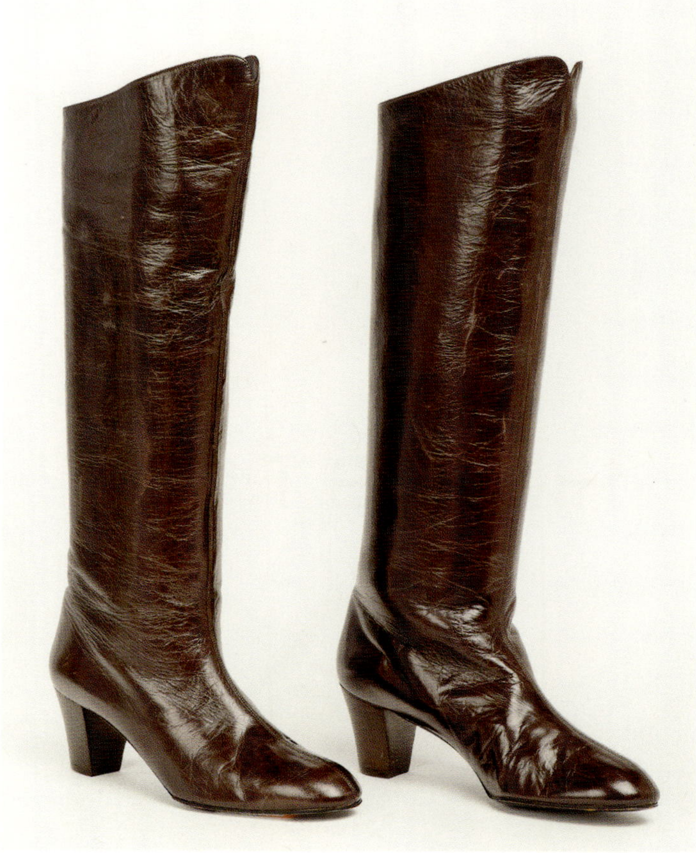

Halston
Boots, 1982
Suede
Photograph by Eve Prime
Collection of Chris Royer

Halston for Garolini Shoes
Boots, 1982
Leather
Photograph by Eve Prime
Collection of Chris Royer

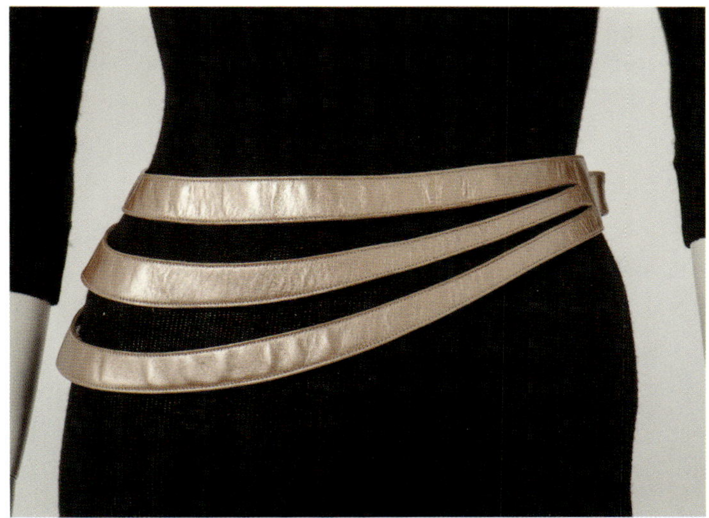

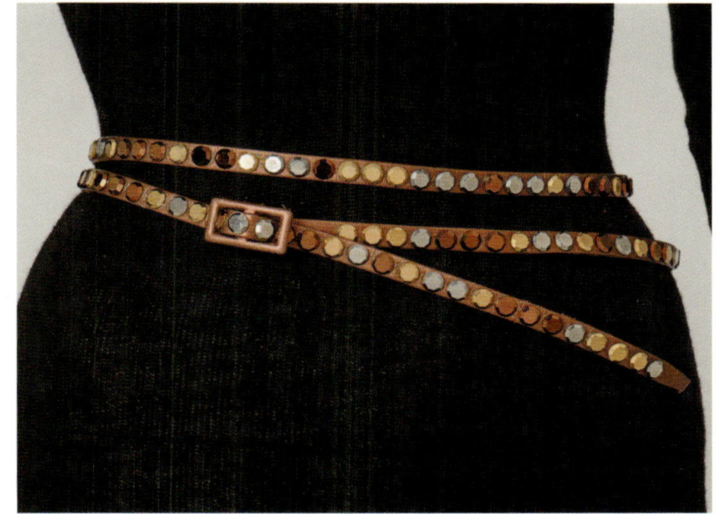

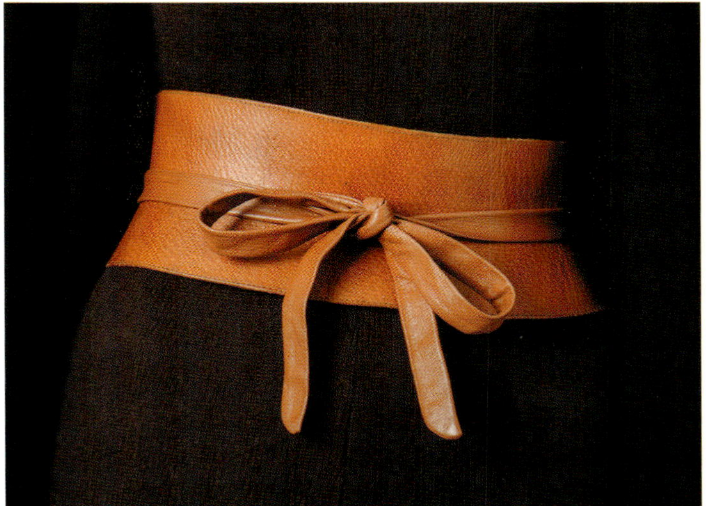

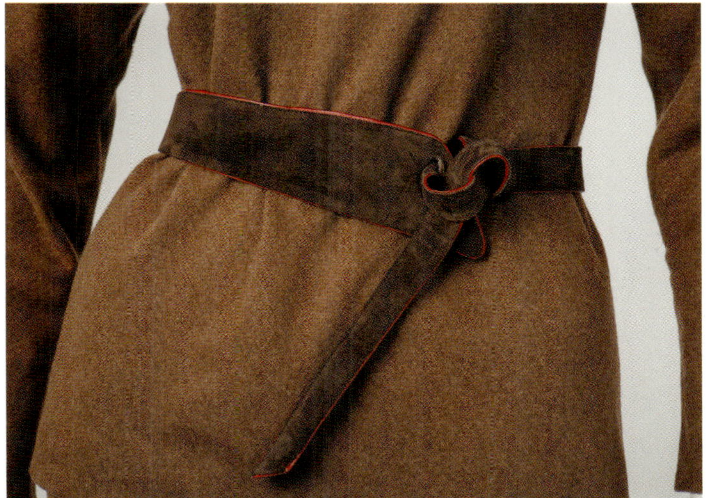

TOP LEFT
Halston
Three-tiered contoured hip belt with slip-through back tie, Metallic Leather Belt Series, Made to Order, 1982–83
Metallic leather
Photograph by Eve Prime
Collection of Chris Royer

BOTTOM LEFT
Halston
Corset-style contour belt with obi tie, Made to Order, 1983
Leather
Photograph by Eve Prime
Collection of Chris Royer

TOP RIGHT
Halston
Double-wrap belt, Crystal Skinny Belt Series, Made to Order, 1982
Metallic leather with applied multicolored crystals
Photograph by Eve Prime
Collection of Chris Royer

BOTTOM RIGHT
Halston
Reversible belt with slip-through tie, Reversible Belt Series, Made to Order, 1983
Suede (shown), leather (reverse)
Photograph by Eve Prime
Collection of Chris Royer

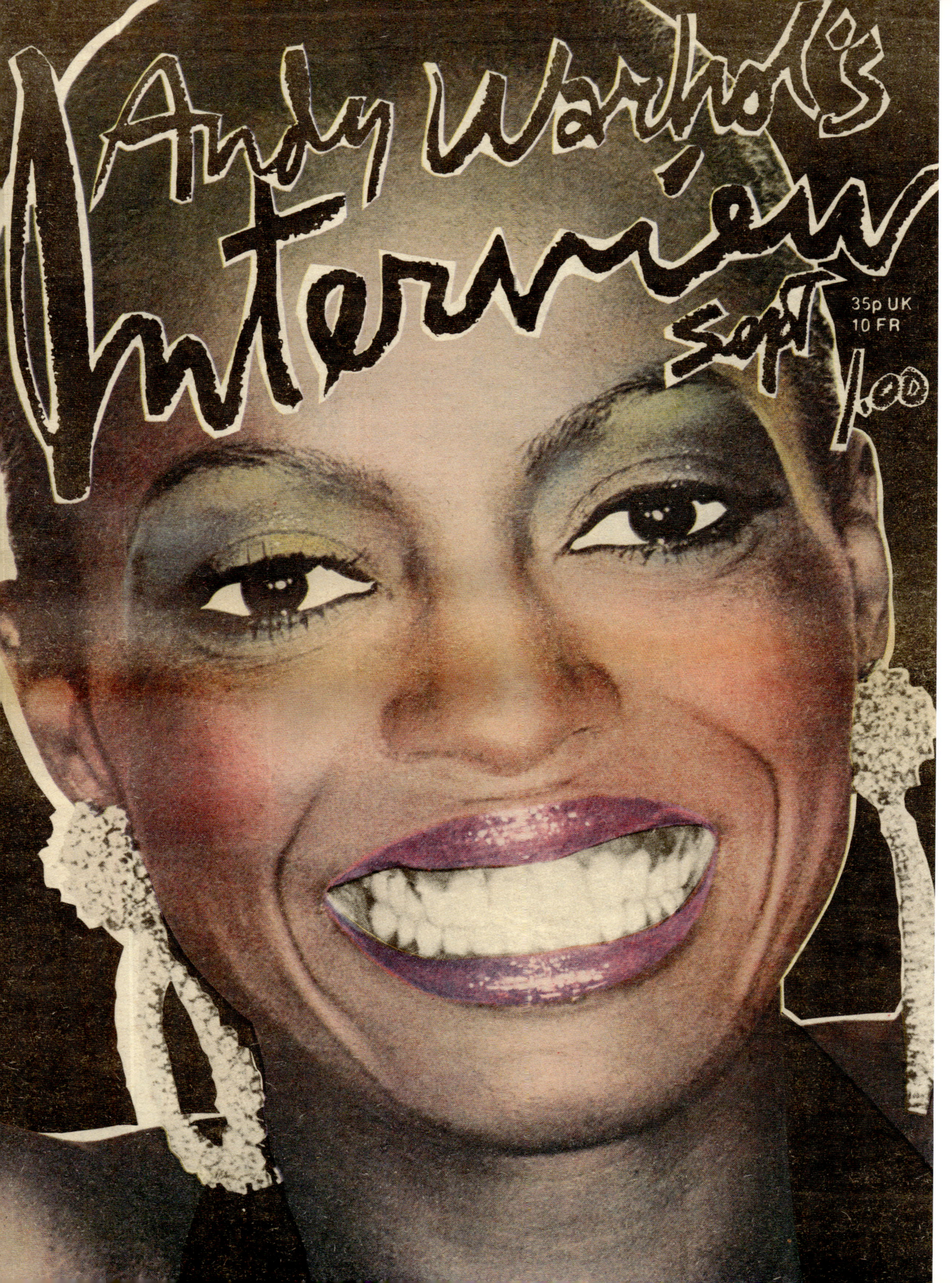

Andy Warhol's
Interview
Sept
35p UK
10 FR
1.00

INTERVIEW MAGAZINE

Interview magazine was started in 1969. The original issues were devoted mainly to film, featuring Warhol's film works, those of other 1960s avant-garde filmmakers, and Hollywood movies of the 1930s and 1940s. The monthly eventually became a chronicle of the worlds of art, fashion, high society, and film. Warhol pioneered the concept of the recorded celebrity-on-celebrity interview, creating an intimate conversational style. Halston was interviewed by Pat Ast in the May 1972 issue. In addition to featuring Halston in *Interview*, Warhol made him the focus of an episode of *Fashion TV*, and he devoted an entire chapter to his friend in his book *Exposures*.

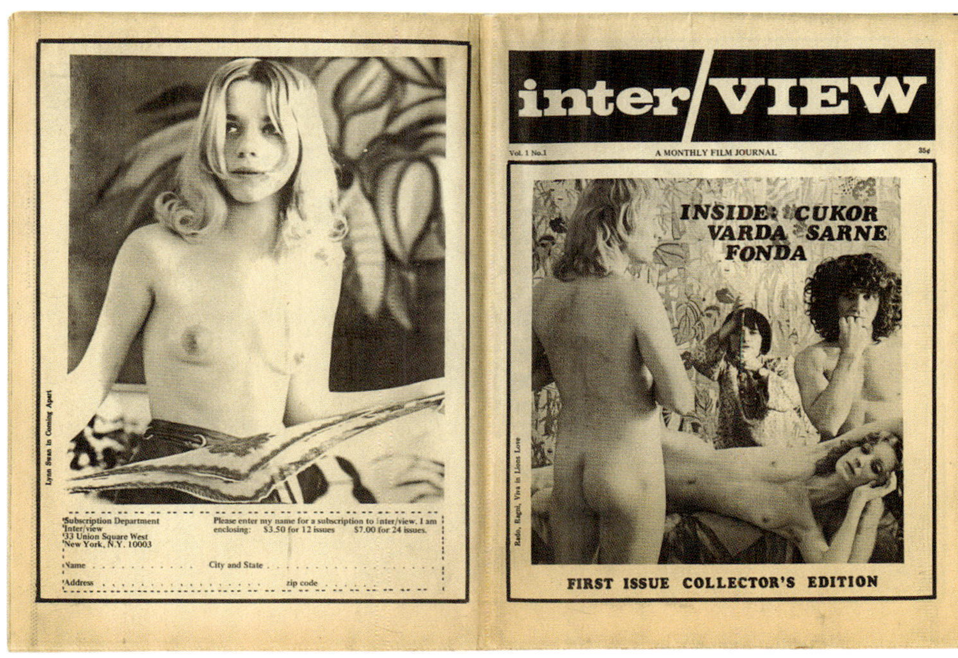

OPPOSITE
Interview, vol. 6, no. 9 (September 1976)
Cover photograph of Diana Ross by Chris von Wangenheim; cover design by Richard Bernstein
Printed ink on newsprint
15 ½ × 11 ¾ × ⅛ in. (39.4 x 29.8 x 0.3 cm)
The Andy Warhol Museum, Pittsburgh; Founding Collection, Contribution The Andy Warhol Foundation for the Visual Arts, Inc., 1998.3.2562.1
Courtesy BMP Media Holdings, LLC

ABOVE
Interview, 1969
Courtesy BMP Media Holdings, LLC

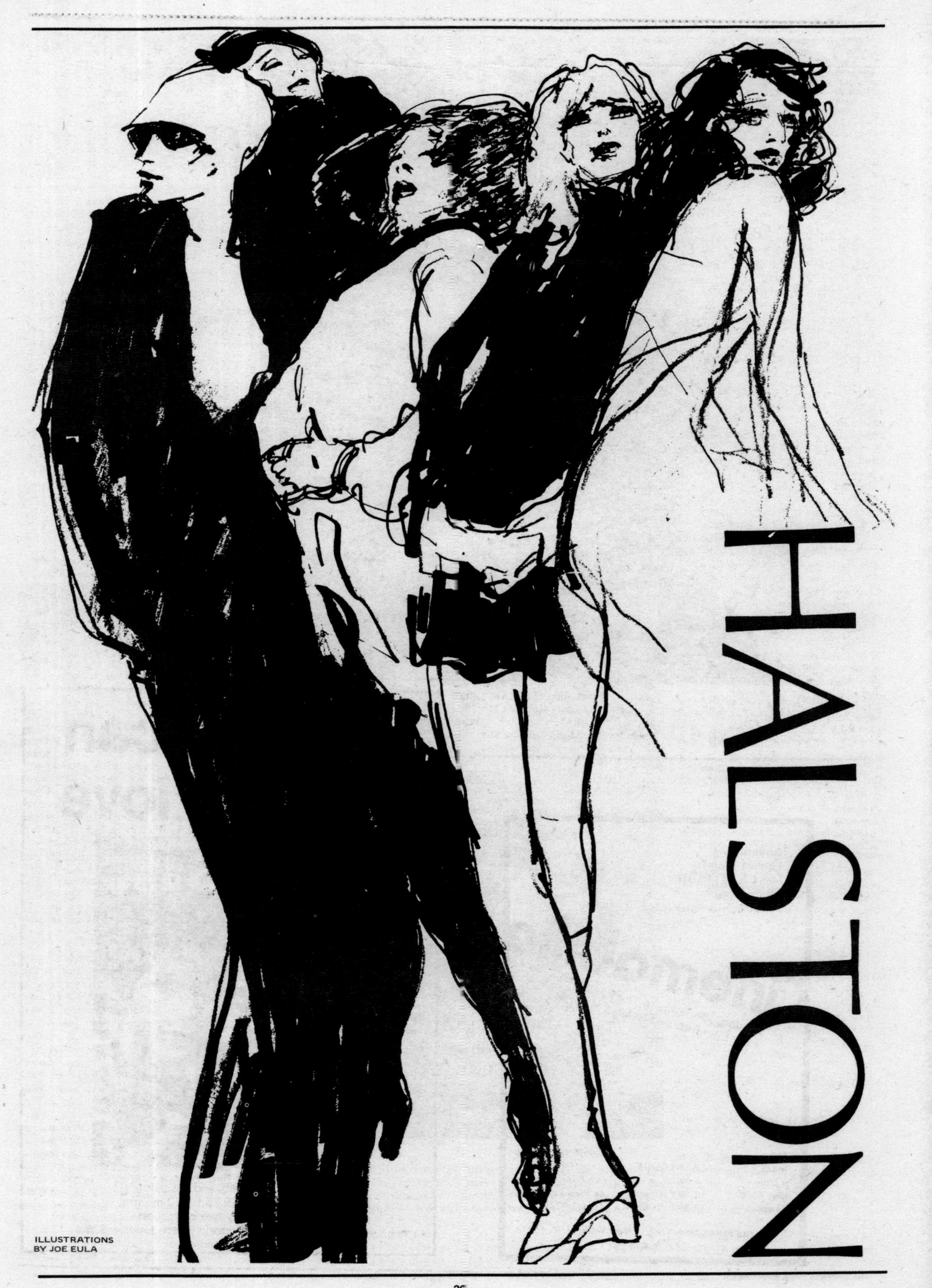
HALSTON
ILLUSTRATIONS
BY JOE EULA
26

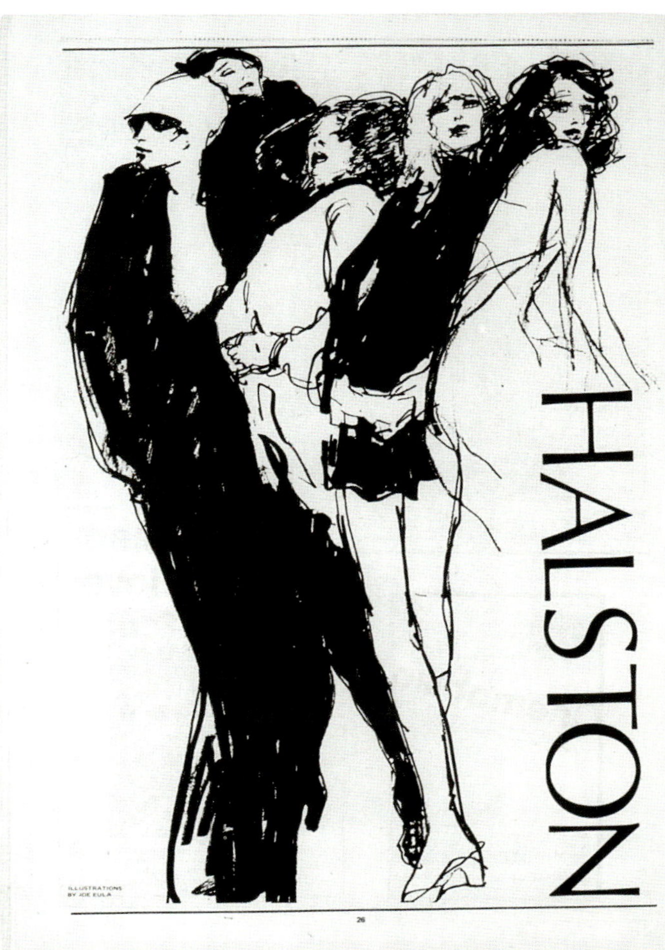

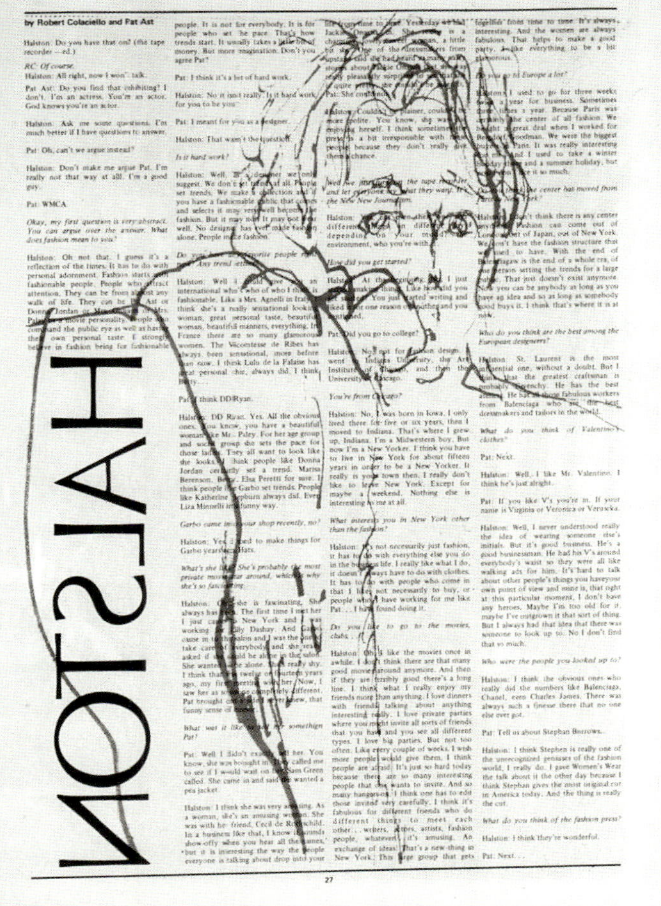

HALSTON

by Robert Colacielllo and Pat Ast

Halston: Do you have that on? (the tape recorder — ed.)

RC: Of course.

Halston: All right, now I won't talk.

Pat Ast: Do you find that inhibiting? I don't. I'm an actress. You're an actor. God knows you're an actor.

Halston: Ask me some questions. I'm much better if I have questions to answer.

Pat: Oh, can't we argue instead?

Halston: Don't make me argue Pat. I'm really not that way at alll. I'm a good guy.

Pat: WMCA.

Okay, my first question is very abstract. You can argue over the answer. What does fashion mean to you?

Halston: Oh not that. I guess it's a reflection of the times. It has to do with personal adornment. Fashion starts with fashionable people. People who attract attention. They can be from almost any walk of life. They can be Pat Ast or Donna Jordan or Mrs. [illegible] or Mrs. Paley or a movie personality. People who command the public eye as well as having their own personal taste. I strongly believe in fashion being for fashionable people. It is not for everybody. It is for people who set the pace. That's how trends start. It usually takes a little bit of money. But more imagination. Don't you agree Pat?

Pat: I think it's a lot of hard work.

Halston: No it isn't really. Is it hard work for you to be you?

Pat: I meant for you as a designer.

Halston: That wasn't the question.

Is it hard work?

Halston: Well, as a designer we only suggest. We don't set trends at all. People set trends. We make a collection and if you have a fashionable public that comes and selects it may very well become the fashion. But it may not. It may not wear well. No designer has ever made fashion alone. People make fashion.

Do you have any favorite people right now? Any trend setters?

Halston: Well I would give you an international who's who of who I think is fashionable. Like a Mrs. Agnelli in Italy. I think she's a really sensational looking woman, great personal taste, beautiful woman, beautiful manners, everything. In France there are so many glamorous women. The Vicomtesse de Ribes has always been sensational, more before than now. I think Lulu de la Falaise has great personal chic, always did. I think, Betty. . .

Pat: I think DD Ryan.

Halston: DD Ryan. Yes. All the obvious ones. You know, you have a beautiful woman like Mrs. Paley. For her age group and social group she sets the pace for those ladies. They all want to look like she looks. I think people like Donna Jordan certainly set a trend. Marisa Berenson. Betty. Elsa Peretti for sure. I think people like Garbo set trends. People like Katherine Hepburn always did. Even Liza Minnelli in a funny way.

Garbo came into your shop recently, no?

Halston: Yes I used to make things for Garbo years ago. Hats.

What's she like? She's probably the most private movie star around, which is why she's so fascinating.

Halston: Oh, she is fascinating. She always has been. The first time I met her I just came to New York and I was working for Lilly Dashay. And Garbo came in to the salon and I was the one to take care of everybody and she really asked if she could be alone in the salon. She wanted to be alone. She's really shy. I think that was twelve or fourteen years ago, my first meeting with her. Now, I saw her as someone completely different. Pat brought out a side I never knew, that funny sense of humor.

What was it like to sell her somethign Pat?

Pat: Well I didn't exactly sell her. You know, she was brought in. They called me to see if I would wait on her. Sam Green called. She came in and said she wanted a pea jacket.

Halston: I think she was very amusing. As a woman, she's an amusing woman. She was with her friend, Cecil de Rothschild. In a business like that, I know it sounds show-offy when you hear all the names, but it is interesting the way the people everyone is talking about drop into your life from time to time. Yesterday we had Jackie Onassis. She is a charming lovely woman, a little bit shy. One of the dressmakers from upstairs said she had heard so many stories about Jackie O and she was really pleasantly surprised . . . she is quite . . .

Pat: She certainly . . .

Halston: Couldn't be plainer, couldn't be more polite. You know, she was enjoying herself. I think sometimes the press is a bit irresponsible with those people because they don't really give them a chance.

Well we just turn on the tape recorder and let everyone say what they want. It's the New New Journalism.

Halston: . . . different . . . in different . . . depending on your mood, . . . environment, who you're with. . .

How did you get started?

Halston: At the beginning . . . I just started making things. Like how did you get started? You just started writing and liked it for one reason or another and you continued.

Pat: Did you go to college?

Halston: No, not for fashion design. I went to Indiana University, the Art Institute of Chicago, and then the University of Chicago.

You're from Chicago?

Halston: No, I was born in Iowa. I only lived there for five or six years, then I moved to Indiana. That's where I grew up, Indiana. I'm a Midwestern boy. But now I'm a New Yorker. I think you have to live in New York for about fifteen years in order to be a New Yorker. It really is your town then. I really don't like to leave New York. Except for maybe a weekend. Nothing else is interesting to me at all.

What interests you in New York other than the fashion?

Halston: It's not necessarily just fashion, it has to do with everything else you do in the business life. I really like what I do, it doesn't always have to do with clothes. It has to do with people who come in that I like, not necessarily to buy, or people who I have working for me like Pat. . . I have found doing it.

Do you like to go to the movies, clubs. . .

Halston: Oh, I like the movies once in awhile. I don't think there are that many good movies around anymore. And then if they are terribly good there's a long line. I think what I really enjoy my friends more than anything. I love dinners with friends talking about anything interesting really. I love private parties where you might invite all sorts of friends that you have and you see all different types. I love big parties. But not too often. Like every couple of weeks. I wish more people would give them. I think people are afraid. It's just so hard today because there are so many interesting people that one wants to invite. And so many hangers-on. I think one has to edit those invited very carefully. I think it's fabulous for different friends who do different things to meet each other . . . writers, actors, artists, fashion people, whatever . . . it's amusing. An exchange of ideas. That's a new thing in New York. This large group that gets together from time to time. It's always interesting. And the women are always fabulous. That helps to make a good party. I like everything to be a bit glamorous.

Do you go to Europe a lot?

Halston: I used to go for three weeks twice a year for business. Sometimes three times a year. Because Paris was certainly the center of all fashion. We bought a great deal when I worked for Bergdorf Goodman. We were the biggest buyers in Paris. It was really interesting for me. And I used to take a winter holiday there and a summer holiday, but now I don't like it so much.

Do you think the center has moved from Paris to New York?

Halston: I don't think there is any center anymore. Fashion can come out of London, out of Japan, out of New York. We don't have the fashion structure that we used to have. With the end of Balenciaga is the end of a whole era, of one person setting the trends for a large public. That just doesn't exist anymore. Now you can be anybody as long as you have an idea and so as long as somebody good buys it. I think that's where it is at now.

Who do you think are the best among the European designers?

Halston: St. Laurent is the most influential one, without a doubt. But I think that the greatest craftsman is probably Givenchy. He has the best atelier. He has all those fabulous workers from Balenciaga who are the best dressmakers and tailors in the world.

What do you think of Valentino's clothes?

Pat: Next.

Halston: Well, I like Mr. Valentino. I think he's just alright.

Pat: If you like V's you're in. If your name is Virginia or Veronica or Veruschka.

Halston: Well, I never understood really the idea of wearing someone else's initials. But it's good business. He's a good businessman. He had his V's around everybody's waist so they were all like walking ads for him. It's hard to talk about other people's things you haveyour own point of view and mine is, that right at this particular moment, I don't have any heroes. Maybe I'm too old for it, maybe I've outgrown it that sort of thing. But I always had that idea that there was someone to look up to. No I don't find that so much.

Who were the people you looked up to?

Halston: I think the obvious ones who really did the numbers like Balenciaga, Chanel, even Charles James. There was always such a finesse there that no one else ever got.

Pat: Tell us about Stephan Burrows.

Halston: I think Stephen is really one of the unrecognized geniuses of the fashion world, I really do. I gave Women's Wear the talk about it the other day because I think Stephan gives the most original cut in America today. And the thing is really the cut.

What do you think of the fashion press?

Halston: I think they're wonderful.

Pat: Next . . .

27

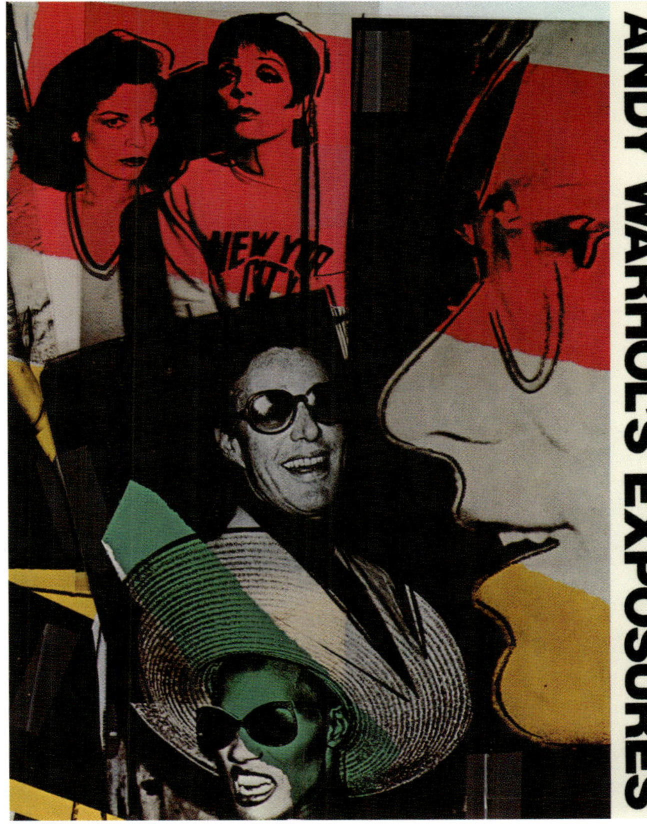

OPPOSITE AND ABOVE
Interview, May 1972
Courtesy BMP Media Holdings, LLC

RIGHT
Andy Warhol with Bob Colacello
Andy Warhol's Exposures, 1979
Published by Grosset & Dunlap,
New York

STUDIO 54

OPPOSITE LEFT
Andy Warhol
Studio 54, 1978
Acrylic and silkscreen ink on linen
26 × 14 × ¾ in. (66 × 35.6 × 1.9 cm)
The Andy Warhol Museum, Pittsburgh; Founding Collection, Contribution The Andy Warhol Foundation for the Visual Arts, Inc., 1998.1.428

OPPOSITE RIGHT (FROM TOP TO BOTTOM)
Andy Warhol
Fred Hughes and Bianca Jagger, ca. 1979
Gelatin silver print
8 × 10 in. (20.3 × 25.4 cm)
The Andy Warhol Museum, Pittsburgh; Contribution The Andy Warhol Foundation for the Visual Arts, Inc., 2001.2.652

Andy Warhol
Halston and Steve Rubell, ca. 1980
Gelatin silver print
8 × 10 in. (20.3 × 25.4 cm)
The Andy Warhol Foundation for the Visual Arts, Inc., FL06.01092

Andy Warhol
Halston and Unidentified Man in Drag, November 3, 1980
Gelatin silver print
8 × 10 in. (20.3 × 25.4 cm)
The Andy Warhol Foundation for the Visual Arts, Inc., FL06.02624

Andy Warhol
Liza Minnelli, 1978
Gelatin silver print
8 × 9⅞ in. (20.3 × 25.1 cm)
The Andy Warhol Museum, Pittsburgh; Contribution The Andy Warhol Foundation for the Visual Arts, Inc., 2001.2.814

Andy Warhol
Andy Warhol and Unidentified Man (detail), n.d.
Gelatin silver print
8 × 10 in. (20.3 × 25.4 cm)
The Andy Warhol Museum, Pittsburgh; Contribution The Andy Warhol Foundation for the Visual Arts, Inc., 2001.2.185

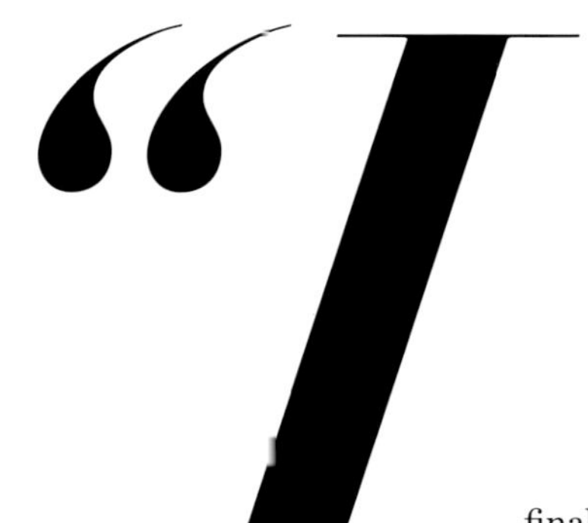

finally decided what I'm going to give all the Halston family for Christmas—Halston and Steve and Dr. Giller and Bianca—paintings of a free drink ticket from 54."

—Andy Warhol, *Diaries*, December 19, 1978

"Studio 54 was such an interesting phenomenon, a sociological phenomenon where people on all levels of society got along together. So I changed my working patterns a bit to see that."

—Halston, quoted by Lisa Belkin, *New York Times*, March 15, 1987

"Every day, I can't wait for the night."

—Steve Rubell, quoted in *Interview*, June 1978

Part impresario, part entrepreneur, part circus master, Steve Rubell and his business partner, Ian Schrager, transformed a former CBS television studio on West 54th Street into the internationally known nightclub whose gilded, drug-fueled energy defined the late 1970s in New York. Opening in April 1977, Studio 54 emerged almost immediately as the late-night playground synonymous with glamorous hedonism.

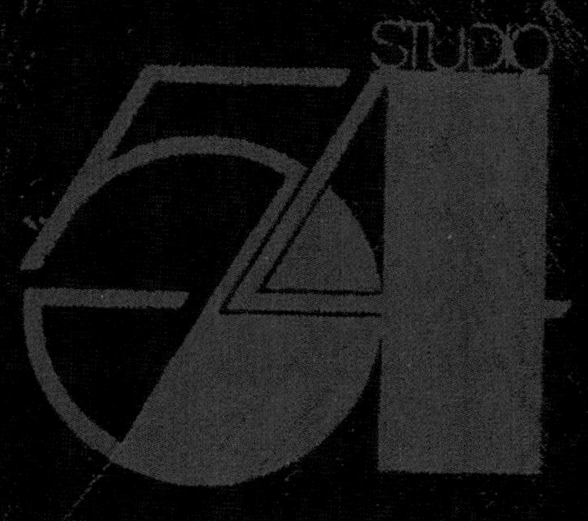

VIP
COMPLIMENTARY
DRINKS
№ 13110

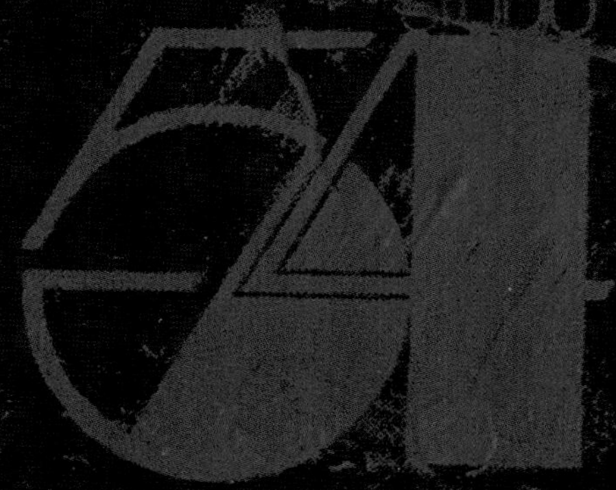

VIP
COMPLIMENTARY
DRINKS
№ 13111

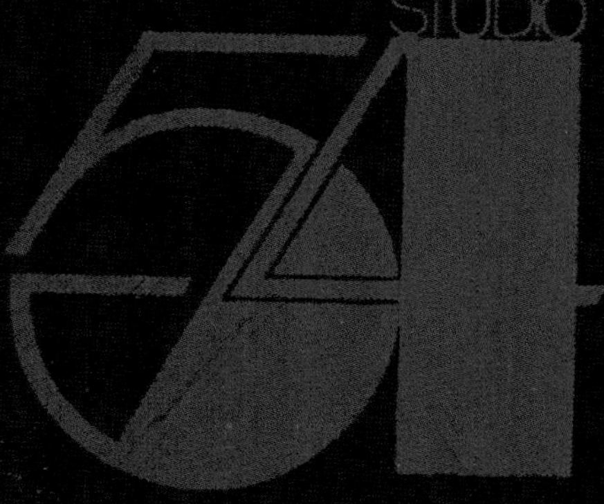

VIP
COMPLIMENTARY
DRINKS
№ 13112

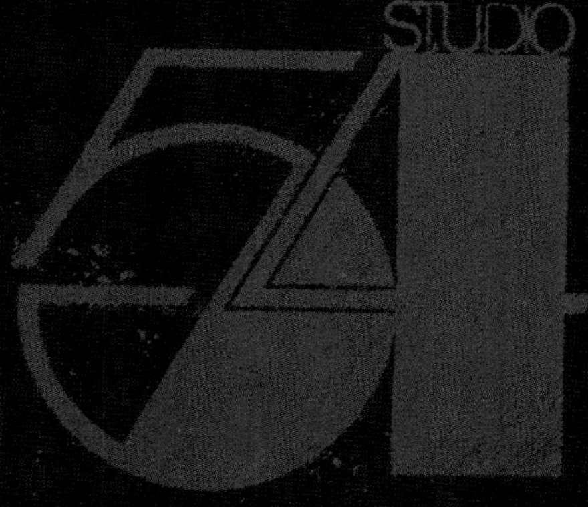

VIP
COMPLIMENTARY
DRINKS
№ 13113

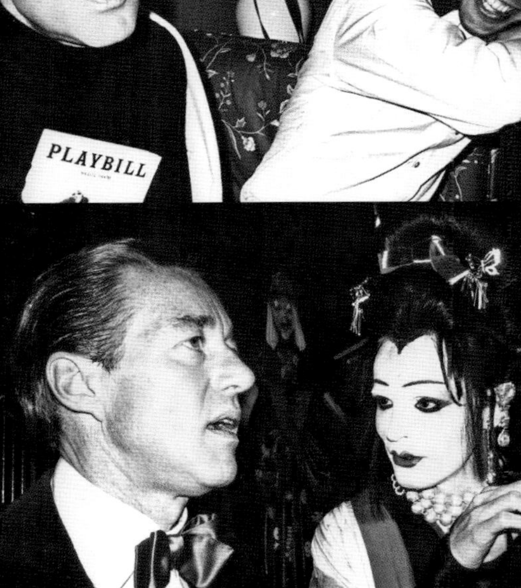

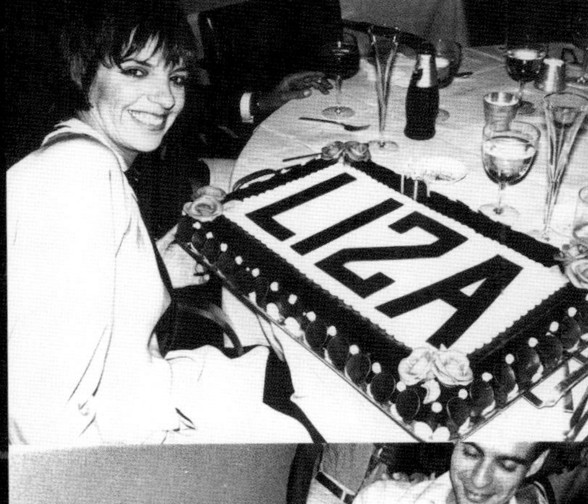

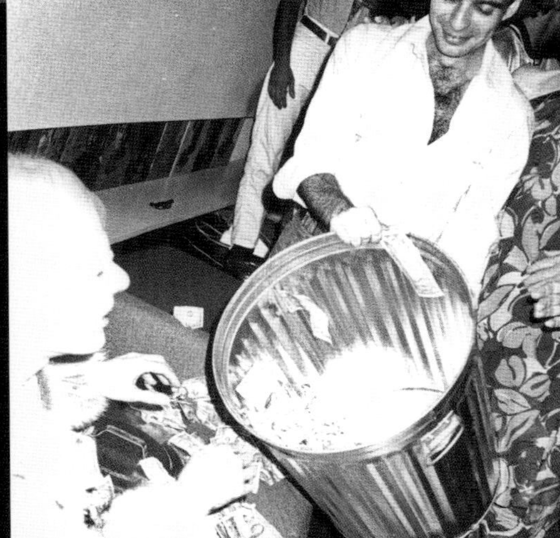

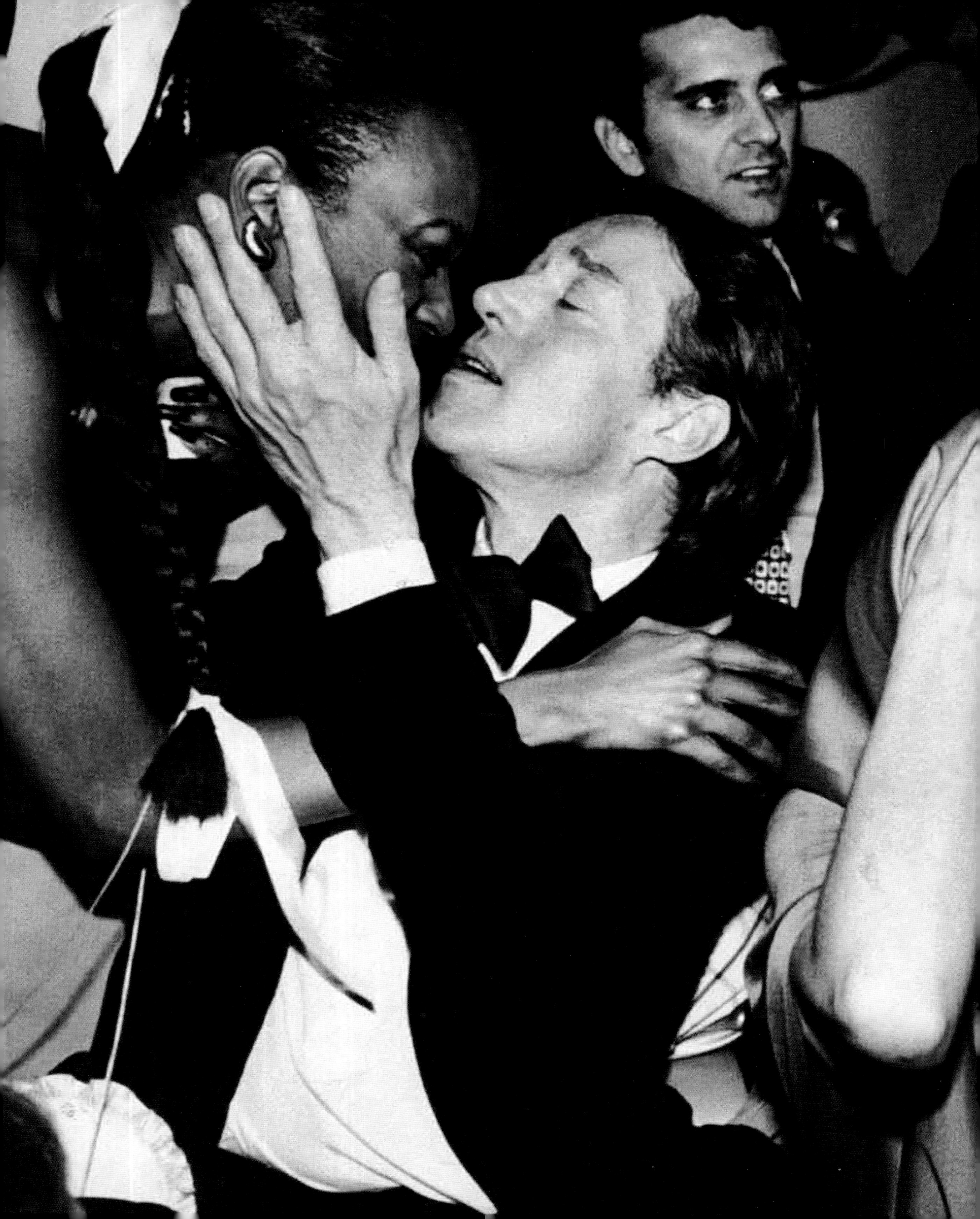

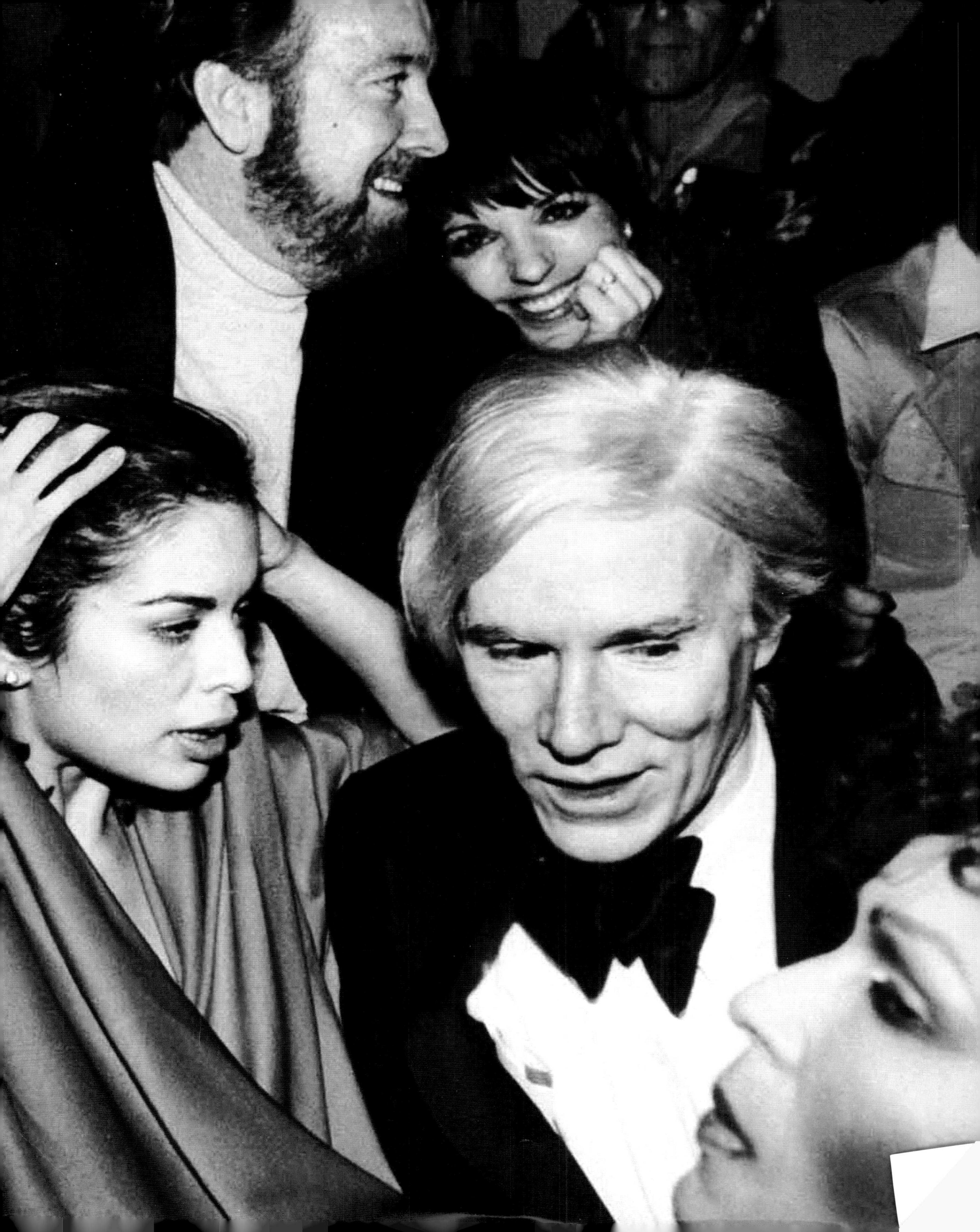

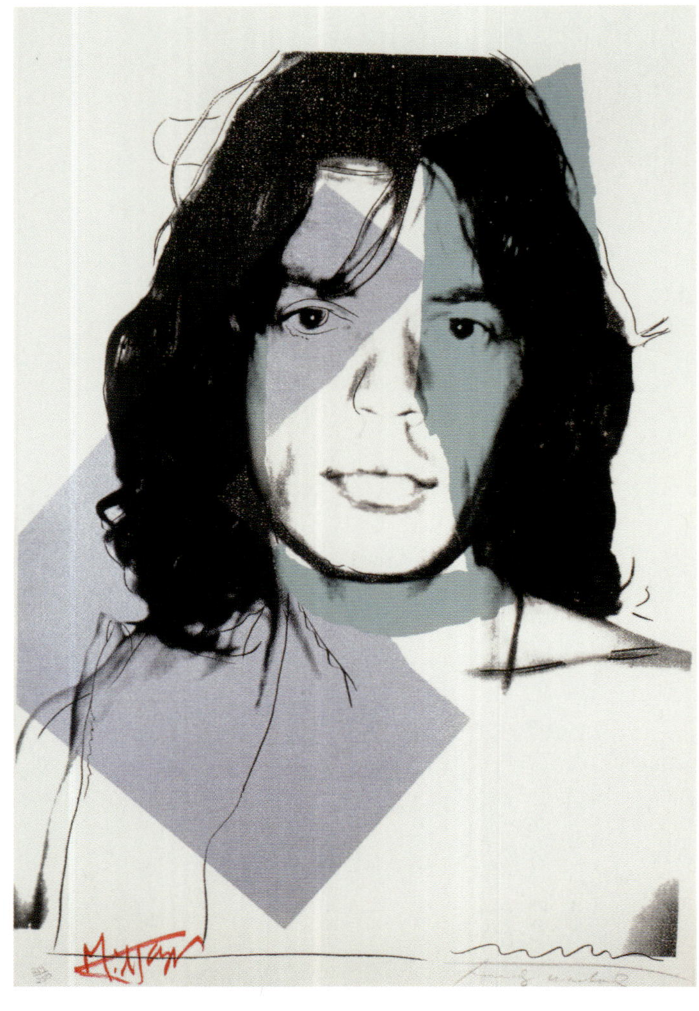

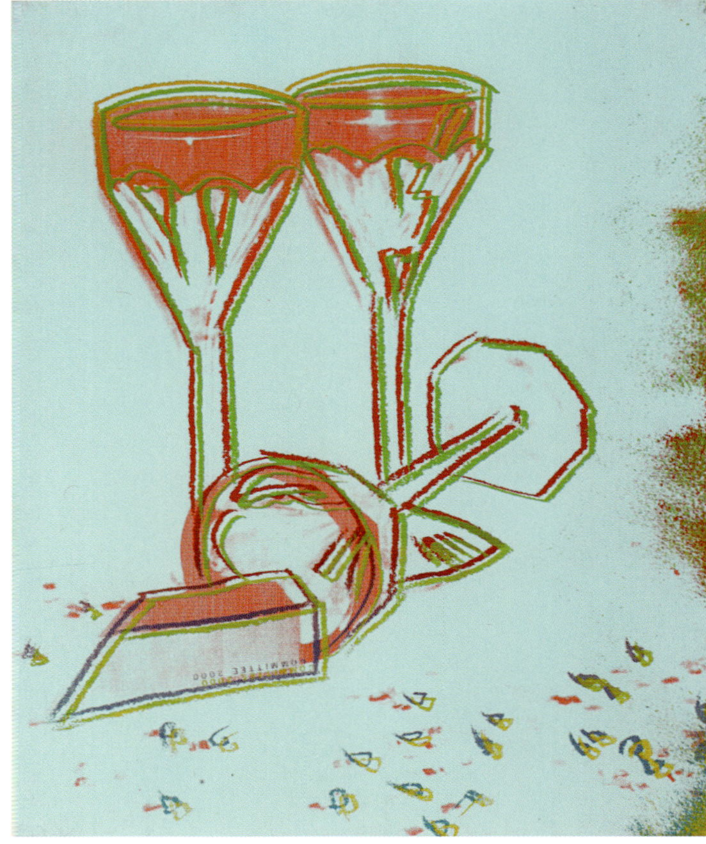

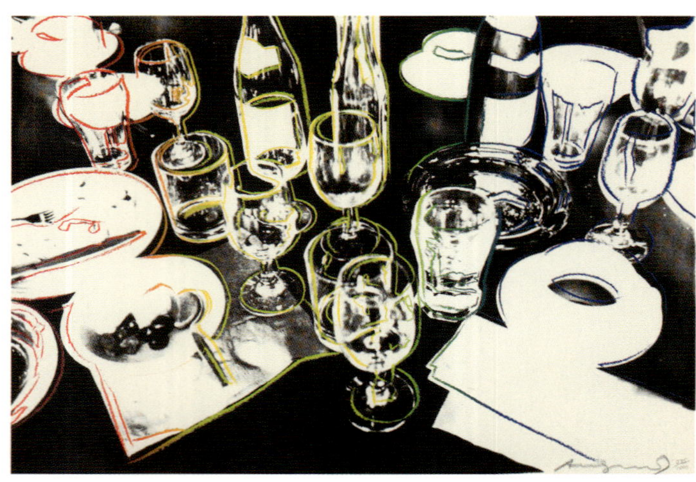

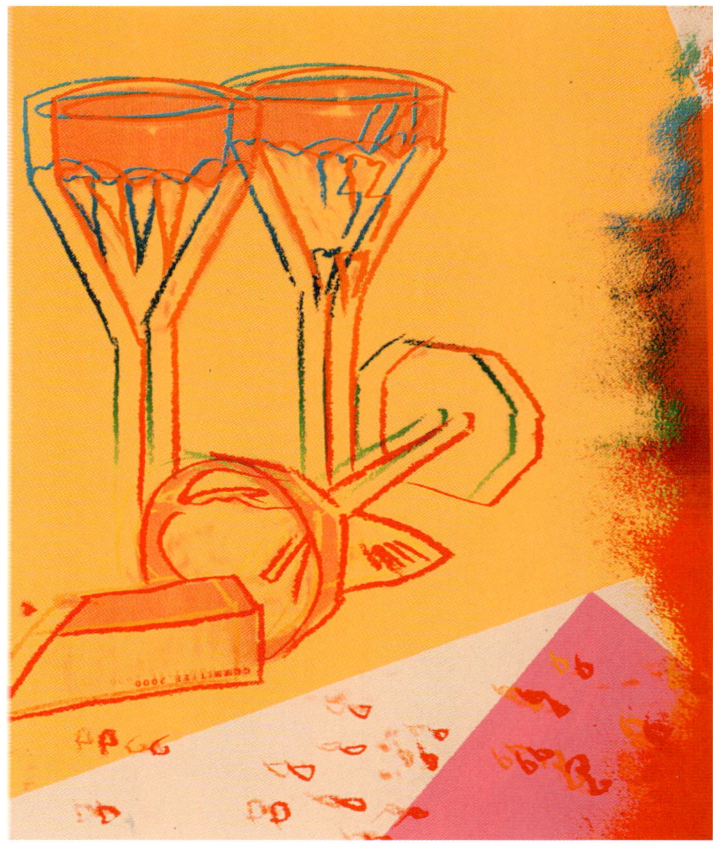

PREVIOUS SPREAD
New Year's Eve party at Studio 54, December 31, 1974: (left to right) Halston, Bianca Jagger, Jack Haley Jr. (background), Liza Minnelli (background), Andy Warhol
Photograph by Robin Platzer
Time & Life Pictures/Getty Images

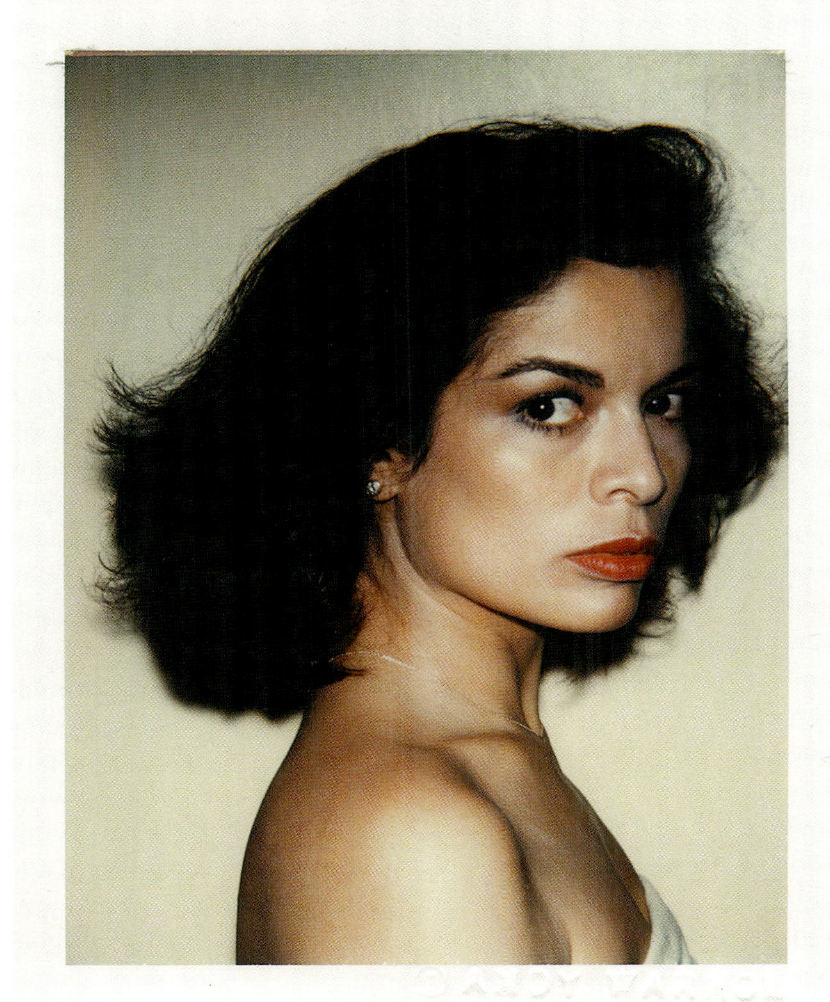

To celebrate Bianca Jagger's twenty-seventh birthday in May 1977, Halston requested that Studio 54's doors be opened on a Monday night so he could host a surprise party for his close friend, the estranged wife of Mick Jagger. The now-legendary event at the recently opened club helped launch Studio 54 as the red-hot center of New York's late-night club scene. Rubell and Schrager arranged for a white horse to be led onto the dance floor by a black couple sheathed only in paint and glitter. Bianca Jagger, wearing a white off-the-shoulder Halston dress, spontaneously mounted the white horse and rode it a short distance. A nearly naked Victor Hugo grabbed the lead. Balloons, confetti, and feathers floated down from the ceiling, and lightbulbs spelled out her name in illuminated letters along one wall.

Many parties attended by Halston and Warhol followed at Studio 54, firmly putting the club at the forefront of New York's social life. The two men, along with Bianca Jagger, Truman Capote, and Liza Minnelli, shaped the core of Studio 54's celebrity guest list.

OPPOSITE TOP LEFT
Andy Warhol
Mick Jagger, 1975
Screen print on Arches Aquarelle (Rough) paper
43½ × 29 in. (110.5 × 73.7 cm)
The Andy Warhol Museum, Pittsburgh; Founding Collection, Contribution The Andy Warhol Foundation for the Visual Arts, Inc., 1998.1.2412.1

OPPOSITE BOTTOM LEFT
Andy Warhol
After the Party, 1979
Screen print on Arches 88 paper
21½ × 30½ in. (54.6 × 77.5 cm)
The Andy Warhol Museum, Pittsburgh; Founding Collection, Contribution The Andy Warhol Foundation for the Visual Arts, Inc., 1998.1.2431

OPPOSITE TOP RIGHT
Andy Warhol
Committee 2000, 1982
Acrylic and silkscreen ink on linen
20 × 16 in. (50.8 × 40.6 cm)
The Andy Warhol Museum, Pittsburgh; Founding Collection, Contribution The Andy Warhol Foundation for the Visual Arts, Inc., 1998.1.387

OPPOSITE BOTTOM RIGHT
Andy Warhol
Committee 2000, 1982
Acrylic and silkscreen ink on linen
20 × 16 in. (50.8 × 40.6 cm)
The Andy Warhol Museum, Pittsburgh; Founding Collection, Contribution The Andy Warhol Foundation for the Visual Arts, Inc., 1998.1.388

ABOVE
Andy Warhol
Bianca Jagger, 1979
Polaroid™ Polacolor Type 108
4¼ × 3⅜ in. (10.8 × 8.6 cm)
The Andy Warhol Museum, Pittsburgh; Contribution The Andy Warhol Foundation for the Visual Arts, Inc., 2000.2.347

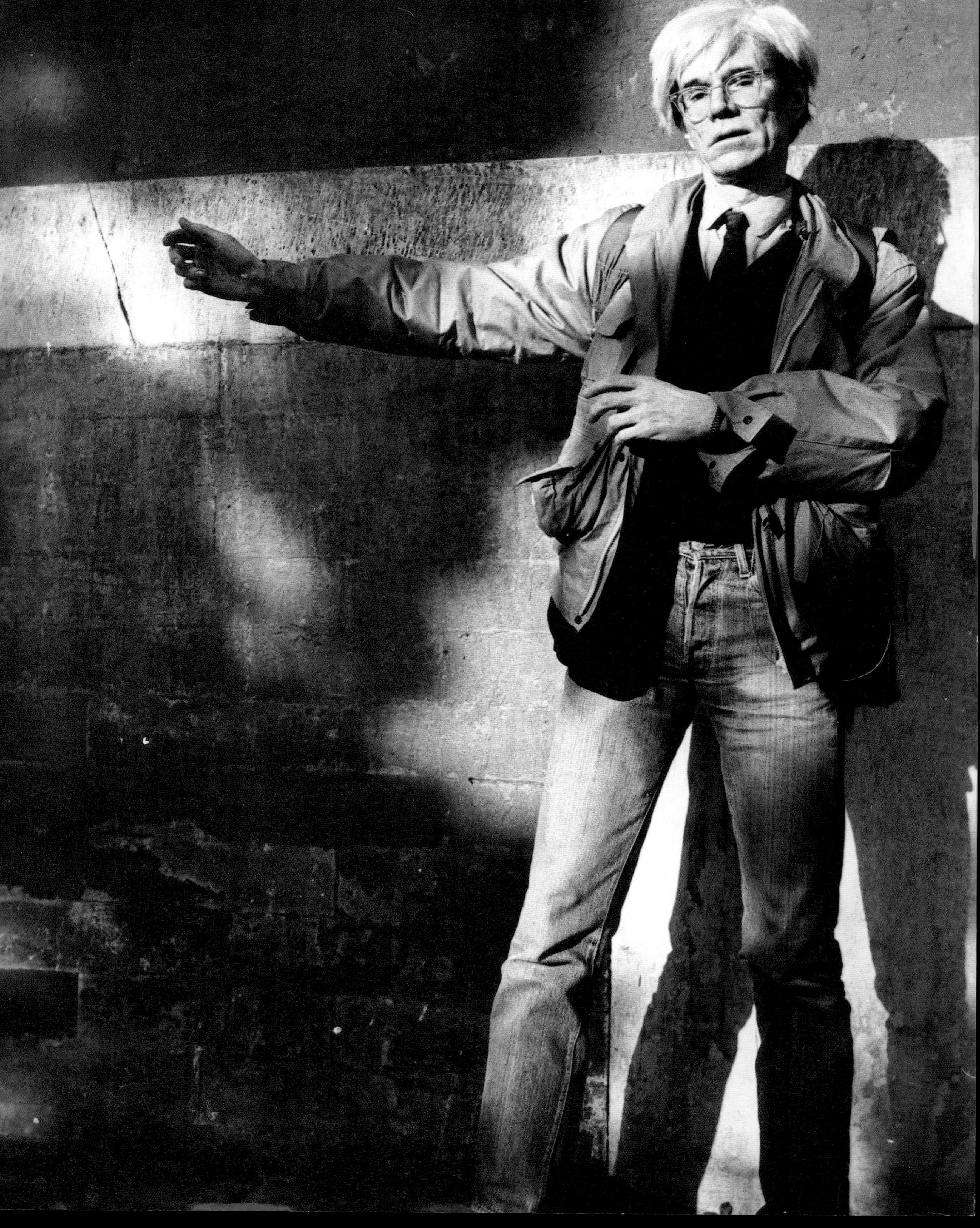

1980s

1980s

RIGHT
Andy Warhol
Camouflage, 1987
Screen print on Lenox Museum Board
38 x 38 in. (96.5 x 96.5 cm)
The Andy Warhol Museum, Pittsburgh; Founding Collection, Contribution The Andy Warhol Foundation for the Visual Arts, Inc., 1998.1.2503.3

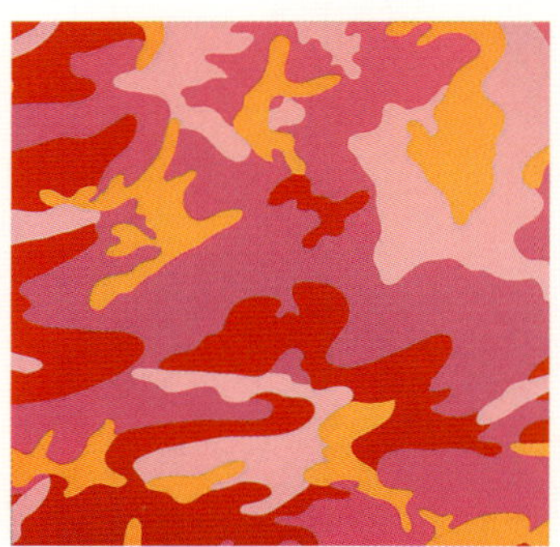

WARHOL

1980
Develops *Andy Warhol's T.V.*, directed by Don Munroe.

POPism: The Warhol '60s, by Warhol and Pat Hackett, is published by Harcourt Brace Jovanovich.

Warhol's photographs are exhibited at the Museum Ludwig in Cologne and the Stedelijk Museum in Amsterdam.

In Vatican City, Warhol and Fred Hughes briefly meet Pope John Paul II.

Paints a diamond-dust portrait of Martha Graham that winds up in Halston's collection.

Photographs his collection of shoes, including many Halston designs, for his series of diamond-dust *Shoe* paintings. Halston purchases a number of these paintings and later donates them to Des Moines Art Center.

1981
Makes *Dollar Signs*, *Knives*, *Crosses*, and *Guns* works.

Produces and stars in three one-minute episodes of *Andy Warhol's T.V.*, directed by Don Munroe, for *Saturday Night Live*.

Begins to be represented by the Zoli modeling agency.

HALSTON

1980
Becomes the first American designer to travel and show in the People's Republic of China. Halston's around-the-world tour begins in September and includes stops in Los Angeles, Tokyo, Kyoto, Beijing, Shanghai, and Paris. He designs coordinating outfits for his entourage of twenty-eight people and choreographs wardrobe changes, often requiring several in one day. A television crew films throughout the trip but the footage is never aired.

Halston Sportswear signs a contract with Kosugi Sangyo Co. Ltd. to manufacture and distribute Halston Sportswear in Japan.

1981
May 2: Appears on the popular ABC television show *The Love Boat*. It is a two-hour "fashion cruise" special, in which he guest stars with the designers Gloria Vanderbilt, Geoffrey Beene, and Bob Mackie.

October 16: "A Halston Night for Martha Graham," a major publicity and charity event held at Bloomingdale's in New York, raises $75,000 for the Martha Graham Center of Contemporary Dance. Halston stages a fashion show for the dinner entertainment, featuring his latest resort collection and costumes he had designed for Martha Graham productions. Members of the dance company model the costumes, Warhol and Victor Hugo model colored Halston jackets, and the Halstonettes model the fashions. Warhol stays onstage to photograph the models as they come down the runway.

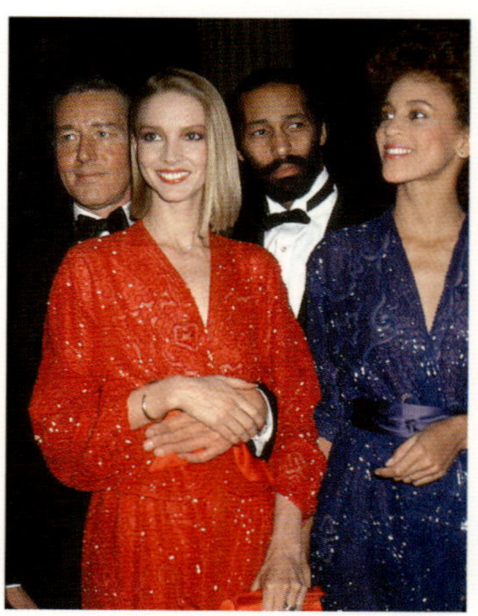

LEFT
Halston with Karen Bjornson, Alva Chinn, and Chinn's former husband
Photograph by Rose Hartman

PREVIOUS SPREAD, LEFT
Andy Warhol
China (Andy Warhol at the Great Wall), 1982
Gelatin silver print
10 × 7 15/16 in. (25.4 × 20.2 cm)
The Andy Warhol Museum, Pittsburgh; Contribution The Andy Warhol Foundation for the Visual Arts, Inc., 2001.2.865

PREVIOUS SPREAD, RIGHT
Andy Warhol
Halston (detail), n.d.
Gelatin silver print
10 x 8 in. (25.4 x 20.3 cm)
The Andy Warhol Museum, Pittsburgh; Contribution The Andy Warhol Foundation for the Visual Arts, Inc., 2001.2.332

RIGHT
Andy Warhol
The Last Supper, 1986
Acrylic and silkscreen ink on linen
78 × 306 × 2 in. (198.1 × 777.2 × 5.1 cm)
The Andy Warhol Museum, Pittsburgh; Founding Collection, Contribution The Andy Warhol Foundation for the Visual Arts, Inc., 1998.1.355

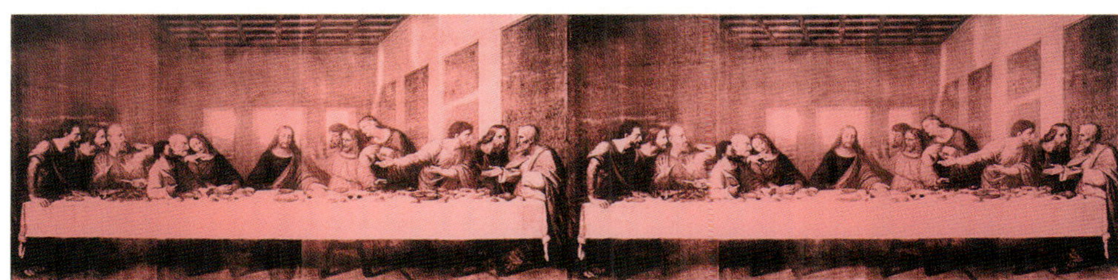

1982

Travels to Hong Kong and Beijing with Fred Hughes and the photographer Christopher Makos.

The Whitney Museum of American Art convinces Warhol to embark on the preservation of his films from the 1960s. In collaboration with the Museum of Modern Art, preservation work on the films commences a few years later.

1983

During this period, Warhol begins a series of works, many of them painted by hand, based on advertisements and corporate logos.

Warhol, Jean-Michel Basquiat, and Francesco Clemente begin collaborating on paintings. Warhol and Basquiat become close friends and work together into 1985.

Appears in a Japanese television commercial for TDK.

1984

With Don Munroe, makes a music video for the Cars' "Hello Again." The video also features Warhol.

The exhibition *Collaborations: Jean-Michel Basquiat, Francesco Clemente, Andy Warhol* is shown at the Bruno Bischofberger Gallery in Zurich.

Moves the Factory and the *Interview* offices to a former Consolidated Edison building at 22 East 33rd Street.

1985

Makes *Absolut Vodka* paintings, which are used in "Absolut Warhol" advertisements, the first in a series created by artists.

Exhibits his *Invisible Sculpture*, consisting of a pedestal, a wall label, and Warhol himself in a showcase, at the nightclub Area. An earlier version consists of motion detectors and alarms.

Andy Warhol's Fifteen Minutes, directed by Don Munroe, airs on MTV from 1985 to 1987.

1982

January: After years of renting Warhol's beachfront house in Montauk, Halston purchases one hundred acres in Montauk with Lauren Hutton. He continues to rent Warhol's house for several more years because his property does not have a house on it.

February: Marisa Berenson, wearing a pink Halston gown, marries Richard Golub in Halston's Olympic Tower showrooms. Warhol attends the ceremony.

September: Announces a six-year, multimillion-dollar licensing deal with JCPenney to design lower-priced fashion for men, women, children, and the home, under the Halston III label.

1983

June 7: Selects the American Museum of Natural History in New York City as the venue for his first runway show for Halston III women's collection for JCPenney.

June 24: Hosts his brother, Bob Frowick, at Warhol's Montauk house. Warhol, who is a guest at the same time, notes in his diary that Bob is there with his wife and children. The children are wearing clothes from Halston's new JCPenney line.

July: Norton Simon Industries is acquired by Esmark, Inc.

Commissions Warhol to create and illustrate a series of four advertisements, each promoting a different category of his licensed fashion and cosmetics lines.

1984

May: Esmark is acquired by Beatrice Foods, Inc.

July: Begins a two-week vacation and never returns to work in his Olympic Tower offices.

October: Tries unsuccessfully to buy back his company.

Continues to design for family and friends.

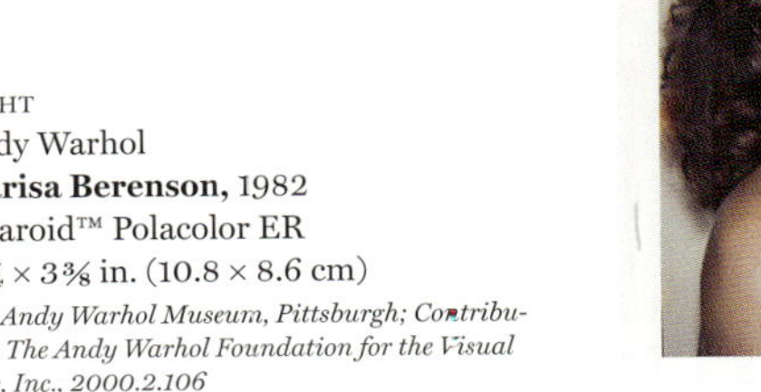

RIGHT
Andy Warhol
Marisa Berenson, 1982
Polaroid™ Polacolor ER
4¼ × 3⅜ in. (10.8 × 8.6 cm)
The Andy Warhol Museum, Pittsburgh; Contribution The Andy Warhol Foundation for the Visual Arts, Inc., 2000.2.106

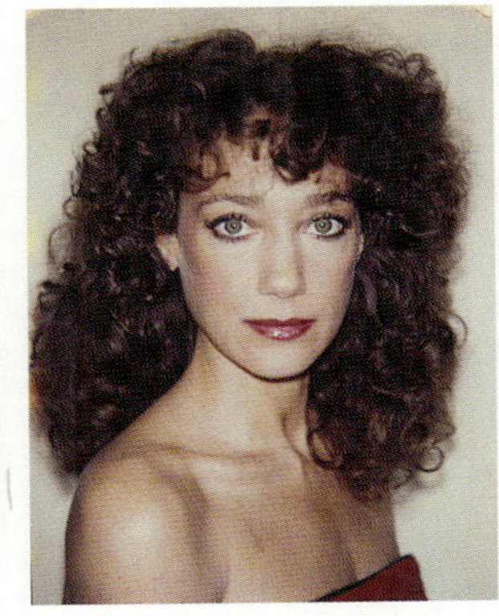

1980s

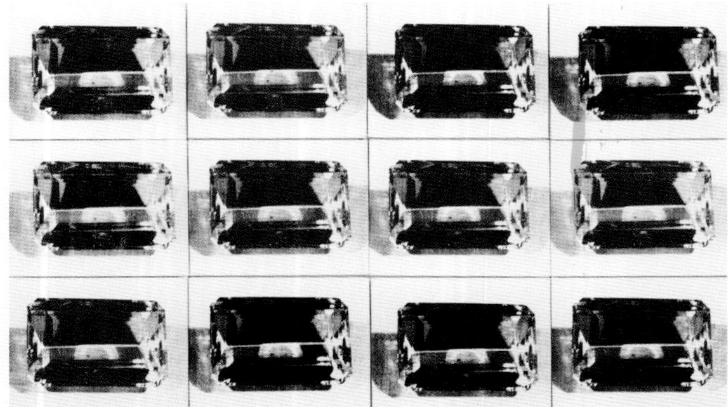

America, with photographs and text by Warhol, is published by Harper and Row.

Appears as a guest star in the 200th episode of the television program *The Love Boat*. Is also featured in a television commercial for Diet Coke.

1986

Makes *Last Supper* and *Camouflage* paintings. Also makes *Self-Portrait* paintings, which are exhibited at the Anthony d'Offay Gallery in London.

Options film and television rights to Tama Janowitz's book *Slaves of New York*.

1987

Sewn Photographs are shown at the Robert Miller Gallery in New York. The *Last Supper* paintings are exhibited at the Palazzo delle Stelline in Milan.

Five days before his death, Warhol models in a fashion show, which also features Miles Davis, at the Tunnel nightclub.

After suffering acute pain for several days, Warhol has gallbladder surgery at New York Hospital. The operation is successful, but complications during recovery cause his death on February 22. He is buried near his parents in St. John Chrysostom Byzantine Catholic Cemetery in Pittsburgh.

1988

The public auction of Warhol's estate is held at Sotheby's in New York over a ten-day period. More than $25 million is raised to benefit the Andy Warhol Foundation for the Visual Arts, Inc., as required by Warhol's will. The five-volume slipcased catalogue becomes a collector's item.

A program of sixteen of Warhol's early films, "The Films of Andy Warhol," is shown at the Whitney Museum of American Art. At the time, these films had not been seen by the public since 1972.

1986

Beatrice is acquired by BCI Holdings in a leveraged buyout deal.

November: Revlon Group purchases Halston Enterprises and Halston Fragrances from BCI Holdings.

Halston tests positive for AIDS.

1987

Designs a pale green chiffon wedding dress for his sister, Sue. Halston returns, after thirty years, to Evansville, Illinois, to attend her wedding to Bud Watkins. Adding his own special touch, Halston has posted on the marquee of the River House Hotel the line: "Hey Sue, This Bud's for You."

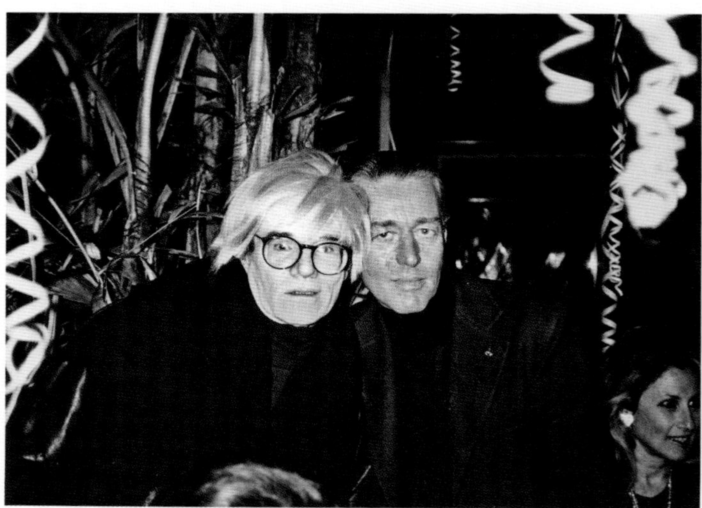

ABOVE
Andy Warhol
Andy and Halston, ca. 1986
Gelatin silver print
8 x 10 in. (20.3 x 25.4 cm)
The Andy Warhol Foundation for the Visual Arts, Inc., FL08.00312

OPPOSITE
Andy Warhol
Diamond Dust Diamonds, 1980
Silkscreen ink and diamond dust on synthetic polymer paint on canvas, twelve panels
Overall: 42 × 72 in. (106.7 × 182.9 cm)
Des Moines Art Center Permanent Collections; Gift of Roy Halston Frowick, New York, 1986.43.1–.12

RIGHT
Andy Warhol
The Andy Warhol Diaries,
edited by Pat Hackett, 1989
Published by Warner Books, New York

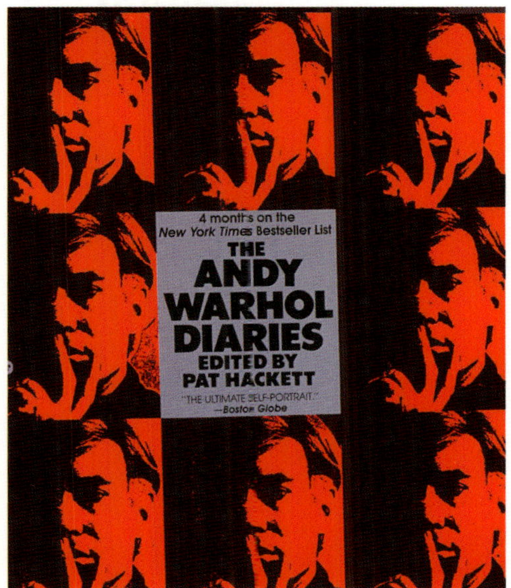

1989

A retrospective of Warhol's painting and sculpture is organized by the Museum of Modern Art; it travels to Chicago, London, Cologne, Venice, and Paris.

A retrospective of Warhol's "pre-Pop" commercial art, *Success Is a Job in New York: The Early Art and Business of Andy Warhol*, is organized by the Grey Art Gallery at New York University; it travels to the Carnegie Museum of Art in Pittsburgh.

An agreement is signed for The Andy Warhol Museum. The partners are The Andy Warhol Foundation, Dia Center for the Arts, and Carnegie Institute. Dia and the Foundation donate hundreds of paintings and works in other media, and the Carnegie operates the museum, located in Pittsburgh.

Pat Hackett condenses more than 20,000 of Warhol's diary pages into an 807-page book titled *The Andy Warhol Diaries*.

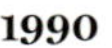

1994

The Andy Warhol Museum opens; at the time it is the largest museum in the world devoted to one artist.

1989

January: Sells his Paul Rudolph townhouse for $5 million. Also sells his land in Montauk.

Donates and sells his collection of Warhol paintings.

Moves to California to be near his family.

Buys a $200,000 Rolls-Royce Corniche to be driven on tours up and down the California coast and through the redwoods. He instructs his family to sell it upon his death and to donate the money to AIDS research.

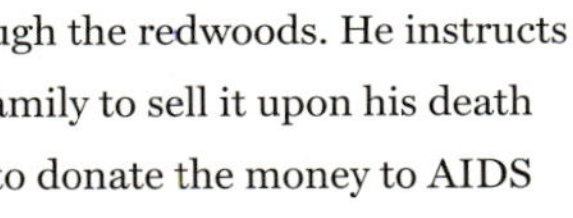

1990

March 26: Halston dies in his sleep at Pacific Presbyterian Hospital in San Francisco of complications from AIDS. He is fifty-seven years old.

March 31: Church services are held at the Calvary Presbyterian Church on Fillmore Street in San Francisco.

June 6: Liza Minelli organizes a memorial for Halston in Alice Tully Hall at Lincoln Center.

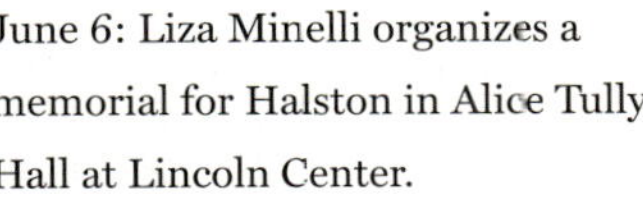

1991

October: The Museum at the Fashion Institute of Technology in New York stages *Halston: Absolute Modernism*, a retrospective exhibition of Halston's work, cocurated by Richard Martin and Harold Koda.

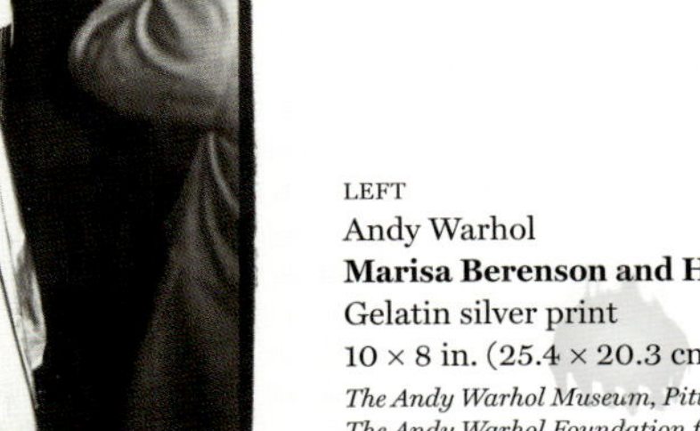

LEFT
Andy Warhol
Marisa Berenson and Halston, n.d.
Gelatin silver print
10 × 8 in. (25.4 × 20.3 cm)
The Andy Warhol Museum, Pittsburgh; Contribution The Andy Warhol Foundation for the Visual Arts, Inc., 2001.2.195

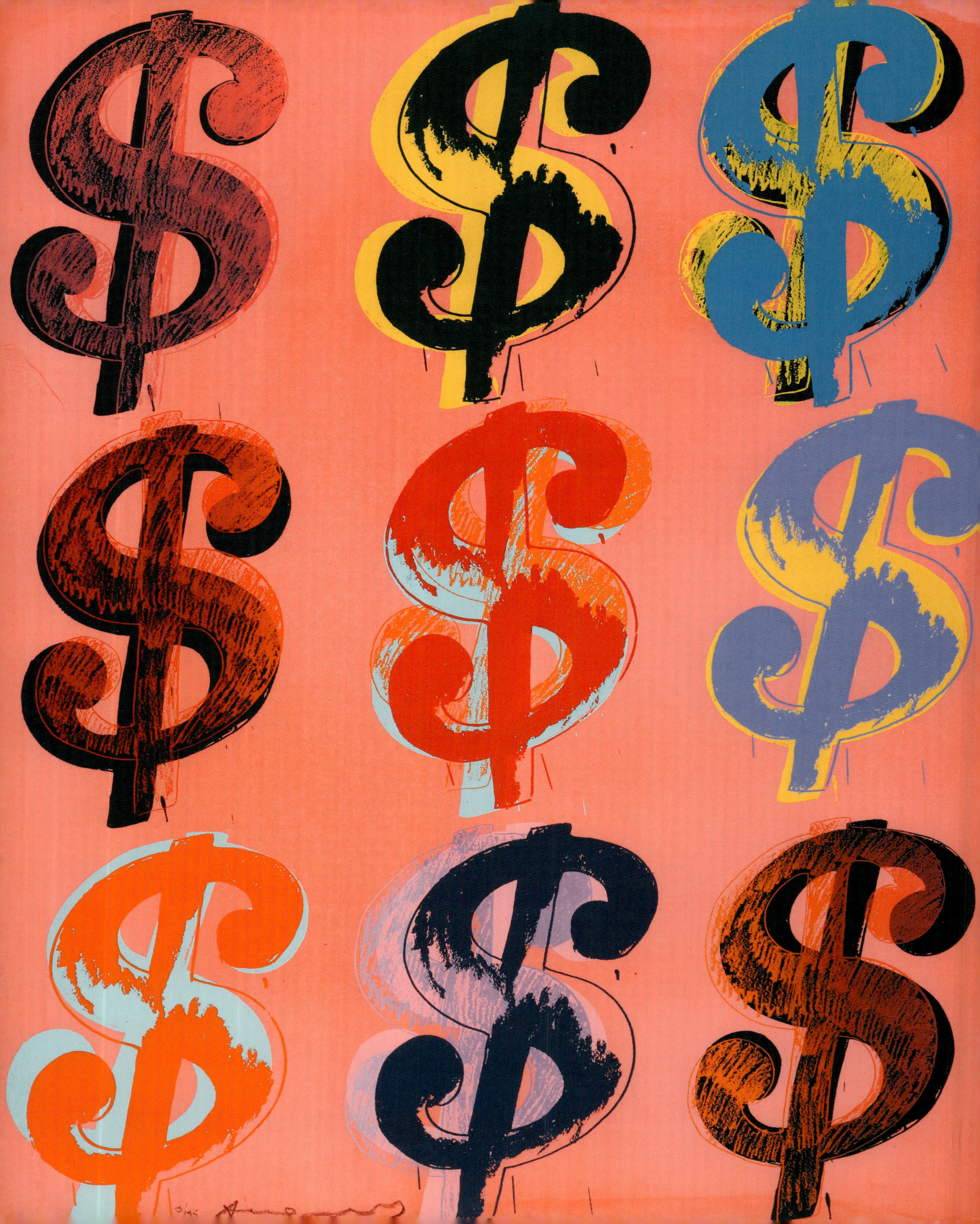

THE BUSINESS OF ART

"Business art is the step that comes after Art. I started as a commercial artist, and I want to finish as a business artist. After I did the thing called 'art' or whatever it's called, I went into business art. I wanted to be an Art Businessman of a Business Artist. Being good in business is the most fascinating kind of art."

—Andy Warhol, *THE Philosophy of Andy Warhol*

Andy Warhol
$ (9), 1982
Screen print on Lenox Museum Board
40 × 32 in. (101.6 × 81.3 cm)
The Andy Warhol Museum, Pittsburgh; Founding Collection, Contribution The Andy Warhol Foundation for the Visual Arts, Inc., 1998.1.2460.1

PORTRAITS

In the 1970s and 1980s Warhol received hundreds of commissions for painted portraits from wealthy socialites, musicians, and stars. These were a significant aspect of his career and a main source of income. Halston commissioned Warhol to create his portrait and encouraged his wealthy clients and friends to do the same.

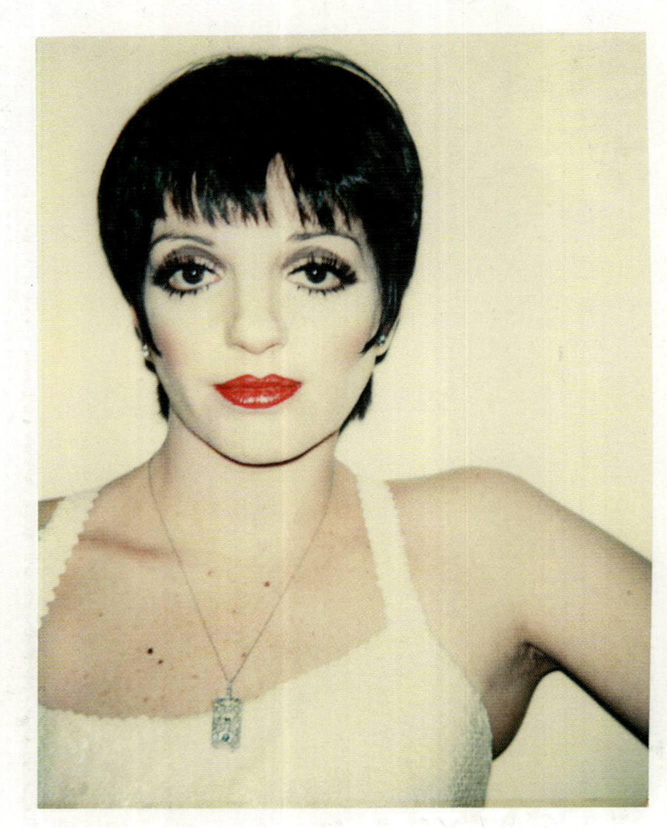

Andy Warhol
Liza Minnelli, 1977
Polaroid™ Polacolor Type 108
4¼ × 3⅜ in. (10.8 × 8.6 cm)
The Andy Warhol Museum, Pittsburgh; Contribution The Andy Warhol Foundation for the Visual Arts, Inc., 2000.2.330

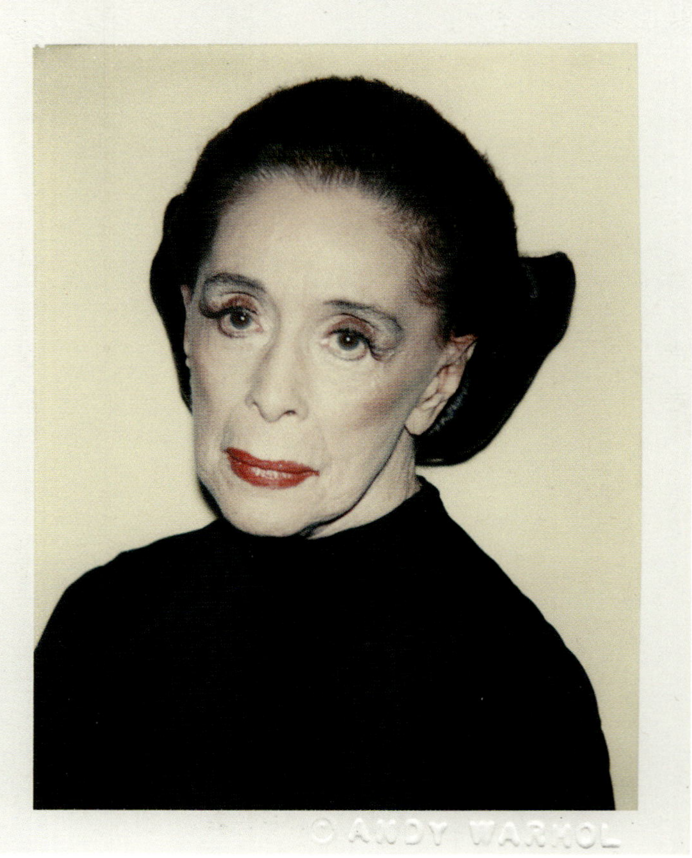

Andy Warhol
Martha Graham, 1979
Polaroid™ Polacolor Type 108
4¼ × 3⅜ in. (10.8 × 8.6 cm)
The Andy Warhol Museum, Pittsburgh; Contribution The Andy Warhol Foundation for the Visual Arts, Inc., 2000.2.335

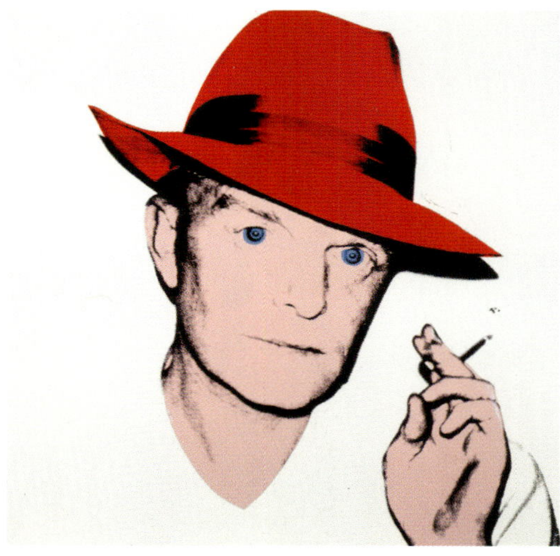
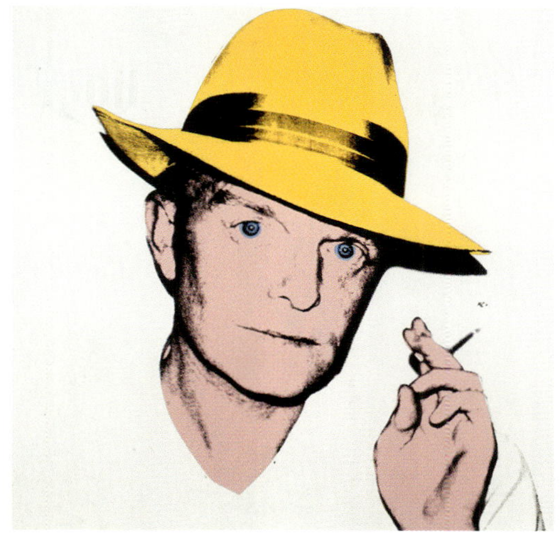
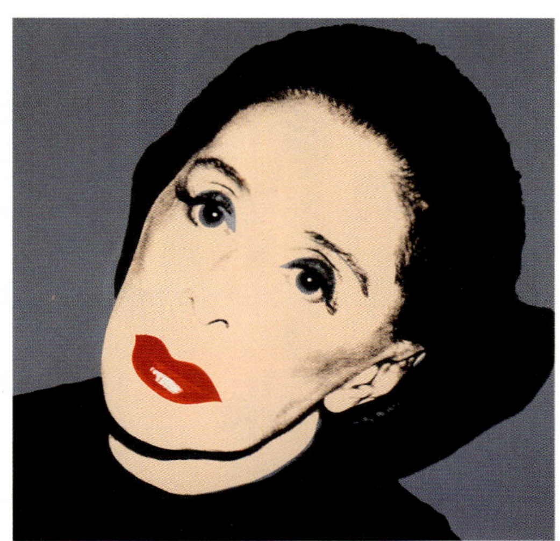
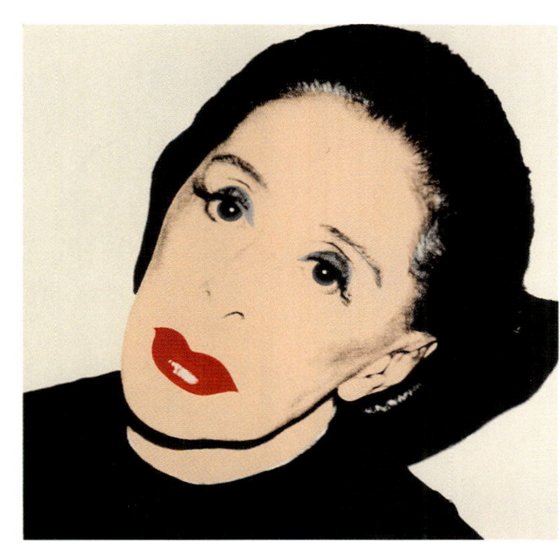
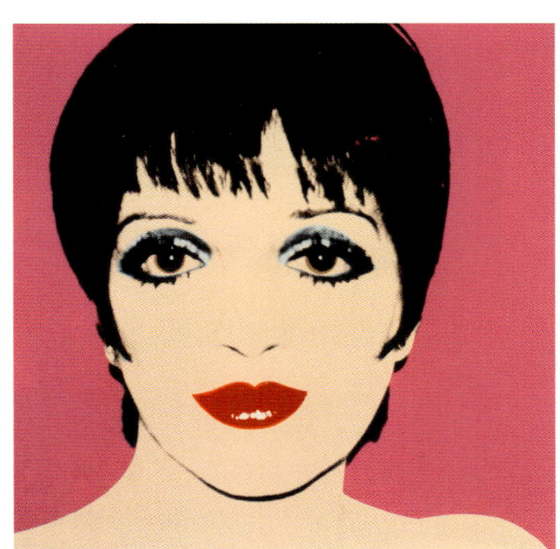
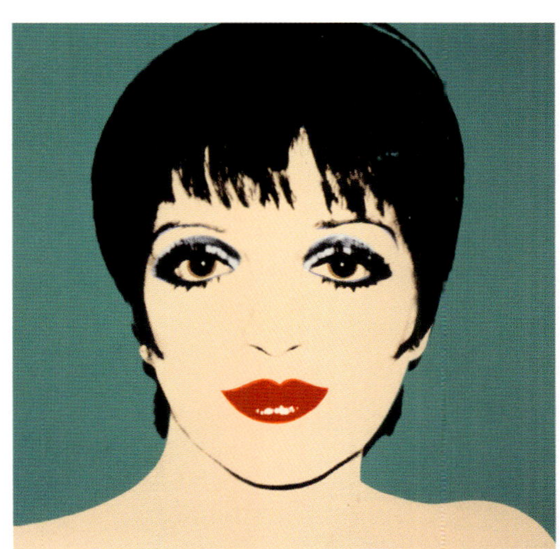

TOP ROW
Andy Warhol
Truman Capote, 1979
Acrylic and silkscreen ink on linen
Each: 40 × 40 in. (101.6 × 101.6 cm)
The Andy Warhol Museum, Pittsburgh; Founding Collection, Contribution Dia Center for the Arts, 1997.1.11a, 1997.1.11b

MIDDLE ROW
Andy Warhol
Martha Graham, 1980
Acrylic and silkscreen ink on linen
Each: 40 × 40 in. (101.6 × 101.6 cm)
The Andy Warhol Museum, Pittsburgh; Founding Collection, Contribution Dia Center for the Arts, 1997.1.13b, 1997.1.13a

BOTTOM ROW
Andy Warhol
Liza Minnelli, 1979
Acrylic and silkscreen ink on linen
Each: 40 × 40 in. (101.6 × 101.6 cm)
The Andy Warhol Museum, Pittsburgh; Founding Collection, Contribution Dia Center for the Arts, 1997.1.10b, 1997.1.10a

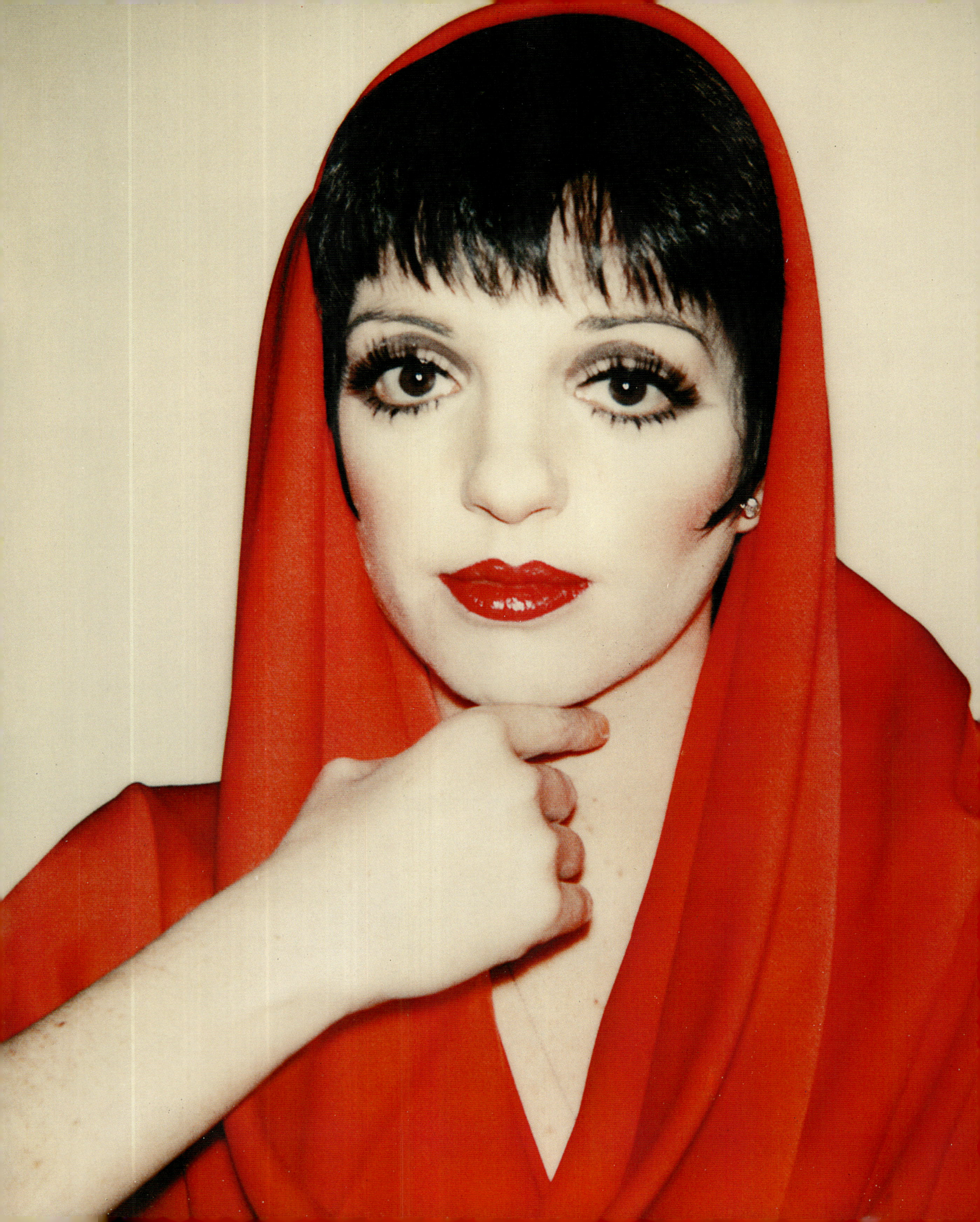

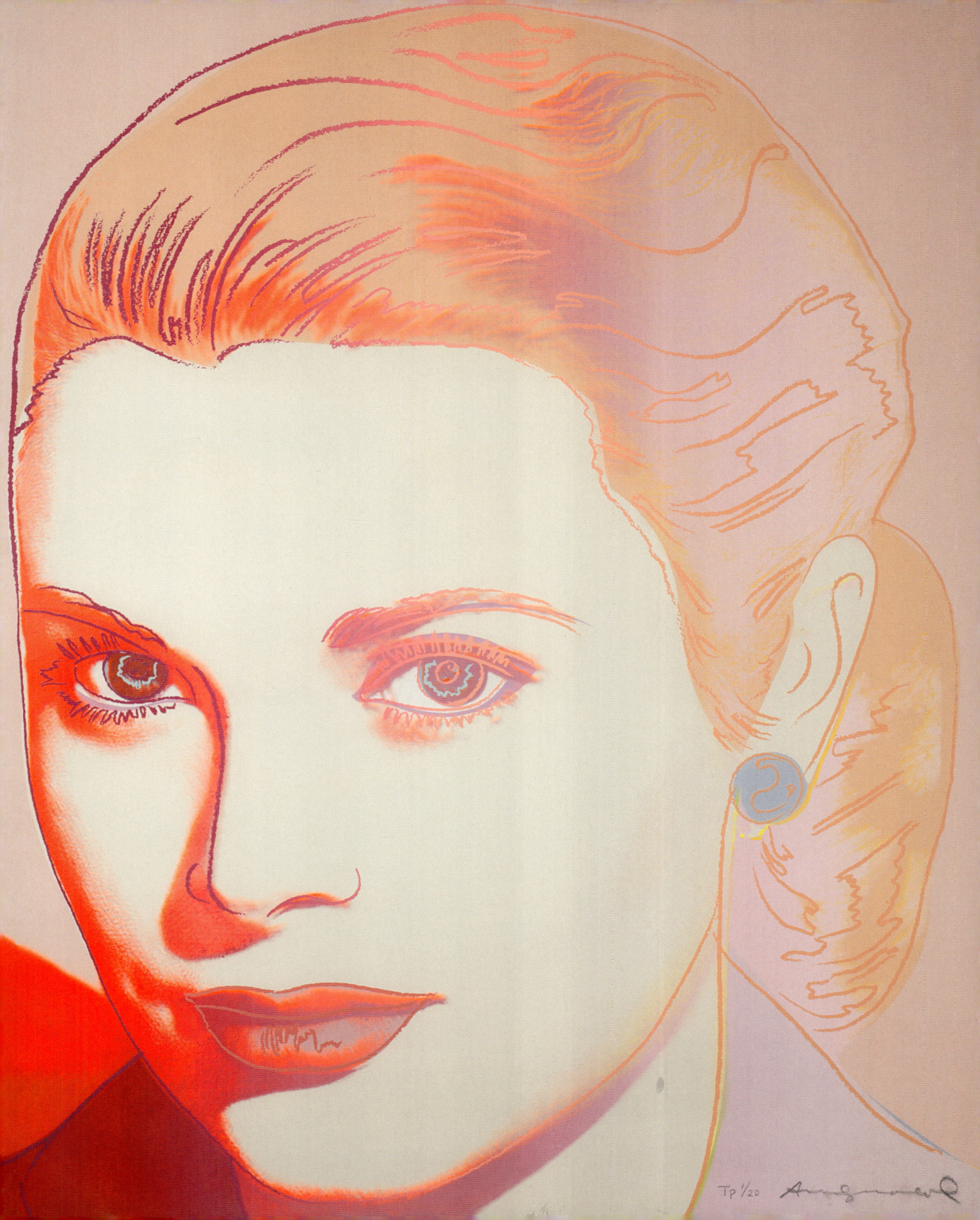
TP 1/20

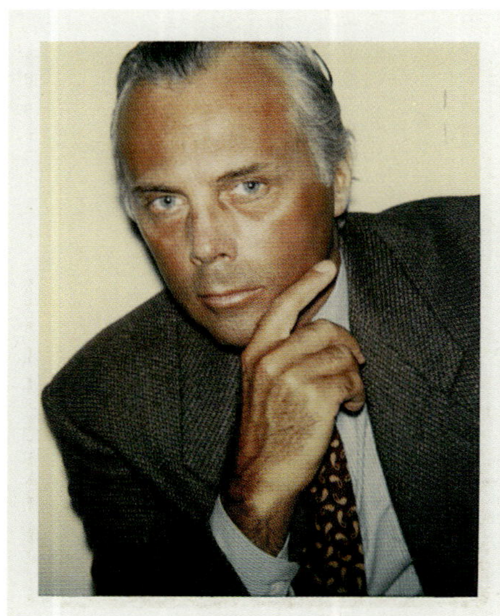

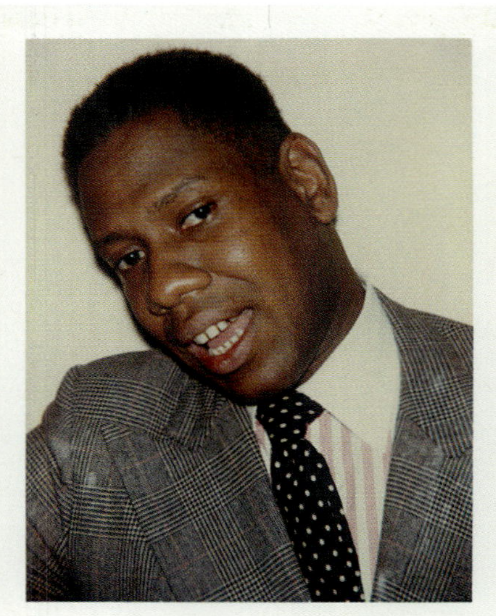

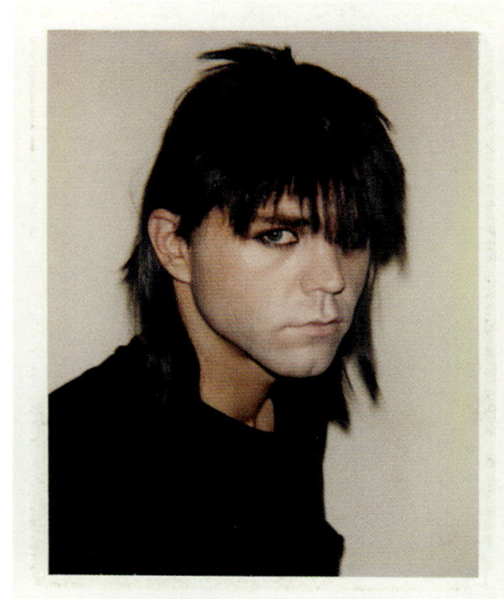

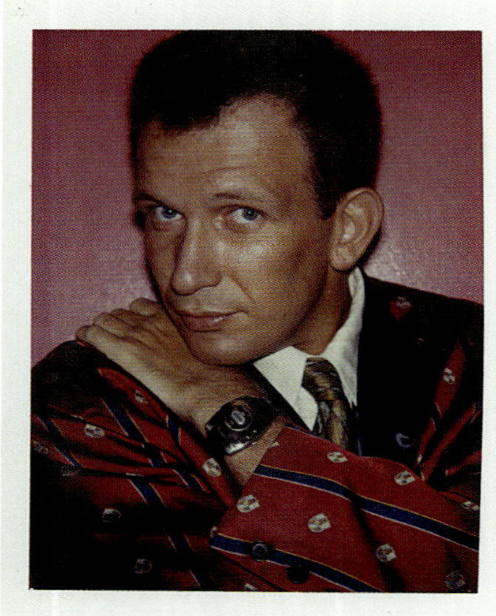

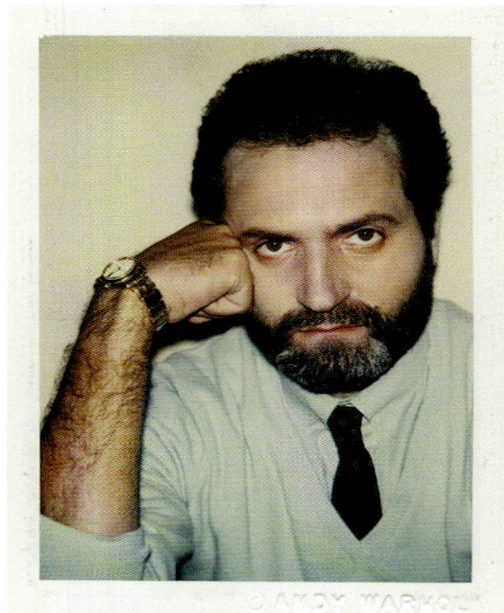

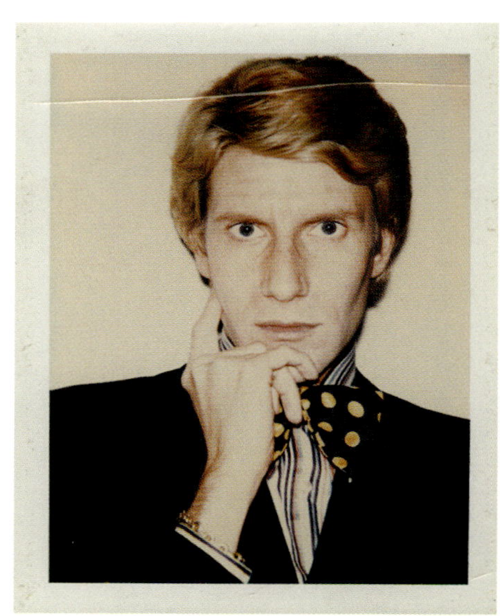

PREVIOUS SPREAD, LEFT
Andy Warhol
Liza Minnelli (wearing Halston) (detail), 1977
Polaroid™ Polacolor Type 108
4 ¼ × 3⅜ in. (10.8 × 8.6 cm)
The Andy Warhol Museum, Pittsburgh; Contribution The Andy Warhol Foundation for the Visual Arts, Inc., 2000.2.328

PREVIOUS SPREAD, RIGHT
Andy Warhol
Grace Kelly, 1984
Screen print on Lenox Museum Board
Sheet: 40 × 31⅞ in. (101.6 × 81 cm)
Des Moines Art Center Permanent Collections; Gift of Roy Halston Frowick, New York, 1986.46

TOP LEFT
Andy Warhol
Giorgio Armani, 1981
Polaroid™ Polacolor 2
4 ¼ × 3⅜ in. (10.8 × 8.6 cm)
The Andy Warhol Museum, Pittsburgh; Contribution The Andy Warhol Foundation for the Visual Arts, Inc., 2000.2.831

BOTTOM LEFT
Andy Warhol
Jean Paul Gaultier, 1984
Polaroid™ Polacolor ER
4 ¼ × 3⅜ in. (10.8 × 8.6 cm)
The Andy Warhol Museum, Pittsburgh; Contribution The Andy Warhol Foundation for the Visual Arts, Inc., 2001.2.1899

TOP MIDDLE
Andy Warhol
André Leon Talley, 1984
Polaroid™ Polacolor ER
4 ¼ × 3⅜ in. (10.8 × 8.6 cm)
The Andy Warhol Museum, Pittsburgh; Contribution The Andy Warhol Foundation for the Visual Arts, Inc., 2000.2.822

BOTTOM MIDDLE
Andy Warhol
Gianni Versace, 1980
Polaroid™ Polacolor Type 108
4 ¼ × 3⅜ in. (10.8 × 8.6 cm)
The Andy Warhol Museum, Pittsburgh; Contribution The Andy Warhol Foundation for the Visual Arts, Inc., 2000.2.835

TOP RIGHT
Andy Warhol
Stephen Sprouse, 1984
Polaroid™ Polacolor ER
4 ¼ × 3⅜ in. (10.8 × 8.6 cm)
The Andy Warhol Museum, Pittsburgh; Contribution The Andy Warhol Foundation for the Visual Arts, Inc., 2000.2.855

BOTTOM RIGHT
Andy Warhol
Yves Saint Laurent, 1972
Polaroid™ Polacolor Type 108
4 ¼ × 3⅜ in. (10.8 × 8.6 cm)
The Andy Warhol Museum, Pittsburgh; Contribution The Andy Warhol Foundation for the Visual Arts, Inc., 2000.2.848

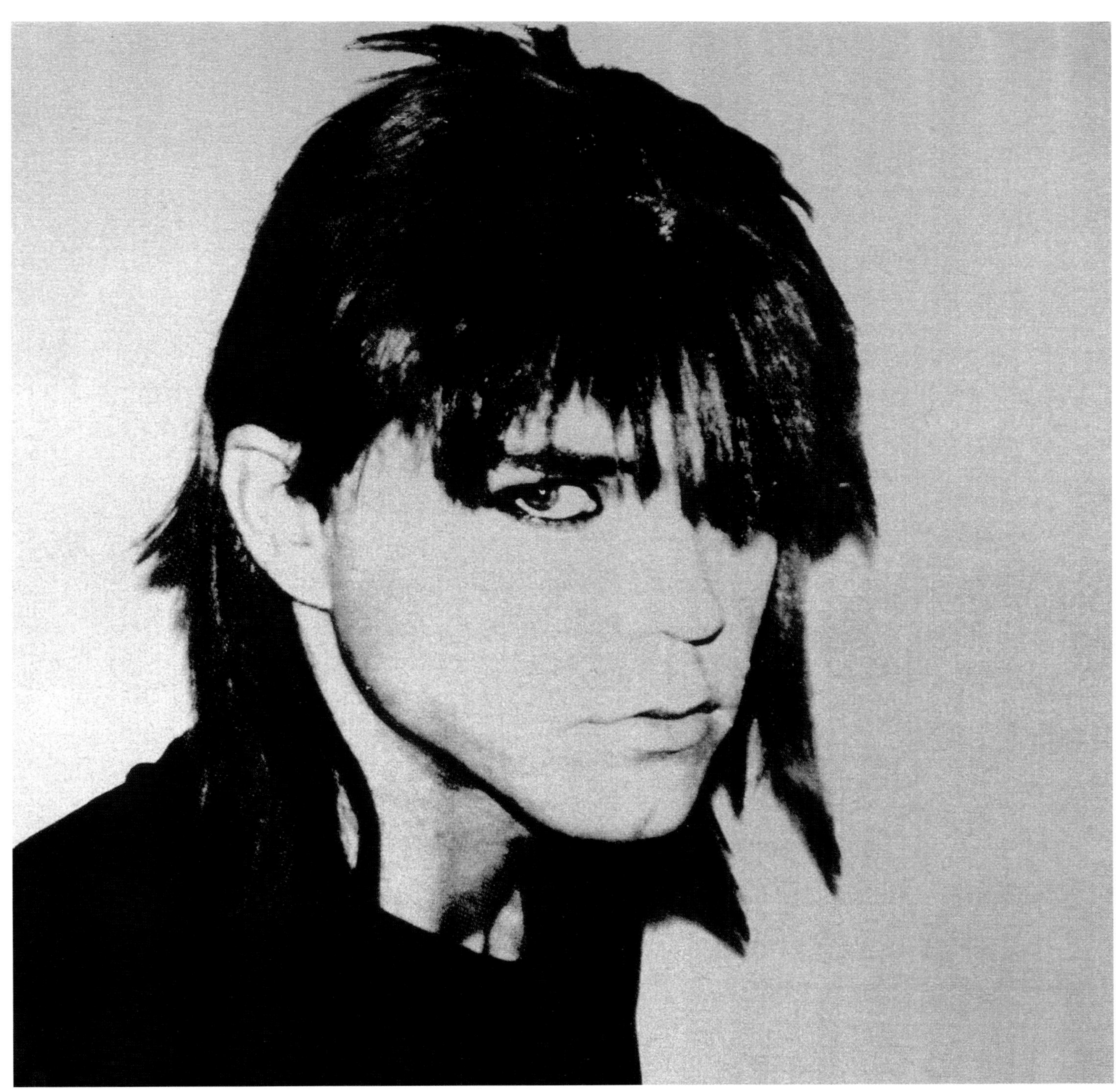

Andy Warhol
Stephen Sprouse, 1984
Acrylic and silkscreen ink on linen
40 × 40 in. (101.6 × 101.6 cm)
The Andy Warhol Museum, Pittsburgh; Founding Collection, Contribution The Andy Warhol Foundation for the Visual Arts, Inc., 1998.1.661

HALSTON'S WARHOLS

"I think everyone should have furs, jewels and Andy Warhol paintings."

—Halston, quoted in Andy Warhol, *Diaries*, December 3, 1978

"Halston gave me a green beaded dress to hang in my closet. It's like a $5,000 dress. It's his art."

—Andy Warhol, *Diaries*, December 24, 1980

Whether purchased or given as gifts, by the mid-1980s Halston had amassed a large collection of Warhol paintings and prints. Halston first bought ten miniature *Mao* paintings for about $2,000 each in the mid-1970s. According to Bob Colacello in *Holy Terror,* "It was the beginning of a long business relationship between him and Andy. He also asked Andy to do his portrait, and came to the Factory a couple of months later for the 'unveiling' lunch and was so pleased by Andy's depiction that he agreed to advertise in *Interview* for the first time." The ad ran in March 1975 on the back cover. "And where Halston led, others followed. Between December 1974 and December 1976 our advertising pages doubled, with most of the increase in the fashion category." Halston's Warhols included a number of works illustrated in this book, such as these three *Mona Lisa* paintings, *Diamon Dust Shoes*, and *Gems*; the *Liz* and *Grace Kelly* prints; and a number from the *Self-Portrait with Skull* series.

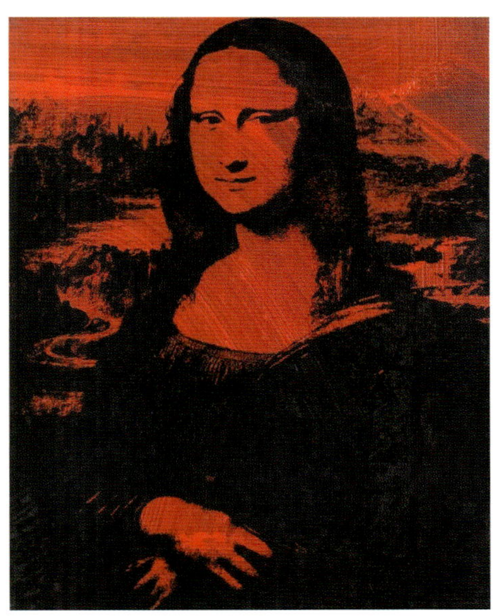

OPPOSITE AND RIGHT
Andy Warhol
Mona Lisa, 1979
Acrylic and silkscreen on canvas
Each: 25 × 20 in. (63.5 × 50.8 cm)
Des Moines Art Center Permanent Collections; Gift of Roy Halston Frowick, New York, 1986.27, 1986.28, 1986.26

HALSTON

Dear Andy-
Each time I get a gift of a painting from you, Halston says "you are a very lucky lady." How right he is! Your gift last week is a real treasure. You are very special and I thank you for being so kind to me.
Love, Faye

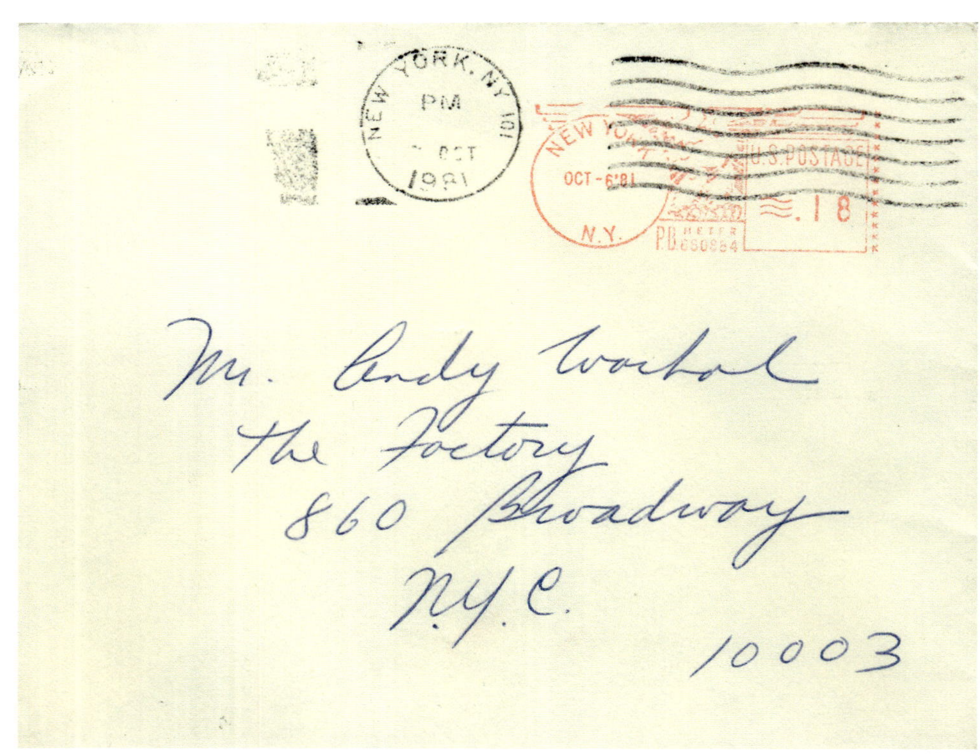

NEW YORK, NY 101
PM
7 OCT
1981

NEW YORK N.Y.
OCT-6'81
U.S. POSTAGE
.18
PB METER 650884

Mr. Andy Warhol
The Factory
860 Broadway
N.Y.C.
10003

Faye Robeson
Envelope and handwritten note to Andy Warhol on Halston embossed stationery card,
postmarked October 6, 1981
From Time Capsule 580
The Andy Warhol Museum, Pittsburgh; Founding Collection, Contribution The Andy Warhol Foundation for the Visual Arts, Inc., TC580.49.1–2

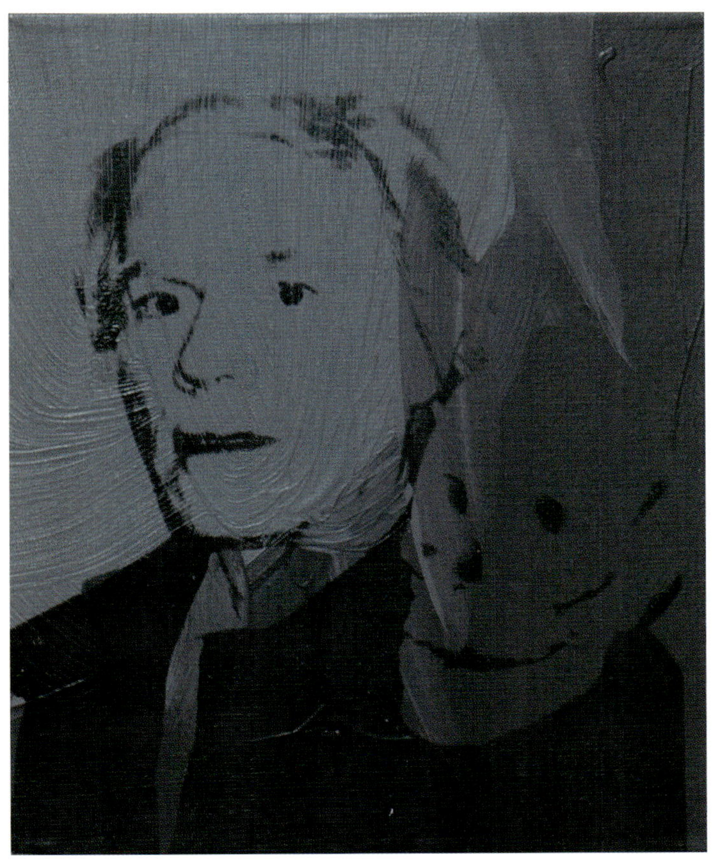

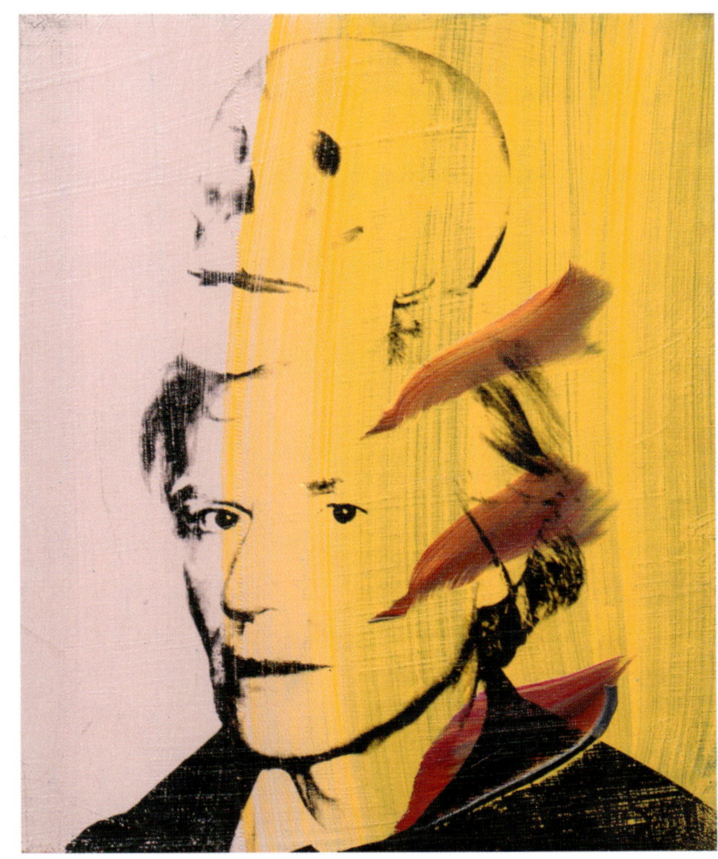

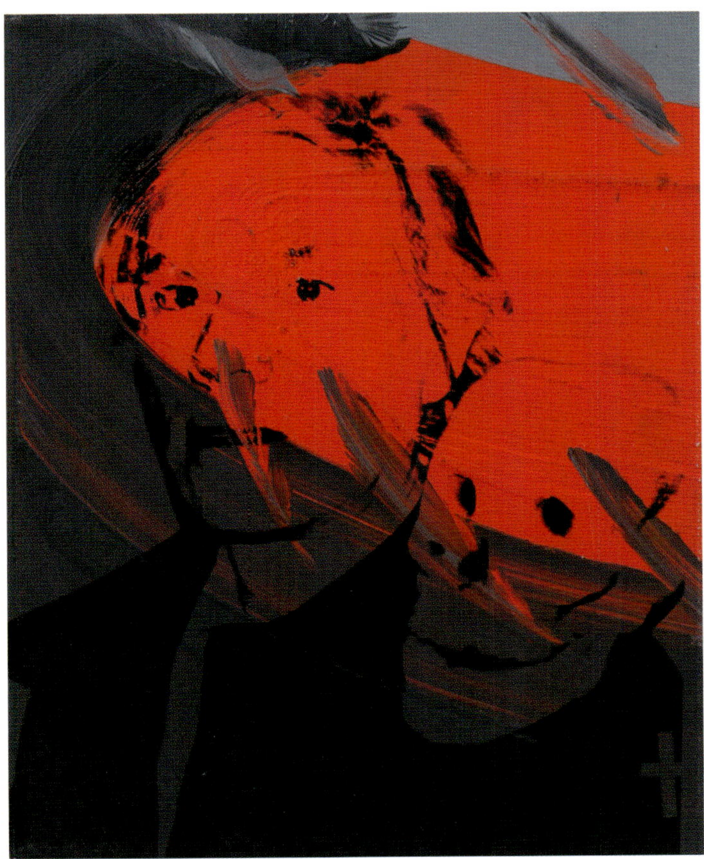

TOP LEFT
Andy Warhol
Self-Portrait with Skull, 1976
Silkscreen ink on synthetic polymer on canvas
16 × 13 in. (40.6 × 33 cm)
Des Moines Art Center Permanent Collections; Gift of Roy Halston Frowick, New York, 1986.32

TOP RIGHT
Andy Warhol
Self-Portrait with Skull, 1978
Silkscreen ink on synthetic polymer on canvas
16 × 13 in. (40.6 × 33 cm)
Des Moines Art Center Permanent Collections; Gift of Roy Halston Frowick, New York, 1986.34

BOTTOM LEFT
Andy Warhol
Self-Portrait with Skull, 1978
Silkscreen ink on synthetic polymer on canvas
16 × 13 in. (40.6 × 33 cm)
Des Moines Art Center Permanent Collections; Gift of Roy Halston Frowick, New York, 1986.33

CHINA

Both Halston and Warhol traveled to China shortly after the U.S. and Chinese governments established full diplomatic relations in 1979. This was the first time that the Communist republic had opened its doors to foreign travelers since 1946, and both men were eager to explore business opportunities in China.

In September 1980, Halston became the first American designer invited to show in China. For the trip, he amassed a group of twenty-eight models, assistants, business colleagues, and friends, for whom he designed outfits in complementary colors for every occasion. Halston directed the clothes his entourage wore for air travel, diplomatic receptions, banquet dinners, and sightseeing, and even supplied them with matching robes to be worn backstage. Halston model Pat Cleveland recalled the experience. "We were like migrating birds, well-choreographed, all color-coordinated."

When Halston presented his designs to 1,400 Chinese designers and manufacturers in Shanghai, the low necklines and diaphanous fabrics shocked his audience into silence. During the question and answer session, he asked his models to remove their jackets so that the audience could examine the construction and materials. "Every seam and fabric was examined by a swarm of China's fashion elite," reported the Associated Press on September 22, 1980. In addition to Shanghai and Beijing, the tour included appearances in Japan and France for Halston to help launch his brands internationally.

Two years later, in 1982, Warhol traveled to Hong Kong and Beijing. Warhol's small group included the photographer Christopher Makos and Fred Hughes, his manager. Hughes helped arrange for Warhol to meet with a Hong Kong industrialist, who was commissioning portraits for his restaurants and clubs. After business in Hong Kong, the group spent three days in Beijing, where Andy toured Tiananmen Square, the Forbidden City, and the Great Wall. As Makos recalled, "The trip was pretty low-key; the only people who recognized Andy were other American tourists. Of course, the Chinese always noticed him in a crowd, but mainly because he looked so unusual, not because he was the guy who painted those portraits of Mao."

OPPOSITE TOP
Halston (center) and a group of models, dressed in his designs made of Chinese silks, on the Great Wall of China, September 17, 1980
Associated Press

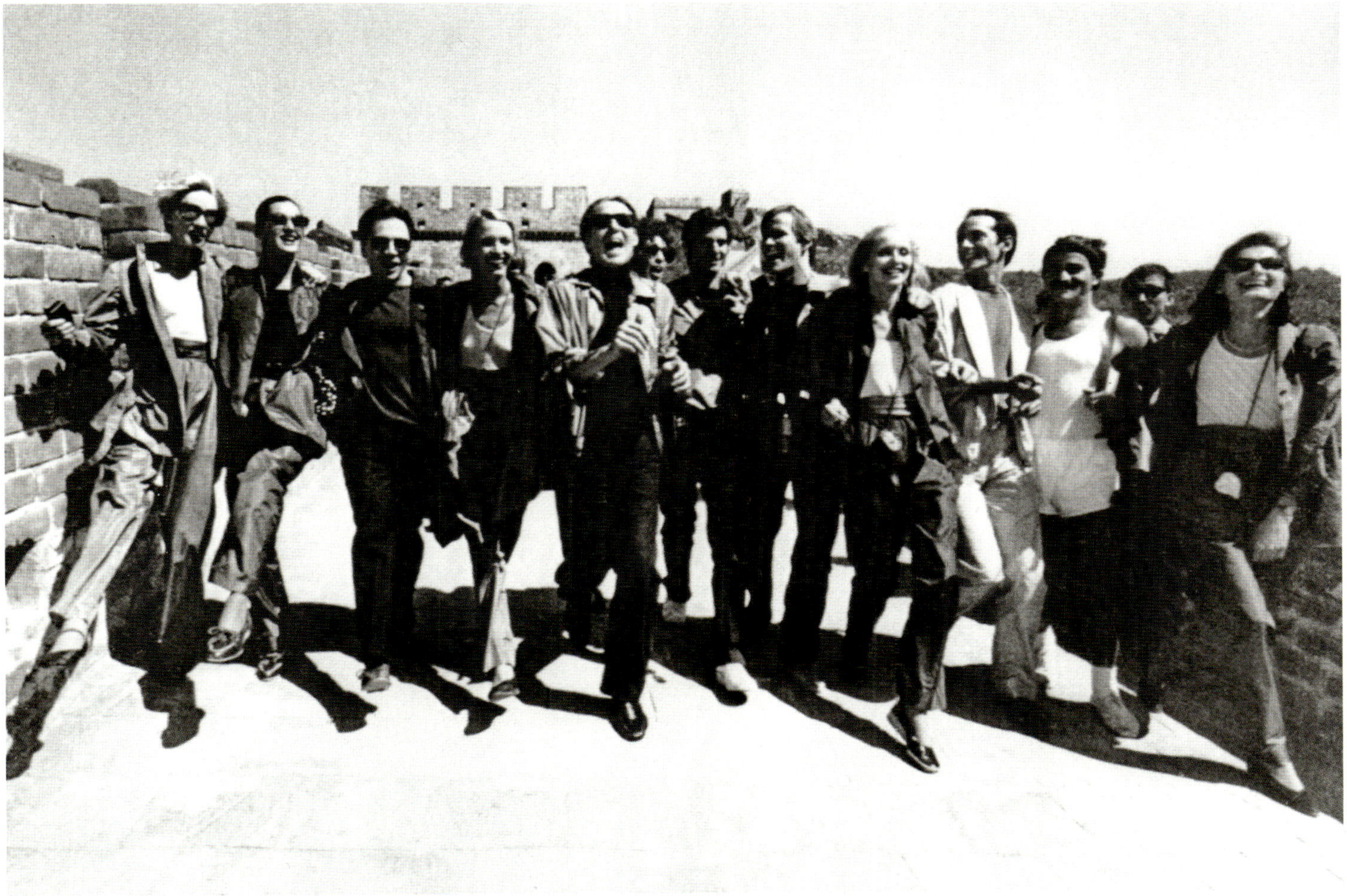

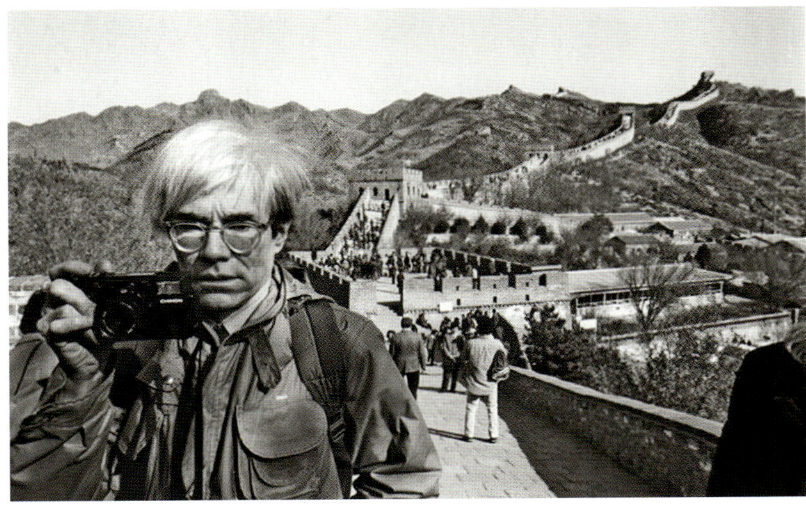

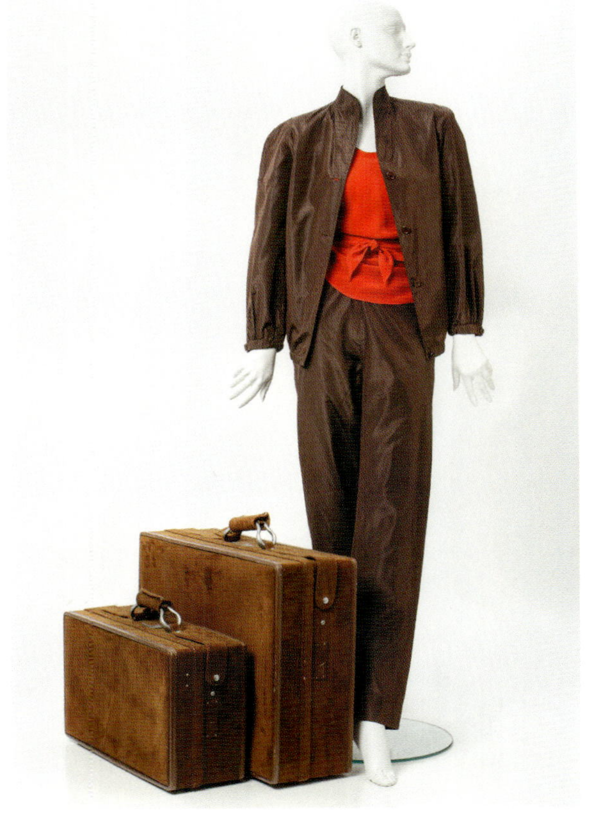

BOTTOM LEFT
Andy with Chinon on the Great Wall, 1982
Photograph by Christopher Makos
makostudio.com

BOTTOM RIGHT
Halston
Travel set: jacket and pants, dolman-style top, created for China trip, 1980
Silk taffeta (pants), silk (shirt)
Halston for Hartman (3-piece Ultrasuede luggage set)
Photograph by Eve Prime
Collection of Chris Royer

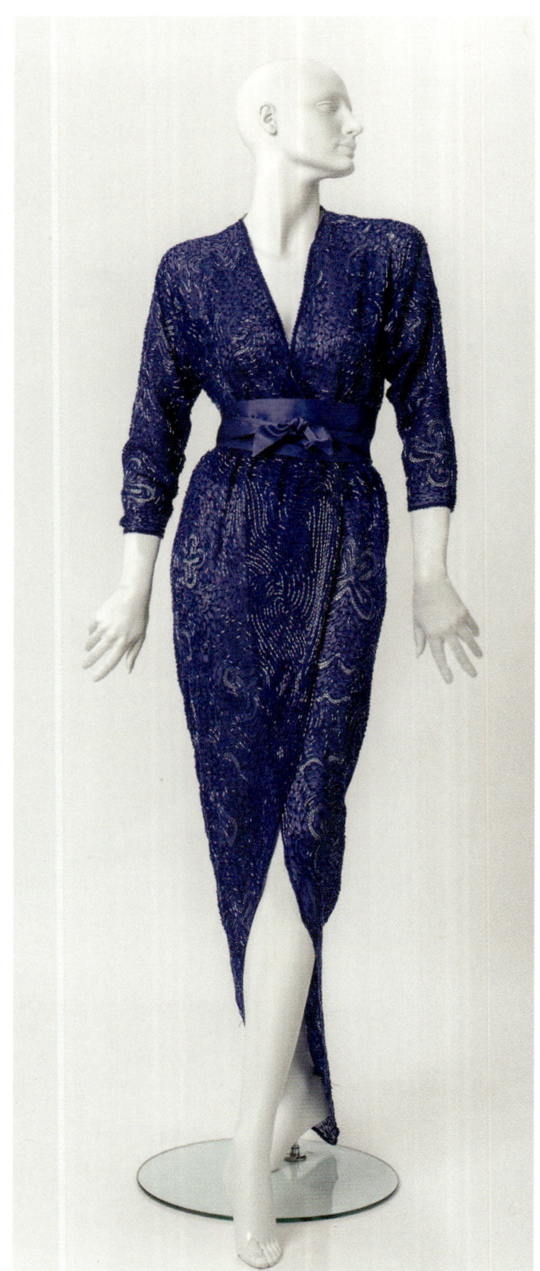

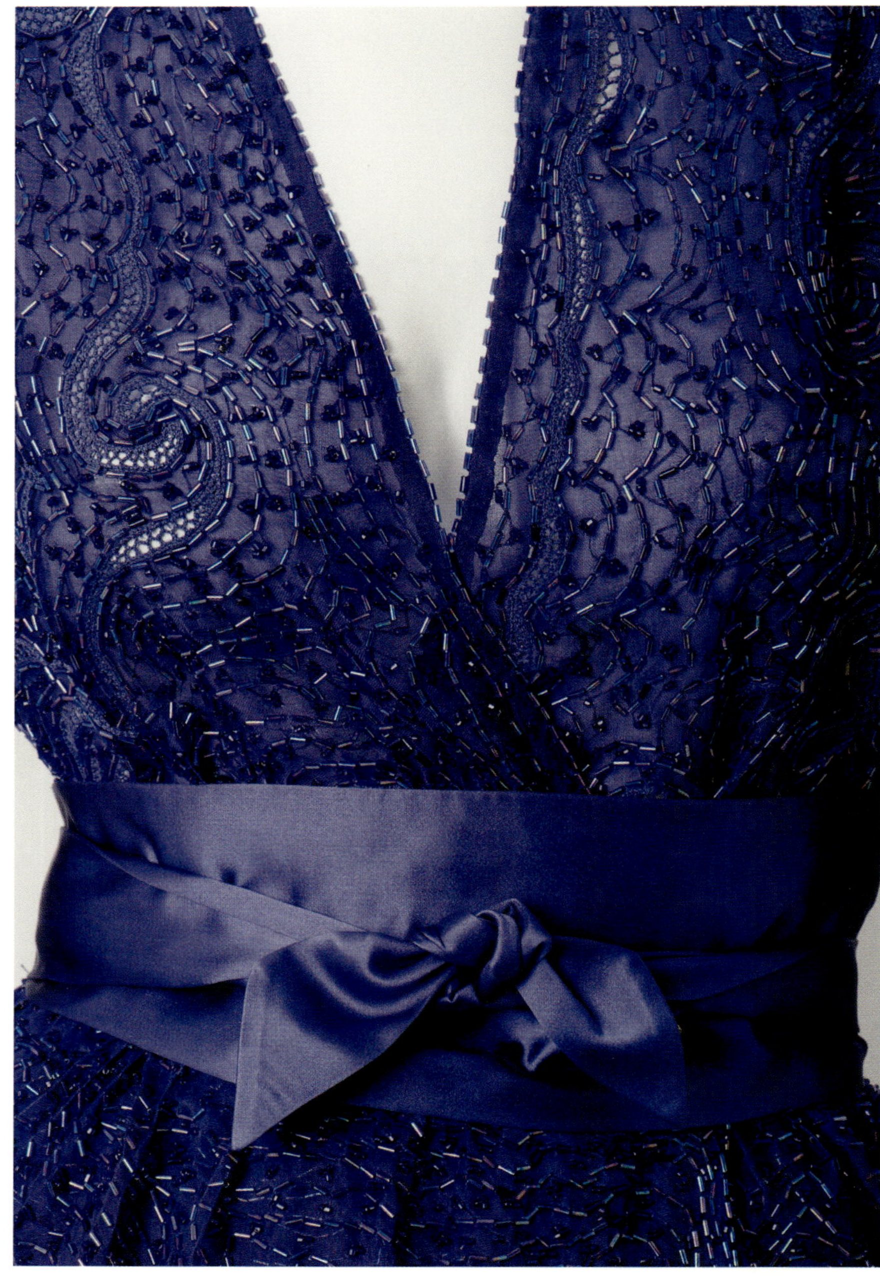

Halston
Beaded evening dress with dolman sleeves and tulip-style skirt, created for China trip, 1980
Silk organza, bugle beads
Photograph by Eve Prime
Collection of Chris Royer

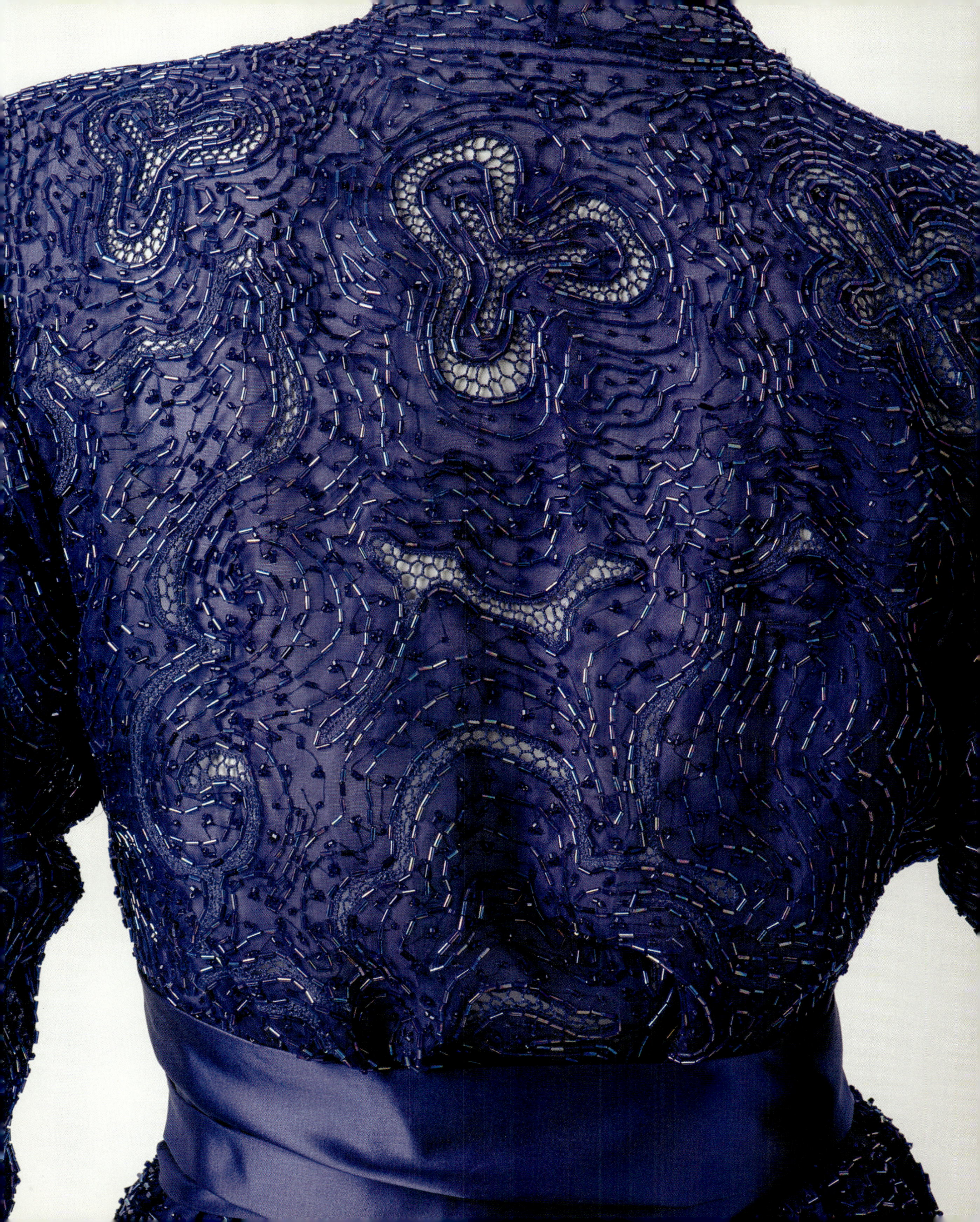

SPARKLE

Warhol and Halston loved silver and shiny, glittery looks, achieved through actual diamonds and metallic paint (in Warhol's case), and metallic threads and beading (in Halston's). Halston employed materials that reflected light to dramatize body movement. In his early collections he used gold lamé and Lurex woven into knit or cut velvet evening pajamas. Later he was famous for sequins by the yard.

Inspired by patterns drawn from nature and themes such as fireworks and city lights, he embellished garments with honeycombs, fringes, feathers, maps, flowers, geometric shapes, and Art Nouveau–style glittery clusters. Liza Minnelli claimed that he designed her clothes with sequins in order to "disguise her glow" (conceal perspiration) while she was performing onstage. Always considering the beauty and comfort of his clients, Halston had found a practical use for sparkle.

OPPOSITE TOP LEFT
Halston
Beaded evening dress,
Made to Order, 1979
Silk and chiffon with bugle beads, scattered paillettes
Photograph by Eve Prime
Collection of Chris Royer

OPPOSITE BOTTOM LEFT
Halston
Beaded evening top with skirt,
Made to Order, 1981
Silk organza, bugle beads, and multicolored paillettes; silk velvet (skirt)
Photograph by Eve Prime
Collection of Chris Royer

OPPOSITE TOP RIGHT
Halston
Beaded and embroidered evening top with skirt, 1981
Silk chiffon with bugle beads, sequins; silk velvet (skirt)
Photograph by Eve Prime
Collection of Chris Royer

OPPOSITE BOTTOM RIGHT
Halston
Two-piece halter, pants, and obi belt,
Starburst Evening Wear Series, 1981
Silk organza, silk satin, bugle beads
Photograph by Eve Prime
Collection of Chris Royer

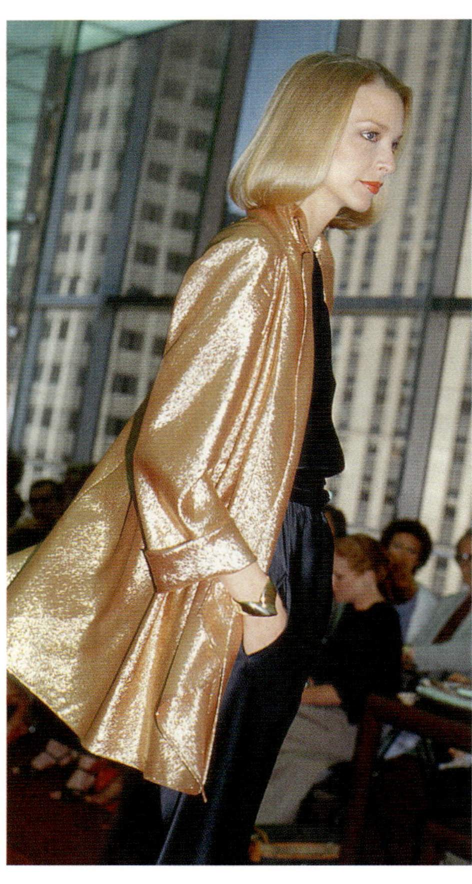

LEFT
Model in a gold jacket by Halston
Photograph by Rose Hartman

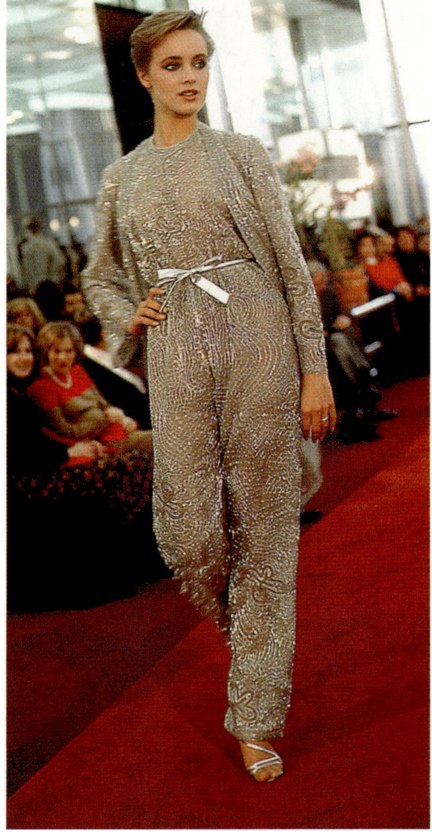

RIGHT
Model wearing a beaded jumpsuit by Halston
Photograph by Rose Hartman

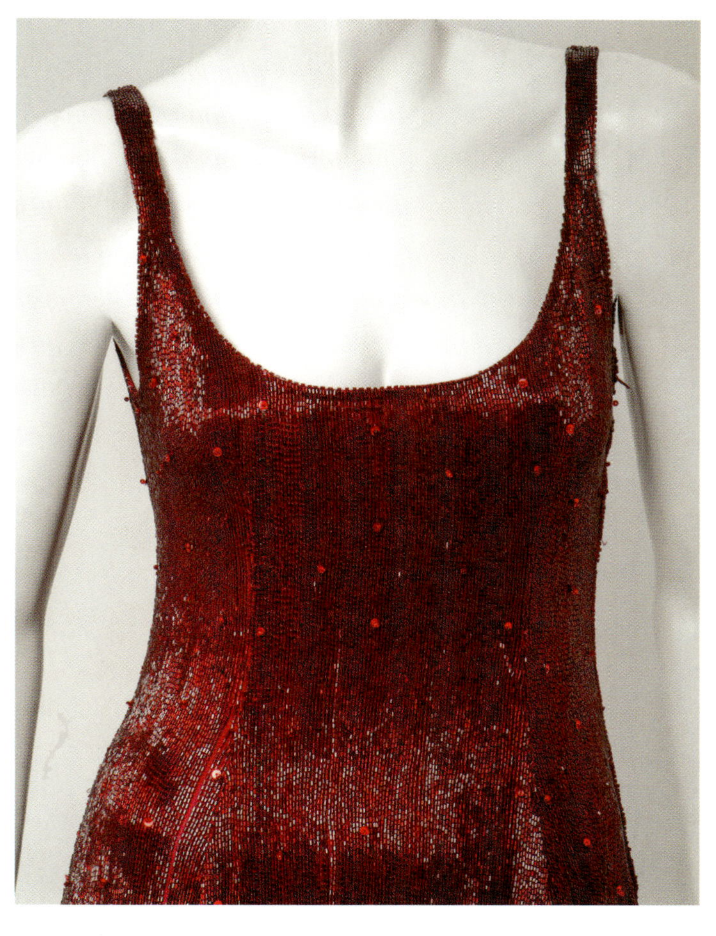

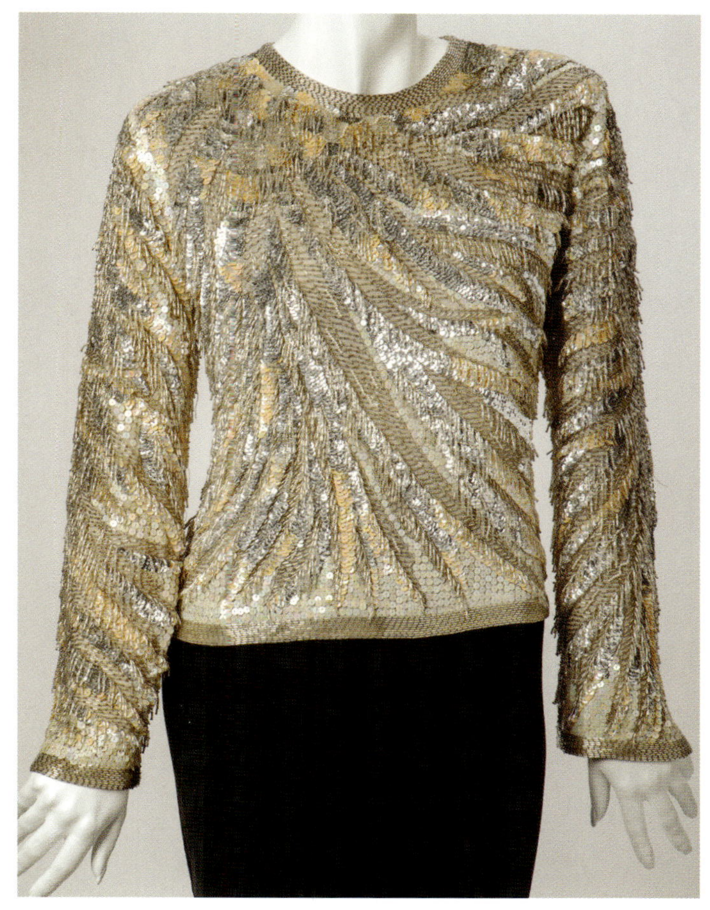

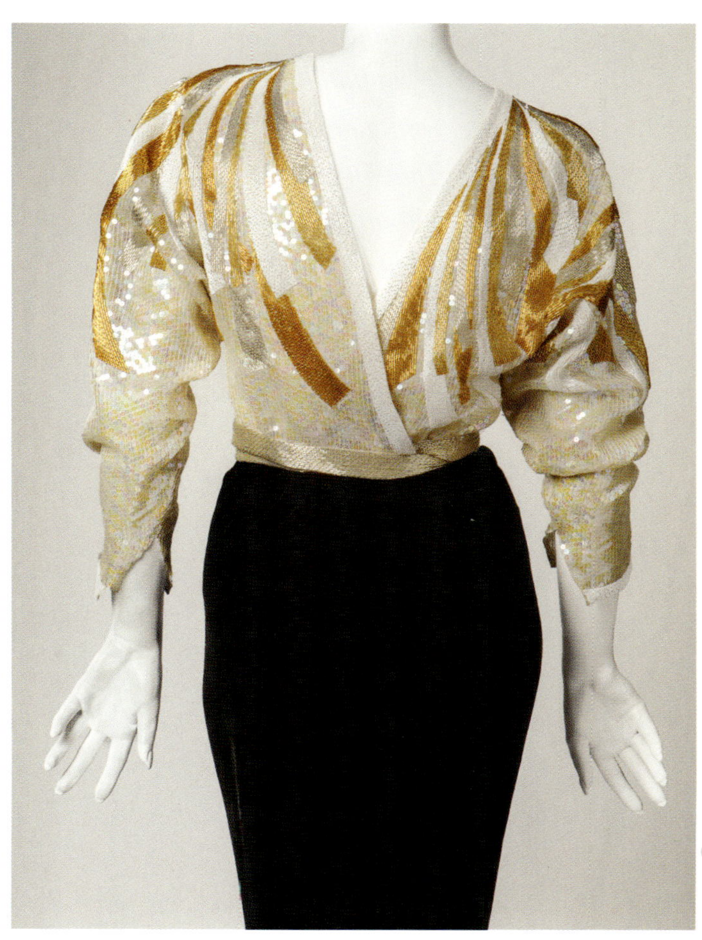

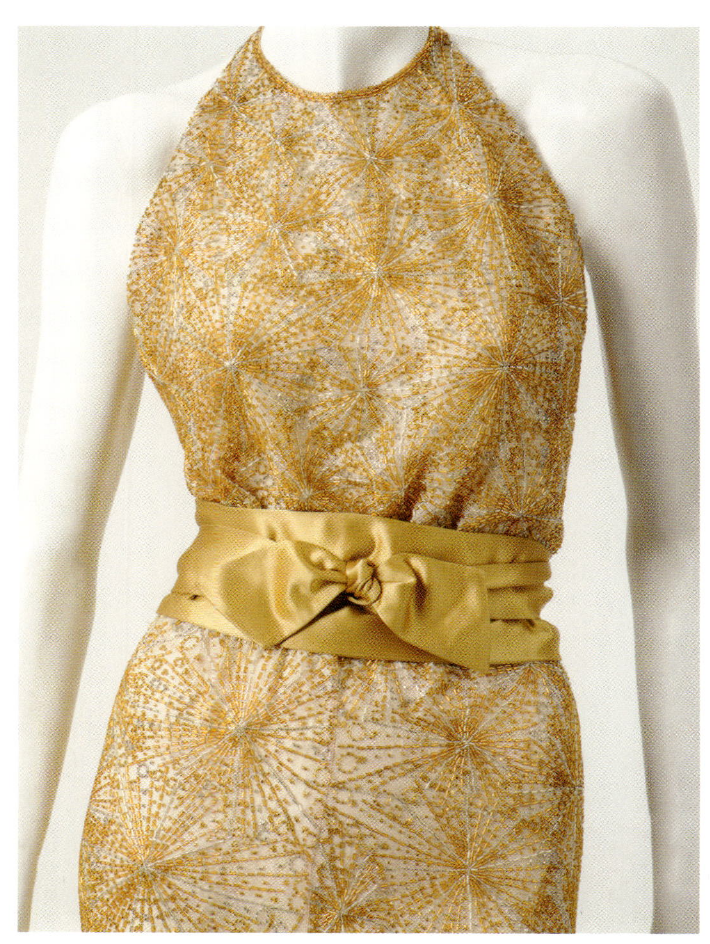

"Halston's show was great. . . . He had this new fabric that's beautiful, that's like paper and silk, and people were feeling it to see what it was. It came in gunmetal grey and gunmetal green and like with a waterfall through it, like iridescent."

—Andy Warhol, *Diaries*, April 22, 1982

Halston
Evening dress with under slip and obi belt, 1983
Silk organza, duchess satin
Photograph by Eve Prime
Collection of Chris Royer

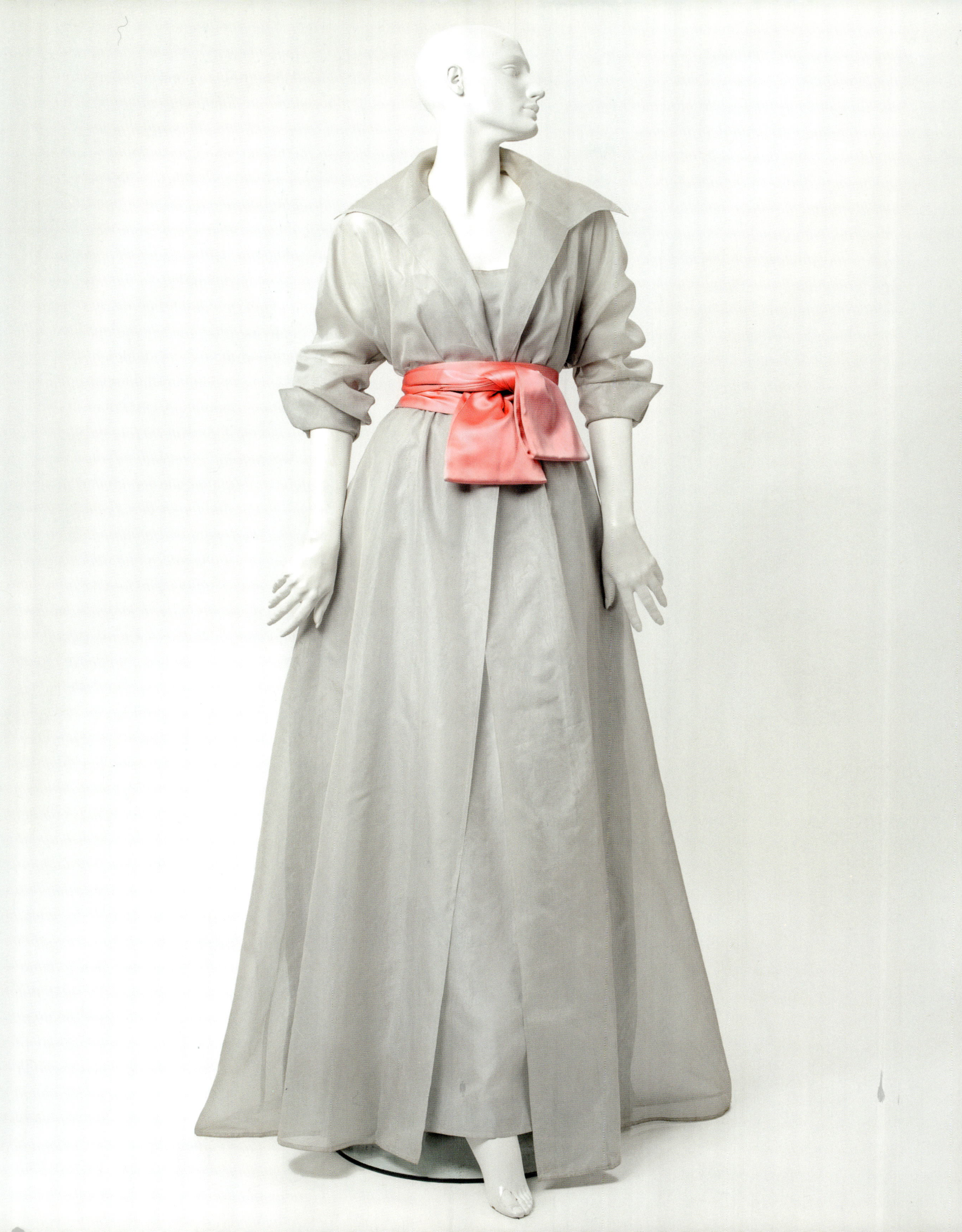

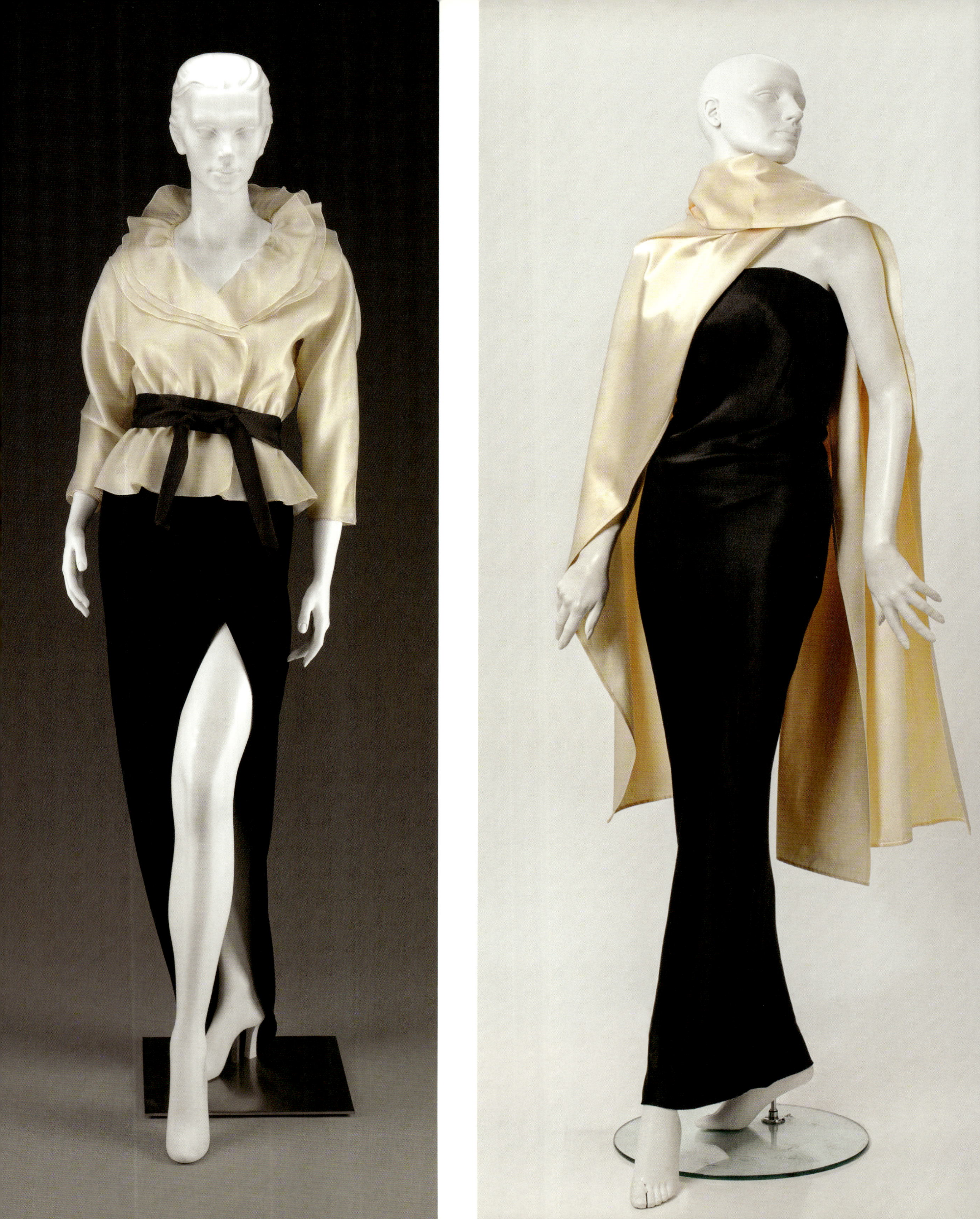

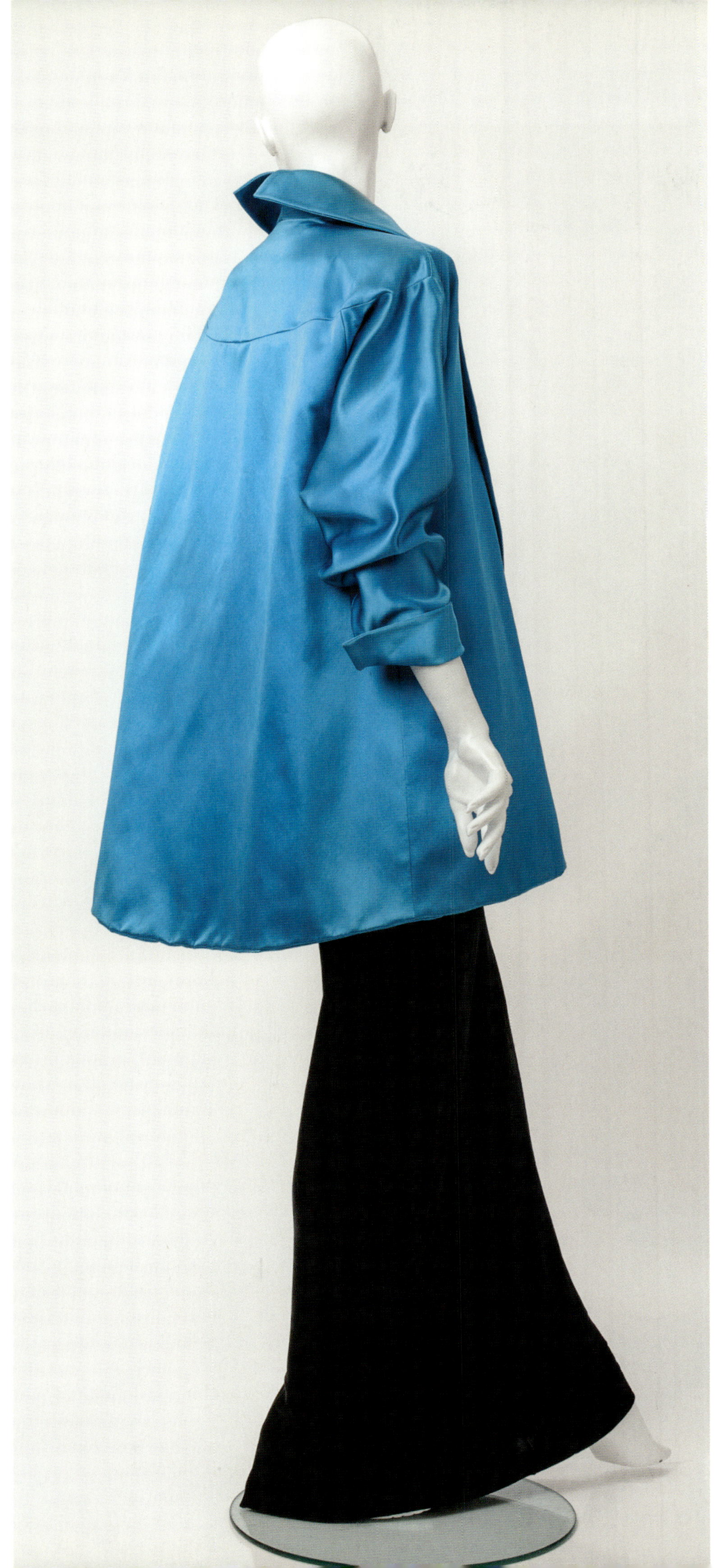

FAR LEFT
Halston
Evening dress with ruffle top and tulip wrap skirt, 1980
Silk organza, velvet
Indianapolis Museum of Art, 80.262A–C

MIDDLE
Halston
Spiral-cut evening dress with shawl, Made to Order, 1984
Silk (dress), silk satin (shawl)
Photograph by Eve Prime
Collection of Chris Royer

LEFT
Halston
Spiral-cut evening dress with evening coat, Made to Order, 1984
Silk (dress), duchess satin (coat)
Photograph by Eve Prime
Collection of Chris Royer

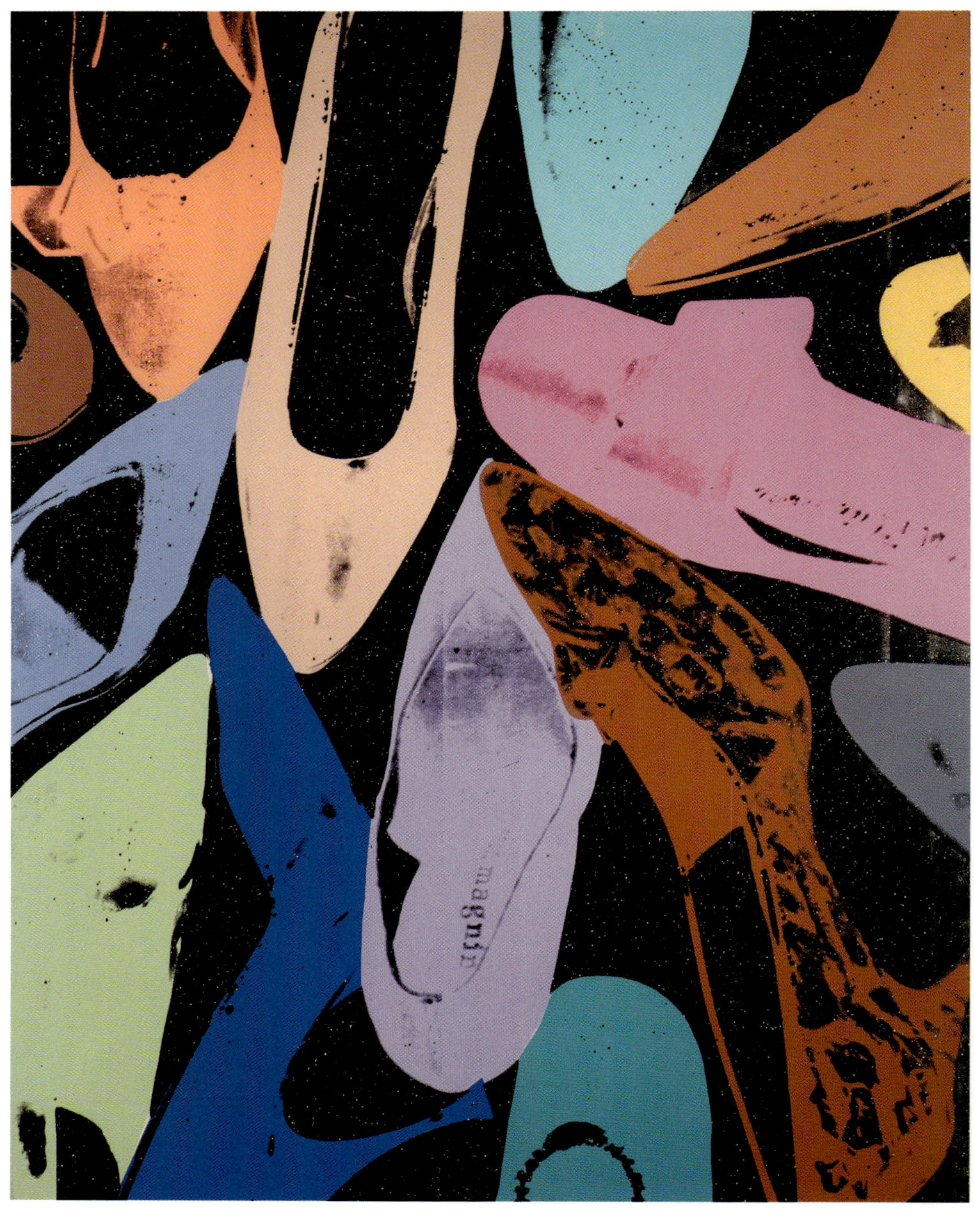

Between 1979 and 1981 Halston created a metallic evening shoe collection under his Garolini shoe license. In 1980 Warhol photographed many of these shoes and created diamond-dust paintings, using actual diamond shavings on top of the silkscreen works.

"Halston gave an autograph party for Andy Warhol at the Garolini Shoe showroom. The occasion was really a presentation of Halston's new shoes for resort, but no one paid the least bit of attention to them. Instead, everyone milled around the huge silk-screen of shoes Mr. Warhol had just run off."

—John Duka, "Notes on Fashion," *New York Times*, August 4, 1981

Andy Warhol
Diamond Dust Shoes (Random), 1980
Acrylic, silkscreen ink, and diamond dust on linen
90 x 70 in. (228.6 x 177.8 cm)
The Andy Warhol Museum, Pittsburgh; Founding Collection, Contribution The Andy Warhol Foundation for the Visual Arts, Inc., 1998.1.237

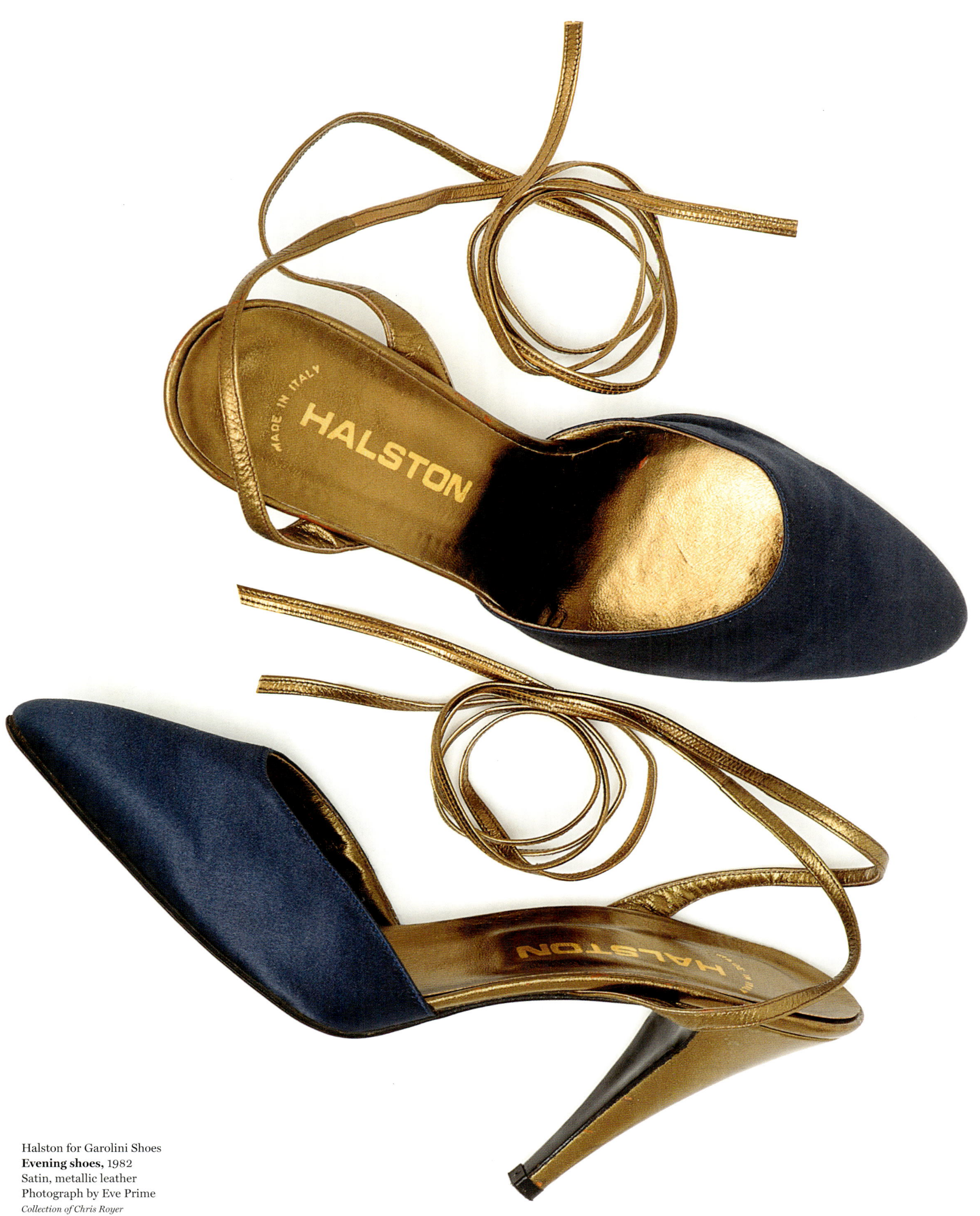

Halston for Garolini Shoes
Evening shoes, 1982
Satin, metallic leather
Photograph by Eve Prime
Collection of Chris Royer

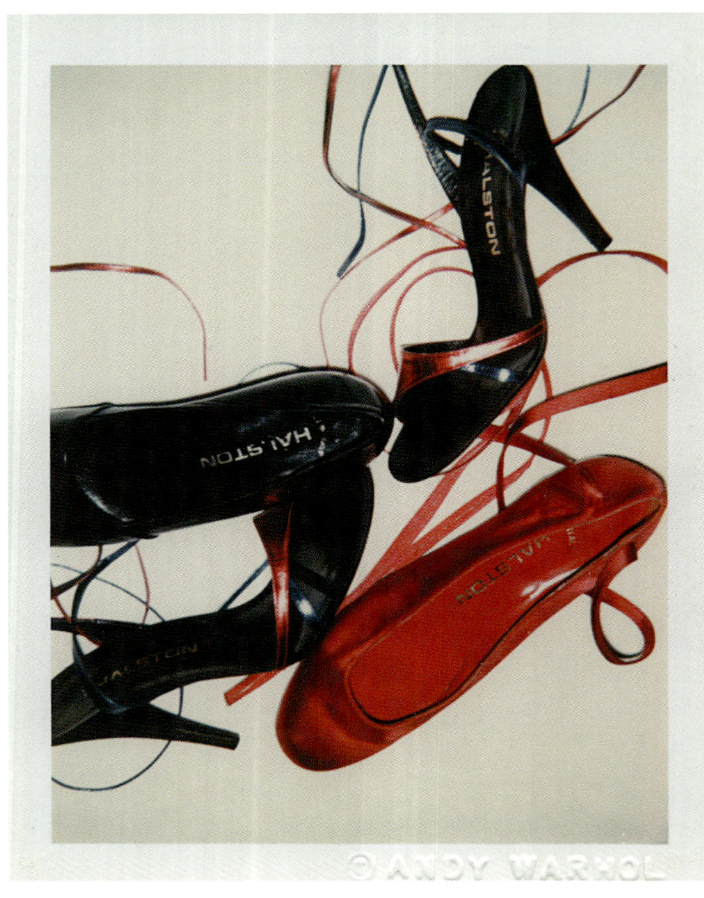

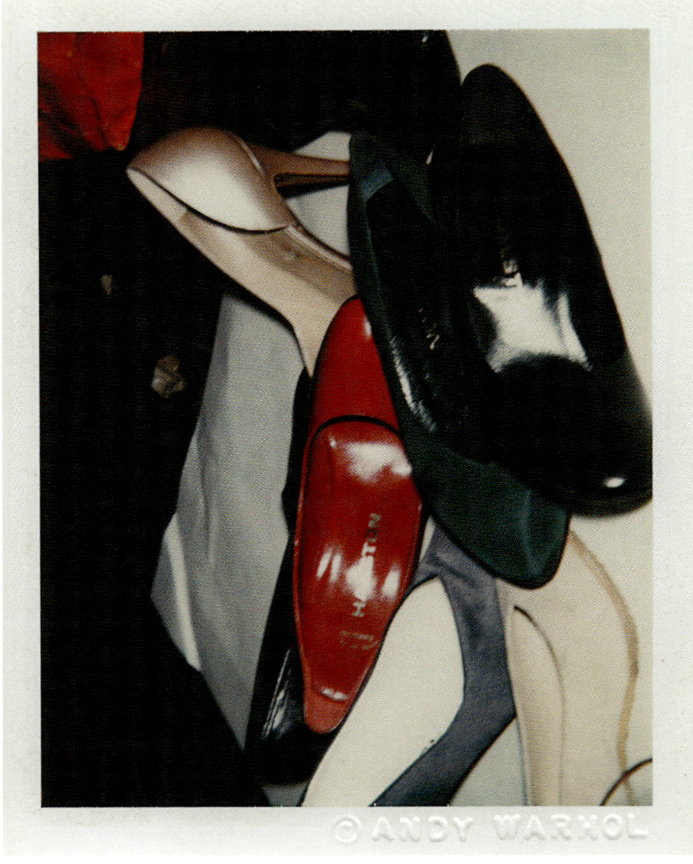

Andy Warhol
Shoes, 1980
Polaroid™ Polacolor 2
4¼ x 3⅜ in. (10.8 x 8.6 cm)
The Andy Warhol Museum, Pittsburgh; Contribution The Andy Warhol Foundation for the Visual Arts, Inc., 2001.2.1611

Andy Warhol
Shoes, 1980
Polaroid™ Polacolor 2
4¼ x 3⅜ in. (10.8 x 8.6 cm)
The Andy Warhol Museum, Pittsburgh; Contribution The Andy Warhol Foundation for the Visual Arts, Inc., 2001.2.1612

OPPOSITE
Andy Warhol
Diamond Dust Shoes (Random), 1980
Acrylic, silkscreen ink, and diamond dust on linen
90 x 70 in. (228.6 x 177.8 cm)
The Andy Warhol Museum, Pittsburgh; Founding Collection, Contribution The Andy Warhol Foundation for the Visual Arts, Inc., 1998.1.243

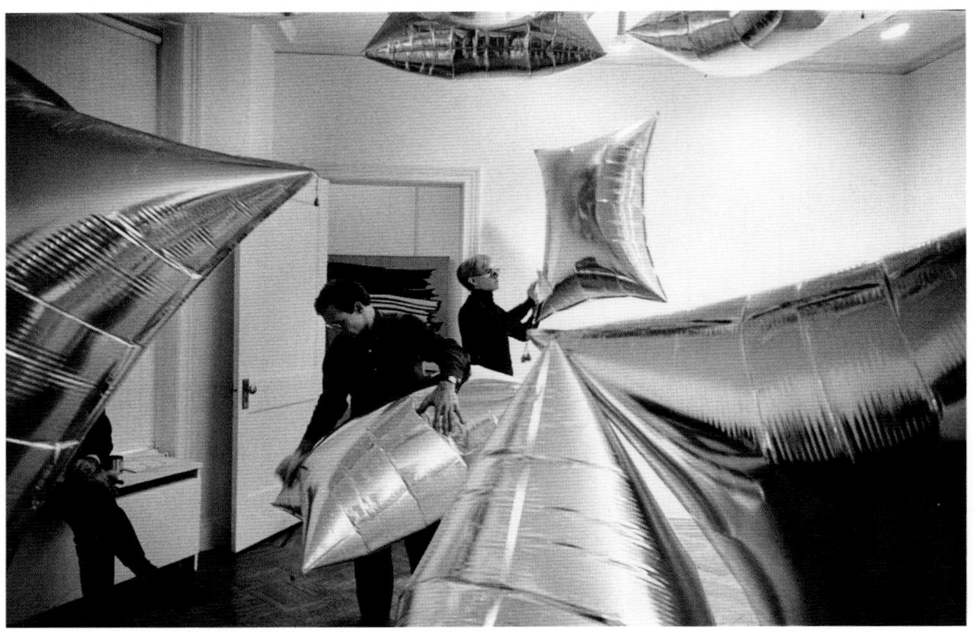

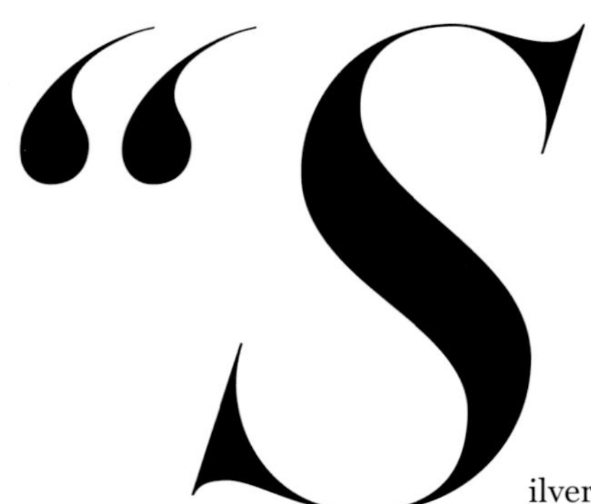

ilver was the future, it was spacey—the astronauts wore silver suits—Shepard, Grissom, and Glenn had already been up in them, and their equipment was silver, too. And silver was also the past—the Silver Screen—Hollywood actresses photographed in silver sets. And maybe more than anything, silver was narcissism—mirrors were backed with silver."

—Andy Warhol and Pat Hackett, *POPism: The Warhol '60s*

Silver Clouds (1964) captured everything Warhol liked about silver. Warhol's use of metallic materials spanned his entire career, from his gold- and silver-leaf drawings in the 1950s to the metallic grounds in his portraits of actors in the 1980s.

After a visit to Japan in 1980, Halston hired a Japanese textile designer named Reiko Sudo to hand paint cloud shapes on silk. Fabric was reproduced from the painted design and iridescent sequins were sewn across the surface of the dress to create a subtle, shiny patina.

TOP RIGHT
Nat Finkelstein
Andy Warhol and Two Unidentified Men, 1966
Gelatin silver print
7⅛ × 9½ in. (18.1 × 24.1 cm)
The Andy Warhol Museum, Pittsburgh; Museum Purchase, 1996.9.29

OPPOSITE
Halston
"Clouds" evening dress, 1982–83
Silk jersey with iridescent sequins
Indianapolis Museum of Art, 2009.556a

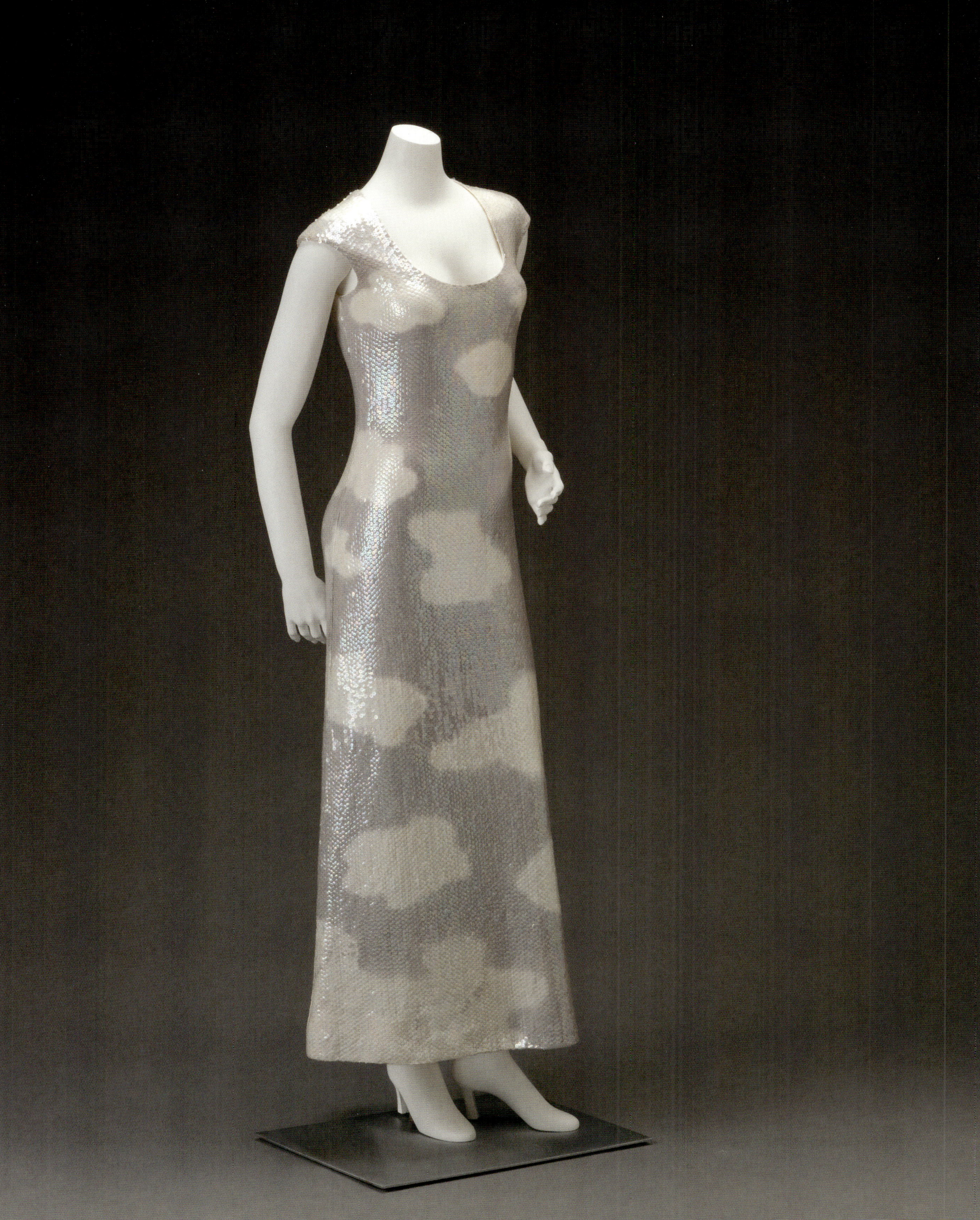

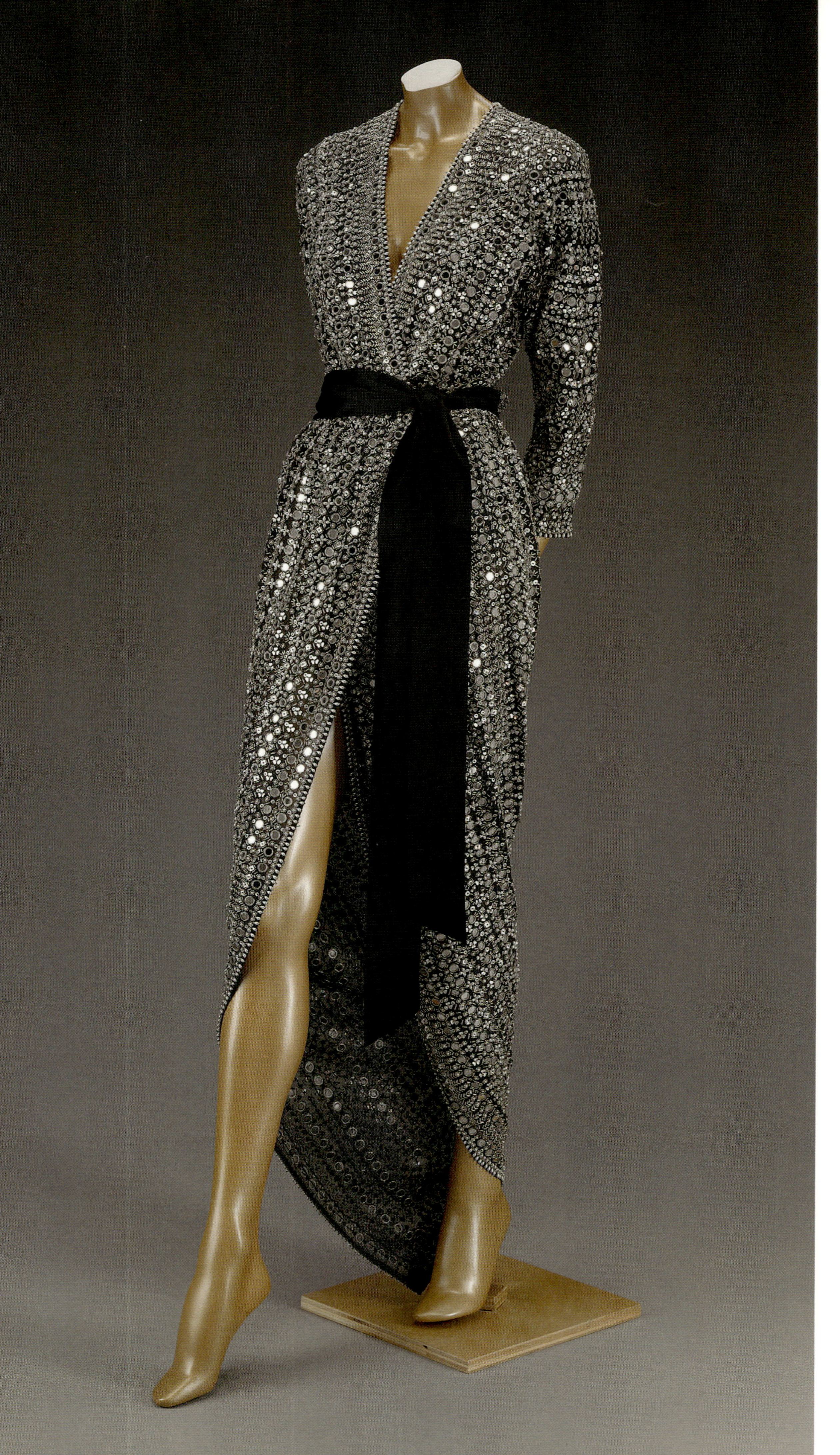

LEFT
Halston
Evening dress, 1981
Silk organza, silk, mirrors, sequins, glass beads, bugle beads, pearl beads, metallic threads
Indianapolis Museum of Art, 82.84A–B

OPPOSITE TOP LEFT
Andy Warhol
Clint Eastwood, ca. 1984
Acrylic and silkscreen ink on canvas
20 × 16 in. (50.8 × 40.6 cm)
The Andy Warhol Museum, Pittsburgh; Founding Collection, Contribution The Andy Warhol Foundation for the Visual Arts, Inc., 1998.1.541

OPPOSITE TOP RIGHT
Andy Warhol
Meryl Streep, ca. 1984
Acrylic and silkscreen ink on canvas
20 × 16 in. (50.8 × 40.6 cm)
The Andy Warhol Museum, Pittsburgh; Founding Collection, Contribution The Andy Warhol Foundation for the Visual Arts, Inc., 1998.1.665

OPPOSITE BOTTOM LEFT
Andy Warhol
Bill Murray, ca. 1984
Acrylic and silkscreen ink on linen
20 x 16 in. (50.8 x 40.6 cm)
The Andy Warhol Museum, Pittsburgh; Founding Collection, Contribution The Andy Warhol Foundation for the Visual Arts, Inc., 1998.1.620

OPPOSITE BOTTOM RIGHT
Andy Warhol
Diane Keaton, ca. 1984
Acrylic and silkscreen ink on canvas
20 x 16 in. (50.8 x 40.6 cm)
The Andy Warhol Museum, Pittsburgh; Founding Collection, Contribution The Andy Warhol Foundation for the Visual Arts, Inc., 1998.1.591

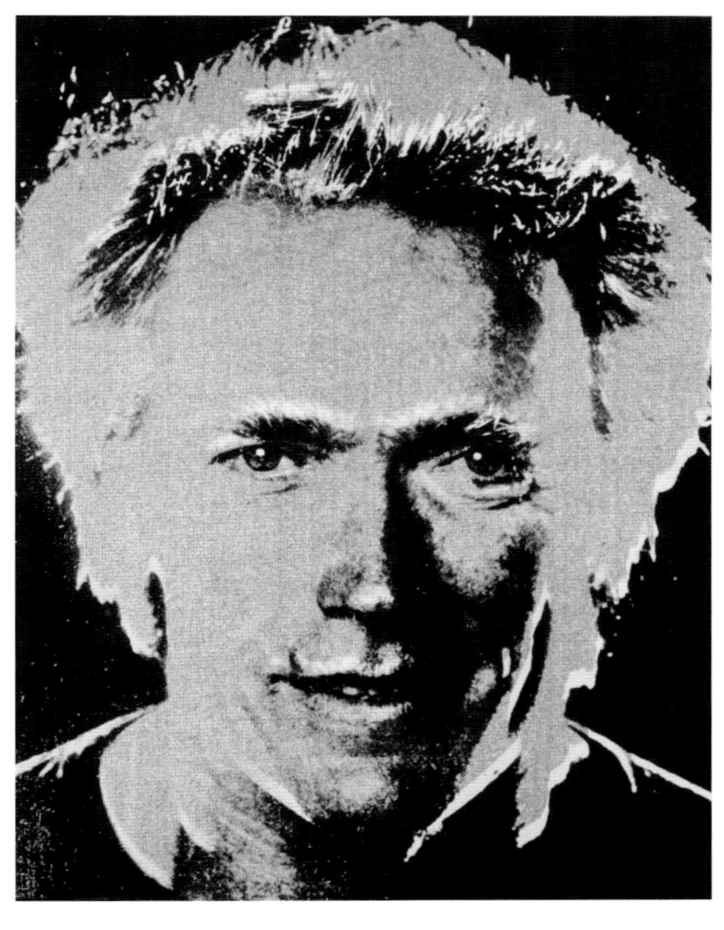
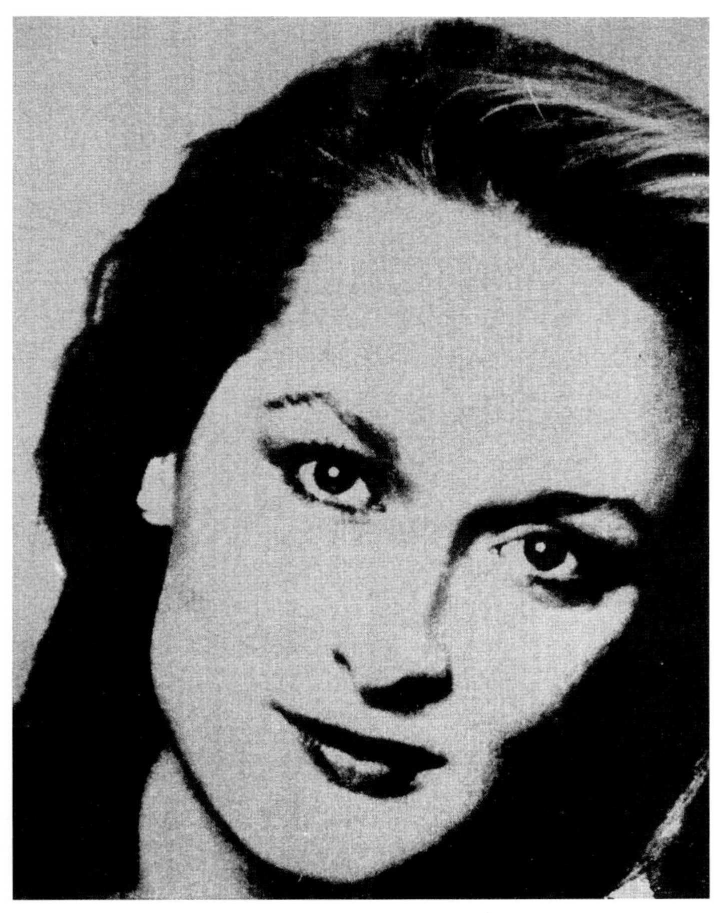
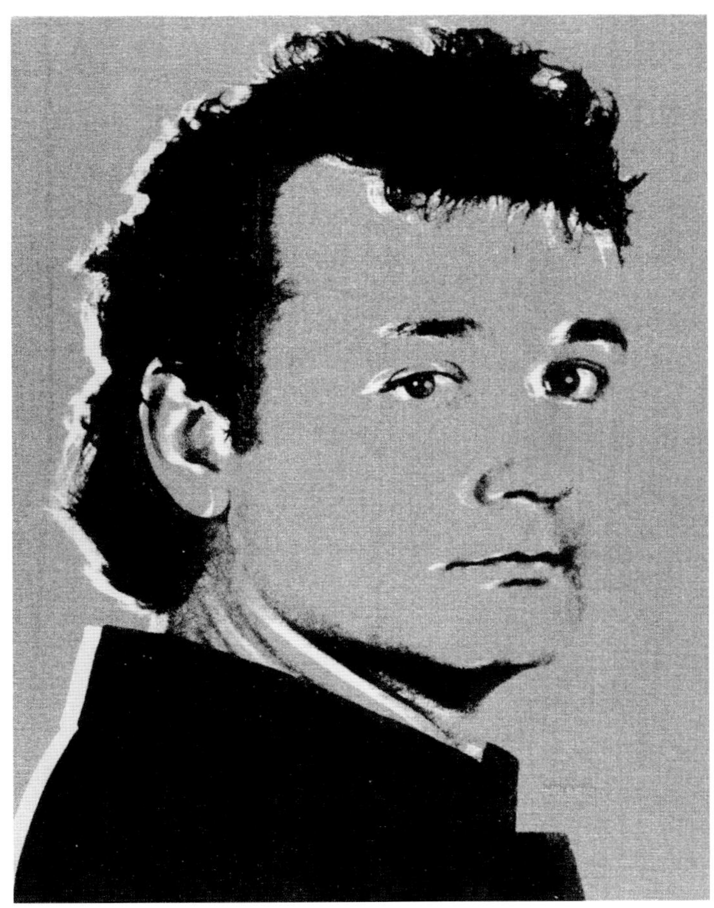
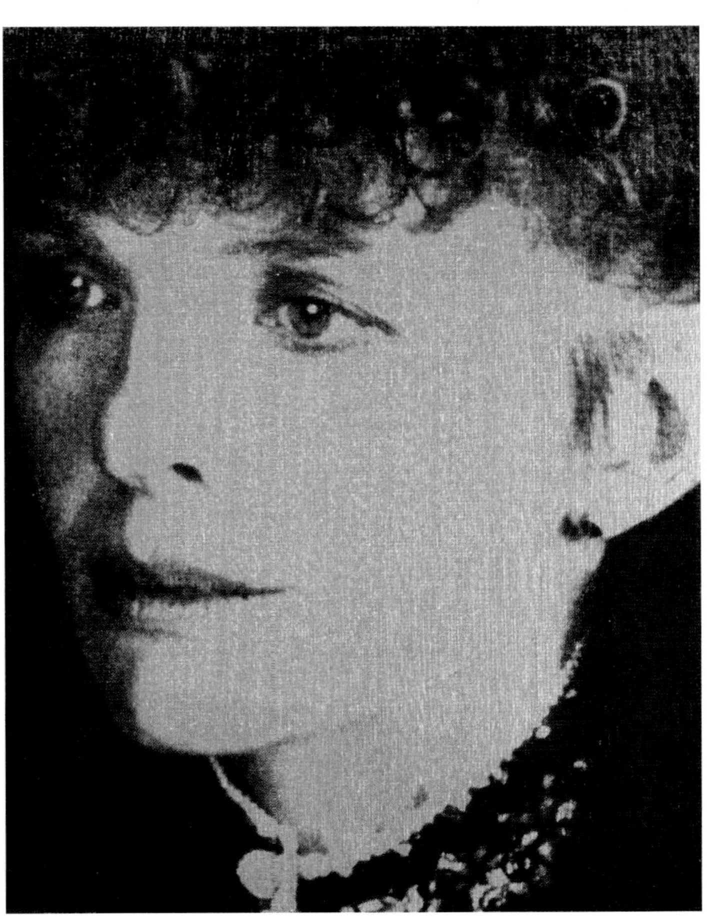

CELEBRITY

"It used to be that when you were famous, you were famous for one thing. John F. Kennedy was President. Elvis was the King of Rock and Roll. Elizabeth Taylor was the world's greatest movie star. But now, it seems like you have to do lots of things really well, and don't get to stay famous for long unless you're always switching."

—Andy Warhol, *America*

"I always like [going to parties at] Halston's [townhouse] when Elizabeth Taylor is there. She has the best personality. She reminds me of my first superstar, Edie Sedgwick. Edie never grew up. Elizabeth is like a big kid too. She always says what she feels like saying."

—Andy Warhol, *Exposures*

Elizabeth Taylor and Halston arrive at St. Bartholomew's Episcopal Church on Park Avenue for the wedding of Liza Minnelli to theatrical manager Mark Gero on Tuesday night, December 4, 1979. Taylor stood in for Minnelli's mother, the late Judy Garland. *Associated Press*

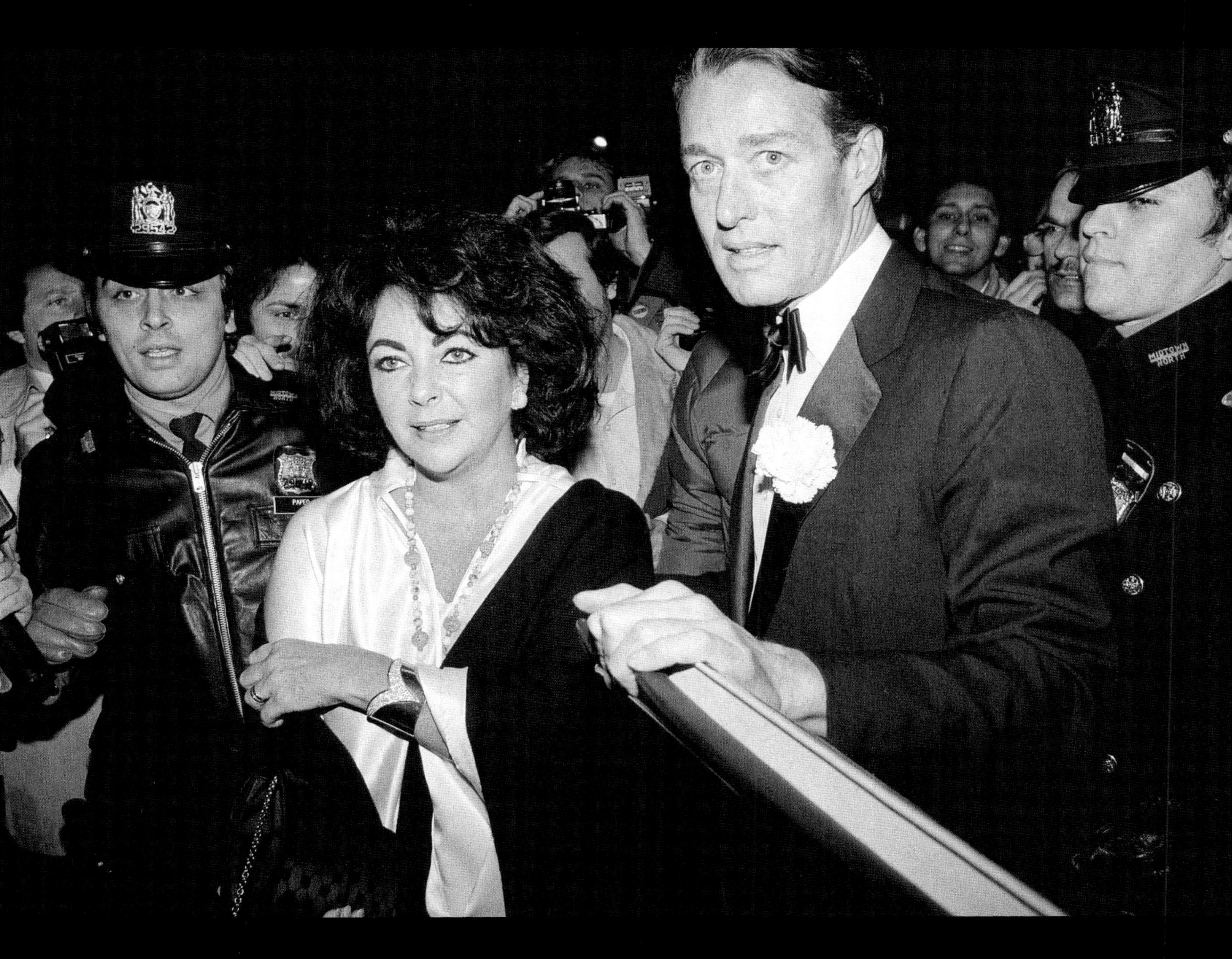
MIDTOWN
NORTH

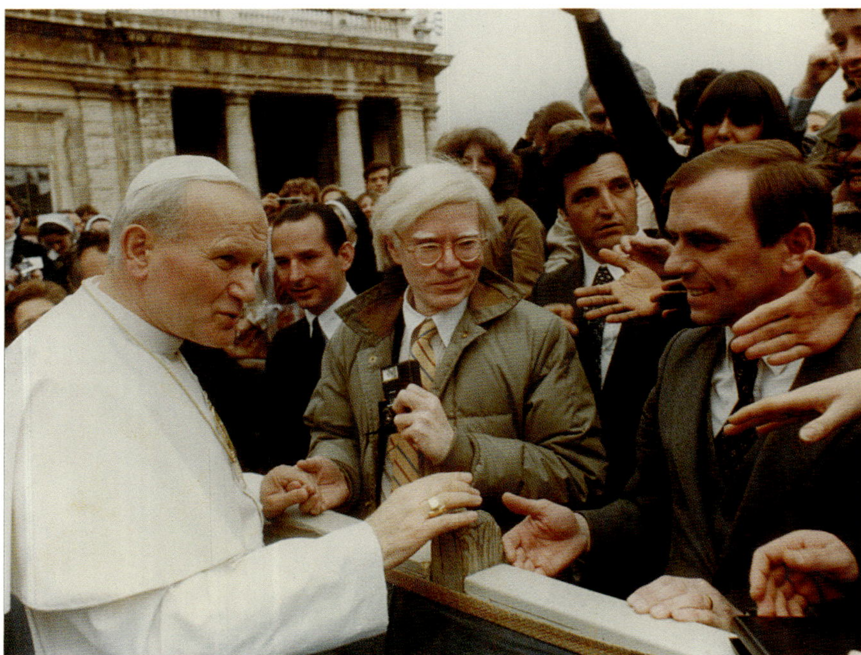

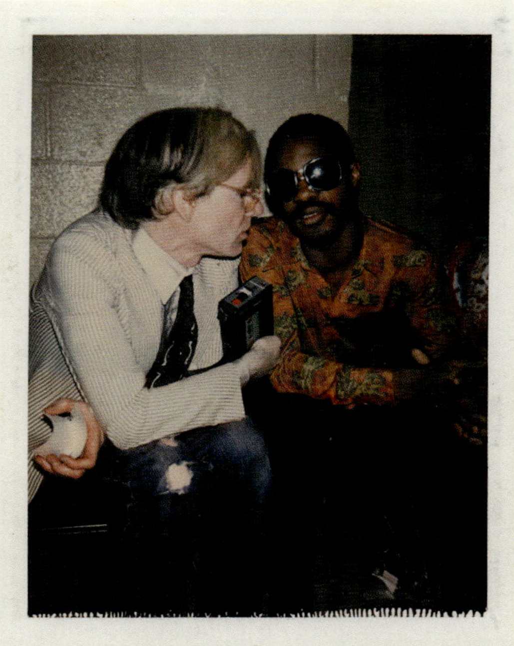

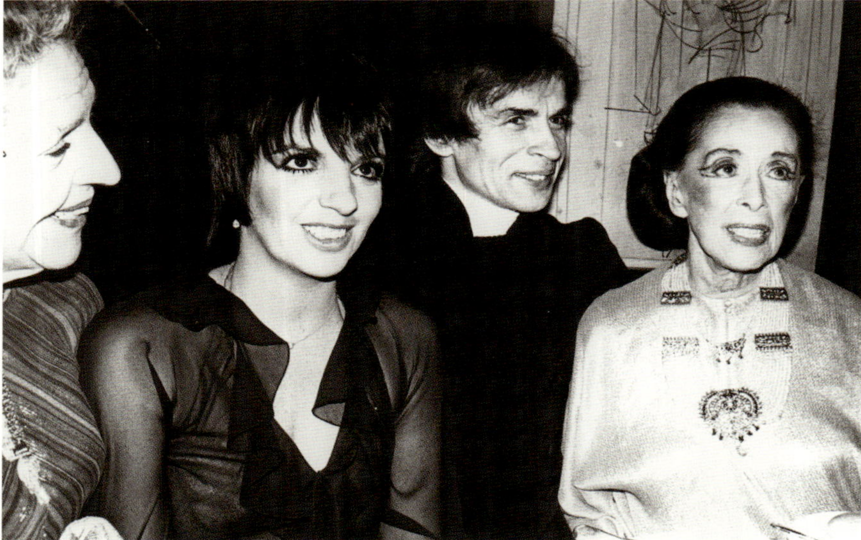

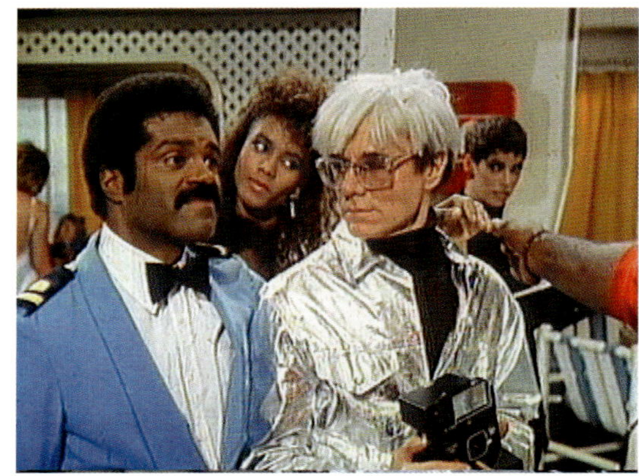

TOP LEFT
Felici
Pope John Paul II, Fred Hughes, and Andy Warhol, 1980
Chromogenic color print
8 × 9⅞ in. (20.3 × 25.1 cm)
The Andy Warhol Museum, Pittsburgh; Founding Collection, Contribution The Andy Warhol Foundation for the Visual Arts, Inc., 1998.3.9434

BOTTOM LEFT
Andy Warhol
Unidentified Female, Liza Minnelli, Rudolf Nureyev, and Martha Graham, ca. 1980
Gelatin silver print
8 × 9⅞ in. (20.3 × 25.1 cm)
The Andy Warhol Museum, Pittsburgh; Contribution The Andy Warhol Foundation for the Visual Arts, Inc., 2001.2.204

TOP RIGHT
Andy Warhol
Self-Portrait with Stevie Wonder, date unknown
Polaroid™
4¼ × 3⅜ in. (10.8 × 8.6 cm)
The Andy Warhol Museum, Pittsburgh; Founding Collection, Contribution The Andy Warhol Foundation for the Visual Arts, Inc., 1998.1.2992.1

BOTTOM RIGHT
***The Love Boat* (Episode 200),** 1985
1 in. videotape, color, sound, 49 minutes
Douglas S. Cramer Productions in association with Aaron Spelling Productions, Inc., Executive producers, Aaron Spelling, Douglas S. Cramer. Producers, Dennis Hammer, William Bickley, and Michael Warren. Director, Richard Kinon. Video still courtesy The Andy Warhol Museum

"Television needs glamour and we can supply it."

—Halston, quoted in *People*, February 23, 1981

As recognizable icons, both Halston and Warhol were invited to appear in episodes of the wildly popular television series *The Love Boat*. Set on a cruise ship, the weekly show featured celebrity guests as characters on vacation. Halston was invited on the show in 1981, Warhol in 1985.

Warhol's television shows, *Andy Warhol's T.V.* and *Andy Warhol's Fifteen Minutes*, were broadcast on New York cable television and nationally on MTV. He created work for *Saturday Night Live* and produced music videos for rock bands such as the Cars. Warhol also signed with a few modeling agencies, appearing in fashion shows and in numerous print and television ads.

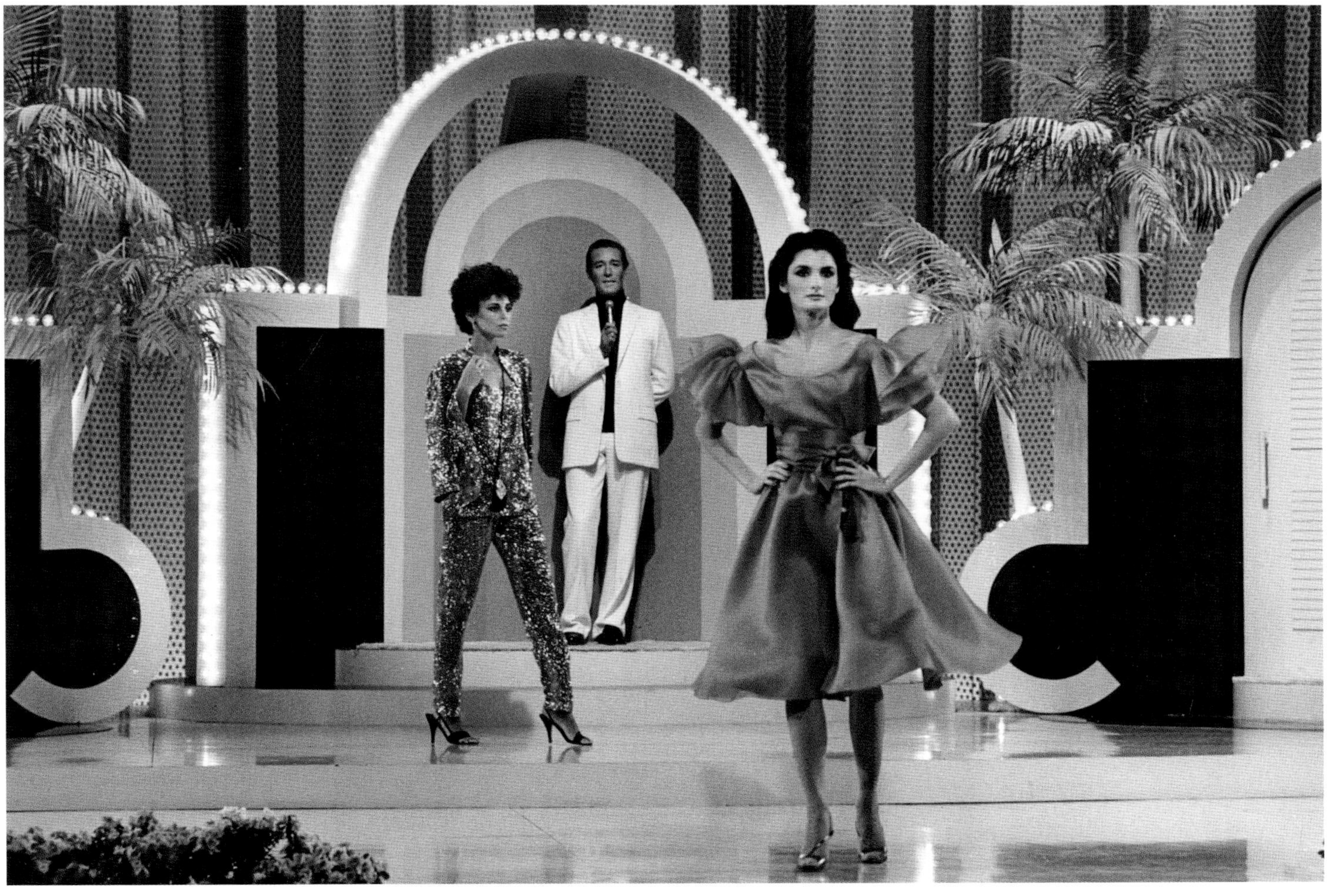

Along with the designers Geoffrey Beene, Bob Mackie, and Gloria Vanderbilt, Halston made a guest appearance on *The Love Boat*, May 2, 1981
ABC Photo Archives

FRIENDSHIP

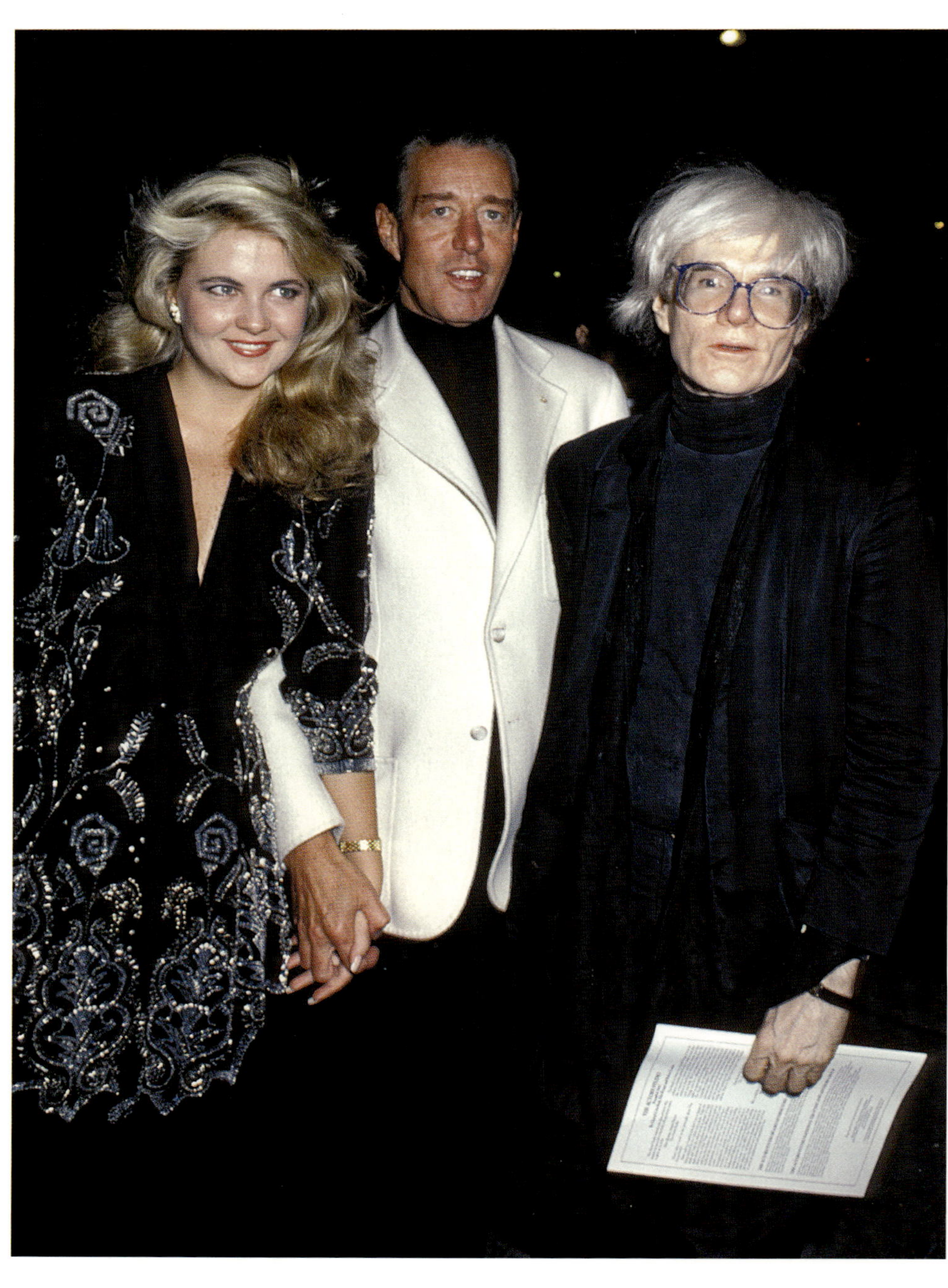

RIGHT
Cornelia Guest, Halston, and Warhol at the New York premiere of *The Color of Money*, October 8, 1986
Photograph by Ron Galella
WireImage/Getty Images

OPPOSITE (CLOCKWISE FROM TOP LEFT)
Andy Warhol
Pat Ast, n.d.
Gelatin silver print
8 × 10 in. (20.3 × 25.4 cm)
The Andy Warhol Museum, Pittsburgh; Founding Collection, Contribution The Andy Warhol Foundation for the Visual Arts, Inc., 1998.1.300827

Andy Warhol
Andy Warhol, Martha Graham, and a birthday cake, 1981
Gelatin silver print
8 × 10 in. (20.3 × 25.4 cm)
The Andy Warhol Museum, Pittsburgh; Contribution The Andy Warhol Foundation for the Visual Arts, Inc., 2001.2.829

Andy Warhol
Bianca Jagger, Halston, and Marisa Berenson, December 6, 1977
Photograph from Time Capsule 577
10 × 8 in. (25.4 × 20.3 cm)
The Andy Warhol Museum, Pittsburgh; Founding Collection, Contribution The Andy Warhol Foundation for the Visual Arts, Inc., TC577.78

Andy Warhol
Marisa Berenson, ca. 1980
Gelatin silver print
10 × 8 in. (25.4 × 20.3 cm)
The Andy Warhol Museum, Pittsburgh; Contribution The Andy Warhol Foundation for the Visual Arts, Inc., 2001.2.70

Andy Warhol
Diana Vreeland, ca. 1979
Gelatin silver print
10 × 8 in. (25.4 × 20.3 cm)
The Andy Warhol Museum, Pittsburgh; Founding Collection, Contribution The Andy Warhol Foundation for the Visual Arts, Inc., 1998.1.3072

Andy Warhol
Halston and Paloma Picasso in Halston's Olympic Tower showroom, New York, n.d.
Photograph from Time Capsule 577
8 x 10 in. (20.3 x 25.4 cm)
The Andy Warhol Museum, Pittsburgh; Founding Collection, Contribution The Andy Warhol Foundation for the Visual Arts, Inc., TC577.106.66

Andy Warhol
Joe Eula, 1978
Gelatin silver print
8 × 10 in. (20.3 × 25.4 cm)
The Andy Warhol Foundation for the Visual Arts, Inc., FL06.00277

Andy Warhol
Catherine Guinness, John Richardson, and Diane von Furstenberg, n.d.
Gelatin silver print
8 × 10 in. (20.3 × 25.4 cm)
The Andy Warhol Museum, Pittsburgh; Contribution The Andy Warhol Foundation for the Visual Arts, Inc., 2001.2.165

OPPOSITE CENTER
Andy Warhol
André Leon Talley, Tina Chow, and Unidentified Man, n.d.
Gelatin silver print
10 x 8 in. (25.4 x 20.3 cm)
The Andy Warhol Museum, Pittsburgh, Contribution The Andy Warhol Foundation for the Visual Arts, Inc., 2001.2.197

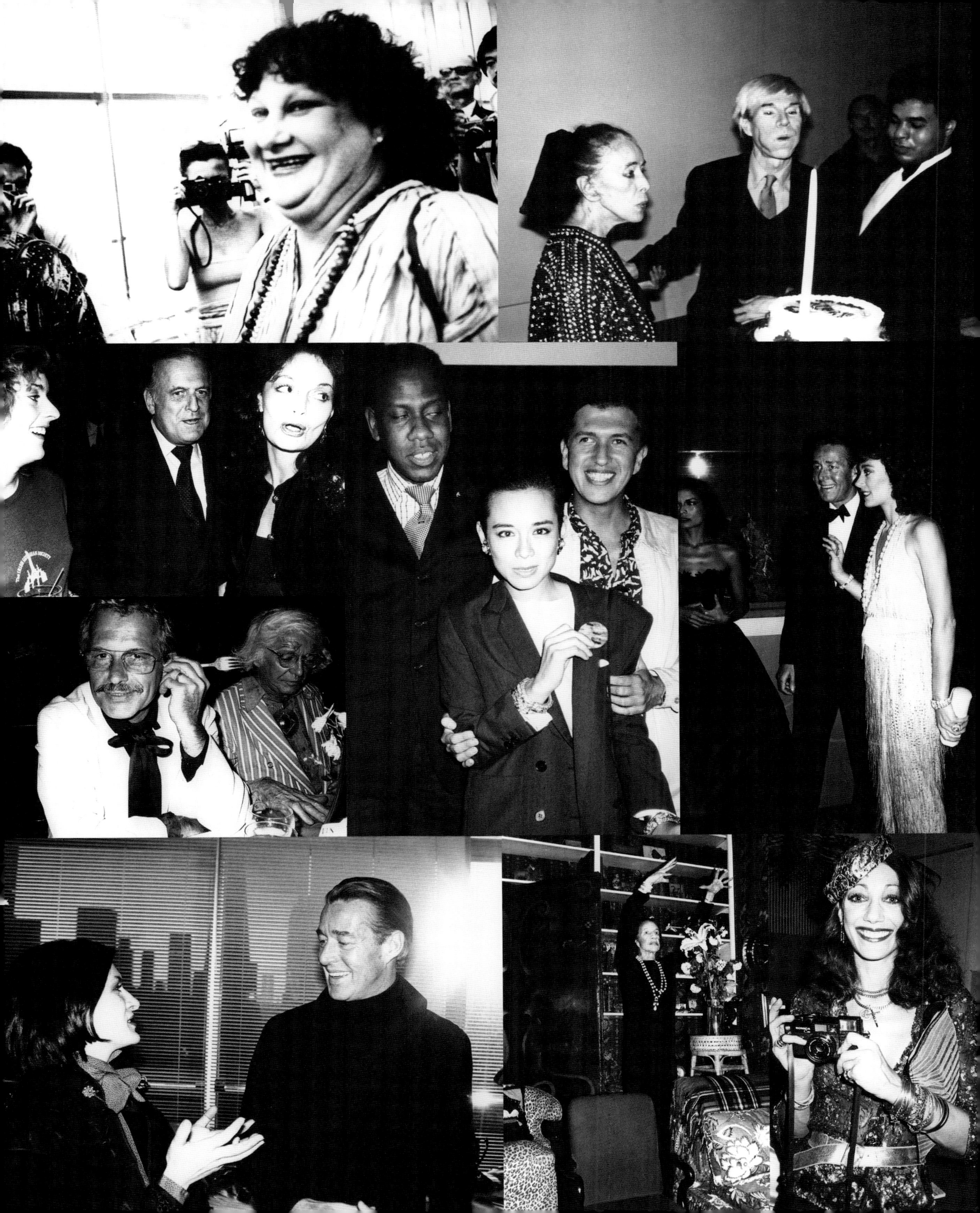

MONTAUK

"Halston invited me to Montauk, so I'm going at 6:30 on Friday with him on his rented plane. It's so nice to be invited to your own house by the person who's renting it—you feel at home and you're still making money."

—Andy Warhol, *Diaries*, July 9, 1981

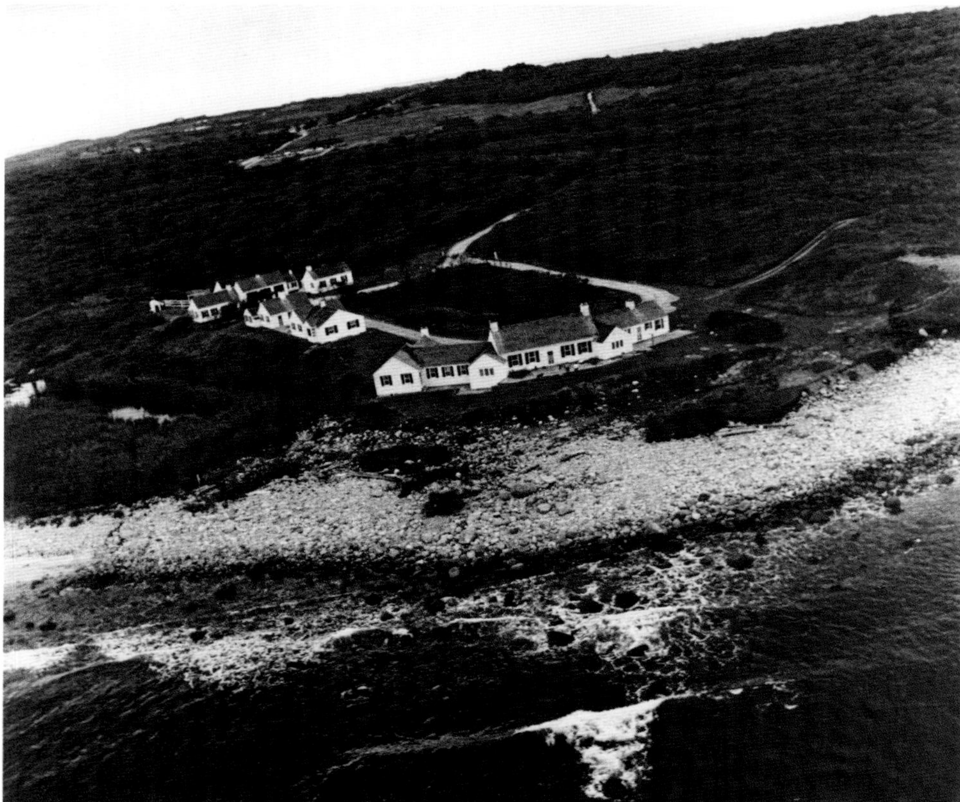

Andy Warhol's beach compound in Montauk, New York, 1971

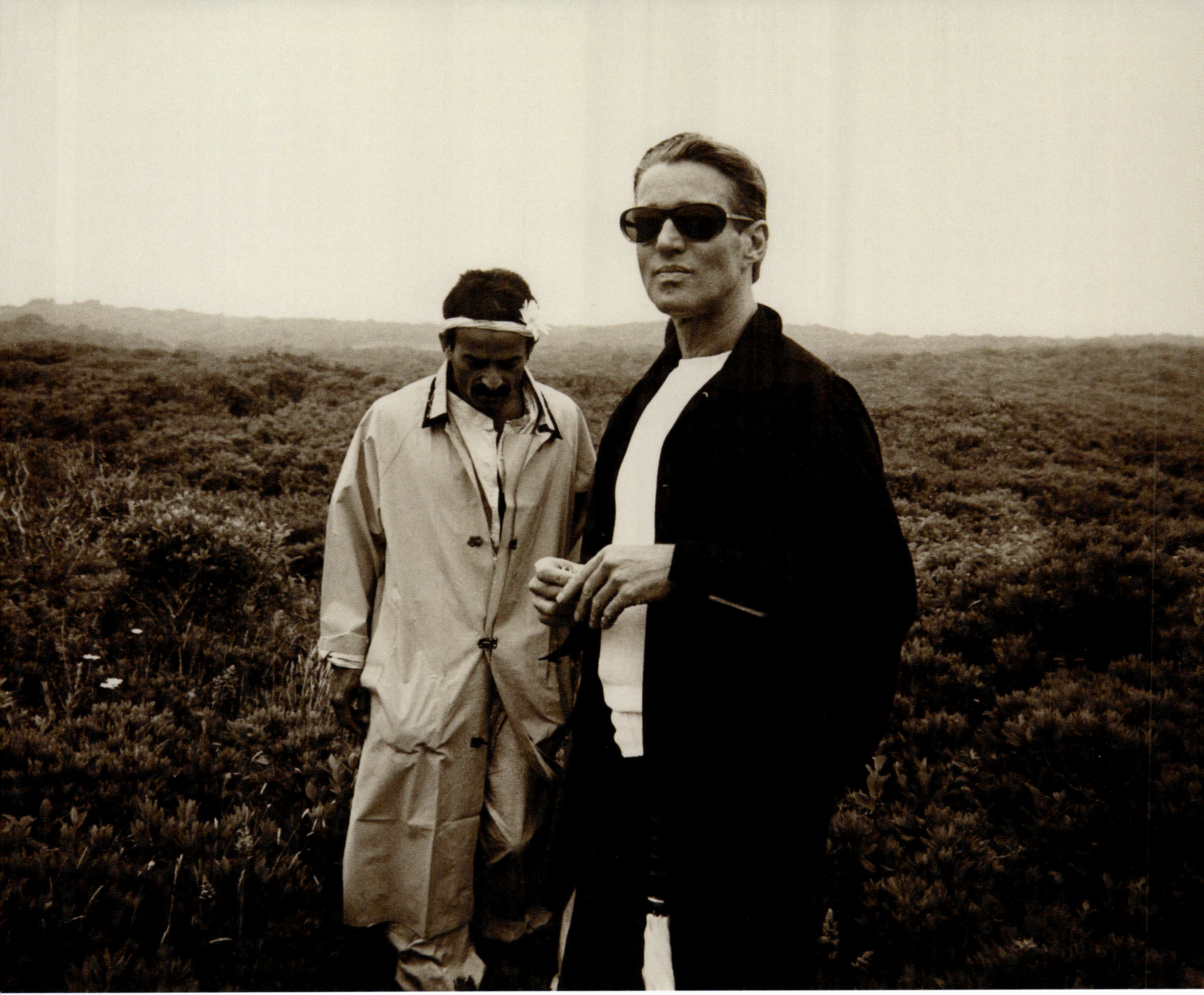

Andy Warhol
Montauk: Victor Hugo and Halston,
1982
Gelatin silver print
8 × 10 in. (20.3 × 25.4 cm)
The Andy Warhol Foundation for the Visual Arts, Inc., FL06.03037

As the 1980s opened, Halston and Warhol shared a great deal of time together, from Thanksgiving and Christmas dinners to weekends at Warhol's compound in Montauk.

In 1972, Warhol purchased an oceanfront compound in Montauk, New York, on the easternmost tip of Long Island. The compound included four white clapboard buildings, the largest of which was a seven-bedroom, four-and-a half-bath house. Lee Radziwill, Jackie Kennedy's sister, rented the Montauk property from Warhol for the first summer, and in her memoir, *Happy Times*, she described the easygoing aura and spaciousness that made Warhol's home such an alluring retreat. "The main house had a floor of huge old flagstones and two enormous fireplaces opposite each other. It smelled of cedar and sea."

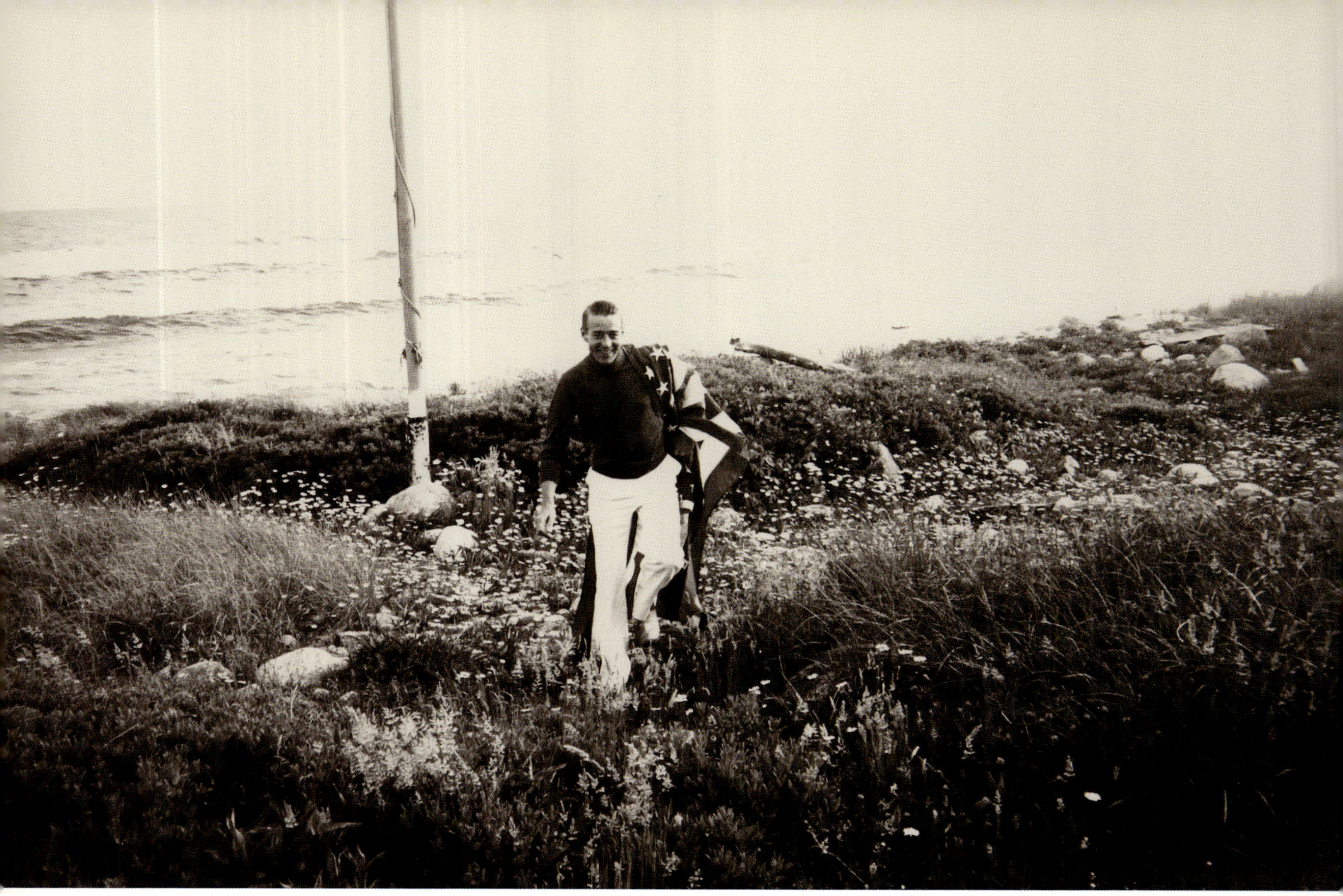

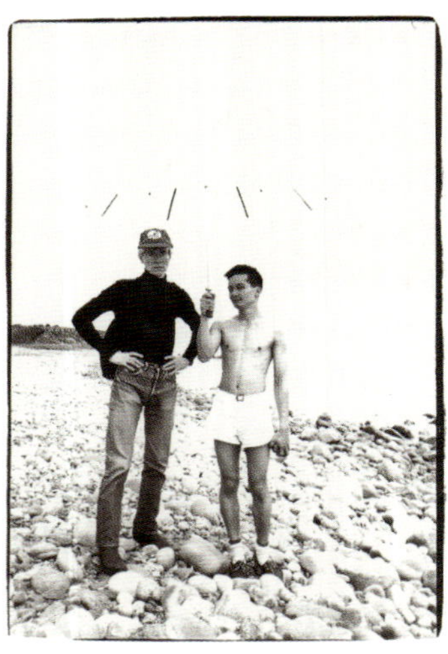

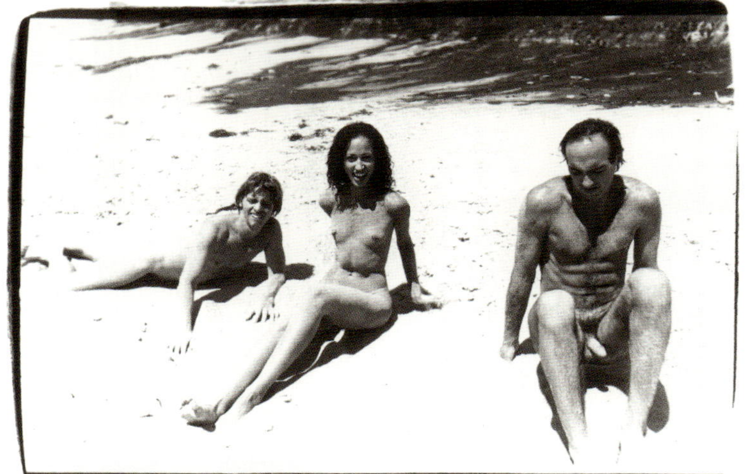

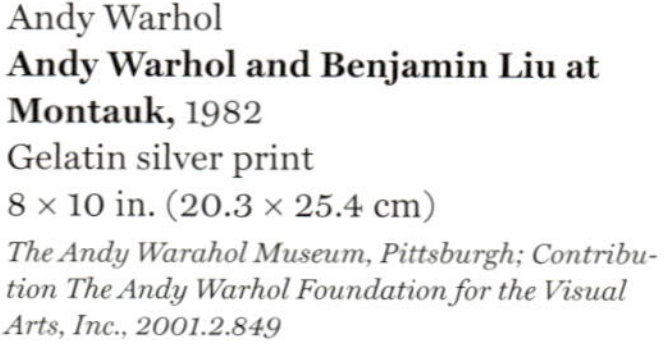

Andy Warhol
Andy Warhol and Benjamin Liu at Montauk, 1982
Gelatin silver print
8 × 10 in. (20.3 × 25.4 cm)
The Andy Warahol Museum, Pittsburgh; Contribution The Andy Warhol Foundation for the Visual Arts, Inc., 2001.2.849

Andy Warhol
Christopher Makos, Pat Cleveland, and Jon Gould at the beach, n.d.
Gelatin silver print
8 × 10 in. (20.3 × 25.4 cm)
The Andy Warhol Museum, Pittsburgh; Contribution The Andy Warhol Foundation for the Visual Arts, Inc., 2001.2.1109

TOP
Andy Warhol
Montauk: Halston, 1982
Gelatin silver print
8 × 10 in. (20.3 × 25.4 cm)
The Andy Warhol Foundation for the Visual Arts, Inc., FL05.04237

The seclusion of the twenty-acre property appealed to Warhol, even though he did not hide his dislike of the sun and water. He leased the beach house in order to pay the mortgage but was a regular guest in his own home. Friends who stayed in Montauk included Halston, Mick and Bianca Jagger, Elizabeth Taylor, John Lennon, Jackie Kennedy, Truman Capote, Liza Minnelli, and others.

For many years, Halston rented Warhol's Montauk compound year-round, finding it a relaxing refuge from New York City. Halston became so enamored of Montauk that he purchased one hundred undeveloped acres with the superstar model Lauren Hutton. However, he did not build on his Montauk property and continued to rent Warhol's home until he moved to California in 1989, shortly before he died.

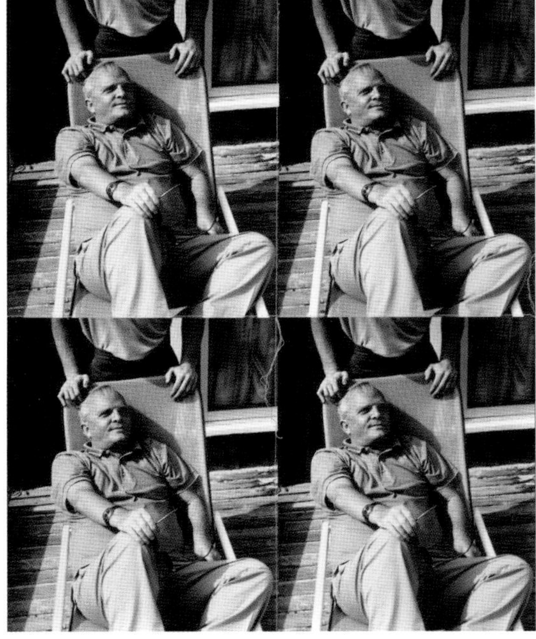

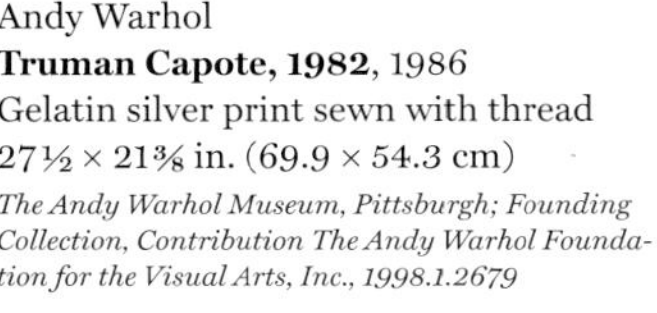

Andy Warhol
Truman Capote, 1982, 1986
Gelatin silver print sewn with thread
27½ × 21⅜ in. (69.9 × 54.3 cm)
The Andy Warhol Museum, Pittsburgh; Founding Collection, Contribution The Andy Warhol Foundation for the Visual Arts, Inc., 1998.1.2679

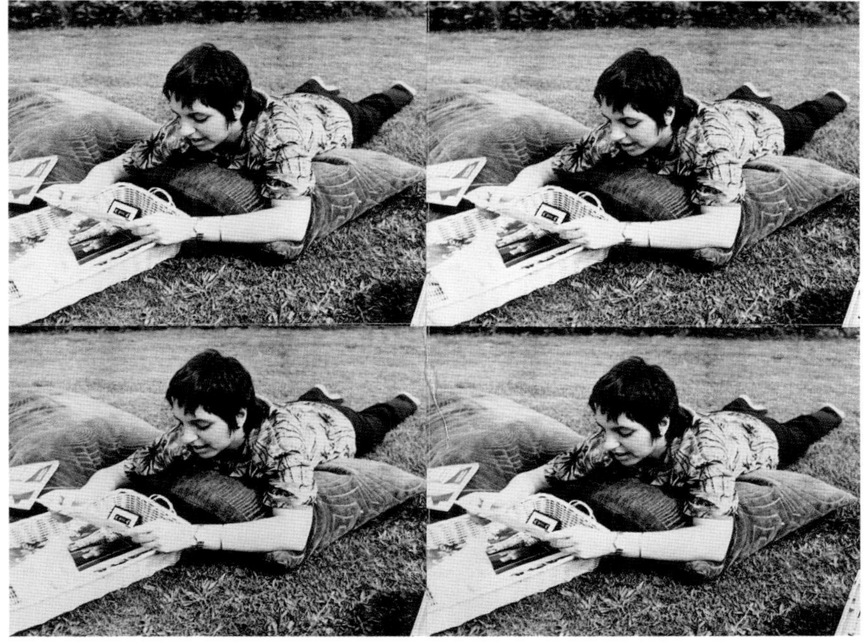

Andy Warhol
Liza Minnelli, ca. 1978, 1986
Gelatin silver print sewn with thread
21⅜ × 27⅝ in. (54.3 × 70.2 cm)
The Andy Warhol Museum, Pittsburgh; Founding Collection, Contribution The Andy Warhol Foundation for the Visual Arts, Inc., 1998.1.2693

AIDS

It is perhaps impossible to overstate the impact of AIDS on the personal, social, and cultural networks of gay men in New York City in the 1980s. AIDS not only struck down Halston, Joe Eula, Victor Hugo, Keith Haring, Jon Gould, Steve Rubell, and a host of other friends and business associates, the disease also destroyed the context that largely inspired Halston's and Warhol's work. The revolutionary nature of New York City in the 1970s was its mixing of worlds, uptown and downtown, gay and straight.

Beginning in the mid-1970s and reaching a peak in the early 1980s, the lifestyle of openly gay men—even the most extreme aspects of the culture they created in lower Manhattan and Fire Island—was seen as aspirational to the straight world. These gay men led the nightlife vanguard at Studio 54, a relatively safe and sanitized vision of debauchery, and opened the world of private downtown clubs to the same famous faces. The stark, industrial design of clubs such as the Saint can be seen echoing through the mirrored, orchid-strewn Halston offices, and the direct and simple sexuality that was so resonant in the chic and sophisticated fashions of the era owed more than a little to gay culture.

This cross-cultural world of risk and experimentation was, seemingly, gone overnight by the late 1980s, due partly to the fact that the first group of gay men to be affected by AIDS was a close-knit and relatively small community. What before had been seen as exhilarating acts of freedom were suddenly cast with darkness, even shame. The truth remains that the era was not so much about self-destruction but about living as fully as possible.

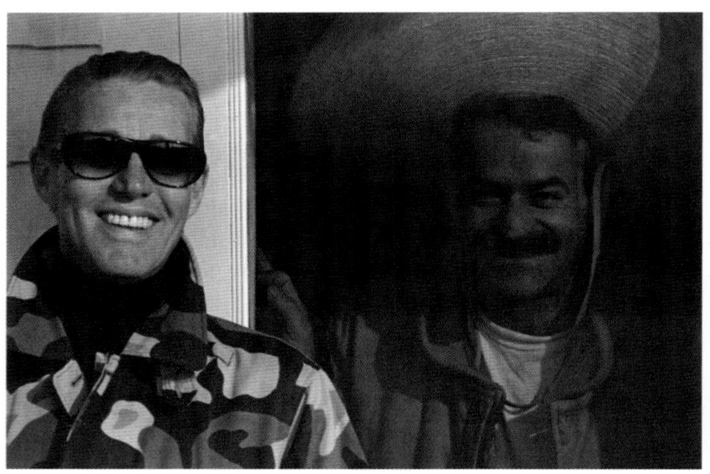

Halston and Victor Hugo at Halston's Montauk retreat, 1987
Courtesy the Lesley Frowick Collection

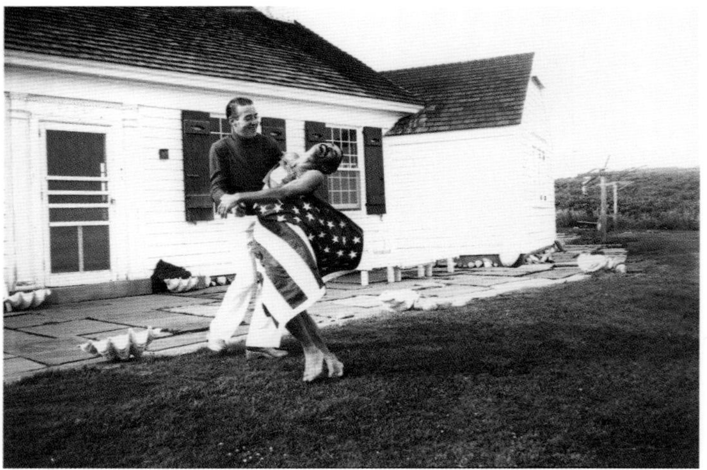

Andy Warhol
Halston and Victor Hugo with American flag, 1982
Gelatin silver print
8 x 10 in. (20.3 x 25.4 cm)
The Andy Warhol Museum, Pittsburgh; Contribution The Andy Warhol Foundation for the Visual Arts, Inc., 2001.2.711

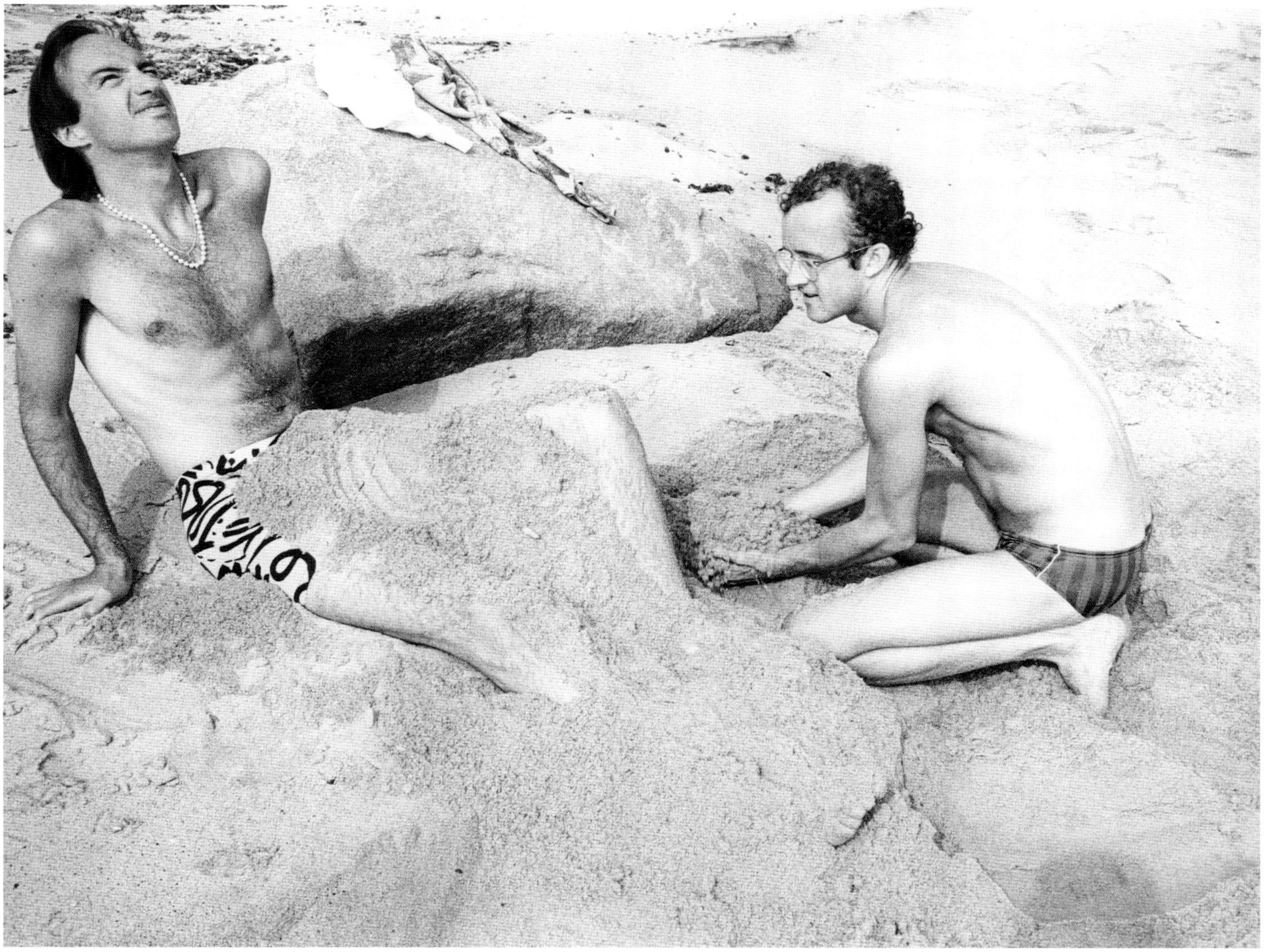

Andy Warhol
Jon Gould and Keith Haring, n.d.
Gelatin silver print
8 × 10 in. (20.3 × 25.4 cm)
The Andy Warhol Museum, Pittsburgh; Contribution The Andy Warhol Foundation for the Visual Arts, Inc., 2001.2.710

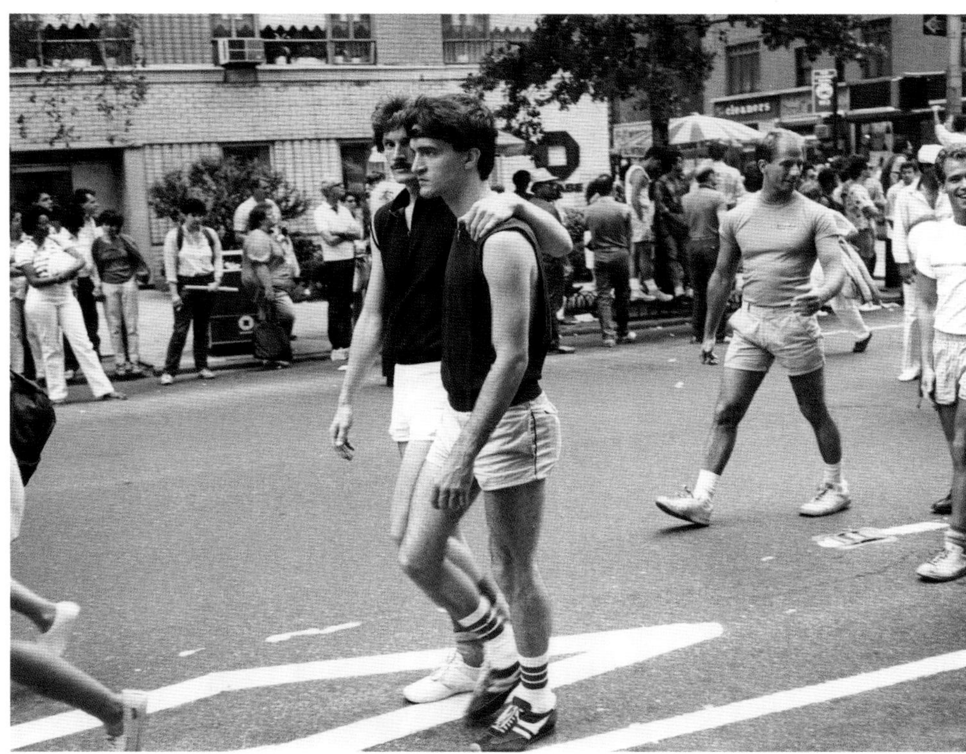

Andy Warhol
Unidentified Men, 1984
Gelatin silver print
8 × 10 in. (20.3 × 25.4 cm)
The Andy Warhol Museum, Pittsburgh; Contribution The Andy Warhol Foundation for the Visual Arts, Inc., 2001.2.252

ENDINGS

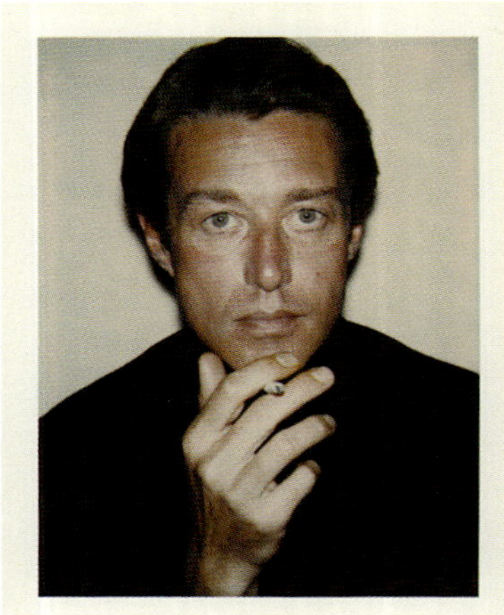

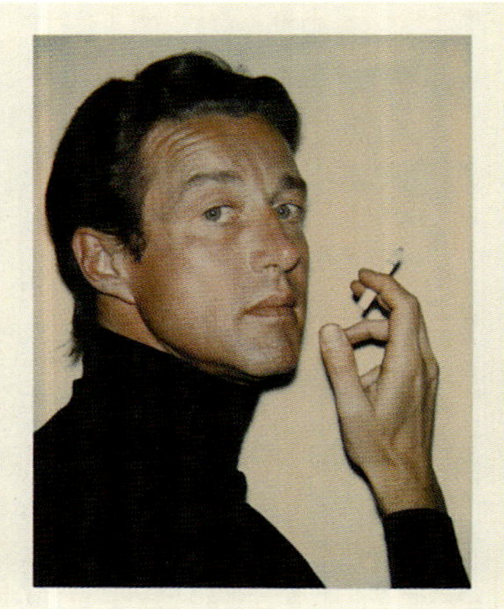

"They're selling Halston's floor in the Olympic Tower out from under him. It's so sad. Where did Halston go so wrong when he sold his name? What should he have done that he didn't? That's what I want to know. And I want to know it from him, I want to sit down and find out what I should do if I ever sell myself. Find out when and where he made his mistakes. In case I ever want to let a big corporation buy me out and just be a figurehead. Because there's got to be a way to do it where you don't lose all your power the way Halston did."

—Andy Warhol, *Diaries*, November 25, 1984

Human beings are complicated, and creative ones can be more complicated than the rest. While Halston and Warhol were friends and ambitious men, they were not without discord or immune from weakness. By many accounts they alternately loved and hated each other, depending on circumstances. Warhol was, as many have put it, jealous of Halston's good looks, easy charm, and extensive social reach. He was also aware of Halston's dark streak, which could end friendships. In like turns they celebrated holidays, birthdays, and big events together, then questioned the other's motives or feelings in private.

It does seem clear that to the end they deeply admired each other. It was a giant blow to Halston when Warhol died in 1987. But the posthumous publication in 1989 of *The Andy Warhol Diaries*, which exposed Halston's drug use, soured the memory of Warhol for Halston. In anguish of being publicly mentioned in less-than-flattering terms, Halston donated and sold off his entire collection of Warhol paintings.

In creating this publication, the aim is neither to whitewash the past, nor to drag out all the sordid details, but instead, with the wisdom of hindsight, to embrace the complexity of these men and their incredible contribution to American fashion and art.

TOP
Andy Warhol
Halston, 1974
Polaroid™ Polacolor Type 108
4 ¼ × 3 ⅜ in. (10.8 × 8.6 cm)
The Andy Warhol Museum, Pittsburgh; Contribution The Andy Warhol Foundation for the Visual Arts, Inc., 2000.2.844

BOTTOM
Andy Warhol
Halston, 1974
Polaroid™ Polacolor Type 108
4 ¼ × 3 ⅜ in. (10.8 × 8.6 cm)
The Andy Warhol Museum, Pittsburgh; Contribution The Andy Warhol Foundation for the Visual Arts, Inc., 2000.2.845

OPPOSITE
Andy Warhol
Halston, n.d.
Graphite on HMP paper
31⅛ × 23⅞ in. (79.1 × 60.6 cm)
The Andy Warhol Museum, Pittsburgh; Founding Collection, Contribution The Andy Warhol Foundation for the Visual Arts, Inc., 1998.1.2254

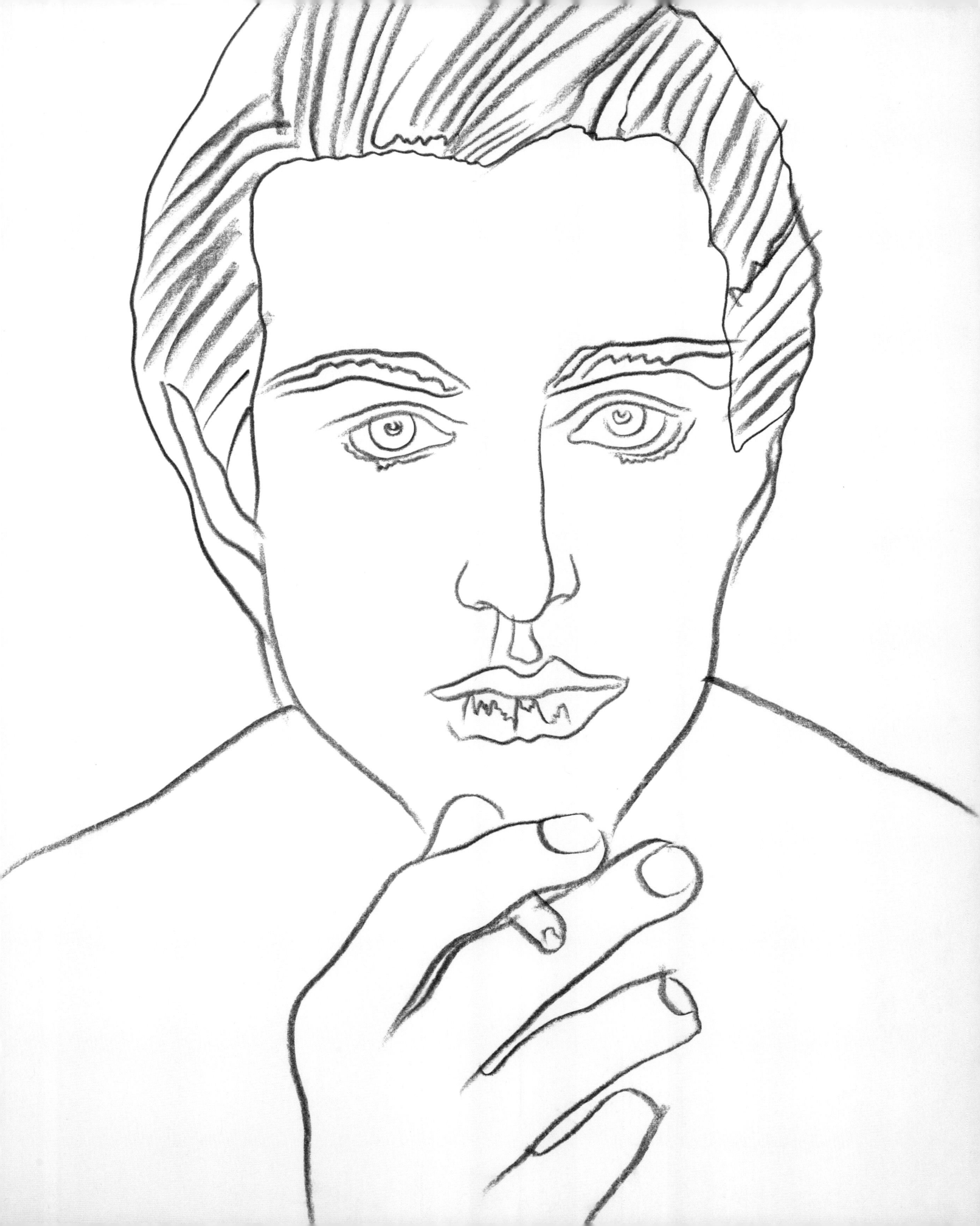

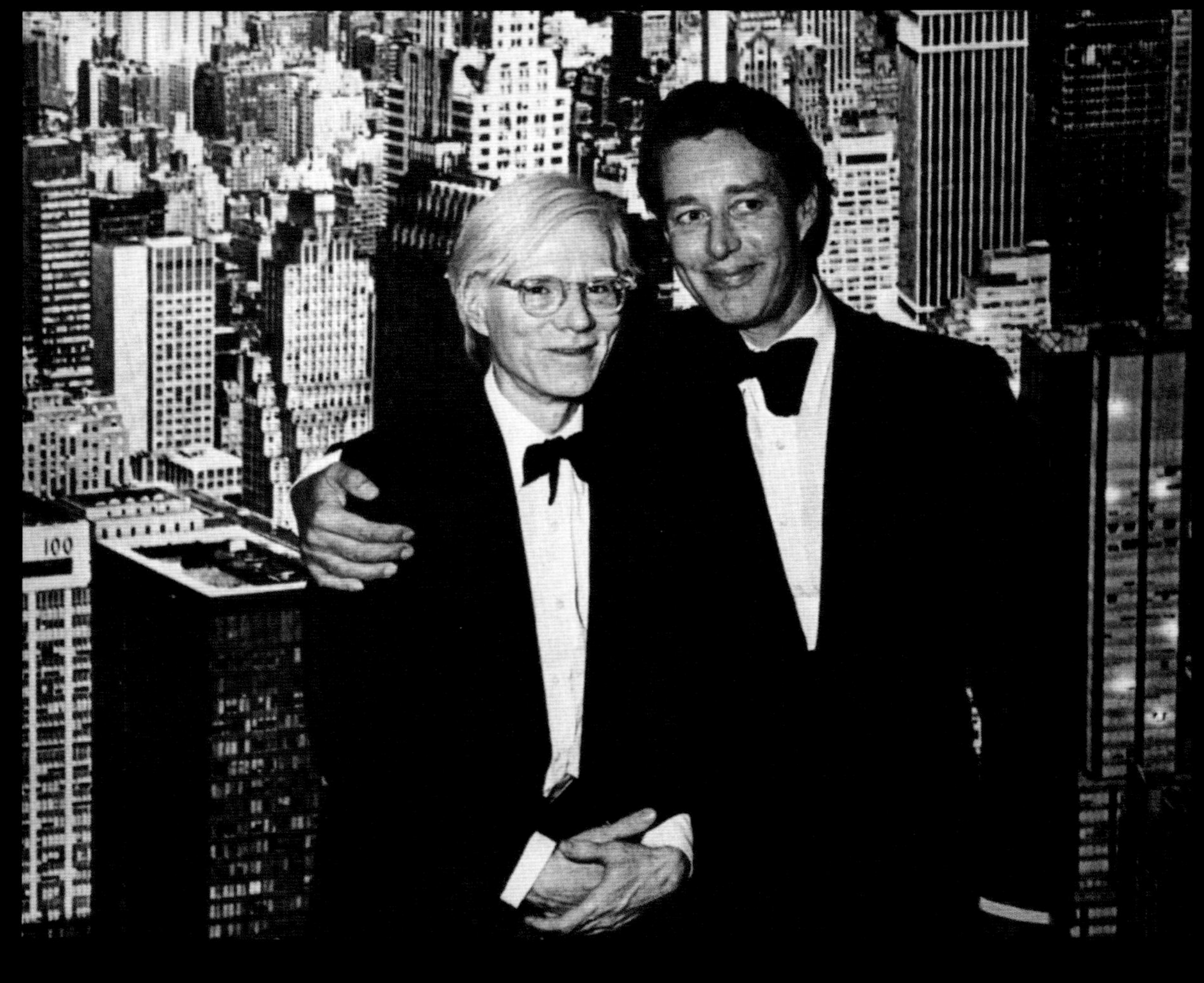
100

NOTES TO PAGES 54–232

54: Halston, quoted in Elaine Gross and Fred Rottman, *Halston: An American Original* (New York: HarperCollins, 1999), 4; Andy Warhol, interview with Gretchen Berg, "Andy Warhol, My True Story," in *I'll Be Your Mirror: The Selected Andy Warhol Interviews, 1962–1987*, edited by Kenneth Goldsmith (New York: Carroll & Graf, 2004), 85.
63: Andy Warhol, *America* (New York: HarperCollins, 1985), 132.
64: Warhol, *America*, 22.
89: Andy Warhol and Bob Colacello, *Andy Warhol's Exposures* (New York: Grosset & Dunlap, 1979), 82.
96: Andy Warhol, interview with G. R. Swenson, *ARTnews* (November 1963), reprinted in Goldsmith, *I'll Be Your Mirror*, 19.
107: Andy Warhol and Pat Hackett, *POPism: The Warhol '60s* (New York: Harcourt Brace Jovanovich, 1990), 137.
109: Andy Warhol, quoted by Gene Youngblood, "New Warhol at Cinémathèque," *L.A. Free Press*, February 16, 1968, cited by Jonas Mekas in *Andy Warhol Film Factory*, edited by Michael O'Pray (London: British Film Publishing, 1989), 33; Jackie Curtis, quoted in Patrick S. Smith, *Andy Warhol's Art and Films* (Ann Arbor, Mich.: UMI Research Press, 1986), 138.
110: Warhol, *America*, 85.
114: Warhol and Hackett, *POPism*, 169.
130: Halston, interview with Eugenia Sheppard, *New York Post*, February 7, 1973; Warhol and Colacello, *Andy Warhol's Exposures*, 39; Andy Warhol, *THE Philosophy of Andy Warhol (from A to B and Back Again)* (New York: Harcourt Brace Jovanovich, 1975), 66.
150: Halston, quoted in "Halston Brings Back the Kneecap with His Skimp," *People*, November 25, 1974, 18.
152: Andy Warhol, *The Andy Warhol Diaries*, edited by Pat Hackett (New York: Warner Books, 1989), entry for March 13, 1978, 117.
158: Warhol, *Diaries*, entry for September 19, 1986, 759; Warhol, *Diaries*, entry for July 2, 1977, 57; Vincent Fremont, interview with Allison Unruh, *Andy Warhol Enterprises*, edited by Sarah Urist Green and Alison Unruh (Ostfildern, Germany: Hatje Cantz Verlag, 2010).
166: Warhol, *THE Philosophy of Andy Warhol*, 150.
178: Warhol, *Diaries*, entry for December 19, 1978, 189; Halston, quoted by Lisa Belkin, *New York Times*, March 15, 1987; Steve Rubell, quoted in "First Anniversary Interview: Steve Rubell," *Interview*, June 1978 (7, no. 6): 19.
191: Warhol, *THE Philosophy of Andy Warhol*, 92.
199: Halston, quoted in Warhol, *Diaries*, entry for December 3, 1978, 186; Warhol, *Diaries*, entry for December 24, 1980, 352; Bob Colacello, *Holy Terror: Andy Warhol Close Up* (New York: HarperCollins, 1990), 260.
202: Pat Cleveland, quoted in Gross and Rottman, *Halston*, 47; Associate Press, "China Shocked by Halston," *Bangor Daily News*, September 22, 1980, 16; Christopher Makos, *Warhol/Makos: A Personal Photographic Memoir* (New York: NAL Books, 1988), 98.
208: Warhol, *Diaries*, entry for April 22, 1982, 44.
212: John Duka, "Notes on Fashion," *New York Times*, August 4, 1981.
216: Warhol and Hackett, *POPism*, 83.
220: Warhol, *America*, 30–31; Warhol and Colacello, *Exposures*, 42.
223: Halston, quoted in Suzy Kalter, "Love Boat Gets Buoyed Up with Some Titanic Egos Like Halston, Gloria & Beene," *People*, February 23, 1981, 99.
226: Warhol, *Diaries*, entry for July 9, 1981, 394.
227: Lee Radziwill, *Happy Times* (New York: Assouline, 2000), 32.
232: Warhol, *Diaries*, entry for November 25, 1984, 617.

Andy Warhol and Halston, n.d.
Photograph by Barbra Walz

CREDITS

INDEX

Page numbers in *italics* refer to images. The letter *n* refers to notes.

A
After the Party (Warhol), *182*, 183
AIDS, 230
American Dream, 49
André Leon Talley (Warhol), 196, *196*
André Leon Talley, Tina Chow, and Unidentified Man (Warhol), 224, *225*
Andy and Halston (Warhol), 188, *188*
Andy and Victor Hugo (Warhol), 30, *30*
Andy Warhol (Shore), 85, *85*, 100, *100*, 127, *127*
Andy Warhol, Martha Graham, and a birthday cake (Warhol), 224, *225*
Andy Warhol and Benjamin Liu at Montauk (Warhol), 228, *228*
Andy Warhol and Chuck Wein (Shore), 98, *98*
The Andy Warhol Diaries (Warhol), 189, *189*, 232
Andy Warhol's Exposures (Warhol), 177, *177*
Andy Warhol's Fifteen Minutes, 223
  debut of, 37
  Jacobs in, 34, *34*
  motto of, 37
Andy Warhol's T.V., *223*
  Cleveland in, 34, *34*
  guests on, 37
  premiere of, 37
  Rhodes in, 34, *34*
Armani, Giorgio, 196, *196*
aspirations, 54–55
Ast, Pat, 17, 23, 36, 40, 44n6, 224, *225*
Avedon, Richard, 19n2, 83

B
Ball, Lucille, 16
Barr, Neal, *80*
Beaded and embroidered evening top with skirt, 1981 (Halston), 206, *207*
Beaded evening dress, 1979 (Halston), 206, *207*
Beaded evening dress with dolman sleeves and tulip-style skirt, 1980 (Halston), 204, *204–5*
Beaded evening top with skirt, 1981 (Halston), 206, *207*
Beard, Peter, 36
Bendel, Henri, 39
Benson, Harry, 2–3, 15, *15*, 42, *42*, 138–39
Berenson, Marisa, 17, *92*, *93*, 187, *187*
  with Halston, 189, *189*, 224, *225*
  with Jagger and Halston, 224, *225*
Bergdorf Goodman, 64
  Halston opening in, 72
  Streisand at, 79, *79*
Bergen, Candice, 84, *84*, 110, *111*, *112–13*
Bianca Jagger (Warhol), 183, *183*
Bianca Jagger draped in leopard print in Halston's studio, 138–39
Bianca Jagger, Halston, and Marisa Berenson (Warhol), 224, *225*
bias cutting, 23
Bill Murray (Warhol), 218, *219*
Bjornson, Karen, 17, 36
  with Halston and Chinn, 186, *186*
Black and White Ball
  Bergen at, 84, *84*, 110, *111*, *112–13*
  Capote at, 110, *111*
  Graham, K., at, 110, *111*
  Paley at, 110
  Vanderbilt at, 110
  Warhol on, 110
BoBo's Hat (Warhol), *94–95*, 95
Bonwit Teller window displays (Warhol), 64, *65*, *66–67*, 67, 68, *68*
Boots (Halston), 172, *172*
Bottomly, Susan "International Velvet," 33, 36, 107, *107*
Braniff Airlines, 162, *162*
Brillo Soap Pads Box (Warhol), 87, *87*
Burrows, Stephen, 40, 44
business art, 191

C
caftan, 23
Camouflage (Warhol), 186, *186*
Camp (Warhol), 33
Campbell's Soup Can (Tomato Rice) (Warhol), 82, *82*
Cap (Halston), 72, *73*
Cape with hood, matching pants, dolman-style top, and obi belt, 1979 (Halston), 140, *140*
Capote, Truman, 193, *193*, 229, *229*
  at Black and White Ball, 110, *111*
Caraballo, Victor, 31
Carson Pirie Scott, 64
Catherine Guinness, John Richardson, and Diane von Furstenberg (Warhol), 224, *225*
celebrity culture
  at Studio 54, 183
  von Furstenberg on, 47
  Warhol on, 220
Channing, Carol, *58*, 60, 136, *137*
  with Graham, M., 152, *153*
Cheetah (boutique), 32
The Chelsea Girls (Warhol), 35, *35*
childhood, 54–55
China (Andy Warhol at the Great Wall) (Warhol), *184*, 186
Chinn, Alva, 17
  with Halston and Bjornson, 186, *186*
Chow, Tina, Talley and, 224, *225*
Christopher Makos, Pat Cleveland, and Jon Gould at the Beach (Warhol), 228, *228*
Clarke, Shirley, 114, *115*
Cleveland, Pat, 17, 20, 36, *45*, 154, *155*
  in *Andy Warhol's T.V.*, 34, *34*
  background of, 39
  on black models, 44
  on career beginnings, 39–40
  in China, 202
  on cooking, 41
  at Coty Awards after party, *38*, 39
  discovery of, 39
  on diversity, 154
  on draping, 136
  on Halston, 40–41
  with Halston in showroom, 42, *42*
  Halston meeting, 40
  interview with, 39–44
  with Makos and Gould, 228, *228*
  modeling sportswear line, 42, *42*
  on success, 43
  on Versailles 1973 fashion show, 43–44
  on Warhol, 41, 43
  Warhol meeting, 40
Clint Eastwood (Warhol), 218, *219*
Clouds evening dress, 1982–83 (Halston), 216, *217*
Committee 2000 (Warhol), 183, *183*
Corset-style contour belt with obi tie (Halston), 173, *173*
costume, 158
Coty American Fashion Critics' Awards 1972, 23, *36*
  Cleveland at after party for, *38*, 39
  Halston at after party for, *38*, 39
Cow Wallpaper [Pink on Yellow] (Warhol), 84, *84*
Curtis, Jackie, 109

D
Daché, Lilly, 61, 72
Darling, Candy, 36, 119
Dejean, Alain, 128, *128*
de la Renta, Oscar, 44
department stores. *See also specific department stores*
  Warhol on, 64
Diamond Dust Diamonds (Warhol), *188*, 189
Diamond Dust Shoes (Random) (Warhol), 212, *212*, 214, *215*
Diana Vreeland (Warhol), 224, *225*
Diana Vreeland and Martha Graham (Warhol), 122, *122*
Diane Keaton (Warhol), 218, *219*
Diane von Furstenberg (Warhol), 47, *47*
di Sant'Angelo, Giorgio, 40
diversity, 154
$ (9) (Warhol), *190*, 191
Dom (nightclub), 32, 114
Donghia, Angelo, 40, 100
Donovan, Carrie, 39
Double-wrap belt (Halston), 173, *173*
draping, 136
Drawings of Halston designs (Eula), 98, *99*
Dress, 1972 (Halston), 20, *21*
Dress, 1973 (Halston), 132, *133*
Dress and sweater set, 1972 (Halston), 134, *134*
Dugan, Bill, 14, 19n1
Duka, John, 212

E
Ebony, 39–40, 44n1
Edelman, Arthur, 93
Edelman, Teddy, 93
Eight Female Heads Wearing Sunglasses (Warhol), 76, *76*
Elvis (Warhol), *96*
Engelhard, Jane, 20
Ensemble, 1970–71 (Halston), 132, *132*
Ensemble, 1972–73 (Halston), 22, *22*
Ensemble, 1974 (Halston), 22, *22*
Erwitt, Elliott, *112–13*
Estévez, Luis, 47, 48
Eula, Joe, 97, *97*, *98*, 146, 224, *225*, 230
  Drawings of Halston designs, 98, *99*
  illustrations by, 19n3
  Skimp drawing, 150, *150*, 151, *151*
Evansville, Indiana, 56, *56*
Evening dress, 1972 (Halston), 22, *22*
Evening dress, 1972–73 (Halston), 24, *25*
Evening dress, 1976 (Halston), 146, *146*
Evening dress, 1981 (Halston), 218, *218*
Evening dress with hand-painted snake, 1971 (Halston), 119, *119*
Evening dress with matching shrug/shawl, 1983 (Halston), *26*, 27
Evening dress with print based on Warhol's *Flowers* painting (Halston), 124, *125*
Evening dress with ruffle top and tulip wrap skirt, 1980 (Halston), *210*, 211
Evening dress with under slip and obi belt, 1983 (Halston), 208, *209*
Evening ensemble: caftan, 1971 (Halston), 143, *144*
Evening ensemble: dress (Halston), 136, *136*
Evening sarong, 1977 (Halston), 147, *147*
Evening shoes, 1982 (Halston), 213, *213*
The Exploding Plastic Inevitable, 84, 100, 114
Eyes and Hat (Warhol), 75, *75*

F
Factory, 103
  Hugo at, 30
  party, 114, *115*
  premiere of, 100
  Silver, 83, 100, *100*, 107, 114
Factory Diary (Warhol), 36
  Kuhn in, 34, *34*
Fashion (Warhol), 36–37
  Halston in, 35, *35*, 37
fashion shows
  Frowick, L., on, 16–17
  Halston, 152, *153*
  Versailles 1973, 20, 43–44, 128, *128*
Fashion: The Empress and the Commissioner (Warhol), 35, *35*, 37
fashion video, 36
Female Costumed Full Figure (Warhol), 61, *61*
Female Fashion Figure (Warhol), 70, *70*, 71, *71*
Female Fashion Model (Halston Show) (Warhol), 152, *153*
Female Head (Warhol), 72, *72*
Fenn, Otto, *78*, 79
Ferro, Shirley, 12, *12*, 150, *150*
50-Dollar Bills Paintbrush (Hugo), 123, *123*
Finkelstein, Nat, 216, *216*
Five Shoes and Three Purses (Warhol), 60, *60*
Fleming-Joffe, Ltd. storefront, 93, *93*
Floor-length dress, 1975 (Halston), 143, *145*
Flowers (Warhol), 125, *125*, 126, *126*
Folding Screen (Warhol), 62, *63*, 68, *69*
Ford, Tom, 27
Forth, Jane, 36
***** [Four Stars]* (Warhol), 32, 33
Fownes (Warhol), 68, *68*
Fred Hughes and Bianca Jagger (Warhol), 178, *179*
Fremont, Vincent, 36, 158
Frowick, Bob, *55*, *55*
Frowick, Hallie Mae, 55, *55*
Frowick, Lesley, 12, *12*, *19*
  birthday of, 14, 16, *16*
  on domestic help, 17
  on fashion shows, 16–17
  on Halston, 14–19
  on made-to-order, 16
Frowick, Margaret, 55, *55*

G
Galella, Ron, *38*, 39, 165, *165*, 224, *224*
Garolini Shoes, 212, 213, *213*
Gaultier, Jean Paul, 196, *196*
gay lifestyle, 230
Gernreich, Rudi, 23
Gianni Versace (Warhol), 196, *196*
Gilded Lily (boutique), 32
Giorgio Armani (Warhol), 196, *196*
glamour, 27, 32
Goldman, Heidi, 85, *85*
Gould, Jon, 18, 230
  with Haring, 231, *231*
  with Makos and Cleveland, 228, *228*
Grace Kelly (Warhol), *195*, 196
Graham, Katharine, 110, *111*

Graham, Martha, 41, 164, *164*, 192, *192*, 193, *193*
with Channing, 152, *153*
with Halston, 165, *165*
with Minnelli and Nureyev, 222, *222*
with Vreeland, 122, *122*
with Warhol and birthday cake, 224, *225*
Guest, Cornelia, 224, *224*
Guinness, Catherine, 224, *225*
Guke, George, 55, *55*

H
Hackett, Pat, 98, 107, 114, 121, 186, 189, 216
Halstead, Dirck, *156*, 157
Halston, *10*, *54*, *55*, *58*, *80*, *117*, 128. *See also specific works*
appearance of, 158
artwork collected by, 17, 199
aspirations of, 54–55
assistants, 98
with Berenson, 189, *189*, 224, *225*
with Berenson and Jagger, 224, *225*
Bergdorf Goodman opening, 72
on bias cutting, 23
birthday of, 14, 16, *16*
with Bjornson and Chinn, 186, *186*
in Braniff Airlines uniforms, 162, *162*
on caftan, 23
on career, 54
on cashmere, 23
childhood of, 54–55
in China, 202, *203*
with Cleveland in showroom, 42, *42*
Cleveland meeting, 40
Cleveland on, 40–41
cooking and, 17
at Coty Awards after party, *38*, 39
domestic help, 17, 43
early success of, 87
entourage of, 20, 28, 36, 103, *104–5*
family of, 18
in *Fashion*, 35, *35*, 37
fashion shows, 152, *153*
Frowick, L., on, 14–19
with Goldman, 85, *85*
Graham, M., with, 165, *165*
with Guest and Warhol, 224, *224*
with Haring in *Interview*, 18
with Hugo, 31, *31*, 227, *227*, 230, *230*
in *Interview*, 18, 175
last portrait at home in New York, 19, *19*
with Liston, 162, *162*
at Magic, Fantasy, and Dreams (costume ball), 163, *163*
Manhattan townhouse designed by Rudolph, 15, *15*, 17
materials of, 130, 206, 208
with Minnelli, 152, *153*, 165, *165*
motto of, 20
nickname for Warhol, 17
perfume by, 166, 167, *167*
perfume promotion by, 166, *166*
with Paloma Picasso, 224, *225*
with police uniform designs, 163, *163*
routine and, 30
Rubell with, 178, *179*
Saint Laurent compared with, 20
selling company, 18, 20, 232
after show, 118, *118*
showroom, 100, 101, *101*
signature look of, 130
on Studio 54, 178
Taylor and, 220, *221*
timeline 1930s–40s, 52–53
timeline 1950s, 60–61
timeline 1960s, 82–85
timeline 1970s, 118–23
timeline 1980s, 186–89
von Furstenberg on, 47
with Warhol, 188, *188*, 224, *224*, *234*, 235
on women, 130
Halston (Warhol), *185*, 186, 232, *232*, *233*
Halston: Absolute Modernism, 25
Halston Advertising Campaign series (Warhol), 170, *170*, 171, *171*
Halston and Paloma Picasso (Warhol), 224, *225*
Halston and Victor Hugo (Warhol), 31, *31*
Halston and Victor Hugo with American Flag (Warhol), 230, *230*
Halston Archives and Study Room at Fashion Institute of Technology, 25
Halstonettes, 20, 28, 36. *See also specific Halstonettes*
in Acapulco, 103, *104–5*
Halston III, 25
Halston with Steve Rubell (Warhol), 178, *179*
Happy's Luggage (Warhol), 95, *95*
Haring, Keith, 18, 230
with Gould, 231, *231*
with Halston in *Interview*, 18
Harper's Bazaar, September 1961, 83, *83*
Hartman, Rose, 42, *42*, 152, *152*, 166, *166*, 186, *186*, 206, *206*
Hat, 1965 (Halston), 75, *75*
Hat, mid-1960s (Halston), 75, *75*
Hat box (Halston), 61, *61*
Henry Hudson Baths, 32
Henson, Jim, 18
high-low collaborations, 25
Hiro, 19n2
Holzer, Baby Jane, 33, 36, 123
Horst, Horst P., 46, *46*
Hughes, Fred, 18
in China, 202
Jagger with, 178, *179*
with Warhol and Pope John Paul II, 222, *222*
Hugo, Victor, 27n4, 28, *28*, *29*, 123, *123*, 146
cooking and, 41
at Factory, 30
with Halston, 31, *31*, 227, *227*, 230, *230*
with Warhol, 30, *30*, 31
Warhol on, 28
window displays by, 28, 30
Huston, Anjelica, 20, 40, 152, *153*
Hutton, Lauren, 130, *131*, 229

I
I. Miller shoes, 70, 71, *71*
Inspiring Beauty: 50 Years of Ebony Fashion Fair, 39–40, 44n1
Interview, 36, 175, *175*
Halston and Haring in, 18
Halston in, 18, 175
May 1972, *176*, 177, *177*
September 1976, *174*, 175
Introduction ("Fleming-Joffe-Goldwyn Present") (Warhol), 95, *95*

J
Jackie (Warhol), 89, *90*, *91*
Jackie's Boots . . . (Warhol), 95, *95*
Jacobs, Marc, 34, *34*
Jagger, Bianca, 138, *138–39*, *183*
with Halston and Berenson, 224, *225*
Hughes with, 178, *179*
at Montauk, 122, 229
parties at Studio 54, 123, 180, *181*, 183
JCPenney, 14, 15, 25, 30, 186, 187
Jean Paul Gaultier (Warhol), 196, *196*
Joe Eula (Warhol), 97, *97*, 224, *225*
John Paul II (Pope), 222, *222*
Johnson, Beverly, *156*, 157
Johnson, Eunice W., 44n1
Johnston, Johnny, 39
Jon Gould and Keith Haring (Warhol), 231, *231*
Jordan, Donna, 36, 40, 44n3

K
Kahn, Naeem, 16, 19n4
Kaleidoscope (boutique), 32
Karan, Donna, 27
Kelly, Grace, *195*, 196
Kempner, Nan, 36
Kennedy, Jacqueline, 11, 20, 31, 72, *90*, *91*, *93*, *95*, 95, 229
in front of White House, 89, *89*
Paris visit, 82, *82*
pillbox hat for, 20, *88*, 89
Kennedy, John F.
assassination of, 89
in front of White House, 89, *89*
Kermit the Frog, 18
Klein, Calvin, 25, 27
Koda, Harold, 25
Kuhn, Evelyn
in *Factory Diary*, 34, *34*
source images for, 36

L
Lady Bird Strickland, 39
The Last Supper (Warhol), 187, *187*, 188, 189
Lauren, Ralph, 27
Legs in Red High Heels (Warhol), 76, *76*
Leopard-patterned evening ensemble, 1970 (Halston), 143, *144–45*
Lesley Frowick (Halston's niece) (Warhol), 12, *12*
lifestyle branding, 27
Lisi, Virna, 74, *74*
Liston, Sonny, 162, *162*
Liu, Benjamin, 228, *228*
Liz (Warhol), 97, *97*
source images for, 96
Liza Minnelli (Warhol), 192, *192*, 193, *193*, 229, *229*
Liza Minnelli (wearing Halston) (Warhol), *194*, 196
Liza Minnelli and Halston at Fashion Show (Warhol), 152, *153*
Long goddess-style dress (Halston), 140, *141*
Lopez, Antonio, 40, 44n4
The Love Boat, 222, *222*, 223, *223*
Luna, Donyale, 33, 44, 154, 157, *157*

M
Machalaba, Nick, 163, *163*
made-to-order. *See also specific made-to-order garments*
Frowick, L., on, 16
Magic, Fantasy, and Dreams (costume ball), 163, *163*
Make Him Want You (Warhol), 96, *96*
Makos, Christopher, 203, *203*
in China, 202
with Cleveland and Gould, 228, *228*
Male Fashion Figure (Warhol), 70, *70*
Mao (Warhol), 119, *119*
Marilyn (Warhol), 96
Marisa Berenson (Warhol), 187, *187*, 224, *225*
Marisa Berenson and Halston (Warhol), 189, *189*
Marisol, 17
Martha Graham (Warhol), 164, *164*, 192, *192*, 193, *193*
Martha Graham, Carol Channing, and Unidentified Woman (Warhol), 152, *153*
Martha Graham: Lamentation (Warhol), 164, *164*
Martha Graham: Letter to the World (The Kick) (Warhol), 164, *164*
Martin, Richard, 25
on fashion, 32
Max Factor, 166
McCardell, Claire, 23
McDarrah, Fred W., 114, *115*, *117*, 118
Mears, Patricia, 49
Mekas, Jonas, 36, 98
Meryl Streep (Warhol), 218, *219*
Mick Jagger (Warhol), *182*, 183
Midi-length collarless coat (Halston), 129, *129*
Midi-length sleeveless dress with mock turtleneck (Halston), 129, *129*
Minnelli, Liza, 43, 192, *192*, 193, *193*, *194*, 196, 229, *229*
in Halston's showroom, 100, 101, *101*
Halston with, 152, *153*, 165, *165*
with Nureyev and Graham, M., 222, *222*
Mirabella, Grace, 23
Miss Dior (Warhol), 68, *68*
Miss Piggy, 18
Model at a fashion show at Halston's Olympic Tower showroom (Warhol), 152, *153*
Mod Wedding, 114, *115*
Mona Lisa (Warhol), *198*, 199, *199*
Montauk: Halston (Warhol), 228, *228*
Montauk house, 226, *226*
Cleveland on, 41
Frowick on, 17, 18
Halston land near, 187, 189
Radziwill on, 227
renters of, 229
Warhol purchase of, 118, 123
Montauk: Victor Hugo and Halston (Warhol), 227, *227*
Morrissey, Paul, 36, 98, 118
Morse, Joan "Tiger," 32, 35, *35*
Munroe, Don, 36, 122, 123, 186, 187

N
Netter, Michael, 36
Nico, 33
Warhol with, 114, *115*
Noa the Boa (Warhol), 93, 95, *95*
Noguchi, Isamu, 17
Norris, Gary, 114
North, Nancy, 17, 19n1, 36
Nureyev, Rudolf, 222, *222*

O
Obama, Michelle, 19n4
100-Dollar Bills Robe (Halston), 123, *123*
"Onstage Happening by Andy Warhol" (Warhol), 23, 36

P
Paley, Babe, 20
at Black and White Ball, 110
Paraphernalia (boutique), 36
Paraphernalia (Warhol), 36
Pashun, Tommy, 37

- *Pat Ast* (Warhol), 224, *225*
- *Pat Cleveland* (Warhol), 44, *45*
- Pearlstein, Phillip, 63
- Peretti, Elsa, 20, 40, 44n5, 146, 152, 170
- perfume
  - by Halston, 166, 167, *167*
  - Halston promoting, 166, *166*
  - Warhol on, 166
- *Perfume Bottle and Lipstick* (Warhol), *168*, 169
- *THE Philosophy of Andy Warhol (from A to B and Back Again)* (Warhol), 121, *121*, 130
- photographic silkscreen, *96*
- Picasso, Paloma, 224, *225*
- pillbox hat (Halston), *88*
  - for Kennedy, Jacqueline, 89
- Pittman, Dustin, *10*, 11, 154, *155*
- Pittsburgh steel mills, 56, *56*
- Platzer, Robin, *180–81*, 182
- Preksta, Mary, 55, *55*
- Prime, Eve, 24, *24*, *26*, 27, 129, *129*, 140, *140*, *141*, 147, *148–49*, 172, *172*, 206, *207*, 208, *209*, 213, *213*
- *Production Title ("The Autobiography of a Snake Called Noa the Boa")* (Warhol), 95, *95*

R

- *Race Riot* (Warhol), 44, 154
- Radziwill, Lee, 118, 123, 227
- Reversible belt with slip-through tie (Halston), 173, *173*
- Rhodes, Zandra, 34, *34*
- Richardson, John, 224, *225*
- Rivers, Larry, 17, 37, 119
- Robeson, Faye, 14, 200, *200*
- Rockefeller, Happy, 31
- Rodriguez, Narciso, 27
- Roehl, Virginia, 64, *65*
- Rooney, John, 152, *153*
- Ross, Diana, *174*, 175
- Rossi, Randi, 114, *115*
- Rothschild, Marie-Hélène de, 128, *128*
- Royer, Chris, 12, *12*, 17, 20
  - on sarong dress, 23, 146
  - in Skimp, 150, *150*
  - at Versailles, 128, *128*
- Rubell, Steve, 41, 178, 230
  - Halston with, 178, *179*
- Rudolph, Paul, 15, *15*, 17
- Ryan, DD, 16

S

- Saint Laurent, Yves, 196, *196*
  - Halston compared with, 20
- *Sandal* (Warhol), 76, *76*
- Sarong, 1981 (Halston), 147, *148–49*
- sarong dress
  - debut of, 121, 130, 146
  - Royer on, 23, 146
- Scavullo, Francesco, 130, *131*
- Schermann, Pierre, 12, *12*, 150, *150*
- Schrager, Ian, 178
- *Screen Test: Donyale Luna* (Warhol), 157, *157*
- *Screen Test: Ivy Nicholson* (Warhol), 33, *33*
- *Screen Test: Lou Reed* (Warhol), *108*, 109
- Sedgwick, Edie, 33, 84, 98
  - as 1965 Girl of the Year, 107
  - Warhol on, 107, 220
  - Warhol with, 106, *106*
- *Self-Portrait (Tuxedo)* (Warhol), *81*, 82
- *Self-Portrait* (Warhol), *81*, 82
- *Self-Portrait with Movie Camera* (Warhol), *116*, 118
- *Self-Portrait with Skull* (Warhol), 122, *122*, 201, *201*
- *Self-Portrait with Stevie Wonder* (Warhol), 222, *222*
- Set, 1972 (Halston), 22, *22*
- *S&H Green Stamps* (Warhol), 83, *83*
- Shiller, Astrid, 86, *86*
- shirtdress, 19, 23, 119
- *Shoe* (Warhol), 76, *76*
- *Shoes* (Warhol), 214, *214*
- Shore, Stephen, 85, *85*, 98, *98*, 100, *100*, 114, *115*, 127, *127*
- Shrimpton, Jean, *102*, 103
- Shrug/Shawl (back and front), 1984 (Halston), *142*, 143, *143*
- *Silk Scarf* (Warhol), 71, *71*
- silver, 206, 216
- *Silver Clouds* (Warhol), 84, 85, *100*, 216
- *Silver Liz [Ferus Type]* (Warhol), 97, *97*
- Simon, Norton, 18, 20
- Sims, Naomi, 17, 40, 44, 154
  - at Lucky Spot Restaurant, 157, *157*
- Singelis, Leila Davis, 64, *65*
- Skimp
  - debut of, 150
  - Eula's drawing of, 150, *150*, 151, *151*
  - Ferro in, 150, *150*
  - Royer in, 150, *150*
- Sklar, Michael, 36
- Sleeveless dress and cardigan set, 1972 (Halston), 24, *24*
- Sleeveless gown with wrap, 1983 (Halston), 157, *157*
- Soumaya, Mohammed, 17, 18, 43
- Spiral-cut evening dress with evening coat, 1984 (Halston), 211, *211*
- Spiral-cut evening dress with shawl, 1984 (Halston), *210–11*, 211
- Sprouse, Stephen, 37, 119, 125, 150, 196, *196*, 197, *197*
- *Stamped Shoes* (Warhol), 77, *77*
- *Stephen Sprouse* (Warhol), 196, *196*, 197, *197*
- Stern, Bert, 72, *73*, *92*, 93
- Stone, Nancy, 19n3
- Strapless tulle dance dress, 1980 (Halston), 157, *157*
- Streisand, Barbra, 79, *79*
- Studio 54, 31, 41
  - celebrity guest list at, 183
  - Halston on, 178
  - Jagger's birthday at, 183
  - New Year's Eve party at, *180–81*, 182
- *Studio 54* (Warhol), 178, *179*
- *Style with Elsa Klensch*, 37
- Sudo, Reiko, 216
- Suit with calla lily collar, sweater, and matching scarf, 1979 (Halston), 134, *134*
- Suit with dirndl skirt, blouse, and obi belt, 1979 (Halston), 134, *134*
- Suit with matching coat and scarf, 1979 (Halston), 134, *135*
- Superstars, 20, 33, 36, 40, 84, 103, 107. *See also specific Superstars*

T

- Talley, André Leon, 196, *196*
  - with Chow, 224, *225*
- Taylor, Elizabeth, *96*, *97*, *97*
  - Halston and, 220, *221*
  - reciting poetry, 43
  - Warhol on, 220
- Teeny Weeny (boutique), 32
- Three-tiered contoured hip belt with slip-though back tie, 1982–83 (Halston), 173, *173*
- Tiffany's, 64
- *Tiger Morse* (Warhol), 35, *35*
- *Time Capsule 21* (Warhol), 120, *120*
- *Time Capsule 471* (Warhol), 16, *16*, 18
- *Trash* (Warhol), 36
- Travel set, 1980 (Halston), 203, *203*
- *Truman Capote* (Warhol), 193, *193*, 229, *229*
- tube dresses, 23
- Two-piece dress, Halston V line, 1975 (Halston), 22, *22*
- Two-piece evening dress, Spring 1981 (Halston), 22, *22*
- Two-piece halter, pants, and obi belt, 1981 (Halston), 206, *207*

U

- uniform, 158
  - Braniff Airlines, 162, *162*
  - Halston with designs for police, 163, *163*

V

- Vanderbilt, Alfred G., 110
- Velvet dress and white mink mask, 1966 (Halston), 84, *84*
- Velvet Underground, 33, 84,100, 114
  - Warhol on, 114
- Versace, Gianni, 196, *196*
- Versailles 1973 fashion show, 20
  - black models at, 44
  - Cleveland on, 43–44
  - models at gala night, 128, *128*
  - Royer at, 128, *128*
- Veruschka, 36
- *Victor Hugo* (Warhol), 28, *28*, *29*
- Vionnet, Madeleine, 23
- von Furstenberg, Diane, *47*
  - background of, 47
  - on celebrity culture, 47
  - on China, 48
  - on freedom, 48
  - with Guinness and Richardson, 224, *225*
  - on Halston, 47
  - at home, 46, *46*
  - on honesty in design, 48
  - interview with, 47–48
  - on wrap dress, 48
- Vreeland, Diana, 224, *225*
  - in *Fashion: The Empress and the Commissioner*, 35, *35*, 37
  - with Graham, M., 122, *122*

W

- Wallen, Eva, 123, *123*
- Walters, Barbara, 31
- Walz, Barbra, *234*, 235
- Wangenheim, Chris von, *174*, 175
- Warhol, Andy, *55*, *85*, *98*, *115*, *121*, *127*. *See also specific works*
  - on appearance, 158
  - appearance of, 32–33, 158
  - aspirations of, 54–55
  - barn studio space, 57, *57*
  - birthday, 18
  - on Black and White Ball, 110
  - on business art, 191
  - on career, 54
  - on celebrity culture, 220
  - childhood, 54–55
  - in China, *184*, 186, 202, 203, *203*
  - Cleveland meeting, 40
  - Cleveland on, 41, 43
  - death of, 18–19, 37, 232
  - on department stores, 64
  - early success of, 87
  - early work of, 70–71
  - entourage of, 20, 33, 103
  - on filming, 109
  - glamour and, 32
  - with Graham, M., and birthday cake, 224, *225*
  - on Halston, 130
  - with Halston, 188, *188*, 224, *224*, *234*, 235
  - with Halston and Guest, 224, *224*
  - Halston's nickname for, 17
  - high school homeroom class picture, *57*, *57*
  - with Hughes and Pope John Paul II, 222, *222*
  - on Hugo, 28
  - on *Jackie* series, 89
  - jeans, 160, *160*
  - last public appearance of, 37
  - with Liu, 228, *228*
  - on look of 1960s, 32
  - on New York City, 63
  - with Nico, 114, *115*
  - passport photo, *59*, 60
  - on perfume, 166
  - process of, 96
  - on Sedgwick, 107
  - with Sedgwick, 106, *106*
  - shirt, 161, *161*
  - shoes, 160, *160*
  - on silver, 216
  - on *Style with Elsa Klensch*, 37
  - subject matter of, 49
  - on Taylor, 220
  - timeline 1930s–40s, 49–53
  - timeline 1950s, 60–61
  - timeline 1960s, 82–85
  - timeline 1970s, 118–23
  - timeline 1980s, 186–89
  - on Ultrasuede, 130
  - on Velvet Underground, 114
  - wig, 158, *159*
- Warhola, John, *55*, *55*
- Warhola, Julia, 55, *55*
- *The Warhol Look*, 27
- Waronov, Mary, 35, *35*
- Wein, Chuck, 98, *98*
- window displays, 32, 64, 79. *See also Bonwit Teller window displays*
  - by Hugo, 28, 30, 31
- Wonder, Stevie, 222, *222*

Y

- Yee, Pui, 19n3
- *You're In* (Warhol), 169, *169*
- *Yves Saint Laurent* (Warhol), 196, *196*

Z

- Zaye, Lisa, 14
- Zhang Haun, 48

ACKNOWLEDGMENTS

The Andy Warhol Museum would like to thank the wide range of people who are responsible for this landmark project.

The personal nature of *Halston and Warhol: Silver and Suede* makes it particularly significant, reflective of the involvement of many people who were close to Halston and Warhol as family, friends, employees, and colleagues. We are particularly indebted to Halston's niece, Lesley Frowick, for bringing the original project concept to us and for sharing not only her knowledge of Halston but also her love for her uncle. We appreciate the generous contribution by Pat Cleveland, whose memories of her friendship with Halston and Warhol give the book depth, and were delighted to work with Corrine LaBalme and Chris Royer, who provided vital information about their time with Halston that would otherwise be lost. We were also fortunate to be able to publish new essays by Valerie Steele, Director at the Museum at the Fashion Institute of Technology, and Geralyn Huxley, The Warhol's Curator of Film and Video. And we are grateful for the enthusiasm and support of Diane von Furstenberg.

The exhibition associated with this volume has been supported by numerous individuals and institutions. In particular, we acknowledge Chris Royer; the Museum at the Fashion Institute of Technology, New York; Des Moines Art Center; Martha Graham School of Dance, New York; Indianapolis Museum of Art; John F. Kennedy Presidential Library and Museum, Boston; the Museum of the City of New York; and the Chicago History Museum.

This publication and exhibition are presented as part of The Warhol's twentieth-anniversary celebration in 2014. Like so many of our exhibitions, *Halston and Warhol: Silver and Suede* would not happen without the support of PNC Financial Services. PNC makes it possible to present world-class exhibitions in Pittsburgh and to tour our exhibitions domestically. We salute PNC for its ongoing support. We also send our thanks to Halston Heritage for its assistance and for its work in continuing to make Halston a part of the global fashion scene.

Without the motivating force of Abigail Franzen-Sheehan, Director of Publications, this publication would not be in print. We thank her for her careful review and oversight of the project while maintaining its vision and meeting its tight deadlines. Special thanks are due to Signe Watson, Research Intern, who tirelessly researched information with industriousness and good cheer. Other members of our internal writing and production team who made this publication possible are: Matt Wrbican, Chief Archivist; Cindy Lisica, Assistant Archivist; Gregory J. Burchard, Senior Manager of Rights, Reproductions and Photographic Services; and additional interns Kristen Whitlinger and Meredith Antle.

We are likewise grateful to other members of our internal staff, who, on a day-to-day basis, provide exceptional support for museum projects like this one.

Our leadership team: Eric Shiner, Director; Patrick Moore, Deputy Director; and Rachel Baron-Horn, Director of Finance & Operations.

Our curatorial and exhibitions teams: Nicholas Chambers, The Milton Fine Curator of Art; Jennifer Melvin, Executive & Curatorial Assistant; Geralyn Huxley, Curator of Film & Video; Gregory Pierce, Assistant Curator of Film & Video; Ben Harrison, Curator of Performing Arts; Jesse Kowalski, Director of Exhibitions; Alissa Osial, Exhibitions Coordinator; Heather Kowalski, Registrar; Amber Morgan, Associate Registrar for Collections; Caitlin Gongas, Assistant Registrar; and John Jacobs, Assistant Registrar for Collections. Also, we thank the cataloguers of the Warhol Time Capsules Cataloguing Project for helping to locate many of the archival objects presented in the exhibition: Erin Byrne, Marie Elia, and Elaina Vitale.

Our external affairs team: Rick Armstrong, Communications Manager; Emily Meyer, Assistant Communications Manager; Josh Jeffery, Manager of Digital Engagement; Jason Fate, Manager Visitor Services; Deanna Zeits, Development Assistant; Paul Matarrese, Museum Store Manager; and Donald Warhola, Liaison to the Andy Warhol Foundation for the Visual Arts.

Our education and interpretation team: Tresa E. Varner, Curator of Education & Interpretation; Nicole Dezelon, Associate Curator of Education; Leah Morelli, School Programs Coordinator; Paul O'Brien, Studio Programs Coordinator; Adil Mansoor, Youth Programs Coordinator; and Heather White, Community Programs Coordinator.

Finally, we thank our publisher, Abrams, and its industrious staff. Elisa Urbanelli, Associate Publisher, has given tremendous support, both in encouragement and editorial review of this publication; and John Gall, Creative Director, has designed a book that is both elegant and evocative.

Editor: Elisa Urbanelli
Designer: John Gall with Sebit Min
Managing Editor: David Blatty
Production Manager: Anet Sirna-Bruder

Library of Congress Control Number: 2013945519

ISBN: 978-1-4197-1095-7

Image credits appear on page 235, which is a continuation of this copyright page.

Printed and bound in the United States
10 9 8 7 6 5 4 3 2 1

Abrams books are available at special discounts when purchased in quantity for premiums and promotions as well as fundraising or educational use. Special editions can also be created to specification. For details, contact specialsales@abramsbooks.com or the address below.

ABRAMS
THE ART OF BOOKS SINCE 1949

The Andy Warhol Museum
One of the four Carnegie Museums of Pittsburgh

115 West 18th Street
New York, NY 10011
www.abramsbooks.com

PAGES 2–3
Four Halstonettes at the Olympic Tower showroom, left to right: Karen Bjornson, Alva Chinn, Connie Cook, and Pat Cleveland
Photograph by Harry Benson

PAGE 4
Andy Warhol
Halston, 1974
Polaroid™ Polacolor Type 108
4 ¼ x 3 ⅜ in. (10.8 x 8.6 cm)
The Andy Warhol Museum, Pittsburgh; Contribution The Andy Warhol Foundation for the Visual Arts, Inc., 2000.2.846

PAGE 5
Andy Warhol
Self-Portrait (Fright Wig), 1986
Polaroid™ Polacolor ER
4 ¼ x 3 ⅜ in. (10.8 x 8.6 cm)
The Andy Warhol Museum, Pittsburgh; Founding Collection, Contribution The Andy Warhol Foundation for the Visual Arts, Inc., 1998.1.2896